Reflections

An Anthology of African American Philosophy

JAMES A. MONTMARQUET

Tennessee State University, Nashville

WILLIAM H. HARDY

Tennessee State University, Nashville

Wadsworth
Thomson Learning

Australia • Canada • Denmark • Japan • Mexico • New Zealand • Philippines
Puerto Rico • Singapore • Spain • United Kingdom • United States

Philosophy Editor: Peter Adams
Assistant Editor: Kerri Abdinoor
Editorial Assistant: Mindy Newfarmer
Marketing Manager: Dave Garrison
Project Editor: Matt Stevens

Print Buyer: Stacey Weinberger
Permissions Editor: Joohee Lee
Production Service/Compositor: Shepherd, Inc.
Cover Designer: Bill Stanton
Printer/Binder: Custom Printing/Von Hoffman Press

Printed in the United States of America
2 3 4 5 6 7 03 02 01 00

ISBN 0534–57393–2

For more information, contact
Wadsworth/Thomson Learning
10 Davis Drive
Belmont, CA 94002-3098
USA
www.wadsworth.com

International Headquarters
Thomson Learning
290 Harbor Drive, 2nd Floor
Stamford, CT 06902-7477
USA

UK/Europe/Middle East/South Africa
Thomson Learning
Berkshire House
168-173 High Holborn
London WC1V 7AA
United Kingdom

Asia
Thomson Learning
60 Albert Street #15-01
Albert Complex
Singapore 189969

Canada
Nelson/Thomson Learning
1120 Birchmount Road
Scarborough, Ontario M1K 5G4
Canada

Library of Congress Cataloging-in-Publication Data

Reflections : an anthology of African American philosophy / [compiled by] James A.
Montmarquet, William H. Hardy.
     p. cm.
  Includes bibliographical references.
  ISBN 0-534-57393-2
  1. Afro-American philosophy. I. Montmarquet, James A. II. Hardy, William H.

B944.A37 R44 2000
191'.089'96073

99-049165

 This book is printed on acid-free recycled paper.

CONTENTS

iii

The fundamental idea behind this collection is to provide the instructor with a sufficient quantity, breadth, and diversity of materials to be the sole text for a course on African American philosophy. To this end—

- We have included a substantial number of classic readings from such authors as Frederick Douglass, Sojourner Truth, W. E. B. DuBois, Marcus Garvey, Ralph Ellison, Malcolm X, and Martin Luther King, Jr. Most instructors should find these sufficient to remove the need for any supplementary readings in this regard.

- We have tried to balance, in our use of more contemporary materials, professional philosophers (Laurence M. Thomas, Lewis R. Gordon, and Bernard Boxill) with other philosophically interesting authors from outside the discipline of philosophy (Patricia J. Williams, Derrick Bell, James H. Cone, and bell hooks).

- We have sought to present side by side contrasting views on perennial issues such as separatism versus assimilation, as well as more contemporary issues such as women's and gay liberation, the message of rap music, and Ebonics. Each chapter contains at least one explicitly indicated contemporary or classic "controversy." This focus on debate and contrast will help instructors with experience in traditional "moral issues" courses but relatively new to African American philosophy courses.

- We have focused not just on issues of race but on gender as well. There is an entire section devoted to this subject, and it also enters heavily into our readings in such areas as the law and theology. For example, our "contemporary issue" in this last area concerns the relation between black "womanists" and the traditional, and generally more conservative, black denominations.

- In addition to materials on the expected subjects of consciousness, political philosophy, and ethics, we have included sections on the law, aesthetics, and theology. These themes not only serve an important intellectual purpose, but also a pedagogical one. At a certain point in one's course, the sheer persistence of certain social issues makes it desirable to have new areas of exploration.

- Even with the diversity of materials contained here, there are certain themes that the instructor can use effectively to achieve a necessary element of unity. One such unifying theme concerns the relation between a certain type of ("nationalist") focus on blackness and the many critics of this focus. This debate, as we point out in our general introduction, embraces a great number of issues and authors: the nineteenth-century colonizers and their critics, Marcus Garvey and his critics, some of the differences between Malcolm X and Martin Luther King, Jr., the Black Arts Movement versus its critics, Cone's black liberation theology versus more moderate voices, and so forth.

We believe, then, that we have put together a collection that is comprehensive, balanced, and diverse. It stresses the vitality of contemporary African American intellectual debate but does not ignore the nineteenth- and early twentieth-century origins of today's controversies.

Of course, no anthology can be "all things to all people"; sacrifices must be made. Here let us acknowledge some of the more important of these:

- Given the recent upsurge of writings by contemporary academic African American philosophers, we could have populated our entire book with these works. Regrettably, we have had to omit many excellent contemporary philosophers to create the kind of balances we have sought.

- Also, the complete story of black philosophy—from ancient Egypt through the Diaspora and into such locales as the Caribbean—is an important one, but it is not ours here. The focus of this collection is African *American* philosophy. Ideally, a course on this subject would be coupled with one on African philosophy.

- Finally, there is an important period in the historical development of professional African American philosophy—roughly, between Alain Locke and the emergence of Cornel West as a leading academic voice in the 1980s—to which we have been unable to do justice. Instead, it has seemed to make a better "teaching volume" to provide from this period other, less narrowly academic writers: Garvey, Malcolm X, King, James Baldwin, Ellison.

Suggestions to the User. The following points might be helpful to instructors:

First, the book is designed to provide more than enough materials for a semester-long introductory course. Although a background in philosophy is always helpful, we think that only the Alain Locke essay, "Values and Imperatives," would be highly difficult reading for such an audience. Occasionally, where an author's heavy use of an unfamiliar term demanded it, we have provided guidance in our brief introduction to each section. The introductions are not meant to do anything more than provide a lead-in to each section, highlighting its main themes and touching on the main points of each essay.

Although we have designed our book in a specific format, some alterations may be very reasonable. Angela P. Harris's article, for example, is part of the section on feminism but could be used in the section on law as well. The one on feminism. The DuBois–Washington debate might be taken up earlier in the course than our location of it suggests. The affirmative action debate might be explored in the section on ethics and values, rather than the one on violence and social justice. More significantly, one might want to begin with the classic readings from Part II (Delaney and Douglass, at least). In fact, one might even want to begin with Part II in its entirety, then move back to the part on racial consciousness. What we would *not* suggest, however, is to try to cover the historical materials in strictly chronological order—for example, beginning with David Walker from Part III, then going back to Delaney and Douglass, and so forth. This would seriously interfere with the basically *thematic* organization of the text.

Each reading includes both "study questions" and "discussion questions." The first are designed simply to guide the students through the more important points and arguments of each reading. Answering these is a way of writing a short summary of the main points in the reading. The discussion questions are more probing. Typically, they challenge the student to come to terms with the weaknesses or especially controversial aspects of the reading. Here we have favored more leading questions and have generally eschewed the timeworn device of simply asking, "What do you think about the author's views on X?" Instructors who find our selections disproportionately favoring viewpoints different from their own may take some comfort in the fact that the vast majority of the discussion questions are critical.

Acknowledgments

Any interdisciplinary undertaking such as ours is bound to draw on many individuals' knowledge. First, we would like to thank the many reviewers of this manuscript whose suggestions we have always taken seriously and in many cases followed: Lewis Gordon, Brown University; Ann Hetzel Gunkel, Columbia College, Chicago; Barbara Hall, Georgia State University; Clevis Headley, Florida Atlantic University; Helen Mitchell, Howard Community College; and Naomi Zack, SUNY, Albany. We would also like to thank our colleagues at Tennessee State University in the English department (especially Helen Houston and Jocelyn Irby), whose counsel, books, and suggestions have been very helpful in regard to the chapter on aesthetics, and our colleagues in Africana Studies, Amiri Al-Hadid and Wosene Yefru, who have been very helpful in suggesting materials on black nationalism and Afrocentrism. Our part-time colleague in this department, Andy Lampkin, has been of assistance on issues pertaining to black theology. Kathy Bryant and especially Andrea Bednar of Shepherd Inc. have lent their editorial skills to the improvement of our often tangled prose. Finally, Peter Adams and Kerri Abdinoor of Wadsworth have been of invaluable assistance in shaping and encouraging this entire project.

INTRODUCTION: WHAT IS AFRICAN AMERICAN PHILOSOPHY?

We can begin by saying that African American philosophy is a *part* of the larger attempt to understand the African American experience: its history, its significance, and its value. In this respect, it is not different from African American history, literature, or other forms of cultural expression. What distinguishes *philosophy* from these is not an absolutely rigid barrier but more a matter of relative emphasis. The discipline of philosophy gives great emphasis to such factors as these:

1. While history or literature often *uses* broad, abstract concepts (such as "self-consciousness" or "justice"), the object in philosophy is to understand these and to be very conscious of one's use of them. Philosophers might typically distinguish several senses of a term such as "consciousness."
2. While other disciplines are certainly concerned with issues of values, philosophy is so in a more direct, *argumentative* fashion. Philosophers defend views on questions of good and bad, right and wrong, and so on—by way of explicit, rational argument.
3. While philosophy may have no distinctive means of expression, in the way that art has "painting," philosophy is unique in embracing *the whole*—that is, the methods, insights, and conclusions of all other disciplines, including not just the arts but the sciences as well. Where other disciplines leave off, one might say that philosophy begins.

African American philosophy, then, applies this kind of thinking and approach to the African American experience in all its dimensions. Obviously, philosophers do not paint pictures, invent, or record stories concerning this experience, although they are liable to be interested in all of these, and much more. Instead, philosophers are focused on certain general concepts implicated in this experience: consciousness, identity, community, alienation, assimilation, separation, justice, and racism, to name but some of the ones of greatest concern in this volume. Philosophers explore these general ideas partly to understand them in their own right, but also because they are interested in practical, "real-life" issues to which such an understanding is central.

African American philosophy involves a sustained, intense reflection on the African American experience, but does this mean that African American philosophy is uniquely the product of African Americans? Typically, it has fallen to members of a given group to take the lead in defining and discussing the nature of that group's experience—after all, it is *their* experience. Still, it would be very wrong and counterproductive, we think, to leap from this to the conclusion that *only* members of a group, or a culture, can have anything important to say concerning their experience. Among other bad consequences, this would *isolate* African American philosophy and philosophers even more than circumstances of history, culture, and prejudice have already done. It would also carry the unfortunate suggestion that African Americans should not seek to understand and define the experience of *others*. On this disturbing idea, everyone becomes walled within the limitations of their own cultural experience. Communication between groups becomes hazardous at best, for one always runs the risk of being denounced as "not being able to understand." With the failure of communication, democracy itself is imperiled.

Another error, we suggest, would be to think of African American philosophy as limited to the writings of *professional* philosophers—persons holding Ph.D.s in this discipline and earning a living teaching it. Although professional philosophers (those possessed of considerable formal training in the academic discipline of philosophy) may properly take the *lead* in this endeavor, it would be wrong to suppose that *only* such individuals have anything philosophically important or profound to say about the African American experience. Although not holding positions within academic philosophy departments, such African American thinkers as Cornel West, Toni Morrison, James Cone, Alice Walker, Henry Louis Gates, Derrick Bell, Patricia Williams, Albert Murray, and, on the more conservative side, Thomas Sowell are indisputably among today's most important *public* intellectuals. Increasingly, they help define our public debate on many issues, some with great philosophical import. In so doing, they carry on the tradition of Hamilton, Madison, Oliver Wendell Holmes, and John Dewey—as well as that of Frederick Douglass, W. E. B. DuBois, and Martin Luther King, Jr. The influence and importance of this tradition rest partly in the fact that it is not confined to one academic discipline—or to the academy at all.

Still a third error, we think, would be to tie the subject matter of African American philosophy *too* closely to "the perennial questions of philosophy" (free will, the existence of God, the foundations of morality, and so forth). To be sure, the concerns of African American philosophy, insofar as it is a form of *philosophy,* should ultimately link up with these perennial issues, but they should *also* connect with the issues of greatest concern to theorists not in philosophy at all. These include scholars working in such areas as gender studies, aesthetics and literary theory, theology, legal theory—and Africana studies. Truly, African American philosophy is *interdisciplinary.*

What, then, are the main issues or concerns of this growing area of philosophy? To begin, there are issues concerned with "consciousness." What is it *like* to be an African American? Here the philosophical discussion has been greatly shaped by W. E. B. DuBois' famous doctrine of "double-consciousness" (basically, that African Americans have a consciousness both of themselves as they are and of themselves as the larger, predominantly white world sees them). Such questions lead to the subject of *racism.* What is racism? How has it shaped the African American consciousness and the larger social world in which African Americans live? Racism, however, is not just a matter of consciousness and history but of social policy. What social policies, we will need to ask, must effectively combat racism? For instance, what is the proper role and importance of *affirmative action?*

These are but some of the core areas of concern in African American philosophy. From these core concerns, African American philosophy extends into such central areas of the black experience as the law and legal philosophy, aesthetics and the arts, and religion and theology. Thinking now of this subject as a *whole,* we think it is helpful to divide African American philosophy into *two* broad traditions.[1]

The first tradition tends to stress the *distinctive* history and culture of African Americans. In that respect, it turns inward and asks African Americans to do so. Its political expression is toward "nationalism" or "separatism" as it focuses on the idea that African Americans—whatever their relations with others—need to build something for themselves. Artistically, as one would expect, it stresses the obligations of the black artist to his or her community. Economically, its focus is on "self-help." Its political ethic focuses not so much on rights as on responsibilities—and especially on empowerment.

The second tradition tends to stress the rightful *place* of African Americans in the larger society in which they exist. Its political expression is toward *equality*—an equal share of the educational and economic opportunities that exist within the larger American society. Artistically, while it, too, celebrates black culture and the black artist, it also wants to be sensitive to the dangers of too narrowly confining the artist to a view of "the black community" and its needs—or of divorcing black art from the Western intellectual tradition. While this second tradition does not necessarily seek—and, in many cases, would even oppose—biological or cultural "assimilation" into the larger society, it would embrace the idea of *belonging* to what ought to become a more culturally diverse society. Economically, while not opposing "self-help," this view insists on the obligations of the larger society *to* the black community. Politically, while not opposing "empowerment," it seeks empowerment in part through coalitions with other disenfranchised groups. Ethically, it embraces—and opposes anyone who disparages—the framework of "rights."

---

[1] For a more complex account, see Cornel West, "The Four Traditions," in Part II, Reading 12 of the text.

PART I

FOUNDATIONS

Race and Racism

It is a peculiar sensation, this double-consciousness, this sense of always looking at one's self through the eyes of others, of measuring one's soul by the tape of a world that looks on in amused contempt and pity. One ever feels his two-ness,—an American, a Negro; two souls, two thoughts, two unreconciled strivings; two warring ideals in one dark body, whose dogged strength alone keeps it from being torn asunder.

W. E. B. DuBOIS

I never felt "two warring souls in one dark body" nor did I experience a conflict over my identity. Since I was a child I have always known that my heritage was not the same as that of whites. I never thought we came over here on the Mayflower.

MOLEFI K. ASANTE

The Negro people, as a race, have a contribution to make to civilization and humanity which no other race can make . . . and it is the duty of Americans of Negro descent, as a body, to maintain their race identity until the mission of the Negro people is accomplished.

W. E. B. DuBOIS

We are still trapped in the rigidity of notions of biological racial difference that presuppose pseudoscientific ideas of race. And the one-drop rule [whereby any black ancestors at all render one "black"] is still public policy. Whites assume that this is how blacks want it, and blacks continue to reproduce it socially for a variety of reasons. . . .

NAOMI ZACK

The antirace people therefore miss the point. Even if they show that race is a social construction, . . . even if they show that races are pseudosocientific fictions, they still need to address the ways in which phenomena understood as racial phenomena are lived. Not all black people know what races are, but they know what hatred of black people is.

LEWIS R. GORDON

If African American philosophy is fundamentally a set of reflections on the meaning of the African American experience, the readings in this chapter are of central importance to this subject, for what they concern is precisely the meaning of the African American experience—seen through the concept of *race.* Certainly, one appropriate beginning for any such reflections is W. E. B. DuBois' idea of the "two-ness" of African American consciousness. Actually, it may be noticed that, in our first reading, DuBois speaks of a *pair* of dualities. First, there is the idea of "double-consciousness": of seeing oneself through the eyes of another versus one's own true consciousness of self. Second, there is the split *within* one's own consciousness—the two warring ideals: "one Negro, one American."

In our second selection, "Racism, Consciousness, and Afrocentricity," Molefi K. Asante, largely credited as the founder and leading advocate of the Afrocentric movement in the United States, is sharply critical of what he calls "the illusion of DuBoisian double-consciousness." Asante records the development of his own consciousness as "unitary and holistic." Whatever the problems of other blacks, Asante describes himself as very clear in his identity: he is black; his whole world is black—not white. Rather than experiencing conflicting feelings of identity and difference, Asante describes his reaction to whites as one of "anger, hostility, and resentment." In the last part of his discussion, Asante addresses his concept of "race." Regardless of the mix of one's genetic background, he says, African Americans must regard themselves as one thing—"black": to speak otherwise is to make a futile attempt to hide from social and political realities.

Theorists have differed in their understanding of "race," emphasizing such different factors as biology, language, nation, and culture. There is a much wider agreement, at least today, that rac*ism*, because it involves the oppression of one race by another, is morally wrong. Our next two readings seek greater philosophical clarity, however, on just what "racism" is and what forms it can take.

In his contribution, Kwame Anthony Appiah—a Ghanian philosopher educated in England and a co-director of Harvard University's Center for Afro-American Studies—distinguishes "racialism" (the view that the world is divided into a small number of "races" distinguished by their unique inherited qualities) from two forms of racism—"extrinsic" and "intrinsic." Extrinsic racists treat race basically as an *indicator* of desirable or undesirable qualities. Appiah writes: "Evidence that there are no such differences in morally relevant characteristics—that Negroes do not necessarily lack intellectual capacities, that Jews are not especially avaricious—should lead people out of racism if it is purely extrinsic." By contrast, intrinsic racists treat race *itself* as making one more or less valuable than members of other races.

In his discussion of the same topic ("The Heart of Racism"), J. L. A. Garcia begins by noting some problems with thinking of racism as distinguished by certain ("prejudiced") *beliefs*. He proposes that, instead, we think of racism not only in terms of beliefs (and their rationality) but also in terms of our "wants, intentions, likes, and dislikes." Thus, Garcia defines *racism* as "a vicious kind of racially based disregard for the welfare of certain people." According to Garcia, racism is "always immoral," and a main virtue of his definition is that it explains *why* this is so: if hate, ill will, or just a lack of concern toward others is wrong, racism is wrong as a form of this. In contrast to

Appiah's view, Garcia would deny that favoritism for one's own group, when not coupled with ill feeling toward others, is racist.

In their contributions, Naomi Zack and Lewis R. Gordon analyze, from somewhat different perspectives, the status of persons of "mixed race"—that is, people whose parents are of different races. Zack begins by alluding to the "myths" surrounding racial classification—especially the so-called one-drop rule, according to which anyone with a single "drop of black blood" is considered black, regardless of whether he or she possesses any heritable "black traits." Strictly speaking, she points out, "race" is not inherited; what is inherited is simply certain traits, such as skin color, which society has used to construct a concept of race. Ultimately, her concern is that persons should not be forced—by the "one-drop rule" or any other official policy—to deny who they are and where they come from.

In his discussion, Lewis R. Gordon—an imortant new voice of the "black existentialist" school[1]—raises a number of skeptical points regarding the mixed race category. For Gordon, this category needs to be understood relative to certain more basic realities governing the present world. In that world, he points out, racial differences are not mere differences; they are *directional.* Insofar as "white" designates a kind of reference point, almost a "god-like perspective," from which *other* races are viewed, to be white (in a white world) means—Gordon points out—precisely to *not* have a race. By contrast, "blackness" is seen as the lowest rung on the social ladder—hence the expression "the untouchables are the blacks of India." From this standpoint, then, Gordon notes, a white and black mixture is metaphysically problematic: if "white" is not a race, the white parent must fundamentally surrender kinship with his or her child. Thus seen, the child "is already black"—especially as blacks constitute a mixed group (with its own internal hierarchy of color) to begin with. In the end, following a close discussion of six points on which the concept of mixed race might be thought to engender a healthy clarity concerning racial matters, Gordon concludes that it will not. In particular, he suggests, if a cardinal principle of the racist outlook is "Don't be black," the idea of mixed race turns out to be very compatible with this outlook.

---

[1] The philosophical movement termed "existentialism" is broadly concerned with the nature of individual human existence, especially with the individual's struggle "to exist" against the various forces—social, political, religious, even philosophical—which may seek to prevent this. The "black existentialist"—following in the steps of anti-colonialist psychologist and philosopher Frantz Fanon—aims to describe the nature of black existence, especially in the face of white racism. Thus, consider Gordon's remarks quoted at the start of the introduction.

1   *From* The Souls of Black Folk

W. E. B. DuBois

Study Questions

1. What experiences led DuBois to understand what it meant "to be a problem"?
2. What is "second sight"?
3. What is "double-consciousness" and is it the same as second sight?
4. What, according to DuBois, is the dilemma faced by African American artisans, artists, and professionals in their work?

Of Our Spiritual Strivings

O water, voice of my heart, crying in the sand,
  All night long crying with a mournful cry,
As I lie and listen, and cannot understand
    The voice of my heart in my side or the
    voice of the sea,
  O water, crying for rest, is it I, is it I?
    All night long the water is crying to me.

Unresting water, there shall never be rest
  Till the last moon droop and the last tide fail,
And the fire of the end begin to burn in the west;
    And the heart shall be weary and wonder
    and cry like the sea,
  All life long crying without avail,
    As the water all night long is crying to me.

ARTHUR SYMONS

Between me and the other world there is ever an unasked question: unasked by some through feelings of delicacy; by others through the difficulty of rightly framing it. All, nevertheless, flutter round it. They approach me in a half-hesitant sort of way, eye me curiously or compassionately, and then, instead of saying directly, How does it feel to be a problem? they say, I know an excellent colored man in my town; or, I fought at Mechanicsville; or, Do not these Southern outrages make your blood boil? At these I smile, or am interested, or reduce the boiling to a simmer, as the occasion may require. To the real question, How does it feel to be a problem? I answer seldom a word.

And yet, being a problem is a strange experience,—peculiar even for one who has never been anything else, save perhaps in babyhood and in Europe. It is in the early days of rollicking boyhood that the revelation first bursts upon one, all in a day, as it were. I remember well when the shadow swept across me. I was a little thing, away up in the hills of New England, where the dark Housatonic winds between Hoosac and Taghkanic to the sea. In a wee wooden schoolhouse, something put it into the boys' and girls' heads to buy gorgeous visiting-cards—ten cents a package—and exchange. The exchange was merry, till one girl, a tall newcomer, refused my card,—refused it peremptorily, with a glance. Then it dawned upon me with a certain suddenness that I was different from the others; or like, mayhap, in heart and life and longing, but shut out from their world by a vast veil. I had thereafter no desire to tear down that veil, to creep through; I held all beyond it in common contempt, and lived above it in a region of blue sky and great wandering shadows. That sky was bluest when I could beat my mates at examination-time, or beat them at a foot-race, or even beat their stringy heads. Alas, with the years all this fine contempt began to fade; for the worlds I longed for, and all their dazzling opportunities, were theirs, not mine. But they should not keep these prizes, I said; some, all, I would wrest from them. Just how I would do it I could never decide: by reading law, by healing the sick, by telling the wonderful tales that swam in my head,—some way. With other black boys the

From *The Souls of Black Folk*, originally published by A. C. McClurg, 1903.

strife was not so fiercely sunny: their youth shrunk into tasteless sycophancy, or into silent hatred of the pale world about them and mocking distrust of everything white; or wasted itself in a bitter cry, Why did God make me an outcast and a stranger in mine own house? The shades of the prison-house closed round about us all: walls strait and stubborn to the whitest, but relentlessly narrow, tall, and unscalable to sons of night who must plod darkly on in resignation, or beat unavailing palms against the stone, or steadily, half hopelessly, watch the streak of blue above.

After the Egyptian and Indian, the Greek and Roman, the Teuton and Mongolian, the Negro is a sort of seventh son, born with a veil, and gifted with second-sight in this American world,—a world which yields him no true self-consciousness, but only lets him see himself through the revelation of the other world. It is a peculiar sensation, this double-consciousness, this sense of always looking at one's self through the eyes of others, of measuring one's soul by the tape of a world that looks on in amused contempt and pity. One ever feels his twoness,—an American, a Negro; two souls, two thoughts, two unreconciled strivings; two warring ideals in one dark body, whose dogged strength alone keeps it from being torn asunder.

The history of the American Negro is the history of this strife,—this longing to attain self-conscious manhood, to merge his double self into a better and truer self. In this merging he wishes neither of the older selves to be lost. He would not Africanize America, for America has too much to teach the world and Africa. He would not bleach his Negro soul in a flood of white Americanism, for he knows that Negro blood has a message for the world. He simply wishes to make it possible for a man to be both a Negro and an American, without being cursed and spit upon by his fellows, without having the doors of Opportunity closed roughly in his face.

This, then, is the end of his striving: to be a co-worker in the kingdom of culture, to escape both death and isolation, to husband and use his best powers and his latent genius. These powers of body and mind have in the past been strangely wasted, dispersed, or forgotten. The shadow of a mighty Negro past flits through the tale of Ethiopia the Shadowy and of Egypt the Sphinx. Throughout history, the powers of single black men flash here and there like falling stars, and die sometimes before the world has rightly gauged their brightness. Here in America, in the few days since Emancipation, the black man's turning hither and thither in hesitant and doubtful striving has often made his very strength to lose effectiveness, to seem like absence of power, like weakness. And yet it is not weakness,—it is the contradiction of double aims. The double-aimed struggle of the black artisan—on the one hand to escape white contempt for a nation of mere hewers of wood and drawers of water, and on the other hand to plough and nail and dig for a poverty-stricken horde—could only result in making him a poor craftsman, for he had but half a heart in either cause. By the poverty and ignorance of his people, the Negro minister or doctor was tempted toward quackery and demagogy; and by the criticism of the other world, toward ideals that made him ashamed of his lowly tasks. The would-be black *savant* was confronted by the paradox that the knowledge his people needed was a twice-told tale to his white neighbors, while the knowledge which would teach the white world was Greek to his own flesh and blood. The innate love of harmony and beauty that set the ruder souls of his people a-dancing and a-singing raised but confusion and doubt in the soul of the black artist; for the beauty revealed to him was the soul-beauty of a race which his larger audience despised, and he could not articulate the message of another people. This waste of double aims, this seeking to satisfy two unreconciled ideals, has wrought sad havoc with the courage and faith and deeds of ten thousand thousand people,—has sent them often wooing false gods and invoking false means of salvation, and at times has even seemed about to make them ashamed of themselves.

Away back in the days of bondage they thought to see in one divine event the end of all doubt and disappointment; few men ever worshipped Freedom with half such unquestioning faith as did the American Negro for two centuries. To him, so far as he thought and dreamed, slavery was indeed the sum of all villainies, the cause of all sorrow, the root of all prejudice; Emancipation was the key to a promised land of sweeter beauty than ever stretched before the eyes of wearied Israelites. In song and exhortation swelled one refrain—Liberty; in his tears and curses the God he implored had Freedom in his right hand. At last it came,—suddenly, fearfully, like a dream. With one wild carnival of blood and passion came the message in his own plaintive cadences:—

> "Shout, O children!
> Shout, you're free!
> For God has bought your liberty!"

Years have passed away since then,—ten, twenty, forty; forty years of national life, forty years of renewal and development, and yet the swarthy spectre sits in its accustomed seat at the Nation's feast. In vain do we cry to this our vastest social problem:—

> "Take any shape but that, and my firm nerves
> Shall never tremble!"

The Nation has not yet found peace from its sins; the freedman has not yet found in freedom his promised land. Whatever of good may have come in these years of change, the shadow of a deep disappointment rests upon the Negro people,—a disappointment all the more bitter because the unattained ideal was unbounded save by the simple ignorance of a lowly people.

The first decade was merely a prolongation of the vain search for freedom, the boon that seemed ever barely to elude their grasp,—like a tantalizing will-o'-the-wisp, maddening and misleading the headless host. The holocaust of war, the terrors of the Ku-Klux Klan, the lies of carpetbaggers, the disorganization of industry, and the contradictory advice of friends and foes, left the bewildered serf with no new watchword beyond the old cry for freedom. As the time flew, however, he began to grasp a new idea. The ideal of liberty demanded for its attainment powerful means, and these the Fifteenth Amendment gave him. The ballot, which before he had looked upon as a visible sign of freedom, he now regarded as the chief means of gaining and perfecting the liberty with which war had partially endowed him. And why not? Had not votes made war and emancipated millions? Had not votes en-franchised the freedmen? Was anything impossible to a power that had done all this? A million black men started with renewed zeal to vote themselves into the kingdom. So the decade flew away, the revolution of 1876 came, and left the half-free serf weary, wondering, but still inspired. Slowly but steadily, in the following years, a new vision began gradually to replace the dream of political power,—a powerful movement, the rise of another ideal to guide the unguided, another pillar of fire by night after a clouded day. It was the ideal of "book-learning"; the curiosity, born of compulsory ignorance, to know and test the power of the cabalistic letters of the white man, the longing to know. Here at last seemed to have been discovered the mountain path to Canaan; longer than the highway of Emancipation and law, steep and rugged, but straight, leading to heights high enough to overlook life.

Up the new path the advance guard toiled, slowly, heavily, doggedly; only those who have watched and guided the faltering feet, the misty minds, the dull understandings, of the dark pupils of these schools know how faithfully, how piteously, this people strove to learn. It was weary work. The cold statistician wrote down the inches of progress here and there, noted also where here and there a foot had slipped or some one had fallen. To the tired climbers, the horizon was ever dark, the mists were often cold, the Canaan was always dim and far away. If, however, the vistas disclosed as yet no goal, no resting-place, little but flattery and criticism, the journey at least gave leisure for reflection and self-examination; it changed the child of Emancipation to the youth with dawning self-consciousness, self-realization, self-respect. In those sombre forests of his striving his own soul rose before him, and he saw himself,—darkly as through a veil; and yet he saw in himself some faint revelation of his power, of his mission. He began to have a dim feeling that, to attain his place in the world, he must be himself, and not another. For the first time he sought to analyze the burden he bore upon his back, that dead-weight of social degradation partially masked behind a half-named Negro problem. He felt his poverty; without a cent, without a home, without land, tools, or savings, he had entered into competition with rich, landed, skilled neighbors. To be a poor man is hard, but to be a poor race in a land of dollars is the very bottom of hardships. He felt the weight of his ignorance,—not simply of letters, but of life, of business, of the humanities; the accumulated sloth and shirking and awkwardness of decades and centuries shackled his hands and feet. Nor was his burden all poverty and ignorance. The red stain of bastardy, which two centuries of systematic legal defilement of Negro women had stamped upon his race, meant not only the loss of ancient African chastity, but also the hereditary weight of a mass of corruption from white adulterers, threatening almost the obliteration of the Negro home.

A people thus handicapped ought not to be asked to race with the world, but rather allowed to give all its time and thought to its own social problems. But alas! while sociologists gleefully count his bastards and his prostitutes, the very soul of the toiling, sweating black man is darkened by the shadow of a vast despair. Men call the shadow prejudice, and learnedly explain it as the natural defence of culture against barbarism, learning against ignorance, purity against crime, the "higher" against the "lower" races. To which the Negro cries Amen! and swears that to so much of this strange prejudice as is founded on just homage to civilization, culture, righteousness, and progress, he humbly bows and meekly does obeisance. But before that nameless prejudice that leaps beyond all this he stands helpless, dismayed, and well-nigh speechless; before that personal disrespect and mockery, the ridicule and systematic humiliation, the distortion of fact and wanton license of fancy, the cynical ignoring of the better and the boisterous welcoming of the worse, the all-pervading desire to inculcate disdain for everything black, from Toussaint to the devil,—before this there rises a sickening despair that would disarm and discourage any nation save that black host to whom "discouragement" is an unwritten word.

But the facing of so vast a prejudice could not but bring the inevitable self-questioning, self-disparagement, and lowering of ideals which ever accompany repression and breed in an atmosphere of contempt and hate. Whisperings and portents came borne upon the four winds: Lo! we are diseased and dying, cried the dark hosts; we cannot write, our voting is vain; what need of education, since we must always cook and serve? And the Nation echoed and enforced this self-criticism, saying: Be content to be servants, and nothing more; what need of higher culture for half-men? Away with the black man's ballot, by force or fraud,—and behold the suicide of a race! Nevertheless, out of the evil came something of good,—the more careful adjustment of education to real life, the clearer perception of the Negroes' social responsibilities, and the sobering realization of the meaning of progress.

So dawned the time of _Sturm und Drang:_ storm and stress to-day rocks our little boat on the mad waters of the world-sea; there is within and without the sound of conflict, the burning of body and rending of soul; inspiration strives with doubt, and faith with vain questionings. The bright ideals of the past,—physical freedom, political power, the training of brains and the training of hands,—all these in turn have waxed and waned, until even the last grows dim and overcast. Are they all wrong,—all false? No, not that, but each alone was over-simple and incomplete,—the dreams of a credulous race-childhood, or the fond imaginings of the other world which does not know and does not want to know our power. To be really true, all these ideals must be melted and welded into one. The training of the schools we need to-day more than ever,—the training of deft hands, quick eyes and ears, and above all the broader, deeper, higher culture of gifted minds and pure hearts. The power of the ballot we need in sheer self-defence,—else what shall save us from a second slavery? Freedom, too, the long-sought, we still seek,—the freedom of life and limb, the freedom to work and think, the freedom to love and aspire. Work, culture, liberty,—all these we need, not singly but together, not successively but together, each growing and aiding each, and all striving toward that vaster ideal that swims before the Negro people, the ideal of human brotherhood, gained through the unifying ideal of Race; the ideal of fostering and developing the traits and talents of the Negro, not in opposition to or contempt for other races, but rather in large conformity to the greater ideals of the American Republic, in order that some day on American soil two world-races may give each to each those characteristics both so sadly lack. We the darker ones come even now not altogether empty-handed: there are to-day no truer exponents of the pure human spirit of the Declaration of Independence than the American Negroes; there is no true American music but the wild sweet melodies of the Negro slave; the American fairy tales and folklore are Indian and African; and, all in all, we black men seem the sole oasis of simple faith and reverence in a dusty desert of dollars and smartness. Will America be poorer if she replace her brutal dyspeptic blundering with light-hearted but determined Negro humility? or her coarse and cruel wit with loving jovial good-humor? or her vulgar music with the soul of the Sorrow Songs?

Merely a concrete test of the underlying principles of the great republic is the Negro Problem, and the spiritual striving of the freedmen's sons is the travail of souls whose burden is almost beyond the measure of their strength, but who bear it in the name of an historic race, in the name of this the land of their fathers' fathers, and in the name of human opportunity.

And now what I have briefly sketched in large outline let me on coming pages tell again in many ways, with loving emphasis and deeper detail, that men may listen to the striving in the souls of black folk.

Discussion Questions

1. DuBois speaks of "warring ideals" within the African American's soul. How would you describe these "ideals"? What relation do they have to "double-consciousness"?
2. DuBois says that "Negro blood has a message for the world." What do you think this message is and in what sense is it a message of all those sharing a common blood, regardless of nationality and differences of culture?
3. He also says that he would not "Africanize America, for America has too much to teach the world and Africa." What do you suppose he has in mind?
4. DuBois suggests that the black scientist (savant) is faced with a choice between pursuing the knowledge needed by his or her people (which is liable to be "old stuff" to the white scientific community) or pursuing the interests of the latter (which is liable to be unintelligible to his or her own people). To what extent is this a valid contrast today? Insofar as it is a valid contrast, what is the black scientist/professional supposed to do?

2   Racism, Consciousness, and Afrocentricity

MOLEFI KETE ASANTE

Study Questions

1. What early experiences shaped Asante's views on race?

2. How did the white view of blacks in Valdosta differ from blacks' view of themselves?
3. Why does Asante reject the Christian church?
4. What does Asante mean by the "terror of reality"?
5. Why is DuBois' idea of "double-consciousness" an illusion, according to Asante?
6. Why does Asante reject the idea of a mixed race designation?

From *Lure and Loathing*, Gerald Early, ed. (New York: Penguin Press, 1993), pp. 127–143.

A Frame of Reference

I was born in Valdosta, Georgia, on August 14, 1942. My great-great-grandmother, Frances Chapman, had given birth to my great-grandfather, Plenty Smith, in 1866. My grandfather Moses Smith had moved his family from Dooly County, Georgia, to Valdosta, in Lowndes County. The Smith family had strong Asante and Mandinka ancestry despite the disruptions of slavery. My father, for whom I was first named, Arthur Lee Smith, married Lillie Wilkson, whose maternal grandmother was Muskogee. I was their first child, although my mother had three daughters, and my father, a son older than me. Eventually between them there were sixteen children in all. I lived in Georgia and Tennessee until May 1960, when I graduated from high school in Nashville, Tennessee.

My early experiences certainly contributed to my racial consciousness by bringing me at once into the quicksand of the social environment that was the United States in the late 1940s and early 1950s. Subsequent events were to underscore the lessons of my ritual of passage into the world of southern racism, where whites often exhibited an anti-African phobia unfathomable to me as a young boy of Valdosta, Georgia, and Nashville, Tennessee. I went to a church boarding school in Nashville when I was eleven years old. Every summer and holiday I would return to Valdosta to crop tobacco and to pick cotton in order to have spending money for the next school year.

Realization

The whites I saw in this small Georgia town in the 1950s were neither more intelligent nor more industrious than the Africans I knew. The whites were wealthier and consequently more powerful by virtue of the false status bestowed by race in America. Living and growing up in Valdosta ruined the self-esteem of some Africans and brought our self-confidence into question. But in the end we were to have no problem of con-

sciousness, the reality of being black in Georgia was too intimate, personal, defining. I did not reject my blackness; I embraced it.

To remind us of just how cruel the whites could be in the South, an African man was killed and his body dragged through the dirt roads of the two black sections of town, Southside and Westside. I was barely six when this happened, but the fumes rising from the anger in the black community colored the mental skies of a thousand children for several years. The damnable deed rained down hatred among us every time the story was told of how the poor victim had pleaded his innocence before they killed him. Whenever I heard the name Kill-Me-Quick, the area in Valdosta that the lynched man is said to have come from, I thought of it as some distant, foreboding community instead of the small satellite community of the Southside it really was. I never knew how it got its name, only that the name conjured up some strange sense of terror.

So lynching registered early and substantially on my mind; the effect of the monstrous crimes against innocent and often defenseless African Americans was permanent. Several years would pass before I understood the extent of the mental chains with which we had been shackled: African men and women harassed, mutilated, murdered in the stark piney-woods country or under the shade of the Spanish-mossed oaks.

The Element of Race

Shaped in the mold of segregation, I knew at a very early age that the world of America was black and white. The technicolor revolution of the Asians and Latinos had not penetrated the thick, gloomy fog of reality that hung over the question of race in Valdosta in those days. It would not be until I attended college in California that I would experience the multicolored reality that was becoming America. Here I was for all practical purposes a made-in-America person. Yet the making itself had not convinced me that I was truly a part of the process that governed the society. Black and white, two colors, two origins, two destinies, that is what intervened in the midst of reflections on place for a young African in the south of Georgia.

We were for all practical purposes the whole world. And when the young people of our church sang, "And he got the whole world in his hands," we knew that it meant both the Southside and the Westside and maybe the white people who occupied those big houses on Ashley and Patterson streets. I was sixteen before I ever knew anything about Chinese or Mexicans. In fact, the only Jew I had ever seen, besides the Nordic Jew Jesus whose picture hung on the wall of the church, was the man who ran Lazarus Brothers Pawn Shop on Ashley Street in Valdosta. This was the one store on the main street of the city that largely catered to a black clientele. Japanese we had heard of because of the war. They had been the comic characters in our books, the wild-eyed killers of the war comics. My impression of the Japanese was certainly warped by the information that went into my young mind. Puerto Ricans did not exist in Valdosta. Blacks and Protestant whites, that was it for the entire city, with the exception of the one Jew.

What I knew about race relations was just about all that the whites knew, too, I suspected. Their world was also black and white. We worked for the whites; they never worked for us. I observed this every time I was awakened at five-thirty in the morning by my mother so that I would not miss the truck that took us young children to the tobacco or cotton fields. A black man usually drove the truck to the farm. It would be an old truck, often a small pickup, loaded with about twenty or twenty-five people. Arriving at the fields before the sun came up, we would all pile out of the truck and put our cotton sacks on or hitch our mules to the sled, depending on whether it was cotton or tobacco. After a full day's work in the fields we were dead tired, dirty, hungry, and ready to be paid. A white man paid our driver, and would pay us when we had weighed the cotton of the day or accounted for the "cropped" tobacco.

Life had been like this since Emancipation. Sharecroppers and tenant farmers and hired laborers served the interests of the white farmers who made the economy of the region. Neither the whites nor we could have given a clear dissertation or disputation on the state of the world, so locked we were into the social cage of our existence.

Being about My Own Business

When I was twelve years old I thought I had to be about my own business. Work had never been far from our house. It sat outside our door at six o'-clock every morning in the summer as a big truck with workers piled on it. Let us say that I had heard about twelve's being the age that a child becomes conscious of right and wrong, and let us say that this had a powerful impact upon my brain. In fact, at church they said Jesus had been about "his father's business" at that age. I had to be baptized and I had to get a job.

Nothing in the Bible my father and mother kept on the small table alongside the wall of the front room could have prepared me for the shape, the deep grooves, of the hatred whites held for us by virtue of our color. Although I was later to be told that it was also because of their fear of Africans, resulting from the five hundred years of war on African people, I am not so sure, however, that the Valdosta whites knew anything about five hundred years of domination. They knew about the whites' place and the blacks' place. It was all about location, and in their minds God had decreed these "places."

By twelve I had mastered the litany of possibilities for the African American: a schoolteacher, a preacher, a funeral-home director, and maybe a lawyer. My family had three or four root men and women and I was said to have been born with a veil over my face, meaning that I would probably be a root doctor or a preacher. Moses Smith, my grandfather, had practiced the roots openly and was known as a strong follower of the spirits. But his father, Plenty, my great-grandfather, carried even more authority in his combination of roots and Baptist tradition. He relied upon his own spiritual sights to heal and counsel people who made pilgrimages to his Dooly County home. Moses had made a convergence between dream books, Christianity in its Church of Christ fundamentalism, roots, hoodoo, and Yoruba. My father, Arthur, only dabbled in the spirits, often being told by his elders that he did not have enough faith in the healing or spiritual powers of the unseen.

With my father's lack of interest in the roots and stubborn rationalism I was not encouraged in the root line of work though it seemed to be a logical path for me. Eager to work and to show my own contribution to the family's economy, I started on the road to my profession with a shoebox that held shoe polish, a rag, and an old brush. I found a white barbershop down on Ashley Street willing to give me a chance to work on the shoes of the white customers. My very first customer, demonstrating for others in the shop his contempt for Africans, even a child, spat on my head as I leaned over his shoes. I knew what had happened. I did not say a word as I gathered up my shoeshine box, forgot about my payment, and walked out of the barbershop to the laughter of the man and a few other customers. My father, I remembered, was proud of me.

Unwelcomed as a child in the most elementary economic position one could have in the Deep South of the late 1950s, I came to expect nothing from whites. In fact, whites in the South were seen as the natural enemies of Africans. One spoke to them as if to strangers from another planet. They could wreak havoc in one's life with a word, a signal, a sign, or a whisper to the sheriff that you were "a bad nigger." I had come from a family of "bad niggers," whose Asante and Creek roots meant that there was a whole history of resistance to white hatred. Our family lived in poverty but never in shame; we were hard workers and prided ourselves on our ability to outwork anyone. If hard physical labor could make one rich, then all of my brothers and sisters would have been millionaires. Discrimination, prejudice, segregation, and the doctrine of white racial supremacy were neither innocuous nor benign in those days; they were real legacies rooted in the

great enslavement of Africans. And often what we thought was benevolence on the part of whites, who would give our church their secondhand clothes, often turned out to be another statement of their alleged superiority.

Insight and Introspection

The tightly knit community of Africans who lived on the dirt roads of Valdosta never saw themselves as intellectually or physically inferior to whites. There existed no reference points outside of ourselves despite the economic and psychological poverty of our situation. Our social, political, and economic situations could be explained in terms of white racial preference. Whether this was true or not in every case, we believed it. For example, if only whites worked in the banks downtown as tellers and managers, we knew that it was because Africans were never given a chance. The proof came later when Africans were given jobs in the banks and department stores; the incredible thing is that whites were amazed that we could be successful in those positions, such was their ignorance. Whatever advantage whites had was directly tied to race. My grandfather Moses, a favorite name for males in my family, had often told us sitting around the fireplace eating boiled peanuts that if they gave a black person a chance to enter any sport—tennis, swimming, or golf—they would do just as well as the whites, if not better. It was a problem of access and money, he would say. Although we recognized our degradation, I do not ever recall wanting to be like whites; they were neither beautiful nor strong nor decent people.

I was a young adult when I really felt the rage against prejudice inside me. But I never allowed it to control me. My father had instructed me too well for that to happen. I controlled and directed the rage with committed vows made in the name of my great-great-grandmother, Frances Chapman, who lived and died in the piney woods of Dooly County, Georgia, about eighty miles north of Valdosta. Among the vows, I remember, was never to allow white racial supremacy to go unchallenged. As a student in elementary and high school in Tennessee, where I had gone from Georgia when I was eleven, my friends looked to me in any confrontation with whites because I maintained an understanding in my relationships with whites that demanded mutual respect. During the school year I attended the Nashville Christian Institute and received religious education. My religious training dampened any desire I had for confrontation, although I was always taught to defend myself.

Becoming a Christian at eleven, I tried preaching, since the ministry was a natural extension of the roots tradition, in which I felt right at home, until I became disenchanted with religion generally and the way it was practiced in the Church of Christ specifically. After several years I gave up the attempt and endeavored rather to demonstrate propriety and good judgment in the face of ignorance. Relocating myself from the Christian religion became a substantive pathway to many future liberations. Whites did not only control the money in the country, they also controlled the religion. I wanted no part of the mind control that went along with a religion that had become the deification of white culture, including white dislike, hatred, and fear of Africa and Africans.

It seemed to me that whites demonstrated their fear of us in their inability to allow us to share space in almost any enterprise. The whites in Valdosta who rose above the petty, pedestrian attitudes toward Africans were often ostracized by their neighbors. A few of them were labeled "nigger lovers" by other whites. One year I saw the Ku Klux Klan marching down the streets in their white robes shouting vile remarks about "nigger lovers" and "niggers." I thought of them, I remember, as a pathetic band of misfits; I was curious, however, about who they were behind those hoods. The Klan was not just against Africans, that little circle of frightened men was against whites who thought Africans were intelligent, human, moral, and equal to whites.

The Terror of Reality

It has taken me considerable time to understand that the fundamental terror which resides in the white mind in terms of black-white relationships is rejection, that is, the fear that we will reject white values, standards, and ideas. But it is a deeper fear than, say, the fear that one might not be able to succeed in some venture; it is an existential fear, the fear that one might cease to exist without us to give them their sense of identity. To me, quite frankly, it mattered little how much whites feared the lack of existence because of their treatment of Africans. Almost every white I met felt some guilt about the condition of Africans but felt helpless to do anything about it. They recognized the historical nature of the racism that was daily poured into the African's cup. Every day brought other revelations, and whether it was social services or education, economics or housing, the situation was the same.

The attack on Africans in the academy, that is, the absolute difficulty some white professors have in granting excellence to African students or the immense problems whites have in giving tenure to African American scholars, is directly related to the fear of rejection. More amazingly, despite the Civil War, whites never allowed or wanted Africans to be truly "free" in America. Physical freedom did not mean psychological freedom, either for blacks or whites. Thus, confrontation is inevitable on almost every front because the white American is stuck with the heritage of the enslavement, unable to let the slave go free, and thereby refusing to see himself or herself alongside the African. They are forced by this position to oppose the African's leadership, creativity, innovation, and direction. Yet the African has vowed to be free. This is the source of conflict. I made that vow of freedom in the sandy pineywoods country when I was fourteen.

The feeling that you are in quicksand is inescapable in the quagmire of a racist society. You think that you can make progress in the interpretation of what's happening now only to discover that every step you take sinks the possibility of escaping. You are a victim despite your best efforts to educate those around you to the obvious intellectual mud stuck in their minds. For me, however, the course has always been rather clear, thanks to Arthur Smith and Lillie Smith's giving me the Francis Chapman and Plenty Smith stories when I grew up in Valdosta, Georgia.

The Illusion of Double-Consciousness

I was never affected by the Du Boisian double-consciousness. I never felt "two warring souls in one dark body" nor did I experience a conflict over my identity. Since I was a child I have always known that my heritage was not the same as that of whites. I never thought we came over here on the *Mayflower*. When I got up in the mornings to go to the cotton and tobacco fields, little white children got up to go fishing in the lakes or to camp. I knew that much from seeing them at the swimming pool, at the lakes, and at the parks as I rode those trucks back and forth to work. That was the experience it seemed of the white children I either saw or heard about; however, certainly somewhere in Georgia there must have been other whites with work experiences similar to mine. The point, though, is that most of the labor in the South during that period was performed by Africans. There were and remain in this country dual societies, one white and richer, one black and poorer. Perhaps in a great number of Africans these societies and the "two warring souls" converge to create a caldron of psychological problems; this was not the case with me or my family even when we were dysfunctional.

Valdosta, in all of its transparency, made my consciousness unitary and holistic. The starkness of the contrast was as evident as the paved streets in the white section of town and the muddy dirt roads on our side. My identity was solid, not fluid. My parents never gave any indication of suffering from low self-esteem or low self-confidence; they suffered from a severe income deficiency. Did I

think that I shared something with these whites? Was I that crazy? Did I believe that I was an American in the same way whites were? Did I want to be like whites? No, we did not even go to the same Christian churches; our religion, although called Christian, was different. It might have been another matter if I had gone to school and to church with whites when I was younger. I might have suffered confusion, double-consciousness, but I did not.

The *orishas* captured us and sent us on a different way. The whites had no *orishas*. Our music was different. Our parties were different. Our clothes were different. Were there then two warring souls in my bosom? No, anger, resentment, and hatred for the people I thought had to be the most callous, inhuman, brutal beings on earth, that was in my heart. Was I conflicted about my identity? Not for one moment did I experience any sense of personal or cultural confusion about my origins, community, and struggle. There were no "two warring souls" in my personality. This is not to say that the hypocrisy of the United States in not living up to its guarantee of African freedom was not often present in my mind, but I was clear about the reality of America.

One discovers in this kind of situation that there is no beginning and no end, or so it seems. To think that a young person growing up in the South could decipher the situation in any realistic way is to attribute too much to experience and not enough to reading history and culture. This I was to come to much later in my life. But I had seen enough, heard enough, and felt enough to understand my predicament. Because I had such an insular upbringing in many respects, that is, the segregated schools kept me away from the longing to be white or to be accepted by whites that Du Bois must have felt in Great Barrington, Massachusetts. My whole world was black except on rare occasions when a lone white would enter our neighborhood to collect the insurance money, to hire an employee, to deliver some secondhand clothes, or to campaign politically.

Avoiding Psychological Trouble

I knew, however, that it would be necessary to avoid becoming either a misoriented African or a disoriented African in the maturing process. One could be misoriented by receiving and accepting false information. I had to cautiously weigh information that was presented to me. I had seen many young people, my own age at the time, totally disoriented about America. Disorientation occurred when a person got the wrong information, accepted it, and tried to act on the basis of it. My reading included everything from the King James version of the Bible to Marx and Fanon. We were into Fanon in the late sixties. His early death gave him a kind of martyr's status with me. Here was this clear mind, this brilliant analyst, who would help Africans to see how to liberate themselves. In a fundamental way, Fanon was one of the guides that I used to chart my own path out of the maze of disinformation and misinformation that surrounded me. Observing as a young man of the sixties, I could see an anti-Africanite in every opposition to our freedom and equality. I could discern the bogus use of equality as it was emerging in the counter use of the term to mean that affirmative action was reverse discrimination. The more sophisticated white reactionaries seemed to call it reverse racism. Of course, it was neither. Affirmative action was a down payment on the reparations that should have been granted to Africans who had worked in this country for 244 years for free. My youth had prepared me for the sixties.

The racist anti-Africanite was clearly in the ascendancy in the South of my youth. Almost every white person who occupied a political position was an anti-Africanite. Sometimes they campaigned for office on the grounds that they would be sure to "keep the niggers in their places." Could I possibly have been confused about where the sheriff of Lowndes County, Georgia, stood on issues of race? Only if I was crazy. This is not to say that "crazy" black people did not exist then. As now, we had individuals who felt that the "Lord gave the whites the power to rule" over us. If it were not so, they argued, then it would not be so. I saw the irrationality of our condition at an early age and was reminded that my great-grandfather, Plenty, did not like fools or ignorant people. His style was to maintain distance from the source of his irritation. I learned that lesson on one of my many visits as a child to my great-grandfather's farm in Dooly County, Georgia.

I am sure that there were misoriented Africans in Valdosta during that time. By *misoriented* I mean Africans who believed that it was better to identify with the "masters" rather than with the "slaves." I remember one black man who went around trying to convince other Africans that a certain white racist was better than another white racist because at least the white racist he was supporting for election "had never beat a Negro." Presumably, the other white racist had physically whipped some of his field hands.

The racist anti-Africanite finds the activities of the misoriented African comforting for his or her anti-Africanism. The misoriented African, much like Sartre's inauthentic Jew, runs away from his or her Africanity by attempting to deny it, conceal it, or attack it. Unlike the Jew, who seldom wishes to destroy his or her Jewishness, the misoriented African assumes that he or she is not African and therefore takes exception to those who remind him or her that he or she bears all of the major characteristics of resemblance to those who are African. Thus, the misoriented African, that is, the inauthentic African, allows the dominance of the single-consciousness of Europe to conquer him or her. At that moment, and not before, the misoriented African becomes for all practical purposes the spitting image of the racist anti-Africanite. Neither a victim of double-consciousness nor attuned to the consciousness of his or her own historical experiences, which would center the person, the misoriented African becomes disoriented and believes that he or she is actually a European.

Since one can only have one heritage despite the multiplicity of cultural backgrounds that go into that heritage, to assume that one possesses more than one heritage is to suggest contradictions in the person's heritage. Actually our heritage might be composed of many backgrounds but in the end we inherit a unified field of culture, that is, one whole fabric of the past rather than split sheets or bits and pieces. Otherwise what we inherit is not very useful.

Despite denial of Africanity, others see the misoriented African as African and box him or her into the existential reality which he or she denies. Denial may take many forms, including the idea that one is indeed different from those Africans who do not deny. A person who denies his historical reality means that he is not confident in his reality. He possesses a fluid identity. This is what I tried to avoid as a young adult in college, this fluid identity. I thank my *ori*, Obatala, for giving me a solid sense of identity. Therefore, I found every opportunity to learn from other Africans with solid identities.

There was always something in me that said you cannot flee from reality, you cannot escape the historical condition and remain sane. Denial assumes a larger and larger portion of the concentration time of those who have fluid identities. What I have seen in their lives is obsession, the obsession with denial-and-discovery. To deny the reality opens the possibility that one may be discovered to be authentically African despite all psychological efforts at denial. There is perhaps nothing worse than seeing an African who looks concretely African and who acts expressively African trying to deny Africanness but who is discovered to be African by the very people he or she is trying to fool.

Consciousness Transformed

In 1972 I visited Ghana during the first of what were to be eighteen trips to Africa over the next twenty years. UCLA had graciously consented to allow me to visit Africa in my capacity as the Director of the Center for Afro-American Studies.

When I finally reached the library at the University of Ghana, Legon, I asked the librarian whether my book *The Rhetoric of Black Revolution* had reached his campus. He replied, "Yes, but I thought the author Arthur Smith was an Englishman." He could not understand how a person with an African phenotype could have an English name or so it seemed to me. Nevertheless, it was a profound encounter for an African American.

I vowed then and there that I would change my name. The name Arthur L. Smith, Jr., inherited from my father, had been betrayed by the dungeon of my American experience. Soon thereafter I took the Sotho name Molefi, which means "One who gives and keeps the traditions" and the Asante last name Asante from the Twi language. My father was elated. He said to me that had he been able to, that is, had he known an African name, he would have changed his name long ago. This made me very proud because I had always been supported by my father's sense of reason. I had no intention of ever masking or wanting to mask. I was straight up and down an African in my consciousness and that fact did not contradict my nationality as an American; it simply threw everything into the most ordered reality possible for me.

The Mask

I could never understand the aim of the Africans who sought to mask. Masking leads to masquerades. The first stage of masking is to cover up, whether sartorially or linguistically. Making certain that you wear the right fashions, have the right hairstyle, and affect the appropriate outward expressions of taste becomes the main preoccupation of masking. "Oh no, I couldn't be seen in those ethnic clothes," a misoriented African American once said to me while dressed in Italian shoes, an English paisley tie, and a French suit. Further masking is effected by using language to befuddle and mislead the potential discoverers. "You see, I'm only part Negro; my father's father was German" may be a correct statement of biological history but it is of no practical value in the American political and social context. There is neither a political nor a social definition within the American society for such masquerade. Neither biracial nor interracial has any political meaning in the contemporary setting of the United States. Thus, to employ the biological argument is to engage in a masquerade because the person seeks to escape the social and political definition for people whose biological history is essentially similar. Most African Americans have mixed gene pools, either one African ethnic group with another or African with some other ethnic and/or racial groups. Nevertheless, we say we are black and mean the word in all of the political and social dimensions it has in this situation. It is like calling the ancient Egyptians "black," which certainly they were in terms that we recognize today. That is, the ancient Egyptians looked no different from the present-day African Americans. In fact, the contemporary Egyptians in the south of Egypt can be mistaken for African Americans!

In the proving ground of America, some of us, and I am one, have been tested in every way. Yet as a lover of harmony I have thought that the most remarkable Maatic achievement of the human personality in this age would be the elimination of racism, prejudice, and discrimination. Perhaps I have wished for this because of the early rites of passage that I went through as a young man, but I would hope that my wish is a part of the celebration of the human possibility. Even from my young adult years I thought a precondition of my fullness, a necessary and natural part of my maturity, was the commitment to be who I am, to be Afrocentric.

One becomes Afrocentric by exploring connections, visiting the quiet places, and remaining connected. The furious pace of our dislocation, mislocation, displacement, off-centeredness, and marginalization, often brought on by the incredible conspiracy of the Eurocentric architecton, drives us further and further away from ourselves, reinforcing us in our dislocation and affirming us

in our out-of-placeness. In such a situation, in the fringes of the European experience, pushed away from the center, we swirl around lost looking for place, for location. Afrocentricity is the active centering of the African in subject place in our historical landscape. This has always been my search; it has been a quest for sanity. Therefore, it was unthinkable for me to entertain ideas of living in the margins, being in the periphery of someone else's historical and cultural experiences. My aim was more fundamental, basic, the essential quality of being normal, uncomplicated. By being normal I do not reject the other; I embrace that which I truly know, i.e., jazz, blues, railroads, Obatala, roots, hoodoo, soul, rhythms, sweet mommas, Dunbar and Hughes, Sanchez, Mari Evans, and Charles Fuller, and so on, in ways that I do not know the products of the other, i.e., country music, mistletoe, Valhalla, Wotan, pale blonds, Frost, and Mailer. I recognize these products as a part of my experience in the large but they do not impact on me in the same way as those which seem to grow from the soil of my ancestors. With my own products I can walk confidently toward the future knowing full well that I can grasp whatever else is out there because my own center is secured.

True, I saw and see many who assume that for an African to strive to be European is the real normalcy. Such "Negroes" are often insane, suffering from a deep sense of self-hatred, which in the end prevents them from having a healthy relationship with the whites whom they admire merely because of their whiteness. Fortunately for me, I have managed to hold back the demons of double-consciousness by being who I am and trying, in Harriet Tubman's name, to be all that I ought to be.

Discussion Questions

1. Asante speaks of problems of self-esteem in Valdosta but says, "In the end we were to have no problem of consciousness." To what extent is he in a position to speak for others?

2. What do you think Asante means to convey by describing himself and others living in Valdosta as "Africans"? What is to be said for and against this mode of description?
3. To what extent is it true that whites fear blacks will "reject white values"? What evidence can you provide for and against this assertion?

4. Asante says in criticism of DuBois that he was never under the illusion that he was white, but does that mean he was never subject to what DuBois calls "double-consciousness"?
5. Do you think that Asante would describe as "misoriented" an African American who is devoted to his career—say, as a research scientist—irrespective of racial issues?

3   Racisms

KWAME ANTHONY APPIAH

Study Questions

1. What is "racialism" and why is it not necessarily a bad or dangerous view?
2. What is the difference between "extrinsic" and "intrinsic" racism?
3. In what way does extrinsic racism involve a "cognitive incapacity"?
4. What is "racial prejudice" (as he defines it) and how does it differ from racism?
5. Why is "intrinsic racism" a moral error, according to Appiah?
6. Why is favoritism for one's family justified in a way that favoritism for one's race is not?

If the people I talk to and the newspapers I read are representative and reliable, there is a good deal of racism about. People and policies in the United States, in Eastern and Western Europe, in Asia and Africa and Latin America are regularly described as "racist." Australia had, until recently, a racist immigration policy; Britain still has one; racism is on the rise in France; many Israelis support Meir Kahane, an anti-Arab racist; many Arabs, according to a leading authority, are

Reprinted by permission of the author and publisher from *Anatomy of Racism,* David Theo Goldberg, ed. (Minneapolis: University of Minnesota Press, 1990), pp. 3–17.

anti-Semitic racists;[1] and the movement to establish English as the "official language" of the United States is motivated by racism. Or, at least, so many of the people I talk to and many of the journalists with the newspapers I read believe.

But visitors from Mars—or from Malawi—unfamiliar with the Western concept of racism could be excused if they had some difficulty in identifying what exactly racism was. We see it everywhere, but rarely does anyone stop to say what it is, or to explain what is wrong with it. Our visitors from Mars would soon grasp that it had become at least conventional in recent years to express abhorrence for racism. They might even notice that those most often accused of it—members of the South African Nationalist party, for example—may officially abhor it also. But if they sought in the popular media of our day—in newspapers and magazines, on television or radio, in novels or films—for an explicit definition of this thing "we" all abhor, they would very likely be disappointed.

Now, of course, this would be true of many of our most familiar concepts. *Sister, chair, tomato*—none of these gets defined in the course of our daily business. But the concept of racism is in worse shape than these. For much of what we say about it is, on the face of it, inconsistent.

It is, for example, held by many to be racist to refuse entry to a university to an otherwise qualified "Negro" candidate, but not to be so to refuse entry to an equally qualified "Caucasian" one. But "Negro" and "Caucasian" are both alleged to be names of races, and invidious discrimination on the basis of race is usually held to be a paradigm case of racism. Or, to take another example, it is widely believed to be evidence of an unacceptable racism to exclude people from clubs on the basis of race; yet most people, even those who think of "Jewish" as a racial term, seem to think that there is nothing wrong with Jewish clubs, whose members do not share any particular religious beliefs, or Afro-American societies, whose members share the juridical characteristic of American citizenship and the "racial" characteristic of being black.

I say that these are inconsistencies "on the face of it," because, for example, affirmative action in university admissions is importantly different from the earlier refusal to admit blacks or Jews (or other "Others") that it is meant, in part, to correct. Deep enough analysis may reveal it to be quite consistent with the abhorrence of racism; even a shallow analysis suggests that it is intended to be so. Similarly, justifications can be offered for "racial" associations in a plural society that are not available for the racial exclusivism of the country club. But if we take racism seriously we ought to be concerned about the adequacy of these justifications.

In this essay, then, I propose to take our ordinary ways of thinking about race and racism and point up some of their presuppositions. And since popular concepts are, of course, usually fairly fuzzily and untheoretically conceived, much of what I have to say will seem to be both more theoretically and more precisely committed than the talk of racism and racists in our newspapers and on television. My claim is that these theoretical claims are required to make sense of racism as the practice of reasoning human beings. If anyone were to suggest that much, perhaps most, of what goes under the name "racism" in our world cannot be given such a rationalized foundation, I should not disagree: but to the extent that a practice cannot be rationally reconstructed it ought, surely, to be given up by reasonable people. The

right tactic with racism, if you really want to oppose it, is to object to it rationally in the form in which it stands the best chance of meeting objections. The doctrines I want to discuss can be rationally articulated: and they are worth articulating rationally in order that we can rationally say what we object to in them.

Racist Propositions

There are at least three distinct doctrines that might be held to express the theoretical content of what we call "racism." One is the view—which I shall call *racialism*[2]—that there are heritable characteristics, possessed by members of our species, that allow us to divide them into a small set of races, in such a way that all the members of these races share certain traits and tendencies with each other that they do not share with members of any other race. These traits and tendencies characteristic of a race constitute, on the racialist view, a sort of racial essence; and it is part of the content of racialism that the essential heritable characteristics of what the nineteenth century called the "Races of Man" account for more than the visible morphological characteristics—skin color, hair type, facial features—on the basis of which we make our informal classifications. Racialism is at the heart of nineteenth-century Western attempts to develop a science of racial difference; but it appears to have been believed by others—for example, Hegel, before then, and many in other parts of the non-Western world since—who have had no interest in developing scientific theories.

Racialism is not, in itself, a doctrine that must be dangerous, even if the racial essence is thought to entail moral and intellectual dispositions. Provided positive moral qualities are distributed across the races, each can be respected, can have its "separate but equal" place. Unlike most Western-educated people, I believe—and I have argued elsewhere[3]—that racialism is false; but by itself, it seems to be a cognitive rather than a moral problem. The issue is how the world is, not how we would want it to be.

Racialism is, however, a presupposition of other doctrines that have been called "racism," and these other doctrines have been, in the last few centuries, the basis of a great deal of human suffering and the source of a great deal of moral error.

One such doctrine we might call "extrinsic racism": extrinsic racists make moral distinctions between members of different races because they believe that the racial essence entails certain morally relevant qualities. The basis for the extrinsic racists' discrimination between people is their belief that members of different races differ in respects that *warrant* the differential treatment, respects—such as honesty or courage or intelligence—that are uncontroversially held (at least in most contemporary cultures) to be acceptable as a basis for treating people differently. Evidence that there are no such differences in morally relevant characteristics—that Negroes do not necessarily lack intellectual capacities, that Jews are not especially avaricious—should thus lead people out of their racism if it is purely extrinsic. As we know, such evidence often fails to change an extrinsic racist's attitudes substantially, for some of the extrinsic racist's best friends have always been Jewish. But at this point—if the racist is sincere—what we have is no longer a false doctrine but a cognitive incapacity, one whose significance I shall discuss later in this essay.

I say that the *sincere* extrinsic racist may suffer from a cognitive incapacity. But some who espouse extrinsic racist doctrines are simply insincere intrinsic racists. For *intrinsic racists*, on my definition, are people who differentiate morally between members of different races because they believe that each race has a different moral status, quite independent of the moral characteristics entailed by its racial essence. Just as, for example, many people assume that the fact that they are biologically related to another person—a brother, an aunt, a cousin—gives them a moral interest in that person,[4] so an intrinsic racist holds that the bare fact of being of the same race is a reason for preferring one person to another. (I shall return to this parallel later as well.)

For an intrinsic racist, no amount of evidence that a member of another race is capable of great moral, intellectual, or cultural achievements, or has characteristics that, in members of one's own race, would make them admirable or attractive, offers any ground for treating that person as he or she would treat similarly endowed members of his or her own race. Just so, some sexists are "intrinsic sexists," holding that the bare fact that someone is a woman (or man) is a reason for treating her (or him) in certain ways.

There are interesting possibilities for complicating these distinctions: some racists, for example, claim, as the Mormons once did, that they discriminate between people because they believe that God requires them to do so. Is this an extrinsic racism, predicated on the combination of God's being an intrinsic racist and the belief that it is right to do what God wills? Or is it intrinsic racism because it is based on the belief that God requires these discriminations because they are right? (Is an act pious because the gods love it, or do they love it because it is pious?) Nevertheless, the distinctions between racialism and racism and between two potentially overlapping kinds of racism provide us with the skeleton of an anatomy of the propositional contents of racial attitudes.

Racist Dispositions

Most people will want to object already that this discussion of the propositional content of racist moral and factual beliefs misses something absolutely crucial to the character of the psychological and sociological reality of racism, something I touched on when I mentioned that extrinsic racist utterances are often made by people who suffer from what I called a "cognitive incapacity." Part of the standard force of accusations of racism is that their objects are in some way *irrational*. The objection to Professor Shockley's claims about the intelligence of blacks is not just that they are false; it is rather that Professor Shockley seems, like many people we call "racist," to be unable to see that the evidence does not support his factual claims and that the connection between his factual claims and his policy prescriptions involves a series of non sequiturs.

What makes these cognitive incapacities especially troubling—something we should respond to with more than a recommendation that the individual, Professor Shockley, be offered psychotherapy—is that they conform to a certain pattern: namely, that it is especially where beliefs and policies that are to the disadvantage of nonwhite people that he shows the sorts of disturbing failure that have made his views both notorious and notoriously unrealiable. Indeed, Professor Shockley's reasoning works extremely well in some other areas: that he is a Nobel Laureate in physics is part of what makes him so interesting an example.

This cognitive incapacity is not, of course, a rare one. Many of us are unable to give up beliefs that play a part in justifying the special advantages we gain (or hope to gain) from our positions in the social order—in particular, beliefs about the positive characters of the class of people who share that position. Many people who express extrinsic racist beliefs—many white South Africans, for example—are beneficiaries of social orders that deliver advantages to them by virtue of their "race," so that their disinclination to accept evidence that would deprive them of a justification for those advantages is just an instance of this general phenomenon.

So too, evidence that access to higher education is as largely determined by the quality of our earlier educations as by our own innate talents, does not, on the whole, undermine the confidence of college entrants from private schools in England or the United States or Ghana. Many of them continue to believe in the face of this evidence that their acceptance at "good" universities shows them to be intellectually better endowed (and not just better prepared) than those who are rejected. It is facts such as these that give sense to the notion of false consciousness, the idea that an ideology can prevent us from acknowledging facts that would threaten our position.

The most interesting cases of this sort of ideological resistance to the truth are not, perhaps, the ones I have just mentioned. On the whole, it is less surprising, once we accept the admittedly problematic notion of self-deception, that people who think that certain attitudes or beliefs advantage them or those they care about should be able, as we say, to "persuade" themselves to ignore evidence that undermines those beliefs or attitudes. What is more interesting is the existence of people who resist the truth of a proposition while thinking that its wider acceptance would in no way disadvantage them or those individuals about whom they care—this might be thought to describe Professor Shockley; or who resist the truth when they recognize that its acceptance would actually advantage them—this might be the case with some black people who have internalized negative racist stereotypes; or who fail, by virtue of their ideological attachments, to recognize what is in their own best interests at all.

My business here is not with the psychological or social processes by which these forms of ideological resistance operate, but it is important, I think, to see the refusal on the part of some extrinsic racists to accept evidence against the beliefs as an instance of a widespread phenomenon in human affairs. It is a plain fact, to which theories of ideology must address themselves, that our species is prone both morally and intellectually to such distortions of judgment, in particular to distortions of judgment that reflect partiality. An inability to change your mind in the face of appropriate[5] evidence is a cognitive incapacity; but it is one that all of us surely suffer from in some areas of belief; especially in areas where our own interests or self-images are (or seem to be) at stake.

It is not, however, as some have held, a tendency that we are powerless to resist. No one, no doubt, can be impartial about everything—even about everything to which the notion of partiality applies; but there is no subject matter about which most sane people cannot, in the end, be persuaded to avoid partiality in judgment. And it may help to shake the convictions of those whose incapacity derives from this sort of ideological defense if we show them how their reaction fits into this general pattern. It is, indeed, because it generally *does* fit this pattern that we call such views "racism"—the suffix "-ism" indicating that what we have in mind is not simply a theory but an ideology. It would be odd to call someone brought up in a remote corner of the world with false and demeaning views about white people a "racist" if that person gave up these beliefs quite easily in the face of appropriate evidence.

Real live racists, then, exhibit a systematically distorted rationality, the kind of systematically distorted rationality that we are likely to call "ideological." And it is a distortion that is especially striking in the cognitive domain: extrinsic racists, as I said earlier, however intelligent or otherwise well informed, often fail to treat evidence against the theoretical propositions of extrinsic racism dispassionately. Like extrinsic racism, intrinsic racism can also often be seen as ideological; but since scientific evidence is not going to settle the issue, a failure to see that it is wrong represents a cognitive incapacity only on controversially realist views about morality. What makes intrinsic racism similarly ideological is not so much the failure of inductive or deductive rationality that is so striking in someone like Professor Shockley but rather the connection that it, like extrinsic racism, has with the interests—real or perceived—of the dominant group.[6] Shockley's racism is in a certain sense directed *against* non-white people: many believe that his views would, if accepted, operate against their objective interests, and he certainly presents the black "race" in a less than flattering light.

I propose to use the old-fashioned term "racial prejudice" in the rest of this essay to refer to the deformation of rationality in judgment that characterizes those whose racism is more than a theoretical attachment to certain propositions about race.

Racial Prejudice

It is hardly necessary to raise objections to what I am calling "racial prejudice"; someone who exhibits such deformations of rationality is plainly in trouble. But it is important to remember that propositional racists in a racist culture have false moral beliefs but may not suffer from racial prejudice. Once we show them how society has enforced extrinsic racist stereotypes, once we ask them whether they really believe that race in itself, independently of those extrinsic racist beliefs, justifies differential treatment, many will come to give up racist propositions, although we must remember how powerful a weight of authority our arguments have to overcome. Reasonable people may insist on substantial evidence if they are to give up beliefs that are central to their cultures.

Still, in the end, many will resist such reasoning; and to the extent that their prejudices are really not subject to any kind of rational control, we may wonder whether it is right to treat such people as morally responsible for the acts their racial prejudice motivates, or morally reprehensible for holding the views to which their prejudice leads them. It is a bad thing that such people exist; they are, in a certain sense, bad people. But it is not clear to me that they are responsible for the fact that they are bad. Racial prejudice, like prejudice generally, may threaten an agent's autonomy, making it appropriate to treat or train rather than to reason with them.

But once someone has been offered evidence both (1) that their reasoning in a certain domain is distorted by prejudice, and (2) that the distortions conform to a pattern that suggests a lack of impartiality, they ought to take special care in articulating views and proposing policies in that domain. They ought to do so because, as I have already said, the phenomenon of partiality in judgment is well attested in human affairs. Even if you are not immediately persuaded that you are yourself a victim of such a distorted rationality in a certain domain, you should keep in mind always that this is the usual position of those who suffer from such prejudices. To the extent that this line of thought is not one that itself falls within the domain in question, one can be held responsible for not subjecting judgments that *are* within that domain to an especially extended scrutiny; and this is a fortiori true if the policies one is recommending are plainly of enormous consequence.

If it is clear that racial prejudice is regrettable, it is also clear in the nature of the case that providing even a superabundance of reasons and evidence will often not be a successful way of removing it. Nevertheless, the racist's prejudice will be articulated through the sorts of theoretical propositions I dubbed extrinsic and intrinsic racism. And we should certainly be able to say something reasonable about why these theoretical propositions should be rejected.

Part of the reason that this is worth doing is precisely the fact that many of those who assent to the propositional content of racism do not suffer from racial prejudice. In a country like the United States, where racist propositions were once part of the national ideology, there will be many who assent to racist propositions simply because they were raised to do so. Rational objection to racist propositions has a fair chance of changing such people's beliefs.

Extrinsic and Intrinsic Racism

It is not always clear whether someone's theoretical racism is intrinsic or extrinsic, and there is certainly no reason why we should expect to be able to settle the question. Since the issue probably never occurs to most people in these terms, we cannot suppose that they must have an answer. In fact, given the definition of the terms I offered, there is nothing barring someone from being both an intrinsic and an extrinsic racist, holding both that the bare fact of race provides a basis for treating members of his or her own race differently from others and that there are morally relevant characteristics that are differentially distributed among the races. Indeed, for reasons I shall discuss in a moment, *most* intrinsic racists are likely to express extrinsic racist beliefs, so that we should not be surprised that many people seem, in fact, to be committed to both forms of racism.

The Holocaust made unreservedly clear the threat that racism poses to human decency. But it also blurred our thinking because in focusing our attention on the racist character of the Nazi atrocities, it obscured their character as atrocities. What is appalling about Nazi racism is not just that it presupposes, as all racism does, false (racialist) beliefs—not simply that it involves a moral incapacity (the inability to extend our moral sentiments to all our fellow creatures) and a moral failing (the making of moral distinctions without moral differences)—but that it leads, first, to oppression and then to mass slaughter. In recent years, South African racism has had a similar distorting effect. For although South African racism has not led to killings on the scale of the Holocaust—even if it has both left South Africa judicially executing more (mostly black) people per head of population than most other countries and led to massive differences between the life chances of white and nonwhite South Africans— it *has* led to the systematic oppression and economic exploitation of people who are not classified as "white," and to the infliction of suffering on citizens of all racial classifications, not least by the police state that is required to maintain that exploitation and oppression.

Part of our resistance, therefore, to calling the racial ideas of those, such as the Black Nationalists of the 1960s, who advocate racial solidarity, by the same term that we use to describe the attitudes of Nazis or of members of the South African Nationalist party, surely resides in the fact that they largely did not contemplate using race as a basis for inflicting harm. Indeed, it seems to me that there is a significant pattern in the modern rhethoric of race, such that the discourse of racial solidarity is usually expressed through the language of *intrinsic* racism, while those who have used race as the basis for oppression and hatred have appealed to *extrinsic* racist ideas. This point is important for understanding the character of contemporary racial attitudes.

The two major uses of race as a basis for moral solidarity that are most familiar in the West are varieties of Pan-Africanism and Zionism. In each case it is presupposed that a "people," Negroes or Jews, has the basis for shared political life in the fact of being of the same race. There are varieties of each form of "nationalism" that make the basis lie in shared traditions; but however plausible this may be in the case of Zionism, which has in Judaism, the religion, a realistic candidate for a common and nonracial focus for nationality, the peoples of Africa have a good deal less in common culturally than is usually assumed. I discuss this issue at length in *In My Father's House: Essays in the Philosophy of African Culture,* but let me say here that I believe the central fact is this: what blacks in the West, like secularized Jews, have mostly in common is that they are perceived—both by themselves and by others—as belonging to the same race, and that this common race is used by others as the basis for discriminating against them. "If you ever forget you're a Jew, a goy will remind you." The Black Nationalists, like some Zionists, responded to their experience of racial discrimination by accepting the racialism it presupposed.[7]

Although race is indeed at the heart of Black Nationalism, however, it seems that it is the fact of a shared race, not the fact of a shared racial character, that provides the basis for solidarity. Where racism is implicated in the basis for national solidarity, it is intrinsic, not (or not only) extrinsic. It is this that makes the idea of fraternity one that is naturally applied in nationalist discourse. For, as I have already observed, the moral status of close family members is not normally thought of in most cultures as depending on qualities of character; we are supposed to love our brothers and sisters in spite of their faults and not because of their virtues. Alexander Crummell, one of the founding fathers of Black Nationalism, literalizes the metaphor of family in these startling words:

Races, like families, are the organisms and ordinances of God; and race feeling, like family feeling, is of divine origin. The extinction of race feeling is just as possible as the extinction of family feeling. Indeed, a race *is* a family.[8]

It is the assimilation of "race feeling" to "family feeling" that makes intrinsic racism seem so much less objectionable than extrinsic racism. For this metaphorical identification reflects the fact that, in the modern world (unlike the nine-

teenth century), intrinsic racism is acknowledged almost exclusively as the basis of feelings of community. We can surely, then, share a sense of what Crummell's friend and co-worker Edward Blyden called "the poetry of politics," that is, "the feeling of race," the feeling of "people with whom we are connected."[9] The racism here is the basis of acts of supererogation, the treatment of others better than we otherwise might, better than moral duty demands of us.

This is a contingent fact. There is no logical impossibility in the idea of racialists whose moral beliefs lead them to feelings of hatred for other races while leaving no room for love of members of their own. Nevertheless most racial hatred is in fact expressed through extrinsic racism: most people who have used race as the basis for causing harm to others have felt the need to see the others as independently morally flawed. It is one thing to espouse fraternity without claiming that your brothers and sisters have any special qualities that deserve recognition, and another to espouse hatred of others who have done nothing to deserve it.[10]

Many Afrikaners—like many in the American South until recently—have a long list of extrinsic racist answers to the question why blacks should not have full civil rights. Extrinsic racism has usually been the basis for treating people worse than we otherwise might, for giving them less than their humanity entitles them to. But this too is a contingent fact. Indeed, Crummell's guarded respect for white people derived from a belief in the superior moral qualities of the Anglo-Saxon race.

Intrinsic racism is, in my view, a moral error. Even if racialism were correct, the bare fact that someone was of another race would be no reason to treat them worse—or better—than someone of my race. In our public lives, people are owed treatment independently of their biological characters: if they are to be differently treated there must be some morally relevant difference between them. In our private lives, we are morally free to have aesthetic preferences between people, but once our treatment of people raises moral issues, we may not make arbitrary distinctions. Using race in itself as a morally relevant distinction strikes most of us as obviously arbitrary. Without associated moral characteristics, why should race provide a better basis than hair color or height or timbre of voice? And if two people share all the properties morally relevant to some action we ought to do, it will be an error—a failure to apply the Kantian injunction to universalize our moral judgments—to use the bare facts of race as the basis for treating them differently. No one should deny that a common ancestry might, in particular cases, account for similarities in moral character. But then it would be the moral similarities that justified the different treatment.

It is presumably because most people—outside the South African Nationalist party and the Ku Klux Klan—share the sense that intrinsic racism requires arbitrary distinctions that they are largely unwilling to express it in situations that invite moral criticism. But I do not know how I would argue with someone who was willing to announce an intrinsic racism as a basic moral idea; the best one can do, perhaps, is to provide objections to possible lines of defense of it.

De Gustibus

It might be thought that intrinsic racism should be regarded not so much as an adherence to a (moral) proposition as the expression of a taste, analogous, say, to the food prejudice that makes most English people unwilling to eat horse meat, and most Westerners unwilling to eat the insect grubs that the IKung people find so appetizing. The analogy does at least this much for us, namely, to provide a model of the way that *extrinsic* racist propositions can be a reflection of an underlying prejudice. For, of course, in most cultures food prejudices are rationalized: we say insects are unhygienic and cats taste horrible. Yet a cooked insect is no more health-threatening than a cooked carrot, and the unpleasant taste of cat meat, far from justifying our prejudice against it, probably derives from that prejudice.

But there the usefulness of the analogy ends. For intrinsic racism, as I have defined it, is not simply a taste for the company of one's "own kind," but a moral doctrine, one that is supposed to underlie differences in the treatment of people in contexts where moral evaluation is appropriate. And for moral distinctions we cannot accept that "de gustibus non est disputandum." We do not need the full apparatus of Kantian ethics to require that public morality be constrained by reason.

A proper analogy would be with someone who thought that we could continue to kill cattle for beef, even if cattle exercised all the complex cultural skills of human beings. I think it is obvious that creatures that shared our capacity for understanding as well as our capacity for pain should not be treated the way we actually treat cattle—that "intrinsic speciesism" would be as wrong as racism. And the fact that most people think it is worse to be cruel to chimpanzees than to frogs suggests that they may agree with me. The distinction in attitudes surely reflects a belief in the greater richness of the mental life of chimps. Still, I do not know how I would *argue* against someone who could not see this; someone who continued to act on the contrary belief might, in the end, simply have to be locked up.

The Family Model

I have suggested that intrinsic racism is, at least sometimes, a metaphorical extension of the moral priority of one's family; it might, therefore, be suggested that a defense of intrinsic racism could proceed along the same lines as a defense of the family as a center of moral interest. The possibility of a defense of family relations as morally relevant—or, more precisely, of the claim that one may be morally entitled (or even obliged) to make distinctions between two otherwise morally indistinguishable people because one is related to one and not to the other—is theoretically important for the prospects of a philosophical defense of intrinsic racism. This is because such a defense of the family involves—like intrinsic racism—a denial of the basic claim expressed so clearly by Kant, that from the perspective of morality, it is as rational agents *simpliciter* that we are to assess and be assessed. For anyone who follows Kant in this, what matters, as we might say, is not who you are but how you try to live. Intrinsic racism denies this fundamental claim also. And, in so doing, as I have argued elsewhere, it runs against the mainstream of the history of Western moral theory.[11]

The importance of drawing attention to the similarities between the defense of the family and the defense of the race, then, is not merely that the metaphor of family is often invoked by racism; it is that each of them offers the same general challenge to the Kantian stream of our moral thought. And the parallel with the defense of the family should be especially appealing to an intrinsic racist, since many of us who have little time for racism would hope that the family is susceptible to some such defense.

The problem in generalizing the defense of the family, however, is that such defenses standardly begin at a point that makes the argument for intrinsic racism immediately implausible: namely, with the family as the unit through which we live what is most intimate, as the center of private life. If we distinguish, with Bernard Williams, between ethical thought, which takes seriously "the demands, needs, claims, desires, and generally, the lives of other people,"[12] and morality, which focuses more narrowly on obligation, it may well be that private life matters to us precisely because it is altogether unsuited to the universalizing tendencies of morality.

The functioning family unit has contracted substantially with industrialization, the disappearance of the family as the unit of production, and the increasing mobility of labor, but there remains that irreducible minimum: the parent or parents with the child or children. In this "nuclear" family, there is, of course, a substantial body of shared experience, shared attitudes, shared knowledge and beliefs; and the mutual

psychological investment that exists within this group is, for most of us, one of the things that gives meaning to our lives. It is a natural enough confusion—which we find again and again in discussions of adoption in the popular media—that identifies the relevant group with the biological unit of *genitor, genetrix,* and *offspring* rather than with the social unit of those who share a common domestic life.

The relations of parents and their biological children are of moral importance, of course, in part because children are standardly the product of behavior voluntarily undertaken by their biological parents. But the moral relations between biological siblings and half-siblings cannot, as I have already pointed out, be accounted for in such terms. A rational defense of the family ought to appeal to the causal responsibility of the biological parent and the common life of the domestic unit, and not to the brute fact of biological relatedness, even if the former pair of considerations defines groups that are often coextensive with the groups generated by the latter. For brute biological relatedness bears no necessary connection to the sorts of human purposes that seem likely to be relevant at the most basic level of ethical thought.

An argument that such a central group is bound to be crucially important in the lives of most human beings in societies like ours is not, of course, an argument for any specific mode of organization of the "family": feminism and the gay liberation movement have offered candidate groups that could (and sometimes do) occupy the same sort of role in the lives of those whose sexualities or whose dispositions otherwise make the nuclear family uncongenial; and these candidates have been offered specifically in the course of defenses of a move toward societies that are agreeably beyond patriarchy and homophobia. The central thought of these feminist and gay critiques of the nuclear family is that we cannot continue to view any one organization of private life as "natural," once we have seen even the broadest outlines of the archaeology of the family concept.

If that is right, then the argument for the family must be an argument for a mode of organization of life and feeling that subserves certain positive functions; and however the details of such an argument would proceed it is highly unlikely that the same functions could be served by groups on the scale of races, simply because, as I say, the family is attractive in part exactly for reasons of its personal scale.

I need hardly say that rational defenses of intrinsic racism along the lines I have been considering are not easily found. In the absence of detailed defenses to consider, I can only offer these general reasons for doubting that they can succeed: the generally Kantian tenor of much of our moral thought threatens the project from the start; and the essentially unintimate nature of relations within "races" suggests that there is little prospect that the defense of the family—which seems an attractive and plausible project that extends ethical life beyond the narrow range of a universalizing morality—can be applied to a defense of races.

Conclusions

I have suggested that what we call "racism" involves both propositions and dispositions.

The propositions were, first, that there are races (this was *racialism*) and, second, that these races are morally significant either (a) because they are contingently correlated with morally relevant properties (this was *extrinsic racism*) or (b) because they are intrinsically morally significant (this was *intrinsic racism*).

The disposition was a tendency to assent to false propositions, both moral and theoretical, about races—propositions that support policies or beliefs that are to the disadvantage of some race (or races) as opposed to others, and to do so even in the face of evidence and argument that should appropriately lead to giving those propositions up. This disposition I called "racial prejudice."

I suggested that intrinsic racism had tended in our own time to be the natural expression of feelings of community, and this is, of course, one of the reasons why we are not inclined to call it racist. For, to the extent that a theoretical position is not associated with irrationally held beliefs that tend to the *dis*advantage of some group, it fails to display the *directedness* of the distortions of rationality characteristic of racial prejudice. Intrinsic racism may be as irrationally held as any other view, but it does not *have* to be directed *against* anyone.

So far as theory is concerned I believe racialism to be false: since theoretical racism of both kinds presupposes racialism, I could not logically support racism of either variety. But even if racialism were true, both forms of theoretical racism would be incorrect. Extrinsic racism is false because the genes that account for the gross morphological differences that underlie our standard racial categories are not linked to those genes that determine, to whatever degree such matters are determined genetically, our moral and intellectual characters. Intrinsic racism is mistaken because it breaches the Kantian imperative to make moral distinctions only on morally relevant grounds—granted that there is no reason to believe that race, *in se,* is morally relevant, and also no reason to suppose that races are like families in providing a sphere of ethical life that legitimately escapes the demands of a universalizing morality.

Discussion Questions

1. If intrinsic racists simply want to help and support members of their own race more than others but do not want to harm others, is there anything wrong with this?
2. If extrinsic racists are sincere in their conviction, on what grounds can they be faulted for their *beliefs?* Can it ever be wrong simply to have a particular belief?
3. Why has "extrinsic" rather than "intrinsic" racism been historically connected to the infliction of harms?

4. Do you agree with Appiah's contention that what blacks mostly have in common is that others have perceived them to be a group and have been subject, on this basis, to common discrimination?

Notes

1. Bernard Lewis, *Semites and Anti-Semites* (New York: Norton, 1986).

2. I shall be using the words "racism" and "racialism" with the meanings I stipulate: in some dialects of English they are synonyms, and in most dialects their definition is less than precise. For discussion of recent biological evidence see M. Nei and A. K. Roychoudhury, "Genetic Relationship and Evolution of Human Races," *Evolutionary, Biology,* vol. 14 (New York: Plenum, 1983), pp. 1–59; for useful background see also M. Nei and A. K. Roychoudhury, "Gene Differences between Caucasian, Negro, and Japanese Populations," *Science,* 177 (August 1972), pp. 434–35.

3. See my "The Uncompleted Argument: Du Bois and the Illusion of Race," *Critical Inquiry,* 12 (Autumn 1985); reprinted in Henry Louis Gates (eds.), *"Race," Writing, and Difference* (Chicago: University of Chicago Press, 1986), pp. 21–37.

4. This fact shows up most obviously in the assumption that adopted children intelligibly make claims against their natural siblings: natural parents are, of course, causally responsible for their child's existence and that could be the basis of moral claims, without any sense that biological relatedness entailed rights or responsibilities. But no such basis exists for an interest in natural *siblings;* my sisters are not causally responsible for my existence. See "The Family Model," later in this essay.

5. Obviously what evidence should *appropriately* change your beliefs is not independent of your social or historical situation. In mid-nineteenth-century America, in New England quite as much as in the heart of Dixie, the pervasiveness of the institutional support for the prevailing system of racist belief—the fact that it was reinforced by religion and state, and defended by people in the universities and colleges, who had the greatest cognitive authority—meant that it would have been appropriate to insist on a substantial body of evidence and argument before giving up assent to racist propositions. In California in the 1980s, of course, matters stand rather differently. To acknowledge this is not to admit to a cognitive relativism; rather, it is to hold that, at least in some domains, the fact that a belief is widely held—and especially by people in positions of cognitive authority—may be a good prima facie reason for believing it.

6. Ideologies, as most theorists of ideology have admitted, standardly outlive the period in which they conform to the objective interests of the dominant group in a society; so even someone who thinks that the dominant group in our society no longer needs racism to buttress its position can see racism as the persisting ideology of an earlier phase of society. (I say "group" to keep the claim appropriately general; it seems to me a substantial further claim that the dominant group whose interests an ideology serves is always a class.) I have argued, however, in "The Conservation of 'Race' " that racism continues to serve the interests of the ruling classes in the West; in *Black American Literature Forum,* 23 (Spring 1989), pp. 37–60.

7. As I argued in "The Uncompleted Argument: Du Bois and the Illusion of Race." The reactive (or dialectical) character of this move explains why Sartre calls its manifestations in Négritude an "antiracist racism"; see "Orphée Noir," his preface to Senghor's *Anthologie de la non velle poésie nègre et malagache de langue française* (Paris: PUF, 1948). Sartre believed, of course, that the synthesis of this dialectic would be the transcendence of racism; and it was his view of it as a stage—the antithesis—in that process that allowed him to see it as a positive advance over the original "thesis" of European racism. I suspect that the reactive character of antiracist racism accounts for the tolerance that is regularly extended to it in liberal circles; but this tolerance is surely hard to justify unless one shares Sartre's optimistic interpretation of it as a stage in a process that leads to the end of all racisms. (And unless your view of this dialectic is deterministic, you should in any case want to play an argumentative role in moving to this next stage.)

For a similar Zionist response see Horace Kallen's "The Ethics of Zionism," *Maccabaeen,* August 1906.

8. "The Race Problem in America," in Brotz's *Negro Social and Political Thought* (New York: Basic Books, 1966), p. 184.

9. *Christianity, Islam and the Negro Race* (1887; reprinted Edinburgh: Edinburgh University Press, 1967), p. 197.

10. This is in part a reflection of an important asymmetry: loathing, unlike love, need justifying; and this, I would argue, is because loathing usually leads to acts that are *in se* undesirable, whereas love leads to acts that are largely *in se* desirable—indeed, supererogatorily so.

11. See my "Racism and Moral Pollution," *Philosophical Forum,* 18 (Winter-Spring 1986–87) pp. 185–202.

12. *Ethics and the Limits of Philosophy* (Cambridge, Mass.: Harvard University Press, 1985) p. 12. I do not, as is obvious, share Williams's skepticism about morality.

4   The Heart of Racism

J. L. A. GARCIA

Study Questions

1. What are some problems with the view that racism pertains to a belief in racial superiority?
2. What is Garcia's definition of *racism* and how does it pass the test that it be able to make clear what is wrong with racism?
3. How are individual and institutional racism connected on Garcia's account?
4. Why is prejudice not essential to racism?
5. How do Appiah and Garcia differ regarding intrinsic racism and preferential treatment?

The phenomenon of racism having plagued us for many centuries now, it is somewhat surprising to learn that the concept is so young. The second edition of *The Oxford English Dictionary* (1989) dates the earliest appearances of the term 'racism' only to the 1930s.[1] During that decade, as the shadow of Nazism lengthened across Europe, social thinkers coined the term to describe the ideas and theories of racial biology and anthropology to which the Nazi movement's intellectual defenders appealed in justifying its political program. Thus, Ruth Benedict, in a book published in 1940, called racism "the dogma that one ethnic group is condemned by nature to congenital inferiority and another group is destined to congenital superiority"[2] (Benedict, 1940).

These origins are reflected in the definition that the *O.E.D.* still offers: "The theory that distinctive human characteristics and abilities are determined by race."[3] Textbook definitions also echo this origin: "Racism—a doctrine that one race is superior" (Schaefer, 1990: p. 27). Recently,

however, some have argued that these definitions no longer capture what people mean when they talk of racism in the moral and political discourse that has become the term's primary context. Some on the political left argue that definitions reducing racism to people's beliefs do not do justice to racism as a sociopolitical reality. Robert Miles records the transition in the thought of Ambalvaner Sivanandan, director of Britain's Institute of Race Relations, who abandoned his earlier account of racism (1973) as "an explicit and systematic ideology of racial superiority" because later (1983) he came to think that "racism is about power not prejudice." Eventually (1985), he saw racism as "structures and institutions with power to discriminate" (1985). (Quoted at Miles, 1989: p. 54.)[4] From the right, the philosopher Antony Flew has suggested that, to identify racism with "negative beliefs" about "actual or alleged matters of fact" is a "sinister and potentially dangerous thing"—it "is to demand, irrespective of any evidence which might be turned up to the contrary, that everyone must renounce certain disapproved propositions."[5] Flew worries that this poses a serious threat to intellectual freedom, and proposes a behavioral understanding of 'racism' as "meaning the advantaging or disadvantaging of individuals for no better reason than that they happen to be members of this racial group rather than that."

I agree with these critics that in contemporary moral and political discourse and thought, what we have in mind when we talk of racism is no longer simply a matter of beliefs.[6] However, I think their proposed reconceptions are themselves inadequate. In this paper, I present an account of racism that, I think, better reflects contemporary usage of the term, especially its primary employment as both descriptive and evaluative; and I sketch some of this view's implications for the morality of race-sensitive discrimination in private and public life. I will also briefly point out some

From the *Journal of Social Philosophy* 28 (1997), pp. 5–16. Reprinted by permission.

of this account's advantages over various other ways of thinking about racism that we have already mentioned—racism as a doctrine, as a socioeconomic system of oppression, or as a form of action. One notable feature of my argument is that it begins to bring to bear on this topic in social philosophy points made in recent criticisms of modernist moral theory offered by those who call for increased emphasis on the virtues. (This voice has hitherto largely been silent in controversies within practical social philosophy.)

I. A Volitional Conception of Racism

Kwame Anthony Appiah rightly complains that, although people frequently voice their abhorrence of racism, "rarely does anyone stop to say what it is, or what is wrong with it" (Appiah, 1990: 3). This way of stating the program of inquiry we need is promising, because, although racism is not essentially "a moral doctrine," *pace* Appiah, it is always a moral evil[7] (Appiah, 1990: 13). No account of what racism is can be adequate unless it at the same time makes clear what is wrong with it. How should we conceive racism, then, if we follow Appiah's advice "to take our ordinary ways of thinking about race and racism and point up some of their presuppositions" (Appiah, 1990: 4)? My proposal is that we conceive of racism as fundamentally a vicious kind of racially based disregard for the welfare of certain people. In its central and most vicious form, it is a hatred, ill-will, directed against a person or persons on account of their assigned race. In a derivative form, one is a racist when one either does not care at all or does not care enough (i.e., as much as morality requires) or does not care in the right ways about people assigned to a certain racial group, where this disregard is based on racial classification. Racism, then, is something that essentially involves not our beliefs and their rationality or irrationality, but our wants, intentions, likes, and dislikes and their distance from the moral virtues.[8] Such a view helps explain racism's conceptual ties to various forms of *hatred* and contempt. (Note that

'contempt' derives from 'to contemn'—not to care (about someone's needs and rights.)

It might be objected that there can be no such thing as racism because, as many now affirm, "there are no races." This objection fails. First, that 'race' is partially a social construction does not entail that there are no races. One might even maintain, though I would not, that race-terms, like 'person,' 'preference,' 'choice,' 'welfare,' etc., and, more controversially, such terms as 'reason for action,' 'immoral,' 'morally obligatory,' etc. may be terms that, while neither included within nor translatable into, the language of physics, nevertheless arise in such a way and at such a fundamental level of social or anthropological discourse that they should be counted as real, at least, for purposes of political and ethical theory.[9] Second, as many racial anti-realists concede, even if it were true that race is unreal, what we call racism could still be real (Appiah, 1992: p. 45). What my account of racism requires is not that there be races, but that people make distinctions in their hearts, whether consciously or not on the basis of their (or others') racial classifications. That implies nothing about the truth of those classifications.[10]

Lawrence Blum raises a puzzling question about this. We can properly classify a person S as a racist even if *we* do not believe in races. But what if S herself does not believe in them? Suppose S is a White person who hates Black people, but picks them out by African origin, attachment to African cultures, residence or rearing in certain U.S. neighborhoods, and so on. Should we call S racist if she does not hate Black people *as such* (i.e., on the basis of her assigning them to a Black race), but hates all people she thinks have been corrupted by their internalizing undesirable cultural elements from Harlem or Watts, or from Nairobi, or the Bunyoro? I think the case underdescribed. Surely, a person can disapprove of a culture or a family of cultures without being racist. However, cultural criticism can be a mask for a deeper (even unconscious) dislike that is defined by racial classifications. If the person transfers her disapproval of the group's culture to contempt or disregard for those designated as the group's members, then she is already doing something morally vicious. When she assigns all the groups disliked to the same racial classification, then we are entitled to suspect racism, because we have good grounds to suspect that her disavowals of underlying racial classifications are false. If S hates the cultures of various Black groups for having a certain feature, but does not extend that disapproval to other cultures with similar features, then that strongly indicates racism.

Even if she is more consistent, there may still be racism, but of a different sort. Adrian Piper suggests that, in the phenomenon she calls 'higher order discrimination,' a person may claim to dislike members of a group because she thinks they have a certain feature, but really disapprove of the feature because she associates it with the despised group. This 'higher order discrimination' would, of course, still count as racist in my account, because the subject's distaste for the cultural element derives from and is morally infected by race-based disregard.

We should also consider an additional possibility. A person may falsely attribute an undesirable feature to people she assigns to a racial group because of her disregard for those in the group. This will often take the forms of exaggeration, seeing another in the worst light, and withholding from someone the benefit of the doubt. So, an anti-Semite may interpret a Jew's reasonable frugality as greed; a White racist may see indolence in a Black person's legitimate resistance to unfair expectations of her, and so on.

Thinking of racism as thus rooted in the heart fits common sense and ordinary usage in a number of ways. It is instructive that contemptuous White racists have sometimes called certain of their enemies 'Nigger-lovers.' When we seek to uncover the implied contrast-term for this epithet, it surely suggests that enemies of those who "love" Black people, as manifested in their efforts to combat segregation, and so forth, are those who hate Black people or who have little or no human feelings toward us at all. This is surely born out by the behavior and rhetoric of paradigmatic White racists.

This account makes racism similar to other familiar forms of inter-group animosity. Activists in favor of Israel and of what they perceive as Jewish interests sometimes call anti-Semites 'Jewhaters.' Wistrich, for example, says that " 'anti-Semitism,' which never really meant hatred of [all] Semites, but rather hatred of Jews, has come to be accepted in general usage as denoting all forms of hostility toward Jews and Judaism throughout history" (Wistrich, 1992: p. xv). He opposes this expansion of meaning, especially extending the term to cover opposition to the religion of Judaism. According to him, those who coined the term for their own doctrines were "not opposed to Jews on religious grounds, but claimed to be motivated by social, economic, political, or 'racial' considerations."[11] What is important for us is to note that *hostility* toward Jews is the heart of anti-Semitism.

It is also worth noting that, immediately prior to the coining of the term 'racism,' even some of the early anti-Nazi polemicists referred to their subject as 'race hatred.'[12] This suggests such thinkers may have realized that the true problem was not so much the doctrines of the scientists of race-biology and race-anthropology, but the antipathy these doctrines rationalized and encouraged.

Racism also seems, intuitively, to be structurally similar to xenophobia and the anti-homosexual malice sometimes called 'homophobia.' However, xenophobia is commonly understood not primarily as consisting in holding certain irrational beliefs about foreigners, but in *hatred* or disregard of them. This suggests that racism should, as I here claim, be considered a form of disaffection.[13] The gay activists Kirk and Madsen urge that we reclassify some so-called 'homophobes' as 'homohaters.' They cite studies indicating that many people who detest homosexuals betray none of the telltale physiological signs of phobia, and remind us that what is at stake is primarily a hostility toward homosexual persons on account of their homosexuality.[14] Again, by analogy, racism should be deemed a form of disregard.

On my account, racism retains its strong ties to intolerance. This tie is uncontroversial. Marable, for example, writes of "racism, and other types of intolerance, such as anti-Semitism . . . [and]

homophobia . . ." (Marable, 1992: 3, 10). Intolerant behavior is to be expected if racism is hatred.[15] How, after all, can one tolerate those whom one wants to injure, and why ought one to trouble oneself to tolerate those whom one disregards?

Such an account of racism as I propose can both retain and explain the link between the two "senses of" racism found in some dictionaries: (i) belief in superiority of R1s to R2s, and (ii) interracial 'antagonism.'[16] I suggest that we think of these as two elements within most common forms of racism. In real racists, I think, (ii) is normally a ground of (i) (though sometimes the reverse is true), and (i) is usually a rationalization of (ii). What is more important is that (i) may not be logically *necessary* for racism. (In some people, it may nonetheless be a psychological necessity.) However, even when (ii) is a result of (i), it is (ii) and not (i), that makes a person a racist. (Logically, not causally.)

My view helps explain why racism is always immoral. As Stephen Nathanson says, "Racism, as we ordinarily speak of it, . . . implies . . . a special disregard for other groups. Hence, there is a sense in which racism is necessarily immoral" (Nathanson, 1992: p. 9).[17] Its immorality stems from its being opposed to the virtues of benevolence and justice. Racism is a form of morally insufficient (i.e., vicious) concern or respect for some others. It infects actions in which one (a) tries to injure people assigned to a racial group because of their XXXXX, or (b) objectionably fails to take care *not* to injure them (where the agent accepts harm to R1s because she disregards the interests and needs of R1s because they are R1s). We can also allow that an action is racist in a derivative and weaker sense when it is less directly connected to racist disregard, for example, when someone (c) does something that (regardless of its intended, probable, or actual effects) stems in significant part from a belief or [an] apprehension about other people, that one has (in significant part) because of one's disaffection toward them because of (what one thinks to be their) race. Racism, thus, will often offend against justice, not just against benevolence, be-

cause one sort of injury to another is withholding from her the respect she is owed and the deference and trust that properly express that respect. Certain forms of paternalism, while benevolent in some of their goals, may be vicious in the means employed. The paternalist may deliberately choose to deprive another of some goods, such as those of (licit) freedom and (limited) self-determination in order to obtain other goods for her. Here, as elsewhere, the good end need not justify the unjust means. Extreme paternalism constitutes an instrumentally malevolent benevolence: one harms A to help her. I return to this below in my discussion of 'Kiplingesque' racism.

If, as I maintain, racism is essentially a form of racially focused ill-will or disregard (including disrespect), then that explains why " 'racism' is inescapably a morally loaded term. To call a person a racist is to impugn his character by suggesting deliberate, malign discrimination . . ." (Lichtenberg, 1992: p. 5).

My account of racism suggests a new understanding of racist behavior and of its immorality. This view allows for the existence of both individual racism and institutional racism. Moreover, it makes clear the connection between the two, and enables us better to understand racism's nature and limits. Miles challenges those who insist on talking only of 'racisms' in the plural to "specify what the many different racisms have in common" (Miles, 1989: p. 65). This may go too far. Some philosophers have offered respected accounts of common terms that seem not to require that every time A is an F and B is an F, then A and B must have some feature in common (other than that of being-an-F, if that *is* a feature). Nominalism and Wittgenstein's "family resemblance" view are two examples. However, if we are not dealing with two unrelated concepts the English terms for which merely happen to have the same spelling and pronunciation (like the 'bank' of a river and the 'bank' that offers loans), then we should be able to explain how the one notion develops out of the other.

Some think that institutions, etc., are racist when they are structures of racial domination, and that individual beliefs, etc. are racist when they express, support, or justify racial superiority. Both, of course, involve denying or violating the equal dignity and worth of all human beings independent of race. This sort of approach contains some insight. However, it leaves unclear how the two levels or types of racism are related, if they are related at all. Thus, such views leave us rather in the dark about what it is in virtue of which each is a form of racism. Some say that institutional racism is what is of central importance; individual racism, then, matters only inasmuch as it perpetuates institutional racism. I think that claim reverses the order of moral importance, and I shall maintain that the individual level has more explanatory importance.

At the individual level, it is in desires, wishes, intentions, and the like that racism fundamentally lies, not in actions or beliefs. Actions and beliefs are racist in virtue of their *coming from* racism in the desires, wishes, and intentions of individuals, not in virtue of their *leading to* these or other undesirable effects. Racism is, for this reason, an interesting case study in what we might call 'infection' (or 'input-centered' or backward-looking) models of wrongdoing, in contrast to the more familiar consequentialist and other result-driven approaches. Infection models of wrongdoing—according to which an action is wrong because of the moral disvalue of what goes into it rather than the nonmoral value of what comes out of it—seem the best approach within virtues-based ethics. In such ethical systems, actions are immoral insofar as they are greedy, arrogant, uncaring, lustful, contemptuous, or otherwise corrupted in their motivational sources.[18] Finally, desires, wishes, and intentions *are* racist when they either are, or in certain ways reflect, attitudes that withhold from people, on the basis of their being assigned to a particular race, levels or forms of good-will, caring, and well-wishing that moral virtue demands.[19] At its core, then, racism consists in vicious attitudes toward people based on their assigned race. From there, it extends to corrupt the people, individual actions, institutional behavior, and systemic operations it infects. Some, however, seem not to think of racism in this way, as something that, like cruelty or stupidity, can escalate from its primary occurrence in individual people to infect collective thought and decision-making of organizations and, from there, to contaminate the behavior of institutions as well. So to think of it is to see the term as not merely descriptive and evaluative, but also as having some explanatory force.

How is institutional racism connected to racism within the individual? Let us contrast two pictures. On the first, institutional racism is of prime moral and explanatory importance. Individual racism, then, matters (and, perhaps, occurs) only insofar as it contributes to the institutional racism which subjugates a racial group. On the second, opposed view, racism within individual persons is of prime moral and explanatory import, and institutional racism occurs and matters because racist attitudes (desires, aims, hopes, fears, plans) infect the reasoning, decision-making, and action of individuals not only in their private behavior, but also when they make and execute the policies of those institutions in which they operate. I take the second view. Institutional racism, in the central sense of the term, occurs when institutional behavior stems from (a) or (b) above or, in an extended sense, when it stems from (c). Obvious examples would be the infamous Jim Crow laws that originated in the former Confederacy after Reconstruction. Personal racism exists when and insofar as a person is racist in her desires, plans, aims, etc., most notably when this racism informs her conduct. In the same way, institutional racism exists when and insofar as an institution is racist in the aims, plans, etc., that people give it, especially when their racism informs its behavior. Institutional racism begins when racism extends from the hearts of individual people to become institutionalized. What matters is that racist attitudes contaminate the operation of the institution; it is irrelevant what its original point may have been, what its designers meant it to do. If it does not operate from those motives (at time T1), then it does not embody institutional racism (at T1). On this view, some phenomena sometimes described as institutionally racist will turn out not to be properly so describable, but others not normally considered to be institutionally racist will fit the description. (I return to this below.)

Not only is individual racism of greater explanatory import, I think it also more important morally. Those of us who see morality primarily as a matter of suitably responding to other people and to the opportunities they present for us to pursue value will understand racism as an offense against the virtues of benevolence and justice in that it is an undue restriction on the respect and goodwill owed people. (Ourselves as well as others; racism, we must remember, can take the form of self-hate.) Indeed, as follows from what I have elsewhere argued, it is hard to render coherent the view that racist hate is bad mainly for its bad effects. The sense in which an action's effects are bad is that they are undesirable. But that it is to say that these effects are evil things to want and thus things the desire for which is evil, vicious. Thus, any claim that racial disadvantage is a bad thing presupposes a more basic claim that race-hatred is vicious. What is more basic morally is also morally more important in at least one sense of that term.[20] Of course, we should bear in mind that morality is not the same as politics. What is morally most important may not be the problem whose rectification is of greatest political urgency.

II. Implications and Advantages

There are some noteworthy implications and advantages of the proposed way of conceiving of racism.

First, it suggests that prejudice, in its strict sense of 'pre-judgment,' is not essential to racism, and that some racial prejudice may not be racist, strictly speaking. Racism is not, on this view, primarily a cognitive matter, and so it is not in its essence a matter of how or when one makes one's judgments. Of course, we can still properly call prejudiced-based beliefs racist in that they *characteristically* either are rooted in prior racial disregard, which they rationalize, or they foster such

disregard.[21] Whether having such a belief is immoral in a given case will depend in large part on whether it is a rationalization for racial disaffection. It may depend on *why* the individual is so quick to think the worst of people assigned to the other racial group. Of course, even when the order is reversed and the prejudice does not whitewash a prior and independent racial disaffection, but causes a subsequent one, the person will still be racist because of that disaffection, even if she is not racist in holding that belief, that is, even if she does not hold it for what we might call 'racist reasons.' My guess is that, in most people who have been racists for some expanse of time, the belief and the disregard will reinforce each other.

A person may hold prejudices about people assigned to a race without herself being racist and without it being racist of her to hold those prejudices.[22] The beliefs themselves can be called 'racist' in an extended sense because they are characteristically racist. However, just as one may make a wise move without acting wisely (as when one makes a sound investment for stupid reasons), so one may hold a racist belief without holding it for racist reasons. One holds such a belief for racist reasons when it is duly connected to racial disregard: when it is held in order to rationalize that disaffection or when contempt inclines one to attribute undesirable features to people assigned to a racial group. One whose racist beliefs have no such connection to any racial disregard in her heart does not hold them in a racist way and if she has no such disregard, she is not herself a racist, irrespective of her prejudices.

Second, when racism is so conceived, the person with racist feelings, desires, hopes, fears, and dispositions is racist even if she never acts on these attitudes in such a way as to harm people designated as members of the hated race. (This is not true when racism is conceived as consisting in a system of social oppression.) It is important to know that racism can exist in (and even pervade) societies in which there is no systematic oppression, if only because the attempts to oppress fail. Even those who think racism important primarily because of its effects should find this possibility of inactive racism worrisome for, so long as this latent racism persists, there is constant threat of oppressive behavior.

Third, on this view, race-based preference (favoritism) need not be racist. *Preferential* treatment in affirmative action, while race-based, is not normally based on any racial disregard. This is a crucial difference between James Meredith's complaint against the University of Mississippi and Allan Bakke's complaint against the University of California at Davis Medical School (see Appiah, 1990: p. 15). Appiah says that what he calls "extrinsic racism has usually been the basis [1] for treating people worse than we otherwise might, [2] for giving them less than their humanity entitles them to" (Appiah, 1992: 18). What is important to note here is that (1) and (2) are not at all morally equivalent. Giving someone less than her humanity entitles her to is morally wrong. To give someone less than we could give her, and even to give her less than we would if she (or we, or things) were different is to treat her "worse [in the sense of 'less well'] than we otherwise might." However, the latter is not normally morally objectionable. Of course, we may not deny people even gratuitous favors out of hatred or contempt, whether or not race-based, but that does not entail that we may not licitly choose to bestow favors instead on those to whom we feel more warmly. That I feel closer to A than I do to B does not mean that I feel hatred or callousness toward B. I may give A more than A has a claim to get from me and more than I give B, while nevertheless giving B everything to which she is entitled (and even more). Thus, race-based favoritism does not have to involve (2) and need not violate morality.

Appiah recognizes this fact, saying that 'intrinsic racism,' because of its ties to solidarity, fraternity, and even "family feeling," is often merely "the basis for acts of supererogation, the treatment of others better than we otherwise might, better than moral duty demands of us" (Appiah, 1990: 11). However, he warns ominously, "This is a contingent fact. There is no logical impossibility in the idea of racialists whose moral beliefs lead them to feelings of hatred for other races while leaving them no room

for love for members of their own" (Appiah, 1990: 12). But why should the fact that this remains a logical possibility incline us to condemn racial preference? When the possibility is actualized, and someone feels, not special regard for those who share assignment to her own racial group (along with adequate affection for people assigned to other groups), but hatred for those allocated to other groups (whether or not there is affection for people allocated to her own), then we have illicit antipathy not licit favoritism. When this ugly possibility is not actualized, however, then we need some independent argument against favoritism.[23] Appiah invokes Kant for this purpose (Appiah, 1992: 18; 1990: 14,15). However, the invocation is insufficient. There is no obvious inconsistency in willing that a moderate form of race preference, like other moderate forms of kinship preference, should be a universal law of nature, as Kant's own principal test of universalization requires.[24]

Discrimination *on the basis of* race, then, need not be immoral. It is discrimination *against* people because of their racial assignment that cannot but be immoral. Christopher Jencks says "we need formal discrimination in favor of blacks to offset the effects of persistent informal discrimination against them."[25] Suppose Jencks' claim about our need for discrimination is true. Can racial favoritism ever be justified? It will help to remind ourselves that discriminating *in favor of* R1s need not entail discriminating *against* R2s.[26] The latter consists in acting either (i) with intention of harming R2s, or (ii) with hard-hearted racist indifference to the action's foreseeable ill effects on R2s,[27] or (iii) from racist beliefs held because of racist disaffection. Similarly, racial self-segregation need not be immoral. It may be especially suspect when White people do it, because we have good historical reason to be suspicious that what is presented as merely greater-than-morally-required concern for fellow White people really involves less-than-morally-required concern for Black people. It may also be ill-advised even when it is Black people who do it. However, in neither case must it be immoral.[28] In neither case must it be racist.

According to this conception of racism, *de jure racial segregation* violates political morality primarily because (and, therefore, when) it expresses a majority's (or minority's) racial indifference, contempt, or ill-will. It is therein vicious, offending against the virtues of both benevolence and justice. However, it need not have such origin, a fact illustrated by recent suggestions to establish separate academies to deal with the educational challenges confronting young Black males, and by efforts to control the racial demography of public housing projects in order to avoid problems that have sometimes arisen when such projects became virtually all-Black or virtually all-White. Whatever the social merit of such proposals, in cases like these, even if the segregation in the end proves immoral, this is not intrinsic. There must be some special additional factor present that makes it immoral. De facto racial segregation (mere separation or disproportional representation) need not be morally problematic at all when it happens to result from decently and responsibly motivated individual or social actions.[29] However, it will be immoral if its bad effects on, say, R1s are accepted out of racist hardheartedness, that is, out of racist indifference to the harm done R1s. This will sometimes, but not always, be the case when harms are disproportionally distributed across the various racial groupings to which people are assigned.

Fourth, on this view of racism, racist discrimination need not always be conscious. The real reason why person P1 does not rent person P2 a room may be that P1 views P2 as a member of a racial group R2, to whose members P1 has an aversion. That may be what it is about P2 that turns P1 off, even if P1 convinces herself it was for some other reason that she did not rent. As racist discrimination need not always be conscious, so it need not always be intended to harm. Some of what is called 'environmental racism,' especially the location of waste dumps so as disproportionally to burden Black people, is normally not intended to harm anyone at all. Nevertheless, it is racist if, for example, the dumpers regard it as less important if it is 'only,' say, Black people who suffer. However, it will

usually be the case that intentional discrimination based on racist attitudes will be more objectionable morally, and harder to justify, than is unintentional, unconscious racist discrimination. Rac*ial* discrimination is not always rac*ist* discrimination. The latter is always immoral, because racism is inherently vicious and it corrupts any differentiation that it infects. The former—racial discrimination—is not inherently immoral. Its moral status will depend on the usual factors—intent, knowledge, motive, and so on—to which we turn to determine what is vicious.

This understanding of racism also offers a new perspective on the controversy over efforts to restrict racist "hate speech." Unlike racially *offensive* speech, which is defined by its (actual or probable) effects, racist *hate* speech is defined by its origins, i.e., by whether it expresses (and is thus an act of) racially directed hate. So we cannot classify a remark as racist hate speech simply on the basis of *what* was said; we need to look to *why* the speaker said it. Speech laden with racial slurs and epithets is presumptively hateful, of course, but merely voicing an opinion that members of R1 are inferior (in some germane way) will count as racist (in any of the term's chief senses, at least) only if, for example, it expresses an opinion held from the operation of some predisposition to believe bad things about R1s, which predisposition itself stems in part from racial disregard.[30] This understanding of racist hate speech should allay the fears of those who think that racial oversensitivity and the fear of offending the oversensitive will stifle the discussion of delicate and important matters beneath a blanket of what is called 'political correctness.' Racist hate speech is defined by its motive forces and, given a fair presumption of innocence, it will be difficult to give convincing evidence of ugly motive behind controversial opinions whose statement is free of racial insults.

I am grateful to many people who discussed these matters with me. Henry Richardson, Martha Minow, David Wilkins, David Wong, Anthony Appiah, Susan Wolf, Dennis Thompson, Glenn Loury, and Judith Lichtenberg offered thoughtful comments on earlier drafts of some of this material. Discussions with Russell Hittinger, Ken Taylor, and others also profited me greatly. I am especially indebted to Lawrence Blum for repeated acts of encouragement and assistance, including reading and discussing my manuscripts and letting me read from his unpublished work, and I thank him and an audience at Rutgers' 1994 conference on philosophy and race, for making suggestions and raising forceful objections.

My work was made possible by generous sabbatical support from Georgetown University, by research assistance from Rutgers University, and by grants from the National Endowment for the Humanities and from Harvard's Program in Ethics and the Professions. This paper would not have been written without the stimulation and the opportunity for reflection afforded me at the annual Ford Foundation Fellows conferences. To all these institutions I am indebted.

Discussion Questions

1. Must racism involve ill will? Might not a racist be strongly in favor of his or her own group and neutral about others? Doesn't this amount to the same as being neutral about one's own group and strongly against others?
2. Suppose a Jew bears ill will toward Germans on the grounds that the German nation was responsible for the Holocaust (in which most of her family was killed). Is this "racist" by Garcia's definition? Is it morally wrong?
3. Is it possible to hate members of a race, believing them to be superior (and hating them for it)? Does this qualify as racism?

Notes

1. The same dictionary dates the cognate 'racist,' as both adjective and noun, to the same period, but places the first appearances of 'racialism' and 'racialist' three decades earlier.
2. Miles begins a summary of his review of the first uses of the term in the effort of certain intellectuals to attack the pseudo-scientific defenses of the Nazi movement by saying that "the concept of racism was forged largely in the course of a conscious attempt to withdraw the sanction of science from a particular

meaning of the idea of 'race' "; and he chides these early critics on the grounds that their interpretation of racism, "by focusing on the product of nineteenth century scientific theorizing, tended to presume that racism was always, and therefore was only, a structured and relatively coherent set of assertions. . . . Such a definition [is problematic insofar as it] excludes less formally structured assertions, stereotypical ascriptions and symbolic representations . . ." (Miles, 1986: 47, 48).

3. Merriam-Webster's *Ninth New Collegiate Dictionary* offers a secondary definition: "racial prejudice or discrimination."

4. For a negative appraisal of Sivanandan's thought, see David Dale, "Racial Mischief: The Case of Dr. Sivanandan," in Palmer, 1986: pp. 82–94.

5. Discussing an account of racism offered by Britain's Commission for Racial Equality, Flew writes: "[a] sinister and potentially dangerous thing here is the reference to actual or alleged matters of fact—to 'negative beliefs' . . . . For this is to demand, irrespective of any evidence which might be turned up to the contrary, that everyone must renounce certain disapproved propositions about average or universal differences and similarities as between races and racial groups: difference and similarities, that is, either in respect of biology or in respect of culture. To concede such a demand to the often Marxist militants of race relations is to open the door to purges: not only of libraries and of textbooks and of curricula; but also of people. It is not ten years since many a campus in the U.S.A. was ringing with calls to 'Sack' and even to 'Kill Jensen'—Jensen being a psychologist who dared to publish evidence suggesting that there may be genetically determined average differences between different races and racial groups in respect of other than their racial defining characteristics" (Flew, 1986: 22).

6. Banton suggests that we should restrict our usage of the term, withholding its application from many people we nowadays call racists. In his view, these people are not racists because they use arguments of cultural superiority in preference to the doctrines of biologically based superiority the term was coined to pick out (Banton, 1970). This proposal is unrealistic, and serves to illustrate what makes unacceptable the excessively conservative approach to word meaning of those who still insist that racism consists solely in certain beliefs, ideology, doctrines, and theories.

7. That is not to say that its definition must include a moral evaluation. The act-utilitarian must hold that nonoptimific behavior is always wrong simply in virtue of what it is and what morality is, but she need not think the term 'nonoptimific' includes a moral evaluation in its definition. Similarly, a divine command

theorist may judge every act against God's will to be immoral *eo ipso,* without thinking this wrongness analytically derivable from the meaning of 'against God's will.'

8. According to Miles, the term 'racism' originally denoted certain pseudo-scientific doctrines. I think the term changed its meaning, and speculate that this change occurred as race became important less for the discredited beliefs than for attitudes and resultant social practices. (See Miles, 1989: chaps. 2, 3.) On the linguistic history, also see the *Oxford English Dictionary,* 2nd ed.

9. Compare David Wiggins and John McDowell on Kantian moral realism. (See Wiggins, "Truth, Invention, and the Meaning of Life," in Wiggins, 1987; and McDowell, 1986).

Although in conversation with me he has denied any such dependence, there is reason to worry that Appiah's position may covertly rely on a form of scientism, the supposition that no serious use of a once-pseudo-scientific term is permissible if it plays no role within legitimate science. In any case, he seems to allow that neither the fact that the concept of 'race' is inexact in its criteria and extension, nor the fact that it was the subject of a discredited science, nor the fact that it was used to justify unjust social practices, is by itself sufficient to show that the notion must be banished from speech. (Perhaps he thinks they are jointly sufficient, but that remains to be shown.) Moreover, he is willing to talk informally of this person being Black and that one White, so he and I are not so far apart. I do not see why this informal, but acceptable, way of speaking cannot be extended to allow us to call such talk acceptable (albeit informal) racial classifications. Of course, informal talk of races cannot be accepted if racial terms must really be scientific. That, however, returns us to our question why anyone should think that.

Appiah's criticism of talk of races on the grounds that there are no "racial essences" suggests that he may presuppose a metaphysical essentialism that does not count against using racial terms on the looser bases of Wittgensteinian "family resemblances": perhaps a combination of surface and ancestral features, ordered in no one way, underlies the legitimate application of race terms to many but not all persons.

10. Miles objects to some early accounts of the nature of racism on the grounds that they "tended to remain inextricably entangled with, and consequently to legitimate, the idea of 'race' " (Miles, 1989: 48).

11. After an Arab dismissed a charge of anti-Semitism by the late Meir Kahane, on the grounds that Arabs are themselves a Semitic people, I once heard Kahane sensibly (if not necessarily accurately) respond by amending his charge to that of 'Jew-hater.' Of course, Kahane himself was often described, with some justification, as an Arab-hater. The connection between racism and anti-Semitism may be more than analogical. It is sometimes said that anti-Semitism is itself a type of racism. Thus, Miles writes of "that form of racism which others label anti-Semitism" (Miles, 1989: 68).

It is worth remarking that, whereas Wistrich thinks anti-Semitism "the longest hatred," Castoriadis claims that the Hebrew Bible is, because of its exaltation of the Jews, the oldest extant racist document (Castoriadis, 1992: 3). I think that Castoriadis' view serves as a *reductio* of understanding racism as a matter of beliefs. Whether or not one thinks God selected the Jews for a special role in human salvation, this election hardly constitutes the sort of contemptuous or aversive dismissal of others that properly counts as racist.

12. "Critics of scientific theories of race prior to this decade [the 1930s] did not use a concept of racism to identify their ideological object. For example, in a wide-ranging critique published in the late 1920s, Friedrich Hertz referred to 'race hatred' " (Miles, 1989: 42).

13. As I said at the outset, the term 'xenophobia' also suggests that this aversion to others is accompanied or caused by fear of them, but I do not think this association carries over to 'racism.'

14. They write, " 'Homophobia' is a comforting word, isn't it? It suggests that . . . all who oppose, threaten, and persecute us [that is, homosexuals] are actually scared of us! [However, f]ear need have nothing to do with it. A well-designed study . . . demonstrat[ed] that although some 'homonegative' males respond to homosexual stimuli with the 'tell-tale racing heart' of phobia, plenty of others don't." Kirk and Madsen condemn "the specious 'diagnosis' " of homophobia as a "medically exculpatory euphemism," and offer a proposal: "Let's reserve the term 'homophobia' for the psychiatric cases to which it really applies, and find a more honest label for the attitudes, words, and acts of hatred that are, after all, the real problem." As for their own linguistic procedure, "when we really do mean 'fear of homosexuals,' [then] 'homophobia' it will be; when we're talking about hatred of homosexuals, we'll speak (without the hyphen) of 'homohatred,' 'homohating,' and 'homohaters.' We urge the reader to follow suit." (See Kirk and Madsen, 1989: xxii–xxiii.) This is sensible advice, though some caveats are in order. First, we should bear in mind that not every fear is a phobia. Second, even the quasi-scientific term "homonegative" tends to lump together such very different matters as (i) a person's personal aversion to her own engaging in homosexual activities, (ii) her concern over perceived social effects of other peoples' homosexual conduct, and (iii) her holding the belief that such conduct is morally impermissible. Hatred of ho-

mosexual persons is immoral (although, as Kirk and Madsen point out, to see it simply as a medical condition tends to exculpate). Moral disapproval of homosexual practices, whether on medical, moral, or religious grounds, is a different matter, however, and it may often be an unrelated one. Third, to use the prefix 'homo' to mean 'homosexual' is objectionable for obvious reasons, so it seems preferable to speak of 'homosexual-haters' and 'homosexual-hatred,' retaining the hyphen. This would also make it clear, as the term 'homophobia' does not, that what is to be condemned is an attitude of ill-will or contempt toward certain people, and not a moral judgment on certain practices.

15. The Freudian theorist Elizabeth Young-Bruehl, in an unpublished paper, argues that anti-Semitism differs from racism in that anti-Semitism, which she thinks rooted in a combination of assumed male Gentile sexual superiority and economic and intellectual inferiority, aims to exterminate its targets, while racism, which she thinks rooted in assumed White male sexual inferiority, seeks to keep its victims around for humiliation (Young-Bruehl, 1992). I suspect all this wrong-headed. For our purposes, what is important is that no such causality is essential to racism or anti-Semitism, because we should label haters of Jews or Black people anti-Semite and racists even if we knew their hatred had different causes.

16. I shall use such terms as 'R1' and 'R2' to refer to racial groups, and such expression as 'R1s' and 'R2s' to refer to people assigned to such groups. This usage holds potential for some confusion, since the plural term 'R1s' is not the plural of the singular term 'R1', but I think the context will always disambiguate each instance of this usage.

17. Two caveats. First, since our interest is in the central sense(s) of the term 'racism', I see little reason to add Cottingham's qualifier "there is a sense in which" to our claim that racism must be illicit. Any sense of the term in which racism is not illicit must be decidedly peripheral. Second, Cottingham seems to think of this "disregard" as primarily a matter of negative evaluative beliefs, while I reject any such doxastic account and construe 'disregard' as disaffection or malice.

18. See Slote, 1994, and Garcia, forthcoming.

19. I will not try to identify minimal levels of good will such that having less is against the virtue of benevolence, nor minimal levels of respect such that less offends against justice. I doubt these levels can be identified in abstraction, and it will be difficult or impossible for us to determine them even in minutely described particular situations. Throughout, I generally restrict my talk of disrespect and other forms of disregard to cases where the levels are morally vicious, offending against the moral virtues of benevolence and justice, respectively.

20. See Garcia, 1986, and Garcia, 1987.

21. In a way similar to my nondoxastic account of racism, John Dewey seems to have offered an account of race-prejudice that is nondoxastic. Recent scholarship reminds us that, for Dewey, prejudice was not primarily a matter of hasty judgment, but of a fear of, and aversion to what is unfamiliar. Gregory Pappas expounded Dewey's view in his paper, "Dewey's Philosophical Interpretation of Racial Prejudice," presented at a session of the 1992 Ford Fellows Conference in Irvine, California.

22. See Appiah, 1992.

23. Iris Young offers the interesting suggestion that modernist moral theory's aversion to partiality, like its aversion to appeals to feelings and its insistence on the irrelevance of gender, ethnicity, and other aspects of personal or groups experience, history, and situatedness, originates as part of an endeavor to eliminate from the viewpoint of the moral judge those factors that are deemed inessential to her as a rational agent and that serve to differentiate her from others. This effort is perhaps most evident in Kant's famous insistence that an agent's moral requirements be rooted in her (universal) reason, and not to be contingent upon her desires (unlike "hypothetical imperatives"), lest the requirements vary across persons and times, as he thought all substantive desired did. Young also thinks the impartialist unfairly presents impartiality as the only alternative to egoism (see Young, 1990: chap. 4). If that is right, then the impartialist position rests upon several dubious assumptions, most notably, assumptions about the constituents of the moral agent's identity (or "essence"), about the irreducible variability of desires and feelings, and about the supposed gap between human passions and desires on the one had and abstract reason on the other. All these assumptions are currently undergoing philosophical reconsideration. (See, especially, Blum, 1994.)

24. Note that action from maxims that pass Kant's universalizability test is therein permissible, not necessarily obligatory.

25. Quoted in Hacker, "The New Civil Way," p. 30

26. Arguing against some writers who use the slogan "Preference is not prejudice" is support their view that moderate racial preference is permissible, Miles complains, "[To] prefer is to rank and to choose to value something or person or group, and therefore necessarily to preclude some other thing, person or group." (Miles, 1989: 8) What Miles says is true, but does nothing to prove the controverted point that excluding person S1 in the course of expressing greater-than-morally-required regard for S2 is the moral equivalent of excluding S1 out of less-than-morally-required concern for S1. That said, I do certainly not wish to associate myself with the further doctrines of the thinkers Miles is

criticizing, who use the inflammatory example of preferring to marry within one race as an example of supposedly innocent preference. In a society such as ours, any such "preference" is likely to be informed by and to result in part from an aversion to interracial marriage as 'race-treachery' or 'miscegenation'. Such a preference is not at all innocent, in my view, having roots in deep-seated racial antipathy.

In personal correspondence, Glenn Loury has expressed misgivings about my view, reminding me that "what ends in personal viciousness towards the 'other' finds its beginning in the more benign celebration of the virtues of one's 'own kind.'" I wonder whether, in fact, racial antipathy does *always* begin in such a benign attitude. However, even if it does, the danger that it may lead to racial antipathy is a reason to be cautious of racial favoritism. It is not a reason to condemn this partiality as malign nor, more to the point, as racist. Even the framers of a recent California measure proposing to outlaw racial preferences observe a distinction between discriminating against A and according B a preference. "The anti-affirmative action measure is essentially a simple declaration: 'Neither the State of California nor any of its political subdivisions shall use race, sex, color, ethnicity, or national origin as a criterion for either discriminating against or granting preferential treatment to, any individual or group in the operation of the state's system of public employment, public education, or public contracting," (Schrog 1995, p. 18). The drafters may, however, make the distinction merely to close a possible linguistic loophole, and not deem it a distinction that marks any genuine and morally significant difference. With that, of course, I disagree.

27. I say 'foreseeable' efffects rather than 'foreseen' because S's racists contempt may be the reason she does not bother to find out, and thus does not foresee some of the bad effects of her behavior.

28. I think this undermines an argument recently offered by Gomberg. He argues against what has been called "moderate patriotism," which "includ[es limited] preference for fellow nationals," on the grounds that any argument in defense of it will also legitimize what he calls "moderate racism," which allows someone to "discriminate against black or Hispanic people or against immigrants" so long as one is careful not to "violate their fundamental rights (p.147). Assuming that such "moderate racism" is unjustifiable, then so too is moderate patriotism or any form of preference. The problem is that it is hard to see why Gomberg's "moderate racism" need be unjustifiable, or even why it is racism. His analogy with patriotism suggests that what Gomberg has in mind is merely a mild form of preference for people of one's own racist group. This will sometimes be suspicious morally, especially when the one discriminating on the basis of race belongs to a group that has enforced and benefited from forms of

discrimination that are racist, that is, that are driven by racial disaffection. However, it is unclear that there is anything morally troubling in the same-race favoritism by those on the bottom, or by those who live in a situation, unlike ours, where favoritism has been historically divorced from race hatred. Similarly, there seems to be nothing morally troubling in other-race favoritism; at least, there is nothing morally troubling where favoritism is likely to be divorced from hatred of one's own racial group, as in the case with other-race favoritism by those from historically oppressing groups.

Indeed, while same-race favoritism by people considered members of the oppressing group and other-race favoritism by those allocated to the oppressed group are disturbing morally, I think that, to the extent this discomfort is legitimate, it will be rooted in our suspicion that it is really race-hatred masking as mere favoritism, or in our worry that such a practice, should it become widespread, will have the bad effect of exacerbating the comparatively disadvantaged position of those assigned to the historically oppressed group. The latter worry may be serious, but it is a concern about the general effects of a social (or personal) policy, not a concern that individuals may be treated unjustly. As such, it is much less significant morally.

(Since first writing this, I have seen a similar point made in Stephen Nathanson's response to Gomberg. Nathanson sensibly writes that "a racial preference might not be inherently wrong or evil. American Blacks have been an oppressed group that has needed special attention. Whites are not similarly oppressed as a group. Thus, a person with a special affection and concern for whites might not be equally justified in promoting their interests. . . ." Actions done from such favoritism will even "be wrong if they require neglect of the much more pressing need of others" (Nathanson, 1992: 10, 11).

In this connection, it is worth noting that Appiah rejects what he calls "intrinsic speciesism," adherents of which think it would be morally permissible "to kill cattle for beef, even if cattle exercised all the complex cultural skills of human beings" (Appiah, 1992: 19). Such a position is to be condemned, of course, but we can condemn it without necessarily rejecting the view ("moderate speciesism"?) that even in the world of Appiah's cosmopolitan cattle, we may, and perhaps even should, show greater concern for members of our own species simply because of their relation to us. The impermissibility of such favoritism does not follow from the recognition that there are moral limits on the ways in which we may treat the various others outside the favored group. I can think morality allows and even demands that I care specially for my family without thereby committing myself to thinking that we may slaughter, butcher, and eat the folks next door.

29. See Carter, 1991.

30. For a helpful discussion of the controversy surrounding efforts to identify and regulate hate speech, and of the different grounds offered for these restrictions, see Simon, 1991.

References

Appiah, Anthony. "Racisms." In *Anatomy of Racism,* pp. 3–17. Ed. D. T. Goldberg. Minneapolis: University of Minnesota Press, 1990.

Banton, Michael. "The Concept of Racism." In *Race and Racialism,* pp. 17–34. Ed. Sami Zubaida. New York: Barnes & Noble, 1970.

Carter, Stephen. *Reflections of an Affirmative Action Baby.* New York: Basic Books, 1991.

Flew, Antony. "Clarifying the Concepts." In Palmer, 1986, pp. 15–31.

Gomberg, Paul. "Patriotism Is Like Racism." *Ethics* 101 (1990): 144–50.

Kirk, Marshall, and Hunter Madsen. *After the Ball: How America Will Conquer Its Fear and Hatred of Gays in the '90s.* New York: Doubleday, 1989.

McDowell, John. "Values and Secondary Qualities." In *Morality and Objectivity,* pp. 110–29. Ed. Ted Honderich. London: Humanities, 1985.

Miles, Robert. *Racism.* London: Routledge, 1989.

Nathanson, Stephen. "Is Patriotism Like Racism?" *APA Newsletter on Philosophy and the Black Experience* 91 (1992): 9–11.

Palmer, Frank ed. *Anti-Racism: An Assault on Education and Value.* London: Sherwood, 1986.

Simon, Thomas. "Fighting Racism: Hate Speech Detours." In *An Ethical Education: Community and Morality in the Multicultural University.* Ed. Mortimer Sellers. Oxford: Berg, 1994.

Wiggins, David. *Needs, Value, Truth.* New York: Blackwell, 1987.

Young-Bruehl, Elizabeth. "Kinds of Types of Prejudices." 1992. Unpublished.

Contemporary Issue: Views on "Mixed Race"

---

5 Mixed Black and White Race and Public Policy

NAOMI ZACK

Study Questions

1. What is the "one-drop rule"?
2. According to Zack, why is race not a meaningful biological classification?
3. Explain the connection Zack outlines between the classification "slave" and "negro."
4. According to Zack, why are we "still trapped in the rigidity of notions of biological racial difference that presuppose pseudoscientific ideas of race"?
5. What ultimately is Zack's answer to the question of whether there should be a socially allowed category of "mixed race"?

Reprinted by permission of the author from *Hypatia* 10 (1995), pp. 119–132.

There is so much myth involved in the classification of Americans into black and white racial categories that the facts about race are part of the subject of Racial Theory. Racial Theory is the intellectual structure within which it is possible to develop an understanding of how *race* is socially constructed. In that theoretical context, the ordinary concept of race in the United States, which purports to be about something hereditary and physical, has no scientific foundation; neither does this concept have an ethical rationale that ensures just treatment for individuals or a maximization of benefits for all concerned groups. In this essay, I mean to sketch the historical, empirical, and emancipatory context for permitting American individuals of mixed black and white race to identify themselves racially. Such permission would be a matter of future public policy in many different political, intellectual, scientific, and educational contexts—it would reflect a massive paradigm shift in emancipatory black and white racial thought and action, just as the historical denial of permission has reflected white racism and racial oppression. Because the case of black and white racial mixture has always been the site of the most stringent impositions of racial purity in American culture, argument for self-identification in that case is an important beginning for unraveling racial mythology in general.

The One-Drop Rule

The racial categories of black and white race form a rigid, asymmetrical classification system in the United States. On a folk level, it is assumed that an individual is either black or white, but not both.[1] However, there have been individuals acknowledged as having both black and white ancestors since seventeenth-century colonial days, so something besides the facts of heredity as they are understood in other cases of ancestral diversity must be at work here.[2] At work is the one-drop rule, which has been reflected in the United States census since 1920. According to the one-drop rule, an individual is racially black if he or she has one black ancestor anywhere in her genealogical line of descent, and this holds regardless of whether, or how many, white, Asian, or Native American ancestors were also present. By contrast, a person is white only if she has no nonwhite ancestors. That is the logic behind American racial designations, and its only basis is the public policy that was associated with black chattel slavery. Nevertheless, Americans assume that there are biological foundations for racial classifications. That there are no such foundations is worth a few minutes to review.

The Biology of Race

First of all, the drop in the-one-drop rule refers to a drop of blood. It used to be believed that ancestors literally passed their blood on to their descendants and that this blood mixed with the blood of other ancestors whenever a child was conceived. We now know that this is nonsense: maternal and fetal blood circulate separately; blood is not passed on, but its type is copied genetically; there are no general racial blood types—human blood types are distinguished for transfusion purposes, and full siblings may have incompatible blood types.[3]

According to biological anthropologists, the racial unit is not an individual but a population that has more of some physical traits than other populations. There probably never have been pure races because racial populations have rarely been isolated from members of other racial populations. Social taboos may substitute for geographical isolation in breeding populations, but no such taboo has ever been completely effective; and even if such a taboo were effective, the physical traits that would be designated as racial traits would be a matter of cultural choice and not biology.[4] Biologically, there is no *general* genetic marker for race. There are genes associated with particular physical traits that have been socially designated as racial traits, but no gene for white race, black race, Asian race, or any other race has been scientifically identified during the centuries in which the modern idea of race has been in circulation.[5] It is important, in this regard, to note the contrast with sex. Although all individuals do not neatly divide into XX or XY on a chromosomal level because of borderline and more complex combinations of X and Y, nevertheless, X and Y are identifiable as general sexual markets that determine more specific sexual characteristics.[6] Even after all social constructions of sex and gender are filtered out, the overwhelming majority of individuals are XX or XY. This general XX-ness or XY-ness causes or explains less general physical characteristics, which themselves have underlying genes. For example, the presence of XX predicts the presence of the gene for ovaries. If it were the case that all of the specific physical sexual characteristics varied along continua and that XX and XY did not exist, then there would be no general genetic basis for sex. That is the situation with race. The specific physical characteristics that different cultures have designated as racial in different ways, vary, without any underlying general genetic marker that causes them or that can be used to explain their presence. Once one realizes this, it becomes clear that *race* is what cultures take it to be. As a *general* biological characteristic, which is how racist cultures construct race, race does not exist. But given racist constructions, race has a powerful social reality, and it is therefore an extraordinarily complex subject to both refer to and dissolve at the same time.

Due to the one-drop rule, an American classified as black may have more genes that cause physical characteristics considered to be white than an American classified as white. The presence of a black ancestor does not ensure the presence of any of the genes of that ancestor beyond the second generation. This is because individuals get one-half of their genes from each parent, and there is no guarantee that they have genes from all four grandparents—the "racial" genes, that is, the genes underlying perceptible traits that the culture has designated as "racial" traits, might be just as likely to drop out as the nonracial ones. Lest it seem contradictory to speak—even in quotes—of racial genes in the same breath as a claim that there are no genes for race, it should be remembered that a racial gene is a gene for a trait that has been *culturally* determined to be a racial trait. There is nothing specifically racial in a biological sense about a "racial" gene. "Racial" genes are genes that underlie skin color, hair texture, and other physical characteristics of human beings. They otherwise have nothing extra, physically or genetically, to distinguish them from other "nonracial" genetic differences, except that these "racial" genes have been designated, picked out, identified, as "racial." Finally, it should also be noted that so-called racial genes do not get inherited in clumps. Most genes are subject to dispersal and recombination at conception, and the genes behind the physical traits that society has picked out as racial are no more likely to get passed on together than are genes for traits to which society attaches no racial significance.[7] This is why individuals who are other-

wise presumed to be of the same race do not all have the same racial traits.

Groups of individuals from the same geographical area, such as a part of precolonial Africa, may share some biological traits among their members, such as dark brown skin and curly hair. But the designation of these traits as racial is a purely cultural construction. Ever since the colonial period racial designation has accompanied the oppression and exploitation, or domination, of the groups so designated. During the seventeenth, eighteenth, and nineteenth centuries, the domination of what are now called third world populations was practiced by Europeans on a global scale. The physical differences from Europeans of these third world peoples and the assumed difference in geographical origins of their ancestors became the basis of modern European concepts of race. Until the 1920s, social scientists also assumed that cultural differences among racially designated groups were physically inherited.[8]

The American History of the One-Drop Rule

In colonial America, prisoners from Africa were worked as slaves, along with Europeans and Native Americans. By the end of the eighteenth century, these African slaves were known as "n"egroes—the 'n' was always lowercase until the Harlem Renaissance—and only "n"egroes could be enslaved in the United States.[9] By that time, those individuals who were then called "negroes" and who historians after the 1930s refer to as "Negroes," but who should probably be referred to as American slaves, had been conceptualized as a distinct race from whites, lower in biological hierarchy and intellectually and morally inferior to whites (Zack 1993, 116–122). So, first African prisoners were made slaves and then they were defined as a "race" of "negroes." Every member of this "race" of "negroes" was posited as having the characteristics of a population that was essentially different from the "white" population. (Unfortunately, the limitations of this essay preclude investigation of the development of cultural constructions of racial whiteness, not to mention the racialization of the indigenous American population.) Why was it necessary to posit that difference as a matter of public policy? Because the white population, as a matter of public policy, based on Enlightenment political theory, was constructed as having a human birthright of freedom (Immerwahr and Burke 1993, 26–7). The next conceptual step in the American racializing program, insofar as it was connected with the institution of slavery, entailed an identification of enslavement itself as a determinant of race.

The common assumption among contemporary historians is that in English North America, "Negroes" were enslaved because they were "n"egroes.[10] In fact, the situation was worse than that: African prisoners and their descendants were enslaved and kept in slavery for the simple reason that they or their ancestors were first enslaved. This was accomplished through the mediating concept of race, specifically the concept of "negro race."

The final North American public policy regarding the children of female slaves was beneficial to the economic interests of the owners of female slaves. As owners of living things, these owners wanted to have secure ownership of the offspring of what they already owned. Since only "n"egroes could be owned as slaves, the only way that they could own the children of their slaves were if those children were "n"egroes. As everyone has always known, the fathers of many children of women slaves were not slaves or "n"egroes. Therefore, to protect the economic interests of slave owners in English North America, the institution of slavery gave birth to the one-drop rule, as a matter of public policy. By contrast, in Louisiana under French rule and throughout Latin America, manumission of children with slave mothers and free white fathers was common all through the period of slavery. Those children were recognized as mixed black and white race.[11]

It became illegal to import slaves into the United States, in the 1830s. Then the cotton gin increased the speed with which cotton could be processed, and the need for slave labor to grow cotton increased. The large-scale miscegenation of the slave population due to generations of sexual exploitation of female slaves by free whites, as well as intraracial miscegenation within the "n"egro population, resulted in an otherwise embarrassing number of "whiter" slave offspring, who, if they were not automatically designated "n"egroes, because only negroes could be enslaved, would have presented a disastrous loss of capital for the slave economy. After Louisiana came under the rule of Anglo-Americans, and throughout slavery in the United States after the 1850s, all the children of slave mothers, regardless of their paternity, were assumed to have the racial status of their mothers. This was of course contrary to English custom and law, which supported patriarchal descent in all other matters of lineage and property (Zack 1993, 57–61).

Even though, originally, the economics of slavery determined the public policy of the one-drop rule, the abolition of slavery did not mitigate the application of this rule. Between the Civil War and 1915 the one-drop rule became the law in most states, where it was expressed in so-called anti-miscegenation laws that proscribed interracial marriage (Zack 1993, 79–82).[12] Ironically, this policy was locked in place among African Americans during the Harlem Renaissance, when many prominent mixed-race black spokespersons explicitly took up Negro identities to the conceptual obliteration of their white ancestors. At the time, there was no choice in the matter because the United States census no longer recognized a category of mixed race; so anyone who was "black" according to the one-drop rule was not accepted as white in American society (Zack 1993, 95–112). Even though the antimiscegenation laws were struck down by the United States Supreme Court in 1967, the one-drop rule has never been successfully challenged as a basis for racial classification. Officially, and according to custom, an American is black given one black ancestor, no matter how many white ancestors she has and regardless of her social experiences.

Mixed Black and White Race and Present Public Policy: In Principle

The American history of racial categorization was unjust. Against the widespread understanding that the United States has a long history of racial injustice, this might occasion a yawn. However, we are still trapped in the rigidity of notions of biological racial difference that presuppose pseudo-scientific ideas of race. And the one-drop rule is still public policy. Whites assume that this is how blacks want it, and blacks continue to reproduce it socially for a variety of reasons, including the preservation of hard-won affirmative action benefits that reinforce "pure" racial identities, family and community loyalty, and the continuing devaluation and oppression of individuals with African ancestry by individuals without African ancestry.

Nonetheless, many individuals of mixed black and white race, especially of first generation "mixture," experience the one-drop rule not only as racist in itself, against them, but as fundamentally supportive of the false categories of race. The whole idea of race requires an assumption of a population stable in certain physical characteristics, which will "breed true." That is, the idea of race rests on fantasies of racial purity.

The question is not whether it is better for an individual with black and white ancestors to be designated white, or partly black and partly white, than all black, because addressing the question in those terms accepts a foundation of the unjust treatment of blacks by whites. Rather, these are the pertinent questions: Since there is no such thing as race and our present legacy of racial categories is shot through with pseudo-science and racist habits and beliefs, how should "race" be determined? Who should decide what race I am to myself? How should anyone determine the "race" of another person? Notice that there are two levels to these questions. If race is a fiction, then the person of pure race is in the same position regarding these questions as the person of mixed race. But, if race is accepted or recognized as a social reality, then, in the context

of the nonsense of the one-drop rule, the person of mixed black and white race presents a special problem to herself and others.

I would like to stay on the level that all notions of race are fictions, but I don't think that is yet feasible at this time in American culture. Therefore, I am provisionally going to go along with the fiction that there are such things as black and white race, as a basis on which to consider the ongoing one-drop rule from the standpoint of an individual of mixed black and white race. How should mixed black and white individuals identify themselves and be racially identified by others at this time?

I think that the only emancipatory answer to that question has to be provided by the individuals themselves. It has been estimated that between 75 percent and 90 percent of all African Americans have some white ancestry. Within this group, the group likely to self-identify as mixed race is probably no more than 10 percent or 15 percent (Williamson 1980, 9–16, 125). If, however, there is no scientific foundation to the concept of race, that is, if races do not exist, then neither do mixed races exist. The facts of racial mixture, namely the existence of individuals of mixed race, undermine the very notion of race, which presupposes racial "purity." Since there never have been pure races, it is impossible to calculate degrees of racial mixture. Still, despite these puzzles, on a folk level, Americans take race very seriously, and it is only fair that those individuals who do not fit into any one of the recognized racial categories have an opportunity to identify themselves, that is, to choose their own racial identities.

As it stands now, most people "choose" a racial identity after they have learned how others identify them. This is a passive process of choice, closer to socially approved assent than free choice. Children with a black parent and a white parent, and even greater degrees of racial diversity, are now obligated to "choose" which box to check as they move through the various institutional processes of racial identification in the culture. They choose the box that "best" applies to them, but nothing in official or social reality permits them a choice of *everything* that applies to them in racial terms.

Broadly speaking; even given the racial fictions in place, every person defines for herself what it means to be what she is racially by learning about her family history. Using present energy and making commitments for the future, she invents her racial identity at the same time that she tells herself she is discovering it. This is an existential point. The person of mixed race is as entitled to this existential process, with its self-defining illusion of invention masquerading as discovery, as is the person of presumptively pure race. In the present case, she has a right to be mixed race rather than black race or white race. At present, she can be white only if she lies about the presence of a black ancestor. And she can only eschew all racial identity, should she choose to invent herself on the ground of her discovery that race is a fiction, if she refuses to participate in many cultural contexts that might other wise benefit her. This right for a mixed race person to be mixed race seems to be a fundamental requirement for psychological and social health, but it is as difficult to create a general justification for it as it is to justify the right of human beings to selfhood. In fact, the generality of the justification can only be anchored by something beyond American law and culture, as I will try to do in a moment. United States federal racial classification systems presently allow for only four racial categories—black, white, Asian and Native American, with an added ethnic rider of Hispanic or non-Hispanic. Where categories of "other" have been added to state forms, according to "Directive 15," the components of "other" in individual cases are reassessed, and if an individual has a black ancestor, the individual is reclassified as black (see Fernández 1995; Graham 1995).

In June 1993 the United States House of Representatives Subcommittee on Census, Statistics, and Postal Personnel heard public testimony concerning the inclusion of a multiracial category in the U.S. census. As of this writing, the outcome of those hearings is inconclusive. It is not merely that even liberal public record keeping is constrained by outmoded concepts of race in the population at large. The inconclusiveness is further diffused by the expressed concern of African American interest groups that if part of their presently designated constituency of African Americans redesignates itself as multiracial, the remaining constituency will lose affirmative action gains (see Wright 1994). Nonetheless, many black and white mixed-race Americans continue to wonder whether one-drop black racial identification, based on biological fiction, should be supported at the expense of more accurate description and record keeping. It is difficult to see how anyone except the mixed-race individuals themselves would have a right to decide that matter.

According to international moral-political rights theories, as stated in the United Nations Charter, the right of Americans of mixed race to identify themselves and be identified, that is, recognized, as a distinct racial category would seem to be related to other social and political rights of self-determination. The analogue to national self-determination in this political sense, for mixed black and white Americans, is racial self-identification. As with emerging nations, united within themselves by geography, self-identification precedes identification and recognition by others.

Mixed-race people do not constitute geographically continuous, potentially sovereign entities as groups, so there is no issue of political independence at stake. But, neither do racially pure groups present a basis for national sovereignty—except within separatist movements, which in the United States, at least, have been motivated by extremist and supremacist ideologies. There has been, of course, some geographically based political districting of black racial interests in the United States in recent years for the presumed benefit of blacks. If some of the people in those districts revise their identification as racially mixed and not-black, there is concern that the remaining blacks would not benefit as much as when the group was larger (Wright 1994). But, the resulting groups could form coalitions. And, the racism against blacks that presupposes nonexistent general differences among all members of racially designated populations will have been undermined to the extent that everyone publicly acknowledges that some American blacks have white ancestors and are therefore not, strictly speaking, "black." If all blacks are not black because some of them are also white, then the rigid differences that people mistakenly assume have a biological foundation would begin to soften in American folk thought. This would in turn undermine racism as a psychological attitude based on an assumption of strong physical difference.

Furthermore, the United Nations Charter expresses an international moral-political consensus that all individuals are entitled to the same rights, regardless of race and color (Article 2). If blacks and whites have a right to identify themselves as such, then so do mixed black and white individuals. The United Nations Charter also stipulates that no one may be compelled to belong to an association (Article 20, #2). If the one-drop rule does not have the biological foundation it has been assumed to have in American history, then no one should be compelled to be black. And, if race itself is a fiction, then no one should be compelled to identify herself or be identified by others in any way at all racially, if she so chooses. Failure to identify in some specific way racially, or in any way racially, ought not to put anyone at a disadvantage compared to those who do so identify.

In the context of freedom of association as stipulated by the United Nations Charter, racial identification has not yet been addressed because it has been assumed up to now that racial identification has a neutral, factual foundation. Indeed, the international theoretical work on race has primarily focused on the promulgation of the findings of the social and biological sciences of the first half of the twentieth century, which concluded that cultural differences among racial groups are matters of historical contingency rather than physical heredity.[13] But, since there is no empirical, factual foundation for the American one-drop rule of black racial classification, in many cases of mixed race, there are no neutral, factual determinants for racial identification. Given this absence of an assumed biological foundation for racial identification, if it is, for

whatever reason, necessary that mixed-race individuals be identified by race, those individuals have a right to choose their racial identifications, based on the United Nations Charter right to freedom of association.

In situations where an individual's chosen racial designation is at odds with how others classify her, care should be taken by those others to refine the empirical basis on which they make their identifications. And in many cases, the reliance on socially coerced self-identification, that is, the one-drop rule, is so strong that experts will have to dispense with racial categories altogether. An interesting example of this is found in recent American Medical Association policy recommendations for the detection of sickle-cell anemia in infants. It was formally believed that infants of nonwhite racial groups were at higher risk for this disease; however, medical practitioners have come to realize that they have no reliable criteria for identifying all infants racially, so the recommended procedure for detection is to test all infants for sickle-cell anemia, regardless of the racial group to which they seem to belong or are said to belong (Clinton 1991, 2158).

Mixed-race individuals would also have a right to reject all racial identification, just as a full right to freedom in religious affiliation would include the choice of no religious affiliation, or the choice of atheism. I have so far been suggesting that black and white mixed-race Americans would chose to identify as mixed race or nonracial. But even that is too stringent a projection once the false categories begin to crumble. Some people who are mixed black and white race will choose to be black. Others will choose to be white. And still others will choose to identify based on Asian or Native American ancestry.

Mixed Black and White Race and Present Public Policy: In Fact

Parallel to the foregoing theoretical justification for self-identification for individuals of mixed race, there is a demographic and grass-roots basis for such self-identification that public policy theorists and planners need to allow into their awareness as specific contexts make relevant. Statistically, mixed-race births in the United States have increased 26 times as much as pure-race births over recent decades.[14] And now, for the first time in American history, due to the success of the Civil Rights movement, albeit incomplete and begrudged, there is a generation of mixed black and white individuals who are not ashamed of their racial origins, and whose parents do not experience a need to apologize for having brought them into the world.

Project RACE (Reclassify All Children Equally), an organization originating from efforts to change racial designations of school children in Georgia, has been lobbying legislatures in recent years to include multiracial categories on the U.S. census and in local record keeping. The membership of the Association of MultiEthnic Americans consists of mixed-race families and their children; they actively support one another through social and cultural events and newsletters in which they share their experiences in the larger society that does not recognize their existence as mixed race.[15]

When people from different racial categories have children, as they always have done despite the existence of social or legal strictures, and whether they do so as a result of exploitation, accident, ignorance, or love, fairness in a racial society requires that those children receive the same degree of racial respect as presumptively racially pure children, especially since it is widely assumed that racial identities are constructed in childhood in ways closely connected with self-esteem on deep motivational levels. It is not known to what extent the importance of a child's positive feelings about race is a result of racism in the culture. Neither is it known whether it would be consistent with other aspects of mental health and social adjustment for individuals to eschew all racial identity—even in a racist society. Before the studies can be conducted that will provide empirical answers to these questions, however, the conceptual framework or theoretical assumptions that would otherwise underlie such studies must be reexamined. There is no

reason to believe that social scientists are not as burdened by racial mythology as other people.

At this time, for the first time in American academic letters, a small, rapidly increasing number of scholars from varied disciplines are beginning to discuss these issues of microdiversity, and the subject of mixed race is becoming a recognized addition to curricula that address diversity and multiculturalism: Paul Spickard (1989), F. James Davis (1991), Maria P. P. Root (1992), and I (1993, 1995) have recently published book-length works on the topic of mixed race in the United States; and further work is in press as of this writing. (The popular print media and commercial publishing houses are not far behind, or ahead, as the case may be.) The general scholarly topic is *Racial Theory*, the specialization at issue is *Mixed Race* (or *Multirace*), but in practical policy-making contexts, the facts that need to be addressed are the facts of *microdiversity*. The term "microdiversity" points to the reality that many individuals are racially diverse within themselves and not merely diverse as members of groups that are believed, in often erroneous ways, to be racially different from other groups.

The map of the emancipatory scholarship of microdiversity is now on the drawing board: it may be filled in by tracing out the complex varieties of microdiversity which exist in reality; or it may blaze a route to a neo-universalist rejection of the concept of race in both scholarly and popular culture. In historical analyses, microdiversity intersects with critiques of patriarchy because the one-drop rule is a legacy of white male slave owners; and in feminist analyses of contemporary culture, microdiversity intersects with gender because mixed-race women are still stereotyped as exotic, erotic, and morally defective.

In terms of present practice and policy, microdiversity has indeterminate connections with affirmative action. Since the aim of both affirmative action and the scholarship of microdiversity is to improve the institutional situations of individuals who would otherwise be overlooked or abused, both become redundant if they succeed. In the meantime, if affirmative action is just and effective, the facts of microdiversity strengthen its mandate because people of mixed race have never before been positively acknowledged to exist. So long as Americans believe in races, they will believe in racial whiteness, and whites will probably continue to be generally better off than nonwhites. And if affirmative action programs continue to be the chosen strategy for achieving equality, then mixed-race individuals, insofar as they do not belong to the white, privileged, dominant group, would continue to qualify as affirmative action clients (or "patients").

I want to close with a word of caution. Tigers have to be dismounted with great care. It's one thing to understand within a safe forum that race is a biological fiction. In American culture at large, the fiction of race continues to operate as fact, and in situations of backlash against emancipatory progress, the victims of racial oppression, nonwhites, are insulted and injured further for their progress against oppression. If those who practice such second-order oppression begin to employ the truth that race is a fiction, gains already secured against first-order oppression (or in redress of it) could be jeopardized. This is a risk many will find daunting, but the answer is not to back off from the truth but to realize that it will take a while to replace the fictitious cultural realities. If the truth about mixed black and white race and race in general were to be (affirmatively) taught throughout the American educational system, it would take about two generations to have a real effect on the culture—the first generation would learn it in school and teach it to their children.

Discussion Questions

1. Let us allow that each individual has the moral right to define his or her identity. Does it follow that *society* has the obligation to recognize this identity as a social category?

2. If race is supposed to be a cultural rather than a biological classification, what implications does this have for the classification of "mixed race"? For instance, does "mixed race" correspond to a culture?

3. Insofar as the one-drop rule is the product of white racism, are blacks today entitled to appeal to it in order to argue against a new social category, which, many believe, would seriously dilute black political power?

4. What would be the likely effects of a "mixed race" or "biracial" category in the United States? Do you agree with Zack's contention that a recognition of a "mixed race" category would have generally positive effects in terms of undermining racism?

5. Which ought to have priority (in the event that these conflict)—individuals' right to have a socially recognized identity or disadvantaged groups' right to achieve the greatest possible advancement?

Notes

1. For more comprehensive discussions of the inadequacy of the American folk concepts of black and white race, see Zack (1993, 1994).

2. For a book-length treatment of the history of mixed black and white race in the United States, conducted within the traditional racial paradigm, see Williamson (1980).

3. For the facts on blood and race, see Zack (1993, chap. 2 and references).

4. For a discussion of race and breeding, see Zack (1993, chap. 4).

5. For an argument about the *modernity* of contemporary concepts of race, see Bernal (1987, 439–45,454–5). See also Zack (1996, chap. 12).

6. For a discussion of the development of X and Y as chromosomal markers of sex, see Kevles (1985, 238–50).

7. For discussions of variations in racial genes, see Dubinin (1965, 68–83) and Dunn (1965, 61–67).

8. For accounts and discussions of the history of the concept of race in the social sciences see Leiris (1965) and Wacker (1983).

9. For descriptions of nineteenth-century racial hierarchies and source references, see Zack (1993, 58–61, 78–79).

10. For example, Immerwahr and Burke write, "Only blacks were slaves and slaves were slaves *because* they were black" (1993, 27).

11. The classic comparison of North and South America on this issue is Degler (1971).

12. For further details on the history of antimiscegenation laws, see Sickels (1972).

13. For the United Nations positions on race, culture, and heredity, see "Four Statements on the Race Question" (drafted at Unesco House, Paris) in Kuper (1965, 344–364).

14. For the statistics on the increase of mixed-race marriages and births, see Special Reports (1993, 20–21).

15. See Project Race Newsletter, April 1993 (Roswell, Georgia).

References

Bernal, Martin. 1987. *Black Athena.* New Brunswick: Rutgers University Press.

Clinton, Jarrett J. 1991. From the agency for health care policy and research. *Journal of the American Medical Association* 70 (18): 2158.

Davis, F. James. 1991. *Who is black?* University Park: Penn State Press.

Degler, Carl N. 1971. *Neither black nor white: Slavery and race relations in Brazil and the United States.* New York: Macmillan.

Dubinin, N. P. 1965. Race and contemporary genetics. In *Race, science, and society.* See Kuper 1965.

Dunn, L. C. 1965. Race and biology. In *Race, science, and society.* See Kuper 1965.

Fernández, Carlos A. 1995. Testimony of the Association of MultiEthnic Americans. In *American mixed race: The culture of microdiversity.* See Zack 1995.

Graham, Susan. 1995. The grass roots advocacy. In *American mixed race: Exploring microdiversity.* See Zack 1995.

Immerwahr, John and Michael Burke. 1993. Race and the modern philosophy course. *Teaching Philosophy* 16 (1): 26–27.

Kevles, Daniel J. 1985. *In the name of eugenics.* Berkeley: University of California Press.

Kuper, Leo, ed. 1965. *Race, science, and society.* New York: Columbia University Press.

Leiris, Michael. 1965. Race and culture. In *Race, science, and society.* See Kuper 1965.

Root, Maria P. P. 1992. *Racially mixed people in America.* Newbury Park: Sage.

Sickels, Robert J. 1972. *Race, marriage and the law.* Albuquerque: University of New Mexico Press.

Special Reports. 1993. *I-Pride Newsletter* 15(January): 20–21.

Spickard, Paul. 1989. *Mixed blood: Inter-marriage and ethnic identity in twentieth-century America.* Madison: University of Wisconsin Press.

Wacker, R. Fred. 1983. *Ethnicity, pluralism and race.* Westport: Greenwood.

Williamson, Joel. 1980. *New people.* New York: Free Press.

Wright, Lawrence. 1994. One drop of blood. *New Yorker,* 25 July, 46–55.

Zack, Naomi. 1993. *Race and mixed race.* Philadelphia: Temple University Press.

———. 1994. Race and philosophic meaning. *APA Newsletter on Philosophy and the Black Experience* 93: 2.

———. 1995. *American mixed race: The culture of microdiversity.* Lanham: Roman and Littlefield.

———. 1996. *Bachelors of science: Seventeenth century identity then and now.* Philadelphia: Temple University Press.

6   Race, Biraciality, and Mixed Race—In Theory

LEWIS R. GORDON

Study Questions

1. Explain Omi and Winant's view and Gordon's objection to it.
2. How does Gordon define *racism?* How does racism, then, relate to Pico's *Oration on the Dignity of Man?*

3. What is the connection between domination and racelessness?
4. Is there discrimination within the black community against those perceived as being "mixed," or is the reverse true?
5. Why are blacks suspicious of the mixed-race category?
6. What does Gordon mean by the "suicidal irony of a critical mixed race theory"?

Reprinted by permission of the publisher and author from *Her Majesty's Other Children* (Lanham, MD: Rowman and Littlefield, 1997), pp. 51–71.

"You, who are a doctor," said I to my [American] interlocutor, "you do not believe, however, that the blood of blacks has some specific qualities?"

He shrugged his shoulders: "There are three blood types," he responded to me, "which one finds nearly equally in blacks and whites."

"Well?"

"It is not safe for black blood to circulate in our veins."

JEAN-PAUL SARTRE, "RETURN FROM THE UNITED STATES"

An African American couple found themselves taking their child, a few months of age, to a physician for an ear infection. Since their regular physician was out, an attending physician took their care. Opening the baby girl's files, he was caught by some vital information. The charts revealed a diagnosis of "H level" alpha thalassemia, a genetic disease that is known to afflict 2 percent of northeast Asian populations. He looked at the couple.

The father of the child, noticing the reticence and awkwardness of the physician, instantly spotted a behavior that he had experienced on many occasions.

"It's from me," he said. "She's got the disease from me."

"Now, how could she get the disease from you?" the physician asked with some irritation.

"My grandmother is Chinese," the father explained.

The physician's face suddenly shifted to an air of both surprise and relief. Then he made another remark. "Whew!" he said. "I was about to say, 'But—you're *black*.'"

The couple was not amused.

Realizing his error, the physician continued. "I mean, I shouldn't have been surprised. After all, I know Hispanics who are also Asians, so why not African Americans?"

Yes. Why not?

The expression "mixed race" has achieved some popularity in contemporary discussions of racial significations in the United States, Canada,

and the United Kingdom.[1] It is significant that these three countries are marked by the dominance of an Anglo-cultural standpoint. In other countries, particularly with Spanish, Portuguese, and French influences, the question of racial mixture has enjoyed some specificity and simultaneous plurality. For the Anglos, however, the general matrix has been in terms of "whites" and "all others," the consequence of which has been the rigid binary of whites and nonwhites. It can easily be shown, however, that the specific designations in Latin and Latin American countries are, for the most part, a dodge and that, ultimately, the primary distinctions focus on being either white or at least not being black.

We find in the contemporary Anglophone context, however, a movement that is not entirely based on the question of racial mixture per se. The current articulation of racial mixture focuses primarily upon the concerns of *biracial* people. Biracial mixture pertains to a specific group within the general matrix of racial mixing, for a biracial identity can only work once, as it were. If the biracial person has children with, say, a person of a supposedly pure race, the "mixture," if you will, will be between a biracial "race" and a pure one. But it is unclear what race the child will then designate (a mixture of biraciality and *X*, perhaps, which means being a new biracial formation?).

To understand both mixed race and its biracial specification and some of the critical race theoretical problems raised by both, we need first to understand both race and racism in contemporary race discourse.

Much of contemporary race discourse is muddled, confusing, and premised on an ongoing project of evading the core issues of race and racism. Texts that racialize everyone with equal-opportunity racism tend to achieve some popularity because of the carrot they offer the contemporary sentiment on race matters. There is desire to speak about race, that is, but not about racism. Consequently, as race is spoken of in ways that offer multiple sites of oppression (consider the current vogue of the term *racisms*), we find persistent racializing of every site of oppression. Thus, even where race isn't the proper marker nor concern, the terms *race* and *racism* are evoked as legitimating expressions for acts of condemnation. One reason for this tendency is the historic role race and racism have played in the construction of oppression in Anglo societies. For example, given the historical significance of slavery and the civil rights struggle in the United States, the operating metaphor for oppression has been and continues to be race and racism. Thus, race discourse is projected onto any location of group oppression, the consequence of which is that race and racism are spoken of in contexts ranging from Irish-Anglo conflicts to black-Korean conflicts.

Yet, if we were to deconstruct the order of racial signifiers in these contexts, we will notice the persistence of the metaphor "the blacks of . . . ." If one has to be "the black" in or of a particular context in order to designate a racial and a racist formation, then the rug that slips away beneath one's feet becomes apparent with the Fanonian historical "lived-experience" *(l'expérience vécue)* of the black: Although there are people who function as "the blacks" of particular contexts, there is a group of people who function as the blacks everywhere.[2] They are called, in now-archaic language—*Negroes.* Negroes are the blacks of everywhere, the black blacks, the blackest blacks.

Blackness functions as the prime racial signifier. It is, the element that enters a room and frightens Reason out. The popular effort to articulate racial specificity through rubrics such as "racial formation," as emerged in the 1980s in work like that of Michael Omi and Howard Winant, fails, then, to address the lived reality of what race and racism are about.[3] Their theory, which they call racial formation, is premised on the view that race must now be analyzed beyond its historical associations with ethnicity, class, or nation.[4] The biological paradigm of racial formation is limited and limiting, they argue, because it supposedly presumes a static meaning to a historically shifting concept. "*Race is*," they claim, "*a*

concept which signifies and symbolizes social conflicts and interests by referring to different types of human bodies. . . . We define *racial formation* as the sociohistorical process by which racial categories are created, inhabited, transformed, and destroyed" (p. 55, emphasis in original). They define racism thus: "A racial project can be defined as *racist* if and only if it *creates or reproduces structures of domination based on essentialist categories of race*" (p. 71). Fanon's sociogenic turn supports this interpretation. But the historical specificity of blackness as a point *from which* the greatest distance must be forged entails its status as metaphor. The formal structure of racism could be articualted thus:

$$\underline{\qquad} < \!\!-\!\!-\!\!- \underline{\qquad}$$

The underlined blanks are asymmetric points. The arrow points to a direction at which to aim. That direction goes away from the direction to avoid. Color contingently occupies these relations. Distance is relationally understood here, as are race and racism. This distance transcends logic ironically through a logic of its own. For instance, the call for black existence as unjustified existence need not appeal to essentialist racial categories.[5] Couldn't a structure of domination based on an *absence of essential categories* emerge—especially where an essential category is "humanness"?

Note further that the concept of racial formation is based on a distinction between social constructivity (which is an ontological claim about reference) and racial meaning (which pertains to the concept of race and is a claim about sense). Omi and Winant are antipathetic, on social constructivist grounds, to biological interpretations of race, even though a social construction can have biological connotations or senses. It is like a physicist who claims that what is meant by "table" is its collection of atoms. It may be correct that physical particles comprise a table, but that in no way determines the table's meanings. Thus, although meaning may be a function of societal conditions—how, for example, language is manifested—it doesn't follow that what is "meant" is social. Think of the distinction between a belief and a belief about or on the basis of that belief. Both race and racism, for instance, emerge when the physical or the biological is invoked. Groups are therefore racialized at the point at which the values attributed to them are treated as material attributes of who or "what" they are. There are formations that will not collapse into the "racial" category without a special set of signifiers, which the racial formation theory was designed to reject.[6]

In his famous *Oration on the Dignity of Man,* Pico Della Mirandola constructed a schema that is instructive for the understanding of race and racism.[7] According to Pico, the human being stood between the gods above and animals below. Although racism is generally spoken about in terms of hatred of other races, one should note the difference between hatred of other races and racism. One can hate another race on the basis of the conviction that that other race is one's racial superior. With such hatred there is no construction of the other race as less than human. In fact, with such a construction, there is danger of one's own race being less so. To be more precise on our use of the term *racism,* then, we shall use racism to refer to (1) the conviction that there is a race that is superior to other races and (2) the institutional practice of treating that race as superior to others. Pico's schema becomes instructive, in that the implications of a superior race and an inferior race fall onto the schema, in terms of which each group is pushed in relation to the gods and animals. The teleological implication of a superior race is its closer place to the gods, and the implication of an inferior race is its closer place to animals.[8]

The consequence of such a schema is that the conditions of being human are transformed into conditions of being gods or at least godlike. An instructive example of such conditions is Hitler's logic in *Mein Kampf.*[9] There, Hitler argues that the proof of a superior group's superiority is its ability to exercise its will over inferior groups. Thus, a superior group "is" superior by virtue of its place under the status quo. An implication of this superiority is its freedom from constraints. The superior group is literally boundless. It thus

serves as the criterion for its own justification, whereas the inferior groups can only be "justified" in terms of the superior group. In effect, then, the category of superiority demands the impossible of the inferiors. They are to prove the validity of their existence, which, in effect, means to demonstrate, beyond using themselves as justification, that their existence is justified. Recall that Fanon identified this phenomenon in *Les damnés de la terre* when he writes:

Because it is a systematic negation of the other, a resolute decision to refuse the other all the attributes of humanity, colonialism compels the dominated people constantly to ask the question: In reality, who am I? (p. 300).

Although Fanon is talking about colonialism, his points have a corollary in racism. For racism compels the designated inferior race to ask constantly not only in reality who am I, but also, "In reality, *what* am I?"

Without the transition of an interrogated "what," a what that signals a call for one's place in the scheme of human identification, neither racism nor race is born. On the same page, Fanon adds a distinction between domination and colonialism. To be dominated is not identical with being colonized, for it is still possible for one's humanity to be acknowledged (as, for example, in the case of being under the authority of a legitimate government). It is when one's humanity is wiped out of the scheme of human affairs, to the point of functioning as a natural phenomenon among other natural phenomena—in other words, among the land, plants, and animals—that the racist schema evinces itself. Both race and racism, then, are functions below the sphere of normativity. The consequence is that the dominant "race" is, as it were, *raceless.*

Race-neutrality is loaded with coded racial designations. If the standpoint of "man" is the dominant group, then that group stands as the leitmotif of all human significations. If white stands at the top of the value scheme of a society, we will find that many supposedly racially neutral terms also carry a white subtext. Arguably, in most of the world, except northeast Asia and India, the terms *man, woman, person, child,* and a host of other supposedly racially neutral terms, usually mean white man, white woman, white person, and white child.[10] Thus, to be equal to white means to be raceless. Race, then, is a feature of all other groups, and racism becomes a uniquely white possibility and perspective on these groups.

We can now explore the question of how both mixed race and biraciality can be understood in this context. In the United States, the significant factor of differentiation is premised on whites in an epicenter of swirling colors. In effect, then, to be "mixed" is a function of colored realities, not white ones, on the level of "race." Although whites may speak of being "mixed" with various European ethnicities and religions, racial mixture and white identity are antipathetic to each other. Whiteness, in other words, usually signifies purity. The "child," if you will, of white-nonwhite liaisons exists as an onto-biological point of difference from at least one parent. One finds, in such circumstances, a rigid order of hierarchies according to social subordination. Thus, in all matrices it is the white parent who loses onto-racial connection to her or his offspring. But in other matrices—for example, Northeast Asians ("mongoloids") with blacks—it is the Asian parent who loses the connection.[11] In terms of membership, then, the black parent finds a permanent racial connection with the child. (Of course, there are children who reject the racial designation and, in effect, reject, although not intentionally, their parents. But our concern here is the social reality of the hierarchies.)

One finds, then, that offsprings who are biracial mixtures with blacks are pretty much excluded from most racial categories except for black. Although it can be shown that among Native Americans the story differs—for Native American and African American offsprings are often both (Native American and black)—there is still the social reality of the different quality of life available for a child who is a result of Native American unions with whites or Asians versus blacks. I recall speaking at a state university in Tennessee. A member of the audience introduced himself as a redneck with a Confederate flag on his truck. He also identified himself as part Cherokee by virtue of his grandmother, and he added that that has posed no problem at efforts to recruit him at Ku Klux Klan and right-wing militia rallies. I asked him to consider what his affiliations may have been if his grandmother were black or Asian. I also asked him to think about the significance of his Confederate flag as a sign of willingness to join right-wing and racist organizations. And finally, I asked him why he was so proud of being taken by such people as someone who is ideologically in their camp. Before he could respond, a woman in the audience, who announced herself as part Cherokee as well, voiced her objection. "Indians aren't white," she said. "There are whites with some Indian in them. But to be Indian, that's another story. Go to the reservations. You'll see."

Later that year, I found myself having lunch with a prominent couple from Toronto, Canada, one of whom regarded herself as being a biracial mixture of European and Chinese parentage. Her husband was white. As we discussed matters of race and theory, I eventually asked her and her husband to consider this: Most racially mixed marriages in North America occur between white men and Asian women. I recall a Chinese male associate in San Francisco lamenting that, in order to marry an Asian woman in California, he would have to find a way to become white. If the possibility of having children is still a central concern in most marriages, and if people also consider the possibility of desirable children in their choice of matrimonial partners, why don't white men seem to worry about having children with Asian women? Why is the least mixture between blacks and every other group, and the highest mixture between whites and every other group except blacks?[12] And finally, why is there such a qualitatively different life in racial terms for Asians who are mixed with blacks versus Asians mixed with whites? Do we find Asians (and Latin Americans) rushing to wed blacks to uplift their gene pool, as seems to be the case with their marrying whites? Blackness, in the end, functions as a constant, underlying mark of racialization as does no other racial designation. Its persistence suggests that the fluidity of racial identities points upward in continuing spirals of potential whiteness.

But blackness also points to a history of mixed racialization that, although always acknowledged among blacks, is rarely understood or seen among other groups. I have argued elsewhere, for instance, that to add the claim of "mixture" to blacks in both American continents would be redundant, because blacks are their primary "mixed" populations to begin with. Mixture among blacks, in particular, functions as an organizing aesthetic, as well as a tragic history. On the aesthetic level, it signifies the divide between beauty and ugliness. On the social level, the divide is between being just and unjust, virtuous and vicious; "fair skin" is no accidental, alternative term for "light skin." And on the historical level, the divide signifies concerns that often are denied. Consider the striking similarity of the subtext of the following two observations—the first by El-Haji Malik El-Shabazz and the second by Frantz Fanon:

Out in the world later, in Boston and New York, I was among the millions of Negroes who were insane enough to feel that it was some kind of status symbol to be light-complexioned—that one was actually fortunate to be born thus. But, still later, I learned to hate every drop of that white rapist's blood that is in me.[13]

And Mayotte Capécia has [a good] reason [for being elated at having a white grandmother]: It is an honor to be the daughter of a white woman. That shows that she was not "made in the bushes." (This expression is reserved for all the illegitimate children of the upper class in Martinique. They are known to be extremely numerous: Aubery, for example, is reputed to have fathered fifty.) (*Peau noire,* p. 37, n. 5)

In these two passages, we find both an aesthetic and moral tale that is indicative of the dynamics that emerge on questions of racial mixture. On the one hand, there is the prevailing significance of what Fanon calls "denegrification" *(dénégrification),* the phenomenon in which blackness is treated as a Manichæan quantity to be either eliminated from one's body or at least reduced. But on the other hand, there are the facts of historical social reality. In the El-Shabazz/Malcolm X passage, there is the histori-

cal reality of rape that signals the wisdom of the contemporary black expression, "All of us have a little bit of white in us." In Fanon's discussion, however, there is the more nuanced reality of the dynamics of power and gender difference. For Fanon's point is not only that social status enables one to "have one's way" with groups of lower social status, but that even among the upper classes, gender genealogies are of differing significance.[14] A white female parent or grandparent shifts the meaning of the source of whiteness. It is not that one's genesis cannot have a history of violence (for the source of violence could also be from the black father and forefathers), but that if violence were present against a white forebear, consequences would have been different. The victimological narrative on both rape and lynching are so focused on white females for the former and black males for the latter in the Americas that an invisible history of predatory white males reaping the advantages of legally rejected black female bodies became the organizing principles behind any social consciousness of interracial realities. We find, then, a history of a touch of whiteness being a mark of blackness in the Americas.[15] As one U.S. woman of African descent puts it:

While some have recently overthrown this term [Black American] in favor of African American, I have not. I find it too simplistic. I am not an African with American citizenship. Please do not misunderstand. I embrace my African roots. However, the term African American excludes the Native American, White Protestant, and Jewish components of my distant ancestry. And, I identify most strongly with a culture rooted in the American South. Since I have not yet thought up a term that I like better, I still call myself Black.[16]

This woman makes no denial of being "mixed." Yet she defines herself as black, and she uses the term *black* in the way most U.S. blacks actually use the term. (In countries like Brazil, however, blackness refers to a mythical, "pure" blackness because of the existence of the various populations of recognized mixtures that differentiate themselves from blacks. To this point we shall return.) In the North American context, then, awareness of being mixed has taken on a kind of banality in black communities. What is often overlooked, however, is the extent to which mixture-in-itself also has functioned as a site of value. The general view is that people of color's preferential treatment for lightness of skin and eyes and straightness of hair are signs of their preference for or desire to become white. Consider Fanon's rather pithy observation:

For several years, some laboratories have been trying to discover a serum for "denegrification"; these laboratories, with all the seriousness in the world, have rinsed their test tubes, checked their scales, and begun research that might make it possible for the miserable Negroes to whiten themselves and thus to throw off the burden of that corporeal malediction. (*Peau noire*, pp. 89–90)

These remarks on the technology of denegrification signal the matrices of value in a world that is conditioned by two fundamental convictions: (1) it is best to be white, and (2) it is worst to be black. The logic leads to obvious conclusions of rational action. Failing to become white, one can at least increase the distance between oneself and blackness. Thus, there are skin creams for lighter skin, hair devices and chemicals for straight, "pretty," more "manageable" hair, blue- and hazel-eyed contact lenses, and surgical techniques for the transformation of lips, hips, thighs, and any dimension of the body that is interpreted as a signifier of blackness.[17] Yet in spite of the seemingly obvious aim of becoming white, I suggest that another step in the analysis is needed to understand how such phenomena are, in phenomenological terms, *lived.* The way such phenomena are lived alludes less to becoming white than to gaining certain aesthetic and political-economic resources that pertain to being white. Many blacks, in short, simply want to be beautiful and successful. But because no black can be white, it follows that there must be some *other,* achievable point of being beautiful and successful that is aimed at in such activity, and I have argued that that achievable point is ironically one that is already embodied by the people trying to achieve it. One has, in other words, a phenomenon of black people aiming not to pass for being white, but instead to pass for being *mixed,* which is ironic because most people of color in North

and South America as well as Europe and Australia, are, in fact, already mixed. That being mixed needs to be made apparent—that is, it is important to *look* like one's mixture, to be, in a word, "authentically" mixed—provides a demand for the technology of mixed-race constructions.[18] Within the white social sphere, the technological innovation is ironically similar: The objective, whether in Bo Derek's wearing corn-rows or the current wave of hairstyle and tanning techniques to don the *look* of mixed race, is not to be taken for being mixed in the sense of parentage or heredity, but in the sense of *playing* mixture—literally, wearing it.

Appearing mixed offers something for both poles of the racial matrix. A touch of mixedness, which announces blackness, functions like black leather or lingerie in a bedroom—wearing it elicits associations and desires that are necessary but purged and relegated elsewhere in a bad-faith social order.[19] If blacks are socially acceptable sites of sexual and biological release, then one needs to wear one's blackness to be set "free."[20] The mixture emerges, then, as whiteness in colored clothing. In popular culture, examples abound: Whites in "darky" or blackface makeup, superheroes and heroines who don dark garbs, sexy vampire ghouls in dark clothing, or even the recent popular film, *The Mask* (1994), in which the personality released by the protagonist's wearing the possessed mask during the night abounds with peculiarly African American and Afro-Caribbean cultural formations, music such as jazz, rhumba, salsa, and the language of hipsters' like Cab Calloway and the youthful Detroit Red (Malcolm X). The libidinous release achieved through rock 'n' roll has its genesis, after all, in white participation in black musical productions.[21]

In black communities, power and superiority have long been invested in children whose mixture was, let us say, phenomenologically apparent. To wear one's mixedness offered instant satisfaction. Even if one were not affluent or successful, simply appearing mixed signaled that one ought to have been so. One's existence takes on that added, almost-human element that shifts one's condition from the banal to the unjust and eventually to the tragic—as in the case of the "tragic mulatto."

Recall our discussion of Pico's schema. Individuals who are a mixture of white and black find themselves in more than a construction of mixture in and of itself. They find themselves lacing a mixture of clearly unequal terms. For even if their whiteness is toppled from the stage of whiteness, it will stand, nevertheless, on the level of a human existence. But the prevailing ideology offers no hope in the other direction, where blackness is located on a lower point of the evolutionary scale. The conclusion is devastating: One is more of a human being to the extent to which one is less black.

The consequence of such an ideology is a set of existential and political considerations that provide tensions in the current movements of mixed-race identifications, to which we shall now turn.

Race talk is dirty business, primarily because race discourse exists in a racist context, a context that is occasioned by such a desire to deny what it is that its mode of operation is to play on ambiguities of the human condition in order to avoid getting to the heart of the matter. Consequently, diversions constitute a vast body of the literature. One is on the road to sobriety, however, when one begins to interrogate the keepers of the gate, for at least then one can discern the purpose of the practice.

Race discourse today can be divided into groups who find the very concept of race repugnant and groups who find race itself to be less an issue and racism to be the primary concern.[22] Between these two groups of theorists, however, I would add a group I shall call *everyday people.* For the most part, everyday people do not think about races. They instead think about groups of people who are identified as races by people who theorize about what human beings are and what they do. Thus, for the typical antiblack racist, it is not races that bother him. It is *the blacks. The blacks* are an idealization that is seen in the body of certain people throughout the day. *The blacks* signal the extreme category of the nonwhites. As a character announced in a wonderful German cinematic allegory on racism and immigration: "As if it weren't bad enough that we had the Italians and the Turks. Now we have the Africans!"[23] Similarly, children learn about groups to hate, although they have no clue about what races are. I make these remarks because it is important to understand the extent to which race is a designation that usually emerges in contexts of explanation, whereas racism is simply the lived, ongoing practice that stimulates such explanation. The antirace people therefore miss the point. Even if they show that race is a social construction, even if they show that races are no more than cultural or social formations, even if they show that races are pseudoscientific fictions, they still need to address the ways in which phenomena understood as racial phenomena are lived. Not all black people know what races are, but they know what hatred of black people is. They read it in the symbols of value and the objective sites of power and lack thereof in which they are immersed in their waking moments, and even in their dreams. Even if every scientific claim about the existence of races is true, the antiracism people can retort, and rightly I would say, that such claims will have no impact on the task of fighting racism.[24] The fight against racism is an existential/moral phenomenon. Proof is found in the nineteenth century, when people who actually believed in the scientific validity of the concept of race simultaneously fought against slavery, genocide, and exploitation, and the myriad of ways in which *racism* is made manifest. Against Anthony Appiah's position then, where it is claimed that racism needs to be rejected because of the scientific invalidity (which for him constitutes the ontological illegitimacy) of the concept of race, the obvious conclusion here is that the scientific invalidity of races is not the relevant point.[25]

The antirace gatekeepers have had an unfortunate relationship with the evolution of one dimension of mixed-race movements and contemporary biracial politics. As we've seen, the whole point is not to be the darkest/most inferior.

So, given the existential dimensions of what we have discussed thus far, what, may we say, are the goals and possibilities available for a critical theory of mixed race?

Some claims that can be asserted in favor of a critical race theory premised on mixed-race identity are:

1. Accuracy and consistency of racial ideology demand a mixed-race standpoint, for if whites and blacks are "pure," then mixtures signify "other" forms of race. (This argument supports the reasoning behind constructing separate racial categories for mixed-race people.)

2. The question of accuracy raises questions of affiliation: Filial recognition plays an important role in our self-identities. The need to recognize fully one's ancestry calls for recognition of mixture. Saying that one's ancestry is all-black because of the "one-drop rule," for instance, fails to identify relatives whose lineage is multiracial beyond their African ancestry.

3. On the biracial end, there is the fact of converging embodiments to consider: A biracial offspring "is" biologically and often culturally both of her or his parents.

4. If race *means* black or white, then mixture becomes an enigma. It signifies "racelessness." (This argument goes both ways. In favor of a separate category for mixed-race people, it is advanced as a way of eliminating their exclusion from racial matrices by making such a provision. Against a category of mixed-race people, it is advanced to claim that even a racial designation will be an inaccurate articulation of their reality. And there are those who argue that it provides a critique of racial categories to begin with and perhaps point to a [raceless] future.)[26]

5. On the practical end, biraciality and mixed-race designations can serve an antiracist strategy: recognition of racial mixture dilutes identities premised on conceptions of "purity" and can therefore be an important stage on the road to a raceless or more racially free future.

6. And finally, but not exhaustively, there is the existential claim: Mixed and biracial people have unique experiences that can be shared and cultivated through a recognized group identification. (This existential turn is also, of course, support for the political implications designated by the first claim.)

Now, recall my point about the two dominant principles of racist ideology: (1) be white, but above all, (2) don't be black. We can call the first *the principle of white supremacy;* and we can call the second *the principle of black inferiority.* Given these two principles, the following responses can be made to our six aforementioned claims.

First, we have already shown that to be racialized means not to be "white." And in fact, when white is spoken of as a race, many whites experience discomfort for good reason; it violates their place in the social order. Thus, when all is said and done, the question of mixed-race people being an "other" race is only significant in regard to principle (2), which signifies the importance of not being black. Now, although this principle doesn't apply to biracial and mixed people along Euro-Asian or Euro-Native American lines—and given the racial hierarchies, it is rare, very rare indeed, that we find principle (2) being articulated in relation to any group other than blacks—it becomes clear that the "other" race argument is really about not being black.[27] Since the practice is geared toward adhering to principle (2), the political consequence will be an institutionalization of a certain place in the racial hierarchy. There will, in short, be an institutionally recognized group of nonblacks. One can readily see why certain groups of blacks are very suspicious of such a move, for its consequence is, after all, a quantitative reduction, by a legal stroke, of the population of designated black people. A whole group of black people will, that is, legally disappear.

Perhaps the best critical response to this move stems from our articulation of racism as a desire for black people to disappear. The first claim about accuracy requiring a mixed-race standpoint has the consequence of facilitating such a process, at least in terms of legal measures that can be taken. Such a consequence clearly violates W. E. B. Du Bois' famous admonition against problematizing people instead of responding to the social problems that people experience.[28] There is nothing in the first claim that can reject the conclusion that the world will be better off if it had a lot less black folks, especially since the number of white people in the world will in no way diminish from such a move.

The second claim about affiliation seems to me to be correct but also in need of other considerations, for the question of filial recognition pertains primarily to *white* affiliation. The history of ancestral denial and rejecting descendants hasn't been a problem of colored folks. It is a white problem. There are whites who deny black ancestry and whites who reject black descendants; the issue pertains to the principle of white supremacy. But the principle of black inferiority also emerges through the lack of appreciation of black filial recognition. In black communities, for instance, talk of ancestry nearly always pertains to non-black ancestry. It was only during brief moments of African ancestral pride, periods under attack today as "nationalist" and "Afrocentric," that a search for specificity of African lineage emerged. There are, however, surprising sites of such recognition. On a research visit to Cuba, for instance, my U.S. colleagues and I were astonished by a tour guide's response to a question raised by a member of our delegation: "Are there any Cuban Indians still around?" The guide, without missing a beat, responded, "Native Caribbeans were killed off within a century of Columbus's landing. All Cubans are of African and European ancestry." Because Cubans, at least the Cubans who remain on the island, are for the most part a "colored" people, the point of colored recognition is here affirmed. But even in Cuba, there are clearly black-designated people. There, as in most of the Caribbean, Central America, and South America, such people hardly stand as racially superior. The project of the ancestral claim, then, is to affirm *mixture* itself, which is to establish the force of the principle of black inferiority.

The third claim is clearly true. Biracial offsprings are from both parents biologically and often culturally. But again, once one introduces a racial designation other than white, the principle of black inferiority becomes the dominant factor. The biracial person can embody white superiority if the current group of people who are designated white people disappear. But in that case, whoever is next on the racial hierarchical scale will become white people. This turn, then, affirms the principle of black inferiority only because of the *current* limitations of embodying the principle of superior whiteness. In countries such as Brazil and Mexico, this is exactly what occurs. I recall a colleague of mine being shocked, for instance, while staying with a family in Guatemala. The family, whom he saw as not only colored but "mixed," categorically hated black people. What were they? Their answer was simple: white.

Moreover, the biracial offspring who attempts to affirm both identities faces the social reality of both identities existing on unequal terms. In short, to affirm whiteness on the level of blackness has the consequence of equalizing whiteness, which, in effect, is to "blacken" it. There is thus the catch-22 of being unable to affirm their white side *as white* without encountering two perversions of reality: Either the white side is treated as superior or it is treated as a form of nonwhite whiteness; as, in a word, colored. These considerations bring us to the fourth claim, which addresses the supposed racelessness of mixed groups.

The fourth claim is subject to all the criticisms of race-neutrality. Since whites function as normative standpoints of humanity, they normally live as raceless. Angela Y. Davis, in a public lecture, phrased the situation thus: If colored means not to be white, then white means to be colorless.[29] Thus, to declare, as Michael Jackson did in his song "Black or White," "I don't want to spend my life being a color," means, in effect, to spend one's life surreptitiously being white. The problem with using this route as a means to a raceless future, then, is that it affirms a future premised on both principles by ultimately advocating the elimination of black people.

In an essay entitled, "White Normativity and the Racial Rhetoric of Equal Protection," Robert Westley unmasks some insidious dimensions of racelessness in the present age.[30] When the search for a legal remedy to racism took the form of *equal* protection, many whites suddenly gained the consciousness of being *racialized*. In the previous world, there were only human beings and coloreds—at the bottom of which were *the blacks.* Today, the law says that blacks are equal to every other group, which for these groups means that the law considers them equal to blacks. A strange equality: blacks move up while everyone else moves "down." For many whites, the metaphor of being treated "like the blacks" became a source of deeply rooted anxiety. In effect, social policy demanded that they . . . take, as Adam and Eve apparently did, a "fall." Needless to say, many whites couldn't take it, and a full-scale attack on affirmative action and an array of antirace and so-called reverse-discrimination constructions emerged. The goal of this attack is supposedly a raceless future, but because racism can persist without race, such a future holds the key to a special nightmare of exploitation and invisibility without reference. It problematizes race, ultimately, to preserve racism.

The fifth claim, which sees an antiracist strategy in which racelessness is the carrot at the end of the rod, is problematic for the same reasons as the fourth one: It portends a world without blacks.

The sixth claim, that biracial and mixed-race people have a unique existential situation, strikes me as correct. Mixed-race and biracial people do have unique experiences that are functions of their existential situation. For the biracial child, the anonymous white man may be, in his specific instantiation, Daddy. And all the literature and cultural knowledge of victimized feminity—white, pure, rapable—may be Mommy. Similarly, the complex social forces that say that one is more one's black parent than one's white parent (or one's Asian or Native American parent) raises a complex question of who one is by virtue of one's choice and that choice's relation to one's

social situation. Since black Americans and Native Americans are already mixed peoples (what is a "pure" New World black and Native American today?), the question relates, mostly, to people of color elsewhere: African Americans, for example, experience a profound anxiety when they travel to "black" countries; they seem, in those places, to be the least or lesser blacks; they carry with them, that is, the United States as a history of white domination and, for the most part, the masculine history of white "insemination."

On the existential level, biracial people at least have the unique experience of living the racial realities of more than one group in the course of their innermost private lives. That reality alone substantiates something unique, since among all other groups, "others" function anonymously. "God knows what they do in their homes!" is not a rhetorical appeal in biracial people's lived realities.

The question of the political significance of the sixth claim is undermined, however, by our critique of the other claims, especially the first. After all, having a unique situation does not mean that the principle of white superiority and the principle of black inferiority should be affirmed. For the biracial child stands below whiteness and, by virtue of biraciality, in affirmation of black inferiority. The impact of building policy on the uniqueness of biracial people, then, is that it fails to account for political realities that are already in place against people who are clear and present violators of the principle against blackness—in a word, *blacks*.

In spite of contemporary resistance to "binary" analyses, a critical discussion of mixed-race categories calls for an understanding of how binary logic functions in discourses on race and racism. Without binaries, no racism will exist. We have seen the politics of mixed-racialization come to the fore, for instance, on matters of legal recognition of multiple categories. There, principle (2), which affirms the importance of not being black, is the most significant principle. That is because there are social benefits in not being designated black. It is a waste of time to discuss the social losses of being designated white, since the distribution of resources on a global scale falls disproportionately in favor of whites. Affirming principle (2), therefore, affirms the whole racist hierarchy that we may be attempting to avoid. It solidifies the significance of the expression, "Well, at least you're not black."

The struggle against racism from a mixed-race critical position cannot work, then, through simply a rejection of principle (1). To reject the importance of being white in no way addresses the social revulsion with being black. A mixed-race racial position is compatible with the rejection of principle (1), but it is not compatible with the rejection of principle (2). That is because there is no way to reject the thesis that there is something wrong with being black beyond the willingness to "be" black—not in terms of convenient fads of playing blackness, but by paying the social costs of anti-blackness on a global scale. Against the raceless credo, then, racism cannot be rejected without a dialectic in which humanity experiences a blackened world. But therein lies the suicidal irony of a *critical* mixed-race theory.

Discussion Questions

1. Compare Gordon's definition of *racism* with Garcia's.
2. How is Gordon arguing that the category of "mixed race" will ultimately promote racism? How would Zack reply?
3. How does the recognition of mixed race violate one, but not the other, basic principle of racist ideology?

Notes

1. See, for example, Naomi Zack's *Race and Mixed Race* (Philadelphia: Temple University Press, 1993) and her edited volume *American Mixed Race* (Lanham, MD: Rowman and Littlefield, 1995), as well as the February 13, 1995, issue of *Newsweek* for some discussion of this phenomenon. One also can argue that the popularity of the term *hybridity* in postmodern and postcolonial cultural studies is indicative of this phenomenon, where, in an effort to evade the peculiarly biological dimensions of race, *cultural* mixture becomes the focus in a tale of political ambiguity. That cultures are not homogeneous is not new to cultural anthropologists. Its contemporary popularity is premised on a false academic history of hegemonic purity. For discussion, see Paul Gilroy's *The Black Atlantic; Modernity and Double Consciousness* (Cambridge, MA: Harvard University Press, 1993). Although Gilroy's position is a sound critique of cultural reductionism and cultural purity (homogeneity may have been a value of cultures, but not a reality of their evolution), some of his readers' interests stem not from the social logic of his argument but from a fascination with a form of privileged hybridity or mixture. One need only consult the contemporary mystique of mixture, particularly of the female biracial variety in British popular films over the past two decades. For discussion, see Joy Ann James, *Resisting State Violence in U.S. Culture* (Minneapolis: University of Minnesota Press, 1996) and Lisa Anderson, *Mammies No More!* (Lanham, MD: Rowman & Littlefield, 1997). Finally, on the matter of political ambiguity, I think context and relevance are the best appeals. Sometimes, circumstances are without ambiguity. Only those with tenuous access to power can afford ambiguity in their political relations.

2. See Fanon, *Peau noire, masques blancs,* chap. 5. For discussion, see *Bad Faith and Antiblack Racism,* part III.

3. Michael Omi and Howard Winant, *Racial Formations in the United States: From the 1960s to the 1990s,* 2nd ed. (New York and London: Routledge, 1994).

4. We argue that sex and gender are two categories that also apply.

5. I discuss this dimension of antiblack racism in parts III and IV of *Bad Faith and Antiblack Racism.* See also "Introduction: Black Existential Philosophy" in *Existence in Black.*

6. For discussion, see treatments of the spirit of seriousness in chap. 6 and the discussion of "meaning" and racism in Parts II and III of *Bad Faith and Antiblack Racism,* as well as the critique, in *Fanon and the Crisis of European Man,* chap. 3, of the current misuse of the term *social construction.* See also Fanon's discussion of blacks as an "*objet phobogène*" (phobogenic object) and the point at which "*commence le cycle du biologique*" (the cycle of the *biological* begins) in *Peau noire,* pp. 123, 131. For critical discussion of Omi and Winant's notion of a racial formation, see also David Theo Goldberg's *Racist Culture: Philosophy and the Politics of Meaning* (Oxford: Blackwell, 1993), especially p. 88.

7. See Count Giovanni Pico Della Mirandola, *Oration on the Dignity of Man,* trans. by Elizabeth L. Forbes, in *The Renaissance Philosophy of Man,* ed. by Ernst Cassirer, Paul Oskar Kristeller, and John Herman Randall, Jr. (Chicago: University of Chicago Press, 1939).

8. For some readers, Lovejoy's discussion of the Great Chain of Being may come to mind. For discussion of that ontological schema, see Daniel Wideman, "The 'African Origin' of AIDS: De-constructing Western Biomedical Discourse," in *Black Texts and Textuality: Constructing and De-Constructing Blackness,* ed. with an intro. by Lewis R. Gordon and Renée T. White (Lanham, MD: Rowman & Littlefield, forthcoming). See also Robert Westley, "White Normativity and the Rhetoric of Equal Protection" in *Existence in Black.*

9. For discussion of this "logic," see C. W. Cassinelli, *Total Revolution: A Comparative Study of Germany under Hitler, the Soviet Union under Stalin, and China under Mao* (Santa Barbara and Oxford: Clio Books, 1976), part II.

10. One can argue that they mean these categories in those other societies as well, but the argument requires a demonstration of the relation between historical reality and phenomenology of "race seeing." For such a phenomenology, see *Bad Faith and Antiblack Racism,* chaps. 13–14.

11. For some discussion of Afro-Asian dynamics, see Ernest Allen, Jr., "When Japan Was 'Champion of the Darker Races': Satokata Takahashi and the Flowering of Black Messianic Nationalism," *The Black Scholar* 24, no. 1 (Winter 1994): 23–46, and Joy Ann James, *Resisting State Violence in U.S. Culture* (Minneapolis: University of Minnesota Press, 1996), chap. 15. For specifically Northeast Asian encounters with racial mixture in the United States, see Stephen Satris, " 'What Are They?' " in *American Mixed Race: The Culture of Microdiversity,* ed. by Naomi Zack (Lanham, MD: Rowman and Littlefield, 1995), pp. 53–60. Satris argues that children of European (caucasion) and Northeast Asian (mongoloid) descent tend to be regarded as Asian only when mongoloid morphology is visually apparent. Children who don't appear as such are regarded and treated by the white and Asian communities as white.

12. According to the U.S. Census, as of 1993, only 2% of interracial marriages were between blacks and "other" races, 20% between blacks and whites, but the number of interracial marriages between whites and non-black "others" was 77%. See also Connie Leslie, Regina Elam, Allison Samuels, and Danzy Senna, "The Loving Generation: Biracial Children Seek Their Own Place," *Newsweek* (February 13, 1995), p. 72, where these figures also are cited.

13. From *The Autobiography of Malcolm X as Told to Alex Haley* (New York: Ballentine Books, 1965), p. 2.

14. The impact of class on interracial relationships hasn't received significant study. And in fact, most of the constructions of interracial liaisons are premised on either a white male boss with a colored female subordinate, or affluent men of color with affluent white women. But note: relationships are most likely to occur where people are compelled to live. Because the black poor and the white poor have few options over where they can live, and because the urban poor tend to be located in black areas of cities, it follows that interracial relationships should have a greater probability of emerging in poor or working-class communities: In fact, there are no black American communities that have not had a white population, however small.

15. For discussion, see Fanon's essay "Antillais et africains" in his *Pour la révolution africaine: Écrits politiques* (Paris: François Maspero, 1979), pp. 22–31. The essay appears as "West Indians and Africans" in the English edition, *Toward the African Revolution: Political Essays,* trans. by Haakon Chevalier (New York: Grove Press, 1967), pp. 17–27. See also our chap. 4 below.

16. Victoria Holloway, "President's Message," *The Drum: The SNMA-Yale Chapter Newsletter* (October 1991): 1.

17. The question of transforming the body takes special forms with Northeast Asians. There is, for instance, the phenomenon of surgically "fixing" the eyes. But note, the normative point is white eyes. The probability of Asians transforming their bodies to look more "black" is very small. For discussion of Northeast Asian Americans' identity formations, see Brian Locke, "The Impact of the Black-White Binary on Asian American Identity," *Radical Philosophy Review* 1 no. 2 (1998). Locke argues that an apocalyptic subtext of the U.S. black-white binary structures Asian Americans as foreign.

18. In this regard, the appeal to mixed race as a model for resisting appeals to racial and cultural "authenticity" appears misguided, for the problem of authenticity—as "being *authentically* mixed" demonstrates—is quite resilient.

19. For more discussion of playing blackness, see bell hooks, *Black Looks: Race and Representation* (Boston: South End Press, 1992), chap. 1.

20. See, for example, bell hooks' criticism of Camille Paglia: " 'Black' Pagan or White Colonizer?" chap. 7 of hooks' *Outlaw Culture* (New York and London: Routledge, 1994).

21. One also finds the phenomenon of mixture in philosophy itself, where there is antipathy on the part of the dominant, Anglo-Analytical philosophy toward any of the pluralistic, "mixed" conceptions of philosophy ranging from pragmatism and European continental philosophy, on the one hand, to Africana philosophies and Eastern philosophies on the other. Departments that offer both are "mixed." Interestingly enough, certain "mixtures" exist in the form of Anglo-Analytical approaches to Africans philosophy, the most noted proponent of which is Kwame Anthony Appiah and the analytical race theorists who follow his path.

22. Theorists who focus on the concept of race are Michael Omi and Howard Winant, K. Anthony Appiah, Jorge Klor de Alva, and Naomi Zack. Theorists who focus on racism are Lucius Outlaw, Paget Henry, David Theo Goldberg, Cornel West, and myself, among others. This distinction doesn't mean, however, that the two groups do not touch on dimensions of each other's position. The former group argues that the elimination of the discourse of race is a necessary step toward the elimination of racism. The latter takes two stands on that issue. First, some argue for the existential complexity of race. Second, some argue that racism can exist without race. In either event, both groups end up addressing race and racism, but the first group, unlike the second, wants to eliminate both categories.

23. *Schwartzfarhen* (1992). In contemporary Eastern Europe (and Europe generally), the digression seems to take a definite form: first, xenophobic (anti-immigration) and, eventually, racist (antiblack). The argument is that immigration policies pollute the state by leading to an influx of blacks. For discussion, see Paul Hockenos, *Free to Hate: The Rise of the Right in Post-Communist Eastern Europe* (New York and London: Routledge, 1993). We also may note that in California the pattern is strikingly similar: Proposition 187 is anti-immigrants legislation that has been followed by a so-called Civil Rights Initiative, which is an anti-Affirmative Action legislation that is primarily antiblack.

24. A classic instance of a thinker and activist against racism who nevertheless believes in races is Franz Boas. Boas believed not only in the existence of races, but also that blacks were to some extent less intellectually capable than whites, yet he fought vehemently against the status of second-class citizenship of blacks. For discussion, see Vernon Williams, Jr., *Re-thinking Race: Franz Boas and His Contemporaries* (Lexington: University of Kentucky Press, 1996). See also Amy Guttman's "Responding to Racial Injustice" in Anthony Appiah and Amy Guttman, *Color Conscious: The Political Morality of Race,* with an intro. by David B. Wilkins (Princeton: Princeton University Press, 1996), p. 64.

25. For discussion, see K. Anthony Appiah's "Racisms" in *Anatomy of Racism,* ed. by David Theo Goldberg (Minneapolis: University of Minnesota Press, 1990), pp. 3–17; Appiah's *In My Father's House: Africa in the Philosophy of Culture* (New York and Oxford: Oxford University Press), pp. 13–15; and "Race, Culture, and Identity: Misunderstood Connections" in *Color Conscious.* We return to Appiah and scientific criteria of meaning in chap. 6, below.

26. All of these possibilities are discussed in Naomi Zack's *Mixed Race and American Mixed Race.*

27. On the nonracial level, a correlative is in religious-cultural affiliation, where the goal of the assimilating Jew is not to be Jewish. The closest similarity to the racial question emerges when the assimilating Jew of "mixed" Gentile-Jewish parentage experiences this question through having a Jewish mother. We return to this question in chap. 6, below.

28. W. E. B. Du Bois, *The Souls of Black Folks,* with introductions by Nathan Hare and Alvin F. Poussaint, revised and updated bibliography (New York and Scarborough, Ontario: New American Library, 1982 [originally published, 1903]), chap. 1.

29. Angela Y. Davis, Keynote Address, *10th Annual Empowering Women of Color Conference: Reaping Fruit, Throwing Seed* (22 April 1995), University of California at Berkeley.

30. Robert Westley, "White Normativity and the Rhetoric of Equal Protecting" in *Existence in Black.*

PART II

MORAL AND POLITICAL PHILOSOPHY

Nationalism, Separatism, and Assimilation

It is idle to talk about rights, it is mere chattering for the sake of being seen and heard—like the slave, saying something because his so called "master" said it.

MARTIN R. DELANEY

My strongest conviction as to the future of the Negro therefore is, that he will not be expatriated nor annihilated, nor will he forever remain a separate and distinct race from the people around him, but that he will be absorbed, assimilated, and will only appear finally, as the Phoenicians now appear on the shores of the Shannon, in the features of a blended race.

FREDERICK DOUGLASS

The whole of mankind is a vast representation of the Deity. Therefore we cannot extinguish any race either by conflict or amalgamation without serious responsibility.

EDWARD BLYDEN

Frantz Fanon may have expressed himself too succinctly but it is all there in his words. "There is no Negro mission; there is no white burden . . . I have one right alone: That of not renouncing my freedom through my choices—I am not a prisoner of history. I should not seek there for the meaning of my destiny."

BERNARD BOXILL

To answer the question of "Who am I?" correctly, then, is to know and live one's history and practice one's culture.

MAULANA RON KARENGA

T his chapter develops certain important aspects of two African American paradigms, or fundamental ways of seeing and organizing reality. One paradigm is separatist—or, at any rate, nationalist. (Not all nationalists are separatists, for one may believe in a "black nation" without advocating physical separation.) The other paradigm is assimilationist—or, at any rate, anti-separatist and to some extent anti-nationalist. (One may oppose separation without endorsing biological or even cultural assimilation, for distinct cultures may live in physically the same area.)

The idea of *nationalism* has a long and an important history specifically for African Americans. Writing before the Civil War, Martin R. Delaney spoke of persons of African descent in this country, both slave and free, as a "nation within a nation," united by common culture and opposed by a common foe, the larger, white society. For Delaney, this status—coupled with the futility of petitioning for one's rights within the larger nation—meant that *colonization* was the only feasible expression of nationhood. Rejecting the idea of emigration to Liberia, he favored a number of other possible sites. By contrast, his fellow advocate of colonization, Edward W. Blyden, spoke passionately of the "thousands and thousands of Negroes in the South . . . longing to go to the land of their fathers"—that is, back to Africa.

In the twentieth century, West Indian political theorist and activist Marcus Garvey emerged as the leading advocate of the ideas of black nationalism and possible colonization. In the selections from his writings included here, Garvey speaks to the perennial issues of racial pride, religious faith, and especially power.

Of course, one may believe in the imperatives of struggle *without* accepting either colonization or separatism. It was, after all, Frederick Douglass—the greatest *opponent* of colonization and separatism—who lived by these words: "Power concedes nothing without a fight; it never has and it never will." In our selections, Douglass attacks both separatism and colonization and even predicts the eventual assimilation of the black race into the general U.S. population. Douglass, however, did not advocate intermarriage or the deliberate biological assimilation of African Americans. Instead, his vision was of one of social and political assimilation but, above all else, of democracy. The real question, Douglass wrote, was whether "the white and colored people of this country [can] be blended into a common nationality and enjoy together, in the same country, under the same flag, the inestimable benefits of life, liberty, and the pursuit of happiness, as neighborly citizens of a common country." Answering his own question, Douglass said, "I believe they can."

In the past two decades, a perceptible change has occurred in black nationalist thought. Although black nationalism remains a potent political force, certainly in the figure of Louis Farrakhan and in the Nation of Islam, with the rise of black studies departments in universities it has become an educational/intellectual movement as well. With this change has come an important new term in African American philosophy: *Afrocentrism*.

Maulana Karenga is probably the most influential figure uniting the black nationalism of the 1960s and 1970s and the Afrocentric movement of the 1980s and 1990s. His "Seven Principles" are an attempt to define an African-based value system and to provide the philosophical basis of the African American holiday Kwanzaa, devised by Karenga himself. In the 1990s, Molefi K. Asante, whose critique of DuBois was included in Part I, has emerged as a leading exponent of "Afrocentricity." Asante conceives of this as a thoroughgoing alternative to prevailing "Eurocentric" paradigms—in education, social science, and historical research. In the reading included here, Asante characterizes the "Afrocentric idea" in education. In his view, a student is best served by educational methods that "place his or her group within the center of the context of knowledge." His objection to the U.S. system of education basically is that this has been done only for whites. Others, and especially African Americans, are educated from a perspective in which

African people are the objects, not the subjects, of history. That is, they are studied from the perspective of the doings of Europeans and the effect of Europeans on people of color. They are not, Asante points out, studied as historical subjects (agents) in their own right.

The object of Afrocentrism, then, is to correct this serious injustice. Where Afrocentrism is especially controversial, however, is in its tendency to divide world cultural history into very separate, seemingly isolated streams, based on race. It is also controversial in its tendency to present these traditions, and especially the African ones, seemingly in a romanticized way—wherein all that is bad, or perceived bad, such as homosexuality, becomes a matter of "decadent" European influences.

Cornel West's synoptic discussion of the "four responses" (to white supremacism) may be read as, in part, a criticism of some tendencies within Afrocentrism. [What West terms the "exceptionalist" tradition is most like Afrocentrism in upholding the uniqueness and unique contributions of African civilization.] The "humanist" tradition, with which West is evidently most in sympathy, while upholding these values, does so by emphasizing the analogies of African American culture with other cultural forms and their "universal human content." West writes of the humanist tradition that it "neither romanticizes nor rejects" Afro-American culture.

One important contemporary application of the nationalist/assimilation divide concerns the use of Black English (Ebonics) in school. A recent focus of debate has been a proposal of the Oakland School Board in 1996, which asserted the validity of Ebonics as the primary language of black students and proposed that standard English be taught them as a second language. For some—including Professor Smitherman, whose reflections on Ebonics are included here—this proposal was liberating. Others, including many prominent black leaders, voiced their opposition. Smitherman, a prominent black linguist, argues the scientific case for Ebonics. Milton Baxter, whose background is in educational theory, raises questions mainly concerned with the social impact of Ebonics.

7 The Condition, Elevation, Emigration, and Destiny of the Colored People of the United States

MARTIN R. DELANY

Study Questions

1. What basic similarity exists between the colored people of the United States and such groups as the Poles in Russia and the Hungarians in Austria?
2. What is the "great mistake" of the colored peoples and how does it relate to the three fundamental laws?
3. What, according to Delaney, must be the "means of elevation"?
4. Why is it useless to talk of "rights"? What solution does Delaney suggest instead?

I. Condition of Many Classes in Europe Considered

That there have been in all ages and in all countries, in every quarter of the habitable globe, especially among those nations laying the greatest claim to civilization and enlightenment, classes of people who have been deprived of equal privileges, political, religious and social, cannot be denied, and that this deprivation on the part of the ruling classes is cruel and unjust, is also equally true. Such classes have ever been looked upon as inferior to their oppressors, and have ever been mainly the domestics and menials of society, doing the low offices and drudgery of those among whom they lived, moving about and existing by mere sufferance, having no rights nor privileges but those conceded by the common consent of their political superiors. These are historical facts that cannot be controverted, and therefore proclaim in tones more eloquently than

thunder, the attention of every oppressed man, woman, and child under the government of the people of the United States of America.

In past ages there were many such classes, as the Israelites in Egypt, the Gladiators in Rome, and similar classes in Greece; and in the present age, the Gipsies in Italy and Greece, the Cossacs in Russia and Turkey, the Sclaves and Croats in the Germanic States, and the Welsh and Irish among the British, to say nothing of various other classes among other nations.

That there have in all ages, in almost every nation, existed a nation within a nation—a people who although forming a part and parcel of the population, yet were from force of circumstances, known by the peculiar position they occupied, forming in fact, by the deprivation of political equality with others, no part, and if any, but a restricted part of the body politic of such nations, is also true.

Such then are the Poles in Russia, the Hungarians in Austria, the Scotch, Irish, and Welsh in the United Kingdom, and such also are the Jews, scattered throughout not only the length and breadth of Europe, but almost the habitable globe, maintaining their national characteristics, and looking forward in high hopes of seeing the day when they may return to their former national position of self-government and independence, let that be in whatever part of the habitable world it may. This is the lot of these various classes of people in Europe, and it is not our intention here, to discuss the justice or injustice of the causes that have contributed to their degradation, but simply to set forth the undeniable facts, which are as glaring as the rays of a noonday's sun, thereby to impress them indelibly on the mind of every reader of this pamphlet.

It is not enough, that these people are deprived of equal privileges by their rulers, but, the more effectually to succeed, the equality of these

From *The Condition, Elevation, Emigration, and Destiny of the Colored People of the United States,* originally appeared in 1852, privately printed in Philadelphia.

classes must be denied, and their inferiority by nature as distinct races, actually asserted. This policy is necessary to appease the opposition that might be interposed in their behalf. Wherever there is arbitrary rule, there must of necessity, on the part of the dominant classes, superiority be assumed. To assume superiority, is to deny the equality of others, and to deny their equality, is to premise their incapacity of self-government. Let this once be conceded, and there will be little or no sympathy for the oppressed, the oppressor being left to prescribe whatever terms at discretion for their government, suits his own purpose.

Such then is the condition of various classes in Europe; yes, nations, for centuries within nations, even without the hope of redemption among those who oppress them. And however unfavorable their condition, there is none more so than that of the colored people of the United States.

II. Comparative Condition of the Colored People of the United States

The United States, untrue to her trust and unfaithful to her professed principles of republican equality, has also pursued a policy of political degradation to a large portion of her native born countrymen, and that class is the Colored People. Denied an equality not only of political, but of natural rights, in common with the rest of our fellow citizens, there is no species of degradation to which we are not subject.

Reduced to abject slavery is not enough, the very thought of which should awaken every sensibility of our common nature; but those of their descendants who are freemen even in the non-slaveholding States, occupy the very same position politically, religiously, civilly and socially, (with but few exceptions,) as the bondman occupies in the slave States.

In those States, the bondman is disfranchised, and for the most part so are we. He is denied all civil, religious, and social privileges, except such as he gets by mere sufferance, and so are we. They have no part nor lot in the government of the country, neither have we. They are ruled and governed without representation, existing as mere nonentities among the citizens, and excrescences on the body politic—a mere dreg in community, and so are we. Where then is our political superiority to the enslaved? None, neither are we superior in any other relation to society, except that we are defacto masters of ourselves and joint rulers of our own domestic household, while the bondman's self is claimed by another, and his relation to his family denied him. What the unfortunate classes are in Europe, such are we in the United States, which is folly to deny, insanity not to understand, blindness not to see, and surely now full time that our eyes were opened to these startling truths, which for ages have stared us full in the face.

It is time that we had become politicians, we mean, to understand the political economy and domestic policy of nations; that we had become as well as moral theorists, also the practical demonstrators of equal rights and self-government. Except we do, it is idle to talk about rights, it is mere chattering for the sake of being seen and heard—like the slave, saying something because his so called "master" said it, and saying just what he told him to say. Have we got now sufficient intelligence among us to understand our true position, to realise our actual condition, and determine for ourselves what is best to be done? If we have not now, we never shall have, and should at once cease prating about our equality, capacity, and all that. . . .

IV. Our Elevation in the United States

That very little comparatively as yet has been done, to attain a respectable position as a class in this country, will not be denied, and that the successful accomplishment of this end is also possible, must also be admitted; but in what manner, and by what means, has long been, and is even now, by the best thinking minds among the colored people themselves, a matter of difference of opinion.

We believe in the universal equality of man, and believe in that declaration of God's word, in which it is there positively said, that "God has made of one blood all the nations that dwell on the face of the earth." Now of "the nations that dwell on the face of the earth," that is, all the people—there are one thousand millions of souls, and of this vast number of human beings, two-thirds are colored, from black, tending in complexion to the olive or that of the Chinese, with all the intermediate and admixtures of black and white, with the various "crosses" as they are physiologically, but erroneously termed, to white. We are thus explicit in stating these points, because we are determined to be understood by all. We have then, two colored to one white person throughout the earth, and yet, singular as it may appear, according to the present geographical and political history of the world, the white race predominates over the colored; or in other words, wherever there is one white person, that one rules and governs two colored persons. This is a living undeniable truth, to which we call the especial attention of the colored reader in particular. Now there is a cause for this, as there is no effect without a cause, a comprehensible remediable cause. We all believe in the justice of God, that he is impartial, "looking upon his children with an eye of care," dealing out to them all, the measure of his goodness; yet, how can we reconcile ourselves to the difference that exists between the colored and the white races, as they truthfully present themselves before our eyes? To solve this problem, is to know the remedy; and to know it, is but necessary, in order successfully to apply it. And we shall but take the colored people of the United States, as a fair sample of the colored races everywhere of the present age, as the arguments that apply to the one, will apply to the other, whether Christians, Mahommedans, or pagans.

The colored races are highly susceptible of religion; it is a constituent principle of their nature, and an excellent trait in their character. But unfortunately for them, they carry it too far. Their hope is largely developed, and consequently, they usually stand still—hope in God, and really expect Him to do that for them, which it is necessary they should do themselves. This is their great mistake, and arises from a misconception of the character and ways of Deity. We must know

God, that is understand His nature and purposes, in order to serve Him; and to serve Him well, is but to know him rightly. To depend for assistance upon God, is a *duty* and right; but to know when, how and in what manner to obtain it, is the key to this great Bulwark of Strength, and Depository of Aid.

God himself is perfect; perfect in all his works and ways. He has means for every end; and every means used must be adequate to the end to be gained. God's means are laws—fixed laws of nature, a part of His own being, and as immutable, as unchangeable as Himself. Nothing can be accomplished but through the medium of, and comformable to these laws.

They are *three*—and like God himself, represented in the three persons in the God-head—the *Spiritual, Moral* and *Physical* Laws. That which is Spiritual, can only be accomplished through the medium of the Spiritual law; that which is Moral, through the medium of the Moral law; and that which is Physical, through the medium of the Physical law. Otherwise than this, it is useless to expect any thing. Does a person want a spiritual blessing, he must apply through the medium of the spiritual law—*pray* for it in order to obtain it. If they desire to do a moral good, they must apply through the medium of the moral law—exercise their sense and feeling of *right* and *justice,* in order to effect it. Do they want to attain a physical end, they can only do so through the medium of the physical law—go to *work* with muscles, hands, limbs, might and strength, and this, and nothing else will attain it.

The argument that man must pray for what he receives, is a mistake, and one that is doing the colored people especially, incalculable injury. That man must pray in order to get to Heaven, every Christian will admit—but a great truth we have yet got to learn, that he can live on earth whether he is religious or not, so that he conforms to the great law of God, regulating the things of earth; the great physical laws. It is only necessary, in order to convince our people of their error and palpable mistake in this matter, to call their attention to the fact, that there are no people more religious in this Country, than the colored people, and none so poor and miserable as they. That prosperity and wealth, smiles upon the efforts of wicked white men, whom we know to utter the name of God with curses, instead of praises. That among the slaves, there are thousands of them religious, continually raising their voices, sending up their prayers to God, invoking His aid in their behalf, asking for a speedy deliverance; but they are still in chains, although they have thrice suffered out their three score years and ten. That "God sendeth rain upon the just and unjust," should be sufficient to convince us that our success in life, does not depend upon our religious character, but that the physical laws governing all earthly and temporary affairs, benefit equally the just and the unjust. Any other doctrine than this, is downright delusion, unworthy of a free people, and only intended for slaves. That all men and women, should be moral, upright, good and religious—we mean *Christians*—we would not utter a word against, and could only wish that it were so; but, what we here desire to do is, to correct the long standing error among a large body of the colored people in this country, that the cause of our oppression and degradation, is the displeasure of God towards us, because of our unfaithfulness to Him. This is not true; because if God is just—and he is—there could be no justice in prospering white men with his fostering care, for more than two thousand years, in all their wickedness, while dealing out to the colored people, the measure of his displeasure, for not half the wickedness as that of the whites. Here then is our mistake, and let it forever henceforth be corrected. We are no longer slaves, believing any interpretation that our oppressors may give the word of God, for the purpose of deluding us to the more easy subjugation; but freemen, comprising some of the first minds of intelligence and rudimental qualifications, in the country. What then is the remedy, for our degradation and oppression? This appears now to be the only remaining question—the means of successful elevation in this our own native land? This depends entirely upon the application of the means of Elevation.

V. Means of Elevation

Moral theories have long been resorted to by us, as a means of effecting the redemption of our brethren in bonds, and the elevation of the free colored people in this country. Experience has taught us, that speculations are not enough; that the *practical* application of principles adduced, the thing carried out, is the only true and proper course to pursue.

We have speculated and moralised much about equality—claiming to be as good as our neighbors, and every body else—all of which, may do very well in ethics—but not in politics. We live in society among men, conducted by men, governed by rules and regulations. However arbitrary, there are certain policies that regulate all well organized institutions and corporate bodies. We do not intend here to speak of the legal political relations of society, for those are treated on elsewhere. The business and social, or voluntary and mutual policies, are those that now claim our attention. Society regulates itself—being governed by mind, which like water, finds its own level. "Like seeks like," is a principle in the laws of matter, as well as of mind. There is such a thing as inferiority of things, and positions; at least society has made them so; and while we continue to live among men, we must agree to all *just* measures—all those we mean, that do not necessarily infringe on the rights of others. By the regulations of society, there is no equality of persons, where there is not an equality of attainments. By this, we do not wish to be understood as advocating the actual equal attainments of every individual; but we mean to say, that if these attainments be necessary for the elevation of the white man, they are necessary for the elevation of the colored man. That some colored men and women, in a like proportion to the whites, should be qualified in all the attainments possessed by them. It is one of the regulations of society the world over, and we shall have to conform to it, or be discarded as unworthy of the associations of our fellows.

Cast our eyes about us and reflect for a moment, and what do we behold! Every thing that presents to view gives evidence of the skill of the white man. Should we purchase a pound of groceries, a yard of linen, a vessel of crockeryware, a piece of furniture, the very provisions that we eat,—all, all are the products of the white man, purchased by us from the white man, consequently, our earnings and means, are all given to the white man.

Pass along the avenues of any city or town, in which you live—behold the trading shops—manufactories—see the operations of the various machinery—see the stage-coaches coming in, bringing the mails of intelligence—look at the railroads interlining every section, bearing upon them their mighty trains, flying with the velocity of the swallow, ushering in the hundreds of industrious, enterprising travelers. Cast again your eyes widespread over the ocean—see the vessels in every direction with their white sheets spread to the winds of heaven, freighted with the commerce, merchandise and wealth of many nations. Look as you pass along through the cities, at the great and massive buildings—the beautiful and extensive structures of architecture—behold the ten thousand cupolas, with their spires all reared up towards heaven, intersecting the territory of the clouds—all standing as mighty living monuments, of the industry, enterprise, and intelligence of the white man. And yet, with all these living truths, rebuking us with scorn, we strut about, place our hands akimbo, straighten up ourselves to our greatest height, and talk loudly about being "as good as any body." How do we compare with them? Our fathers are their coachmen, our brothers their cookmen, and ourselves their waiting-men. Our mothers their nurse-women, our sisters their scrub-women, our daughters their maid-women, and our wives their washer-women. Until colored men, attain to a position above permitting their mothers, sisters, wives, and daughters, to do the drudgery and menial offices of other men's wives and daughters; it is useless, it is nonsense, it is pitiable mockery, to talk about equality and elevation in society. The world is looking upon us, with feelings of commiseration, sorrow, and contempt. We scarcely deserve sympathy, if we peremptorily refuse advice, bearing upon our elevation.

We will suppose a case for argument: In this city reside, two colored families, of three sons and three daughters each. At the head of each family, there is an old father and mother. The opportunities of these families, may or may not be the same for educational advantages—be that as it may, the children of the one go to school, and become qualified for the duties of life. One daughter becomes school-teacher, another a mantua-maker, and a third a fancy shop-keeper; while one son becomes a farmer, another a merchant, and a third a mechanic. All enter into business with fine prospects, marry respectably, and settle down in domestic comfort—while the six sons and daughters of the other family, grow up without educational and business qualifications, and the highest aim they have, is to apply to the sons and daughters of the first named family, to hire for domestics! Would there be an equality here between the children of these two families? Certainly not. This, then, is precisely the position of the colored people generally in the United States, compared with the whites. What is necessary to be done, in order to attain an equality, is to change the condition, and the person is at once changed. If, as before stated, a knowledge of all the various business enterprises, trades, professions, and sciences, is necessary for the elevation of the white, a knowledge of them also is necessary for the elevation of the colored man; and he cannot be elevated without them.

White men are producers—we are consumers. They build houses, and we rent them. They raise produce, and we consume it. They manufacture clothes and wares, and we garnish ourselves with them. They build coaches, vessels, cars, hotels, saloons, and other vehicles and places of accommodation, and we deliberately wait until they have got them in readiness, then walk in, and contend with as much assurance for a "right," as though the whole thing was bought by, paid for, and belonged to us. By their literary attainments, they are the contributors to, authors and teachers of, literature, science, religion, law, medicine, and all other useful attainments that the world now makes use of. We have no reference to ancient times—we speak of modern things.

These are the means by which God intended man to succeed: and this discloses the secret of the white man's success with all of his wickedness, over the head of the colored man, with all of his religion. We have been pointed and plain, on this part of the subject, because we desire our readers to see persons and things in their true position. Until we are determined to change the condition of things, and raise ourselves above the position in which we are now prostrated, we must hang our heads in sorrow, and hide our faces in shame. It is enough to know that these things are so; the causes we care little about. Those we have been examining, complaining about, and moralising over, all our life time. This we are weary of. What we desire to learn now is, how to effect a *remedy;* this we have endeavored to point out. Our elevation must be the result of *self-efforts,* and work of our *own hands.* No other human power can accomplish it. If we but determine it shall be so, it will be so. Let each one make the case his own, and endeavor to rival his neighbor, in honorable competition.

These are the proper and only means of elevating ourselves and attaining equality in this country or any other, and it is useless, utterly futile, to think about going any where, except we are determined to use these as the necessary means of developing our manhood. The means are at hand, within our reach. Are we willing to try them? Are we willing to raise ourselves superior to the condition of slaves, or continue the meanest underlings, subject to the beck and call of every creature bearing a pale complexion? If we are, we had as well remained in the South, as to have come to the North in search of more freedom. What was the object of our parents in leaving the South, if it were not for the purpose of attaining equality in common with others of their fellow citizens, by giving their children access to all the advantages enjoyed by others? Surely this was their object. They heard of liberty and equality here, and they hastened on to enjoy it, and no people are more astonished and disappointed than they, who for the first time, on beholding the

position we occupy here in the free North—what is called, and what they expect to find, the free States. They at once tell us, that they have as much liberty in the South as we have in the North—that there as free people, they are protected in their rights—that we have nothing more—that in other respects they have the same opportunity, indeed the preferred opportunity, of being their maids, servants, cooks, waiters, and menials in general, there, as we have here—that had they known for a moment, before leaving, that such was to be the only position they occupied here, they would have remained where they were, and never left. Indeed, such is the disappointment in many cases, that they immediately return back again, completely insulted at the idea, of having us here at the north, assume ourselves to be their superiors. Indeed, if our superior advantages of the free States, do not induce and stimulate us to the higher attainments in life, what in the name of degraded humanity will do it? Nothing, surely nothing. . . .

XVI. National Disenfranchisement of Colored People

The most prominent provisions of the Constitution of the United States, and those which form the fundamental basis of personal security, are they which provide, that every person shall be secure in their person and property: that no person may be deprived of liberty without due process of law, and that for crime or misdemeanor; that there may be no process of law that shall work corruption of blood. By corruption of blood is meant, that process, by which a person is *degraded* and deprived of rights common to the enfranchised citizen—of the rights of an elector, and of eligibility to the office of a representative of the people; in a word, that no person nor their posterity, may ever be debased beneath the level of the recognised basis of American citizenship. This debasement and degradation is "corruption of blood"; politically understood—a legal acknowledgement of inferiority of birth.

Heretofore, it ever has been denied, that the United States recognised or knew any difference between the people—that the Constitution makes no distinction, but includes in its provisions, all the people alike. This is not true, and certainly is blind absurdity in us at least, who have suffered the dread consequences of this delusion, not now to see it.

By the provisions of this bill, the colored people of the United States are positively degraded beneath the level of the whites—are made liable at any time, in any place, and under all circumstances, to be arrested—and upon the claim of any white person, without the privilege, even of making a defence, sent into endless bondage. Let no visionary nonsense about *habeas corpus,* or a *fair trial,* deceive us; there are no such rights granted in this bill, and except where the commissioner is too ignorant to understand when reading it, or too stupid to enforce it when he does understand, there is no earthly chance—no hope under heaven for the colored person who is brought before one of these officers of the law. Any leniency that may be expected, must proceed from the whims or caprice of the magistrate—in fact, it is optional with them; and *our* rights and liberty entirely at their disposal.

We are slaves in the midst of freedom, waiting patiently, and unconcernedly—indifferently, and stupidly, for masters to come and lay claim to us, trusting to their generosity whether or not they will own us and carry us into endless bondage.

The slave is more secure than we; he knows who holds the heel upon his bosom—we know not the wretch who may grasp us by the throat. His master may be a man of some conscientious scruples; ours may be unmerciful. Good or bad, mild or harsh, easy or hard, lenient or severe, saint or satan—whenever that master demands any one of us—even our affectionate wives and darling little children, *we must go into slavery*—there is *no alternative.* The *will* of the man who sits in judgment on our liberty, is the law. To him is given *all power* to say, whether or not we have a right to enjoy freedom. This is the power over the slave in the South—this is now extended to the North. The will of the man who sits in judgment over us is the law; because it is explicitly provided that the *decision* of the commissioner shall be final, from which there can be no appeal.

The freed man of the South is even more secure than the freeborn of the North; because such persons usually have their records in the slave states, bringing their "papers" with them; and the slaveholders will be faithful to their own acts. The Northern freeman knows no records; he despises the "papers."

Depend upon no promised protection of citizens in any quarter. Their own property and liberty are jeopardised, and they will not sacrifice them for us. This we may not expect them to do.

Besides, there are no people who ever lived, love their country and obey their laws as the Americans.

Their country is their Heaven—their Laws their Scriptures—and the decrees of their Magistrates obeyed as the fiat of God. It is the most consummate delusion and misdirected confidence to depend upon them for protection; and for a moment suppose even our children safe while walking in the streets among them.

A people capable of originating and sustaining such a law as this, are not the people to whom we are willing to entrust our liberty at discretion.

What can we do?—What shall we do? This is the great and important question:—Shall we submit to be dragged like brutes before heartless men, and sent into degradation and bondage?—Shall we fly, or shall we resist? Ponder well and reflect.

A learned jurist in the United States, (Chief Justice John Gibson of Pennsylvania,) lays down this as a fundamental right in the United States: that "Every man's house is his castle, and he has the right to defend it unto the taking of life, against any attempt to enter it against his will, except for crime," by well authenticated process.

But we have no such right. It was not intended for us, any more than any other provision of the law, intended for the protection of Americans. The policy is against us—it is useless to contend against it.

This is the law of the land and must be obeyed; and we candidly advise that it is useless for us to contend against it. To suppose its repeal, is to anticipate an overthrow of the Confederative Union; and we must be allowed an expression of opinion, when we say, that candidly we believe, the existence of the Fugitive Slave Law *necessary* to the continuance of the National Compact. This Law is the foundation of the Compromise—remove it, and the consequences are easily determined. We say necessary to the continuance of the National Compact: certainly we will not be understood as meaning that the enactment of such a Law was *really* necessary, or as favoring in the least this political monstrosity of the THIRTY-FIRST CONGRESS of the UNITED STATES of AMERICA—surely not at all; but we speak logically and politically, leaving morality and right out of the question—taking our position on the acknowledged popular basis of American Policy; arguing from premise to conclusion. We must abandon all vague theory, and look at *facts* as they really are; viewing ourselves in our true political position in the body politic. To imagine ourselves to be included in the body politic, except by express legislation, is at war with common sense, and contrary to fact. Legislation, the administration of the laws of the country, and the exercise of rights by the people, all prove to the contrary. We are politically, not of them, but aliens to the laws and political privileges of the country. These are truths—fixed facts, that quaint theory and exhausted moralising, are impregnable to, and fall harmlessly before.

It is useless to talk about our rights in individual States: we can have no rights there as citizens, not recognised in our common country; as the citizens of one State, are entitled to all the rights and privileges of an American citizen in all the States—the nullity of the one necessarily implying the nullity of the other. These provisions then do not include the colored people of the United States; since there is no power left in them, whereby they may protect us as their own citizens. Our descent, by the laws of the country, stamps us with inferiority—upon us has this law worked *corruption of blood*. We are in the hands of the General Government, and no State can rescue us. The Army and Navy stand at the service of our enslavers, the whole force of which, may at any moment—even in the dead of night, as has been done—when sunk in the depth of slumber, be called out for the purpose of forcing our mothers, sisters, wives, and chil-

dren, or ourselves, into hopeless servitude, there to weary out a miserable life, a relief from which, death would be hailed with joy. Heaven and earth—God and Humanity!—are not these sufficient to arouse the most worthless among mankind, of whatever descent, to a sense of their true position? These laws apply to us—shall we not be aroused?

What then shall we do?—what is the remedy—is the important question to be answered?

This important inquiry we shall answer, and find a remedy in when treating of the emigration of the colored people.

XVII. Emigration of the Colored People of the United States

That there have been people in all ages under certain circumstances, that may be benefited by emigration, will be admitted; and that there are circumstances under which emigration is absolutely necessary to their political elevation, cannot be disputed.

This we see in the Exodus of the Jews from Egypt to the land of Judea; in the expedition of Dido and her followers from Tyre to Mauritania; and not to dwell upon hundreds of modern European examples—also in the ever memorable emigration of the Puritans, in 1620, from Great Britain, the land of their birth, to the wilderness of the New World, at which may be fixed the beginning of emigration to this continent as a permanent residence.

This may be acknowledged; but to advocate the emigration of the colored people of the United States from their native homes, is a new feature in our history, and at first view, may be considered objectionable, as pernicious to our interests. This objection is at once removed, when reflecting on our condition as incontrovertibly shown in a foregoing part of this work. And we shall proceed at once to give the advantages to be derived from emigration, to us as a people, in preference to any other policy that we may adopt. This granted, the question will then be, Where shall we go? This we conceive to be all-important—of paramount consideration, and shall endeavor to show the most advantageous locality; and premise the recommendation, with the strictest advice against any countenance whatever, to the emigration scheme of the so called Republic of Liberia.

Discussion Questions

1. Do African Americans constitute "a nation within a nation"? (Define *nation*.)
2. Is there an *alternative* to the very widely rejected ideas of colonization, political separatism, and assimilation? If so, what is it?
3. Compare the attitudes of African Americans in reference to Africa with those of American Jews in reference to Israel—or other ethnic groups in reference to the land of their origin.
4. Delaney suggests that white people have succeeded, despite their wickedness, by being producers (and black people have failed, despite their religion, by being mere consumers). Do you agree?

8 The Future of the Negro, The Future of the Colored Race, The Nation's Problem, and On Colonization

FREDERICK DOUGLASS

Study Questions

1. Why is a separate nation within a nation not a workable idea?
2. Why is Douglass against "racial pride"?
3. Why is racial isolation not a good thing?
4. What is the "worst aspect of the talk of colonization"?

It would require the ken of a statesman and the vision of a prophet combined to tell with certainty what will be the ultimate future of the colored people of the United States, and to neither of these qualifications can I lay claim. We have known the colored man long as a slave, but we have not known him long as a freeman and as an American citizen. What he was as a slave we know; what he will be in his new relation to his fellowmen, time and events will make clear. One thing, however, may safely be laid down as probable, and that is, that the Negro, in one form and complexion or another, may be counted upon as a permanent element of the population of the United States. He is now seven millions, has doubled his number in thirty years, and is increasing more rapidly than the more favored population of the South. The idea of his becoming extinct finds no support in this fact. But will he emigrate? No! Individuals may, but the masses will not. Dust will fly, but the earth will remain. The expense of removal to a foreign land, the difficulty of finding a country where the conditions of existence are more favorable than here, attachment to native land, gradual improvement in moral surroundings, increasing hope of a better future, improvement in character and value by education, impossibility of finding any part of the globe free from the presence of white men,—all conspire to keep

"The Future of the Negro," from *The North American Review,* July 1884; "The Future of the Colored Race," from *The North American Review,* May 1886 pp. 437–440; "The Nation's Problem," a speech before the Bethel Literary and Historical Society, April 1889; "On Colonization" is from an address, "The Lessons of the Hour," delivered in Washington, D.C., 1894.

the Negro here, and compel him to adjust himself to American civilization.

In the face of history I do not deny that a darker future than I have indicated may await the black man. Contact of weak races with strong has not always been beneficent. The weak have been oppressed, persecuted, driven out, and destroyed. The Hebrews in Egypt, the Moors in Spain, the Caribs in the West Indies, the Picts in Scotland, the Indians and Chinese in our own country, show what may happen to the Negro. But happily he has a moral and political hold upon this country, deep and firm, one which in some measure destroys the analogy between him and other weak peoples and classes. His religion and civilization are in harmony with those of the people among whom he lives. He worships with them in a common temple and at a common altar, and to drag him away is to destroy the temple and tear down the altar. Drive out the Negro and you drive out Christ, the Bible, and American liberty with him. The thought of setting apart a State or Territory and confining the Negro within its borders is a delusion. If the North and South could not live separately in peace, and without bloody and barbarous border wars, the white and black cannot. If the Negro could be bottled up, who could or would bottle up the irrepressible white man? What barrier has been strong enough to confine him? Plainly enough, migration is no policy for the Negro. He would invite the fate of the Indian, and be pushed away before the white man's bayonet.

Nor do I think that the Negro will become more distinct as a class. Ignorant, degraded, and repulsive as he was during his two hundred years of slavery, he was sufficiently attractive to make possible an intermediate race of a million, more or less. If this has taken place in the face of those odious barriers, what is likely to occur when the colored man puts away his ignorance and degradation and becomes educated and prosperous? The tendency of the age is unification, not isolation; not to clans and classes, but to human brotherhood. It was once degradation intensified for a Norman to associate with a Saxon; but time and events have swept down the barriers between them, and Norman and Saxon have become Eng-

lishmen. The Jew was once despised and hated in Europe, and is so still in some parts of that continent; but he has risen, and is rising to higher consideration, and no man is now degraded by association with him anywhere. In like manner the Negro will rise in social scale. For a time the social and political privileges of the colored people may decrease. This, however, will be apparent rather than real. An abnormal condition, born of war, carried him to an altitude unsuited to his attainments. He could not sustain himself there. He will now rise naturally and gradually, and hold on to what he gets, and will not drop from dizziness. He will gain both by concession and by self-assertion. Shrinking cowardice wins nothing from either meanness or magnanimity. Manly self-assertion and eternal vigilance are essential to Negro liberty, not less than to that of the white man.

The Future of the Colored Race

It is quite impossible, at this early date, to say with any decided emphasis what the future of the colored people will be. Speculations of that kind, thus far, have only reflected the mental bias and education of the many who have essayed to solve the problem.

We all know what the Negro has been as a slave. In this relation we have his experience of two hundred and fifty years before us, and can easily know the character and qualities he has developed and exhibited during this long and severe ordeal. In his new relation to his environment, we see him only in the twilight of twenty years of semi-freedom; for he has scarcely been free long enough to outgrow the marks of the lash on his back and the fetters on his limbs. He stands before us, to-day, physically, a maimed and mutilated man. His mother was lashed to agony before the birth of her babe, and the bitter anguish of the mother is seen in the countenance of her offspring. Slavery has twisted his limbs, shattered his feet, deformed his body and distorted his features. He remains black, but no longer comely. Sleeping on the dirt floor of the slave cabin in infancy, cold on one side and warm on the other, a forced circulation of blood on the one side and chilled and retarded circulation on the other, it has come to pass that he has not the vertical bearing of a perfect man. His lack of symmetry, caused by no fault of his own, creates a resistance to his progress which cannot well be overestimated, and should be taken into account, when measuring his speed in the new race of life upon which he has now entered. As I have often said before, we should not measure the Negro from the heights which the white race has attained, but from the depths from which he has come. You will not find Burke, Grattan, Curran and O'Connell among the oppressed and famished poor of the famine-stricken districts of Ireland. Such men come of comfortable antecedents and sound parents.

Laying aside all prejudice in favor of or against race, looking at the Negro as politically and socially related to the American people generally, and measuring the forces arrayed against him, I do not see how he can survive and flourish in this country as a distinct and separate race, nor do I see how he can be removed from the country either by annihilation or expatriation.

Sometimes I have feared that, in some wild paroxysm of rage, the white race, forgetful of the claims of humanity and the precepts of the Christian religion, will proceed to slaughter the Negro in wholesale, as some of that race have attempted to slaughter Chinamen, and as it has been done in detail in some districts of the Southern Status. The grounds of this fear, however, have in some measure decreased since the Negro has largely disappeared from the arena of Southern politics, and has betaken himself to industrial pursuits and the acquisition of wealth and education, though even here, if over-prosperous, he is likely to excite a dangerous antagonism; for the white people do not easily tolerate the presence among them of a race more prosperous than themselves. The Negro as a poor ignorant creature does not contradict the race pride of the white race. He is more a source of amusement to that race than an object of resentment. Malignant resistance is augmented as he approaches the plane occupied by the white race, and yet I think that that resistance

will gradually yield to the pressure of wealth, education, and high character.

My strongest conviction as to the future of the Negro therefore is, that he will not be expatriated nor annihilated, nor will he forever remain a separate and distinct race from the people around him, but that he will be absorbed, assimilated, and will only appear finally, as the Phoenicians now appear on the shores of the Shannon, in the features of a blended race. I cannot give at length my reasons for this conclusion, and perhaps the reader may think that the wish is father to the thought, and may in his wrath denounce my conclusion as utterly impossible. To such I would say, tarry a little, and look at the facts. Two hundred years ago there were two distinct and separate streams of human life running through this country. They stood at opposite extremes of ethnological classification: all black on the one side, all white on the other. Now, between these two extremes, an intermediate race has arisen, which is neither white nor black, neither Caucasian nor Ethiopian, and this intermediate race is constantly increasing. I know it is said that marital alliance between these races is unnatural, abhorrent and impossible, but exclamations of this kind only shake the air. They prove nothing against a stubborn fact like that which confronts us daily and which is open to the observation of all. If this blending of the two races were impossible we should not have at least one-fourth of our colored population composed of persons of mixed blood, ranging all the way from a dark-brown color to the point where there is no visible admixture. Besides, it is obvious to common sense that there is no need of the passage of laws, or the adoption of other devices, to prevent what is in itself impossible.

Of course this result will not be reached by any hurried or forced process. It will not arise out of any theory of the wisdom of such blending of the two races. If it comes at all, it will come without shock or noise or violence of any kind, and only in the fullness of time, and it will be so adjusted to surrounding conditions as hardly to be observed. I would not be understood as advocating intermarriage between the two races. I am not a propagandist, but a prophet. I do not say that what I say *should* come to pass, but what I think is likely to come to pass, and what is inevitable. While I would not be understood as advocating the desirability of such a result, I would not be understood as deprecating it. Races and varieties of the human family appear and disappear, but humanity remains and will remain forever. The American people will one day be truer to this idea than now, and will say with Scotia's inspired son:

> A man's a man for a' that.

When that day shall come, they will not pervert and sin against the verity of language as they now do by calling a man of mixed blood, a Negro; they will tell the truth. It is only prejudice against the Negro which calls everyone, however nearly connected with the white race, and however remotely connected with the Negro race, a Negro. The motive is not a desire to elevate the Negro, but to humiliate and degrade those of mixed blood; not a desire to bring the Negro up, but to cast the mulatto and the quadroon down by forcing him below an arbitrary and hated color line. Men of mixed blood in this country apply the name *"Negro"* to themselves, not because it is a correct ethnological description, but to seem especially devoted to the black side of their parentage. Hence in some cases they are more noisily opposed to the conclusion to which I have come, than either the white or the honestly black race. The opposition to amalgamation, of which we hear so much on the part of colored people, is for most part the merest affectation, and will never form an impassable barrier to the union of the two varieties.

The Nation's Problem

. . . I want the colored people of this country to understand the true character of the great race which rules, and must rule and determine the destiny of this republic. Justice and magnanimity are elements of American character. They may do much for us. But we are in no condition to depend upon these qualities exclusively. Depend upon it, whenever the American people shall become convinced that they have gone too far in recognizing the rights of the Negro, they will find some way to abridge those rights. The Negro is great, but the welfare of the nation will be considered greater. They will forget the Negro's service in the late war. They may forget his loyalty to the republic. They may forget the enmity of the old slaveholding class to the government. They may forget their solemn obligations of friendship to the Negro, and press to their bosoms the white enemies of the nation, while they give the cold shoulder to the black friends of the nation. Be not deceived. History repeats itself. The black man fought for American independence. The Negro's blood mingled with the white man's blood at Bunker Hill, and in State Street, Boston. But this sacrifice on his part won for him only temporary applause. He was returned to his former condition. He fought bravely under Gen. Jackson at New Orleans, but his reward was only slavery and chains. These facts speak, trumpet-tongued, of the kind of people with whom we have to deal, and through them we may contemplate the sternest possibilities of the future.

I have said that at no time has the character of the Negro been so generally, seriously and unfavorably discussed as now. I do not regard discussion as an evil in itself. On the contrary I regard it not as an enemy, but as a friend. It has served us well at other times in our history, and I hope it may serve us well hereafter. Controversy, whether of words or blows, whether in the forum or on the battle field, may help us, if we but make the right use of it. We are not, however, to be like dumb driven cattle in this discussion, in this war of words and conflicting theories. Our business is to answer back wisely, modestly, and yet grandly.

While I do not regard discussion as an enemy in itself, I cannot but deem it in this instance as out of place and unfortunate. It comes to us as a surprise and a bitter disappointment. It implies a deplorable unrest and unsoundness in the public mind. It shows that the reconstruction of our national institutions upon a basis of liberty, justice and equality is not yet honestly accepted as a final and irrevocable settlement of the Negro's relation to the government, and of his membership in the body politic. There seems to be in it a lurking disposition, a looking around for some plausible excuse for dispossessing the Negro of some part of his inheritance conceded to him in the generous spirit of the new departure of our government. We seem to be trying how not to do it.

Going back to the early days of the anti-slavery movement, I cannot but remark, and I call upon you to remark, the striking contrast between the disposition which then existed to utterly ignore the Negro and the present disposition to make him a topic of universal interest and deepest concern. When the Negro was a slave and stood outside the government, nobody but a few so-called abolition fanatics thought him worthy of the smallest attention. He was almost as completely outside of the nation's thought as he was outside of the nation's law and the nation's religion. But now all is changed. His freedom makes him discussed on every hand. The platform, the pulpit, the press and the legislative hall regard him and struggle with him as a great and difficult problem, one that requires almost divine wisdom to solve. Men are praying over it. It is always a dangerous symptom when men pray to know what is their duty.

Now it is to this gigantic representation to which I object. I deny that the Negro is correctly represented by it. The statement of it is a prejudice to the Negro's cause. It denotes the presence of the death-dealing shadow of an ancient curse. We had fondly hoped, and had reason to hope, that when the Negro ceased to be a slave, when he ceased to be a thing and became a man, when he ceased to be an alien and became a citizen, when the constitution of the United States ceased to be the charter of slavery and became the charter of liberty, the Negro problem was solved and settled forever. The whole contention now raised over him is an anachronism, a misnomer, a false pretense, a delusion and a sham, a crafty substitution of a false issue for the true one.

I deny and utterly scout the idea that there is now, properly speaking, any such thing as a Negro problem now before the American people. It is not the Negro, educated or illiterate, intelligent or ignorant, who is on trial or whose qualities are giving trouble to the nation. The real problem lies in the other direction. It is not so much what the Negro is, what he has been, or what he may be that constitutes the problem. Here, as elsewhere, the lesser is included in the greater. The Negro's significance is dwarfed by a factor vastly larger than himself. The real question, the all-commanding question, is whether American justice, American liberty, American civilization, American law and American Christianity can be made to include and protect alike and forever all American citizens in the rights which, in a generous moment in the nation's life, have been guaranteed to them by the organic and fundamental law of the land. It is whether this great nation shall conquer its prejudices, rise to the dignity of its professions, and proceed in the sublime course of truth and liberty marked out for itself since the late war or shall swing back to its ancient moorings of slavery and barbarism. The Negro is of inferior activity and power in the solution of this problem. He is the clay, the nation is the potter. He is the subject, the nation is the sovereign. It is not what he shall be or do, but what the nation shall be and do, which is to solve this great national problem.

Speaking for him, I can commend him upon every ground. he is loyal and and patriotic; service is the badge of all his tribe. He has proved it before, and will prove it again. The country has never called upon him in vain. What he has been in the past in this respect that he will be in the future. All he asks now, all he has ever asked, all he will ever ask, is that the nation shall fulfill toward him its own recognized and self-imposed obligations. When he asks for bread he will not accept a stone. When he asks for fish he will not accept a serpent. His protest now is against being cheated by cunningly-devised judicial decisions, by frauds upon the ballot box, or by brutal violence of red-shirted rebels. He only asks the American people to adjust the practice to the justice and wisdom of their laws, and he holds that this is first, midst, and last, and the only problem to be solved.

While, however, the Negro may very properly protest against the popular statement of the question, and while he may insist that the one just stated is the proper one, and the only one; while he may hold that primarily and fundamentally it is an American problem and not a Negro problem, he may materially assist in its solution. He can assume an attitude, develop a character, improve his condition, and, in a measure, compel the respect and esteem of his fellow-men.

In order to do this we have, first of all, to learn and to understand thoroughly the nature of the social, moral, and political forces that surround us, and how to shape our ends and wisely determine our destiny. We should endeavor to discover the true sources of our danger—whether they be within ourselves or in circumstances external to ourselves. If I am here for any useful purpose, it is in some measure to answer the question, "What of the night?"

For the present I have seemed to forget that this is an occasion of joy. I have thus far spoken mainly in sorrow rather than in gladness; in grief rather than in gratitude. Like the resolution of Hamlet, my outlook has been sicklied o'er with the pale cast of thought. I must go on in the same line.

Now, what of the night? What of the night? Is it cheered by the beams of celestial light and hope, or is it saddened by ominous clouds, darkness and distant thunder? The latter, and not the former, is the true answer. You and I should be brave enough to look the facts fairly and firmly in the face.

I profoundly wish I could make a different response to this inquiry. But the omens are against me. I am compelled to say that while we have no longer to contend with the physical wrongs and abominations of slavery; while we have no longer to chill the blood of our hearers by talking of whips, chains, branding irons and blood-hounds; we have, as already intimated, to contend with a foe, which, though less palpable, is still a fierce and formidable foe. It is the ghost of a by-gone, dead and buried institution. It loads the very air with a malignant prejudice of race. It has poisoned the fountains of justice, and defiled the altars of religion. It acts upon the body politic as the leprous distillment acted upon the blood and body of the murdered king of Denmark. In ante-

bellum times it was the standing defense of slavery. In our own times it is employed in defense of oppression and proscription. Until this foe is conquered and driven from the breasts of the American people, our relations will be unhappy, our progress slow, our lives embittered, our freedom a mockery, and our citizenship a delusion.

The work before us is to meet and combat this prejudice by lives and acquirements which contradict and put to shame this narrow and malignant feeling. We have errors of our own to abandon, habits to reform, manners to improve, ignorance to dispel, and character to build up. This is something which no power on earth can do for us, and which no power on earth can prevent our doing for ourselves, if we will.

In pointing out errors and mistakes common among ourselves, I shall run the risk of incurring displeasure; for no people with whom I am acquainted are less tolerant of criticism than ourselves, especially from one of our own number. We have been so long in the habit of tracing our failures and misfortunes to the views and acts of others that we seem, in some measure, to have lost the talent and disposition of seeing our own faults, or of "seeing ourselves as others see us." And yet no man can do a better service to another man than to correct his mistakes, point out his hurtful errors, show him the path of truth, duty and safety.

One of the few errors to which we are clinging most persistently and, as I think, most mischievously has come into great prominence of late. It is the cultivation and stimulation amongst us of a sentiment which we are pleased to call race pride. I find it in all our books, papers and speeches. For my part I see no superiority or inferiority in race or color. Neither the one nor the other is a proper source of pride or complacency. Our race and color are not of our own choosing. We have no volition in the case one way or another. The only excuse for pride in individuals or races is in the fact of their own achievements. Our color is the gift of the Almighty. We should neither be proud of it nor ashamed of it. But we may well enough be proud or ashamed when we have ourselves achieved success or have, by our faults, failed of success. If the sun has curled our hair and tanned our skin let the sun be proud of its achievement, for we have done nothing for it one way or the other. I see no benefit to be derived from this everlasting exhortation by speakers and writers among us to the cultivation of race pride. On the contrary, I see in it a positive evil. It is building on a false foundation. Besides, what is the thing we are fighting against, and what are we fighting for in this country? What is the mountain devil, the lion in the way of our progress? What is it, but American race pride; an assumption of superiority upon the ground of race and color? Do we not know that every argument we make, and every pretension we set up in favor of race pride is giving the enemy a stick to break our own heads?

But it may be said that we shall put down race pride in the white people by cultivating race pride among ourselves. The answers to this is that the devils are not cast out by Beelzebub, the prince of devils. The poorest and meanest white man, drunk or sober, when he has nothing else to commend him, says: "I am a white man, I am." We can all see the low extremity reached by that sort of race pride, and yet we encourage it when we pride ourselves upon the fact of our color. I heard a Negro say: "I am a Negro, I am." Let us away with this supercilious nonsense. If we are proud let it be because we have had some agency in producing that of which we can properly be proud. Do not let us be proud of what we can neither help nor hinder. The Bible puts us in the condition in this respect of the leopard, and says that we can no more change our skin than the leopard his spots. If we are unfortunate in being placed among a people with which our color is a badge of inferiority, there is no need of our making ourselves ridiculous by forever, in words, affecting to be proud of a circumstance due to no virtue in us, and over which we have no control.

You will, perhaps, think this criticism uncalled for. My answer is that truth is never uncalled for. Right thinking is essential to right acting, and I hope that we shall hereafter see the wisdom of basing our pride and complacency upon substantial results accomplished by the race.

The question here raised is not merely theoretical, but is of practical significance. In some of our colored public journals, with a view to crippling my humble influence with the colored race, I have seen myself charged with a lack of race pride. I am not ashamed of that charge. I have no apology or vindication to offer. If fifty years of uncompromising devotion to the cause of the colored man in this country does not vindicate me, I am content to live without vindication.

While I have no more reason to be proud of one race than another, I dare say, and I fear no contradiction, that there is no other man in the United States prouder than myself of any great achievement, mental or mechanical, of which any colored man or woman is the author. This is not because I am a colored man, but because I am a man, and because color is a misfortune, and is treated as a crime by the American people. My sentiments at this point originate not in my color, but in a sense of justice common to all right-minded men. It is not because I am a Negro, but because I am a man. It is that which gives the sympathy of the crowd to the underdog, no matter what may be his color. When a colored man is charged with a want of race pride, he may well ask, What race? for a large percentage of the colored race are related in some degree to more than one race. But the whole assumption of race pride is ridiculous. Let us have done with complexional superiorities or inferiorities, complexional pride or shame. I want no better basis for my activities and affinities than the broad foundation laid by the Bible itself, that "God has made of one blood all nations of men to dwell on all the face of the earth." This comprehends the Fatherhood of God and the brotherhood of man.

I have another criticism to make of a position which, I think, often invites unfavorable comparison and positive disparagement. It is our noisy assertion of equality with the Caucasian race. There are two kinds of equality, one potential and the other actual, one theoretical and the other practical. We should not be satisfied by merely quoting the doctrine of potential equality as laid down in the Declaration of Independence, but we should give it practical illustration. We have to do as well as to be. If we had built great ships, sailed around the world, taught the science of navigation, discovered far-off islands, capes, and continents, enlarged the boundaries of human knowledge, improved the conditions of man's existence, brought valuable contributions to art, science and literature, revealed great truths, organized great States, administered great governments, defined the laws of the universe, formulated systems of mental and moral philosophy, invented railroads, steam engines, mowing machines, sewing machines, taught the sun to take pictures, the lightning to carry messages, we then might claim, not only potential and theoretical equality, but actual and practical equality. Nothing is gained to our cause by claiming for ourselves more than of right we can establish belongs to us. Manly self-assertion, I know, is a power, and I would have that power employed within the bounds of truth and sobriety. We should never forget, in our relations with our fellows, that modesty is also a power.

When it is manifested without any much of servility it is as sure to win respect as unfounded pretension is sure to provoke and receive contempt. We should give our critics no advantage at this point, either by word or by conduct. Our battle with popular prejudice requires on our part the utmost circumspection in word and in deed. Our men should be gentlemen and our women ladies, and we can be neither without a modest reserve in mind and in manners.

Were I not speaking to the most cultivated class of our people, for the Bethel Literary Society comprises that class, I might hesitate to employ this course of remark. You, I am quite sure, will not misapprehend my statements or my motives.

There is one other point worthy of animadversion—it is the error that union among ourselves is an essential element of success in our relations to the white race. This, in my judgment, is a very serious mistake. I can hardly point out one more pregnant with peril. It is contended that we are now eight millions; that we hold the balance of power between the two great political parties of the country, and that, if we were only united in one body, under wise and powerful leaders, we could shape the policy of both political parties, make and unmake parties, control the destiny of the republic, and secure for ourselves a desirable and happy future. They say that in union there is strength; that united we stand and divided we fall, and much else of the same sort.

My position is the reverse of all this. I hold that our union is our weakness. In quoting these wise sayings, colored men seem to forget that there are exceptions to all general rules, and that our position in this country is an exceptional position.

The rule for us is the exception. There are times and places when separation and division are better than union, when to stand apart is wiser than standing together. There are buildings which will hold a few, but which will break down under the weight of a crowd; the ice of the river may be strong enough to bear a man, but would break through under the weight of an elephant. The ice under us in this country is very thin, and is made very weak by the warm fogs of prejudice. A few colored people scattered among large white communities are easily accepted by such communities, and a larger measure of liberty is accorded to the few than would be to the many. The trouble is that when we assemble in great numbers anywhere we are apt to form communities by ourselves, and our occupation of any part of a town or city, apart from the people surrounding us, brings us into separate schools, separate churches, separate benevolent and literary societies, and the result is the adoption of a scale of manners, morals and customs peculiar to our condition and to our antecedents as an oppressed people. When we thus isolate ourselves we say to those around us: "We have nothing in common with you," and, very naturally, the reply of our neighbors is in the same tone and to the same effect; for when a people care for nobody, nobody will care for them. When we isolate ourselves we lose, in a large measure, the common benefit of association with those whose advantages have been superior to ours.

The foundation upon which we stand in this country is not strong enough to make it safe to stand together. A nation within a nation is an anomaly. There can be but one American nation under the American government, and we are Americans. The constitution of the country makes us such, and our lines of activity should accord with our citizenship. Circumstances now compel us in certain directions to maintain separate neighborhoods and separate institutions. But these circumstances should only be yielded to when they are irresistible. A Negro neighborhood depreciates the market value of property. We should distribute ourselves among the people, build our houses where if they take fire other houses will be in danger. Common dangers will create common safeguards.

Our policy should be to unite with the great mass of the American people in all their activities, and resolve to fall or flourish with our common country. We cannot afford to draw the color line in politics, trade, education, manners, religion, fashion, or civilization. Especially, we cannot afford to draw the color line in politics. No folly could be greater. A party acting upon that basis would be not merely a misfortune but a dire calamity to our people. The rule of the majority is the fundamental principle of the American government, and it may be safely affirmed that the American people will never permit, tolerate, or submit to the success of any political device or strategy calculated to circumvent and defeat the just application and operation of this fundamental principle of our government.

It is also fair to state that no part of the American people—Irish, Scotch, Italian, or German—could attempt any such political jugglery with less success than ourselves.

Another popular error flaunted in our faces at every turn, and for most part by very weak and impracticable editors, is the alleged duty of colored men to patronize colored newspapers, and this simply because they happen to be edited and published by colored men, and not because of their intrinsic value. Anybody that can find means to issue a paper with a patent back and hang out a colored flag at the head of its columns, demands support on the ground that it is a colored newspaper. For one, I am not disposed to yield to this demand. A colored newspaper maker has no higher claim upon us for patronage than a col-

ored carpenter, a colored shoemaker, or a colored bricklayer. Whether he should be supported should depend upon the character of the man and the quality of his work. Our people should not be required to buy an inferior article offered by a colored man, when for the same money they can purchase a superior article from a white man. We need, and ought to have, the best supply of mental food that the American market affords.

In saying this I do not forget that an able, sound and decent journal, conducted in a spirit of justice and not made a vehicle of malice or personal favoritism, edited and published by colored men is a powerful lever for the elevation and advancement of the colored race. Such a paper has special claims upon all who desire to raise colored people in the estimation of themselves and their surroundings. But while this is true, it is also true that in the same proportion that an able and influential public journal tends to remove popular prejudice and elevate us in the judgment of those whose good opinion is worth having, a feeble, ungrammatical, indecent and wretchedly conducted public journal tends to lower us in the opinion of good men, besides has a debasing influence upon the minds of its readers. Character and quality should rule here as well as elsewhere. . . .

On Colonization

But I now come to another proposition, held up as a solution of the race problem, and this I consider equally unworthy with the one just disposed of. The two belong to the same low-bred family of ideas.

It is the proposition to colonize the coloured people of America in Africa, or somewhere else. Happily this scheme will be defeated, both by its impolicy and its impracticability. It is all nonsense to talk about the removal of eight millions of the American people from their homes in America to Africa. The expense and hardships, to say nothing of the cruelty attending such a measure, would make success impossible. The American people are wicked, but they are not fools;

they will hardly be disposed to incur the expense, to say nothing of the injustice which this measure demands. Nevertheless, this colonizing scheme, unworthy as it is of American statesmanship, and American honour, and though full of mischief to the coloured people, seems to have a strong hold on the public mind, and at times has shown much life and vigor.

The bad thing about it is, that it has, of late, owing to persecution, begun to be advocated by coloured men of acknowledged ability and learning, and every little while some white statesman becomes its advocate. Those gentlemen will doubtless have their opinion of me; I certainly have mine of them. My opinion is, that if they are sensible, they are insincere; and if they are sincere, they are not sensible. They know, or they ought to know that it would take more money than the cost of the late war, to transport even one half of the coloured people of the United States to Africa. Whether intentionally or not, they are, as I think, simply trifling with an afflicted people. They urge them to look for relief where they ought to know that relief is impossible. The only excuse they can make for the measure is that there is no hope for the Negro here, and that the coloured people in America owe something to Africa.

This last sentimental idea makes colonization very fascinating to the dreamers of both colours. But there is really no foundation for it.

They tell us that we owe something to our native land. This sounds well. But when the fact is brought to view, which should never be forgotten, that a man can only have one native land and that is the land in which he is born, the bottom falls entirely out of this sentimental argument.

Africa, according to her colonization advocates, is by no means modest in her demands upon us. She calls upon us to send her only our best men. She does not want our riff-raff, but our best men. But these are just the men who are valuable and who are wanted at home. It is true that we have a few preachers and laymen with at missionary turn of mind whom we might easily spare. Some who would possibly do as much good by going there as by staying here. By this is not the colonization idea. Its advocates want not only the best, but millions of the best. Better still, they want the United States government to vote the money to send them there. They do not seem to see that if the Government votes money to send the Negro to Africa, that the Government may employ means to complete the arrangement and compel us to go.

Now I hold that the American Negro owes no more to the Negroes in Africa than he owes to the Negroes in America. There are millions of needy people over there, but there are also millions of needy people over here as well, and the millions in America need intelligent men of their number to help them, as much as intelligent men are needed in Africa to help her people. Besides, we have a fight on our hands right here, a fight for the redemption of the whole race, and a blow struck successfully for the Negro in America, is a blow struck for the Negro in Africa. For, until the Negro is respected in America, he need not expect consideration elsewhere. All this native land talk, however, is nonsense. The native land of the American Negro is America. His bones, his muscles, his sinews, are all American. His ancestors for two hundred and seventy years have lived and laboured and died, on American soil, and millions of his posterity have inherited Caucasian blood.

It is pertinent, therefore, to ask, in view of this admixture, as well as in view of other facts, where the people of this mixed race are to go, for their ancestors are white and black, and it will be difficult to find their native land anywhere outside of the United States.

But the worst thing, perhaps, about this colonization nonsense is, that it tends to throw over the Negro a mantle of despair. It leads him to doubt the possibility of his progress as an American citizen. It also encourages popular prejudice with the hope that by persecution or by persuasion the Negro can finally be dislodged and driven from his natural home, while in the nature of the case he must stay here and will stay here, if for no other reason than because he cannot well get away.

I object to the colonization scheme, because it tends to weaken the Negro's hold on one country, while it can give him no rational hope of another. Its tendency is to make him despondent and doubtful, where he should feel assured and confident. It forces upon him the idea that he is forever doomed to be a stranger and a sojourner in the land of his birth, and that he has no permanent abiding place here.

All this is hurtful; with such ideas constantly flaunted before him, he cannot easily set himself to work to better his condition in such ways as are open to him here. It sets him to groping everlastingly after the impossible.

Every man who thinks at all, must know that home is the fountain head, the inspiration, the foundation and main support, not only of all social virtue but of all motives to human progress, and that no people can prosper, or amount to much, unless they have a home, or the hope of a home. A man who has not such an object, either in possession or in prospect, is a nobody and will never be anything else. To have a home, the Negro must have a country, and he is an enemy to the moral progress of the Negro, whether he knows it or not, who calls upon him to break up his home in this country, for an uncertain home in Africa.

But the agitation on this subject has a darker side still. It has already been given out that if we do not go of our own accord, we may be forced to go, at the point of the bayonet. I cannot say that we shall not have to face this hardship, but badly as I think of the tendency of our times, I do not think that American sentiment will ever reach a condition which will make the expulsion of the Negro from the United States by any such means, possible.

Yet, the way to make it possible is to predict it. There are people in the world who know how to bring their own prophecies to pass. The best way to get up a mob, is to say there will be one, and this is what is being done. Colonization is no solution, but an evasion. It is not repentance but putting the wronged ones out of our presence. It is not atonement, but banishment. It is not love, but hate. Its reiteration and agitation only serves to fan the flame of popular prejudice and to add insult to injury.

The righteous judgment of mankind will say if the American people could endure the Negro's presence while a slave, they certainly can and ought to endure his presence as a free man.

If they could tolerate him when he was a heathen, they might bear with him now that he is a Christian. If they could bear with him when ignorant and degraded, they should bear with him now that he is a gentleman and a scholar.

Such a crime against justice, such a crime against gratitude, should it ever be attempted, would certainly bring a national punishment which would cause the earth to shudder. It would bring a stain upon the nation's honor, like the blood on Lady Macbeth's hand. The waters of all the oceans would not suffice to wash out the infamy. But the nation will commit no such crime. But in regard to this point of our future, my mind is easy. We are here and are here to stay. It is well for us and well for the American people to rest upon this as final.

Discussion Questions

1. Today Irish Americans are, in contrast to 150 years ago, much more culturally assimilated into the general population and, by the same token, much more prosperous relative to the same general population. Is there a lesson in this for African Americans—or not?

2. If the main argument against a separate black state is that whites would not tolerate it, how can this argument lead to the conclusion Douglass desires: namely, that the solution is for blacks to secure their rights and achieve prosperity *within* American society? In other words, if whites would not tolerate a separate nation, how would they be expected to grant equal rights?

3. Do you agree with Douglass' contention that "our [African Americans'] union is our weakness"?

9 *From* Philosophy and Opinions of Marcus Garvey

MARCUS GARVEY

Study Questions

1. What is the difference, according to Garvey, between religion and belief in God?
2. Why is the Bible not the solution to the problems of black people?
3. Who is "the most dangerous member of our society" and why?
4. What is Garvey's attitude toward Europe and toward the white race?

HISTORY is the land-mark by which we are directed into the true course of life.

The history of a movement, the history of a nation, the history of a race is the guide-post of that movement's destiny, that nation's destiny, that race's destiny.

What you do to-day that is worthwhile, inspires others to act at some future time.

CHANCE has never yet satisfied the hope of a suffering people.

Action, self-reliance, the vision of self and the future have been the only means by which the oppressed have seen and realized the light of their own freedom.

LIFE is that existence that is given to man to live for a purpose, to live to his own satisfaction and pleasure, providing he forgets not the God who created him and who expects a spiritual obedience and observation of the moral laws that He has inspired.

There is nothing in the world common to man, that man cannot do.

From *Philosophy and Opinions of Marcus Garvey,* Amy Jacques-Garvey, ed. (New York: Atheneum Press, 1977), chapter one (pp. 1–14). Reprinted by permission of Simon and Schuster Publishers.

The ends you serve that are selfish will take you no further than yourself; but the ends you serve that are for all, in common, will take you even into eternity.

It is only the belief and the confidence we have in a God why man is able to understand his own social institutions, and move and live like a rational human being.

Take away the highest ideal—FAITH and CONFIDENCE IN A GOD—and mankind at large is reduced to savagery and the race destroyed.

A race without authority and power, is a race without respect.

CRITICISM is an opinion for good or ill, generally indulged in by the fellow who knows more than any one else, yet the biggest fool. There is no criticism that calls not forth yet another. The last critic is the biggest fool of all, for the world starts and ends with him. He is the source of all knowledge, yet knows nothing, for there is not a word one finds to use that there is not another that hath the same meaning, then wherefore do we criticize?

FEAR is a state of nervousness fit for children and not men. When man fears a creature like himself he offends God, in whose image and likeness he is created. Man being created equal tears not man but God. To fear is to lose control of one's nerves, one's will—to flutter, like a dying fowl, losing consciousness, yet, alive.

AMBITION is the desire to go forward and improve one's condition. It is a burning flame that lights up the life of the individual and makes him see himself in another state. To be ambitious is to be great in mind and soul. To want that which is worth while and strive for it. To go on without looking back, reaching to that which gives satisfaction. To be humanly ambitious is to take in the world which is the province of man;

to be divinely ambitious is to offend God by rivalling him in His infinite Majesty.

ADMIRATION is a form of appreciation that is sometimes mistaken for something else. There may be something about you that suggests good fellowship when kept at a distance, but in closer contact would not be tolerated, otherwise it would be love.

RELIGION is one's opinion and belief in some ethical truth. To be a Christian is to have the religion of Christ, and so to be a believer of Mohammed is to be a Mohammedan but there are so many religions that every man seems to be a religion unto himself. No two persons think alike, even if they outwardly profess the same faith, so we have as many religions in Christianity as we have believers.

DEATH is the end of all life in the individual or the thing; if physical, the crumbling of the body into dust from whence it came. He who lives not uprightly, dies completely in the crumbling of the physical body, but he who lives well, transforms himself from that which is mortal, to immortal.

FAITHFULNESS is actuated by a state of heart and mind in the individual that changes not. No one is wholly faithful to a cause or an object, except his heart and mind remain firm without change or doubt. If one's attitude or conduct changes toward an object, then one has lost in one's faithfulness. It is a wholeness of belief overshadowing all suspicion, all doubt, admitting of no question; to serve without regret or disgust, to obligate one's self to that which is promised or expected, to keep to our word and do our duty well. There are but few faithful people now-a-days.

PROHIBITION—is to abstain from intoxicating liquor, as it makes us morbid and sometimes drunk. But we get drunk every day, nevertheless, not so much by the strength of what we sip from the cup, but that which we eat, the water we drink, and the air we inhale, which at fermentation conspire at eventide to make us so drunk and tired that we lose control of ourselves and fall asleep. Everybody is a drunkard, and if we were to enforce real prohibition we should all be dead.

There is no strength but that which is destructive, because man has lost his virtues, and only respects force, which he himself cannot counteract.

This is the day of racial activity, when each and every group of this great human family must exercise its own initiative and influence in its own protection, therefore, Negroes should be more determined to-day than they have ever been, because the mighty forces of the world are operating against non-organized groups of peoples, who are not ambitious enough to protect their own interests.

Wake up Ethiopia! Wake up Africa! Let us work towards the one glorious end of a free, redeemed and mighty nation. Let Africa be a bright star among the constellation of nations.

A man's bread and butter is only insured when he works for it.

The world has now reached the stage when humanity is really at the parting of the ways. It is a question of "MAN MIND THYSELF."

The political readjustment of the world means that those who are not sufficiently able, not sufficiently prepared, will be at the mercy of the organized classes for another one or two hundred years.

The only protection against INJUSTICE in man is POWER—Physical, financial and scientific.

The masses make the nation and the race. If the masses are illiterate, that is the judgment passed on the race by those who are critical of its existencce[sic].

The function of the Press is public service without prejudice or partiality, to convey the truth as it is seen and understood without favoritism or bias.

EDUCATION is the medium by which a people are prepared for the creation of their own particular civilization, and the advancement and glory of their own race.

NATIONHOOD is the only means by which modern civilization can completely protect itself.

Independence of nationality, independence of government, is the means of protecting not only the individual, but the group.

Nationhood is the highest ideal of all peoples.

The evolutionary scale that weighs nations and races, balances alike for all peoples; hence we feel sure that some day the balance will register a change for the Negro.

If we are to believe the Divine injunction, we must realize that the time is coming when every man and every race must return to its own "vine and fig tree."

Let Africa be our guiding Star—OUR STAR OF DESTINY.

So many of us find excuses to get out of the Negro Race, because we are led to believe that the race is unworthy—that it has not accomplished anything. Cowards that we are! It is we who are unworthy, because we are not contributing to the uplift and up-building of this noble race.

How dare any one tell us that Africa cannot be redeemed, when we have 400,000,000 men and women with warm blood coursing through their veins?

The power that holds Africa is not Divine. The power that holds Africa is human, and it is recognized that whatsoever man has done, man can do.

We of the Negro Race are moving from one state of organization to another, and we shall so continue until we have thoroughly lifted ourselves into the organization of GOVERNMENT.

Be as proud of your race today as our fathers were in the days of yore. We have a beautiful history, and we shall create another in the future that will astonish the world.

Woman

What the night is to the day, is woman to man. The period of change that brings us light out of darkness, darkness out of light, and semi-light out of darkness are like the changes we find in woman day by day.

She makes one happy, then miserable. You are to her kind, then unkind. Constant yet inconstant. Thus we have WOMAN. No real man can do without her.

Love

A happy but miserable state in which man finds himself from time to time; sometimes he believes he is happy by loving, then suddenly he finds how miserable he is. It is all joy, it sweetens life, but it does not last. It comes and goes, but when it is active, there is no greater virtue, because it makes one supremely happy.

We cannot hold our love, but there is one love that never changeth or is mistaken, and that is God's. The longer we hold our love, the nearer we approach like unto our Creator.

The whole world is run on bluff. No race, no nation, no man has any divine right to take advantage of others. Why allow the other fellow to bluff you?

Every student of Political Science, every student of Economics knows, that the race can only be saved through a solid industrial foundation. That the race can only be saved through political independence. Take away industry from a race; take away political freedom from a race, and you have a group of slaves.

Peoples everywhere are travelling toward industrial opportunities and greater political freedom. As a race oppressed, it is for us to prepare ourselves that at any time the great change in industrial freedom and political liberty comes about, we may be able to enter into the new era as partakers of the joys to be inherited.

Lagging behind in the van of civilization will not prove our higher abilities. Being subservient to the will and caprice of progressive races will not prove anything superior in us. Being satisfied to drink of the dregs from the cup of human progress will not demonstrate our fitness as a people to exist alongside of others, but when of our own initiative we strike out to build industries, governments, and ultimately empires, then and only then will we as a race prove to our Creator and to man in general that we are fit to survive and capable of shaping our own destiny.

The world ought to know that it could not keep 400,000,000 Negroes down forever.

There is always a turning point in the destiny of every race, every nation, of all peoples, and we have come now to the turning point of the Negro, where we have changed from the old cringing weakling, and transformed into full-grown men, demanding our portion as MEN.

I am not one of those Christians who believe that the Bible can solve all the problems of humanity.

The Bible is good in its place, but we are men. We are the creatures of God. We have sinned against Him, therefore it takes more than the Bible to keep us in our places.

Man is becoming so vile that to-day we cannot afford to convert him with moral, ethical, physical truths alone, but with that which is more effective—implements of destruction.

LEADERSHIP means everything—PAIN, BLOOD, DEATH.

To be prosperous in whatever we do is the sign of TRUE WEALTH. We may be wealthy in not only having money, but in spirit and health. It is the most helpful agency toward a self-satisfying life. One lives, in an age like this, nearer perfection by being wealthy than by being poor. To the contented soul, wealth is the stepping stone to perfection; to the miser it is the nearest avenue to hell. I would prefer to be honestly wealthy, than miserably poor.

To be free from temptation of other people's property is to reflect the HONESTY of our own souls. There are but few really honest people, in that between the thought and the deed we make ourselves dishonest. The fellow who steals, acts dishonestly. We can steal in thought as well as in deed, therefore to be honest is a virtue that but few indulge. To be honest is to be satisfied, hav-

ing all, wanting nothing. If you find yourself in such a state then you are honest, if not the temptation of your soul is bound to make you dishonest. This applies to the king and the peasant alike.

All peoples are struggling to blast a way through the industrial monopoly of races and nations, but the Negro as a whole has failed to grasp its true significance and seems to delight in filling only that place created for him by the white man.

The Negro who lives on the patronage of philanthropists is the most dangerous member of our society, because he is willing to turn back the clock of progress when his benefactors ask him so to do.

No race in the world is so just as to give others, for the asking, a square deal in things economic, political and social.

Men who are in earnest are not afraid of consequences.

No one knows when the hour of Africa's Redemption cometh. It is in the wind. It is coming. One day, like a storm, it will be here. When that day comes all Africa will stand together.

Any sane man, race or nation that desires freedom must first of all think in terms of blood. Why, even the Heavenly Father tells us that "without the shedding of blood there can be no remission of sins?" Then how in the name of God, with history before us, do we expect to redeem Africa without preparing ourselves—some of us to die.

I pray God that we shall never use our physical prowess to oppress the human race, but we will use our strength, physically, morally and otherwise to preserve humanity and civilization.

For over three hundred years the white man has been our oppressor, and he naturally is not going to liberate us to the higher freedom—the truer liberty—the truer Democracy. We have to liberate ourselves.

Every man has a right to his own opinion. Every race has a right to its own action; therefore let no man persuade you against your will, let no other race influence you against your own.

The greatest weapon used against the Negro is DISORGANIZATION.

If you have no confidence in self you are twice defeated in the race of life. With confidence you have won even before you have started.

At no time within the last five hundred years can one point to a single instance of the Negro as a race of haters.

The Negro has loved even under severest punishment. In slavery the Negro loved his master, he safe-guarded his home even when he further planned to enslave him. We are not a race of Haters, but Lovers of humanity's Cause.

Mob violence and injustice have never helped a race or a nation, and because of this knowledge as gathered from the events of ages, we as a people in this new age desire to love all mankind, not in the social sense, but in keeping with the Divine Injunction "MAN LOVE THY BROTHER."

PREPAREDNESS is the watch-word of this age. For us as a race to remain, as we have been in the past—divided among ourselves, parochializing, insularizing, and nationalizing our activities as subjects and citizens of the many alien races and governments under which we live—is but to hold ourselves in readiness for that great catastrophe that is bound to come—that of racial extermination, at the hands of the stronger race—the race that will be fit to survive.

Humanity takes revenging crime from one age to the next, according to the growth and development of the race so afflicted.

But the perpetuation of crime through revenge and retaliation will not save the human race.

Europe is bankrupt today, and every nation within her bounds is endeavoring to find new openings, new fields for exploitation—that exploitation that will bring to them the resources, the revenue and the power necessary for their rehabilitation and well-being.

We are living in a strenuous, active age, when men see, not through the spectacles of sympathy, but demand that each and every one measures up in proportion to the world's demand for service.

The attitude of the white race is to subjugate, to exploit, and if necessary exterminate the weaker peoples with whom they come in contact.

They subjugate first, if the weaker peoples will stand for it; then exploit, and if they will not stand for SUBJUGATION nor EXPLOITATION, the other recourse is EXTERMINATION.

If the Negro is not careful he will drink in all the poison of modern civilization and die from the effects of it.

There can be no peace among men and nations, so long as the strong continues to oppress the weak, so long as injustice is done to other peoples, just so long will we have cause for war, and make a lasting peace an impossibility.

Hungry men have no respect for law, authority or human life.

I am not opposed to the white race as charged by my enemies. I have no time to hate any one. All my time is devoted to the up-building and developement of the Negro Race.

When nations outgrow their national limits, they make war and conquer other people's territory so as to have an outlet for their surplus populations.

The world does not count races and nations that have nothing.

Point me to a weak nation and I will show you a people oppressed, abused, taken advantage of by others.

Show me a weak race and I will show you a people reduced to serfdom, peonage and slavery.

Show me a well organized nation, and I will show you a people and a nation respected by the world.

The battles of the future, whether they be physical or mental, will be fought on scientific lines, and the race that is able to produce the highest scientific development, is the race that will ultimately rule.

Let us prepare TODAY. For the TOMORROWS in the lives of the nations will be so eventful that Negroes everywhere will be called upon to play their part in the survival of the fittest human group.

Let us in shaping our own Destiny set before us the qualities of human JUSTICE, LOVE, CHARITY, MERCY AND EQUITY. Upon such foundation let us build a race, and I feel that the God who is Divine, the Almighty Creator of the world, shall forever bless this race of ours, and who to tell that we shall not teach men the way to life, liberty and true human happiness?

Day by day we hear the cry of "AFRICA FOR THE AFRICANS." This cry has become a positive, determined one. It is a cry that is raised simultaneously the world over, because of the universal oppression that affects the Negro.

All of us may not live to see the higher accomplishment of an African Empire—so strong and powerful, as to compel the respect of mankind, but we in our life-time can so work and act as to make the dream a possibility within another generation.

Discussion Questions

1. In terms of today's political labels, would Garvey be considered a conservative, a liberal, or a radical?
2. If, as Garvey says, "power is the only protection against injustice," what does this imply about whether human beings, as many philosophers have thought, naturally seek justice?
3. In the context of our time, would Garvey's comments about "woman" and "love" be considered acceptable or not?
4. Garvey says both that "the attitude of the white race is to subjugate, to exploit and if necessary exterminate the weaker people with whom they come in contact" and that "I am not opposed to the white race as charged by my enemies." Is he consistent?

10   The Nguzo Saba (The Seven Principles): Their Meaning and Message

MAULANA KARENGA

Study Questions

1. What, according to Karenga, are the main purposes of the Nguzo Saba?
2. What is "complementarity" and how does it relate to Unity?
3. How does one answer the question "Who am I?"

4. How is the value of cooperation expressed in both Ujima and Ujamaa?

From *The African American Holiday of Kwanzaa* (Los Angeles: University of Sankore Press, 1988), pp. 276–282. Reprinted by permission of the author and publisher.

In terms of the interest and aspirations of African American people, the Nguzo Saba were developed and offered as an Afrocentric value system which would serve the following basic functions: 1) organize and enrich our relations with each other on the personal and community level; 2) establish standards, commitments and priorities that would tend to enhance our human possibilities as persons and a people; 3) aid in the recovery and reconstruction of lost historical memory and cultural legacy in the development of an Afrocentric paradigm of life and achievement; 4) serve as a contribution to a core system of communitarian ethical values for the moral guidance and instruction of the community, especially for children; and 5) contribute to an ongoing and expanding set of Afrocentric communitarian values which would aid in bringing into being a new man, woman and child who self-consciously participate in the ethical project of starting a new history of African people and humankind. With these observations in mind, we can now turn to the rich meaning and message of the Nguzo Saba themselves, both in the context of Kwanzaa and daily life.

Umoja (Unity)

To strive for and maintain unity in the family, community, nation and race.

This is the First and foundational Principle of the Nguzo Saba, for without it, all the other Principles suffer. Unity is both a principle and practice of togetherness in all things good and of mutual benefit. It is a principled and harmonious togetherness not simply a being together. This is why value-rootedness is so important, even indispensable. Unity as principled and harmonious togetherness is a cardinal virtue of both classical and general African societies. In ancient Egypt, harmony was a cardinal virtue of Maat, i.e., righteousness, rightness. In fact, one of the ways to translate Maat is to define it as harmony—harmony on the natural, cosmic and social level. Likewise, cieng among the Dinka, means both morality and harmonious living together. Thus in both ancient Egyptian and Dinka society, one cannot live a moral life without living in harmony with other members of the community.

If unity is in essence a Principle, it is no less a practice as are all the other Principles. For practice is central to African ethics and all claims to ethical living and commitment to moral principles

are tested and proved or disproved in relations with others. Relations, then, are the hinge on which morality turns, the ground on which it rises or falls . . . Character development is not simply to create a good person abstracted from community, but rather a person in positive interaction, a person whose quality of relations with others is defined first of all by a *principled* and *harmonious* togetherness, i.e., a real and practiced unity.

Another way of discussing unity is to see it as active solidarity. This essentially means a firm dependable togetherness that is born, based and sustained in action. It is usually applied to groups, organizations, classes, [and] peoples and expresses itself as building and acting together in mutual benefit. The key here is again practice. In the end practice proves everything. No matter how many books one reads on swimming, sooner or later s/he must get into the water and swim. This may be called, on this level, the priority of practice. Finally, unity means a oneness, a similarity and sameness that gives us an identity as a people, an African people. And inherent in this identity as a people is the ethical and political imperative to self-consciously unite in order to define, defend and develop our interests.

Unity as principle and practice begins in the family but presupposes value-orientation of each member. Adults and children must respect and approach unity as a moral principle of family and community not simply a political slogan. As principle and practice, this means principled and harmonious living with brothers and sisters, mothers and fathers—sharing and acting in unison. It means avoidance of conflict and quick, willing and principled resolution when it occurs . . . The family must reject harshness and practice gentleness, stress cooperation and avoid conflict, and be very attentive to things that would divide or create differences negative to togetherness.

Especially important is the unity of the father and mother, for they are the models for the children and the foundation for the family in every sense of the word. Here the African concept of complementarity of male and female as distinct from and opposed to the concept of conflict of the genders is instructive and of value. As Anna J.

Cooper, educator and social theorist, taught "there is a feminine as well as masculine side to truth (and) these are related not as inferior and superior, not as better or worse, not as weaker or stronger, but as complements—complements in one necessary and symmetric whole." The recognition of this truth and responding creatively to it is necessary, she says, to give balance to the individual, and to save the nation from its extremes. It also is a shield against sexism, i.e., the social practice of using gender to establish and/or justify exploitation, oppression or unequal relations. . . .

Finally the family must be, as in African culture, the focal point of unity not simply of siblings and of genders, but also of generations. One of the most important expressions of family unity is the respect and collective concern and care for the elders. Respect for elders . . . is a cardinal article of the code of behavior of African society. One who does not respect his/her elders is seen as immoral and uncultured. Elders are respected, like the ancestors they will become, for their long life of service to the community, for their achievement, for providing an ethical model and for the richness of their experience and the wisdom this has produced. Thus, elders are seen as judges and reconcilers. It is they who hear cases of conflict and problems and offer solutions. One of the most important aspects of African respect for elders is that it makes them useful and active in the community, unlike the worst of European society which deprives them of meaningful roles and places them to the side, leaving them with only failing memories.

Also, the active participation and involvement of elders in the daily life of the family not only benefits them but the younger people. For it teaches them to understand and appreciate the process of growing old, gives them access to seasoned knowledge and experience and helps prevent the so-called generation gap so evident and advertised in European society. Key to this linking of young and old is the concept of lineage which links all the living, the departed and the yet unborn. This is translated in practice into the extended family and the protocol, ritual, reciprocity

and remembrance this involves and requires. Early in life continental African children are taught to memorize and recite their family tree as far back as any ancestor is known. This keeps historical memory alive and reaffirms respect for those living and departed who contributed to their coming into being and cultural molding.

Now, if one starts with the family when discussing unity, the community becomes of necessity the next level of the concern and practice of unity. The family, as it is written, is the smallest example of how the nation (or national community) works. For the relations, values and practice one has in the family are a reflection and evidence of what one will find in the community. Likewise, the strengths and/or weaknesses of the family are those of the community. Unity in the community, then, begins in the family but it extends to organizational affiliation and then the unity of organizations, i.e., African American united fronts. Malcolm X taught that community unity first depended on everyone's belonging to an organization, then all organizations uniting on the basis of common interests and aspirations. He posed community unity—in its two-level form—as morally compelling. It was for him irresponsible and self-destructive not to unite around common interests and instead glory in differences. What African Americans needed to do, he taught, is to forget their superficial organizational differences and even differences of religion and unite around their common identity as Africans, and their common interests, especially the interests of liberation.

Unity of the nation is unity of the national community as distinct from the local community. The above applies in equal measure to the national community. In terms of "racial" unity, when one says race, one means the world African community. Thus, when Garvey says "Up you mighty race; you can accomplish what you will," he is talking to the world African community. The form of unity this takes is Pan-Africanism, i.e., the struggle to unite all Africans everywhere around the common interests and make African cultural and political presence on the world stage both powerful and permanent. Pan-Africanism requires and urges that we see ourselves and act in history as an African people, belonging to a world community of African peoples. In this way, we self-consciously share in both the glory and burden of our history. And in that knowledge and context act to honor, preserve and expand that history in the struggle for liberation and ever higher levels of human life.

Kujichagulia (Self-Determination)

To define ourselves, name ourselves, create for ourselves and speak for ourselves instead of being defined, named, created for and spoken for by others.

The Second Principle of the Nguzo Saba is self-determination. This too expresses itself as both commitment and practice. It demands that we as an African people define, defend and develop ourselves instead of allowing or encouraging others to do this. It requires that we recover lost memory and once again shape our world in our own image and interest. And it is a call to recover and speak our own special truth to the world and raise images above the earth that reflect our capacity for human greatness and progress. . . .

To answer the question of "Who am I?" correctly, then, is to know and live one's history and practice one's culture. To answer the question of "Am I really who I am?" is to have and employ cultural criteria of authenticity, i.e., criteria of what is real and unreal, what is appearance and essence, what is culturally-rooted and foreign. And to answer the question of "Am I all I ought to be?" is to self-consciously possess and use ethical and cultural standards which measure men, women and children in terms of the quality of their thought and practice in the context of who they are and must become—in both an African and a human sense.

The principle and practice of self-determination carries within them the assumption that we have both the right and responsibility to exist as a people and make our own unique contribution to the forward flow of human history. This principle shelters the assumption that as fathers and moth-

ers of humanity and human civilization in the Nile Valley, we have no business playing the cultural children of the world. So it reminds us of the fact that African people created and introduced the basic disciplines of human knowledge—science, technology, geometry, math, medicine, ethics, advanced architecture, etc. And it urges us as a people not to surrender our historical and cultural identity to fit into the culture of another. Openness to exchange is a given, but it presupposes that one has kept enough of one's culture to engage in exchange, rather than slavishly follow another's lead . . . .

Ujima (Collective Work and Responsibility)

To build and maintain our community together and make our sister's and brother's problems our problems and to solve them together.

The Third Principle is Ujima (Collective Work and Responsibility) which is a commitment to active and informed togetherness on matters of common interest. It is also recognition and respect of the fact that without collective work and struggle, progress is impossible and liberation unthinkable. Moreover, the principle of Ujima supports the fundamental assumption that African is not just an identity, but also a destiny and duty, i.e., a responsibility. In other words, our collective identity in the long run is a collective future. Thus, there is a need and an obligation for us as self-conscious and committed people to shape our future with our own minds and hands and share its hardships and benefits together.

Ujima, as principle and practice, also means that we accept the fact that we are collectively responsible for our failures and setbacks as well as our victories and achievements. And this holds true not only on the national level, but also on the level of family and organization or smaller units. Such a commitment implies and encourages a vigorous capacity for self-criticism and self-correction which is indispensable to our strength, defense and development as a people.

The principle of collective work and responsibility also points to the fact that African freedom is indivisible. It shelters the assumption that as long as any African anywhere is oppressed, exploited, enslaved or wounded in any way in her or his humanity, all African people are. It thus, rejects the possibility or desirability of individual freedom in any unfree context; instead it poses the need for struggle to create a context in which all can be free. Moreover, Ujima rejects escapist and abstract humanism and supports the humanism that begins with commitment to and concern for the humans among whom we live and to whom we owe our existence, i.e., our own people. In a word, real humanism begins with accepting one's own humanity in the particular form in which it expresses itself and then initiating and sustaining exchanges with others in the context of our common humanity. It also posits that the liberation struggle to rescue and reconstruct African history and humanity is a significant contribution to overall struggle for human liberation.

In the context of a communitarian social order, cooperation is another key aspect of Ujima. It is based on the assumption that what one does to benefit others is at the same time a benefit to him/her. Likewise, "one who injures others in the end injures him/herself" as the Yoruba proverb states. In the Lovedu community in South Africa, children are taught not to be aggressive or competitive but to be cooperative and share responsibility. Even their language reflects the cooperative thrust. For even when no one has just been given something, the child says when asking for something, "give me also." Likewise, their prayer is never just for themselves but for all's health, blessing, prosperity. In fact, to ask for the personal without at the same time asking for the collective is both improper and immoral.

The lesson of the Lovedu is that harmonious living, as with the Dinka, is of paramount importance. Thus, being quarrelsome or contentious is one of the worst offenses. And striving for uncoerced or free and willing agreement is the model of behavior. Reconciliation of conflict is patient and never coercive, and always done keeping the person in mind. And the fundamental objective in conflict is not to mechanically apply the rule but to reconcile the people. For they believe that "if people do not agree, there can be no relationship." And if they have to be coerced, there cannot be genuine agreement. In such a context collective work and responsibility is facilitated and sustained.

Finally, collective work and responsibility can be seen in terms of the challenge of culture and history. Work—both personal and collective—is truly at the center of history and culture. It is the fundamental activity by which we create ourselves, define and develop ourselves and confirm ourselves in the process as both persons and a people. And it is the way we create culture and make history. It is for this reason, among others, that the Holocaust of Enslavement was so devastating. For not only did it destroy tens of millions of lives, which is morally monstrous in itself, but it also destroyed great cultural achievements, created technological and cultural arrest and thus eroded and limited the human possibility Africa offered the world. In fact, the effects of this Holocaust are present even today both in terms of the problems of the Continent and those of the Diaspora.

The challenge of history and culture then is through collective work and responsibility, to restore that which was damaged or destroyed and to raise up and reconstruct that which was in ruins as the ancient Egyptians taught. It is also to remember we are each cultural representatives of our people and have no right to misrepresent them or willfully do less than is demanded of us by our history and current situation as a community-in-struggle. We must accept and live the principle of shared or collective work and responsibility in all things good, right and beneficial to the community.

Ujamaa (Cooperative Economics)

To build and maintain our own stores, shops and other businesses and to profit from them together.

The Fourth Principle is Ujamaa (Cooperative Economics) and is essentially a commitment to the practice of shared social wealth and the work necessary to achieve it. It grows out of the fundamental communal concept that social wealth belongs to the masses of people who created it and that no one should have such an unequal amount of wealth that it gives him/her the capacity to impose unequal, exploitative or oppressive relations on others. Sharing wealth is another form of communitarian exchange, i.e., sharing and cooperating in general. But it is essential because without the principle and practice of shared wealth, the social conditions for exploitation, oppression and inequality as well as deprivation and suffering are increased. . . .

Ujamaa also stresses self-reliance in the building, strengthening and controlling of the economics of our own community. President [Julius] Nyerere [of Tanzania] has said self-reliance in Ujamaa means "first and foremost . . . that for our development we have to depend upon ourselves and our own resources." The assumption here is that we must seize and maintain the initiative in all that is ours, and that we must harness our resources and put them to the best possible use in the service of the community. This, he says, does not mean denying all assistance from or work with others but of controlling policy and shouldering the essential responsibility for our own future.

Closely related to this concept of self-reliance and the responsibility it requires is the respect for the dignity and obligation of work. To respect work is to appreciate its value, reject its exploitation and engage in it cooperatively for the common good of the community. Also, inherent in Ujamaa is the stress and obligation of generosity especially to the poor and vulnerable. . . .

. . . In fact, throughout the sacred teachings of ancient Egypt in particular and Africa in general, the ethic of care and responsibility is expressed in the concept of shared social wealth and service to the most disadvantaged. This, of course, finds its modern philosophical expression in our social thought and struggles, as a people, around and for social justice. And this struggle is not simply to be generous to the poor and vulnerable but ultimately to end their poverty and vul-

nerability, so that they too can live a decent, undeprived and meaningful life. For only in such a context will they be able to pursue the truly human without the limitation imposed by poverty, deprivation or the debilitating struggle for just life's basic necessities. To share wealth and work, then, is to share concern, care and responsibility for a new, more human and fulfilling future.

Nia (Purpose)

To make our collective vocation the building and developing of our community in order to restore our people to their traditional greatness.

The Fifth Principle of the Nguzo Saba is Nia (Purpose) which is essentially a commitment to the collective vocation of building, developing and defending our national community, its culture and history in order to regain our historical initiative and greatness as a people. The assumption here is that our role in human history has been and remains a key one, that we as an African people share in the great human legacy Africa has given the world. That legacy is one of having not only been the fathers and mothers of humanity, but also the fathers and mothers of human civilization, i.e., having introduced in the Nile Valley civilizations the basic disciplines of human knowledge. It is this identity which gives us an overriding cultural purpose and suggests a direction. This is what we mean when we say we who are the fathers and mothers of human civilization have no business playing the cultural children of the world. The principle of Nia then makes us conscious of our purpose in light of our historical and cultural identity. . . .

. . . We are both *heirs* and *custodians* of a great legacy. This means first that we must not simply receive the legacy as a formal historical and cultural transmission, but recognize and respect its importance. Secondly, it means that far from being simple heirs we are also custodians. And this implies an even greater obligation.

To inherit is to receive as legacy, place adequate value on and make a part of one's life. But to be a custodian of a great legacy is to guard, preserve, expand and promote it. It is to honor it by building on and expanding it and in turn, leaving it as an enriched legacy for future generations. . . . It is a call for us to see ourselves not as simple ghetto dwellers or newly arrived captives of the suburbs, but more definitively as a world historical people who have made and must continue to make a significant contribution to the forward flow of human history. . . .

Finally, Nia suggests that personal and social purpose are not only non-antagonistic but complementary in the true communitarian sense of the word. In fact, it suggests that the highest form of personal purpose is in the final analysis, social purpose, i.e., personal purpose that translates itself into a vocation and commitment which involves and benefits the community. As we have noted elsewhere, such level and quality of purpose not only benefits the collective whole, but also gives fullness and meaning to a person's life in a way individualistic and isolated pursuits cannot. . . .

. . . For again our purpose is not to simply create money makers, but to cultivate men and women capable of social and human exchange on a larger more meaningful scale, men and women of culture and social conscience, of vision and values which expand the human project of freedom and development rather than diminish and deform it.

Kuumba (Creativity)

To do always as much as we can, in the way we can, in order to leave our community more beautiful and beneficial than we inherited it.

The Sixth Principle is Kuumba (Creativity) and logically follows from and is required by the Principle of Nia. It is a commitment to being creative within the context of the national community vocation of restoring our people to their traditional greatness and thus leaving our community more beneficial and beautiful then we, i.e., each generation, inherited it. The Princi-

ple has both a social and spiritual dimension and is deeply rooted both in social and sacred teachings of African societies.

Nowhere is this principle more clearly expressed than in the literature and culture of ancient Egypt. Creativity here is both an original act or imitation of the Creator and a restorative act also reflective of the Creator constantly pushing back the currents of chaos and decay and revitalizing and restoring the natural, spiritual and cosmic energy of the world. In ancient Egypt, there was a spiritual and ethical commitment and obligation to constantly renew and restore the great works, the legacy of the ancestors, and the creative energy of the leader and nation. This was considered doing Maat, i.e., reaffirming and restoring truth, justice and righteousness, harmony, balance, order, rightness, etc. Each pharaoh saw his or her reign, then, as one of restoration of Maat, i.e., the reaffirmation, reestablishment and renewal of the Good, the Beautiful and the Right. . . .

It is interesting to note here that my creation of Kwanzaa falls within the restorative conception of creativity. For when I say I created Kwanzaa, the term "created" does not imply or mean "made out of nothing," for it is clearly not the case as the above discussion on the Continental African origins of Kwanzaa shows. What one has, then, is rather a *creative restoration* in the African spirit of cultural restoration and renewal in both the ancient Egyptian and African American sense of the practice as used in the 1960's.

It is, in fact, a restoring that which was in ruins or disuse in many parts of Africa, and especially among Africans in America and attempting to make it more beautiful and beneficial than it was before as the Principle of Kuumba (Creativity) requires. This . . . contains the interrelated principles of *restoration* and *progressive perfection.* To restore is what we called in the 60's "to rescue and reconstruct." Progressive perfection is a Kawaida concept that assumes an *ability* and *obligation* to strive always to leave what one inherits (legacy, community, etc.) more beautiful and beneficial than it was before. It is, again, in this context and spirit of the cultural project of recovering and reconstructing African first fruit celebrations that Kwanzaa was conceived and constructed.

The stress, then, is on leaving a legacy which builds on and enriches the legacy before you. It is again stress on generational responsibility. Kwanzaa reminds us of the ancient Egyptian teaching that if we wish to live for eternity we must build for eternity, i.e., do great works or serve the community in a real, sustained and meaningful way. . . .

. . . The lesson here is that creativity is central to the human spirit and human society, that it causes us to grow, restores and revitalizes us and the community and insures our life for eternity. . . .

Imani (Faith)

To believe with all our heart in our people, our parents, our teachers, our leaders and the righteousness and victory of our struggle.

The Seventh Principle is Faith which is essentially a profound belief in and commitment to all that is of value to us as a family, community, people and culture. In the context of African spirituality, it begins with a belief in the Creator and in the positiveness of the creation and logically leads to a belief in the essential goodness and possibility of the human personality. For in all African spiritual traditions, from Egypt on, it is taught that we are in the image of the Creator and thus capable of ultimate righteousness and creativity through self-mastery and development in the context of positive support. Therefore, faith in ourselves is key here, faith in our capacity as humans to live righteously, self-correct, support, care for and be responsible for each other and eventually create the just and good society. . . .

. . . Also, . . . faith in the masses of our people is central to our progress as a people. . . . As a community-in-struggle there is no substitute for belief in our people, in their capacity to take control of their destiny and daily lives and shape them in their own image and interests. This is

fundamental to any future we dare design and pursue.

Especially we must believe in the value and validity, the righteousness and significance of our struggle for liberation and a higher level of human life. This must be tied to our belief in our capacity to assume and carry out with dignity and decisiveness the role [Frantz] Fanon and history has assigned us. And that role is to set in motion a new history of humankind and in the company of other oppressed and Third World peoples pose a new paradigm of human society and human relations. Fanon says we can do anything as long as we don't do two basic things: 1) try to catch up with Europe (after all where is it going—swinging between spiritual and nuclear annihilation); and 2) imitate them so that we become "obscene caricatures" of them. We must, he says, invent, innovate, reach inside ourselves and dare "set afoot a new man and woman." The world and our people are waiting for something new, more beautiful and beneficial from us than what a past of oppression has offered us. Let us not imitate or be taught by our oppressors. Let us dare struggle, free ourselves politically and culturally and raise images above the earth that reflect our capacity for human progress and greatness. This is the challenge and burden of our history which assumes and requires a solid faith.

We must, then, have faith in ourselves, in our leaders, teachers, parents and in the righteousness and victory of our struggle, faith that through hard work, long struggle and a whole lot of love and understanding, we can again step back on the stage of human history as a free, proud and productive people. It is in this context that we can surely speak our own special truth to the world and make our own unique contribution to the forward flow of human history.

Discussion Questions

1. How, on the whole, do these principles differ from the main values of (a) Christianity and (b) contemporary American society?
2. Elsewhere Karenga has spoken of complementarity—as opposed to *equality*—as the

ruling principle between men and women (see the essay by Amiri Baraka in Part II B). Here he speaks of it in opposition to "conflict." Why do you suppose he has changed this?

3. Which principle do you prefer as *foundational* for ethics: what Karenga would call the "abstract humanism" of an equal regard for all human beings or the humanism "that begins with commitment to and concern for the humans among whom we live and to whom we our existence, i.e., our own people"?

4. Does Karenga's principle of Ujamaa imply *socialism*?

11   The Afrocentric Idea in Education

MOLEFI K. ASANTE

Study Questions

1. Why would the assumption that African and European Americans hold the same relation to the realities of America lead to "the psychological and cultural death of the African American population"?

2. What does *centricity* mean?

3. How does Afrocentrism help African American pupils see themselves "as subjects rather than objects of education"?

4. What would be the relationship between an Afrocentric and a multicultural education?

Introduction

Many of the principles that govern the development of the Afrocentric idea in education were first established by Carter G. Woodson in *The Mis-education of the Negro* (1933). Indeed, Woodson's classic reveals the fundamental problems pertaining to the education of the African person in America. As Woodson contends, African Americans have been educated away from their own culture and traditions and attached to the fringes of European culture; thus

From the *Journal of Negro Education* 60 (1991), pp. 170–180.

dislocated from themselves, Woodson asserts that African Americans often valorize European culture to the detriment of their own heritage. Although Woodson does not advocate rejection of American citizenship or nationality, he believed that assuming African Americans hold the same position as European Americans vis-à-vis the realities of America would lead to the psychological and cultural death of the African American population. Furthermore, if education is ever to be substantive and meaningful within the context of American society, Woodson argues, it must first address the African's historical experiences, both in Africa and America. That is why he places on education, and particularly on the traditionally African American colleges, the burden of teaching the African American to be responsive to the long traditions and history of Africa as well as America. Woodson's alert recognition, more than 50 years ago, that something is severely wrong with the way African Americans are educated provides the principal impetus for the Afrocentric approach to American education . . . .

Definitions

. . . In education, *centricity* refers to a perspective that involves locating students within the context of their own cultural references so that they can relate socially and psychologically to other cultural perspectives. Centricity is a concept that can be applied to any culture. The centrist paradigm is supported by research showing that the most productive method of teaching any student is to place his or her group within the center of the context of knowledge. For White students in America this is easy because almost all the experiences discussed in American classrooms are approached from the standpoint of White perspectives and history. American education, however, is not centric; it is Eurocentric. Consequently, non-White students are also made to see themselves and their groups as the "acted upon." Only rarely do they read or hear of non-White people as active participants in history. This is as true for a discussion of the American Revolution as it is for a discussion of Dante's *Inferno;* for instance, most classroom discussions of the European slave trade concentrate on the activities of Whites rather than on the resistance efforts of Africans. A person educated in a truly centric fashion comes to view all groups' contributions as significant and useful. Even a White person educated in such a system does not assume superiority based upon racist notions. Thus, a truly centric education is different from a Eurocentric, racist (that is, White supremacist) education.

Afrocentricity is a frame of reference wherein phenomena are viewed from the perspective of the African person. The Afrocentric approach seeks in every situation the appropriate centrality of the African person. In education this means that teachers provide students the opportunity to study the world and its people, concepts, and history from an African world view. In most classrooms, whatever the subject, Whites are located in the center perspective position. How alien the African American child must feel, how like an outsider! The little African American child who sits in a classroom and is taught to accept as heroes and heroines individuals who defamed African people is being actively de-centered, dislocated, and made into a nonperson, one whose aim in life might be to one day shed that "badge of inferiority": his or her Blackness. In Afrocentric educational settings, however, teachers do not marginalize African American children by causing them to question their own self-worth because their people's story is seldom told. By seeing themselves as the subjects rather than the objects of education—be the discipline biology, medicine, literature, or social studies—African American students come to see themselves not merely as seekers of knowledge but as integral participants in it. Because all content areas are adaptable to an Afrocentric approach, African American students can be made to see themselves as centered in the reality of any discipline.

It must be emphasized that Afrocentricity is *not* a Black version of Eurocentricity. Eurocentricity is based on White supremacist notions whose purposes are to protect White privilege and advantage in education, economics, politics, and so forth. Unlike Eurocentricity, Afrocentricity does not condone ethnocentric valorization at the expense of degrading other groups' perspectives. Moreover, Eurocentricity presents the particular historical reality of Europeans as the sum total of the human experience. It imposes Eurocentric realities as "universal"; i.e., that which is White is presented as applying to the human condition in general, while that which is non-White is viewed as group-specific and therefore not "human." This explains why some scholars and artists of African descent rush to deny their Blackness; they believe that to exist as a Black person is not to exist as a universal human being. They are the individuals Woodson identified as preferring European art, language, and culture over African art, language, and culture; they believe that anything of European origin is inherently better than anything produced by or issuing from their own people. Naturally, the person of African descent should be centered in his or her historical experiences as an African, but Eurocentric curricula produce such aberrations of perspective among persons of color.

Multiculturalism in education is a nonhierarchical approach that respects and celebrates a variety of cultural perspectives on world phenomena. The multicultural approach holds that although European culture is the majority culture in the United States, that is not sufficient reason for it to be imposed on diverse student populations as "universal." Multiculturalists assert that education, to have integrity, must begin with the proposition that all humans have contributed to world development and the flow of knowledge and information, and that most human achievements are the result of mutually interactive, international effort. Without a multicultural education, students remain essentially ignorant of the contributions of a major portion of the world's people. A multicultural education is thus a fundamental necessity for anyone who wishes to achieve competency in almost any subject.

The Afrocentric idea must be the stepping-stone from which the multicultural idea is launched. A truly authentic multicultural education, therefore, must be based upon the Afrocentric initiative. If this step is skipped, multicultural curricula, as they are increasingly being defined by White "resisters" . . . will evolve without any substantive infusion of African American content, and the African American child will continue to be lost in the Eurocentric framework of education. In other words, the African American child will neither be confirmed nor affirmed in his or her own cultural information. For the mutual benefit of all Americans, this tragedy, which leads to the psychological and cultural dislocation of African American children, can and should be avoided. . . .

The Condition of Eurocentric Education

Institutions such as schools are conditioned by the character of the nation in which they are developed. Just as crime and politics are different in different nations, so, too, is education. In the United States a "Whites-only" orientation has predominated in education. This has had a profound impact on the quality of education for children of all races and ethnic groups. The African American child has suffered disproportionately, but White children are also the victims of monoculturally diseased curricula.

The Tragedy of Ignorance

During the past five years many White students and parents have approached me after presentations with tears in their eyes or expressing their anger about the absence of information about African Americans in the schools. A recent comment from a young White man at a major university in the Northeast was especially striking. As he said to me "My teacher told us that Martin Luther King was a commie and went on with the class." Because this student's teacher made no effort to discuss King's ideas, the student maliciously had been kept ignorant. The vast majority of White Americans are likewise ignorant about the bountiful reservoirs of African and African American history, culture, and contributions. For example, few Americans of any color have heard the names of Cheikh Anta Diop, Anna Julia Cooper, C. L. R. James or J. A. Rogers. All were historians who contributed greatly to our understanding of the African world. Indeed, very few teachers have ever taken a course in African American Studies; therefore, most are unable to provide systematic information about African Americans. . . .

Correcting Distorted Information

Hegemonic education can exist only so long as true and accurate information is withheld. Hegemonic Eurocentric education can exist only so long as Whites maintain that Africans and other non-Whites have never contributed to world civilization. It is largely upon such false ideas that invidious distinctions are made. The truth, however, gives one insight into the real reasons behind human actions, whether one chooses to follow the paths of others or not. For example, one cannot remain comfortable teaching that art and philosophy originated in Greece if one learns that the Greeks themselves taught that the study of these subjects originated in Africa, specifically ancient Kemet. The first philosophers were the Egyptians Kagemni, Khun-anup, Ptahhotep, Kete, and Seti; but Eurocentric education is so disjointed that students have no way of discovering this and other knowledge of the organic relationship of Africa to the rest of human history. Not only did Africa contribute to human history, African civilizations predate all other civilizations. Indeed, the human species originated on the continent of Africa—this is true whether one looks at either archaeological or biological evidence.

Two other notions must be refuted. There are those who say that African American history should begin with the arrival of Africans as slaves in 1619, but it has been shown that Africans visited and inhabited North and South America long before European settlers "discovered" the "New World." Secondly, although America became something of a home for those Africans who survived the horrors of the Middle Passage, their experiences on the slave ships and during slavery resulted in their having an entirely different (and often tainted) perspective about America from that of the Europeans and others who came, for the most part, of their own free will seeking opportunities not available to them in their native lands. Afrocentricity therefore seeks to recognize this divergence in perspective and create centeredness for African American students.

Conclusion

The reigning initiative for total curricular change is the movement that is being proposed and led by Africans, namely, the Afrocentric idea. When I wrote the first book on Afrocentricity, now in its fifth printing, I had no idea that in 10 years the idea would both shake up and shape discussions in education, art, fashion, and politics. Since the publication of my subsequent works, *The Afrocentric Idea* and *Kemet, Afrocentricty and Knowledge,* the debate has been joined in earnest. Still, for many White Americans (and some African Americans) the most unsettling aspect of the discussion about Afrocentricity is that its intellectual source lies in the research and writings of African American scholars. Whites are accustomed to being in charge of the major ideas circulating in the American academy. . . .

Afrocentricity provides all Americans an opportunity to examine the perspective of the African person in this society and the world. The resistero claim that Afrocentricity is anti-White; yet, if Afrocentricity as a theory is against anything it is against racism, ignorance, and monoethnic hegemony in the curriculum. Afrocentricity is not anti-White; it is, however, pro-human. Further, the aim of the Afrocentric curriculum is not to divide America, it is to make America flourish as it ought to flourish. This nation has long been divided with regard to the educational opportunities afforded to children. By virtue of the protection provided by society and reinforced by the Eurocentric curriculum, the White child is already ahead of the African American child by first grade. Our efforts thus must concentrate on giving the African American child greater opportunities for learning at the kindergarten level. However, the kind of assistance the African American child needs is as much cultural as it is academic. If the proper cultural information is provided, the academic performance will surely follow suit.

When it comes to educating African American children, the American educational system does not need a tune-up, it needs an overhaul. Black children have been maligned by this system. Black teachers have been maligned. Black history has been maligned. Africa has been maligned. Nonetheless, two truisms can be stated about education in America. First, some teachers *can and do* effectively teach African American children; secondly, if some teachers can do it, others can, too. We must learn all we can about what makes these teachers' attitudes and approaches successful, and then work diligently to see that their successes are replicated on a broad scale. By raising the same questions that Woodson posed more than 50 years ago, Afrocentric education, along with a significant reorientation of the American educational enterprise, seeks to respond to the African person's psychological and cultural dislocation. By providing philosophical and theoretical guidelines and criteria that are centered in an African perception of reality and by placing the African American child in his or her proper historical context and setting, Afrocentricity may be just the "escape hatch" African

Americans so desperately need to facilitate academic success and "steal away" from the cycle of miseducation and dislocation.

Discussion Questions

1. If all knowledge is unavoidably "perspectival" (i.e., from an Afrocentric, a Eurocentric, or another perspective, but not simply from a neutral, objective one), how are we to understand Asante's claims that, for example, philosophy originated in Africa? (Is this being claimed merely as an Afrocentric fact or as an objective one?)

2. How do you understand Afrocentricity as something more than an educational idea? Does it carry with it, for instance, an implied *political* program? If so, what is that program?

3. Do you think that Asante's ideas, judged as an educational program, should be subject to test by social scientists and educators to see whether they work? Or is it self-evident that they must?

4. Insofar as a "multicultural" perspective involves multiple centricities, how is this consistent with an Afrocentric perspective?

12   The Four Traditions of Response

CORNEL WEST

Study Questions

1. What is the difference between the "strong" and "weak" exceptionalist views?

2. In what way has "weak assimilationism" provided the basis of the civil rights movement during the past two decades (the sixties and seventies)?

3. In terms of West's discussion, explain what he means by describing the marginalist tradition as involving "both confinement and creativity, restriction and revolt."

4. Why are Afro-American musicians "Afro-American humanists par excellence"?

Modern racist discourse did not go unanswered by Afro-Americans. In this chapter, I shall put forward an interpretation and a description of the Afro-American experience in the light of the black reactions and responses to the modern justifications of the idea of white supremacy initiated in enlightened Europe and inseminated in the slavery-ridden United States. The interpretation and the description are essentially a reconstruction of the black counter discourse to modern European racist discourse. They present a hermeneutic of Afro-American history that focuses on the diverse conceptions of self-image and self-determination during the prolonged Afro-American entrance into the corridors of modernity: the long-overdue reaping of the harvest that Afro-Americans helped cultivate, the seizing of opportunities previously closed, and the bruising encounter with the emptiness, sterility, and hypocrisy of postmodernity.

When Afro-Americans are viewed as passive objects of history, Afro-American history is a record of the exclusion of a distinct racial group from the economic benefits and cultural dilemmas of modernity. Politically, this exclusion has meant white ownership of Afro-American persons, possessions, and progeny; severe discrimination reinforced by naked violence within a nascent industrial capitalist order; and urban enclaves of unskilled unemployables and semiskilled workers within a liberal corporate

Reproduced from *Prophecy Deliverance!* (Philadelphia: Westminster John Knox Press, 1982), pp. 69–91. © 1982 Cornel West. Reprinted by permission of the publisher.

capitalist regime. Culturally, this has meant continual Afro-American degradation and ceaseless attempts to undermine Afro-American self-esteem.

When Afro-Americans are viewed as active subjects of history, Afro-American history becomes the story of a gallantly persistent struggle, of a disparate racial group fighting to enter modernity on its own terms. Politically, this struggle consists of prudential acquiescence plus courageous revolt against white paternalism; institution-building and violent rebellion within the segregated social relations of industrial capitalism; and cautious reformist strategies within the integrated social relations of "postindustrial" capitalism. Culturally, this has meant the maintenance of self-respect in the face of pervasive denigration.

I will attempt to order and organize some significant aspects of the Afro-American past by delineating four ideal types that embody distinct Afro-American historical traditions of thought and action. These categories incorporate abstract elements of Afro-American historical reality; they are, however, derived from an empirical examination of this reality. Needless to say, they rarely appear empirically in their pure, conceptual form, but may serve as heuristic tools to confer intelligibility on Afro-American history and provide an understanding of this history by revealing its internal rationality.

The four theoretical constructs to be considered are the exceptionalist, assimilationist, marginalist, and humanist traditions in Afro-American history.[1] I shall try to stipulate clear definitions of these traditions so they will not be automatically associated with their previously established meanings within traditional historiography.

The Afro-American exceptionalist tradition lauds the uniqueness of Afro-American culture and personality. It claims a *sui generis* status for Afro-American life in regard to form and content. It stresses what qualitatively distinguishes Afro-Americans from the rest of humanity, especially what sets them apart from white Americans. This tradition contains two types: strong exceptionalism and weak exceptionalism. Strong exceptionalism makes ontological claims about Afro-American superiority; Afro-Americans stand above other racial groups because of their genetic makeup, di-

vine chosenness, or innate endowments. Weak exceptionalism makes sociological claims about Afro-American superiority; Afro-Americans stand above other racial groups because of certain values, modes of behavior, or gifts acquired from their endurance of political oppression, social degradation, and economic exploitation.

The Afro-American assimilationist tradition considers Afro-American culture and personality to be pathological. It rejects any idea of an independent, self-supportive Afro-American culture. It stresses the inability of Afro-Americans to create adequate coping devices to alleviate the enormous pressures caused by their dire condition. This tradition also contains two types: strong assimilationism and weak assimilationism. Strong assimilationism makes ontological claims about Afro-American inferiority; Afro-Americans stand below other racial groups because of their genetic makeup, divine rejection, or innate deficiency. Weak assimilationism makes sociological claims about Afro-American inferiority; Afro-Americans stand below other racial groups because of certain values, modes of behavior, or defects acquired from their endurance of political oppression, social degradation, and economic exploitation.

The Afro-American marginalist tradition posits Afro-American culture to be restrictive, constraining, and confining. It emphasizes the suppression of individuality, eccentricity, and nonconformity within Afro-American culture. This tradition is parasitic in that it rests upon either the assimilationist or humanist tradition.

The Afro-American humanist tradition extolls the distinctiveness of Afro-American culture and personality. It accents the universal human content of Afro-American cultural forms. It makes no ontological or sociological claims about Afro-American superiority or inferiority. Rather, it focuses on the ways in which creative Afro-American cultural modes of expression embody themes and motifs analogous to the vigorous cultural forms of other racial, ethnic, or national groups. This tradition affirms Afro-American membership in the human race, not above it or below it.

My conception of these four traditions in Afro-American thought and action assumes that culture is more fundamental than politics in regard to

Afro-American self-understanding. It presupposes that Afro-American cultural perceptions provide a broader and richer framework for understanding the Afro-American experience than political perceptions. As noted earlier, culture and politics are inseparable, but, as I believe Antonio Gramsci has shown, any political consciousness of an oppressed group is shaped and molded by the group's cultural resources and resiliency as perceived by individuals in it.[2] So the extent to which the resources and resiliency are romanticized, rejected, or accepted will deeply influence the kind of political consciousness that individuals possess.

These four traditions of thought and action in Afro-American history can serve as guides for understanding Afro-American culture and politics. They shall represent distinct Afro-American responses to the challenges of self-image and self-determination; they will also be the alternatives from which we choose a desirable response to these challenges.

Exceptionalist Tradition

The self-image of Afro-Americans in both types of the exceptionalist tradition is one of pride, self-congratulation, and often heroism. Afro-Americans are considered to be more humane, meek, kind, creative, spontaneous, and nonviolent than members of other racial groups; less malicious, mendacious, belligerent, bellicose, and avaricious. This tradition posits Afro-American superiority, not over all others, but specifically over white Americans.

The strong exceptionalist tradition in Afro-American history does not appear in any substantive manner until the rise of a secular Afro-American intelligentsia. The early religious Afro-American intellectuals, though vehemently opposed to black oppression and the doctrine of white supremacy, did not subscribe to any form of strong exceptionalism. Despite the fierce fight continually waged for Afro-American enhancement, they refused to make any ontological claims about Afro-American superiority, primarily because of inhibitory, deep, Christian roots.

The first major formulation of strong exceptionalism in Afro-American thought appeared in

the "germ" theory of New England–born, Harvard-trained W. E. B. Du Bois. Ironically, he borrowed this theory from his teacher at Harvard, Albert Bushnell Hart, who used it to support Teutonic (Anglo-Saxon) superiority. This theory maintained that each race possesses its own "race idea and race spirit" embodying its unique gift to humanity. Du Bois wrote:

At the same time the spiritual and physical differences of race groups which constituted the nations became deep and decisive. The English nation stood for constitutional liberty and commercial freedom; the German nation for science and philosophy; the romance nations stood for literature and art, and the other race groups are striving, each in his own way, to develop for civilization its particular message, its particular ideal. . . . Manifestly some of the great races today—particularly the Negro race—have not as yet given to civilization the full spiritual message which they are capable of giving.[3]

And what was this message? In *The Souls of Black Folk* (1903) and *The Gift of Black Folk* (1924), he suggested that it was essentially that of meekness, joviality, and humility manifest in the Afro-American gift of spirit. His essay "Of Our Spiritual Strivings," found in the earlier work, rhetorically asked,

Will America be poorer if she replace her brutal dyspeptic blundering with light-hearted but determined Negro humility? or her coarse and cruel wit with loving jovial good-humor? or her vulgar music with the soul of the Sorrow Songs?[4]

He ended the latter work casting "the sense of meekness and humility" of Afro-Americans against the white man's "contempt, lawlessness and lynching" for domination of the emerging American spirit. The uniqueness of Afro-Americans was even more explicitly endorsed when he wrote: "Negroes differ from whites in their inherent genius and stages of development."[5] Under the influence of Franz Boas and Marxism, Du Bois abandoned the "germ" theory, yet he planted and nurtured its seed long enough for the strong exceptionalist tradition to establish a continued presence in Afro-American thought and action.

James Weldon Johnson gave the strong exceptionalist tradition new life with his notion of the unique creativity of Afro-Americans. In the famous preface to his well-known anthology of

Afro-American poetry, he claimed that the true greatness of a civilization should be measured by its creative powers in the arts. He then added,

The Negro has already proved the possession of these powers by being the creator of the only things artistic that have yet sprung from American soil and been universally acknowledged as distinctive American products.[6]

He attributed these creative powers to the "racial genius" of Afro-Americans,

. . . us who are warmed by the poetic blood of Africa—old, mysterious Africa, mother of races, rhythmic-beating heart of the world.[7]

And what did this "racial genius" consist of? Like that of Du Bois, it was a God-given (or nature-given) spirit revealed in the pietistic, primitive Christianity of rural Afro-Americans.

The majority of literary works during the Harlem Renaissance mark a shift in the strong exceptionalist tradition. The urban setting and the close interaction with alienated white literary figures groping for the vitality of "noble savages" add new content to Afro-American uniqueness: the primitivism of Afro-Americans manifest in their uninhibited and spontaneous behavior.

In the past decade, the strong exceptionalist tradition has flourished in the religious doctrine of the Black Muslims under the leadership of the late Honorable Elijah Muhammad, the black theology of Joseph Washington, and the Black Arts movement promoted by Imamu Baraka, the late Hoyt Fuller, Addison Gayle, and others. These groups provided ontological justifications for the inhumanity of white Americans, hence Afro-American superiority over these whites. The evidence usually adduced was American history; the conclusion was to deny American (white) values, defy American (white) society, and preserve the small dose of (black) humanity left in America.

The weak exceptionalist tradition began in earnest with the African Methodist Episcopal intelligentsia. The humanity of white people was not denied, but they were relegated to a lower moral status than Afro-Americans. For example, R. R. Wright, a leading intellectual of the African Methodist Episcopal Church at the turn of the century, wrote: "The white man is selfish and the American white man is the most grasping breed of humanity ever made."[8] Wright concluded that whites, because of their materialist greed and moral self-centeredness, have never understood the Christian message. Only the peaceful, loving, and forgiving Afro-Americans can instill the spirit of Christianity in the violent, vicious white race: "African Methodism will carry the Christian message of brotherhood to the white man."[9]

The weak exceptionalist tradition continued with the Garvey movement of the 1920s. Garvey heralded Afro-American pride, beauty, and strength without claiming innate white inferiority. His program of racial purity, black religion (including a black Christ, Mary, and God), and Back-to-Africa doctrine was juxtaposed with, for example, the following judgment on white people:

We are not preaching a propaganda of hate against anybody. We love the white man; we love all humanity, because we feel that we cannot live without the other.[10]

Yet Garvey believed that white people behaved in a demonic fashion within the existing social order:

I regard the Klan as a better friend of the race than all the groups of hypocritical whites put together. You may call me a Klansman, if you will, but potentially every white man is a Klansman, as far as the Negro in competition with whites socially, economically, and politically is concerned, and there is no use lying about it.[11]

The most recent instance of weak exceptionalism is surprisingly the great Martin Luther King's doctrine of nonviolence. This doctrine tends to assume tacitly that Afro-Americans have acquired, as a result of their historical experience, a peculiar capacity to love their enemies, to endure patiently suffering, pain, and hardship and thereby "teach the white man how to love" or "cure the white man of his sickness." King seemed to believe that Afro-Americans possess a unique proclivity for nonviolence, more so than do other racial groups, that they have a certain bent toward humility, meekness, and forbearance, hence are quite naturally disposed toward nonviolent action. In King's broad overview, God is utilizing Afro-Americans—this community of *caritas* (other-directed love)—to bring about "the blessed community." He seemed confident that his nonviolent movement of predominantly Afro-Americans was part of a divine plan. He was the drum major of "this mighty army of love":

I am sure that the entire world now looks to the Negro in America for leadership in the whole task of building a world without want, without hate, and where all men live together in shared opportunity and brotherhood.[12]

The self-image fostered by both types of the exceptionalist tradition is defensive in character and romantic in content. It is a reaction to the doctrine of white supremacy, an attempt to build Afro-American pride and self-worth upon quixotic myths about the past, exaggerated expectations of the present, and chiliastic hopes for the future.

This self-image reveals the real roots of the Afro-American exceptionalist tradition: the rise of the Afro-American petite bourgeoisie. The exceptionalist claim of Afro-American superiority can be seen as a cloak for the repressed self-doubts, fears, and anxieties of an emerging Afro-American middle class. It resulted from the inevitable questioning of personal identity and the belated quest for wealth, status, and prestige among the Afro-American parvenu petite bourgeoisie caused by interacting with a hostile white (American) society.

In the cultural sphere, Afro-American exceptionalism was begun by talented Afro-Americans extolling the cultural achievements of the West, searching for Afro-American achievements commensurate with those of the West, and ending by conjuring up mythologies that put Afro-American achievements on a superior footing with those of the West. Personal identity became cushioned by racial myths of superiority; the search for this identity was motivated primarily by the white opposition. Hence, it was extrinsic, containing no enduring sustenance, potency, or authenticity.

In the political sphere, Afro-American exceptionalism started with ambitious Afro-Americans who pursued wealth, status, and prestige in American society, ran up against racist barriers, then returned to the Afro-American world to continue this pursuit, with an acquired hostility toward the society into which they unsuccessfully sought entrance. They amassed wealth, status, and prestige in this world ("big fish in a little pond") and concerned themselves with helping other ambitious

socially mobile Afro-Americans, sometimes under the banner of antiwhitism, and often at the expense of the Afro-American masses.

The bourgeois roots of the exceptionalist tradition are most clearly seen in its aims and conceptions of political struggle. Its major form is Afro-American vocation ideology: a calling for Afro-Americans to acknowledge their uniqueness, utilize it to organize and mobilize themselves against the white world, and undermine the inhumanity and hypocrisy of this white world. A cursory examination of the Afro-American exceptionalist approach to political struggle substantiates a revised version of Lenin's famous quip: "Scratch an exceptionalist and underneath is a budding bourgeois."

Du Bois' "germ" theory had its political analogue in his doctrine of the Talented Tenth. He promoted both simultaneously. While the Afro-American masses are busy giving the world its meekness, humility, and joviality, the Talented Tenth are providing leadership and guidance for these spiritual masses, a leadership and guidance that presuppose the sustained wealth, status, and prestige of the Talented Tenth. In other words, the Untalented Ninetieth possess the idealized gift of spirit, while the Talented Tenth acquire the essentials of power, namely, education and skills:[13]

The Negro race, like all races, is going to be saved by its exceptional men. The problem of education, then, among Negroes must first of all deal with the Talented Tenth; it is the problem of developing the Best of this race that they may guide the Mass away from the contamination and death of the Worst, in their own and other races.[14]

James Weldon Johnson's important role in the National Association for the Advancement of Colored People, that of being its first black executive secretary, embodied the same relationship, with an integrationist twist: a middle-class approach while idealizing the religious "primitivism" of the Afro-American masses.

The literary artists of the Harlem Renaissance, as well as of the Black Arts movement in the 1960s, represent petit bourgeois fascination with the spontaneity of Afro-American proletarian (and lumpenproletarian) life; the first movement remained much less political than the later one. The Harlem Renaissance writers basically portrayed stereotypical life-styles with which they were scarcely acquainted; the Black Arts figures promoted so-called "black" values that rested completely outside the cultural framework of most Afro-Americans. Both movements produced mediocre art, romanticized the Afro-American lower class, and launched lucrative careers for a few middle-class black artists previously excluded from the white (American) world of art.

R. R. Wright's weak exceptionalist approach culminated in an energetic attempt to organize an Afro-American interest group, an Afro-American political party, and an Afro-American voting bloc: early middle-class attempts to utilize Afro-American cohesion to gain entrance to the political mainstream.

The Garvey movement, after great popular support primarily caused by its powerful reversal of European ideals of beauty and culture, resulted in an aborted trip to Africa. The thousands of dollars that were acquired from Afro-Americans, mainly from small entrepreneurs, who purchased stocks in Garvey's business concerns, were squandered, through ineptitude and graft. The Black Muslims, under the late Honorable Elijah Muhammad, opted for entrepreneurship in urban centers—a gallant yet hapless attempt to secure a notch within a declining entrepreneurial capitalism and an ever-expanding corporate domination of the economy. The same holds for the "black capitalism" promoted in the past decade by some Black Power advocates.[15]

King's early political viewpoint was more candid than that of others: it literally proclaimed its goal to be American middle-class status. After a harsh political struggle, the Federal Government was persuaded to legitimize this pursuit. Federal legislation removed certain racist barriers—e.g., disenfranchisement and segregated housing—which increased the possibility of skilled and educated Afro-Americans' acquiring some degree of wealth, status, and prestige in American society. Results for the Afro-American poor have been minimal.[16]

The exceptionalist response to the challenges of self-image and self-determination is this: a romanticization of Afro-American culture that conceals the social mobility of an emerging opportunistic Afro-American petite bourgeoisie. Afro-American exceptionalism offers symbols and rituals to the Afro-American masses which are useful for enhancing the social mobility of Afro-American professional and business groups.[17] It generates cathartic and amorphous feelings of Afro-American pride, self-congratulation, and heroism that contain little substance.

Afro-American philosophy deems the exceptionalist response undesirable. Such a romanticization of Afro-American culture is an escape from reality. It fosters cultural stagnation and leaves Afro-Americans vulnerable to insidious manipulation by black charismatic figures or socially mobile groups. In other words, it does not enhance the cultural life or ameliorate the socioeconomic conditions of the majority of Afro-Americans.

The hypocrisy of Afro-American exceptionalism is revealed usually ex post facto: when bourgeois nationalists, after acquiring some status, prestige, and wealth, begin to "outgrow their childish past," namely, begin to interact, commune, and even marry the previously "inferior enemy"; and when bourgeois integrationists, after gaining a desired place in American society, remain complacently inert and satisfied in their "promised land," the coveted suburbs. So the Afro-American exceptionalist tradition of both types is a stream of thought and action in Afro-American history which serves principally as a covert strategy for Afro-American entrance into the mainstream of American society.

Assimilationist Tradition

The self-image of Afro-Americans in both types of the assimilationist tradition is one of self-hatred, shame, and fear. Afro-Americans are viewed as morbid subhuman monsters. This tradition posits Afro-American inferiority, not against everyone, but specifically to white Americans.

Like the exceptionalist tradition, this stream of thought and action in Afro-American history did not appear in a significant manner until the rise of a secular Afro-American intelligentsia. Aside from occasional remarks by Alexander Crummell and Edward Blyden regarding missionary emigrationism, the early religious Afro-American intelligentsia refused to engage in any talk about Afro-

American inferiority, primarily because they headed the institutions (churches) around which Afro-American culture evolved.

The unchallenged theoretician of the weak assimilationist tradition in Afro-American history is E. Franklin Frazier.[18] The Chicago school of sociology serves as the context in which his brand of weak assimilationism flourished. Borrowing from the social theory of W. I. Thomas (especially his work on Polish peasants) and Robert Parks (notably his work on urban class and status conflict), Frazier views the history of Afro-American culture as a series of devastating social shocks—the initial act of enslavement from Africa, the cruel voyage across the Atlantic Ocean, the "peculiar institution" of slavery, the vicious postemancipation life, and the disintegration of folk culture in the cities.

In his well-known book, *The Negro Family in the United States* (1939), Frazier suggests that the Afro-American culture basically amounts to superstition, ignorance, self-hatred, and fear. It emanates from political despair and produces a wholly negative self-image. He hopes it will soon disappear.[19]

The weak assimilationist tradition under the aegis of Frazier has provided the theoretical framework for legal and political argumentation of civil rights during the past two decades. The message was clear: Afro-Americans have been environmentally created less equal and normal than whites, so only assimilation with whites can break the circle of political oppression and pathological behavior.

This message contains the chief aim of political struggle in the Afro-American weak assimilationist tradition, an ideology of Afro-American uplift: The only hope for Afro-American enhancement is increased interaction with whites, because only assimilation can civilize, refine, and modernize Afro-Americans. In short, it endorses the viewpoints of Samuel Stanhope Smith and Benjamin Rush which we examined in Chapter 2. Frazier makes this point crystal clear:

If the Negro had undertaken to shut himself off from the white culture about him and had sought light from within his experience, he would have remained on the level of barbarism.[20]

Later in life, Frazier began to recognize the belated consequences of his viewpoint. In his

scathing critique of the Afro-American middle class, *Black Bourgeoisie* (1962), he castigates their aping of white bourgeois society, their fanciful world of status, wealth, and prestige, and their inability to take each other seriously as professionals. In a later essay, he advised Afro-American intellectuals to provide positive self-images for black people and to not confuse assimilation with self-effacement.[21] Yet, despite these late attempts that acknowledge the limitations of the weak assimilationist tradition, Frazier almost singlehandedly set in motion a stream of Afro-American thought and action which remains highly influential today.

Like the exceptionalist tradition, the assimilationist one is a petit bourgeois affair; it promotes a self-image that inheres primarily among an insecure, socially mobile Afro-American middle class (and adopted as true by most misguided white social scientists) and posits this largely negative self-image as the only one for all Afro-Americans. Yet, unlike the exceptionalist tradition, it does not romanticize Afro-American culture; instead, it deprecates this culture.

The assimilationist response to the challenges of self-image and self-determination is this: a rejection of Afro-American culture and total assimilation into American society. It assumes that the universal must wipe clean all particulars, that cosmopolitan society erases all provincialities.

Afro-American critical thought must hold the assimilationist response to be unacceptable. The wholesale renunciation of Afro-American culture only denigrates Afro-Americans. It deprives them of the autonomous elements of their way of life, the genuine creations of their cultural heritage. The assimilationist tradition, like the exceptionalist one, is a rash reaction against a hostile white society rather than a responsible response to particular challenges. Both traditions represent the peculiar predicament of the Afro-American middle class. Just as the exceptionalist tradition looks at Afro-American culture and sees no evil, so the assimilationist tradition looks and sees no good. The major shortcoming of the latter is that it overlooks the possibility of cultural vitality and poverty-ridden living conditions existing simultaneously in Afro-American life.

Marginalist Tradition

The Afro-American marginalist tradition promotes a self-image of both confinement and creativity, restriction and revolt. It encompasses a highly individualistic rebellion of Afro-Americans who are marginal to, or exist on the edges of, Afro-American culture and see little use in assimilating into the American mainstream. It expresses a critical disposition toward Afro-American culture *and* American society.

The early manifestations of Afro-American marginalist thought and action were found in the critical attitudes of religious leaders toward their own church members and American society. But the result was rarely personal rebellion against both, owing to the need for conformity and community under severe oppression.

The marginalist tradition appears more fully in the works of Sutton Griggs and Charles Chesnutt.[22] Central for both of them is the problematic status of the "mulatto" (which derives from the Latin word for mule, *mulus*)—the physically marginal person between Afro-American culture and American society. The authors and their characters maintain a distance and express a denial of Afro-American culture which leaves them uprooted. Their rejection and distrust of American society make them vindictive.

Griggs and Chesnutt were the first archetypes of Afro-American marginalists: individualistic, alienated, searching for a home. Their talent and imagination lifted them above what they conceived to be the uncouth, vulgar, and unrefined Afro-American folk culture, yet this same talent and imagination were denied recognition by whites, hence turned against the white world. In the end, both sought escape from this predicament—Griggs to Africa, Chesnutt ("passing") into the white world he had earlier assailed.

The marginalist tradition blossomed in the works and lives of Nella Larsen and Rudolph Fisher. Both were plagued by the inability to accept themselves and could not find comfort anywhere. Larsen's Helga Crane, the protagonist of *Quicksand* (1928), was an attractive well-bred mulatto who sought to overcome her self-hatred and find herself in a provincial southern Negro college, the urban life of Chicago and Harlem, the cosmopolitan world of Copenhagen, and finally the pietistic Christianity of Afro-American rural life. She—Helga (and Larsen)—was an incessant rebel, unable to come to terms with herself in either world, black or white.

Rudolph Fisher, the talented physician-writer, fostered early in life a deep hatred of the white world. He also found it hard to appreciate anything in Afro-American urban life. He praised the spirituals, but refused to acknowledge similar artistic richness in the blues and jazz. The latter he considered secular vulgarizations evolved from the former; the cruel urban environment destroyed the pure, religious pathos of Afro-American rural life. Fisher was unable to feel at home in the city. This detachment allowed him to portray Afro-American urban life more honestly than his literary contemporaries did during the Harlem Renaissance. He was more conscious than they of the divisions within black city life because these divisions affected him more acutely.[23]

The personal revolt of Wallace Thurman may serve as a turning point in the marginalist tradition. It marked the refusal to escape from self-hatred and shame. Prior to Thurman, Afro-American marginalists imagined heroic self-absorbing events, longed for idyllic life-styles of the rural past, or succumbed to resignation. Thurman candidly confronted his negative view of self, and attempted to see something in it that could help him overcome it. Unfortunately, he discovered little to aid him.

This theme was presented, in embryonic form, in his first novel, *The Blacker the Berry* (1929). The jet-black complexion of Emma Lou, his protagonist, forced her to come to terms with who she was. Only a sincere acceptance of her dark skin color, in contrast to the attitudes of both her own culture and white society, led to personal salvation. In his second novel, *The Infants of the Spring* (1932), Thurman portrayed his own predicament and his efforts to get out of it. He parodied the Harlem Renaissance, its phoniness, self-deception, and barrenness. He depicted how its praise of primitivism concealed self-effacement; how white patrons encouraged literary compromise; how Afro-American pretentiousness hid inferiority complexes. For Thurman, only a Nietzschean *Über-*

mensch or a Dostoevskian Underground Man can avoid these traps. Salvation lies in self-definition through art created out of no illusions about the self. Yet his self-acceptance precluded any usage of the positive aspects of Afro-American culture as ingredients for art. He created from a cultural vacuum, from solely personal despair and self-hatred, resulting in an unusually truncated view of life, an extremely limited vision of human experience.

The Afro-American marginalist tradition reached its zenith in the works and life of Richard Wright. The chief motif that pervaded his writings was personal rebellion, against who he was, the culture that nurtured him, the society that rejected him, and the cosmos that seemed indifferent to his plight. Uprooted from the rural life of Mississippi, disgusted with the black bourgeoisie and the predominantly Jewish Communists in Chicago and New York, alienated within the cosmopolitan world of Paris, and distrustful of emerging African nations, Wright was the marginal man *par excellence.*

Wright tried to create an Afro-American self-image that rested solely upon personal revolt, whether it was couched in the naturalism of Dreiser or crudely guided by the philosophical existentialism of Sartre or Camus. His revolt was intense, but it never crystallized into any serious talk of concerted action, partly because such talk presupposes a community, a set of common values and goals, at which a marginal man like Wright can only sneer.

Wright's attitude toward Afro-American culture was twofold: a conscious embodiment and rejection of it.[24] In his major novel, *Native Son* (1940), Wright linked himself to the Afro-American community by presenting Bigger Thomas, his main character, as a symbol of this community, of its plight and hopes. Bigger gave visibility and recognition to Afro-Americans. Wright's sometimes subtle, and often overt, derogatory remarks about Afro-American culture were integral elements in the exposure of this culture. His own fear, shame, and self-hatred, he believed, made him intuitively close to the culture he rejected and rebellious against the society partially responsible for his negative self-image. Wright seemed to think he would always be a part of the culture from which he

sought escape, and the deeper his repudiation of it, the more tightly he remained tied to it. Why? Because his own negative self-image, he seemed to believe, only mirrored the self-image found in Afro-American culture. Artistic imagination allowed him (only him!) to overcome the deep scars of oppression. These livid scars became, for Wright (who had escaped from the inferno), the chief sources of his art. Hence, the assertions of being in his fiction take the form of violent acts against his culture, society, and world.

The first major critique of Wright's perspective was written by the young James Baldwin. In his influential *Partisan Review* essays (reprinted in *Notes of a Native Son*), he claimed that Wright succumbed to the cold, lifeless, abstract categories of social scientists; in short, Wright endorsed the Afro-American self-image found in the assimilationist tradition. For Baldwin, such a view overlooked the richness and beauty in Afro-American life. Wright adopted a self-image that distorted Afro-American culture, denied Afro-American humanity. Baldwin concluded his remarks stating,

Our humanity is our burden, our life; we need not battle for it; we need only to do what is infinitely more difficult—that is, accept it.[25]

The greatness of Baldwin as a person and the significance of his work as a writer is his candid portrayal of this burdensome acceptance. In his first, and best, work of fiction, *Go Tell It on the Mountain* (1953), Baldwin discovered that the positive side of Afro-American life was much easier for him to talk about in essays than depict in fiction. When he looked closely into his own life, he saw almost precisely what Wright saw—terror, fear, and self-hatred.[26] These qualities evolved from a rigid, fundamentalist Christian home in the heart of urban America—Harlem.

Baldwin's protagonist, John Grimes, had an immense fear of God, his father (Gabriel), and white society. He was plagued by a cosmic terror. He felt trapped. If he revolted against his Superegos, he feared perdition; if he submitted, he suffered frustration. The only way out was through a rebellious act of imagination.

Unlike Wright, Baldwin did not rebel for deeper marginality or further isolation. Instead, his was a search for community, a community of love and tolerance denied him by Afro-American culture. Baldwin did not abhor this culture; he simply could not overlook the stifling effects it had on nonconformists. He wanted desperately to identify with Afro-American culture, but he took seriously the Christian, humanist values it espoused and the artistic imagination (the nonverbal or literate expressions) it suppressed. As with Wright, Baldwin was intuitively close to Afro-American culture and simultaneously on the edge of it. But, in contrast to Wright, this marginality was an interim condition, not a permanent state. Baldwin could envisage an escape from the inferno which leads to salvation, whereas Wright's vision landed him in a perennial limbo.

The most recent exponents in the Afro-American marginalist tradition are Gayl Jones and Toni Morrison. They illustrate the restrictive boundaries that confine and stifle Afro-American women. Jones's novels, *Corregidora* (1975) and *Eva's Man* (1976), are essentially indictments of the Afro-American male's sexual exploitation of Afro-American females. Both novels are literally monologues or dialogues about deranged sexual relations within a repressive culture, a culture shaped by white racism and further reinforced by black machismo. Toni Morrison's first two works of fiction, *The Bluest Eye* (1970) and *Sula* (1974), are lucid portraits of what it is like to be a talented Afro-American woman growing up in a strangling culture which punishes creativity and fears nonconformity. Behavioral patterns for women are rigidly set; violation invariably results in marginality. And marginality for imaginative Afro-American women in a machismo culture and hostile white world often leads to personal rebellion and sometimes self-destruction. Morrison captures this progression in a passage from her second novel:

In a way, her strangeness, her naivete, her craving for the other half of her equation was the consequence of an idle imagination. Had she paints, or clay, or knew the discipline of dance, or strings; had she anything to engage her tremendous curiosity and her gift for metaphor, she might have exchanged the restlessness and preoccupation with whim for an activity that provided her with all she yearned for. And like any artist with no art form, she became dangerous.[27]

It is difficult to discern the conception of political struggle in the marginalist tradition. Given the artistic preoccupation of its members, political matters are secondary. If this tradition contains any conception of political struggle at all, it is a highly moralistic one. For example, the frequently cited last chapter of Wright's *Native Son,* which contains Max's speech, more closely resembles a sermon than a Marxist analysis of society.

Baldwin's masterful essays are grounded in moralism, often echoing the rhythm, syncopation, and appeal of an effective sermon. The salient values are love, mercy, grace, and inner freedom. In his famous work, *The Fire Next Time* (1963), he views the racial problem as stemming from truncated personal relationships, from the refusal of black and white Americans to confront each other as human beings. He sees whites as afraid of being judged by blacks, scared of being seen as they really are; blacks as viewing themselves through white eyes, so they know little of who they really are. Even Baldwin's more vitriolic writings about social change have a deep moral fiber which speaks to the heart of individuals rather than to a community planning to undertake concerted political action.

The marginalist response to the challenges of self-image and self-determination is this: a candid acceptance of personal marginality to both Afro-American culture and American society plus moral sermonizing to all Americans. The basic concern of this tradition is to loosen the constraints on individuality in Afro-American life. Thus, it does not provide acute observations on political struggle. The Afro-American marginalist tradition is parasitic in that its members accept the self-image found in the assimilationist and humanist camps.

Despite this dependence on other traditions, the marginalist response is important because it grapples with a personal torment endemic to modernity. This torment is an inevitable alienation and sense of revolt from one's racial group, society, and world, if felt only for a few moments. This tradition endorses a marginality which serves as an impetus to creativity.

Humanist Tradition

The humanist self-image of Afro-Americans is one neither of heroic superhumans untouched by the experience of oppression nor of pathetic subhumans devoid of a supportive culture. Rather, Afro-Americans are viewed as both meek and belligerent, kind and cruel, creative and dull—in short, as human beings. This tradition does not romanticize or reject Afro-American culture; instead, it accepts this culture for what it is, the expression of an oppressed human community imposing its distinctive form of order on an existential chaos, explaining its political predicament, preserving its self-respect, and projecting its own special hopes for the future.

The best example of the Afro-American humanist tradition is its music. The rich pathos of sorrow and joy which are simultaneously present in spirituals, the exuberant exhortations and divine praises of the gospels, the soaring lament and lyrical tragicomedy of the blues, and the improvisational character of jazz affirm Afro-American humanity. These distinct art forms, which stem from the deeply entrenched oral and musical traditions of African culture and evolve out of the Afro-American experience, express what it is like to be human under black skin in America. Afro-American musicians are Afro-American humanists *par excellence.* They relish their musical heritage and search for ways to develop it. This search proceeds without their having to prove to others that this heritage is worth considering, or that it is superior to any other. Rather, the Afro-American musical heritage develops and flourishes by using both its fertile roots and its elements from other musical traditions—from the first religious hymns and work songs through Scott Joplin, Bessie Smith, Louie Armstrong, Mahalia Jackson, Ella Fitzgerald, Duke Ellington, Coleman Hawkins, Lester Young, Billie Holiday, Charlie Parker, Dizzy Gillespie, Ullyses Kay, Miles Davis, Ornette Coleman, John Coltrane, and contemporary black music.[28] The heritage remains vibrant, with innovation and originality ensuring continual growth. Indeed, it has become one of the definitive elements in American culture.

The chief literary figures of the Afro-American humanist tradition—the young Jean Toomer, Langston Hughes, Zora Neale Hurston, Sterling Brown, and Ralph Ellison—turn to the culture of the Afro-American masses, to blues, jazz, and folklore, as the ingredients of their art. They feel no need to be either superior to whites or marginal to Afro-American culture. They consider themselves relatively secure with their heritage, as well as with those of other groups or nations.

The first major literary expression of Afro-American humanism is found in Jean Toomer's still insufficiently studied *Cane* (1923). This work is a search for Afro-American humanity in the alluring, beautiful, and burdensome black folk culture of the South. This unconventional collage of poignant stories and poems—which defies traditional literary genres—is a gem, a relatively untapped treasure that yields deep insights into Afro-American culture.

Toomer describes the myriad of constraining effects resulting from the attitudes and beliefs of Afro-Americans in rural settings. He portrays lives of spirituality and degradation. Women are objects, sex is sterile, human relationships are exploitative and painful. The innocent Karintha is treated as a commodity; Becky is caught in a web of miscegenation, hypocrisy, and sympathy; Fern's otherworldly life melts into nothingness, dissolves into anomie.

When Toomer shifts to the urban setting, despair persists, but possible liberation looms. This liberation lies in the artistic shaping of the past, the discovery of self by understanding the spiritual riches of this past. The central characters, Dan and Kabnis, are archetypes of the Afro-American artist. Dan, whose roots stem from the rural South, comes to the urban North with a messianic mission: to remind the "New Negroes" of their roots. He pursues the socially pretentious and haughty Muriel, who avoids him and ignores his message. Nevertheless, he emerges from the confining Afro-American urban world of self-hatred and shame, aware of the grand challenge of creating an ordered view of life from a fading folk past.

This theme of candid confrontation with the past is further illustrated in "Kabnis," the last and longest story in *Cane,* Kabnis is self-effacing and uncomfortable with southern culture, a culture he knows little of. He confronts his roots in the person of Father John, a former slave. Kabnis, a mulatto, has denied any links with slavery by disavowing any black ancestors. When Father John utters his long-awaited words of wisdom (Christian quips about the sinfulness and mendaciousness of whites), Kabnis is disappointed and angry. He had expected more than mere small talk about an oppressive past, a past, he believes, filled with black docility fueled by a slave religion. Kabnis is ashamed of this past and looks into the future with perplexed eye.

Toomer's insight is that any acceptable Afro-American self-image begins with unflinching introspection. For an oppressed people, a mere superficial glance will result in self-gratifying celebration of heroic resistance, or self-pitying lament over the great damage done. Toomer opts for neither alternative. Instead, he looks into the Afro-American past and sees the small yet cumulative struggles of human beings against overwhelming odds, the creation of both supportive values and stifling mores.

His profound message to Afro-Americans is that in modernity, where alienation is commonplace, it is important to be aware of roots, but even this provides no assurance of ability to achieve a positive self-image in the ever-changing present. The search for personal identity is never a pleasant one if only because the very need for it connotes a misplacement, dislocation, and homelessness of the self. The act of self-definition forever remains open-ended, with no guarantee of triumph. Indeed, the process takes precedence over the result, since any static self-identity soon disintegrates the self.

Only a person highly knowledgeable of, and sensitive to, the Afro-American past, moved by its many struggles, though not blind to its shortcomings, could give such a sympathetic and credibly convincing portrait of an old, God-fearing, Christian black woman as did Langston Hughes with Aunt Hagar in his only novel, *Not Without Laughter* (1930). Although Hughes unequivocally objects to her orthodox religious beliefs, bourgeois values, and white standards, he admires the perseverance and fortitude of Aunt Hagar. Despite adverse circumstances, she endures, with a joy derived from her Christian faith and its Dionysian rituals. Aunt Hagar triumphs over overwhelming

odds in her own dynamic and flexible way, without self-hatred, self-pity, or self-deception. She overcomes by pure, unabated struggle.

This simple, but profound message of personal and communal struggles—of persistent negation and transformation of prevailing realities—voices the wisdom of Afro-American folklore, blues, and jazz. It guides the con life of Sterling Brown's Slim Greer in *Southern Road* (1932) and the tenuous and ultimately tragic plight of Zora Neale Hurston's Janie in *Their Eyes Were Watching God* (1937).

The Afro-American humanist tradition reached its literary apex in the writings of Ralph Ellison. He stands out among Afro-American humanists, and all Afro-American artists of the other traditions, not only because of the superb mastery of his craft and the acuteness of his mind but also because he takes the Afro-American art forms of the past with more *intellectual seriousness* than do other Afro-American artists. He understands the spirituals, blues, jazz, and folklore of the Afro-American masses to be, not artifacts for self-congratulation or objects of catharsis, but rather aesthetic modes of expression that represent distinctive perceptions of reality. They serve as media of social communication which express the values for the joint communal existence of Afro-Americans. For Ellison, the task of the Afro-American artist is to locate, articulate, and delineate the universal human core of these Afro-American art forms and transform this discovery into a work of art that portrays the complexity and ambiguity of human existence.

In his early Buster-Riley tales and his more sophisticated short stories—especially "Flying Home" (1944) and "King of the Bingo Game" (1944)—Ellison delves into the depths of the Afro-American predicament. Ellison's masterpieces, *Invisible Man* (1952) and *Shadow and Act* (1964)—notwithstanding their exorbitant American optimism and sometimes repetitious themes—remain the most powerful literary works that capture the complexity and diversity of the Afro-American experience. His penetrating portrayal of and profound pronouncements on the Afro-American struggle for freedom presuppose, preserve, and present the humanity of black people; he also displays this struggle in its psychological, political, metaphysical, and cosmic dimensions.

Ellison indeed is more subtle when dealing with the matter of cultural self-identity than with political self-determination. This is so primarily because of the European literary tradition he cherishes, the American ideology to which he subscribes, and the Afro-American cultural forms in which he revels. Yet, ironically, this obsession with cultural self-identity is precisely his strength. The perennial questions of "Who am I?", "What is a human being?", "What is an American?", and "What is an Afro-American?" are central to the predicament of black people. And no one else has grappled more seriously (and productively in the qualitative sense) with these questions than Ralph Ellison.

Ellison's deep yet delightful Hickman stories—which cry out for publication in an accessible edition—further testify to my grandiloquent judgment. These stories exemplify his lifelong dedication and devotion to the demanding and difficult task of making known and making plain what Rev. Hickman means when he eloquently exclaims in the powerful sermonlike story, "Juneteenth":

We know who we are by the way we walk. We know who we are by the way we talk. We know who we are by the way we sing. We know who we are by the way we dance. We know who we are by the way we praise the Lord on high.[29]

In short, Ralph Ellison is the Afro-American literary humanist *par excellence.*

The major aim of political struggle in the Afro-American humanist tradition is found in the works of the young A. Phillip Randolph and Chandler Owen of *The Messenger,* William Jones of the Baltimore *Afro-American* (all three during the 1920s), the later Du Bois, Paul Robeson, post-Mecca Malcolm X, Huey Newton, Angela Davis, the later Amiri Baraka, and the ministry of Rev. Herbert Daughtry.[30] These thinkers share a certain common value: the necessity for the democratic control over institutions in the productive and political processes. The basic assumption of this Afro-American humanist political viewpoint is that the present economic system and social arrangements cannot adequately alleviate the deplorable socioeconomic conditions of the Afro-American masses. This assumption is linked to a corollary claim, namely, that the circumstances of the black poor and those of the black working class (including both blue- and white-collar workers) are qualitatively similar and only quantitatively different. In other words, the Afro-American working class merely (yet significantly, in human terms) have higher-paying jobs than the Afro-American lower class; but neither have any meaningful participation in the decision-making process as to who gets hired or fired, nor any control over the production of goods and services.

The ostensible oppressive circumstances of the Afro-American poor and the less visible ones of the Afro-American working class are both linked to the relative powerlessness of Afro-Americans, not only in the political process *but, more important, in the productive process.* This lack of significant control in the work situation also holds for the white poor and working class. Historically, the white poor and working class have served as formidable obstacles for Afro-American enhancement. Racism has been a source of intra-class conflict. But the future looks different. Expansion of interracial unionization in the South, the radicalization of integrated unions in blue- and white-collar occupations, and the concerted push for federalized policy concerning national problems of unemployment and health care may provide the framework for a new era, an era in which the black and white poor and working classes unite against corporate domination of the economy and government. The Afro-American humanist political viewpoint eagerly endorses and energetically encourages action to make this era a reality.

The humanist political perspective acknowledges the complex interplay between practicality and ideology, electoral politics and structural social change. It discourages ideological programs that have no reasonable chance of succeeding and practical ones that preclude the possibility of fundamentally transforming the present economic system and social arrangements. This perspective supports the continued participation of Afro-Americans in electoral politics, reformist strategies in the political and productive processes, and reasonable radical agitation on persistent issues of common concern.

The humanist response to the challenges of self-image and self-determination is this: a promotion of an individuality strengthened by an honest encounter with the Afro-American past and the expansion of democratic control over the major institutions that regulate lives in America and abroad. This response contrasts sharply with the exceptionalist and assimilationist ones. It neither romanticizes nor rejects Afro-American culture; it also avoids the self-serving pursuit of status, wealth, and prestige. Instead, the humanist response provides a cultural springboard useful in facing the ever-present issue of self-identity for Afro-Americans and joins their political struggle to other progressive elements in American society.

Afro-American philosophy deems the norms of the humanist tradition desirable. These norms of individuality and democratic control of the political and productive processes are acceptable because they promote personal development, cultural growth, and human freedom. They foster the fulfillment of the potentialities and capacities of all individuals, encourage innovation and originality in Afro-American culture, and expand people's control over those institutions which deeply affect their lives.

In this way, Afro-American philosophy reconstructs the Afro-American past and critically evaluates Afro-American responses to crucial challenges in the present. It attempts to understand the Afro-American experience in order to enhance and enrich the lives of Afro-Americans, it demands personal integrity and political action.

Discussion Questions

1. Both the exceptionalist and humanist traditions uphold the "uniqueness" of black culture. But how, then, are they different in this regard?
2. Is West right that an assimilationist must believe in Afro-American inferiority? Might not this simply be an argument that minority cultures are sometimes, and especially in this case, better off assimilating, as opposed to resisting?
3. To what extent is the "marginalist" on to something in positing the restrictiveness of black societal norms for black persons? Are these norms more restrictive than norms imposed by other minority groups on their own members?
4. As West defines the four traditions wouldn't almost anyone today want to be more of a

"humanist" than one who holds any of the three other views? Has West stacked the deck in this regard?
5. To which traditions of the four traditions would belong (a) DuBois, (b) Booker T. Washington, (c) Martin Luther King, Jr., (d) Malcolm X?

Notes

1. These four ideal-types represent the basic responses of any group, community, or nation entering modernity. In the American context, they are found among emerging Irish, Italian, Polish, Jewish, etc., communities beginning to interact with the dominant WASP culture and society. In the European context, these traditions are salient in early nineteenth-century Germany, late nineteenth-century Russia, early twentieth-century Spain, etc. They are presently forming in Third World countries. The best recent studies on this problematic of groups entering modernity are those of John Cuddihy on Jewish intellectuals, Rockwell Gray on Spanish thinkers (esp. Ortega y Gasset), and Elaine Showalter on British women novelists. For samples of their work, see John Cuddihy, *The Ordeal of Civility: Freud, Marx, Lévi-Strauss, and the Jewish Struggle with Modernity* (Basic Books, 1974); Rockwell Gray, "Ortega y Gasset and Modern Culture," *Salmagundi,* No. 35 (Fall 1976), pp. 6–41; Elaine Showalter, *A Literature of Their Own: British Women Novelists from Brontë to Lessing* (Princeton University Press, 1977).

2. Antonio Gramsci defends this viewpoint in his important essay, "Problems of Marxism," in *Selections from the Prison Notebooks,* trans. and ed. Quintin Hoare and Geoffrey Nowell Smith (London: Lawrence & Wishart, 1971).

3. W. E. B. Du Bois, "The Conservation of Races," in *The Seventh Son: The Thought and Writings of W. E. B. Du Bois,* Vol. 1, p. 180.

4. Introduction by Saunders Redding, in Du Bois, *The Souls of Black. Folk,* p. 22.

5. This remark is quoted from S. P. Fullinwider's seminal work, *The Mind and Mood of Black America,* p. 60.

6. *The Book of American Negro Poetry,* ed. James Weldon Johnson (1922), pp. 9–10.

7. Manuscript of speech delivered to the Washington, D.C., branch of the NAACP, 1924, Johnson papers, James Weldon Johnson Collection, Yale University Library. Quoted from Fullinwider, *The Mind and Mood of Black America,* p. 89.

8. R. R. Wright, Jr., "Unlynchable Facts," *Christian Recorder,* Vol. 64 (Nov. 16, 1916), p. 4.

9. R. R. Wright, Jr., "African Methodism and the Second Century," *Christian Recorder,* Vol. 64 (April 13, 1916), p. 4.

10. Amy-Jacques Garvey, *Garvey and Garveyism* (New York: University Place Book Shop, 1963), p. 98.

11. *Black Nationalism in America,* ed. J. H. Bracey and others (Bobbs-Merrill Co., 1970), p. 193.

12. Martin Luther King, Jr., "A Mighty Army of Love," *SCLC Newsletter,* Vol. 2 (Oct.–Nov. 1964), p. 7.

13. This interpretation puts the famous Du Bois-Washington debate in a slightly different light. Du Bois indeed favors struggling for political rights and a liberal education for the Talented Tenth, while Washington pushes for the acquisition of marketable skills and accumulation of property among Afro-Americans. But, in regard to Afro-American leadership, Washington preserves an important place for skilled workers and entrepreneurs, who have close contact with ordinary black people. For Du Bois, at this stage in his long career, only the educated elite could provide leadership, an elite that easily falls prey to idealization of the Afro-American masses.

14. W. E. B. Du Bois, "The Talented Tenth," in *The Seventh Son: The Thought and Writings of W. E. B. Du Bois,* Vol. 1, p. 385.

15. An important note should not be overlooked regarding Afro-American nationalist movements in the exceptionalist tradition, namely, their invariably authoritarian and sexist character. These movements—e.g., Garvey, Black Muslims, Congress of African People—delegate power from top to bottom within a highly rigid hierarchical structure wherein women are relegated to the lowest rungs, the most powerless positions. As Christopher Lasch has suggested, these movements may contain elements of a machismo complex and express assertions of masculinity heretofore ignored. Lasch's insightful essay "Black Power: Cultural Nationalism as Politics" is in his work *The Agony of the American Left* (Vintage Press, 1969), pp. 117–168. See also the provocative book by Michele Wallace, *Black Macho and the Myth of the Superwoman* (Dial Press, 1979).

16. Despite ostensible gains during the past decade by the black white-collar and stable blue-collar working class, the black poor has increased, in numbers and percentage. In the Government Census of 1972, the poor and near-poor represented a staggering 42 percent of all Afro-Americans. See Sar Levitan, William Johnston, and Robert Taggart, *Still a Dream* down. There is the barrier of race, of course, which remarkably is the least of his concerns. His resentment is directed primarily against class distinctions and the pretentions of high-toned Negroes. Thus, Fisher wrote the only novel of the decade that exposed class antagonisms among Harlem blacks." See also Robert Bone's perceptive comments on Fisher's attempts to bridge the gap between other cleavages, e.g., rural vs. urban, artist vs. middle class, West Indian vs. southern black, in his short stories. (Robert A. Bone, *Down Home: A History of Afro-American Short Fiction from Its Beginnings to the End of the Harlem Renaissance,*

pp. 150–159; G. P. Putnam's Sons, 1975.) (Harvard University Press, 1975), Ch. 2, esp. p. 33.

17. Martin Kilson makes this acute observation in his article "Black Power: Anatomy of a Paradox," *The Harvard Journal of Negro Affairs,* Vol. 2, No. 1 (1968), pp. 30–34. He writes: "Some professionals are adopting a Black Power ideological format not with the intent of preparing themselves for service to self-governing urban black communities but to make themselves more visible to the white establishment, which is not at all adverse to offering such persons good jobs as alternatives to Black Power. The more viable Negro businessmen are also simulating the Black Power phenomenon in this way. . . . The Black Power advocates have virtually no control over this use of their political style by the professional and business black bourgeoisie, which means the Black Power advocates will eventually lose the payoff potential of nationalist politics. If so . . . the Negro lower classes, whose riots legitimize Black Power, will be joined by the Black Power advocates in holding the bag—with nothing in it save a lot of therapeutic miscellany" (p. 34).

18. Fortunately, there are no Afro-American strong assimilationists, though there are still a few white ones around, e.g., Shockley and Jensen.

19. This viewpoint has been extremely influential in American sociological studies on Afro-Americans. For example, Gunnar Myrdal's renowned *An American Dilemma* (1944) states, "American Negro culture . . . is a distorted development, or an unhealthy condition of American culture" (p. 928). Glazer and Moynihan's first edition of *The Melting Pot* (1963) reads: "The Negro is only an American, and nothing else. He has no values and culture to guard and protect" (p. 53). And the list goes on and on, e.g., Stanley Elkins' Sambo thesis about slave personality in *Slavery* (1959), the Moynihan report on the Afro-American family (1965), Kenneth Clarke's *Dark Ghetto* (1965), etc.

20. E. Franklin Frazier, "Racial Self-Expression," in *Ebony and Topaz: A Collectionana,* ed. Charles S. Johnson (1927), p. 120.

21. In later life, like most active minds, Frazier makes claims inconsistent with his earlier views and engages in a fruitful exercise of self-criticism. Based on his earlier perspective, it is not surprising the black middle class dangles in a world of make-believe since white society excludes them and they abhor their own culture; Afro-American intellectuals also would be hard put to project positive self-images if Afro-American culture is what the early Frazier suggests it is. For Frazier's later essay on Afro-American intellectuals, see "The Failure of the Negro Intellectual," *Negro Digest,* Feb. 1962.

22. My treatment of Afro-American literary texts is intentionally truncated; it remains at the simplistic level of paraphrase, since such a treatment suits the purpose at hand. In the contemporary scene of Afro-American literary criticism, the major tendencies are the learned yet

aloof cosmopolitanism of Nathan Scott, Jr.; the impressive though flawed structuralisms of Robert B. Stepto and Henry-Louis Gates, Jr.; the refined Black Aesthetics of Stephen Henderson; the equivocal hence mediating cultural anthropological viewpoint of Houston A. Baker, Jr.; and the crude though pregnant Marxism of Amiri Baraka. I prefer a Marxist option that does not simply interpret texts, but, more important, provides a theory about the institution of literature (which makes literary texts possible, defines what it is to be "literary," and circumscribes the perimeters of meanings to be found in such texts) and accents the Afro-American participation therein. I present a sketch of this perspective in my extended critique of Fredric Jameson's trilogy—*Marxism and Form, The Prison-house of Language,* and *The Political Unconscious*—entitled "Fredric Jameson's Marxist Hermeneutics," in *Boundary 2: A Journal of Postmodern Literature,* Special Issue on Marxism and Postmodernism, Winter 1983 (forthcoming). See also my Marxist critique of both Gerald Graff's humanist realism and Jacques Derrida's deconstructionist poststructuralism in my essay "Beyond Realism and Anti-Realism: A Critique of Graff and Derrida," *Bucknell Review,* Special Issue on Literature and Philosophy (forthcoming). The pertinent texts of the aforementioned Afro-American literary critics include Nathan Scott, Jr., "The Dark and Haunted Tower of Richard Wright," in *Five Black Writers,* ed. Donald B. Gibson (New York University Press, 1970), pp. 12–25; Nathan Scott, Jr., "Black Literature," *Harvard Guide to Contemporary American Writing,* ed. Daniel Hoffman (Harvard University Press, 1979), pp. 287–341. Robert B. Stepto, "Teaching Afro-American Literature: Survey or Tradition, The Reconstruction of Instruction," in *Afro-American Literature: The Reconstruction of Instruction,* ed. Dexter Fisher and Robert B. Stepto (Modern Language Association of America, 1979), pp. 8–24; Robert B. Stepto, *From Behind the Veil: A Study of Afro-American Narrative;* Henry-Louis Gates, Jr., "Preface to Blackness: Text and Pretext" and "Dis and Dat: Dialect and the Descent," in *Afro-American Literature: The Reconstruction of Instruction,* pp. 44–69, 88–119; Stephen E. Henderson, "The Forms of Things Unknown," in *Understanding the New Black Poetry: Black Speech and Black Music as Poetic References,* ed. Stephen E. Henderson (William Morrow & Co., 1973), pp. 1–69; Houston A. Baker, J., *The Journey Back: Issues in Black Literature and Criticism* (University of Chicago Press, 1980); Houston A. Baker, Jr., "Generational Shifts and the Recent Criticism of Afro-American Literature," *Black American Literature Forum,* Vol. 15, No. 1 (Spring 1981), pp. 3–21; Amiri Baraka, "The Revolutionary Tradition in Afro-American Literature," *Selected Plays and Prose of Amiri Baraka/LeRoi Jones* (Columbia University Press, 1979), pp. 242–251; Amiri Baraka, "Afro-American Literature and Class Struggle," *Black American Literature Forum,* Vol. 14, No. 1 (Spring 1980), pp. 5–14.

23. Nathan Huggins concurs with this observation in his book *Harlem Renaissance* (Oxford University Press, 1971), p. 119, where, in discussing Rudolph Fisher's novel, *The Walls of Jericho* (1928), he writes: "Joshua 'Shine' Jones, Rudolph Fisher's proletarian hero, has several walls to bring down. There is the barrier of race, of course, which remarkably is the least of his concerns. His resentment is directed primarily against class distinctions and the pretentions of high-toned Negroes. Thus, Fisher wrote the only novel of the decade that exposed class antagonisms among Harlem blacks." See also Robert Bone's perceptive comments on Fisher's attempts to bridge the gap between other cleavages, e.g., rural vs. urban, artist vs. middle class, West Indian vs. southern black, in his short stories. (Robert A. Bone, *Down Home: A History of Afro-American Short Fiction from Its Beginnings to the End of the Harlem Renaissance,* pp. 150–159; G. P. Putnam's Sons, 1975.)

24. My reading of Richard Wright is influenced by Martin Kilson's unpublished paper, "Nationalism and Marginality in Black Writers: The Case of Richard Wright." For his shorter treatment of Wright, see Martin Kilson, "Politics and Identity Among Black Intellectuals," *Dissent,* Summer 1981, pp. 339–349.

25. James Baldwin, "Everybody's Protest Novel," in his *Notes of a Native Son* (Beacon Press, 1955), p. 17.

26. My reading of Baldwin is influenced by Stanley Macebuh's *James Baldwin: A Critical Study* (Third Press, 1973).

27. Toni Morrison, *Sula* (Alfred A. Knopf, 1974), p. 105.

28. For noteworthy treatments of this rich tradition, see Eileen Southern, *The Music of Black Americans: A History* (W. W. Norton & Co., 1971); LeRoi Jones, *Blues People: The Negro Experience in White America and the Music That Developed from It* (William Morrow & Co., 1963); LeRoi Jones, *Black Music* (William Morrow & Co., 1969); Ralph Ellison, *Shadow and Act* (Random House, 1964), pp. 187–250; Albert Murray, *Stomping the Blues* (McGraw-Hill Book Co., 1976); André Hodeir, *Jazz: Its Evolution and Essence,* trans. David Noakes (Grove Press, 1956); Ben Sidran, *Black Talk: How the Music of Black America Created a Radical Alternative to the Values of the Western Literary Tradition* (Holt, Rinehart & Winston, 1971).

29. Ralph Ellison, "Juneteenth," *Quarterly Review of Literature,* 1965, p. 276. For the first full treatment of Ellison's writing career, see Robert O'Meally, *The Craft of Ralph Ellison* (Harvard University Press, 1980).

30. The other important stream of thought and behavior in the Afro-American humanist tradition is reformist. It extends from Frederick Douglass through Booker T. Washington to Benjamin Hooks. This stream is represented by those people who satisfy the

cultural criteria of Afro-American humanism and advocate certain reforms in the capitalist system. They fail to promote structural change in society. The stream of thought and action mentioned above (p. 89) represents those people who satisfy the same cultural criteria, but support the replacement of the capitalist system with one that extends democracy into the institutions of production so that the government and economy are truly "of the people, by the people, and for the people." This replacement constitutes a structural change in society, especially a redistribution of its wealth.

Contempory Issue: "Ebonics"

13   Black English/Ebonics: What It Be Like?

GENEVA SMITHERMAN

Study Questions

1. What does Smitherman understand as the original justification for introducing Ebonics?
2. What are some of the distinctive linguistic features of Ebonics?
3. How does Ebonics differ from just colloquial or slang English?
4. What is "signification"?

I looked at my hands, they looked new
I looked at my feet, and they did too
I got a new way of walkin, and a new
      way of talkin.

TRADITIONAL BLACK GOSPEL SONG

The month after the Oakland school board passed its resolution, the term *Ebonics* turned twenty-four years old. Yeah, dass right, the name is over two decades old. It was coined by a group of Black scholars as a new way of talkin bout the language of African slave descendants. Like the message of that old Gospel tune, "Ebonics" was

about transformation, about intellectuals among the Talented Tenth striking a blow for the linguistic liberation of our people. The guru in this group of scholars at that "Language and the Urban Child" conference, convened in St. Louis, Missouri, in January 1973, was the brilliant clinical psychologist, Dr. Robert L. Williams, now Professor Emeritus, Washington University. In the book of conference proceedings Williams published in 1975, he captures the thinking of that historical moment:

A significant incident occurred at the conference. The black conferees were so critical of the work on the subject done by white researchers, many of whom also happened to be present, that they decided to caucus among themselves and define black language from a black perspective. It was in this caucus that the term *Ebonics* was created. [The term refers to] linguistic and paralinguistic features which on a concentric continuum represent the communicative competence of the West African, Caribbean, and United States slave descendant of African origin. It includes the various idioms, patois, argots, ideolects, and social dialects of black people, especially those who have been forced to adapt to colonial circumstances. (1975, Preface, Introduction)

For this group of scholars, the conceptual framework of "Ebonics" represented an avenue for decolonization of the African-American mind, a way to begin repairing the psycholinguistically maimed psyche of Blacks in America. As

Reprinted by permission of the author and publisher from *The Real Ebonics Debate*, Theresa Perry and Lisa Delpit, eds. (Boston: Beacon Press, 1998), pp. 29–37.

Paulo Freire (1985) would put it twelve years later, "language variations (female language, ethnic language, dialects) are intimately interconnected with, coincide with, and express identity. They help defend one's sense of identity and they are absolutely necessary in the process of struggling for liberation" (p. 186). Ebonics reaffirms the interrelatedness of language and culture and links Africans in America with Africans around the globe.

Ebonics: neither "broken" English, nor "sloppy" speech, nor merely "slang," nor some bizarre lingo spoken only by baggy-pants-wearing Black kids. Rather, the variety of Ebonics spoken in the United States (hereafter USEB) is rooted in the Black American Oral Tradition and represents a synthesis of African (primarily West African) and European (primarily English) linguistic-cultural traditions. The linguistic shape of the words in USEB can readily be identified as Standard English, that is, the Language of Wider Communication here in the United States (hereafter LWC), but these words do not always have the same meaning in USEB as in LWC. Further, there are many words of direct African origin—for example, *okay, gorilla, cola, jazz*—that are now part of LWC (often without props to us African slave descendants). However, what gives Black Language (un-huh, dat ain no typo, I meant "language") its distinctiveness is the nuanced meanings of these English words, the pronunciations, the ways in which the words are combined to form grammatical statements, and the communicative practices of the USEB-speaking community. In short, USEB may be thought of as the Africanization of American English.

Patterns of Ebonics

In the next section, I discuss the following patterns of USEB: (1) aspectual *be;* (2) stressed *been;* (3) multiple negation; (4) adjacency/context in possessives; (5) postvocalic /r/ deletion; (6) copula absence; (7) camouflaged and other unique lexical forms.

Consider this statement, which comes from some Black women just kickin it in the beauty shop (gloss: conversational chit-chat at a hair salon): "The Brotha be lookin good; that's what

got the Sista nose open!" In this statement, *Brotha* is USEB for an African-American man, *lookin good* refers to his style, his attractive appearance (not necessarily the same thing as physical beauty in USEB), *Sista* is USEB for an African-American woman, and her passionate love for the Brotha is conveyed by the phrase *nose open* (in USEB, the kind of passionate love that makes you vulnerable to exploitation). *Sista nose* is standard USEB grammar for denoting possession, indicated by adjacency/context (that is, rather than the LWC/'s, s'/). The use of *be* means that the quality of *lookin good* is not limited to the present moment but reflects the Brotha's past, present, and future essence. As in the case of Efik and other Niger-Congo languages, USEB has an aspectual verb system, conveyed by the use of the English verb *be* to denote iterativity (that is, a recurring or habitual state-of-affairs; contrast *He be lookin good* with *He lookin good,* which refers to the present moment only—not the kind of *lookin good* that opens the nose!). Note further that many Black writers and Rap artists employ the spellings "Brotha" and "Sista." Now, they ain just tryin to be cute. These orthographic representations are used to convey a phonological pattern derived from the influence of West African languages, many of which do not have an /r/ sound. Also in these language communities, kinship terms may be used when referring to African people, whether biologically related or not.

Of course there is overlap between USEB and colloquial, everyday American English—for example, use of "ain't," ending sentences with prepositions, double negatives. However, there are critical distinctions that separate linguistically competent USEB speakers from the wannabes. For example, the colloquial speaker says *gonna* or *goin to* for the LWC form *going to.* But the USEB speaker uses the nasalized vowel form, producing a sound close to, but not identical with, LWC *gone,* thus: "What she go (n) do now?," that is, in LWC, "What is she going to do now?" Another example is in negation patterns. While those obsessed with the "national mania for correctness" often rail against colloquial speakers' double negatives, USEB is distinctive not only for its negative inversion, but also for its *multiple* negatives, that is, three or more negatives formed from combinations of indefinite pronouns and/or adjectives. Check out this exclamation of complex negative inversion from a devout churchgoer: "Don't nobody don't know God can't tell me nothin!," that is, in LWC, "A person who doesn't believe in God and isn't saved has no credibility with me."

As mentioned above, USEB words may look like mainstream American English, but the usage and meaning are different. This is the source of a good deal of miscommunication and misunderstanding between USEB and LWC speakers. In response to the question, "Is she married?," the USEB speaker may answer "She been married." If the speaker pronounces *been* without stress, it means the woman in question was once married but is now divorced. If the speaker pronounces *been* with stress, it means she married a long time ago and is still married. Another example is the use of LWC words that are "camouflaged" (Spears, 1982). For example, in the USEB statement, "She come tellin me I'n [didn't] know what I was talkin bout," the verb *come* does not denote motion as in LWC. Rather the meaning of *come* in this context is one of indignation, that is, in LWC, "She had the audacity to tell me that I didn't know what I was talking about. How dare she!" Yet another kind of cross communication example comes from semantic inversion. Due to crossover and the popular appeal of Michael Jackson, most people are aware that *bad* in USEB translates to *good* in LWC; however, lexical items that haven't enjoyed such a high degree of crossover are problematic in these crosscultural exchanges. For example, consider the following form of address common among many Black males: "Yo, Dog!" *Dog* is a linguistic symbol of male bonding, most likely derived from the African-American fraternity tradition of referring to pledges as *dogs. Yo, Dog!* was used by a Brotha on lock down (gloss: imprisoned) to address his European-American male psychiatrist as an expression of camaraderie. Turns out, though, that this white psychiatrist was not yet down (gloss: hip, understanding of the Black Cultural framework). He misinterpreted the Brotha's greeting and made an issue of the "insult."

The above are only some of the patterns in the grammatical, phonological, and semantic systems of USEB. To explore the full 360 degrees of USEB, we need to move on to styles of speaking. In fact, it is the area of communicative practices—rhetorical strategies and modes of discourse—that cuts across gender, generation, and class in the African-American community. USEB speech acts may be classified as follows: (1) Call-Response; (2) Tonal Semantics; (3) Narrativizing; (4) Proverb Use/ Proverbializing; (5) Signification/Signifyin; (6) The Dozens/Snappin/ Joanin. Discussion of two of these discourse modes follows.

Signification or, more commonly, *signifyin,* which can be rendered with or without the phonological and morphosyntactical patterns of USEB, is a form of ritualized insult in which a speaker puts down, talks about, needles—signifies on—other speakers. In this communicative practice, the speaker deploys exaggeration, irony, and indirection as a way of saying something on two different levels at once. It is often used to send a message of social critique, a bit of social commentary on the actions or statements of someone who is in need of a wake-up call. When signifyin is done with verbal dexterity, it avoids the creation of social distance between speaker and audience because the rich humor makes you laugh to keep from crying. Like Malcolm X who once began a speech with these words: "Mr. Moderator, Brother Lomax, Brothas and Sistas, friends and enemies." Now, you don't usually begin a speech by addressing your enemies. Thus, Malcolm's signifyin statement let his audience know that he knew inimical forces were in their midst. Or like one of the deacons at this Traditional Black Church, where the preacher would never deal with the problems and issues folk were facing on a daily basis. Rather, he was always preachin bout the pearly gates and how great thangs was gon be at dat home up in the sky. So one day this deacon said to the preacher, "Reb, you know, I got a home in Heaven, but I ain't homesick!"

Signifyin is engaged in by all age groups and by both males and females in the Black community. It has the following characteristics: (1) indirection, circumlocution; (2) metaphorical-imagistic (images rooted in the everyday real world); (3) humorous, ironic; (4) rhythmic fluency; (5) teachy, but not preachy; (6) directed at person(s) present in the speech situation (signifiers do not talk behind your back); (7) punning, play on words; (8) introduction of the semantically or logically unexpected.

Types of Signification

There are two types of Signification. One type is leveled at a person's mother (and occasionally at other relatives). Traditionally, this first type was referred to as "The Dozens"/"playin The Dozens." The second type of signifyin is aimed at a person, action, or thing, either just for fun or for corrective criticism. Today, the two types of Signification are being conflated under a more general form of discourse, referred to as "snappin."

To fully appreciate the skill and complexity of Signification, we shall analyze in some detail a conversational excerpt involving two Sistas in a group of several at a wedding shower:

Linda: Girl, what up with that head? [Referring to her friend's hairstyle.]
Betty: Ask yo momma. [Laughter from all the Sistas on this conversational set.]
Linda: Oh, so you going there, huh? Well, I *DID* ask my momma. And she said, "Cain't you see that Betty look like her momma spit her out?" [Laughter from all, including Betty.]

Betty and Linda signify on each other. Instead of answering Linda's question directly, Betty decides to inform Linda that the condition of her hairstyle is none of Linda's business by responding with "Ask yo momma." The usual expectation in a conversation is that a speaker's question will be answered honestly and sincerely; thus Betty's unexpected indirection produces laughter from the listeners.

Speech act theory indicates that communication succeeds or fails as a result of the illocutionary (that is, intended) and perlocutionary (that is, received) effects of a message. The surface meaning of "yo momma" for those outside the USEB speech community is simply "your mother/mom." However, within the Black speech community, the utterance immediately signals that an insult has been hurled. The intended and received meaning of *yo momma* is invective; the game of ritual insult begins with participants creating the most appropriate, humorous, spontaneous, creative, exaggerated/untrue retorts that they can come up with.

The source of the retort "Ask yo momma" probably stems from family patterns in which mothers are consulted ("asked") about all kinds of things, great or small. Fathers may even respond to their children's questions or requests by saying "Ask your mother." In USEB, the speaker does not intend the direct meaning, "You should go and ask your mother about this situation." Rather, given the conversational context, the speaker is indirectly saying "Let the game of The Dozens begin." Linda clearly recognizes the entry into this game as indicated by her response, "Oh, so you going there, huh?" Unskilled players, lacking a spontaneous, apposite, humorous retort, would have let the conversation end at this point. However, Linda shows adeptness in playing the game. She regroups momentarily ("Oh, so you going there, huh?") and fires back skillfully. In fact, she "caps" (gloss: wins) this exchange with a more clever retort. Although Betty's use of the intragroup expression, *ask yo momma,* is humorous and sets up a challenge, it is formulaic, simplistic, and stylized. In this instance, it cannot, and does not, beat: "Well, I *DID* ask my momma. And she said, 'Cain't you see that Betty look like her momma spit her out?' " (Troutman-Robinson and Smitherman, 1997).

Although Rev. Jesse Jackson and Sista Maya Angelou came out in the national news and dissed the Oakland school board's resolution, they are well versed in USEB. Twenty years ago, in my first major work on USEB, *Talkin and Testifyin,* I quoted both at length and lauded them as linguistic role models, who are adept at capitalizing on the forms of Black Language to convey profound political messages. Like Jesse who is down wit Signification: "Pimp, punk, prostitute, preacher, Ph.D.—all the P's, you still in slavery!" Thus he conveys the message that all members of the African-American community, regardless of their social status, are marginalized and disempowered, by virtue of U.S. historically institutionalized racism and skin color bias. (Jesse also uses copula absence here—"you still in slavery"—which has not been found in any of the dialects of British English that came over on the *Mayflower,* but which is used widely in the languages of West Africa.)

The Dozens

As mentioned above, The Dozens is one of several significant speech acts in USEB. This ritualized game of insult has analogues in West African communicative practices (see Smitherman, 1995, and the several references cited there). Also referred to as "snappin" by many members of the Hip Hop Nation, The Dozens is like "Yo momma so dumb she thought a quarterback was a refund!"

Sista Maya Angelou is so bad she don't play The Dozens, she play The Thirteens! She uses this USEB discourse mode to critique the actions of Blacks and whites. Here how she do it:

> (The Thirteens Black):
> Your Momma took to shouting
> Your Poppa's gone to war,
> Your sister's in the streets
> Your brother's in the bar,
> The thirteens. Right On . . .
> And you, you make me sorry
> You out here by yourself,
> I'd call you something dirty,
> But there just ain't nothing left,
> cept
> The thirteens. Right On . . .
> (The Thirteens White):
> Your daughter wears a jock strap,
> Your son he wears a bra
> Your brother jonesed your cousin
> in the back seat of the car.
> The thirteens. Right On . . .
> Your money thinks you're something
> But if I'd learned to curse,
> I'd tell you what your name is
> But there just ain't nothing worse
> than
> The thirteens. Right On.

(ANGELOU, 1971)

African-French psychiatrist Frantz Fanon (1967) taught that "every dialect, every language, is a way of thinking. To speak means to assume a culture." To speak Ebonics is to assume the cultural legacy of U.S. slave descendants of African origin. To speak Ebonics is to assert the power of this tradition in the quest to resolve the unfinished business of being African in America. While years of massive research (done in the 1960s and early 1970s) on the language of this group (mostly by white scholars) did indeed debunk cognitive-linguistic deficiency theory, in its place arose social inadequacy theory. Although the language was shown to be systematic and rule-governed, since it is not accepted by the white mainstream, difference became deficit all over again, and in the process, Africans in America suffered further dislocation. To speak (of/on/about) Ebonics, to consciously employ this terminology and conceptual framework, as those Black scholars did back in 1973, and as the Oakland school board has done a generation later, is to be bout the business of relocating African Americans to subject position. Large and in charge, as the Hip Hoppers say, Ebonics, then and now, symbolizes a new way of talkin the walk about language and liberatory education for African Americans.

Discussion Questions

1. Is the issue of Ebonics primarily political or linguistic?
2. To what extent is the use or approval of rhetorical activities, such as "the dozens," separate from the question of validating black language itself?
3. Would an emphasis on teaching or using Ebonics in schools be "liberating" or further disadvantaging?
4. Isn't the question of the Africans *origins* of Ebonics separate from the question of whether, and how, it should be taught in schools?

14   Educating Teachers about Educating the Oppressed

MILTON BAXTER

Study Questions

1. What are the main points made in the CCCC document?
2. What is the importance of the difference between spoken and written English in terms of the student's identity?
3. What is the difference between a social and a regional dialect?
4. How does the failure to attend to the social status of BEV, in Baxter's view, explain many of the practical difficulties of implementing it in the classroom?
5. What considerations beyond linguistic training enter into a teacher's ability to use Black English in the classroom?

I. Introduction

The role of dialects which students bring with them into the classroom has been at the center of much controversy among the linguists and English instructors. Recently it has flourished in the form of a radical resolution adopted by members of the Conference on College Composition and Communication:

We affirm the students' right to their own patterns and varieties of language—the dialects of their nurture or whatever dialects in which they find their own identity and style. Language scholars long ago denied that the myth of a standard American dialect has any validity. The claim that any one dialect is unacceptable amounts to an attempt of one social group to exert its dominance over another. Such a claim leads to false advice for speakers and writers, and immoral advice for humans. A nation proud of its diverse heritage and its

cultural and racial variety will preserve its heritage of dialects. We affirm strongly that teachers must have experiences and training that will enable them to respect diversity and uphold the right of students to their own language.[1]

Clearly the statement of the CCCC has important implications today for the education of many black children who are desperately floundering in an educational system that unfortunately has been for them alienating, constricting, irrelevant, and uncompromising.

There is a grave danger, however, that the CCCC resolution will be propagated without concern for its implications as to actual classroom policy. This danger stems from the failure to spell out explicitly what is meant by the students' right to their own language. The purpose of this paper is to discuss these implications so that educators can gain a much needed perspective for the implementation of this resolution in the English curriculum. There are three crucial areas in which the CCCC statement can be considered undeveloped:

1. It ignores the distinction between spoken expression and written expression.
2. It ignores the social aspect of social dialects.
3. It ignores the network of speech-related behavior that is an integral part of the communication process; that is, it ignores the fact that dialects are enmeshed in a cultural context.

II. Spoken Versus Written Expression in the Dialect

Many educators today will agree that language patterns or dialects are intricately a part of the

---

From *College English* 37 (1976), pp. 677–681. Copyright 1976 by the National Council of Teachers of English. Reprinted with permission.

[1] The resolution, adopted by the Executive Committee of the Conference on College Composition and Communication in 1972, was supported by a position statement published in a Special Fall Issue of *College Composition and Communication* in 1974.

students' identity, and will also acknowledge that much of the students' resistance to adopting classroom Standard American English (hereafter SAE) at the expense of discarding the native dialect, stems from the unwillingness of students to acquire any speech patterns which might set them apart from peers and, more importantly, for which they can perceive no immediate relevance at home or in their community.

These same educators will quickly point out, however, that dialect speaking students want to attain proficiency in written SAE grammar and compositional skills to enable them to pursue their careers successfully. In other words, although many students resist adopting the SAE speech patterns used by teachers, they do not necessarily resist the learning of SAE written usage and conventions (generally referred to as "Edited American English," and hereafter as EAE). Some teachers who would like to change the students' spoken language to more closely approximate SAE have therefore had to adjust their priorities, giving highest priority to the students' attainment of EAE. The statement of the CCCC ignores this important distinction that many educators and students have made between speaking and writing in dialect.

Since it is generally agreed that dialect users must learn to write EAE, the CCCC statement could head off some opposition if it limited itself clearly to spoken language. Even here, it will meet resistance enough, for many teachers who stubbornly resist the intrusion of dialects in their classroom and who painstakingly attempt to erase the various dialect patterns in their students' speech, do so in keeping with the belief that SAE is the superior form of English—a belief which was cultivated during *their own* education when they learned to reject *their own* local dialects.

III. Social Parameters of a Dialect

Another pitfall of the CCCC statement is that it ignores the differences in attitudes that people have about social dialects and regional dialects. Regional dialects are generally regarded with less disdain than social dialects, particularly when a social dialect is associated with a lower socioeconomic group of people, as is the case with that variety of English spoken by many blacks in America. That social dialect, which we will refer to as Black English Vernacular (or BEV), is spoken by lower class, uneducated (or undereducated), poor, largely ghettoized blacks. These social factors are important considerations upon which linguists come to label BEV as a *social* dialect, rather than as a *regional* dialect. While linguists and enlightened educators can acknowledge the theoretical validity of a social dialect such as BEV, they know full well that the acceptance of BEV by the intellectual community will not ameliorate the disdain with which BEV is generally regarded, for our society's intolerance of social dialectal differences can be clearly understood only within the broader pattern of racial and social discrimination. The rejection of BEV is just one manifestation of the racial and class prejudice that permeates our society.

To date, our understanding and treatment of BEV as a social dialect has been myopic in that a great deal of attention has been focused on the *dialect* aspect (i.e., on the nature of the systematic differences between SAE and BEV phonological and syntactic rules, as well as on vocabulary differences) while the *social* aspect has been neglected or willfully ignored, particularly when pedagogical implications are considered. When dialect-enlightened linguists and educators address meetings and conferences, they too often focus most of their attention on grammatical aspects of the dialect, ignoring the association of BEV with stigmatized social status. After the conference fanfare, those teachers influenced by the conference speakers are left with the arduous task of implementing in their curriculum and classroom practices these newfound notions of dialect relativity and, more importantly, but not how to combat the social attitudes held toward the general standard varieties of speech by colleagues, students, and the general community, many of whom are irreconcilably opposed to the very notion of BEV.

One cannot introduce BEV into the English curriculum as just another variety of English with pronunciation and grammatical differences (accountable for by perhaps some later ordered, over generalized rules or perhaps decreolization rules). An educator may be backed by a body of research to support his judgment that the difficulties students are having acquiring EAE are a result of cross-dialectal interference patterns (i.e., BEV influences on the learning of SAE); but this is usually not enough to withstand opposition by persons unable to transcend the social stigma of the dialect and accept BEV as a valid language system. It is, then, the failure to address the *social* aspect of a social dialect such as BEV that threatens to undermine any serious attempts educators might make to implement—in the form of innovative curriculum and pedagogic approaches—their newfound awareness of the need to uphold the students' right to their own language in the classroom.

It is, no doubt, the social stigmatization of BEV that has prompted many middle class blacks to oppose the recognition of BEV as a bona fide dialect. But can we blame the educated middle class blacks for the school system's blatant opposition to dialect-oriented curricula? Not unless they are also to blame for the more pervasive discrimination that exists in this society against lower class, poor, and undereducated people, whatever their speech patterns. We are involved in a form of prejudice that is larger in scope than language; it resides in the social system itself. Although BEV is a full fledged dialect with systematic phonological and grammatical rules, it is perhaps doomed to be shunned by many educators, parents, and even students themselves as an inferior variety of English because of its association with lower class, poor, undereducated black people.

Those black parents who in their lifetime have experienced the degradation of having lower socio-economic status want their children not only to learn SAE, but also to be rid of any remnants of a social dialect that will possibly hamper their success. Many students under pressure from parents, teachers, and their own individual needs to succeed will pursue the acquisition of SAE. But at the same time, they remain cognizant of the need to retain those BEV speech patterns that will

foster their acceptance and participation in peer group situations. From such parents and students little argument, if any, will be found about the ultimate purpose of education: to provide upward social mobility. In this perspective we must examine more closely the social implications of any systematic attempt by educators to permit students, in the province of the classroom, a right to their own language. Such an attempt is always susceptible to being interpreted as institutionally promoting a veneer of cultural diversity, while actually condoning the stigma of lower socio-economic citizenry in the midst of a society in which socially upward aspiring Americans are the norm.

Perhaps implicit in the CCCC's statement is the belief that the classroom acceptance of language diversity among the students will be a catalyst for ultimately bringing about general acceptance of social class and cultural differences. If, however, the introduction of BEV into the classroom is really to be used as a means of exposing and eliminating the various forms of societal prejudice against lower social class behavioral differences, then it is inappropriate and deceitful to disguise these goals.

IV. BEV as a Communication System

If the English class is to be the battleground for the struggle to uphold cultural diversity and pluralism in America, then English teachers will need to do more than involve themselves in in-service teacher training programs dealing with dialect variation. They will need to become sensitized to other communicative behavior of BEV speakers, including gestures, intonation patterns, and various sorts of body language. For example, the common use of falsetto voice among blacks has stirred much informal discussion among linguists about BEV intonational patterns and pitch ranges, some of which have been linked with African sources. Unfortunately, when educators envision the classroom use of a dialect such as BEV, they have in mind BEV speaking students who will utter their dialect patterns with SAE mannerisms, gestures, pitch ranges, intonational patterns, etc.—no doubt to facilitate the teachers' understanding of BEV. Surely the CCCC statement does not call for such a restricted conception of the students' language. Yet, no specific mention is made of these paralinguistic elements. We cannot afford to ignore them. Teachers whose cultural backgrounds are different from the students' will find it hard to interpret these communicative elements used by their students in the classroom.

Along with phonological suprasegmental differences such as pitch ranges and intonational patterns, there are differences in gesticulation (e.g., hand movements, body stances). No doubt many of the gestures used by BEV speakers can be found also among speakers of other varieties of English—in the same way that many of the grammatical features of BEV appear in other dialects. What is important here is that such gestures are important for the speech act itself, because they facilitate communication. Examples are "slapping five" to express acceptance, support, or approval, or perhaps "eyeballing" to indicate derision.

Should teachers allow such speech-related behaviorisms in the classroom? If not, are we promoting what may be an artificial situation in which dialect speakers are granted the right to talk in dialect, but only with SAE speech-related mannerisms (which are in keeping with established "classroom decorum")? If, on the other hand, we permit these dialect-related mannerisms, will we not be asking teachers to go beyond a narrow conception of the linguistic retraining required of them?

V. Educating Teachers about Educating the Oppressed

Granting students a right to their own language in the classroom places a great deal of responsibility on teachers' shoulders, if indeed the CCCC statement is not to become a meaningless catch phrase. Teachers can give life and substance to the CCCC statement not only by acknowledging

dialect differences in the classroom, but also by developing and using curricula that are based on linguistically sound analyses of the English language varieties, and more specifically, that utilize cross-dialectal contrastive methodology for teaching SAE or EAE.

Unless teachers are provided retraining which focuses not only on grammatical characteristics of BEV, but also on culturally defined speech-related behavior, many unwittingly will be exposing their ignorance of important subtleties in their students' communication patterns.

Most important, however, it will be necessary to provide training which will increase the teachers' sensitivity to the apprehensions of students who are speakers of social dialects which carry no prestige in the society, and the use of which in the classroom may be regarded by the students and their parents as a constant reminder of their "inferiority" and lower class status. Each student must be considered individually to determine his or her particular sensitivities. No presumptions can be made about the homogeneity of the student population in its attitudes toward classroom use of dialect-oriented materials, just as it should not be assumed that all BEV speakers use the dialect to the same degree. If we are to seriously advocate the students' right to their own language in the classroom we, as educators, must insure a constant dialogue with our students. We will run the risk of learning their language, just as they will run the risk of learning ours.

Discussion Questions

1. Baxter seems to suggest that Black English should be allowed, if not encouraged, as a spoken but not as a written language. Is this a workable distinction, though?
2. Baxter stresses the social stigma associated with Black English. How would Smitherman respond to this point?
3. If the goal of the Oakland School Board proposal is to use Ebonics as a way of ultimately making students proficient in standard English, don't critics who stress the lower-class associations of Ebonics miss the point?

Feminism, Womanism, and Gender Relations

Womanist: 1. From womanish *(opp. of "girlish," i.e., frivolous, irresponsible, not serious) A black feminist of color. . . . Usually referring to outrageous, audacious, courageous or* willful *behavior. Wanting to know more or in greater depth than is considered "good" for one. . . . 2. Also: A woman who loves other women sexually and/or nonsexually. Appreciates and prefers women's culture, women's emotional flexibility (values tears as natural counterbalance of laughter), and women's strength. Sometimes loves individual men sexually and/or nonsexually.*

ALICE WALKER

Today when many white feminists think of black women, they too often think of faceless masses of welfare mothers and rape victims to flesh out their statistical studies of woman's plight.

MICHELLE WALLACE

All social thought, including white masculinist and black feminist, reflects the interests and standpoint of its creators.

PATRICIA HILL COLLINS

The relation of black women to the ideal of white beauty is not a more intense form of white women's frustration: It is something other, a complex mingling of racial and gender hatred from without, self-hatred from within.

ANGELA P. HARRIS

Equality is false; it's the devil's concept. Our concept is complementarity. Complementarity means you complete or make perfect that which is imperfect.

MAULANA RON KARENGA

They [certain black nationalists and Afrocentrists] have invented an African past to suit their conservative agenda on gender and sexuality.

E. FRANCES WHITE

The authors of the readings in this section start from a general view that racism and sexism are both wrong: insofar as racism and sexism are the work of, and reflect the distinct interests of, white males, the authors' stance toward white males is oppositional. This chapter, however, also explores subtler issues concerning the relation between, on one hand, black women and white female advocates of "feminism" and, on the other hand, black women and black males, especially those of a black nationalist perspective.

The term *feminist* is traditionally applied to (and accepted by) advocates of equal rights for women. Our first author in this section, Sojourner Truth, would qualify, then, as very much a feminist. This movement, which arose out of the nineteenth-century struggle for such basic rights as the vote for women, gained momentum in the 1960s and 1970s. Many African American women, however, while generally sharing its goals, remained alienated from the feminist movement for a number of reasons, the most basic of which was that it did not seem to speak to *their* interests and needs. Thus, when African American novelist Alice Walker introduced the term *womanist*, this struck a responsive chord with many.[1] Regardless of the label, many African American women have felt the need to voice their own distinctive perspective.

In her contribution, Patricia Hill Collins offers some of the elements of an "Afrocentric feminist epistemology." An epistemology is a theory of what constitutes knowledge, how knowledge is attained, and the limits to which its attainment is subject. Her epistemology, then, would address some or all of these general concerns, but from the distinctive experiential base of black women. Another important term Collins uses is *positivism*—a philosophy she opposes. The positivist holds that only testable scientific statements are meaningful—hence, questions of values—of good and bad, right and wrong—are not meaningful. This exclusion, Collins holds, forces African American women to devalue their own deepest emotions and confront the "white masculinist" elite, in a contest where that elite sets the rules.

In her essay, activist and English professor bell hooks ponders the long and deep connection between racism and sexism in this country's history. Racial domination, she contends, has always carried with it sexual domination. Opposition to racism, she insists, must never be allowed to take on a sexist form, nor should the injustice of violence against women ever be obscured by racial injustice.

In the next selection, Angela P. Harris, a law professor at the University of California, mounts a subtle attack on the "gender essentialism" inherent in much contemporary discourse. By the logic of this discourse, all women are oppressed as women, all blacks are oppressed as blacks, and all black women, therefore, are "doubly oppressed" separately as women and as blacks. The fallacy in this, Harris points out, is that there is an "oppression of women" purely as such and in abstraction from such other factors as race and social class.

The term *essentialism* is used in a number of essays in this volume. It is typically used in criticism of those who appear to postulate a fixed, unchanging reality, not susceptible to social or environmental influence. This supposed reality (or "essence"), these critics say, often masks an agenda of the theorist (e.g., the agenda of white feminists, according to Harris).

---

[1]Cleonora Hudson-Weems advocates an "Africana Womanism," critical not only of white feminism but of Walker's relegation of racial issues to a secondary status. See her *Africana Womanism: Reclaiming Ourselves* (Troy, MI: Beford, 1994).

In their different ways, then, Collins, Harris, and hooks articulate a distinctly black female perspective, partly in opposition to the feminist idea that there is a universal female or feminine viewpoint. Some might worry, however, about the opposite danger: that, in postulating a separate black female perspective, they have now postulated two *separate* female essences—one black and one white—with all the attendant difficulties of bringing the two together around issues of mutual concern.

In his contribution, philosophy professor Charles Mills reflects on the emotionally charged question of whether black men have a moral obligation to marry black women. With a skillful hand, he guides the reader through the thicket of "racial purity," "sleeping with the enemy," and "Jungle Fever," among other issues. In the end, he leaves us with the ultimate question of what, if anything, the decision to intermarry signifies about oneself and one's attitudes toward one's own race.

Still, a different controversy involves advocates of gay and lesbian rights, versus at least some black nationalists. In a strongly worded piece, E. Frances White attacks Maulana Karenga, among others, for, in effect, trying to appeal to "an African past" to justify conservative views on questions of gender and sexual orientation in today's world. Poet, essayist, and political activist Amiri Baraka (previously "LeRoi Jones"), in an essay reflective of the excitement and limitations of the period of its composition (the late 1960s), vigorously advocates Karenga's viewpoint.

15   A'n't I a Woman?

SOJOURNER TRUTH

Study Questions

1. What is Sojourner Truth's response to the notion that women, as "the weaker sex," need to be helped into carriages (and the like)?
2. What is her response concerning limitations of "intellect"?
3. What is her view of religion?
4. What conclusion does she come to?

Wall, chilern, whar dar is so much racket dar must be somethin' out of kilter. I tink dat 'twixt de niggers of de Souf and de womin at de Norf, all talkin' 'bout rights, de white men will be in a fix pretty soon. But what's all dis here talkin' 'bout?

Dat man ober dar say dat womin needs to be helped into carriages and lifted ober ditches, and to hab de best place everywhar. Nobody eber helps me into carriages, or ober mud puddles, or gibs me any best place! And a'n't I a woman? Look at my arm! I have ploughed, and planted, and gathered into barns, and no man could head me! And a'n't I a woman? I could work as much and eat as much as a man—when I could get it—and bear de lash as well! And a'n't I a woman? I have borne thirteen chilern, and seen 'em mos' all sold off to slavery, and

---

Originally appeared in the *National Anti-Slavery Standard,* June 1, 1867.

when I cried out with my mother's grief, none but Jesus heard me! And a'n't I a woman?

Den dey talks 'bout dis ting in de head; what dis dey call it? ("intellect," whispered some one near.) Dat's it, honey. What dat got to do wid womin's rights or nigger's rights? If my cup won't hold but a pint, and yourn holds a quart, wouldn't ye be mean not to let me have my little half-measure full?

Den dat little man in black dar, he say women can't have as much rights as men, 'cause Christ wan't a woman! Whar did your Christ come from? Whar did your Christ come from? From God and a woman! Man had nothin' to do wid Him!

If de fust woman God ever made was strong enough to turn de world upside down all alone, dese women togedder (and she glanced her eye over the platform) ought to be able to turn it back, and get it right side up again! And now dey is asking to do it, de men better let 'em.

Discussion Questions

1. Although her argument addresses the rights of all women, in what way is it pitched to the distinctive experiences of black women?
2. Is her response on the question of "intellect" a fully satisfactory one?
3. What do you suppose she means by the first woman having turned the world upside down?

16   The Social Construction of Black Feminist Thought

PATRICIA HILL COLLINS

Study Questions

1. What is the difference between "a black woman's" and a "black feminist" standpoint?
2. In what ways are the knowledge claims put forward by black female scholars likely to be suppressed (or undervalued)?
3. What is "positivism" and why would it not be in favor with many African American women researchers?
4. What is "epistemology"? What are the main elements of an Afrocentric feminist epistemology?
5. In what ways does an Afrocentric feminist epistemology "value the concrete"?

Sojourner Truth, Anna Julia Cooper, Ida Wells-Barnett, and Fannie Lou Hamer are but a few names from a growing list of distinguished African American women activists. Although their sustained resistance to black women's victimization within interlocking systems of race, gender, and class oppression is well known, these women did not act alone.[1] Their actions were nurtured by the support of countless, ordinary African American women who, through strategies of everyday resistance, created a powerful foundation for this more visible black feminist activist tradition.[2] Such support has been essential to the shape and goals of black feminist thought.

The long-term and widely shared resistance among African American women can only have been sustained by an enduring and shared standpoint among black women about the meaning of oppression and the actions that black women can and should take to resist it. Efforts to identify the

central concepts of this black women's standpoint figure prominently in the works of contemporary black feminist intellectuals.[3] Moreover, political and epistemological issues influence the social construction of black feminist thought. Like other subordinate groups, African American women not only have developed distinctive interpretations of black women's oppression, but have done so by using alternative ways of producing and validating knowledge itself.

A Black Women's Standpoint

The Foundation of Black Feminist Thought

Black women's everyday acts of resistance challenge two prevailing approaches to studying the consciousness of oppressed groups.[4] One approach claims that subordinate groups identify with the powerful and have no valid independent interpretation of their own oppression.[5] The second approach assumes that the oppressed are less human than their rulers and, therefore, are less capable of articulating their own standpoint.[6] Both approaches see any independent consciousness expressed by an oppressed group as being not of the group's own making and/or inferior to the perspective of the dominant group.[7] More important, both interpretations suggest that oppressed groups lack the motivation for political activism because of their flawed consciousness of their own subordination.

Yet African American women have been neither passive victims of nor willing accomplices to their own domination. As a result, emerging work on black women's studies contends that black women have a self-defined standpoint on their own oppression.[8] Two interlocking components characterize this standpoint. First, black women's political and economic status provides them with a distinctive set of experiences that offers a different view of material reality than that available to

Reprinted by permission of the author and the University of Chicago Press from *Signs* 17 (1992), pp. 745–773.

other groups. The unpaid and paid work that black women perform, the types of communities in which they live, and the kinds of relationships they have with others suggest that African American women, as a group, experience a different world than those who are not black and female.[9] Second, these experiences stimulate a distinctive black feminist consciousness concerning that material reality.[10] In brief, a subordinate group not only experiences a different reality than a group that rules, but a subordinate group may interpret that reality differently than a dominant group.

Many ordinary African American women have grasped this connection between what one does and how one thinks. Hannah Nelson, an elderly black domestic worker, discusses how work shapes the standpoints of African American and white women: "Since I have to work, I don't really have to worry about most of the things that most of the white women I have worked for are worrying about. And if these women did their own work, they would think just like I do—about this, anyway."[11] Ruth Shays, a black inner city resident, points out how variations in men's and women's experiences lead to differences in perspective: "The mind of the man and the mind of the woman is the same. But this business of living makes women use their minds in ways that men don't even have to think about."[12] Finally, elderly domestic worker Rosa Wakefield assesses how the standpoints of the powerful and those who serve them diverge: "If you eats these dinners and don't cook 'em, if you wears these clothes and don't buy or iron them, then you might start thinking that the good fairy or some spirit did all that. . . . Blackfolks don't have no time to be thinking like that. . . . But when you don't have anything else to do, you can think like that. It's bad for your mind, though."[13]

While African American women may occupy material positions that stimulate a unique standpoint, expressing an independent black feminist consciousness is problematic precisely because more powerful groups have a vested interest in suppressing such thought. As Hannah Nelson notes, "I have grown to womanhood in a world where the saner you are, the madder you are made to appear."[14] Nelson realizes that those

who control the schools, the media, and other cultural institutions are generally skilled in establishing their view of reality as superior to alternative interpretations. While an oppressed group's experiences may put them in a position to see things differently, their lack of control over the apparatuses of society that sustain ideological hegemony makes the articulation of their self-defined standpoint difficult. Groups unequal in power are correspondingly unequal in their access to the resources necessary to implement their perspectives outside their particular group.

One key reason that standpoints of oppressed groups are discredited and suppressed by the more powerful is that self-defined standpoints can stimulate oppressed groups to resist their domination. For instance, Annie Adams, a southern black woman, describes how she became involved in civil rights activities.

When I first went into the mill we had segregated water fountains. . . . Same thing about the toilets. I had to clean the toilets for the inspection room and then, when I got ready to go to the bathroom, I had to go all the way to the bottom of the stairs to the cellar. So I asked my boss man, "What's the difference? If I can go in there and clean them toilets, why can't I use them?" Finally, I started to use that toilet. I decided I wasn't going to walk a mile to go to the bathroom.[15]

In this case, Adams found the standpoint of the "boss man" inadequate, developed one of her own, and acted upon it. In doing so, her actions exemplify the connections between experiencing oppression, developing a self-defined standpoint on that experience, and resistance.

The Significance of Black Feminist Thought

The existence of a distinctive black women's standpoint does not mean that it has been adequately articulated in black feminist thought. Peter Berger and Thomas Luckmann provide a useful approach to clarifying the relationship between a black women's standpoint and black feminist thought with the contention that knowledge exists on two levels.[16] The first level includes the everyday, taken-for-granted knowledge shared by members of a given group, such as the ideas expressed by Ruth Shays and

Annie Adams. Black feminist thought, by extension, represents a second level of knowledge, the more specialized knowledge furnished by experts who are part of a group and who express the group's standpoint. The two levels of knowledge are interdependent; while black feminist thought articulates the taken-for-granted knowledge of African American women, it also encourages all black women to create new self-definitions that validate a black women's standpoint.

Black feminist thought's potential significance goes far beyond demonstrating that black women can produce independent, specialized knowledge. Such thought can encourage collective identity by offering black women a different view of themselves and their world than that offered by the established social order. This different view encourages African American women to value their own subjective knowledge base.[17] By taking elements and themes of black women's culture and traditions and infusing them with new meaning, black feminist thought rearticulates a consciousness that already exists.[18] More important, this rearticulated consciousness gives African American women another tool of resistance to all forms of their subordination.[19]

Black feminist thought, then, specializes in formulating and rearticulating the distinctive, self-defined standpoint of African American women. One approach to learning more about a black women's standpoint is to consult standard scholarly sources for the ideas of specialists on black women's experiences.[20] But investigating a black women's standpoint and black feminist thought requires more ingenuity than that required in examining the standpoints and thought of white males. Rearticulating the standpoint of African American women through black feminist thought is much more difficult since one cannot use the same techniques to study the knowledge of the dominated as one uses to study the knowledge of the powerful. This is precisely because subordinate groups have long had to use alternative ways to create an independent consciousness and to rearticulate it through specialists validated by the oppressed themselves.

The Eurocentric Masculinist Knowledge-Validation Process[21]

All social thought, including white masculinist and black feminist, reflects the interests and standpoint of its creators. As Karl Mannheim notes, "If one were to trace in detail . . . the origin and . . . diffusion of a certain thought-model, one would discover the affinity it has to the social position of given groups and their manner of interpreting the world."[22] Scholars, publishers, and other experts represent specific interests and credentialing processes and their knowledge claims must satisfy the epistemological and political criteria of the contexts in which they reside.[23]

Two political criteria influence the knowledge-validation process. First, knowledge claims must be evaluated by a community of experts whose members represent the standpoints of the groups from which they originate. Second, each community of experts must maintain its credibility as defined by the larger group in which it is situated and from which it draws its basic, taken-for-granted knowledge.

When white males control the knowledge-validation process, both political criteria can work to suppress black feminist thought. Since the general culture shaping the taken-for-granted knowledge of the community of experts is one permeated by widespread notions of black and female inferiority,[24] new knowledge claims that seem to violate these fundamental assumptions are likely to be viewed as anomalies.[25] Moreover, specialized thought challenging notions of black and female inferiority is unlikely to be generated from within a white-male-controlled academic community because both the kinds of questions that could be asked and the explanations that would be found satisfying would necessarily reflect a basic lack of familiarity with black women's reality.[26]

The experiences of African American women scholars illustrate how individuals who wish to rearticulate a black women's standpoint through black feminist thought can be suppressed by a white-male-controlled knowledge-validation process. Exclusion from basic literacy, quality educational experiences, and faculty and administrative positions has limited black women's access to influential academic positions.[27] Thus, while black women can produce knowledge claims that contest those advanced by the white male community, this community does not grant that black women scholars have competing knowledge claims based in another knowledge-validation process. As a consequence, any credentials controlled by white male academicians can be denied to black women producing black feminist thought on the grounds that it is not credible research.

Those black women with academic credentials who seek to exert the authority that their status grants them to propose new knowledge claims about African American women face pressures to use their authority to help legitimate a system that devalues and excludes the majority of black women.[28] One way of excluding the majority of black women from the knowledge-validation process is to permit a few black women to acquire positions of authority in institutions that legitimate knowledge and to encourage them to work within the taken-for-granted assumptions of black female inferiority shared by the scholarly community and the culture at large. Those black women who accept these assumptions are likely to be rewarded by their institutions, often at significant personal cost. Those challenging the assumptions run the risk of being ostracized.

African American women academicians who persist in trying to rearticulate a black women's standpoint also face potential rejection of their knowledge claims on epistemological grounds. Just as the material realities of the powerful and the dominated produce separate standpoints, each group may also have distinctive epistemologies or theories of knowledge. It is my contention that black female scholars may know that something is true but be unwilling or unable to legitimate their claims using Eurocentric masculinist criteria for consistency with substantiated knowledge and Eurocentric masculinist criteria for methodological adequacy.

For any particular interpretive context, new knowledge claims must be consistent with an existing body of knowledge that the group controlling the interpretive context accepts as true. The methods used to validate knowledge claims must also be acceptable to the group controlling the knowledge-validation process.

The criteria for the methodological adequacy of positivism illustrate the epistemological standards that black women scholars would have to satisfy in legitimating alternative knowledge claims.[29] Positivist approaches aim to create scientific descriptions of reality by producing objective generalizations. Since researchers have widely differing values, experiences, and emotions, genuine science is thought to be unattainable unless all human characteristics except rationality are eliminated from the research process. By following strict methodological rules, scientists aim to distance themselves from the values, vested interests, and emotions generated by their class, race, sex, or unique situation and in so doing become detached observers and manipulators of nature.[30]

Several requirements typify positivist methodological approaches. First, research methods generally require a distancing of the researcher from her/his "object" of study by defining the researcher as a "subject" with full human subjectivity and objectifying the "object" of study.[31] A second requirement is the absence of emotions from the research process.[32] Third, ethics and values are deemed inappropriate in the research process, either as the reason for scientific inquiry or as part of the research process itself.[33] Finally, adversarial debates, whether written or oral, become the preferred method of ascertaining truth—the arguments that can withstand the greatest assault and survive intact become the strongest truths.[34]

Such criteria ask African American women to objectify themselves, devalue their emotional life, displace their motivations for furthering knowledge about black women, and confront, in an adversarial relationship, those who have more social, economic, and professional power than they. It seems unlikely, therefore, that black women would use a positivist epistemological stance in rearticulating a black women's standpoint. Black women are more likely to choose an alternative epistemology for assessing knowledge claims, one using standards that are consistent with black women's criteria for substantiated knowledge and with black women's criteria for methodological adequacy. If such an epistemology exists, what are its contours? Moreover, what is its role in the production of black feminist thought?

The Contours of an Afrocentric Feminist Epistemology

Africanist analyses of the black experience generally agree on the fundamental elements of an Afrocentric standpoint. In spite of varying histories, black societies reflect elements of a core African value system that existed prior to and independently of racial oppression.[35] Moreover, as a result of colonialism, imperialism, slavery, apartheid, and other systems of racial domination, blacks share a common experience of oppression. These similarities in material conditions have fostered shared Afrocentric values that permeate the family structure, religious institutions, culture, and community life of blacks in varying parts of Africa, the Caribbean, South America, and North America.[36] This Afrocentric consciousness permeates the shared history of people of African descent through the framework of a distinctive Afrocentric epistemology.[37]

Feminist scholars advance a similar argument. They assert that women share a history of patriarchal oppression through the political economy of the material conditions of sexuality and reproduction.[38] These shared material conditions are thought to transcend divisions among women created by race, social class, religion, sexual orientation, and ethnicity and to form the basis of a women's standpoint with its corresponding feminist consciousness and epistemology.[39]

Since black women have access to both the Afrocentric and the feminist standpoints, an alternative epistemology used to rearticulate a black

women's standpoint reflects elements of both traditions.[40] The search for the distinguishing features of an alternative epistemology used by African-American women reveals that values and ideas that Africanist scholars identify as being characteristically "black" often bear remarkable resemblance to similar ideas claimed by feminist scholars as being characteristically "female."[41] This similarity suggests that the material conditions of oppression can vary dramatically and yet generate some uniformity in the epistemologies of subordinate groups. Thus, the significance of an Afrocentric feminist epistemology may lie in its enrichment of our understanding of how subordinate groups create knowledge that enables them to resist oppression.

The parallels between the two conceptual schemes raise a question: Is the worldview of women of African descent more intensely infused with the overlapping feminine/Afrocentric standpoints than is the case for either African American men or white women?[42] While an Afrocentric feminist epistemology reflects elements of epistemologies used by blacks as a group and women as a group, it also paradoxically demonstrates features that may be unique to black women. On certain dimensions, black women may more closely resemble black men, on others, white women, and on still others, black women may stand apart from both groups. Black feminist sociologist Deborah K. King describes this phenomenon as a "both/or" orientation, the act of being simultaneously a member of a group and yet standing apart from it. She suggests that multiple realities among black women yield a "multiple consciousness in black women's politics" and that this state of belonging yet not belonging forms an integral part of black women's oppositional consciousness.[43] Bonnie Thornton Dill's analysis of how black women live with contradictions, a situation she labels the "dialectics of black womanhood," parallels King's assertions that this "both/or" orientation is central to an Afrocentric feminist consciousness.[44] Rather than emphasizing how a black women's standpoint and its accompanying epistemology are different from those in Afrocentric and feminist analyses, I use black women's experiences as a point of contact between the two.

Viewing an Afrocentric feminist epistemology in this way challenges analyses claiming that black women have a more accurate view of oppression than do other groups. Such approaches suggest that oppression can be quantified and compared and that adding layers of oppression produces a potentially clearer standpoint. While it is tempting to claim that black women are more oppressed than everyone else and therefore have the best standpoint from which to understand the mechanisms, processes, and effects of oppression, this simply may not be the case.[45]

African American women do not uniformly share an Afrocentric feminist epistemology since social class introduces variations among black women in seeing, valuing, and using Afrocentric feminist perspectives. While a black women's standpoint and its accompanying epistemology stem from black women's consciousness of race and gender oppression, they are not simply the result of combining Afrocentric and female values—standpoints are rooted in real material conditions structured by social class.[46]

Concrete Experience as a Criterion of Meaning

Carolyn Chase, a thirty-one-year-old inner city black woman, notes, "My aunt used to say, 'A heap see, but a few know.'"[47] This saying depicts two types of knowing, knowledge and wisdom, and taps the first dimension of an Afrocentric feminist epistemology. Living life as black women requires wisdom since knowledge about the dynamics of race, gender, and class subordination has been essential to black women's survival. African American women give such wisdom high credence in assessing knowledge.

Allusions to these two types of knowing pervade the words of a range of African American women. In explaining the tenacity of racism, Zilpha Elaw, a preacher of the mid-1800s, noted: "The pride of a white skin is a bauble of great value with many in some parts of the United States, who readily sacrifice their intelligence to

their prejudices, and possess more knowledge than wisdom."[48] In describing differences separating African American and white women, Nancy White invokes a similar rule: "When you come right down to it, white women just *think* they are free. Black women *know* they ain't free."[49] Geneva Smitherman, a college professor specializing in African American linguistics, suggests that "from a black perspective, written documents are limited in what they can teach about life and survival in the world. Blacks are quick to ridicule 'educated fools,' . . . they have 'book learning,' but no 'mother wit,' knowledge, but not wisdom."[50] Mabel Lincoln eloquently summarizes the distinction between knowledge and wisdom: "To black people like me, a fool is funny—you know, people who love to break bad, people you can't tell anything to, folks that would take a shotgun to a roach."[51]

Black women need wisdom to know how to deal with the "educated fools" who would "take a shotgun to a roach." As members of a subordinate group, black women cannot afford to be fools of any type, for their devalued status denies them the protections that white skin, maleness, and wealth confer. This distinction between knowledge and wisdom, and the use of experience as the cutting edge dividing them, has been key to black women's survival. In the context of race, gender, and class oppression, the distinction is essential since knowledge without wisdom is adequate for the powerful, but wisdom is essential to the survival of the subordinate.

For ordinary African American women, those individuals who have lived through the experiences about which they claim to be experts are more believable and credible than those who have merely read or thought about such experiences. Thus, concrete experience as a criterion for credibility frequently is invoked by black women when making knowledge claims. For instance, Hannah Nelson describes the importance that personal experience has for her: "Our speech is most directly personal, and every black person assumes that every other black person has a right to a personal opinion. In speaking of grave matters, your personal experience is considered very good evidence. With us, distant statistics are certainly not as important as the actual experience of a sober person."[52] Similarly, Ruth Shays uses her concrete experiences to challenge the idea that formal education is the only route to knowledge: "I am the kind of person who doesn't have a lot of education, but both my mother and my father had good common sense. Now, I think that's all you need. I might not know how to use thirty-four words where three would do, but that does not mean that I don't know what I'm talking about . . . I know what I'm talking about because I'm talking about myself. I'm talking about what I have lived."[53] Implicit in Shays's self-assessment is a critique of the type of knowledge that obscures the truth, the "thirty-four words" that cover up a truth that can be expressed in three.

Even after substantial mastery of white masculinist epistemologies, many black women scholars invoke their own concrete experiences and those of other black women in selecting topics for investigation and methodologies used. For example, Elsa Barkley Brown subtitles her essay on black women's history, "how my mother taught me to be a historian in spite of my academic training."[54] Similarly, Joyce Ladner maintains that growing up as a black woman in the South gave her special insights in conducting her study of black adolescent women.[55]

Henry Mitchell and Nicholas Lewter claim that experience as a criterion of meaning with practical images as its symbolic vehicles is a fundamental epistemological tenet in African American thought-systems.[56] Stories, narratives, and Bible principles are selected for their applicability to the lived experiences of African Americans and become symbolic representations of a whole wealth of experience. For example, Bible tales are told for their value to common life, so their interpretation involves no need for scientific historical verification. The narrative method requires that the story be "told, not torn apart in analysis, and trusted as core belief, not admired as science."[57] Any biblical story contains more than characters and a plot—it presents key ethical issues salient in African American life.

June Jordan's essay about her mother's suicide exemplifies the multiple levels of meaning that can occur when concrete experiences are used as a criterion of meaning. Jordan describes her mother, a woman who literally died trying to stand up, and the effect that her mother's death had on her own work:

> I think all of this is really about women and work. Certainly this is all about me as a woman and my life work. I mean I am not sure my mother's suicide was something extraordinary. Perhaps most women must deal with a similar inheritance, the legacy of a woman whose death you cannot possibly pinpoint because she died so many, many times and because, even before she became your mother, the life of that woman was taken. . . . I came too late to help my mother to her feet. By way of everlasting thanks to all of the women who have helped me to stay alive, I am working never to be late again.[58]

While Jordan has knowledge about the concrete act of her mother's death, she also strives for wisdom concerning the meaning of that death.

Some feminist scholars offer a similar claim that women, as a group, are more likely than men to use concrete knowledge in assessing knowledge claims. For example, a substantial number of the 135 women in a study of women's cognitive development were "connected knowers" and were drawn to the sort of knowledge that emerges from firsthand observation. Such women felt that since knowledge comes from experience, the best way of understanding another person's ideas was to try to share the experiences that led the person to form those ideas. At the heart of the procedures used by connected knowers is the capacity for empathy.[59]

In valuing the concrete, African American women may be invoking not only an Afrocentric tradition, but a women's tradition as well. Some feminist theorists suggest that women are socialized in complex relational nexuses where contextual rules take priority over abstract principles in governing behavior. This socialization process is thought to stimulate characteristic ways of knowing.[60] For example, Canadian sociologist Dorothy Smith maintains that two modes of knowing exist, one located in the body and the space it occupies and the other passing beyond it. She asserts that women, through their child-rearing and nurturing activities, mediate these two modes and use the concrete experiences of their daily lives to assess more abstract knowledge claims.[61]

Amanda King, a young black mother, describes how she used the concrete to assess the abstract and points out how difficult mediating these two modes of knowing can be:

The leaders of the ROC [a labor union] lost their jobs too, but it just seemed like they were used to losing their jobs. . . . This was like a lifelong thing for them, to get out there and protest. They were like, what do you call them—intellectuals. . . . You got the ones that go to the university that are supposed to make all the speeches, they're the ones that are supposed to lead, you know, put this little revolution together, and then you got the little ones . . . that go to the factory everyday, they be the ones that have to fight. I had a child, and I thought I don't have the time to be running around with these people. . . . I mean I understand some of that stuff they were talking about, like the bourgeoisie, the rich and the poor and all that, but I had surviving on my mind for me and my kid.[62]

For King, abstract ideals of class solidarity were mediated by the concrete experience of motherhood and the connectedness it involved.

In traditional African American communities, black women find considerable institutional support for valuing concrete experience. Black extended families and black churches are two key institutions where black women experts with concrete knowledge of what it takes to be self-defined black women share their knowledge with their younger, less experienced sisters. This relationship of sisterhood among black women can be seen as a model for a whole series of relationships that African American women have with each other, whether it is networks among women in extended families, among women in the black church, or among women in the African American community at large.[63]

Since the black church and the black family are both woman-centered and Afrocentric institutions, African American women traditionally have found considerable institutional support for this dimension of an Afrocentric feminist epistemology in ways that are unique to them. While white women may value the concrete, it is questionable whether white families, particularly middle-class nuclear ones, and white community institutions provide comparable types of support. Similarly, while black men are supported by Afrocentric institutions, they cannot participate in black women's sisterhood. In terms of black women's relationships with one another then, African American women may indeed find it easier than others to recognize connectedness as a primary way of knowing, simply because they are encouraged to do so by black women's tradition of sisterhood.

Epistemology and Black Feminist Thought

Living life as an African American woman is a necessary prerequisite for producing black feminist thought because within black women's communities thought is validated and produced with reference to a particular set of historical, material, and epistemological conditions.[64] African American women who adhere to the idea that claims about black women must be substantiated by black women's sense of their own experiences, and who anchor their knowledge claims in an Afrocentric feminist epistemology, have produced a rich tradition of black feminist thought.

Traditionally, such women were blues singers, poets, autobiographers, storytellers, and orators validated by the larger community of black women as experts on a black women's standpoint. Only a few unusual African American feminist scholars have been able to defy Eurocentric masculinist epistemologies and explicitly embrace an Afrocentric feminist epistemology. Consider Alice Walker's description of Zora Neale Hurston: "In my mind, Zora Neale Hurston, Billie Holiday, and Bessie Smith form a sort of unholy trinity. Zora *belongs* in the tradition of black women singers, rather than among 'the literati.' . . . Like Billie and Bessie she followed her own road, believed in her own gods, pursued her own dreams, and refused to separate herself from 'common' people."[65]

Zora Neale Hurston is an exception for, prior to 1950, few black women earned advanced degrees, and most of those who did complied with Eurocentric masculinist epistemologies. While these women worked on behalf of black women, they did so within the confines of pervasive race and gender oppression. Black women scholars were in a position to see the exclusion of black women from scholarly discourse, and the thematic content of their work often reflected their interest in examining a black women's standpoint. However, their tenuous status in academic institutions led them to adhere to Eurocentric masculinist epistemologies so that their work would be accepted as scholarly. As a result, while they produced black feminist thought, those black women most likely to gain academic credentials were often least likely to produce black feminist thought that used an Afrocentric feminist epistemology.

As more black women earn advanced degrees, the range of black feminist scholarship is expanding. Increasing numbers of African American women scholars are explicitly choosing to ground their work in black women's experiences, and, by doing so, many implicitly adhere to an Afrocentric feminist epistemology. Rather than being restrained by their "both/ and" status of marginality, these women make creative use of their outsider-within status and produce innovative black feminist thought. The difficulties these women face lie less in demonstrating the technical components of white male epistemologies than in resisting the hegemonic nature of these patterns of thought in order to see, value, and use existing alternative Afrocentric feminist ways of knowing.

In establishing the legitimacy of their knowledge claims, black women scholars who want to develop black feminist thought may encounter the often conflicting standards of three key groups. First, black feminist thought must be validated by ordinary African American women who grow to womanhood "in a world where the saner you are, the madder you are made to appear."[66] To be credible in the eyes of this group, scholars must be personal advocates for their material, be accountable for the consequences of their work, have lived or experienced their material in some fashion, and be willing to engage in dialogues about their findings with ordinary, everyday people. Second, if it is to establish its legitimacy, black feminist thought also must be accepted by the community of black women scholars. These scholars place varying amounts of importance on rearticulating a black women's standpoint using an Afrocentric feminist epistemology. Third, black feminist thought within academia must be prepared to confront Eurocentric masculinist political and epistemological requirements.

The dilemma facing black women scholars engaged in creating black feminist thought is that a knowledge claim that meets the criteria of adequacy for one group and thus is judged to be an acceptable knowledge claim may not be translatable into the terms of a different group. Using the example of Black English, June Jordan illustrates the difficulty of moving among epistemologies: "You cannot 'translate' instances of Standard English preoccupied with abstraction or with nothing/ nobody evidently alive into Black English. That would warp the language into uses antithetical to the guiding perspective of its community of users. Rather you must first change those Standard English sentences themselves into ideas consistent with the person-centered assumptions of Black English."[67] While both worldviews share a common vocabulary, the ideas themselves defy direct translation.

Once black feminist scholars face the notion that, on certain dimensions of a black women's standpoint, it may be fruitless to try to translate ideas from an Afrocentric feminist epistemology into a Eurocentric masculinist epistemology, then the choices become clearer. Rather than trying to uncover universal knowledge claims that can withstand the translation from one epistemology to another, time might be better spent rearticulating a black women's standpoint in order to give African American women the tools to resist their own subordination. The goal here is not one of integrating black female "folk culture" into the substantiated body of academic knowledge, for that substantiated knowledge is, in many ways, antithetical to the best interests of black women. Rather, the process is one of rearticulating a pre-existing black women's standpoint and recentering the language of existing academic discourse to accommodate these knowledge claims. For those black women scholars engaged in this rearticulation process, the social construction of black feminist thought requires the skill and sophistication to decide which knowledge claims can be validated using the epistemological assumptions of one but not both frameworks, which claims can be generated in one framework and only partially accommodated by the other, and which claims can be made in both frameworks without violating the basic political and epistemological assumptions of either.

Black feminist scholars offering knowledge claims that cannot be accommodated by both frameworks face the choice between accepting the taken-for-granted assumptions that permeate white-male-controlled academic institutions or leaving academia. Those black women who choose to remain in academia must accept the possibility that their knowledge claims will be limited to their claims about black women that are consistent with a white male worldview. And yet those African American women who leave academia may find their work is inaccessible to scholarly communities.

Black feminist scholars offering knowledge claims that can be partially accommodated by both epistemologies can create a body of thought that stands outside of either. Rather than trying to synthesize competing worldviews that, at this point in time, defy reconciliation, their task is to point out common themes and concerns. By making creative use of their status as mediators, their thought becomes an entity unto itself that is rooted in two distinct political and epistemological contexts.[68]

Those black feminists who develop knowledge claims that both epistemologies can accommodate may have found a route to the elusive goal of generating so-called objective generalizations that can stand as universal truths. Those ideas that are validated as true by African American women, African American men, white men, white women, and other groups with distinctive standpoints, with each group using the epistemological approaches growing from its unique standpoint, thus become the most objective truths.[69]

Alternative knowledge claims, in and of themselves, are rarely threatening to conventional knowledge. Such claims are routinely ignored, discredited, or simply absorbed and marginalized in existing paradigms. Much more threatening is the challenge that alternative epistemologies offer to the basic process used by the powerful to legitimate their knowledge claims. If the epistemology used to validate knowledge comes into question, then all prior knowledge claims validated under the dominant model become suspect. An alternative epistemology challenges all certified knowledge and opens up the question of whether what has been taken to be true can stand the test of alternative ways of validating truth. The existence of an independent black women's standpoint using an Afrocentric feminist epistemology calls into question the content of what currently passes as truth and simultaneously challenges the process of arriving at that truth.

Discussion Questions

1. How does Collins support her claim that "all social thought . . . reflects the interests and standpoint of its creators"? Is there a difference between this idea and the idea that all attempts to "credential" something as knowledge (e.g., to get it approved for publication) will reflect the interests of the credentialing group?

2. If knowledge, as Collins suggests, is relative to categories of race and gender, must there be separate "white male" and "black female" (etc.) sciences?

3. If the stereotype of women is that they are more "emotional" and less "abstract" in their

thinking than men, doesn't Collins' epistemology reinforce this stereotype?

4. Is there a way of not reinforcing the stereotype described in question 3, while having distinctively "feminist" epistemology?

5. Collins speaks not simply of an African American feminist epistemology but of an "Afrocentric" one. Has she substantiated her claim that there is a way of knowing common to all African people?

Notes

1. For analyses of how interlocking systems of oppression affect black women, see Frances Beale, "Double Jeopardy: To Be Black and Female," in *The Black Woman,* ed. Toni Cade (New York: Signet, 1970); Angela Y. Davis, *Women, Race, and Class* (New York: Random House, 1981); Bonnie Thornton Dill, "Race, Class, and Gender: Prospects for an All-Inclusive Sisterhood," *Feminist Studies* 9, no. 1 (1983): 131–50; bell hooks, *Ain't I a Woman? Black Women and Feminism* (Boston: South End Press, 1981); Diane Lewis, "A Response to Inequality: Black Women, Racism, and Sexism," *Signs: Journal of Women in Culture and Society* 3, no. 2 (Winter 1977): 339–61; Pauli Murray, "The Liberation of Black Women," in *Voices of the New Feminism,* ed. Mary Lou Thompson (Boston: Beacon Press, 1970), 87–102; and the introduction in Filomina Chioma Steady, *The Black Woman Cross-Culturally* (Cambridge, MA: Schenkman, 1981), 7–41.

2. See the introduction in Steady for an overview of black women's strengths. This strength-resiliency perspective has greatly influenced empirical work on African American women. See, e.g., Joyce Ladner's study of low-income black adolescent girls, *Tomorrow's Tomorrow* (New York: Doubleday, 1971); and Lena Wright Myers's work on black women's self-concept, *Black Women: Do They Cope Better?* (Englewood Cliffs, NJ: Prentice-Hall, 1980). For discussions of black women's resistance, see Elizabeth Fox-Genovese, "Strategies and Forms of Resistance: Focus on Slave Women in the United States," in *In Resistance: Studies in African, Caribbean and Afro-American History,* ed. Gary Y. Okihiro (Amherst: University of Massachusetts Press, 1986), 143–65; and Rosalyn Terborg-Penn, "Black Women in Resistance: A Cross-Cultural Perspective," in Okihiro, *In Resistance,* 188–209. For a comprehensive discussion of everyday resistance, see James C. Scott, *Weapons of the Weak: Everyday Forms of Peasant Resistance* (New Haven, CT: Yale University Press, 1985).

3. See Patricia Hill Collins's analysis of the substantive content of black feminist thought in "Learning from the Outsider Within: The Sociological Significance of Black Feminist Thought," *Social Problems* 33, no. 6 (1986): 14–32.

4. Scott describes consciousness as the meaning that people give to their acts through the symbols, norms, and ideological forms they create.

5. This thesis is found in scholarship of varying theoretical perspectives. For example, Marxist analyses of working-class consciousness claim that "false consciousness" makes the working class unable to penetrate the hegemony of ruling-class ideologies. See Scott's critique of this literature.

6. For example, in Western societies, African Americans have been judged as being less capable of intellectual excellence, more suited to manual labor, and therefore less human than whites. Similarly, white women have been assigned roles as emotional, irrational creatures ruled by passions and biological urges. They too have been stigmatized as being less than fully human, as being objects. For a discussion of the importance that objectification and dehumanization play in maintaining systems of domination, see Arthur Brittan and Mary Maynard, *Sexism, Racism and Oppression* (New York: Basil Blackwell, 1984).

7. The tendency for Western scholarship to assess black culture as pathological and deviant illustrates this process. See Rhett S. Jones, "Proving Blacks Inferior: The Sociology of Knowledge," in *The Death of White Sociology,* ed. Joyce Ladner (New York: Vintage, 1973), 114–35.

8. The presence of an independent standpoint does not mean that it is uniformly shared by all black women or even that black women fully recognize its contours. By using the concept of standpoint, I do not mean to minimize the rich diversity existing among African American women. I use the phrase "black women's standpoint" to emphasize the plurality of experiences within the overarching term "standpoint." For discussions of the concept of standpoint, see Nancy M. Hartsock, "The Feminist Standpoint: Developing the Ground for a Specifically Feminist Historical Materialism," in *Discovering Reality,* ed. Sandra Harding and Merrill Hintikka (Boston: D. Reidel, 1983), 283–310; *Money, Sex, and Power* (Boston: Northeastern University Press, 1983); and Alison M. Jaggar, *Feminist Politics and Human Nature* (Totowa, NJ: Rowman & Allanheld, 1983), 377–89. My use of the standpoint epistemologies as an organizing concept in this essay does not mean that the concept is problem-free. For a helpful critique of standpoint epistemologies, see Sandra Harding, *The Science Question in Feminism* (Ithaca, NY: Cornell University Press, 1986).

9. One contribution of contemporary black women's studies is its documentation of how race, class, and gender have structured these differences. For representative works surveying African American women's experiences, see Paula Giddings, *When and Where I Enter: The Impact of Black Women on Race and Sex in America* (New York: William Morrow, 1984); and Jacqueline Jones, *Labor of Love, Labor of Sorrow: Black Women, Work, and the Family from Slavery to the Present* (New York: Basic Books, 1985).

10. For example, Judith Rollins, *Between Women: Domestics and Their Employers* (Philadelphia: Temple University Press, 1985); and Bonnie Thornton Dill, " 'The Means to Put My Children Through': Child-Rearing Goals and Strategies among Black Female Domestic Servants," in *The Black Woman,* ed. LaFrances Rodgers-Rose (Beverly Hills, CA: Sage Publications, 1980), 107–23, report that black domestic workers do not see themselves as being the devalued workers that their employers perceive and construct their own interpretations of the meaning of their work. For additional discussions of how black women's consciousness is shaped by the material conditions they encounter, see Ladner, *Tomorrow's Tomorrow;* Myers, *Black Women;* and Cheryl Townsend Gilkes, " 'Together and in Harness': Women's Traditions in the Sanctified Church," *Signs* 10, no. 4 (Summer 1985): 678–99. See also Marcia Westkott's discussion of consciousness as a sphere of freedom for women in "Feminist Criticism of the Social Sciences," *Harvard Educational Review* 49, no. 4 (1979): 422–30.

11. John Langston Gwaltney, *Drylongso: A Self-Portrait of Black America* (New York: Vintage, 1980), 4.

12. Ibid., 33.

13. Ibid., 88.

14. Ibid., 7.

15. Victoria Byerly, *Hard Times Cotton Mill Girls: Personal Histories of Womanhood and Poverty in the South* (New York: ILR Press, 1986), 134.

16. See Peter L. Berger and Thomas Luckmann, *The Social Construction of Reality* (New York: Doubleday, 1966), for a discussion of everyday thought and the role of experts in articulating specialized thought.

17. See Michael Omi and Howard Winant, *Racial Formation in the United States* (New York: Routledge & Kegan Paul, 1986), especially 93.

18. In discussing standpoint epistemologies, Hartsock, in *Money, Sex, and Power,* notes that a standpoint is "achieved rather than obvious, a mediated rather than immediate understanding" (132).

19. See Scott, *Weapons of the Weak;* and Hartsock, *Money, Sex, and Power.*

20. Some readers may question how one determines whether the ideas of any given African American woman are "feminist" and "Afrocentric." I offer the following working definitions. I agree with the general definition of feminist consciousness provided by black feminist sociologist Deborah K. King: "Any purposes, goals, and activities that seek to enhance the potential of women, to ensure their liberty, afford them equal opportunity, and to permit and encourage their self-determination represent a feminist consciousness, even if they occur within a racial community" (in "Race, Class and Gender Salience in Black Women's Womanist Consciousness" [typescript, Dartmouth College, Department of Sociology, Hanover, NH, 1987], 22). To be black or Afrocentric, such thought must not only reflect a similar concern for the self-determination of African American people, but must in some way draw upon key elements of an Afrocentric tradition as well.

21. The Eurocentric masculinist process is defined here as the institutions, paradigms, and any elements of the knowledge-validation procedure controlled by white males and whose purpose is to represent a white male standpoint. While this process represents the interests of powerful white males, various dimensions of the process are not necessarily managed by white males themselves.

22. Karl Mannheim, *Ideology and Utopia: An Introduction to the Sociology of Knowledge* (1936; reprint, New York: Harcourt, Brace & Co., 1954), 276.

23. The knowledge-validation model used in this essay is taken from Michael Mulkay, *Science and the Sociology of Knowledge* (Boston: Allen & Unwin, 1979). For a general discussion of the structure of knowledge, see Thomas Kuhn, *The Structure of Scientific Revolutions* (Chicago: University of Chicago Press, 1962).

24. For analyses of the content and functions of images of black female inferiority, see Mae King, "The Politics of Sexual Stereotypes," *Black Scholar* 4, nos. 6–7 (1973): 12–23; Cheryl Townsend Gilkes, "From Slavery to Social Welfare: Racism and the Control of Black Women," in *Class, Race, and Sex: The Dynamics of Control,* ed. Amy Smerdlow and Helen Lessinger (Boston: G. K. Hall, 1981), 288–300; and Elizabeth Higginbotham, "Two Representative Issues in Contemporary Sociological Work on Black Women," in *All the Women Are White, All the Blacks Are Men, but Some of Us Are Brave,* ed. Gloria T. Hull, Patricia Bell Scott, and Barbara Smith (Old Westbury, NY: Feminist Press, 1982).

25. Kun, *The Structure.*

26. Evelyn Fox Keller, *Reflections on Gender and Science* (New Haven, CT: Yale University Press, 1985), 167.

27. Maxine Baca Zinn, Lynn Weber Cannon, Elizabeth Higginbotham, and Bonnie Thornton Dill, "The Cost of Exclusionary Practices in Women's Studies," *Signs* 11, no. 2 (Winter 1986): 290–303.

28. Berger and Luckmann (in *The Social Construction of Reality*) note that if an outsider group, in this

case African American women, recognizes that the insider group, namely, white men, requires special privileges from the larger society, a special problem arises of keeping the outsiders out and at the same time having them acknowledge the legitimacy of this procedure. Accepting a few "safe" outsiders is one way of addressing this legitimation problem. Collins's discussion (in "Learning from the Outsider Within") of black women as "outsiders within" addresses this issue. Other relevant works include Frantz Fanon's analysis of the role of the national middle class in maintaining colonial systems, *The Wretched of the Earth* (New York: Grove, 1963); and William Tabb's discussion of the use of "bright natives" in controlling African American communities, *The Political Economy of the Black Ghetto* (New York: W. W. Norton, 1970).

29. While I have been describing Eurocentric masculinist approaches as a single process, there are many schools of thought or paradigms subsumed under this one process. Positivism represents one such paradigm. See Harding, *The Science Question*, for an overview and critique of this literature. The following discussion depends heavily on Jaggar, *Feminist Politics*, 355–58.

30. Jaggar, *Feminist Politics*, 356.

31. See Keller, *Reflections on Gender*, 67–126, especially her analysis of static autonomy and its relation to objectivity.

32. Ironically, researchers must "objectify" themselves to achieve this lack of bias. See Arlie Russell Hochschild, "The Sociology of Feeling and Emotion: Selected Possibilities," in *Another Voice: Feminist Perspectives on Social Life and Social Science,* ed. Marcia Millman and Rosabeth Kanter (Garden City, NY: Anchor, 1975), 280–307. Also, see Jaggar, *Feminist Politics.*

33. See Norma Haan, Robert Bellah, Paul Rabinow, and William Sullivan, eds., *Social Science as Moral Inquiry* (New York: Columbia University Press, 1983), especially Michelle Z. Rosaldo's "Moral/Analytic Dilemmas Posed by the Intersection of Feminism and Social Science," 76–96; and Robert Bellah's "The Ethical Aims of Social Inquiry," 360–81.

34. Janice Moulton, "A Paradigm of Philosophy: The Adversary Method," in Harding and Hintikka, *Discovering Reality,* 149–64.

35. For detailed discussions of the Afrocentric worldview, see John S. Mbiti, *African Religions and Philosophy* (London: Heinemann, 1969); Dominique Zahan, *The Religion, Spirituality, and Thought of Traditional Africa* (Chicago: University of Chicago Press, 1979); and Mechal Sobel, *Trabelin' On: The Slave Journey to an Afro-Baptist Faith* (Westport, CT: Greenwood Press, 1979), 1–76.

36. For representative works applying these concepts to African American culture, see Niara Sudarkasa, "Interpreting the African Heritage in Afro-American Family Organization," in *Black Families,* ed. Harriette Pipes McAdoo (Beverly Hills, CA: Sage Publications, 1981); Henry H. Mitchell and Nicholas Cooper Lewter, *Soul Theology: The Heart of American Black Culture* (San Francisco: Harper & Row, 1986); Robert Farris Thompson, *Flash of the Spirit: African and Afro-American Art and Philosophy* (New York: Vintage, 1983); and Ortiz M. Walton, "Comparative Analysis of the African and the Western Aesthetics," in *The Black Aesthetic,* ed. Addison Gayle (Garden City, NY: Doubleday, 1971), 154–64.

37. One of the best discussions of an Afrocentric epistemology is offered by James E. Turner, "Foreword: Africana Studies and Epistemology; a Discourse in the Sociology of Knowledge," in *The Next Decade: Theoretical and Research Issues in Africana Studies,* ed. James E. Turner (Ithaca, NY: Cornell University Africana Studies and Research Center, 1984), v–xxv. See also Vernon Dixon, "World Views and Research Methodology," summarized in Harding, *The Science Question,* 170.

38. See Hester Eisenstein, *Contemporary Feminist Thought* (Boston: G. K. Hall, 1983). Nancy Hartsock's *Money, Sex, and Power,* 145–209, offers a particularly insightful analysis of women's oppression.

39. For discussions of feminist consciousness, see Dorothy Smith, "A Sociology for Women," in *The Prism of Sex: Essays in the Sociology of Knowledge,* ed. Julia A. Sherman and Evelyn T. Beck (Madison: University of Wisconsin Press, 1979); and Michelle Z. Rosaldo, "Women, Culture, and Society: A Theoretical Overview," in *Woman, Culture, and Society,* ed. Michelle Z. Rosaldo and Louise Lamphere (Stanford, CA: Stanford University Press, 1974), 17–42. Feminist epistemologies are surveyed by Jaggar, *Feminist Politics.*

40. One significant difference between Afrocentric and feminist standpoints is that much of what is termed womens culture is, unlike African American culture, treated in the context of and produced by oppression. Those who argue for a women's culture are electing to value, rather than denigrate, those traits associated with females in white patriarchal societies. While this choice is important, it is not the same as identifying an independent, historical culture associated with a society. I am indebted to Deborah K. King for this point.

41. Critiques of the Eurocentric masculinist knowledge-validation process by both Africanist and feminist scholars illustrate this point. What one group labels "white" and "Eurocentric," the other describes

as "male-dominated" and "masculinist." Although he does not emphasize its patriarchal and racist features, Morris Berman's *The Reenchantment of the World* (New York: Bantam Books, 1981) provides a historical discussion of Western thought. Afrocentric analyses of this same process can be found in Molefi Kete Asante, "International/Intercultural Relations," in *Contemporary Black Thought,* ed. Molefi Kete Asante and Abdulai S. Vandi (Beverly Hills, CA: Sage Publications, 1980), 43–58; and Dona Richards, "European Mythology: The Ideology of 'Progress,' " in Asante and Vandi, *Contemporary/Black Thought,* 59–79. For feminist analyses, see Hartsock, *Money, Sex, and Power.* Harding also discusses this similarity (see Chap. 7, "Other 'Others' and Fractured Identities: Issues for Epistemologists," 63–96).

42. Harding, *The Science Question,* 166.

43. D. King, "Race, Class and Gender Salience."

44. Bonnie Thornton Dill, "The Dialectics of Black Womanhood," *Signs* 4, no. 3 (Spring 1979): 543–55.

45. One implication of standpoint approaches is that the more subordinate the group, the purer the vision of the oppressed group. This is an outcome of the origins of standpoint approaches in Marxist social theory, itself a dualistic analysis of social structure. Because such approaches rely on quantifying and ranking human oppressions—familiar tenets of positivist approaches—they are rejected by blacks and feminists alike. See Harding, *The Science Question,* for a discussion of this point. See also Elizabeth V. Spelman's discussion of the fallacy of additive oppression in "Theories of Race and Gender: The Erasure of Black Women," *Quest* 5, no. 4 (1982): 36–62.

46. Class differences among black women may be marked. For example, see Paula Giddings's analysis (in *When and Where I Enter*) of the role of social class in shaping black women's political activism; or Elizabeth Higginbotham's study of the effects of social class in black women's college attendance in "Race and Class Barriers to Black Women's College Attendance," *Journal of Ethnic Studies* 13, no. 1 (1985): 89–107. Those African American women who have experienced the greatest degree of convergence of race, class, and gender oppression may be in a better position to recognize and use an alternative epistemology.

47. Gwaltney, *Drylongso,* 83.

48. William L. Andrews, *Sisters of the Spirit: Three Black Women's Autobiographies of the Nineteenth Century* (Bloomington: Indiana University Press, 1986), 85.

49. Gwaltney, *Drylongso,* 147.

50. Geneva Smitherman, *Talkin and Testifyin: The Language of Black America* (Detroit: Wayne State University Press, 1986), 76.

51. Gwaltney, *Drylongso,* 68.

52. Ibid., 7.

53. Ibid., 27, 33.

54. Elsa Barkley Brown, "Hearing Our Mothers' Lives" (paper presented at the Fifteenth Anniversary Faculty Lecture Series, African American and African Studies, Emory University, Atlanta, 1986).

55. Ladner, *Tomorrow's Tomorrow.*

56. Mitchell and Lewter, *Soul Theology.* The use of the narrative approach in African American theology exemplifies an inductive system of logic alternately called "folk wisdom" or a survival-based, need-oriented method of assessing knowledge claims.

57. Ibid., 8.

58. June Jordan, *On Call: Political Essays* (Boston: South End Press, 1985), 26.

59. Mary Belenky, Blythe Clinchy, Nancy Goldberger, and Jill Tarule, *Women's Ways of Knowing* (New York: Basic Books, 1986), 113.

60. Hartsock, *Money, Sex, and Power,* 237; and Nancy Chodorow, *The Reproduction of Mothering* (Berkeley and Los Angeles: University of California Press, 1978).

61. Dorothy Smith, *The Everyday World as Problematic* (Boston: Northeastern University Press, 1987).

62. Byerly, *Hard Times Cotton Mill Girls,* 198.

63. For black women's centrality in the family, see Steady, *The Black Woman;* Ladner, *Tomorrow's Tomorrow;* Brown, "Hearing Our Mothers' Lives"; and McAdoo, *Black Families.* See Gilkes, " 'Together and in Harness,' " for black women in the church; and chapter 4 of Deborah Gray White, *Ar'n't I a Woman? Female Slaves in the Plantation South* (New York: W. W. Norton, 1985). See also Gloria Joseph, "Black Mothers and Daughters: Their Roles and Functions in American Society," in *Common Differences: Conflicts in Black and White Feminist Perspectives,* ed. Gloria Joseph and Jill Lewis (Garden City, NY: Anchor, 1981), 75–126. Even though black women play essential roles in black families and black churches, these institutions are not free from sexism.

64. Black men, white women, and members of other race, class, and gender groups should be encouraged to interpret, teach, and critique the black feminist thought produced by African American women.

65. Walker, *In Search of Our Mothers' Gardens* (New York: Harcourt Brace Jovanovich, 1974), 91.

66. Gwaltney, *Drylongso.*

67. Jordan, *On Call,* 130.

68. Collins, "Learning from the Outsider Within."

69. This point addresses the question of relativity in the sociology of knowledge and offers a way of regulating competing knowledge claims.

17   Reflections on Race and Sex

bell hooks

Study Questions

1. According to hooks, what is the relationship between racial and sexual domination?
2. In what way is hooks critical of the "discourse of black resistance"? How does hooks see this discourse as related to traditional fears of black males as rapists?
3. In what ways is hooks critical of the public coverage of the Central Park rape case?

Race and sex have always been overlapping discourses in the United States. That discourse began in slavery. The talk then was not about black men wanting to be free so that they would have access to the bodies of white women—that would come later. Then, black women's bodies were the discursive terrain, the playing fields where racism and sexuality converged. Rape as both right and rite of the white male dominating group was a cultural norm. Rape was also an apt metaphor for European imperialist colonization of Africa and North America.

Sexuality has always provided gendered metaphors for colonization. Free countries equated with free men, domination with castration, the loss of manhood, and rape—the terrorist act re-enacting the drama of conquest, as men of the dominating group sexually violate the bodies of women who are among the dominated. The intent of this act was to continually remind dominated men of their loss of power; rape was a gesture of symbolic castration. Dominated men are made powerless (i.e., impotent) over and over again as the women they would have had the right to possess, to control, to assert power over, to dominate, to fuck, are fucked and fucked over by the dominating victorious male group.

There is no psychosexual history of slavery that explores the meaning of white male sexual exploitation of black women or the politics of sexuality, no work that lays out all the available information. There is no discussion of sexual sado-masochism, of the master who forced his wife to sleep on the floor as he nightly raped a black woman in bed. There is no discussion of sexual voyeurism. And what were the sexual lives of white men like who were legally declared "insane" because they wanted to marry black slave women with whom they were sexually and romantically involved? Under what conditions did sexuality serve as a force subverting and disrupting power relations, unsettling the oppressor/oppressed paradigm? No one seems to know how to tell this story, where to begin. As historical narrative it was long ago supplanted by the creation of another story (pornographic sexual project, fantasy, fear, the origin has yet to be traced). That story, invented by white men, is about the overwhelming desperate longing black men have to sexually violate the bodies of white women. The central character in this story is the black male rapist. Black men are constructed, as Michael Dyson puts it, as "peripatetic phalluses with unrequited desire for their denied object—white women." As the story goes, this desire is not based on longing for sexual pleasure. It is a story of revenge, rape as the weapon by which black men, the dominated, reverse their circumstance, regain power over white men.

Oppressed black men and women have rarely challenged the use of gendered metaphors to describe the impact of racist domination and/or black liberation struggle. The discourse of black resistance has almost always equated freedom with manhood, the economic and material domination of black men with castration, emasculation. Accepting these sexual metaphors

Reprinted by permission of the publisher from *Yearnings* (Boston: South End Press, 1990), pp. 57–64.

forged a bond between oppressed black men and their white male oppressors. They shared the patriarchal belief that revolutionary struggle was really about the erect phallus, the ability of men to establish political dominance that could correspond to sexual dominance. Careful critical examination of black power literature in the sixties and early seventies exposes the extent to which black women and men were using sexualized metaphors to talk about the effort to resist racist domination. Many of us have never forgotten that moment in *Soul on Ice* when Eldridge Cleaver, writing about the need to "redeem my conquered manhood," described raping black women as practice for the eventual rape of white women. Remember that readers were not shocked or horrified by this glamorization of rape as a weapon of terrorism men might use to express rage about other forms of domination, about their struggle for power with other men. Given the sexist context of the culture, it made sense. Cleaver was able to deflect attention away from the misogynist sexism of his assertions by poignantly justifying these acts as a "natural" response to racial domination. He wanted to force readers to confront the agony and suffering black men experience in a white supremacist society. Again, freedom from racial domination was expressed in terms of redeeming black masculinity. And gaining the right to assert one's manhood was always about sexuality.

During slavery, there was perhaps a white male who created his own version of *Soul on Ice,* one who confessed how good it felt to assert racial dominance over black people, and particularly black men, by raping black women with impunity, or how sexually stimulating it was to use the sexual exploitation of black women to humiliate and degrade white women, to assert phallocentric domination in one's household. Sexism has always been a political stance mediating racial domination, enabling white men and black men to share a common sensibility about sex roles and the importance of male domination. Clearly both groups have equated freedom with manhood, and manhood with the right of men to have indiscriminate access to the bodies of women. Both groups have been socialized to con-

done patriarchal affirmation of rape as an acceptable way to maintain male domination. It is this merging of sexuality with male domination within patriarchy that informs the construction of masculinity for men of all races and classes. Robin Morgan's book, *The Demon Lover: On The Sexuality of Terrorism,* begins with rape. She analyses the way men are bonded across class, race, and nationalities through shared notions of manhood which make masculinity synonymous with the ability to assert power-over through acts of violence and terrorism. Since terrorist acts are most often committed by men, Morgan sees the terrorist as "the logical incarnation of patriarchal politics in a technological world." She is not concerned with the overlapping discourses of race and sex, with the interconnectedness of racism and sexism. Like many radical feminists, she believes that male commitment to maintaining patriarchy and male domination diminishes or erases difference.

Much of my work within feminist theory has stressed the importance of understanding difference, of the ways race and class status determine the degree to which one can assert male domination and privilege and most importantly the ways racism and sexism are interlocking systems of domination which uphold and sustain one another. Many feminists continue to see them as completely separate issues, believing that sexism can be abolished while racism remains intact, or that women who work to resist racism are not supporting feminist movement. Since black liberation struggle is so often framed in terms that affirm and support sexism, it is not surprising that white women are uncertain about whether women's rights struggle will be diminished if there is too much focus on resisting racism, or that many black women continue to fear that they will be betraying black men if they support the feminist movement. Both these fears are responses to the equation of black liberation with manhood. This continues to be a central way black people frame our efforts to resist racist domination; it must be critiqued. We must reject the sexualization of black liberation in ways that support and perpetuate sexism, phallocentrism, and male domination. Even though Michele Wallace tried to expose the fallacy of equating black liberation with the assertion of oppressive manhood in *Black Macho and the Myth of the Superwoman,* few black people got the message. Continuing this critique in *Ain't I a Woman: Black Women and Feminism,* I found that more and more black women were rejecting this paradigm. It has yet to be rejected by most black men, and especially black male political figures. As long as black people hold on to the idea that the trauma of racist domination is really the loss of black manhood, then we invest in the racist narratives that perpetuate the idea that all black men are rapists, eager to use sexual terrorism to express their rage about racial domination.

Currently we are witnessing a resurgence of such narratives. They are resurfacing at a historical moment when black people are bearing the brunt of more overt and blatant racist assaults, when black men and especially young black men are increasingly disenfranchised by society. Mainstream white supremacist media make it appear that a black menace to societal safety is at large, that control, repression, and violent domination are the only effective ways to address the problem. Witness the use of the Willie Horton case to discredit Dukakis in the 1988 Presidential election. Susan Estrich in her post-campaign articles has done a useful job of showing how racist stereotypes were evoked to turn voters against Dukakis, and how Bush in no way denounced this strategy. In all her articles she recounts the experience of being raped by a black man fifteen years ago, describing the way racism determined how the police responded to the crime, and her response. Though her intent is to urge societal commitment to anti-racist struggle, every article I have read has carried captions in bold print emphasizing the rape. The subversive content of her work is undermined and the stereotype that all black men are rapists is re-inscribed and reinforced. Most people in this society do not realize that the vast majority of rapes are not inter-racial, that all groups of men are more likely to rape women who are the same race as themselves.

Within popular culture, Madonna's video "Like a Prayer" also makes use of imagery which links black men with rape, reinforcing this representation in the minds of millions of viewers—even though she has said that her intention is to be anti-racist, and certainly the video suggests that not all black men who are accused of raping white women are guilty. Once again, however, this subversive message is undermined by the overall focus on sexually charged imagery of white female sexuality and black male lust. The most subversive message in the video has nothing to do with anti-racism; it has to do with the construction of white females as desiring subjects who can freely assert sexual agency. Of course the taboo expression of that agency is choosing to be sexual with black men. Unfortunately this is a continuation of the notion that ending racist domination is really about issues of inter-racial sexual access, a myth that must be critiqued so that this society can confront the actual material, economic, and moral consequences of perpetuating white supremacy and its traumatic genocidal impact on black people.

Images of black men as rapists, as dangerous menaces to society, have been sensational cultural currency for some time. The obsessive media focus on these representations is political. The role it plays in the maintenance of racist domination is to convince the public that black men are a dangerous threat who must be controlled by any means necessary, including annihilation. This is the cultural backdrop shaping media response to the Central Park rape case, and the media has played a major role in shaping public response. Many people are using this case to perpetuate racial stereotypes and racism. Ironically, the very people who claim to be shocked by the brutality of this case have no qualms about suggesting that the suspects should be castrated or killed. They see no link between this support of violence as a means of social control and the suspects' use of violence to exercise control. Public response to this case highlights the lack of understanding about the interconnectedness of racism and sexism.

Many black people, especially black men, using the sexist paradigm that suggests rape of white women by black men is a reaction to racist domination, view the Central Park case as an indictment of the racist system. They do not see sexism as informing the nature of the crime, the choice of victim. Many white women have responded to the case by focusing solely on the brutal assault as an act of gender domination, of male violence against women. A piece in the *Village Voice* written by white female Andrea Kannapell carried captions in bold print which began with the statement in all capitals for greater emphasis, "THE CRIME WAS MORE SEXIST THAN RACIST . . ." Black women responding to the same issue all focused on the sexist nature of the crime, often giving examples of black male sexism. Given the work black women have done within feminist writing to call attention to the reality of black male sexism, work that often receives little or no attention or is accused of attacking black men, it is ironic that the brutal rape of a white woman by a group of young black males serves as the catalyst for admission that sexism is a serious problem in black communities. Lisa Kennedy's piece, "Body Double: The Anatomy of a Crime," also published in the *Village Voice,* acknowledges the convergence of racism and sexism as politics of domination that inform this assault. Kennedy writes:

If I accept the premise of the coverage, that this rape is more heartbreaking than all the rapes that happen to women of color, then what happens to the value of my body? What happens to the quality of my blackness?

These questions remain unanswered, though she closes with "a call for a sophisticated feminist offensive." Such an offensive should begin with cultivating critical awareness of the way racism and sexism are interlocking systems of domination.

Public response to the Central Park case reveals the extent to which the culture invests in the kind of dualistic thinking that helps reinforce and maintain all forms of domination. Why must people decide whether this crime is more sexist than racist, as if these are competing oppressions? Why do white people, and especially feminist white women, feel better when black people, especially black women, disassociate themselves from the plight of black men in white supremacist capitalist patriarchy to emphasize opposition to

black male sexism? Cannot black women remain seriously concerned about the brutal effect of racist domination on black men and also denounce black male sexism? And why is black male sexism evoked as though it is a special brand of this social disorder, more dangerous, more abhorrent and life-threatening than the sexism that pervades the culture as a whole, or the sexism that informs white male domination of women? These questions call attention to the either/or ways of thinking that are the philosophical underpinning of systems of domination. Progressive folks must then insist, wherever we engage in discussions of this crime or of issues of race and gender, on the complexity of our experience in a racist sexist society.

The Central Park crime involves aspects of sexism, male domination, misogyny, and the use of rape as an instrument of terror. It also involves race and racism; it is unlikely that young black males growing up in this society, attacking a white woman, would see her as "just a woman"—her race would be foremost in their consciousness as well as her sex, in the same way that masses of people hearing about this crime were concerned with identifying first her race. In a white supremacist sexist society all women's bodies are devalued, but white women's bodies are more valued than those of women of color. Given the context of white supremacy, the historical narratives about black male rapists, the racial identities of both victim and victimizers enable this tragedy to be sensationalized.

To fully understand the multiple meanings of this incident, it must be approached from an analytical standpoint that considers the impact of sexism and racism. Beginning there enables many of us to empathize with both the victim and the victimizers. If one reads *The Demon Lover* and thinks again about this crime, one can see it as part of a continuum of male violence against women, of rape and terror as weapons of male domination—yet another horrific and brutal expression of patriarchal socialization. And if one considers this case by combining a feminist analysis of race and masculinity, one sees that since male power within patriarchy is relative, men from poorer groups and men of color are not able to reap the material and social rewards for their participation in patriarchy. In fact they often suffer from blindly and passively acting out a myth of masculinity that is life-threatening. Sexist thinking blinds them to this reality. They become victims of the patriarchy. No one can truly believe that the young black males involved in the Central Park incident were not engaged in a suicidal ritual enactment of a dangerous masculinity that will ultimately threaten their lives, their well-being.

If one reads again Michael Dyson's piece "The Plight of Black Men," focusing especially on the part where he describes the reason many young black men form gangs—"the sense of absolute belonging and unsurpassed love"—it is easy to understand why young black males are despairing and nihilistic. And it is rather naive to think that if they do not value their own lives, they will value the lives of others. Is it really so difficult for folks to see the connection between the constant pornographic glorification of male violence against women that is represented, enacted, and condoned daily in the culture and the Central Park crime? Does racism create and maintain this blindspot or does it allow black people and particularly black men to become the scapegoats, embodying society's evils?

If we are to live in a less violent and more just society, then we must engage in anti-sexist and anti-racist work. We desperately need to explore and understand the connections between racism and sexism. And we need to teach everyone about those connections so that they can be critically aware and socially active. Much education for critical consciousness can take place in everyday conversations. Black women and men must participate in the construction of feminist thinking, creating models for feminist struggle that address the particular circumstances of black people. Still, the most visionary task of all remains that of re-conceptualizing masculinity so that alternative, transformative models are there in the culture, in our daily lives, to help boys and men who are working to construct a self, to build new identities. Black liberation struggle must be re-visioned so

that it is no longer equated with maleness. We need a revolutionary vision of black liberation, one that emerges from a feminist standpoint and addresses the collective plight of black people.

Any individual committed to resisting politics of domination, to eradicating sexism and racism, understands the importance of not promoting an either/or competition between the oppressive systems. We can empathize with the victim and the victimizers in the Central Park case, allowing that feeling to serve as a catalyst for renewed commitment to anti-sexist and anti-racist work. Yesterday I heard this story. A black woman friend called to say that she had been attacked on the street by a black man. He took her purse, her house keys, her car keys. She lives in one of the poorest cities in the United States. We talked about poverty, sexism, and racial domination to place what had happened in a perspective that will enable both individual healing and political understanding of this crime. Today I heard this story. A white woman friend called to say that she had been attacked in her doorway by a black man. She screamed and he ran away. Neighbors coming to her aid invoked racism. She refused to engage in this discussion even though she was shocked by the intensity and degree of racism expressed. Even in the midst of her own fear and pain, she remained politically aware, so as not to be complicit in perpetuating the white supremacy that is the root of so much suffering. Both of these women feel rage at their victimizers; they do not absolve them even as they seek to understand and to respond in ways that will enrich the struggle to end domination—so that sexism, sexist violence, racism, and racist violence will cease to be an everyday happening.

Discussion Questions

1. In her first book, *Ain't I a Woman?: Black Women and Feminism,* hooks was critical of the often held view that slavery was "emasculating" (that it robbed the slave of his masculinity). Based on what she says in this essay, can you see why hooks would be critical of

this view? (In answering this, you may want to consider *ways* in which something might or might not be emasculating.)

2. To what extent is contemporary American society "emasculating" for the black male?

3. hooks identifies much of the reaction to the Central Park case as "racist." To what extent is it racist for white women to be afraid of black males (under some circumstances)?

4. hooks maintains that the fight against racism and sexism must go hand in hand. Which fight, in your view, is closer to being won? Is it not conceivable that this fight could be largely won—without the other being so?

18   Race and Essentialism in Feminist Legal Theory

ANGELA P. HARRIS

Study Questions

1. What is "gender essentialism"?

2. What is the result of essentialism generally (e.g., for a black lesbian)?

3. What criticisms does Harris make of Catherine MacKinnon's "dominance theory"?

4. How does the case of *Martinez v. Santa Clara Pueblo* highlight some of the differences between MacKinnon's and Harris' legal theories?

5. How does the character of Pecola Breedlove point to a fundamental error in MacKinnon's view of beauty and black women?

6. How does the issue of rape point to a further division between white and black women?

In *Funes the Memorious,* Borges tells of Ireneo Funes, who was a rather ordinary young man (notable only for his precise sense of time) until the age of nineteen, when he was thrown by a half-tamed horse and left paralyzed but possessed of perfect perception and a perfect memory.

After his transformation, Funes

knew by heart the forms of the southern clouds at dawn on the 30th of April, 1882, and could compare them in his memory with the mottled streaks on a book in Spanish binding he had only seen once and with the outlines of the foam raised by an oar in the Río Negro the night before the Quebracho uprising. These memories were not simple ones; each visual image was linked to muscular sensations, thermal sensations, etc. He could reconstruct all his dreams, all his half-dreams. Two or three times he had reconstructed a whole day; he never hesitated, but each reconstruction had required a whole day.[1]

Funes tells the narrator that after his transformation he invented his own numbering system. "In place of seven thousand thirteen, he would say (for example) *Máximo Pérez;* in place of seven thousand fourteen, *The Railroad;* other numbers were Luis Melián Lafinur, Olimar, sulphur, the reins, the whale, the gas, the caldron, Napoleon, Agustín de Vedia."[2] The narrator tries to explain to Funes "that this rhapsody of incoherent terms was precisely the opposite of a system of numbers. I told him that saying 365 meant saying three hundreds, six tens, five ones, an analysis which is not found in the 'numbers' *The Negro Timoteo* or *meat blanket.* Funes did not understand me or refused to understand me."[3]

In his conversation with Funes, the narrator realizes that Funes' life of infinite unique experiences leaves Funes no ability to categorize: "With no effort, he had learned English, French, Portuguese and Latin. I suspect, however, that he was not very capable of thought. To think is to forget differences, generalize, make abstractions.

Reprinted from the *Stanford Law Review* 42 (1990), pp. 581–616.

In the teeming world of Funes, there were only details, almost immediate in their presence."[4] For Funes, language is only a unique and private system of classification, elegant and solipsistic. The notion that language, made abstract, can serve to create and reinforce a community is incomprehensible to him.

"We the People"

Describing the voice that speaks the first sentence of the Declaration of Independence, James Boyd White remarks:

It is not a person's voice, not even that of a committee, but the "unanimous" voice of "thirteen united States" and of their "people." It addresses a universal audience—nothing less than "mankind" itself, located neither in space nor in time—and the voice is universal too, for it purports to know about the "Course of human events" (all human events?) and to be able to discern what "becomes necessary" as a result of changing circumstances.[5]

The Preamble of the United States Constitution, White argues, can also be heard to speak in this unified and universal voice. This voice claims to speak

for an entire and united nation and to do so directly and personally, not in the third person or by merely delegated authority. . . . The instrument thus appears to issue from a single imaginary author, consisting of all the people of the United States, including the reader, merged into a single identity in this act of self-constitution. "The People" are at once the author and the audience of this instrument.[6]

Despite its claims, however, this voice does not speak for everyone, but for a political faction trying to constitute itself as a unit of many disparate voices; its power lasts only as long as the contradictory voices remain silenced.

In a sense, the "I" of Funes, who knows only particulars, and the "we" of "We the People," who know only generalities, are the same. Both voices are monologues; both depend on the silence of others. The difference is only that the first voice knows of no others, while the second has silenced them.

The first voice, the voice of Funes, is the voice toward which literature sometimes seems driven. Law, however, has not been much tempted by the sound of the first voice. Lawyers are all too aware that legal language is not a purely self-referential game, for "legal interpretive acts signal and occasion the imposition of violence upon others."[7] In their concern to avoid the social and moral irresponsibility of the first voice, legal thinkers have veered in the opposite direction, toward the safety of the second voice, which speaks from the position of "objectivity" rather than "subjectivity," "neutrality" rather than "bias." This voice, like the voice of "We the People," is ultimately authoritarian and coercive in its attempt to speak for everyone.

We are not born with a "self," but rather are composed of a welter of partial, sometimes contradictory, or even antithetical "selves." A unified identity, if such can ever exist, is a product of will, not a common destiny or natural birthright. Thus, consciousness is "never fixed, never attained once and for all";[8] it is not a final outcome or a biological given, but a process, a constant contradictory state of becoming, in which both social institutions and individual wills are deeply implicated. A multiple consciousness is home both to the first and the second voices, and all the voices in between. Mari Matsuda, while arguing that in the legal realm "[h]olding on to a multiple consciousness will allow us to operate both within the abstractions of standard jurisprudential discourse, *and* within the details of our own special knowledge,"[9] acknowledges that "this constant shifting of consciousness produces sometimes madness, sometimes genius, sometimes both."[10]

Race and Essentialism in Feminist Legal Theory

In feminist legal theory, the move away from univocal toward multivocal theories of women's experience and feminism has been slower than in other areas. In feminist legal theory, the pull of the second voice, the voice of abstract categorization, is still powerfully strong: "We the People" seems in danger of being replaced by "We the Women." And in feminist legal theory, as in the dominant culture, it is mostly white, straight, and socioeconomically privileged people who claim to speak for all of us.[11] Not surprisingly, the story they tell about "women," despite its claim to universality, seems to black women to be peculiar to women who are white, straight, and socioeconomically privileged—a phenomenon Adrienne Rich terms "white solipsism."[12]

Elizabeth Spelman notes:

[T]he real problem has been how feminist theory has confused the condition of one group of women with the condition of all.

. . . A measure of the depth of white middle-class privilege is that the apparently straightforward and logical points and axioms at the heart of much of feminist theory guarantee the direction of its attention to the concerns of white middle-class women.[13]

The notion that there is a monolithic "women's experience" that can be described independent of other facets of experience like race, class, and sexual orientation I refer to in this essay as "gender essentialism." A corollary to gender essentialism is "racial essentialism"—the belief that there is a monolithic "Black Experience," or "Chicano Experience." The source of gender and racial essentialism (and all other essentialisms, for the list of categories could be infinitely multiplied) is the second voice, the voice that claims to speak for all. The result of essentialism is to reduce the lives of people who experience multiple forms of oppression to addition problems: "racism + sexism = straight black women's experience," or "racism + sexism + homophobia = black lesbian experience." Thus, in an essentialist world, black women's experience will always be forcibly fragmented before being subjected to analysis, as those who are "only interested in race" and those who are "only interested in gender" take their separate slices of our lives.

Moreover, feminist essentialism paves the way for unconscious racism. Spelman puts it this way:

[T]hose who produce the "story of woman" want to make sure they appear in it. The best way to ensure that is to be the storyteller and hence to be in a position to decide which of all the many facts about womens lives ought to go into the story, which ought to be left out. Essentialism works well in behalf of these aims, aims that subvert the very process by which women might come to see where and how they wish to make common cause. For essentialism invites me to take what I understand to be true of me "as a woman" for some golden nugget of womanness all women have as women; and it makes the participation of other women inessential to the production of the story. How lovely: the many turn out to be one, and the one that they are is me.[14]

In a racist society like this one, the storytellers are usually white, and so "woman" turns out to be "white woman."

Why, in the face of challenges from "different" women and from feminist method itself, is feminist essentialism so persistent and pervasive? I think the reasons are several. Essentialism is intellectually convenient, and to a certain extent cognitively ingrained. Essentialism also carries with it important emotional and political payoffs. Finally, essentialism often appears (especially to white women) as the only alternative to chaos, mindless pluralism (the Funes trap), and the end of the feminist movement. In my view, however, as long as feminists, like theorists in the dominant culture, continue to search for gender and racial essences, black women will never be anything more than a crossroads between two kinds of domination, or at the bottom of a hierarchy of oppressions; we will always be required to choose pieces of ourselves to present as wholeness.

Modified Women and Unmodified Feminism: Black Women in Dominance Theory

Catharine MacKinnon[15] describes her "dominance theory," like the Marxism with which she likes to compare it, as "total": "[T]hey are both theories of the totality, of the whole thing, theories of a fundamental and critical underpinning of the whole they envision."[16] Both her dominance theory (which she identifies as simply "feminism") and Marxism "focus on that which is most one's own, that which most makes one the being the theory addresses, as that which is most taken away by what the theory criticizes. In each theory you are made who you are by that which is taken away from you by the social relations the theory criticizes."[17] In Marxism, the "that" is work; in feminism, it is sexuality.

MacKinnon defines sexuality as "that social process which creates, organizes, expresses, and directs desire, creating the social beings we know as women and men, as their relations create society."[18] Moreover, "the organized expropriation of the sexuality of some for the use of others defines the sex, woman. Heterosexuality is its structure, gender and family its congealed forms, sex roles its qualities generalized to social persona, reproduction a consequence, and control its issue."[19] Dominance theory, the analysis of this organized expropriation, is a theory of power and its unequal distribution.

In MacKinnon's view, "[t]he idea of gender difference helps keep the reality of male dominance in place."[20] That is, the concept of gender difference is an ideology which masks the fact that genders are socially constructed, not natural, and coercively enforced, not freely consented to. Moreover, "the social relation between the sexes is organized so that men may dominate and women must submit and this relation is sexual—in fact, is sex."[21]

For MacKinnon, male dominance is not only "perhaps the most pervasive and tenacious system of power in history, but . . . it is metaphysically nearly perfect."[22] The masculine point of view is point-of-viewlessness; the force of male dominance "is exercised as consent, its authority as participation, its supremacy as the paradigm of order, its control as the definition of legitimacy."[23] In such a world, the very existence of feminism is something of a paradox. "Feminism claims the voice of women's silence, the sexuality of our eroticized desexualization, the fullness of 'lack,' the centrality of our marginality and exclusion, the public nature of privacy, the presence of our absence."[24] The wonder is how feminism can exist in the face of its theoretical impossibility.

In MacKinnon's view, men have their foot on women's necks, regardless of race or class, or of mode of production: "Feminists do not argue that it means the same to women to be on the bottom in a feudal regime, a capitalist regime, and a socialist regime; the commonality argued is that, despite real changes, bottom is bottom."[25] As a political matter, moreover, MacKinnon is quick to insist that there is only one "true," "unmodified" feminism: that which analyzes women *as women,* not as subsets of some other group and not as gender-neutral beings.

Despite its power, MacKinnon's dominance theory is flawed by its essentialism. MacKinnon assumes, as does the dominant culture, that there is an essential "woman" beneath the realities of differences between women—that in describing the experiences of "women" issues of race, class, and sexual orientation can therefore be safely ignored, or relegated to footnotes. In her search for what is essential womanhood, however, MacKinnon rediscovers white womanhood and introduces it as universal truth. In dominance theory, black women are white women, only more so.

Essentialism in feminist theory has two characteristics that ensure that black women's voices will be ignored. First, in the pursuit of the essential feminine, Woman leached of all color and irrelevant social circumstance, issues of race are bracketed as belonging to a separate and distinct discourse—a process which leaves black women's selves fragmented beyond recognition. Second, feminist essentialists find that in removing issues of "race" they have actually only managed to remove black women—meaning that white women now stand as the epitome of Woman. Both processes can be seen at work in dominance theory.

Dominance Theory and the Bracketing of Race

MacKinnon repeatedly seems to recognize the inadequacy of theories that deal with gender while ignoring race, but having recognized the problem, she repeatedly shies away from its implications. Thus, she at times justifies her essentialism by pointing to the essentialism of the dominant discourse: "My suggestion is that what we have in common is not that our conditions have no particularity in ways that matter. But we are all measured by a male standard for women, a standard that is not ours."[26] At other times she deals with the challenge of black women by placing it in footnotes. For example, she places in a footnote without further comment the suggestive, if cryptic, observation that a definition of feminism "of coalesced interest and resistance" has tended both to exclude and to make invisible "the diverse ways that many women—notably Blacks and working-class women—have *moved* against their determinants."[27] In another footnote generally addressed to the problem of relating Marxism to issues of gender and race, she notes that "[a]ny relationship *between* sex and race tends to be left entirely out of account, since they are considered parallel 'strata,' "[28] but this thought simply trails off into a string cite to black feminist and social feminist writings.

Finally, MacKinnon postpones the demand of black women until the arrival of a "general theory of social inequality"; recognizing that "gender in this country appears partly to comprise the meaning of, as well as bisect, race and class, even as race and class specificities make up, as well as cross-cut, gender,"[29] she nevertheless is prepared to maintain her "colorblind" approach to women's experience until that general theory arrives (presumably that is someone else's work).

The results of MacKinnon's refusal to move beyond essentialism are apparent in the most tentative essay in *Whose Culture? A Case Note on Martinez v. Santa Clara Pueblo.*[30] Julia Martinez sued her Native American tribe, the Santa Clara Pueblo, in federal court, arguing that a tribal ordinance was invalid under a provision of the Indian Civil Rights Act guaranteeing equal protection of the laws. The ordinance provided that if women married outside the Pueblo, the children of that union were not full tribal members, but if men married outside the tribe, their children were full tribal members. Martinez married a Navajo man, and her children were not allowed to vote or in-

herit her rights in communal land. The United States Supreme Court held that this question was a matter of Indian sovereignty to be resolved by the tribe.[31]

MacKinnon starts her discussion with an admission: "I find *Martinez* a difficult case on a lot of levels, and I don't usually find cases difficult."[32] She concludes that the Pueblo ordinance was wrong, because it "did nothing to address or counteract the reasons why Native women were vulnerable to white male land imperialism through marriage—it gave in to them, by punishing the *woman,* the Native person."[33] Yet she reaches her conclusion, as she admits, without knowledge other than "word of mouth" of the history of the ordinance and its place in Santa Clara Pueblo culture.

MacKinnon has Julia Martinez ask her tribe, "Why do you make me choose between my equality as woman and my cultural identity?"[34] But she, no less than the tribe, eventually requires Martinez to choose; and the correct choice is, of course, that Martinez's female identity is more important than her tribal identity. MacKinnon states,

[T]he aspiration of women to be no less than men—not to be punished where a man is glorified, not to be considered damaged or disloyal where a man is rewarded or left in peace, not to lead a derivative life, but to do everything and be anybody at all—is an aspiration indigenous to women across place and across time.[35]

What MacKinnon does not recognize, however, is that though the aspiration may be everywhere the same, its expression must depend on the social historical circumstances. In this case, should Julia Martinez be content with struggling for change from within, or should the white government have stepped in "on her behalf"? What was the meaning of the ordinance within Pueblo discourse, as opposed to a transhistorical and transcultural feminist discourse? How did it come about and under what circumstances? What was the status of women within the tribe, both historically and at the time of the ordinance and at the present time, and was Martinez's claim heard and understood by the tribal authorities or simply ignored or derided? What were the Pueblo traditions about children of mixed parentage, and how were those traditions changing? In a jurisprudence based on multiple consciousness, rather than the unitary consciousness of MacKinnon's dominance theory, these questions would have to be answered before the ordinance could be considered on its merits and even before the Court's decision to stay out could be evaluated. MacKinnon does not answer these questions, but leaves the essay hanging with the idea that the male supremacist ideology of some Native American tribes may be adopted from white culture and therefore invalid.[36] MacKinnon's tentativeness may be due to not wanting to appear a white cultural imperialist, speaking for a Native American tribe, but to take up Julia Martinez's claim at all is to take that risk. Without a theory that can shift focus from gender to race and other facets of identity and back again, MacKinnon's essay is ultimately crippled. Martinez is made to choose her gender over her race, and her experience is distorted in the process.

Dominance Theory and White Women as All Women

The second consequence of feminist essentialism is that the racism that was acknowledged only in brackets quietly emerges in the feminist theory itself—both a cause and an effect of creating "Woman" from white woman. In MacKinnon's work, the result is that black women become white women, only more so.

In a passage in *Signs I,* MacKinnon borrows a quote from Toni Cade Bambara describing a black woman with too many children and no means with which to care for them as "grown ugly and dangerous from being nobody for so long," and then explains:

By using her phrase in altered context, I do not want to distort her meaning but to extend it. Throughout this essay, I have tried to see if women's condition is shared, even when contexts or magnitudes differ. (Thus, it is very different to be "nobody" as a Black woman than as a white lady, but neither is "somebody"

by male standards.) This is the approach to race and ethnicity attempted throughout. I aspire to include all women in the term "women" in some way, without violating the particularity of any woman's experience. Whenever this fails, the statement is simply wrong and will have to be qualified or the aspiration (or the theory) abandoned.[37]

I call this the "nuance theory" approach to the problem of essentialism: by being sensitive to the notion that different women have different experiences, generalizations can be offered about "all women" while qualifying statements, often in footnotes, supplement the general account with the subtle nuances of experience that "different" women add to the mix. Nuance theory thus assumes the commonality of all women—differences are a matter of "context" or "magnitude"; that is, nuance.

The problem with nuance theory is that by defining black women as "different," white women quietly become the norm, or pure, essential Woman. Just as MacKinnon would argue that being female is more than a "context" or a "magnitude" of human experience, being black is more than a context or magnitude of all (white) women's experience. But not in dominance theory.

For instance, MacKinnon describes how a system of male supremacy has constructed "woman":

Contemporary industrial society's version of her is docile, soft, passive, nurturant, vulnerable, weak, narcissistic, childlike, incompetent, masochistic, and domestic, made for child care, home care, and husband care. . . . Women who resist or fail, including those who never did fit—for example, black and lower-class women who cannot survive if they are soft and weak and incompetent, assertively self-respecting women, women with ambitions of male dimensions—are considered less female, lesser women.[38]

In a peculiar symmetry with this ideology, in which black women are something less than women, in MacKinnon's work black women become something more than women. In MacKinnon's writing, the word "black," applied to women, is an intensifier: If things are bad for everybody (meaning white women), then they're even worse for black women. Silent and suffering, we are trotted onto the page (mostly in footnotes) as the ultimate example of how bad things are.

Thus, in speaking of the beauty standards set for (white) women, MacKinnon remarks, "Black women are further from being able concretely to achieve the standard that no woman can ever achieve, or it would lose its point."[39] The frustration of black women at being unable to look like an "All-American" woman is in this way just a more dramatic example of all (white) women's frustration and oppression. When a black woman speaks on this subject, however, it becomes clear that a black woman's pain at not being considered fully feminine is different qualitatively, not merely quantitatively, from the pain MacKinnon describes. It is qualitatively different because the ideology of beauty concerns not only gender but race. Consider Toni Morrison's analysis of the influence of standards of white beauty on black people in *The Bluest Eye*.[40] Claudia MacTeer, a young black girl, muses, "Adults, older girls, shops, magazines, newspapers, window signs—all the world had agreed that a blue-eyed, yellow-haired, pink-skinned doll was what every girl child treasured." Similarly, in the black community, "high yellow" folks represent the closest black people can come to beauty, and darker people are always "lesser. Nicer, brighter, but still lesser." Beauty is whiteness itself; and middle-class black girls

go to land-grant colleges, normal schools, and learn how to do the white man's work with refinement: home economics to prepare his food; teacher education to instruct black children in obedience; music to soothe the weary master and entertain his blunted soul. Here they learn the rest of the lesson begun in those soft houses with porch swings and pots of bleeding heart: how to behave. The careful development of thrift, patience, high morals, and good manners. In short, how to get rid of the funkiness. The dreadful funkiness of passion, the funkiness of nature, the funkiness of the wide range of human emotions.

Wherever it erupts, this Funk, they wipe it away; where it crusts, they dissolve it; wherever it drips, flowers, or clings, they find it and fight it until it dies. They fight this battle all the way to the grave. The laugh that is a little too loud; the enunciation a little too

round; the gesture a little too generous. They hold their behind in for fear of a sway too free; when they wear lipstick, they never cover the entire mouth for fear of lips too thick, and they worry, worry, worry about the edges of their hair.[41]

Thus, Pecola Breedlove, born black and ugly, spends her lonely and abused childhood praying for blue eyes. Her story ends in despair and the fragmentation of her mind into two isolated speaking voices, not because she's even further away from ideal beauty than white women are, but because Beauty *itself* is white, and she is not and can never be, despite the pair of blue eyes she eventually believes she has. There is a difference between the hope that the next makeup kit or haircut or diet will bring you salvation and the knowledge that nothing can. The relation of black women to the ideal of white beauty is not a more intense form of white women's frustration: It is something other, a complex mingling of racial and gender hatred from without, self-hatred from within.

MacKinnon's essentialist, "color-blind" approach also distorts the analysis of rape that constitutes the heart of *Signs II*. By ignoring the voices of black female theoreticians of rape, she produces an ahistorical account that fails to capture the experience of black women.

MacKinnon sees sexuality as "a social sphere of male power of which forced sex is paradigmatic."[42] As with beauty standards, black women are victimized by rape just like white women, only more so: "Racism in the United States, by singling out Black men for allegations of rape of white women, has helped obscure the fact that it is men who rape women, disproportionately women of color."[43] In this peculiar fashion MacKinnon simultaneously recognizes and shelves racism, finally reaffirming that the divide between men and women is more fundamental and that women of color are simply "women plus." MacKinnon goes on to develop a powerful analysis of rape as the subordination of women to men, with only one more mention of color: "[R]ape comes to mean a strange (read Black) man knowing a woman does not want sex and going ahead anyway."[44]

This analysis, though rhetorically powerful, is an analysis of what rape means to white women masquerading as a general account; it has nothing to do with the experience of black women. For black women, rape is a far more complex experience, and an experience as deeply rooted in color as in gender.

For example, the paradigm experience of rape for black women has historically involved the white employer in the kitchen or bedroom as much as the strange black man in the bushes. During slavery, the sexual abuse of black women by white men was commonplace. Even after emancipation, the majority of working black women were domestic servants for white families, a job which made them uniquely vulnerable to sexual harassment and rape.

Moreover, as a legal matter, the experience of rape did not even exist for black women. During slavery, the rape of a black woman by any man, white or black, was simply not a crime.[45] Even after the Civil War, rape laws were seldom used to protect black women against either white or black men, since black women were considered promiscuous by nature. In contrast to the partial or at least formal protection white women had against sexual brutalization, black women frequently had no legal protection whatsoever. "Rape," in this sense, was something that only happened to white women; what happened to black women was simply life.

Finally, for black people, male and female, "rape" signified the terrorism of black men by white men, aided and abetted, passively (by silence) or actively (by "crying rape"), by white women. Black women have recognized this aspect of rape since the nineteenth century. For example, social activist Ida B. Wells analyzed rape as an example of the inseparability of race and gender oppression in *Southern Horrors: Lynch Law in All Its Phases,* published in 1892. Wells saw that both the law of rape and Southern miscegenation laws were part of a patriarchal system through which white men maintained their control over the bodies of all black people: "[W]hite men used their ownership of the body of the white female as a terrain on which to lynch the black male."[46] Moreover, Wells argued, though many white women encouraged interracial sexual relationships, white women, protected by the patriarchal idealization of white womanhood, were able to remain silent, unhappily or not, as black men were murdered by mobs. Similarly, Anna Julia Cooper, another nineteenth-century theorist, "saw that the manipulative power of the South was embodied in the southern patriarch, but she describes its concern with 'blood,' inheritance, and heritage in entirely female terms and as a preoccupation that was transmitted from the South to the North and perpetuated by white women."[47]

Nor has this aspect of rape become purely a historical curiosity. Susan Estrich reports that between 1930 and 1967, 89 percent of the men executed for rape in the United States were black;[48] a 1968 study of rape sentencing in Maryland showed that in all 55 cases where the death penalty was imposed the victim had been white, and that between 1960 and 1967, 47 percent of all black men convicted of criminal assaults on black women were immediately released on probation.[49] The case of Joann Little is testimony to the continuing sensitivity of black women to this aspect of rape. As Angela Davis tells the story:

Brought to trial on murder charges, the young Black woman was accused of killing a white guard in a North Carolina jail where she was the only woman inmate. When Joann Little took the stand, she told how the guard had raped her in her cell and how she had killed him in self-defense with the ice pick he had used to threaten her. Throughout the country, her cause was passionately supported by individuals and organizations in the Black community and within the young women's movement, and her acquittal was hailed as an important victory made possible by this mass campaign. In the immediate aftermath of her acquittal, Ms. Little issued several moving appeals on behalf of a Black man named Delbert Tibbs, who awaited execution in Florida because he had been falsely convicted of raping a white woman.

Many Black women answered Joann Littles appeal to support the cause of Delbert Tibbs. But few white women—and certainly few organized groups within the anti-rape movement—followed her suggestion that they agitate for the freedom of this Black man who had been blatantly victimized by Southern racism.[50]

The rift between white and black women over the issue of rape is highlighted by the contemporary feminist analyses of rape that have explicitly relied on racist ideology to minimize white women's complicity in racial terrorism.[51]

Thus, the experience of rape for black women includes not only a vulnerability to rape and a lack of legal protection radically different from that experienced by white women, but also a unique ambivalence. Black women have simultaneously acknowledged their own victimization and the victimization of black men by a system that has consistently ignored violence against women while perpetrating it against men. The complexity and depth of this experience is not captured, or even acknowledged, by MacKinnon's account.

MacKinnon's essentialist approach re-creates the paradigmatic woman in the image of the white woman, in the name of "unmodified feminism." As in the dominant discourse, black women are relegated to the margins, ignored or extolled as "just like us, only more so." But "Black women are not white women with color."[52] Moreover, feminist essentialism represents not just an insult to black women, but a broken promise—the promise to listen to women's stories, the promise of feminist method.

Discussion Questions

1. How can one vigorously pursue both "women's rights" and "African American rights" without falling into the kind of gender essentialism to which Harris objects?
2. Why, in practice, is prejudice not necessarily additive (i.e., prejudice against black women equal to prejudice against women plus prejudice against blacks)? Might there be, for instance, in certain cases, *less* prejudice against a black lesbian than against a black male heterosexual?
3. Who is right in the disagreement between MacKinnon and Harris over standards of beauty? Are black women, as MacKinnon suggests, doubly oppressed, or is their resent-

ment, as Harris suggests, specifically against white female standards of beauty?
4. What would be a fair decision in the *Martinez* case?

Notes

1. Jorge Luis Borges, Labyrinths: Selected Stories and Other Writings 59, 63–64 (D. Yates & J. Irby eds., 1964).
2. *Id.* at 64.
3. *Id.* at 65.
4. *Id.* at 66.
5. James Boyd White, When Words Lose Their Meaning 232 (1984).
6. *Id.* at 240.
7. Robert M. Cover, *Violence and the Word,* 95 Yale L. J. 1601, (1986); *see also* Robert Weisberg, *The Law-Literature Enterprise,* 1 Yale J. L. & Humanities 1, 45 (1988) (describing how students of legal interpretation are initially drawn to literary interpretation because of its greater freedom, and then almost immediately search for a way to reintroduce constraints).
8. Teresa de Lauretis, *Feminist Studies/Critical Studies: Issues, Terms, and Contexts,* in Feminist Studies/Critical Studies 1, 8 (T. de Lauretis ed., 1986).
9. Mari J. Matsuda, *When the First Quail Calls: Multiple Consciousness as Jurisprudential Method,* 11 Womens Rts. L. Rep. 7, 9 (1989).
10. *Id.* at 8.
11. *See, e.g.,* Catharine A. MacKinnon, *On Collaboration,* in Feminism Unmodified 198, 204 (1987) ("I am here to speak for those, particularly women and children, upon whose silence the law, including the law of the First Amendment, has been built") [hereinafter Feminism Unmodified].
12. Rich defines white solipsism as the tendency to "think, imagine, and speak as if whiteness described the world." Adrienne Rich, *Disloyal to Civilization: Feminism, Racism, Gynephobia, in* On Lies, Secrets, and Silence 275, 299 (1979).
13. Elizabeth V. Spelman, Inessential Woman: Problems of Exclusion in Feminist Thought 3, 4 (1988).
14. *Id.* at 159.
15. In my discussion I focus on Catharine A. MacKinnon, *Feminism, Marxism, Method, and the State: An Agenda for Theory,* 7 Signs 515 (1982) [hereinafter MacKinnon, Signs I], and Catharine A. MacKinnon, *Feminism, Marxism, Method, and the State: Toward Feminist Jurisprudence,* 8 Signs 635 (1983) [hereinafter MacKinnon, Signs II], but I make reference to the essays in MacKinnon, Feminism Unmodified, *supra* note 11, as well.

16. MacKinnon, *Desire and Power, in* Feminism Unmodified, *supra* note 11, at 46, 49.

17. *Id.* at 48.

18. MacKinnon, *Signs I, supra* note 15, at 516 (footnote omitted).

19. *Id.*

20. MacKinnon, *Desire and Power, supra* note 11, at 3.

21. *Id.* Thus, MacKinnon disagrees both with feminists who argue that women and men are really the same and should therefore be treated the same under the law, and with feminists who argue that the law should take into account women's differences. Feminists who argue that men and women are "the same" fail to take into account the unequal power relations that underlie the very construction of the two genders. Feminists who want the law to recognize the "differences" between the genders buy into the account of women's "natural difference," and therefore (inadvertently) perpetuate dominance under the name of inherent difference. *See id.* at 32–40, 71–77.

22. MacKinnon, *Signs II, supra* note 15, at 638.

23. *Id.* at 639.

24. *Id.*

25. MacKinnon, *Signs I, supra* note 15, at 523.

26. MacKinnon, *On Exceptionality: Women as Women in Law, in* Feminism Unmodified, *supra* note 11, at 70, 76.

27. MacKinnon, *Signs I, supra* note 15, at 518 & n.3.

28. *Id.* at 537 n.54.

29. MacKinnon, *supra* note 11, at 2–3.

30. MacKinnon, *Whose Culture? A Case Note on Martinez v. Santa Clara Pueblo, in* Feminism Unmodified, *supra* note 11, at 63.

31. *Santa Clara Pueblo v. Martinez,* 436 U.S. 49, 71–72 (1978).

32. MacKinnon, *Whose Culture? supra* note 30, at 66.

33. *Id.* at 68.

34. *Id.* at 67.

35. *Id.* at 68.

36. *Id.* at 69.

37. MacKinnon, *Signs I, supra* note 15, at 520 n.7.

38. *Id.* at 530. Yet, having acknowledged that black women have never been "women," MacKinnon continues in the article to discuss "women," making it plain that the "women" she is discussing are white.

39. *Id.* at 540 n.59. Similarly, in Feminism Unmodified, MacKinnon reminds us that the risk of death and mutilation in the course of a botched abortion is disproportionately borne by women of color, MacKinnon, *Not by Law Alone: From a Debate with Phyllis Schlafly, in* Feminism Unmodified, *supra* note 11, at 21, 25, but only in the context of asserting that "[n]one of us can afford this risk," *id.*

40. Toni Morrison, The Bluest Eye (1970).

41. *Id.* at 64.

42. MacKinnon, *Signs II, supra* note 15, at 646.

43. *Id.* at 646 n.22; *see also* MacKinnon, *A Rally Against Rape, in* Feminism Unmodified, *supra* note 11, at 81, 82 (black women are raped four times as often as white women); Diana Russell, Sexual Exploitation 185 (1984) (black women, who comprise 10 percent of all women, accounted for 60 percent of rapes reported in 1967).

Describing Susan Brownmiller, Against Our Will: Men, Women and Rape (1976), MacKinnon writes, "Brownmiller examines rape in riots, wars, pogroms, and revolutions; rape by police, parents, prison guards; and rape motivated by racism—seldom rape in normal circumstances, in everyday life, in ordinary relationships, by men as men." MacKinnon, *Signs II, supra* note 15, at 646.

44. MacKinnon, *Signs II, supra* note 15, at 653; *cf.* Susan Estrich, Real Rape 3 (1987) (remarking, while telling the story of her own rape, "His being black, I fear, probably makes my account more believable to some people, as it certainly did with the police."). Indeed. Estrich hastens to assure us, though, that "the most important thing is that he was a stranger." *Id.*

45. *See* Jennifer Wriggins, *Rape, Racism, and the Law,* 6 Harv. Womens L. J. 103, 118 (1983).

46. Hazel V. Carby, *"On the Threshold of Woman's Era": Lynching, Empire, and Sexuality in Black Feminist Theory, in* "Race," Writing, and Difference, 301, 309 (Henry L. Gates, Jr., ed., 1985).

47. Carby, *supra* at 306 (discussing Anna Julia Cooper, *A Voice from the South* (1892)). Carby continues:

By linking imperialism to internal colonization, Cooper thus provided black women intellectuals with the basis for an analysis of how patriarchal power establishes and sustains gendered and racialized social formations. White women were implicated in the maintenance of this wider system of oppression because they challenged only the parameters of their domestic confinement; by failing to reconstitute their class and caste interests, they reinforced the provincialism of their movement.

Id. at 306–07.

48. Estrich, *supra* note 44, at 107 n.2.

49. Wriggins, *supra* note 45, at 121 n.113. According to the study, "the average sentence received by Black men, exclusive of cases involving life imprisonment or death, was 4.2 years if the victim was Black, 16.4 years if the victim was white." *Id.* I do not know whether a white man has ever been sentenced to death for the rape of a black woman, although I could make an educated guess as to the answer.

50. Angela Davis, Women, Race, and Class 174 (1981).

51. For example, Susan Brownmiller describes the black defendants in publicized Southern rape trials as "pathetic, semiliterate fellows," Brownmiller, *supra* note 43, at 237, and the white female accusers as innocent pawns of white men, *see, e.g., id.* at 233 ("con-

fused and fearful, they fell into line"). *See also* Davis, *supra* note 50, at 196–99.

52. Barbara Omolade, *Black Women and Feminism, in* The Future of Difference 247, 248 (H. Eisenstein & A. Jardine eds., 1980).

19   Do Black Men Have a Moral Duty to Marry Black Women?

CHARLES W. MILLS

Study Questions

1. Why does Mills regard it as worthwhile to focus on the case of black men and white women?
2. How does he respond to the "racial purity" argument?
3. Why does the claimed shortage of eligible black males not yield a moral prohibition against black males marrying white females?
4. What are some of the bad motives alleged by the opponents of interracial marriage and what conclusions does Mills reach regarding them?
5. In Mills' view, what ultimately is the strongest argument against interracial marriages?

It is a measure of the continuing social distance between the races that the average white liberal, I am sure, would automatically assume that only a racist could think that the answer to this question is anything but an obvious "No!" The answer may, of course, still be "No," but it might not be quite so obvious. At any rate, I want to suggest that this issue—a major point of contention in the black community for decades, particularly among black women—is worthy of philosophical investigation. What arguments could there be for such a duty? On what axio-

logical foundation would it be based? How strong would it be?

I.

Let me begin with some brief remarks about the framing of the question itself. It is not just a particularistic variant of the general "Do all people have a duty to marry within their race?" because I think that the answer to *this* question is obviously "No." In other words, as will become clearer below, I am claiming that the differential social status of subordinated and dominant races, especially blacks and whites, generates *moral* asymmetries, so that whereas the claim, e.g., that "whites should only marry whites" *will* in general be based on philosophically uninteresting racist reasons, the case for black endogamy is (at least in some versions) more respectable.

Some other points. (i) Because of the ideological symbolism of marriage as an institution, and the material property considerations involved, this will be the special target of critics of interracial relationships. But many of the arguments against such unions would also be made (and hold as well or as badly) for common-law cohabitation, or just long-term relationships in general (or, for the most militant opponents, even short-term relationships and one-night stands). (ii) I focus on black men/white women relationships rather than also including black women/white men relationships because of another set of

Reprinted by permission of the publisher from the *Journal of Social Philosophy* 25 (1994), pp. 131–153.

asymmetries: that in a sexist society, it is the economically privileged male who usually gets to choose; that most interracial marriages *are* of the black male/white female variety; and that it is this kind which has historically stirred most controversy in the black community. (Since white men have historically had sexual access to black women, the motivations involved are usually significantly different in such cases.) (iii) Finally, it should be noted that though I have put the question in the strong, and positive, form, it is sometimes the case that what opponents really have in mind is the weaker (in the sense of ruling out less), but more pointed, *negative* injunction that black men should (above all) not marry *white* women. Other "women of color" may sometimes be deemed acceptable, or at least less unacceptable.

II.

That there could be such antipathies in the black community will come as a revelation to many whites, who will, of course, be used to thinking of the prohibitions going the other way. The famous line challenging would-be integrationists, after all, was always "But would you let one marry your daughter?" Indeed in the biracial coalitions of the civil rights movements, both communist and liberal, of the 1930s—1960s, acceptance of such relationships was often seen as a kind of ultimate test of good faith, a sign of whether or not whites had genuinely overcome their racist socialization.

This final intimacy (as the Klan warned: let 'em in the classroom and they'll end up in the bedroom) has assumed such significance because of the deep connection between racism and sex. Various theories have been put forward to explain white racism: that it is just "primordial" ethnocentrism writ large and backed by the differential technological and economic power of the European conquest (so *all* human groups would have been equally racist had they gotten the chance); the "culturalist" explanations that tie it, more specifically, to militant Christianity's *jihad* against non-European infidels and heathens, and the Manichaean white/good black/evil color symbolism in many Eu-

ropean languages, particularly English; Marxist economic explanations that see it basically as an ideological rationalization of expansionist colonial capitalism (so that a naive ethnocentrism, and admitted cultural predispositions, would easily have been *overcome* had it not been for the need to justify conquest, expropriation, and enslavement); and psycho-sexual explanations focusing on the anal and genital regions, with their powerful associations of desire and shame, and their perceived link with dirt, blackness, and the dark body. But all theories have had to come to grips—some more, some less, successfully—with the peculiar horror that black male/white female couplings have aroused in the European imagination, the fear, as in *Othello*, that "Even now . . . an old black ram/Is tupping your white ewe."[1]

In the United States in particular, there were widespread laws against what used to be (and is sometimes still) called "miscegenation," and for many of the thousands of black men lynched in the post–Civil War decades, the pretext was the accusation of raping a white woman, with prolonged torture and castration often preceding the final killing. The fact that a black man with a white wife could gain conservative support for a seat on the Supreme Court (including backing from such well-known historical champions of the black civil-rights struggle as Senator Strom Thurmond of South Carolina) is an indicator that times have somewhat changed in the intervening century.[2] But it is by no means the case that such unions are now routine, raising only the occasional eyebrow. As late as the 1960s, in deference to white sensibilities, media representations shied away from depictions of interracial sex. Even the "trail-blazing" 1967 integrationist drama *Guess Who's Coming to Dinner* did not dare to show "Super-Negro" Sidney Poitier exchanging anything more than a chaste kiss (and in the safely diminished frame of a cab's rearview mirror) with white fiancée Katharine Houghton,[3] and, as William Shatner has recently revealed in his autobiography, *Star Trek's* boast that it had the "first interracial kiss" on television was actually false, real lip contact between Captain Kirk (boldly going where no white man had gone before—on television, that is) and Uhura (Nichelle

Nichols) being avoided so as not to offend white viewers.[4] Many pornography catalogs have a specialty section of black-on-white videos where "big black studs meet blonde sluts," (How do I know this?, you casually inquire; a friend of a friend, I quickly reply), a testimony to the familiar Freudian point that revulsion and attraction often co-exist, or even merge. So for many this is truly, as some have called it, "the last taboo," and in a world where we're trying to eliminate racism, it would seem that interracial unions should be welcomed as a sign of progress.

Yet many blacks, particularly women, are hostile to such relationships. Perhaps the single most celebrated scene from Spike Lee's recent *Jungle Fever* (1991), an exploration of an interracial affair between a black man and a white woman, was the "war council" where the bereaved wife is consoled by her black women friends, and black men's alleged desire for "white pussy" is excoriated. (Anybody reading this article who has so far been completely bewildered by what I'm talking about could do worse than beginning by renting this video.[5]) Similarly, in a class on African-American Philosophy I taught this year, this question came up in discussions, and, when I decided to pose it as an essay question, was far and away the most popular topic, the majority of students arguing for "Yes." If this notion seems strange and bizarre to most liberal white philosophers, then, this simply reflects the fact that, while the black male voice is still underrepresented in the academy, the black female voice has until recently been silenced altogether. (In discussions of racism, the black man is the paradigm subject, and in discussions of sexism the white woman is the paradigm subject, so that, as one book title aptly puts it, the result is *All the Women Are White, All the Blacks Are Men*, going on defiantly to assert, however, *But Some of Us Are Brave*.[6]) This paper is, in part, an attempt to reconstruct—doubtless somewhat presumptuously—some of the possible arguments from this usually neglected perspective. So this is one for the sisters. I will go through what I take to be the most popular arguments, dealing with the weaker ones first and leaving the most interesting and challenging ones to the end.[7]

III.

1. The Racial Purification, or "Let's Get the Cream Out of the Coffee," Argument

This argument is basically consequentialist in form, and obviously wouldn't apply to couples who are not planning to have children, or to short-term relationships in general. In its classic version, the Racial Purification Argument is straightforwardly biologistic, with culture, where it is invoked, being envisaged as tied to race by hereditarian links. (Where the connection is somewhat more attenuated, this shades over into what I will distinguish as a separate argument, the Racial Solidarity Argument.) The claim here is that (i) there is such a thing as a "pure" race, (ii) racial "purity" is good, either in itself and/or as a means to other ends, such as cultural preservation and future racial achievement, and (iii) members of the race should therefore regard themselves as having a duty to foster purity, or—when it has already been vitiated—to girding up their loins to restore it.

The structure of the argument is unhappily familiar from its better-known white supremacist version, Klan or Nazi. This version will include corollary racist eugenic notions of degraded "mongrel" types produced by racial interbreeding. However, since blacks are the subordinated rather than dominant race, the boundaries here are perforce drawn so as to *include* rather than exclude those of "mixed" race (the "one-drop" rule—some "black" blood makes you black, whereas some "white" blood *doesn't* make you white). For white racists, then, the emphasis would originally have been on *maintaining* purity against black and/or Jewish "pollution" (seen—in the times when black/Jewish relations were somewhat happier than they are now—as collaborating on this joint contaminatory project: bring on those white Christian virgins!). For blacks, on the other hand, because of the myriad rapes and economically-coerced sexual transactions of slavery and post-slavery, the emphasis is usually on *restoring* a lost purity, getting rid of the "pollution" of *white* blood. Those of mixed race are counted, sometimes reluctantly, as black, but the idea is that they should try to darken their progeny. (So for light-skinned black men, the injunction is sometimes put in the stronger terms of marrying *dark* black women.)

This argument is, of course, multiply vulnerable. To be convincing, it would really have to presuppose polygenism, the heretical hypothesis that popped up repeatedly in racist thought in the 18th and 19th centuries (and was endorsed by such Enlightenment luminaries as Hume and Voltaire) that, *contra* Christian orthodoxy, there were really separate creations for the races, so that blacks and whites were different species.[8] The theology of the black version will necessarily be different (for example, the original Black Muslim claim that whites were created by the evil scientist Yacub[9]), but the logic, with the terms inverted, is the same. In a post-Darwinian framework that assumes a common humanity, it is harder to defend (which has not, of course, stopped 20th-century white racists), though of course one can, and people still do, talk about "higher" and "lower," "more" and "less" evolved, races. However, most biologists and anthropologists would today agree that there are no such things as races in the first place, so that, *a fortiori*, there cannot be "pure" races (this is, to use old-fashioned Rylean language, a kind of "category mistake"). Instead what exists are "clines," gradients of continuously-varying (i.e., *not* discretely-differentiated) phenotypical traits linked with clumpings of genetic patterns.[10] Humans share most of their genes, and, as ironists have pointed out, if you go back far enough, it turns out that we're all originally African anyway, so that even those blond-haired, blue-eyed Nordic types just happen to be grandchildren who left the continent earlier.

Moreover, even if there were natural ontological divisions between different branches of humanity, an auxiliary argument would still obviously be needed to establish why maintaining these particular configurations of genes *would* be a good thing, and such a good thing that the duty to realize it overrides other claims. Culture is not tied to genotype—the familiar point that children of different "races" would, if switched at birth, take on the cultural traits of their new home. So

the argument can only really plausibly get off the ground on the assumption, clearly racist whether in its white or black version, that moral character and/or propensity for intellectual achievement and/or aesthetic worth is genetically racially encoded, *and* of such a degree of difference that promoting it outweighs other considerations such as freedom of choice, staying with the person that you love, and so forth. (The character claim, less often made these days even by white racists [though some sociobiologists *are* now arguing for a hereditarian explanation of black crime rates], is somewhat more defensible as a basis for endogamy, since it has a moral dimension built into it. The black version will, of course, presuppose the innate evil of *whites.* The claim of differential intellectual ability, on the other hand, [more often made by whites than blacks, since the black version of the Racial Purification Argument usually credits whites with a real, if devious, intelligence] runs into the following set of objections. Suppose it were even true, which it isn't, that races are biologically discrete entities, and that members of race R2 are on average less intelligent than members of race R1. In the first place, *intra*-racial differences would still be greater than interracial differences; we would have overlapping normal distribution curves, slightly displaced from each other on the horizontal axis, with some members of R2 being *more* intelligent than some members of R1.[11] In the second place, do people, in searching for a marital partner, always require that their spouse be just as intelligent as they are? Obviously not; there can be all kinds of facets to a person that make him/her sexually attractive, with intelligence just being one of them. On the whole, human intelligence is a good thing, but why should promoting it be such an imperative as to generate overriding moral duties, especially when our inherited educational and cultural legacy, "social" intelligence, is what is really crucial in distinguishing us from our ancestors?[12]

Finally, as a fallback position, there is the defiant assertion—what Anthony Appiah calls "intrinsic racism"[13]—that one race is better than another in complete *independence* of these contestable claims about ability and character, so that it is just good *in itself* that there be more pure whites (or more pure blacks). And here one would simply point out that this is not so much an argument, as a concession that there *is* no argument.

2. The Racial Caution, or "Don't Get the White Folks Mad," Argument

Another kind of consequentialist argument involves quite different kinds of considerations, not questionable claims about racial purity but pragmatic points about strategy. This rests on the uncontroversial factual claim that, as mentioned, many, indeed the majority, of whites are disturbed and angered by such unions,[14] so that entering into them will increase white hostility and opposition to integration. (As surveys during the period of civil rights activism showed, many whites were convinced that integration of the bedroom was in fact the *main thing* on the minds of blacks who were pressing for "civil rights," so that this would just confirm their worst fears.) The principle would not, of course, be that one should avoid white anger at all costs (since the advance of the black liberation struggle will *necessarily* anger some whites, and this would certainly not be a moral reason for abandoning it). Rather, the idea would be that black-on-white relationships *unnecessarily* infuriate whites. So since such unions stir up great passion, and are not a necessary component of the struggle, they should be eschewed. (Some versions might then leave it open for them to be permissible in the future non-racist society, or at least when racism has considerably diminished.)

This argument is obviously somewhat more respectable. It does, however, rest on the assumption that either no point of moral principle is involved, or that breach of the principle is justified by the overwhelmingly negative consequences for achieving black liberation of stirring such passions. The reply to the first might take the anti-utilitarian, let-the-heavens-fall line that individual rights to choice trump such considerations, and that if two people love one another, they should

not forsake their relationship for the sake of expediting a cause. (Or, less nobly, it might just take the in-your-face form of the joys of *épater*-ing Whitey.) It could also be argued that such an approach panders to racism, and as such is immoral in its failure to confront it, since asserting full black personhood means exercising all the rights white persons have. Alternatively, on the second point (that any such principle is in this case overridden by likely negative repercussions), it might be conceded that a greater good sometimes requires restraint, discretion, and so forth, but denied that at this particular time, the consequences are likely to be so horrendous (so the viability of the argument may be in part conjunctural, depending on the situation, e.g., 1920s Mississippi vs. 1990s New York). Or it might be claimed that those who will be infuriated by "miscegenation" will be infuriated by the civil rights struggle *anyway,* so that it is not clear that there is a discrete differential increment of outrage which can be placed in the consequentialist balance pan, or maybe it's not clear how big it will be. (And it could be argued that the allegations of interracial sex will be made whether it's taking place or not.) Nevertheless, I think it is clear that this argument, unlike the first, does have something to be said for it, though there could be debate over how much. Note that here, of course, it will be the negative prohibition ("stay away from white women!") rather than the positive duty that is involved.

3. The Racial Solidarity, or "No Sleeping with the Enemy," Argument

This argument usually accompanies, or is actually conflated with, the Racial Purification Argument, but it's obviously conceptually distinct, if for no other reason than that it can be addressed to couples who don't plan to have children, or to those in short-term relationships. Both consequentialist and deontological versions are possible, cast in terms of the imperative to promote black liberation (and the putatively inhibitory effect of such unions on this project) or one's general duty to the race (to be elaborated on later). Note that because of the *defensibility* of this consequential-ist goal, the black version of the Racial Solidarity Argument is not as immediately and clearly flawed as the corresponding white version, with the goal of preserving white *supremacy,* would be.

Let me run through the important variants, moving, as before, from less to more plausible. To begin with, there are those resting on straight-forwardly racist *innatist* theses, whether in theo-logical guise (whites as "blue-eyed devils"—the reactive black counterpart to the traditional claim that blacks are descendants of Ham's accursed son Canaan) or pseudo-scientific guise (whites as biologically evil "ice people" damned by melanin deficiency—the reactive black counterpart[15] to the post-Darwinian "scientific racism" of the late 19th–early 20th centuries). So the idea is that all whites are intrinsically evil, not to be associated with except out of necessity (e.g., in the work-place), and certainly not to be sought out as sex-ual partners. They are collectively, racially re-sponsible for the enslavement of blacks (the thesis of innate evil implies that though *these* whites are not literally responsible, they would have acted just the same had they been around at the time), so that willingly sleeping with them is like Jews voluntarily sleeping with Nazis. Both for the con-sequences and for the preservation of one's moral character, then, one has a duty not to enter inter-racial relationships.

Since moral character and responsibility are *not* genetically encoded in this way (even the claims of sociobiologists wouldn't stretch to this kind of reasoning), this variant is easily dismiss-able. The more interesting version need not make any such fantastic assumptions. The argu-ment here readily, or maybe grudgingly, admits that whites are just humans like all of us, born as fairly plastic entities who will both be shaped by, and in turn shape, a particular socio-cultural environment. But it will be pointed out that their socialization in a white-supremacist soci-ety makes them ineluctably beneficiaries and perpetrators of the system of oppression respon-sible for keeping blacks down, so that they are all, or mostly (claims of differing strength can be made), the enemy, whether through active

policy or passive complicity. Even if they seem to show good faith, the entering of a social "whiteness" into their personal identity means that they will never, or only very rarely (again, claims of differing strength can be made), be able to overcome their conditioning: sooner or later, their "true colors" are going to come out. If nothing else, because of the numerous affec-tive and cognitive ties—family, friendship, cul-tural attachment—that link them to this white world, and help to constitute their being, they will naturally be less sensitive to its racist char-acter, and more reluctant to confront the radical changes that have to be made to bring about a truly just society.

In the absence of hypotheses about innate evil, the deontological version gets less of a foothold (though argument on page 171 can be seen as partially falling under this category), and the consequentialist version is the one which would have to be run. The idea would be that, given these empirical claims, blacks in such unions are likely to find their efforts to attack white supremacy subtly (maybe even uncon-sciously) resisted and diverted, so that the long-term consequences will be to compromise black struggles. Since it is often the more successful black men (prominent black businessmen, lawyers, entertainers, intellectuals) who marry white women, such unions usually lead to a de-parture from the black world of the elite who (at least on some theories) are precisely the most potentially threatening to the status quo, and their entry into an immensely seductive white world of wealth, comfort and glamour where black problems, e.g., the misery of the inner cities, will gradually seem more and more re-mote. (This inflection of the argument makes the class dimension of black oppression particularly salient. It has traditionally been claimed that blacks have a general duty to "uplift the race," and it is sometimes pointed out in addition that by marrying a white woman, the economic and status resources of the successful black male [material and cultural/symbolic capital] are likely to be removed from the black commu-nity.) Without even realizing it, and through familiar processes of self-deception and motivated inattention, one will gradually "sell out" to the white establishment.

Unlike the innatist version, with its dubious biology, or biotheology, this version has the merits of being more in touch with social reality, and indeed of telling a not-implausible psychological tale. One response is the blunt *denial* that blacks should regard themselves as having any particular duty to combat white supremacy, the individualist every-man-for-himself solution, though this will, of course, rarely be said out loud (as against secretly practiced). A more defensible approach might be to accept the existence of this duty while simultaneously arguing, as some contemporary ethicists have done, for a *restricted* role for consequentialist moral demands.[16] So the idea would be that of course you do have *some* free-floating obligation to resist racism, but this can't be a full-time job invading every aspect of one's life, and unless one's white wife is actually a Klan member or a Nazi (obviously somewhat unlikely), one's personal life is one's own business. (Often this is accompanied by the universalist/humanist claim that in the end, color doesn't matter, we're all just human beings, and so forth.)

Another tack would be to challenge the crucial empirical premise that whites cannot *ever* purge themselves of a whiteness committed to racial supremacy (or the weaker version that their doing so is rare enough that the injunction is warranted on Bayesian grounds). It would be pointed out that people can resist and overcome their socialization, proving by their deeds that they are committed to eradicating racism. For those white women who are naive about the pervasiveness of racism, even among their own family and friends, embarking on an interracial relationship may actually have a salutary cognitive effect, the latter's hostile response awakening her to realities to which she would otherwise have been blind. An abstract opposition to racism might then assume a more visceral force, so that the net result would be a gain for the forces of anti-racism. Once the innatist framework has been abandoned, the biological link between race and character severed, and the Racial Solidarity Argument put on the

consequentialist foundation of ending white supremacy, there is the danger (for its proponents) of the argument being turned on its head. Since not all *black* women will automatically be activist foes of racism (they may have succumbed to racist socialization, or, like the vast majority of human beings, just be trying to get along without heavy-duty political commitments), the question of which spouse will be of more assistance in fighting racism might then come down to simple empirical questions, rather than *a priori* assumptions. If other kinds of arguments are excluded, the foe of interracial marriages would then have to show why, in each case, the overall outcome is likely to be a debit for the anti-racism struggle. (For short-term relationships and one-night stands, neither side will be able to make much of a case for long-term consequentialist repercussions, so—if the premises are not innatist ones—the argument will usually shift to more symbolic issues, as discussed in #6, on page 171.)

4. The Racial Demographics, or "Where Are All the Black Men?," Argument

The Racial Demographics Argument is interesting because, of those we have looked at so far, it is least tied to the explicit political project of fighting white racism, with its accompanying ideological assumptions. This argument simply points to the relatively uncontroversial statistical fact that, because of the disproportionate numbers of black men in jail, unemployed, or dead at an early age (which may or may not be attributed to white racism), there is a significant imbalance of females to "marriageable" black males.[17] ("Marriageable" may itself, of course, seem to have classist overtones, and it is true that this complaint comes most often from middle-class, or upwardly-mobile, black women,[18] but the problem is more general.) William Julius Wilson is famous for his claim that this putative shortage is in part responsible for the perpetuation of the underclass, since single black women of poorer backgrounds will then fall into poverty if they have children.[19] (Some left critics have accused Wilson of sexism on this point, arguing that the real political demand should be for women to get what is now reserved as a "male" wage.) The traditional race/gender status hierarchy in the United States is structured basically as: white men, white women, black men, black women. Because of this low prestige, black women have not generally been sought out as *respectable* partners (as against concubines, mistresses, prostitutes) by white men and men of other races. So if eligible black men differentially seek non-black, particularly white, women, then things will be made even worse for black women, who will then have been rejected both by their own men and the men of other races.[20]

If black men therefore have a duty arising out of this fact, what would its foundation be? Since we are considering arguments in isolation from one another, we need to differentiate this conceptually from the Racial Solidarity Argument as such, though it can obviously be seen in terms of racial solidarity. The argument would not be the *general* one, corollary of #3, to "sleep with the friend," but the claim that in *these* contingent circumstances black men have such a duty. This could be defended in deontological or utilitarian terms, i.e., as a remediable unhappiness which imposes some sort of obligation on us to relieve it. (So this, unlike the previous three arguments, does require more than just *not* marrying white women.)

How plausible is this? Note, to begin with that, as mentioned, no questionable racist claims about whites' innate characters are being made, so it is not vulnerable on that score. But one obviously unhappy feature it has is that, as a putative duty, it seems to be naturally assimilable to duties of *charity*, i.e., the standing obligations most moral theorists think we have (and invested with greater or lesser degrees of stringency) to relieve distress, e.g., through giving to the homeless, to Third World famine relief, and so forth. Isn't it insulting to the person to think that sexual relationships, or marriages, should be generally entered into on these grounds? How would one react to the declaration, or inadvertent discovery, that one had been sought out as a *charitable* obligation? (The argument for endogamous marriage on the

grounds of black self-respect is different, and will be discussed later.) So this seems a bit problematic from the start. There is also the question of how strong this putative obligation is supposed to be. For Kant and most other deontologists, charity is an "imperfect" duty, compliance with which leaves considerable latitude for choice (timing, beneficiary, extent of commitment, and so forth). In the case of something so central to one's life-plans as a choice of partner, rights of individual autonomy and personal freedom would easily override an alleged charitable claim of this sort. Utilitarianism is in general, of course, more demanding, with—depending on the variety—less or no room for what are sometimes called agent-relative "options," if welfare can be maximized through the policy in question. In this case, then, strategies of response would have to defend (non-black) commonsense morality against utilitarianism's demands, or make a case that such a policy, if taken seriously, would be more likely to promote net *un*happiness (through the constraints on the freedoms of black men, and the demeaning knowledge or uncertainty in the minds of black women as to why they had really been chosen). Nevertheless, it is clearly possible that some opponents of interracial marriage would be prepared to bite the bullet and insist on such a duty, arguing perhaps that the situation of black women is now so dire as to easily *outweigh* black male unhappiness at restriction of choice, and that as an entry in the welfare calculus, this unhappiness is not to be taken too seriously anyway, since it is likely, or necessarily, the result of a brainwashed preference for white women, and could be removed with a Brandtian "cognitive psychotherapy."[21] So this argument could be reinforced with considerations we shall look at later.

5. The Tragic Mulattos-to-be, or "Burden on the Children," Argument

Another possible consequentialist argument is that the mixed racial and presumably (though not necessarily) cultural legacy of such unions will impose a differential burden on children of such households, who will be caught between two worlds and fully accepted by neither. This argument is often put forward hypocritically, with the actually-motivating considerations being along the lines of #1–4. Nevertheless, it should obviously still be examined.

To begin with, of course, it only gets off the ground if the couple *do* plan to have children. It could also be argued that it presupposes the continuation of racist attitudes, and that in a non-racist world such children would be completely accepted by both sides of the family. However, since there does not seem to be much likelihood of such a world coming into existence in the near future, this objection could not plausibly carry much weight.

(I have encountered an interesting inversion of this argument, put forward perhaps only semi-seriously, that could be termed the Racial Elimination, or "Browning of the World," Argument. The thesis is that if the bottom line is indeed fighting white racism, and/or racism in general, then interracial unions are not merely morally *permissible,* but *desirable,* to be positively encouraged as a long-term strategy for eliminating racism by making everybody some shade of brown. Unfortunately, I think this underestimates human ingenuity in finding differences upon which to erect comparative aesthetic, moral, and intellectual claims. For many decades after the 19th-century abolition of slavery in the Americas, there were elaborate color hierarchies in the black communities in the United States, the Caribbean, and South America, structured according to one's shade and presumed degree of "white" blood, e.g., octoroon, quadroon, mulatto, Negro, and these persist today in a continuing preference in the West for light-skinned blacks.[22] Even if [which seems genetically impossible, given the normal human variation even in the children of *one* set of parents] all of us were to become a uniform brown, there would still be differences in hair texture and facial features which could be traced back to differential racial ancestry, and which could be used as grounds for discriminatory sorting. In general, I would suggest that the notion that mere somatic difference is the suffi-cient, or major, cause of racism is historically and anthropologically naive. I am sympathetic to the general left position that if politico-economic differences require "racial" differentiation, then the categorization will be generated accordingly even if people are much closer somatically than they currently are. It's worth remembering that in 19th-century Europe, the white working class was sometimes thought of as a separate "race." Where there's a political will, it could be said, there's a conceptual way.)

But back to the burden on the children. One obvious reply would be that some parents-to-be will be able to speak with authority about the non-racist character of their side of the family. But what about those who can't? And even those who do sincerely give such assurances about others' feelings may, of course, be self-deceived, or even deceived by their relatives (whether through disingenuousness, and the fact that racism is no longer respectable, or by normal human self-opacity, and the genuine non-awareness of one's actual gut responses when faced with a flesh-and-blood "mixed" grandson or niece). The way to argue around this might be to insist that extra-loving parental care can make up for any family hostility. However, there is also the set of problems the child will face in the larger society, e.g., growing up in a school and neighborhood environment where racial polarization may lead to partial ostracism by other children of both races. So I think that this does raise genuine concerns, and even if they are outweighed by other factors, they should be given their due. (A magazine called *Interrace* addresses these and other problems of interracial couples.)

6. The Questionable Racial Motivations, or "Maybe You Can Fool That Stupid White Bitch, Nigger, and Maybe You Can Fool Yourself, but You're Not Fooling Anybody Else," Argument

I have left to the last what I consider to be the most interesting argument, or set of arguments. This is the claim that black men who enter such unions, particularly with white women (as against women of other races), are either always, or usually (the claim can be made with differing strengths), motivated by questionable considerations. The argument tends to be deontological in form, the presumption being that some set of normative criteria can be imposed to assess the appropriate motivations for entering a marriage—these days, basically revolving around romantic love—and that, absent these motives, and/or present some other set, the decision to marry is wrong. Since motivation is unlikely ever to be pure, and we are not completely, or at all, self-transparent anyway, one might have to talk about the *preponderance,* and the *likelihood,* of certain kinds of motivations. In addition, there is the separate moral issue of the woman's awareness or non-awareness of the nature of the motivation. Thus one would have to distinguish cases of ignorance and deception, where the white woman doesn't know what is really driving her male spouse-to-be, from cases where both parties know what's going on. (In other kinds of non-romantic marriages, for example marriages of convenience for immigration reasons, or the standard pragmatic tradings of financial security for youthful beauty, both parties often know the score, so that if these unions are wrong, it is not because of *deception.*)

Now obviously interracial marriages have no monopoly on questionable motivations, but the claim of opponents would be that they are *more* likely to be present (or, more strongly, *always* present) in such unions. What is the basis of this claim? The argument is that because of the central historic structuring of the American polity by white racism,[23] the psychology of both whites and blacks has been negatively affected, and that this has ramifications for human sexuality. (Or, as initially mentioned, there is the more radically foundational claim that sex is in fact at the root of racism in the *first* place, so the whole thing *starts* there.) In a patriarchal society, sexuality is distorted by sexism as well as racism, so that male sexuality characteristically involves the notion of conquest, sexual competition, and a proving of one's manhood by securing the woman, or the

series of women, more highly ranked in the established hierarchy of desirability. But *white women* will in general represent the female somatic ideal in our society: they are preeminently the beauty queens, fashion models, movie goddesses, magazine centerfolds, porn stars, whose images are displayed from a billion magazine covers, billboards, television screens, videos, and movie theaters.[24] Black males will inevitably be influenced by this, so that a wide range of potentially questionable motivations is generated:

   (i) sexual exoticism and forbidden fruit-picking,
  (ii) racial revenge,
 (iii) racially-differentiated aesthetic attraction, and
 (iv) racial status-seeking and personhood by proxy.

(i) Sexual exoticism *per se*—the lure of the different—obviously has no intrinsic connection to black and white relations, and indeed need not involve *racial* difference at all, being felt across cultural, ethnic, and class lines. Moreover, on its own it would not really seem to raise any moral problems; people are sexually attracted to each other for all kinds of reasons, and if the strangeness of the Other is what is turning them on, there seems no harm in this—whatever gets you through the night, and so forth. The real concern here would be the prudential one that this is unlikely to prove a reliable foundation for a long-term relationship or marriage, exoticism rapidly being demystified in the quotidian domestic irritations of house-cleaning manias and toilet seats left up. It is really the coincidence of the exotic with the black-white racial taboo, the fact that this strange fruit is *forbidden,* that gives rise to what Spike Lee calls "jungle fever." But again, assuming a liberal view of sexuality, which would deny the legitimacy of such taboos, and taking for granted that both parties know what's going on, no moral, as against prudential, questions would really seem to be raised. I think when people advance this as a moral argument they are either unconsciously conflating it with one or more of the *other* possibilities ([ii] to [iv]), which we'll examine separately, or assuming that one party, e.g., the white woman, doesn't realize the real source of her appeal. So insofar as this is a successful moral argument, it would really just be subsumable under the general proscription against deceit in interpersonal relationships, perhaps with the added *a priori* reminder that, given people's capacity for self-deception, black men are not likely to be willing to face the fact that this *is* really what's driving them (a point we'll encounter again). For (i), then, if there is a duty, it is derivable, given certain empirical assumptions, from the conventional set of duties to the other person, which can be founded either on welfare or Kantian grounds.

(ii) By contrast, racial revenge as a motivation is clearly and uncontroversially immoral. The idea here (though this will not usually be said out loud, or at least within earshot of whites) is that marriage to, or sometimes just sex with, a white woman (or, better, *many* white women), is an appropriate form of revenge, conscious or unconscious, upon white men. This is linked, obviously, to acceptance of a sexist framework in which male combat, here interracial, takes place in part across the terrain of the female body, so that masculinity and honor are fused with ability to appropriate the woman. Sex with the enemy's woman then becomes a symbolic retribution both specific—for the thousands of rapes and other sexual abuses visited upon black women over the hundreds of years of slavery and its aftermath, which black men were in general powerless to stop—and general—for the systematic humiliations of the denial to black men of their manhood in a society created by white men. Obviously black men who enter unions with white women for such purposes are just using them.

(iii), (iv) I will discuss these together since, though the details are different, the root issue is arguably the same. Thus far the duty, insofar as it exists, has been easily derivable from standard prohibitions against deceiving and using others. These final two subsets of allegedly questionable motives are to my mind the most interesting because they raise the possibility of duties to oneself and/or duties to the race.

First, the aesthetic question. As pointed out, in this country the white woman has traditionally represented the somatic norm of beauty.[25] It's true this has recently begun to expand somewhat, with black Miss Americas (including one chosen just this year, 1993), and some preference in the fashion industry for "ethnic" models. But the first black Miss America, 1983 queen (though later deposed) Vanessa Williams, was so fair-skinned that the Congress of Racial Equality refused to recognize her as black, and the black models used in MTV videos will usually be light-skinned, Caucasoid blacks. White or light skin, long non-kinky hair, "fine" noses and narrow non-everted lips remain the norm, and as such are difficult or impossible to achieve without artificial assistance for black women of non-mixed heritage: hence the long-established cosmetic industry in the black community of skin bleaches, hair straighteners, wigs and hair extensions, and more recently (for those who can afford it) chemical peels, dermabrasion and plastic surgery. The argument is, then, that in choosing to marry white women, black men are admitting by this deed their acceptance of a white racist stereotype of beauty, and rejecting their own race. (Obviously there is a feminist, and indeed even more general humanist, argument that stereotypical physical attractiveness should not be the major criterion for marriageability *anyway*, but I am not endorsing these norms but merely outlining their logic. This *is* in fact what motivates most men, and pending the advent of a utopia where physical appearance becomes unimportant, to be systematically disadvantaged by race seems unfair. In other words, I am assuming, though I will not try to show this, that this racial dimension inflicts an *additional* unfairness on top of the normal genetic lottery by which, within a race, "plain" or "ugly" people are socially disadvantaged through not meeting *intra*-racial standards of attractiveness.)

The other set of motives is conceptually distinct, though in practice it will usually go with the aesthetic set, and the ultimate source of both is arguably the same.[26] This is the project of achieving social status through one's white wife. White women are then a kind of prize who can both affirm one's self-esteem, and help to provide an entree (at least in liberal circles) to the still largely white world of status and power of the upper echelons of society. Bluntly, a white woman on your arm shows that you have made it. As such, this is separate from the aesthetic argument, since the idea would be that even a white woman plain by conventional white standards of attractiveness will still provide the aura of social prestige radiating from white-skin privilege. Indeed, one of the arguments that black women who object to such unions frequently use is that black men go out or end up with white women whom they would never consider if they were black and of the same comparative degree of attractiveness (assuming that some kind of interracial translation of such measurements is possible, i.e., a 6 on a white 10-point scale becoming an equivalent 6 on a black 10-point scale, somehow relativized to different phenotype). Under these circumstances in particular, the claim will be made that "it's only because she's white" that the black man is going out with her.

The more radical version of this accusation is that one is actually trying to achieve some kind of derivative personhood, personhood by proxy, in such marriages, insofar as black personhood is systematically denied in a racist society and the black man is likely to have internalized this judgment. (Personhood and status are linked, but separate, since obviously whites can have the former while still wanting to increase their ranking by some metric of the latter, e.g., through climbing the corporate hierarchy.)

For both these sets of motivations, then, duties would arise *in addition* to the obvious ones of not using the white partner. (The latter set of duties is still pertinent since, while people don't usually object to having been chosen at least in part on the basis of their looks, they would presumably *not* want to be chosen merely on the basis of being an abstract representative of an instrumental whiteness.) And these could perhaps be construed as duties to *oneself,* or duties to the *race* (or perhaps this could be collapsed into duties to oneself *insofar as* one is a member of the race, a subset of the more general duties we have to ourselves as humans). In modern moral theory, the notion of duties to oneself is found most famously, of course, in Kant. His idea was that in general we owe respect to all persons, a respect generating duties of differing degrees of stringency, and since we are persons ourselves, this means we have duties to *our*selves (so that certain actions are wrong because we are *using* that self). The idea has been judged problematic by most contemporary philosophers, but some, for example, Thomas Hill, Jr., think that it is in fact a defensible and fruitful way of explicating the internal moral logic of the notion of self-respect.[27] So respecting ourselves precludes acting out of certain kinds of motivation. Applying this to the case of interracial marriage for reasons of types (iii) and (iv), then, the implication is that *even if the white woman is fully aware of, and has no problem with, the black man's motivation,* such marriage would be wrong because it endorses a racist set of values and as such implies a lack of respect for oneself and one's own race.

I think that, though the other arguments I have discussed are also employed, and taken seriously, this really captures the essential objection that many black women have to interracial relationships. And it coheres nicely with the interpretation of racism as an ideology which, in anti-Kantian fashion, systematically *denies* full personhood to certain groups of humans—in effect, the whole race is thought of as sub-persons, *Untermenschen.* The Jamaican activist Marcus Garvey, one of the most famous black leaders of the twentieth century, is celebrated for his insight that white supremacy had left blacks as "a race without respect," and correspondingly the notion of "dissin'" someone, so central to black popular culture, is arguably a recognition, on the level of folk wisdom, of the danger of this diminished moral standing.[28]

Could this then be seen as a friendly amendment to Kant? (I really mean "Kantianism" rather than Kant; in general Kant's own views on sexuality can't be taken seriously.) The immediate obstacle is that race is part of the phenomenal self deemed morally irrelevant, so how could we have duties to ourself based on racial membership? Or how could we have duties to the race that are differentiated from duties to abstract noumenal (and hence raceless) persons? But I think this objection can be finessed in the following way. The claim is not that, *because* we're black (or white, or any other race) we're *differentially* deserving of respect; this would indeed be inconsistent with Kantian principles, presupposing hierarchy rather than equality of value for different persons. So the argument is not that race does enter at the noumenal level. The claim is rather that the historic legacy of white racism has been a social ontology in which race has *not* been abstracted from, but used as an indicator of one's personhood, so that those with a certain "phenomenal" phenotype have been seen as less than human and so undeserving of full (or any) respect. *Resistance* to this legacy therefore requires that one affirm one can be *both* black and a person, that the phenomenal does not correlate with a sub-par noumenal self. Retreat into typical philosophical abstraction ("we're all human— race doesn't matter") evades confronting this, since the terms on which humanity will have been defined will be *white* ones. So the "person" is tacitly constructed as white in the first place, which is why this hidden moral architecture, this colorlessness which is really colored white, has to be exposed to the light. Because of black socialization into this system of values, the fact is that marriage to a white woman *will* often be based on the continuing, if not consciously acknowledged, submission to this racist social ontology, and when it is, *will* imply lack of racial self-respect, respect for one's race (as all other races) as equally entitled to take the full status of

personhood. It is, finally, I believe, something like this moral perception which, even if not always clearly articulated, underlies many black women's intuition that there is often something questionable about these relationships.

But what—the obvious reply will be—if one is quite sure, or as sure as one can be about anything, that one is *not* marrying for such motivations? Here, the opponent of interracial marriages has at least two interesting fallback positions (as distinct, that is, from any of the other arguments previously discussed). First, what the critic may do is introduce an auxiliary *epistemic* thesis (our knowledge of our motivation) as distinct from the *substantive* thesis itself (what our motivation is). The argument would then be that, though in some cases (a minority) black men's motivation might be pure, the combined effects of standard human self-opacity and the cognitive interference produced in these particular circumstances by the strong motivations for self-deception (who will want to admit to himself he's really trying to whiten his being?), mean that they can never *know* that it is pure, so the safest thing to do is to eschew such unions. If this fails, then there is, secondly, the ultimate fallback position of re-introducing a consequentialist framework to argue that even if (a) one's motivation is pure, *and* (b) one knows one's motivation is pure, there is always (c) the fact that, whatever one's motivation, one will be *perceived* by other blacks as having married out of racial self-contempt, thus reinforcing white superiority. And this (as one of my black female students coldly informed me when I was trying to defend a liberal position on the issue) will be "a slap in the face of black women everywhere." So the bottom line for critics is that one's actions will be perceived as being motivated by these self-despising beliefs, and— especially if one is a prominent black figure of high status, with a correspondingly enhanced range of racial spousal selection—this action will be sending a message to the world that, once you *do* have this option to choose: *black women just ain't good enough.*

IV.

I have no neat, wrap-up conclusion to offer, since I think the issue is a complicated one about which a lot more could be said. Rather, my basic aim has been to demonstrate this complexity, and, as a corollary, to show the mistakenness of the knee-jerk white liberal (or, for that matter, black liberal) response that no defensible case could possibly be made for the existence of such a duty. Some of the arguments *are* obviously weak (e.g., #1), but others are stronger, though they may be of conjunctural strength (e.g., #2), involve empirical and normative claims which may or may not hold true (#3, 4, 5), or rest on speculative claims about motivation which are hard to disprove, with a consequentialist fallback line which may seem illegitimately to hold us hostage to others' perceptions (#6). Whether singly or in combination (to the extent that this is possible, bearing in mind that *different* normative frameworks have sometimes been used) they do yield at least a presumptive duty I will leave, perhaps somewhat evasively, for the reader to decide, and if so what kind of a duty it is. At the very least I think I have shown that—using conventional moral theories, and without making racist assumptions about whites, or even appealing to any controversial separatist ideology—an interesting case can in fact be built for a position quite widespread in the "common-sense morality" of the black community.

One common, misguided white liberal reaction to racism has been to move from the anthropological premise that "race" (in the biological sense) doesn't exist, to the conclusion that "race" (in the social sense) doesn't exist either, so that the solution is to proclaim an (ostensibly) colorless universalism in which we pay no attention to race. Sometimes this is expressed in the claim that race is "constructed" (true enough) and therefore unreal. But neither conclusion follows (try walking through the next constructed brick wall you encounter). As Aristotle pointed out long ago, treating people equally doesn't necessarily mean treating them the same, and one could argue analogously that genuine race-neutrality actually requires not *blindness* to race but close attention to

the difference race makes. The subtleties of unraveling and re-weaving conventional morality in a white-supremacist society gradually transforming itself have only just begun to be worked on by philosophers. If discussions such as this one have rarely, if ever, graced the pages of philosophy journals, this is arguably a consequence not of the unimportance of such debates but of the demographics of the profession, and the absence of voices speaking from the day-to-day lives and concerns of a significant sector of the population. We can expect that, with the demographic "browning" of America that is under way, leading to a minority white population some time late in the next century, and perhaps even (dare one hope . . . ?) some more non-white faces around APA meetings, such issues will increasingly begin to appear in these formerly cloistered white pages.

Acknowledgment

I would like to acknowledge the support of the Institute for the Humanities, University of Illinois at Chicago.

Discussion Questions

1. Doesn't the argument that, in intermarrying, a black man is showing a lack of respect for himself and his race apply to *all* interracial unions?
2. In his discussion of "sleeping with the enemy," Mills concludes that the question of what kind of wife would best serve the anti-racism cause should be decided on an individual basis (rather than by a blanket exclusion of whites). How would a black nationalist like Garvey reply?
3. Must the act of a black man marrying a white woman display a lack of due regard for his race, *regardless* of that individual's motives or intentions?
4. Isn't it enough to say that people should marry only for love and compatibility?
5. If it is wrong for black men to marry white women, is it also wrong for them to have ca-

sual sex with them—i.e., more wrong than it would be for them to have casual sex with black women?

Notes

1. For discussions of racism in general, and racism and sex in particular, see, for example: Winthrop D. Jordan, *White Over Black: American Attitudes Toward the Negro, 1550–1812* (1968; rpt. New York and London: W. W. Norton, 1977); St. Clair Drake, *Black Folk Here and There,* vol. I (Los Angeles: Center for Afro-American Studies, UCLA, 1987); John D'Emilio and Estelle B. Freedman, *Intimate Matters: A History of Sexuality in America* (New York: Harper & Row, 1988), chapter five; Calvin C. Hernton, *Sex and Racism in America* (1966; rpt. New York: Grove Press, 1988).

2. As Judge A. Leon Higginbotham, Jr. sardonically pointed out to Clarence Thomas, admonishing him for his cavalier disparagement of the work of civil rights activists, had it not been for their efforts, "if you and your present wife decided that you wanted to reside in Virginia [their present home], you would . . . have been violating the Racial Integrity Act of 1924, which the Virginia Supreme Court as late as 1966 said was consistent with the federal Constitution because of the overriding state interest in the institution of marriage. . . . [Y]ou could have been in the penitentiary today rather than serving as an Associate Justice of the United States Supreme Court." "An Open Letter to Justice Clarence Thomas from a Federal Judicial Colleague," *University of Pennsylvania Law Review,* 140 (1992); reprinted in Toni Morrison, ed., *Race-ing Justice, En-gendering Power: Essays on Anita Hill, Clarence Thomas, and the Construction of Social Reality* (New York: Pantheon Books, 1992), pp. 24–25.

3. For changing (and unchanging) depictions of blacks in United States cinema, see Donald Bogle, *Toms, Coons, Mulattoes, Mammies & Bucks: An Interpretive History of Blacks in American Films* (New York: Viking Press, 1973).

4. William Shatner, with Chris Kreski, *Star Trek Memories* (New York: HarperCollins Publishers, 1993). Nichols disgustedly describes the backstage drama: "[The network suits were] telling me that the kiss would make the show impossible to air. . . . I mean, they even went so far as to suggest changing the scene so that Kirk gets paired off with Nurse Chapel and Spock ends up with me. Somehow, I guess, they found it more acceptable for a Vulcan to kiss me, for this alien to kiss this black woman, than for two humans with different coloring to do the same thing." *Star Trek Memories,* pp. 284–285. The network arranged for the scene to be shot twice, the first take showing actual lip contact, the second take positioning the camera behind Shatner's back at the crucial moment, so that an actual kiss did not have to be shown—and did not in fact occur. The second take was the one eventually aired.

5. For an interesting discussion, see also the *Newsweek* cover story (June 10, 1991) on the movie, "Tackling a Taboo."

6. Gloria T. Hull, Patricia Bell Scott, and Barbara Smith, eds., *All the Women Are White, All the Blacks Are Men, but Some of Us Are Brave: Black Women's Studies* (Old Westbury, New York: The Feminist Press, 1982).

7. I should record here the fact that I have greatly benefited from exposure to, even when I have not always agreed with, the arguments put forward by my students in classroom discussion and essays submitted in the "African-American Philosophy" course I taught in Spring 1993.

8. For a discussion, see, for example, Stephen Jay Gould, *The Mismeasure of Man* (New York and London: W. W. Norton, 1981).

9. See, for example, chapter 10, "Satan," of *The Autobiography of Malcolm X,* as told to Alex Haley, (1965; rpt. New York: Ballantine Books, 1973).

10. "There are no races, there are only clines." Frank B. Livingstone, "On the Nonexistence of Human Races" (1962); rpt. in Sandra Harding, ed., *The "Racial" Economy of Science: Toward a Democratic Future* (Bloomington and Indianapolis: Indiana University Press, 1993).

11. The more radical objection made by some theorists is that the whole idea of quantifying intellectual ability as a single reified number, and then ranking people on a unilinear scale, is inherently incoherent: again, see Gould, *The Mismeasure of Man.* This is sometimes summed up in the *bon mot* that the only thing IQ tests measure is the ability to do well on IQ tests.

12. I have benefited here from Joyce Trebilcot's argument opposing sex roles: "Sex Roles: The Argument from Nature," *Ethics,* 85 (April 1975); rpt. in Garry Brodsky, John Troyer, and David Vance, eds., *Contemporary Readings in Social and Political Ethics* (Buffalo, New York: Prometheus Books, 1984).

13. Kwame Anthony Appiah, *In My Father's House: Africa in the Philosophy of Culture* (New York and Oxford: Oxford University Press, 1992), pp. 13–15.

14. As late as 1978, a national survey showed that "70% of whites . . . rejected interracial marriage on principle": cited in Douglas S. Massey and Nancy A. Denton, *American Apartheid: Segregation and the Making of the Underclass* (Cambridge, Mass.: Harvard University Press, 1993), p. 95.

15. Though contemporary "melanin theory" is indigenous to the black community, the notion of "sun

people" and "ice people" actually comes from the white Canadian author Michael Bradley's *The Iceman Inheritance: Prehistoric Sources of Western Man's Racism, Sexism, and Aggression* (New York: Kayode, 1978).

16. See, for example, Samuel Scheffler, *Human Morality* (New York: Oxford University Press, 1992).

17. Black unemployment rates in recent decades have been at least twice as high as white unemployment rates, and for the category of young black men in the inner cities the rate approaches catastrophic proportions. Another tragic figure frequently cited is the 1990 study that showed that, on any given day in 1989, nearly 1 in 4 black men from the ages of 20 to 29 were either in prison, on parole, or on probation. The leading cause of death for black men 15–34 is homicide. For some of these frightening statistics, see William Julius Wilson, *The Truly Disadvantaged: The Inner City, the Underclass, and Public Policy* (Chicago and London: The University of Chicago Press, 1987) and Andrew Hacker, *Two Nations: Black and White, Separate, Hostile, Unequal* (New York: Charles Scribner's Sons, 1992).

18. Terry McMillan's recent bestseller, *Waiting to Exhale* (1992; rpt. New York: Pocket Starbooks, 1993), revolves in large part around this theme.

19. Wilson, *The Truly Disadvantaged.*

20. I have worked throughout within a heterosexual, and, some gays might say, heterosexist, framework. Why, it may be asked, should black women wait for black, or any other, men? Why shouldn't they embrace their sisters? I certainly don't mean to impugn the legitimacy of lesbian relationships—I think that gay relationships and marriages should be recognized—but, on established assumptions about people's sexual orientation, there will still be a majority of *straight* women for whom this is not an attractive solution. If these assumptions are wrong, of course, so that the whole concept of a basic sexual orientation is misleading in the first place, and sexuality is radically plastic, then some of these arguments won't work. But the *general* issue of racism and sex obviously isn't just an issue for straights.

21. See Richard Brandt, *A Theory of the Good and the Right* (New York: Oxford University Press, 1979).

22. For a fascinating discussion of the psychological ramifications of this, see Kathy Russell, Midge Wilson, and Ronald Hall, *The Color Complex: The Politics of Skin Color Among African Americans* (New York: Harcourt Brace Jovanovich, 1992).

23. And many other countries too, of course. Though I have implicitly focused on the United States throughout, many of these arguments would be applicable elsewhere also.

24. A quick riddle for the reader: name a black female movie star other than Whoopi Goldberg (pop singer Whitney Houston's one-shot appearance in *The Bodyguard* doesn't count). My guess is that the average white reader will come up empty. Now think how remarkable this is in a country where for most of the century movies have epitomized American popular culture, and blacks make up 12% of the population. (Goldberg, by the way, is the exception that proves the rule, in the original sense of that expression, now largely forgotten, of *testing* the rule so that an explanation for the anomaly is called for. At least until lately, she has standardly appeared as a de-sexed comic grotesque. After I completed the original draft of this article, Angela Bassett was nominated for a "Best Actress" Academy Award for her role as Tina Turner in *What's Love Got to Do with It.* So that's one more black actress the white reader is now likely to know. But my general point obviously still stands.)

25. The following discussion draws on *The Color Complex.* The notion of a racial "somatic norm" was first put forward by the Dutch sociologist Harmannus Hoetink; see, for example, *Caribbean Race Relations: A Study of Two Variants* (London: Oxford University Press, 1962).

26. It should be noted, though, that some researchers have argued, on anthropological evidence, that there is a pro-light skinned aesthetic bias in *all* societies, which pre-existed, though of course it will be reinforced by, colonialism and white racism.

27. Thomas E. Hill, Jr., *Autonomy and Self-Respect* (Cambridge: Cambridge University Press, 1991), especially chapters 1 and 2.

28. Likewise, it is no accident that the work of black philosophers has so often focused on the particular importance of *self-respect* for blacks; see, for example, Laurence Thomas, "Self-Respect: Theory and Practice," and Bernard Boxill, "Self-Respect and Protest," both in Leonard Harris, ed., *Philosophy Born of Struggle: Anthology of Afro-American Philosophy from 1917* (Dubuque, Iowa: Kendall/Hunt Publishing Co., 1983).

Contemporary Issue: Women's Rights and Black Nationalism

20 Africa on My Mind: Gender, Counterdiscourse, and African American Nationalism

E. FRANCES WHITE

Study Questions

1. According to White, in what way have certain nationalists invented an African past to suit their conservative agenda?
2. According to White, in what way does Asante's world view involve an "untenable binary opposition"?
3. What would be the difference between "complementarity" and "equality" between the sexes?
4. What is wrong with the idea that Africans lived "simply and harmoniously until the evil Europeans upset their happy life"?

Equality is false; it's the devil's concept. Our concept is complementarity. Complementarity means you complete or make perfect that which is imperfect.

The man has the right that does not destroy the collective needs of his family.

The woman has the two rights of consultation and then separation if she isn't getting what she should be getting.

M. RON KARENGA, *THE QUOTABLE KARENGA*

The African past lies camouflaged in the collective African American memory, transformed by the middle passage, sharecropping, industrializa-

tion, urbanization. Few material goods from Africa survived this difficult history, but Africans brought with them a memory of how social relations should be constructed that has affected African American culture to the present. Although the impact of these African roots are difficult to assess, few historians today deny the importance of this past to African American culture.

But the memories I seek to interrogate in this essay have little to do with "real" memories or actual traditions that African Americans have passed along through blood or even practices. Rather, I am concerned with the way African Americans in the late twentieth century construct and reconstruct collective political memories of African culture to build a cohesive group that can shield them from racist ideology and oppression. In particular it is the political memories of African gender relations and sexuality that act as models for African American social relations that will serve as this paper's focus.

Below I will focus on black nationalism as an oppositional strategy that both counters racism and constructs conservative utopian images of African American life. I will pay close attention to the intertwined discussions on the relationship of the African past to present-day culture and to attempts to construct utopian and repressive gender relations. After situating my work theoretically in the next section, I return to an examination of Afrocentric paradigms that support nationalist discourse on gender and the African past. Finally I look at the emergence of a black feminist discourse that attempts to combine nationalist and feminist insights in a way that counters racism but tries to avoid sexist pitfalls.

Reprinted from the *Journal of Women's History* 2 (1990), pp. 73–97.

Throughout the essay, I choose examples from across the range of nationalist thinking. Some of this writing is obviously narrow and sexist. Other works have influenced my thinking deeply and have made significant contributions to understanding African American women's lives. I argue, however, that all fail to confront the sexist models that ground an important part of their work. I imagine that my criticisms will be read by some as a dismissal of all Afrocentric thinking. Nothing could be further from my intentions. It is because I value the contributions of nationalists that I want to engage them seriously. Yet it is the kind of feminism that demands attention to internal community relations that leads me to interrogate this discourse even while acknowledging its ability to undermine racist paradigms. This kind of black feminism recognizes the dangers of criticizing internal relations in the face of racist attacks but also argues that we will fail to transform ourselves into a liberated community if we do not engage in dialogue on the difficult issues that [confront] us.[1]

African American nationalists have taken the lead in resurrecting and inventing African models for the African diaspora in the United States. They recognize that dominant, negative images of Africa have justified black enslavement, segregation, and continuing impoverishment.[2] Accordingly, nationalists have always argued persuasively that African Americans deny their connections to Africa at the peril of allowing a racist subtext to circulate without serious challenge. At the same time, nationalists have recognized that counterattacks on negative portrayals of Africa stimulate political mobilization against racism in the United States. The consciously identified connections between African independence and the United States Civil Rights movements and, more recently, between youth rebellion in South Africa and campus unrest in the United States stand out as successful attempts to build a Pan-African consciousness.

The construction of Pan-African connections can have its problems, however. At times it depends on the search for a glorious African past while accepting dominant European notions of what that past should look like. As I have argued

elsewhere,[3] proving that Africans created "civilizations" as sophisticated as those in Europe and the Near East has concerned nationalists too much.[4] In the process of elevating Egypt, for example, they have often accepted as uncivilized and even savage primitives the majority of Africans who lived in stateless societies, but whose past deserves respect for its complex relationship to the world around it.[5]

Perhaps more importantly, the nationalist or Afrocentric construction of a political memory attempts to set up standards of social relations that can be both liberating and confining. The quotation at the beginning of this essay by the "inventor" of Kwanza traditions, Ron Karenga, illustrates this point. Building off conservative concepts of "traditional" African gender relations before colonial rule, he argues that the collective needs of black families depend on women's complementary and unequal roles. As I shall make clear below, Karenga has significantly modified his sexist ideas about gender relations, but the ideology of complementarity and collective family needs continues to work against the liberation of black women.

In addition, many nationalists, both male and female, remain openly hostile to any feminist agenda. In a paper arguing that black people should turn to African polygamous and extended family forms to solve the "problem" of female-headed households, Larry Delano Coleman concludes:

> The "hyperliberated" black woman is in fact so much a man that she has no need for men, however wimpish they may be; and the "hyperemasculated" black man is so much a woman, that he has no need for women. May each group of these hyper-distorted persons find homosexual heaven among the whites, for the black race would be better served without them.[6]

Coleman defines "the race" in a way that excludes feminists, lesbians, and gay men from community support—a terrifying proposition in this age of resurgent racism.[7]

In advocating polygamous families, Nathan and Julia Hare, the influential editors of *Black Male/Female Relationships,* link homosexuality with betrayal of the race:

Just as those black persons who disidentify with their race and long to alter their skin color and facial features to approximate that of the white race may be found to suffer a racial identity crisis, the homosexual individual who disidentifies with his/her biological body to the point of subjecting to the surgery of sex-change operations similarly suffers a gender identity confusion. to say the least.[8]

Both the Hares' and Coleman's standards of appropriate gender relations depends on a misguided notion of African culture in the era before "the fall"—that is, before European domination distorted African traditions. These nationalists have idealized polygamous and extended families in a way that stresses both cooperation among women and male support of wives but ignores cross-generational conflict and intrafamily rivalry also common in extended, polygamous families. They have invented an African past to suit their conservative agenda on gender and sexuality.

In making appeals to conservative notions of appropriate gender behavior, African American nationalists reveal their ideological ties to other nationalist movements, including European and Euro-American bourgeois nationalists over the past 200 years. These parallels exist despite the different class and power bases of these movements. European and Euro-American nationalists turned to the ideology of respectability to help them impose the bourgeois manners and morals that attempted to control sexual behavior and gender relations. This ideology helped the bourgeoisie create a "private sphere" that included family life, sexual relations, and leisure time. Respectability set standards of proper behavior at the same time that it constructed the very notion of private life. Nationalism and respectability intertwined as the middle class used the nation-state to impose its notions of the private sphere's proper order on the upper and lower classes. Through state-run institutions, such as schools, prisons, and census bureaus the bourgeoisie disciplined people and collected the necessary information to identify and control them.[9]

Often African Americans have served as a model of abnormality against which nationalism in the United States was constructed. White bourgeois nationalism has often portrayed African Americans as if they threatened respectability. Specifically, white nationalists have described both black men and women as hypersexual. Moreover, black family life has consistently served as a model of abnormality for the construction of the ideal family life. Black families were matriarchal when white families should have been male-dominated. Now they are said to be female-headed when the ideal has become an equal heterosexual pair.[10]

As I have suggested, black people have developed African American nationalism as an oppositional discourse to counter such racist images. Ironically, though not surprisingly, this nationalism draws on the ideology of respectability to develop a cohesive political movement. The African American ideology of respectability does not always share the same moral code with western nationalism. Some Afrocentric thinkers, such as Larry Coleman, turn to Africa for models of gender relations and call for polygamy as an appropriate form of marriage between black men and women. More crucially, black nationalists did not and cannot call on state power to enforce their norms. Their opposition to abortion carries very different weight from the campaign of the Christian right, whose agenda includes making a bid for control of state institutions.

It is this lack of access to state power and African American nationalists' advocacy of an oppressed people that gives Afrocentric ideology its progressive, radical edge and ultimately distinguishes it from European and Euro-American bourgeois nationalism Paradoxically then, Afrocentric ideology can be radical and progressive in relation to white racism and conservative and repressive in relation to the internal organization of the black community. Clearly, nationalists struggle in a way that can deeply threaten white racism. Both the open repression and the ideological backlash against nationalists indicate that their discourse strikes at the heart of black oppression. Yet I often find too narrow black nationalist efforts to define what the community or nation should be. In particular many nationalists attempt to construct sexist and heterosexist ideal models for appropriate behavior.

The Dialectics of Discursive Struggle

How does one prove strength in oppression without overstating the case, diluting criticism of the system and absolving the oppressor in the process? Likewise, the parallel dilemma is how does one critique the system and state of things without contributing to the victimology school, which thrives on litanies of lost battles and casualty lists, while omitting victories and strengths and the possibilities for change inherent in both black people and society?[11]

Karenga has identified a key dilemma facing black scholarship: how do black scholars take into account the possibilities of liberation at the same time that they balance a sense of strength against the realities of victimization? One strategy for moving beyond this dilemma to what Karenga calls an "emancipatory Black science" is to examine the ideological battles in which black people engage, exploring both the racist discourse that they struggle against and the oppositional language constructed in the process of this struggle. As a site of ideological battles, discourses intertwine with the material conditions of our lives. They help organize our social existence and social reproduction through the production of signs and practices that give meaning to our lives.[12] Closely tied to the socioeconomic and political institutions that enable oppressive relations, discourses are often reflected in a variety of forms. For example, the dominant discourse on Africa includes multilayered interventions that are knitted together from scholarly literature, fiction, art, movies, television, media, travel books, government documents, folklore, jokes, and more. The discourse that relies on these interventions creates an image of Africa that reinforces the continent's subordinate power relations to the West. Dominant discursive practice depends on more than lies and myths, although misrepresentation and deception do have roles to play in its strategy. Instead, the West's will to knowledge about Africa has been inextricably bound up with imperialist relations.

It is impossible for people's thoughts on Africa to be unencumbered by this discourse. None of us—not even Africans—can come to the study of Africa without being influenced by its negative image. Accordingly, dominant discourse attempts to blind both the oppressor and the oppressed by setting up smokescreens between people and reality. As Said argues for the Middle East, ". . . for a European or American studying the Orient there can be no disclaiming the main circumstance of his actuality: that he comes up against the Orient as a European or American first, as an individual second."[13] One way that dominant discourse sets up a smokescreen is to make arbitrary categories appear natural and normal. For example, it makes us think that race is a natural category by taking minor biological differences and infusing them with deep symbolic meanings that affect all our lives. Race, then, is a social construction that feels real to us and has significant consequences. . . .

The very nature of dominant discourse leads it to be contested by subordinate groups whose daily experiences help penetrate and demystify its hegemony.[14] This "dialectic of discursive struggle" reveals the vulnerabilities of hegemonies.[15] As part of the same dialectic, counterdiscourses operate on the same ground as dominant ideology. Scott argues:

The crucial point is rather that the very process of attempting to legitimate a social order by idealizing it always provides its subjects with the means, the symbolic tools, the very ideas for a critique that operates entirely within the hegemony. For most purposes, then, it is not at all necessary for subordinate classes to set foot outside the confines of the ruling ideals in order to formulate a critique of power.[16] . . .

The writings of certain feminists of color reveal the Janus-faced nature of counterdiscourse as these women search for allies among the male-dominated nationalist and white-dominated feminist movements. For example, women of color offered challenges within the feminist movement that forced women to acknowledge the problems with an undifferentiated category, Woman. Many of these theorists highlighted the complexities of human identity in recognition of the reality that women have ethnic/race and class positions, inter alia, that interact with gender and sexuality to influence their lives. Accordingly, feminists of color pushed for a movement whose discursive practices opposed sexism and racism simultaneously.[17] For example, Audre Lorde has asked, how does horizontal hostility keep women from ending their oppression? She argued that women need to celebrate their differences and use difference for creative dialogue.[18] Outside a narrow band of bourgeois or separatist-feminists, few United States white feminists today write without giving at least token acknowledgment to Lorde's call to recognize difference.[19]

At the same time, women of color challenged their various ethnic communities to become conscious of sexism at home. Cherríe Moraga problematizes the meaning of home and community as she sensitively explores the way her education and light skin pushed her away from other Chicanos. "I grew white," she acknowledged.[20] But she also stressed that her community forced her to leave home because of her feminism and lesbianism, Feeling betrayed by a mother who accepted the ideology that males were better than females, she fled from those who told her, you are a traitor to your race if you do not put men first. She watched the rise of the Chicano nationalist movement, La Raza, alienated on the sidelines. Yet she found herself increasingly uncomfortable in her nearly all-white surroundings.

Ultimately, she concluded that to be critical of one's race is not to betray it. She joined with other Chicana feminists to turn around the traditional interpretation of Malinche's life, which traces the birth of the Mexican people to Malinche's betrayal of her people. Instead, Moraga and others expose a prior betrayal of Malinche, who had been sold into slavery by her own people.[21] By refusing to accept the terms of a Chicago nationalist movement that brands her a traitor because she publicly criticizes gender relations, Moraga demands a place for herself and other lesbians within Chicano communities.

It is not surprising that feminists such as Audre Lorde and Cherrie Moraga challenge both feminists and nationalist communities. As women with strong lesbian political consciences, they confront homophobia in nationalist movements. Locked in struggle against heterosexism in their own communities, it is very difficult for them to maintain an image of their communities as harmonious. Cheryl Clarke has specifically accused nationalists of increasing the level of homophobia in African American communities during the 1960s and 1970s. She argues persuasively that homophobia limits the political struggle of African Americans:

> The expression of homophobic sentiments, the threatening political postures assumed by black radicals and progressives of the nationalist/communist ilk, and the seeming lack of any willingness to understand the politics of gay and lesbian liberation collude with the dominant white male culture to repress not only gay men and lesbians, but also to repress a natural part of all human beings, namely the bisexual potential in us all. Homophobia divides black people as political allies, it cuts off political growth, stifles revolution, and perpetuates patriarchal domination.[22]

In *Reconstructing Womanhood,* Hazel Carby goes even further when she finds fault with some African American feminists for failing to recognize that even their writings form part of a multi-accented counterdiscourse. She cautions black feminist literary critics to be historically specific when they write about black women's fiction and to recognize competing interests among African American women. She asserts, "in these terms black and feminist cannot be absolute, transhistorical forms (or form) of identity."[23] Black feminists do not have an essential, biologically-based claim on understanding black women's experience since we are divided by class, region, and sexual orientation. Even we have multiple identities that create tensions and contradictions among us. We need not all agree nor need we all speak with one voice. As with all counterdiscourses, the assumption that there exists one essential victim suppresses internal power divisions. To Terdiman's "no discourse is ever a monologue," we should add, the site of counterdiscourse is itself contested terrain.

Inventing African Tradition

The contemporary African American woman must recognize that, in keeping with her African heritage and legacy, her most important responsibilities are to the survival of the home, the family, and its children.[24]

It is out of the feminist tradition of challenging the oppositional discourses that are meaningful to women of color that I interrogate the significance of black nationalism for African American women's lives. Like Sylvia Yanagisako, "I treat tradition as a cultural construction whose meaning must be discovered in present words no less than past acts."[25] As I have suggested, the traditions revealed in nationalist discursive practices are Janus-faced—turned toward struggle with oppressive forces and contesting for dominance within black communities.

This discourse can be represented by Molefi Kete Asante's writings and the journal he edits, *Journal of Black Studies.* Asante recognizes the importance of developing a counterdiscourse within the privileged arena of academia and has consistently published a high quality journal. He is also responsible for developing the first Ph.D. program in African American studies at Temple University.

The focus of his work and his journal is an Afrocentric one because it places "Africans and the interest of Africa at the center of our approach to problem solving."[26] By African, he means both people from the African continent and its diaspora. Although he has collapsed the distinction between African Americans and Africans, he avoids the traps many nationalists fall into when they posit a simplistic, mystical connection between African and African Americans. Unlike earlier nationalists who appealed to a natural, essential element in African culture, he argues that culture "is the product of the material and human environment in which people live."[27] In an editor's note introducing a special issue of the *Journal of Black Studies,* "African Cultural Dimensions," he continues:

As editor I seek to promulgate the view that all culture is cognitive. The manifestations of culture are the artifacts, creative solutions, objects, and rituals that are created in response to nature. Thus, the manuscripts which have been scrupulously selected for this issue are intended to continue the drama of cultural discussion of African themes.[28]

Africans, he argues, have constructed a culture that stands in opposition to Eurocentric culture. He develops a convincing critique of a Eurocentric worldview. For Asante, Eurocentric culture is too materialistic, and the social science that has evolved from this culture in academe too often assumes an objective, universal approach that ultimately suffers from positivism. He argues that neither Marxism nor Freudianism escapes from this shortcoming though he acknowledges that the Frankfurt School's criticisms of positivism has influenced his work.

According to Asante, the task for African Americans is to move beyond the Eurocentric idea to a place where transcultural, Afrocentric analysis becomes possible. He cautions against using a Eurocentric mode that accepts oppositional dichotomies as a reflection of the real world.[29] His critique of the positivist tendency to split mind and body is cogent. Unfortunately, his theory also relies on a false dichotomy. Essentially, his categories, Afrocentric and Eurocentric, form an untenable binary opposition: Europeans are materialistic while Africans are spiritual; Europeans abort life while Africans affirm it.

He is quite right to recognize the existence of a protest discourse that counters racist ideology. But he denies the way that these discourses are both multivocal and intertwined. As suggested above, the dialectic nature of discursive struggle requires that counter- and dominant discourses contest the same ideological ground.

This point can be better understood by examining the roots of Asante's Afrocentric thought. He consciously builds off Negritude and authenticity, philosophies devised explicitly to counter racist ideology and develop nationalist cohesion. V. Y. Mudimbe (1988) has exposed the nature of the binary opposition used by cultural nationalists of the 1930s and 1940s who explored their difference as blacks. Leopold Senghor and Aimé Césaire and other Francophone Africans and African Caribbeans relied on the spiritual/materialistic dichotomy. Turned on its head, this is the opposition used against Africans during the late nineteenth century. As many have pointed out, this reversal of paradigms owed much to the celebration of the "noble savage" by such interwar European writers as Jean-Paul Sartre. Ironically, Western anthropologists, whom nationalists often disparage, also took an active role in this ideological "flip." It was anthropologists such as Michel Griaule and Melville J. Herskovits who revealed to Western-educated intellectuals the internal coherence of African systems of thought.[30] Equally important was the cross-fertilization of ideas between Africans, African Caribbeans, and African Americans. As a result of these three influences, "African experiences, attitudes, and mentalities became mirrors of a spiritual and cultural richness."[31] Far from cultureless savages, Africans had built the essence of spiritual culture.

This reversal of the racist paradigms on Africa accompanied and contributed to the growth of the nationalist movements that ultimately freed the continent from formal colonial rule. The nature of African independence reflects the double-edged character of this nationalism. On the one hand, nationalism helped build the political coherence necessary to threaten European rule; on the other hand, it obscured class and gender divisions in a way that prevented them from being addressed fairly. Clearly, this nationalism shared much with a European brand of nationalism that envisioned a culture unequally divided along gender and class lines.

Similarly, Asante does little to take us beyond the positivism that he criticizes, and his schema assumes a universality as broad as the Eurocentric discourse he shuns. Moreover, the Afrocentric ideology he uses depends on an image of black people as having a culture that has little or nothing to do with white culture. This is one of its major contradictions. On the one hand, nationalists like Asante have to prove to African Americans that Afrocentric ways are different from and better than Euro-American ways. Nationalists try to convince black people that they should begin to live their lives by this Afrocentric ideology. For example, some nationalists argue that African

Americans should turn away from materialism to focus on the spiritual needs of the black community. Yet on the other hand, Asante and others argue that black culture is already based on an Afrocentric worldview that distinguishes it from Euro-American culture. Rather than being an ideology that African Americans must turn to, Afrocentric thought becomes inherent in black culture, and black people already live by these ways in opposition to dominant culture.

I would argue instead that African American culture constantly interacts with dominant culture. Of course, black people do have their own ways not only because they protect themselves from penetration by white culture but also because they are creative. Nonetheless, blacks and whites all live together in the same society, and culture flows in both directions. Like the dominant culture, most African Americans believe that spirituality has a higher value than materialism at the same time that most of these people pursue material goals. If materialism were not considered crass by dominant society, Afrocentric critique would have little value. It is also important to note the extent to which white culture is influenced by African Americans. At an obvious level, we see black influence on white music with the most recent appearance of rap music on television and radio commercials. At a less obvious level, Afrocentric critiques compel hegemonic forces to work at covering the reality of racist relations. Far from being an ideology that has no relationship to Eurocentric thought, nationalist ideology is dialectically related to it.

What I find most disturbing about Asante's work is his decision to collapse differences among black people into a false unity that only a simplistic binary opposition would allow. The focus on similarities between Africans and African Americans at the expense of recognizing historical differences can only lead to a crisis once differences are inevitably revealed. Moreover, his binary opposition cannot account for differences among Africans. Many eloquent African writers have warned us about the problems that came from accepting a false unity during the decolonization phase that has led to the transfer of local power from an expatriate elite to an indigenous one. Ngugi wa Thiongo, Sembene Ousmane, and Chinua Achebe would all warn us against such pitfalls.

And, of course, we cannot face sexism with this false unity, as Buchi Emecheta, Sembene Ousmane, and Mariama Bâ movingly show. Asante does tell us that along with the move beyond the Eurocentric idea, "we can develop a post-male ideology as we unlock creative human potential."[32] Yet he has nothing more to say about gender in the entire book. It is hard to believe that this gesture toward black feminists needs to be taken seriously. It is to other Afrocentric thinkers that we must turn to understand more clearly what this discourse has to say about women.

Among the most important nationalists the *Journal of Black Studies* publishes is Ron Karenga, the founder of *Us*. Some readers will remember him for his leadership role among cultural nationalists in ideological battles against the Black Panthers in the 1960s and 1970s and for this pamphlet, *The Quotable Ron Karenga*. In *Black Awakening in Capitalist America*, Robert Allen quoted a critical excerpt from Karenga's book, exposing its position on women and influencing many young black women (including myself) to turn away from this nationalist position.[33]

Perhaps the key word in Karenga's early analysis of utopian gender relations is complementarity. In this theory, women should complement male roles and, therefore, share the responsibilities of nation building. Of course, in this formulation, complementary did not mean equal. Instead, men and women were to have separate tasks and unequal power. Indeed, in much of Africa today, women give more to men than they get in return in their complementary labor exchange. This is not to suggest that African women are only victims in their societies; nonetheless, sexism based on a complementary model severely limits the possibilities of many women's lives.

It is important to note that Karenga has reformed his position on women. Apparently, he used the time he spent in jail during the 1970s ef-

fectively by spending much of his time studying. It is from his jail cell that he published influential pieces in *Black Scholar* and the *Journal of Black Studies.* He began to articulate more clearly a critique of hegemonic culture, showing the impact of reading Lukacs, Gramsci, Cabral, and Touré. And though he does not say so explicitly, he begins to respond to black feminist critics of his work. Indeed, I find the change in his position on women impressive. Although he remains mired in heterosexist assumptions and never acknowledges his change of heart, he drops his explicit arguments supporting the subordination of women. The new Ron Karenga argues for equality in the heterosexual pair despite his continued hostility to feminists.[34]

Unfortunately, too few nationalists have made this transition with him. Male roles remain defined by conventional, antifeminist notions that fail to address the realities of black life. For example, articles in Nathan and Julia Hare's journal, *Black Male/Female Relationships,* consistently articulate such roles. Charlyn A. Harper-Bolton begins her contribution, "A Reconceptualization of the African American Woman" by examining "traditional African philosophy, the nature of the traditional African woman, and the African American slave woman."[35] She uses African tradition as her starting point because she assumes an essential connection between the African past and African American present:

The contemporary African American woman carries within her very essence, within her very soul, the legacy that was bequeathed to her by the traditional African woman and the African American slave woman.[36]

She leaves unproblematic the African legacy to African Americans as she presents an ahistorical model of African belief systems that ignores the conflict and struggle over meaning so basic to the making of history. This model assumes a harmonious spirituality versus conflicting materialism dichotomy that grounds the work of Asante and her major sources, John Mbiti and Wade Nobles.[37]

It is a peculiarly Eurocentric approach that accepts conflict and competing interests in a Western context but not in an African one. Harper-Bolton never moves beyond the mistaken notion that Africans lived simply and harmoniously until the evil Europeans upset their happy life. Ironically, as I have been arguing, such an image of Africans living in static isolation from historical dynamics supports racist ideals and practices and conveniently overlooks the power dynamics that existed in precolonial Africa like anywhere else in the world. In addition, her model portrays African women as a monolithic and undifferentiated category with no competing interests, values, and conflicts. The power of older women over younger women that characterizes so many African cultures becomes idealized as a vision of the elders' wisdom in decision making. It accepts the view of age relations presented by more powerful older women whose hidden agenda often is to socialize girls into docile daughters and daughters-in-law. . . .

Discussion Questions

1. Even if we suppose that, during the centuries before the Europeans arrived, African men and women lived in complete and total harmony, what implications would this have regarding relations between African American men and women today?

2. Some Afrocentrists have held that homosexuality is a "European perversion"—a sign of European decadence. In your opinion, is this true? Is it fair to criticize this as but another instance of the bipolar thinking of Afrocentrism (African = good; European = bad)?

3. Is the case of polygamy (for African American males in the United States) made stronger for its African heritage?

Notes

1. See Cheryl Clarke, "The Failure to Transform: Homophobia in the Black Community," in *Home Girls: A Black Feminist Anthology,* ed. Barbara Smith (New York: Kitchen Table Press, 1983), 197–208; and Audre Lorde, *Sister Outsider: Essays and Speeches* (Trumansburg, NY: Crossing Press, 1984).

2. They only need point to the racist scientific theories that AIDS began in Central Africa from people who ate [subtext: had sex with] green monkeys to prove this point. Spread by the popular and scientific media, this theory appealed to a white culture that still believes that black sexuality is out of control and animalistic. The scientific evidence contributed to the racist subtext of the anti-AIDS hysteria. See Evelynn Hammonds, "Race, Sex, AIDS: The Construction of 'Other,' " *Radical America* 20, no. 6 (1986); and Evelynn Hammonds and Margaret Cerullo, "AIDS in Africa: The Western Imagination and the Dark Continent," *Radical America* 21, nos. 2–3 (1987).

3. E. Frances White, "Civilization Denied: Questions on *Black Athena,*" *Radical America* 18, nos. 2–3 (1987): 5.

4. See, for example, Cheikh Anta Diop, *The African Origins of Civilization: Myth or Reality,* trans. Mercer Cook (New York: Lawrence Hill, 1974).

5. Chancellor Williams, *The Destruction of African Civilization: Great Issues of a Race from 4500 B.C. to 200 A.D.* (Chicago: Third World Press, 1974).

6. Larry Delano Coleman, "Black Man/Black Woman: Can the Breach Be Healed?" *Nile Review* 2, no. 7: 6.

7. Cheryl Clarke, "The Failure to Transform," has raised similar objections in this thoughtful essay. She argues that leftist male intellectuals have helped to institutionalize homophobia in the black community. I refer to this essay in more detail below.

8. Nathan Hare and Julia Hare, "The Rise of Homosexuality and Other Diverse Alternatives," *Black Male/Female Relationships* 5 (1981): 10.

9. George Mosse, *Nationalism and Sexuality, Respectability and Abnormal Sexuality in Modern Europe* (New York: H. Fertig Publishers, 1985).

10. According to George Mosse, ibid., German nationalists label certain people as "outsiders" who did not live up to the norms set up by nationalism and respectability. By labeling homosexuals, prostitutes, Jews, etc. as perverts who lived outside the boundaries of acceptable behavior, nationalists helped build cohesion. Jewish men, for example, were said to epitomize all that was unmanly and unvirile. By contrast, a good, manly German looked suspiciously at Jewish men. Many of the newly evolving negative identities and classifications fused with the stereotypes of Jews. In this way the rise of National Socialism was inextricably tied to the increase in anti-Semitism.

11. Ron M. Karenga, *Introduction to Black Studies* (Los Angeles: Kawaida Publications, 1982), 213.

12. See Richard Terdiman, *Discourse/Counter-Discourse: The Theory and Practice of Symbolic Resistance in Nineteenth-Century France* (Ithaca: Cornell University Press, 1985).

13. Edward W. Said, *Orientalism* (New York: Vintage, 1978), 11.

14. See James C. Scott, *Weapons of the Weak: Everyday Forms of Peasant Resistance* (New Haven: Yale University Press, 1985). Scott, however, may underemphasize the extent to which people are influenced by dominant hegemonies.

15. Terdiman, *Discourse/Counter-Discourse,* 68.

16. Scott, *Weapons of the Weak,* 338.

17. For further exploration of these ideas, see E. Frances White, "Racisme et sexisme: La confrontation des féministes noires aux formes conjointes de l'oppression," *Les Temps Modernes* 42, no. 485 (December 1986); 173–84.

18. See Lorde, *Sister Outsider.*

19. For examples of white feminists who have been influenced by Audre Lorde's insights, see Barbara Johnson, *A World of Difference* (Baltimore and London: Johns Hopkins University Press, 1987); Teresa de Lauretis, "Feminist Studies/ Critical Studies: Issues, Terms and contexts," in *Feminist Studies/Critical Studies,* ed. T. de Lauretis (Bloomington: Indiana University Press, 1986), 1–19; and de Lauretis, *Technologies of Gender: Essays on Theory, Film, and Fiction* (Bloomington: Indiana University Press, 1987).

20. Cherríe Moraga, *Loving in the War Years: lo que nunca pasa por sus labios* (Boston: South End Press, 1983), 99.

21. See also Gloria Anzaldúa, *Borderlands/La Frontera: The New Mestiza* (San Francisco: Spinster/Aunt Lite, 1987); and Norma Alarcón, "Chicana's Feminist Literature: A Re-vision Through Malintzin or Malintzin:

Putting Flesh Back on the Object," in *This Bridge Called My Back: Writings by Radical Women of Color,* ed. Cherríe Moraga and Gloria Anzaldúa (Watertown, MA: Persephone Press, 1981), 182–90.

22. Clarke, "The Failure to Transform," 207.

23. Carby, *Reconstructing Womanhood,* 17.

24. Charlyn A. Harper-Bolton, "A Reconceptualization of the Black Woman," *Black Male/Female Relationships* 6 (1982): 42.

25. Sylvia Junko Yanagisako, *Transforming the Past: Traditions and Kinship Among Japanese Americans* (Stanford: Stanford University Press, 1985), 18.

26. Molefi Kete Asante, *The Afrocentric Idea* (Philadelphia: Temple University Press, 1987), 8, note 3.

27. Molefi Kete Asante, "Editor's Note," *Journal of Black Studies* 8, no. 2 (1977): 123.

28. Ibid., 123.

29. See Asante, *The Afrocentric Idea.*

30. V. Y. Mudimbe, *The Invention of Africa: Gnosis, Philosophy, and the Order of Knowledge* (Bloomington: Indiana University Press, 1985), 75–92.

31. Ibid., 89.

32. Asante, *Afrocentric Idea,* 8.

33. Allen, *Black Awakening in Capitalist America.*

34. See Karenga, *Introduction to Black Studies.*

35. Harper-Bolton, "A Reconceptualization of the Black Woman," 32.

36. Ibid., 40.

37. See John Mbiti, *African Religion and Philosophy* (Garden City, NY: Doubleday 1970) and Wade Nobles, "Africanity: Its Role in Black Families," *Black Scholar* 5, no. 9 (1974).

21 Black Woman

AMIRI BARAKA

Study Questions

1. How is the separation caused by slavery to be healed?

2. What activities are natural and proper to black women, according to Baraka?

3. What activities are more proper to men?

4. What is the role of white women in the revolution?

From *Raise Race Rays Raze: Essays Since 1965* (New York: Random House, 1969), pp. 147–153.

We are self conscious now, because we are slaves trying to break from slavery. Trying to destroy slavery in the world, and in our own minds. If we could destroy it in our minds, *our love for it,* i.e., if we could see it continuously as evil, as the devil collecting and using our energies to pervert the world . . . then there would be no pause, no rhetoric, only action, which is divine. Maulana has said, "Words are wonderful, but deeds are divine."

We talk about the black woman and the black man like we were separate because we have been separated, our hands reach out for each other, for the closeness, the completeness we are for each other, the expansion of consciousness that we provide for each other. We were separated by the deed and process of slavery. We internalized the process, permitting it to create an alien geography in our skulls, a wandering of spirit that had us missing each other, and never never understanding just what it was. After we were gone from each other. My hand might rest on yours, and still you would be gone. And I, of course, not there, out wandering, among the rogues and whores of the universe.

And so this separation is the cause of our need for self consciousness, and eventual healing. But we must erase the separateness by providing ourselves with healthy African identities. By embracing a value system that knows of no separation but only of the divine complement the black woman is for her man. For instance we do not believe in "equality" of men and women. We cannot understand what devils and the devilishly influenced mean when they say equality for women. We could never be equals . . . nature has not provided thus. The brother says, "Let a woman be a wo-man . . . and let a man be a ma-an . . ." But this means that we will complement each other, that you, who I call my house, because there is no house without a man and his wife, are the single element in the universe that perfectly completes my essence. You are essential to the development of any life in the house because you are that house's completion.

When we say complement, completes, we mean that we have certain functions which are more natural to us, and you have certain graces that are yours alone.

We say that a black woman must first be able to inspire her man, then she must be able to teach our children, and contribute to the social development of the nation.

How do you inspire black man; by being the conscious rising essence of Blackness. Blackness conscious of itself, which is what we mean by *cultured.* Blackness, conscious of itself. Blackness, Maulana has said, is Color, Culture, and Consciousness. By race, by identity, and by action. You inspire Black Man by being Black Woman. By being the nation, as the house, the smallest example of how the nation should be. So you are my "house," I live in you, and together we have a house, and that must be the microcosm, by example, of the entire black nation. "Our nation is our selves."

> What ever we are doing, is what the nation
> is
> doing
> or
> not doing
> is what the nation
> is
> being
> or
> not being

You inspire the man by creating with him this new world we seek. By *being* this new life that must be provided for, at all costs. By being a breath of the future as well as living manifestation of our traditional greatness. Everything we do must be toward fashioning a new way, rededicating our selves to a black value system. The house we live in, the clothes we wear, the food we eat, the words we speak, must reinforce our move for National Liberation and the new consciousness of the million year old African personality, and it is the woman who must reinforce these thrusts. She is the creator of the environment, if she is conscious. The need to expand this environment, to control our space, so that we will be able to create a complementary, beneficial environment for black people and a new world consciousness is the path of National Liberation. Inspire, to raise the spirit of, to constantly lift us to what we have to do. To inspire is to *be* the new consciousness, so that we must be defenders and developers of this new consciousness. You must be what we *need,* to survive . . . the strength, the health, the dignity, which is this *new,* millennia old, raging beauty.

To inspire, is to *be* consciousness, and this act alone is teaching. To teach the children . . . what? To teach them this new consciousness. To give them a value for black liberation, for National Liberation. To teach them to keep their spirits free of the alien value system: to shape them in the master teachings of African Nationalism, the new nationalism, called Kawaida. The doctrine of Maulana Karenga.

Education is the root of development, it is also defense. When we speak of Black Power we mean, Self Respect, Self Determination, and Self Defense. To Teach the children, to educate the children, is to make our future predictable, and positive. Our children are our future. Who controls your children's minds controls your life even after the death of your body. We must make sure our children are Black . . . not only by Race, and Culture, but through Consciousness. Education is the development of consciousness.

If the brothers are to fly in the face of, and confront, finally, to defeat, evil . . . our sisters, in that same struggle, must know the reasons we are struggling, and they must continue to teach, even if we are gone, whether our absence is temporary or permanent. It must be black consciousness that is given to our babies with their milk, and with the warmth of the black woman's loving body. Black consciousness, survival training, inspiration. It must be their natural heritage, and earliest environmental vibration . . . provided for, and emphasized by the woman.

Our women have organized The African Free School here in Newark, named after the first public school in America. It is to project our children in our own image. From 4 to 14 they are taught Sifa Ote Mtu Weusi . . . All Praises To The Black Man. They are taught who they are and what they must grow up to do. What is provided is identity, purpose and direction. A Black Value System of which their mothers must be the earliest examples they are conscious of. *The future black nation is composed of children. Who is in control of their minds?* Each day many black people send their children to school for six hours to learn white racism. Finally at the end of this training they learn, and many submit, and become white racists themselves. It is Black Fathers who must teach Black Mothers, and Black Families, but it is Black Mothers, who are from the earliest living memory closest, therefore, of perhaps deepest value as teachers. It must be survival and liberation that you teach sister.

Inspiration, to provide us with energy to reshape the world. The teaching of the children, so that they will understand, and take up the task.

When we say Social Development, we are talking about the evolution of the living together process, the communing of the community, and how that is manifested. How do we live together . . . is it beneficial? The community itself is an intelligence, it is a living entity, shaped by and shaping its external environment. But by what internal laws do we cohere, as a people? By what organic laws of consciousness, that we actually subscribe to, actually live according to, by what real laws do we arrange ourselves in awe of, in response to.

Despite, but even so, because of, and also, in spite of, The Devil, we are organized among ourselves (even in our lack of Organization) as a people. A captive people. Captive people have an organization, not necessarily in the actual framework of the colonizer's program, but developed in some terrifying measure because of it . . . i.e., because we are slaves. We have relationships with each other that exist exclusively because of the devil. The arc of our consciousness expansion is sometimes confined to narrow explosive bursts, because we cannot grow in absolute openness and health to completely express the black magic of our million year experience on this planet. We are schizophrenic-manic/depressive-paranoid in our everyday world, in varying degrees, to different ends, for different reasons, depending on where we are in the devil's frame, but we have a community any way. For some it is brief memory, a blind snag of melody, perhaps jiggling their leg some funny way even tied up in NudeModSick High "Life." Hippie Nigger, Edwardian Nigger, Twiggy Nigger (ress), AT&T Nigger, Scared Nigger, Preacher

Nigger, Anti-Poverty Nigger (Excuse me TJ) . . . and so forth, along every imaginable string tied up to the devil's shriveling plant. But we have a nation, anyway. Our men are our men. Our women are our women. The smoke filled miniature cosmic toilet is America. That's why we cant always *see* each other. That's why we cant always really be in tune. But we have the racial memory of organization & nationhood and an actual living structure now, as a nation. But a nation in bondage.

We are saying that we gotta get a betta structure. Tradition and reason. Memory and fact. Our life style should be finally beautiful despite any interference. The resistance we turn into light and heat. The liberating consciousness consciously evolved. Consciously developed. Made stronger. The woman must encourage the seeds of liberation in her every act. Social Development means education, health, the home, the community—how it relates to the theme of National Liberation, how they can be drawn into it as contributors—their own consciousness evolving, what you call politicizing, nationalizing. What is a nationalist lifestyle and ethos? Sister you in your dealing with the creative (the baby comes out of your body), the submissive, so enveloping, intelligence, must re-create this world pattern by an act of will.

We are fighting a war, yes, but the most crucial part of that war now is the developing of the army's consciousness. To give them the will, hence the time, to resist & survive, and finally make change. To finally re-exist as a whole people. However that must be done. We must develop a value for re-creating the political intelligence of that nation. *Social development means to re-create the life style of a free people,* evolving it from the life style of a conquered, colonized, people. Every breath must be a bullet, every step an attack. Woman learn the priorities of nation building, and be an example of why we want a nation, in-the-first-place. But you must complement us, complete us, so we are whole. What we do, all our energy, is to be the male part of a free people. All that love and faith (imani) must be the connector the reconnector,

as national purpose, or thru national purpose of black woman to black man, forever: the questions gone, the answers a living creation called nation.

The Leftists have reintroduced the white woman for the precise purpose of stunting the nation, and changing the young black would be "revolutionary" into a snarling attachment of jewish political power. Must it be our fate to be the police dogs of "revolutionary white boys," egged on by Sheena (Tarzan's spare part) the blonde jungle queen. Black women understand that there is no future for the black nation addicted to the integrated political consciousness! That is just the newest order of white rule. Another group, we shuffle to the wdbe music of. With another jargon, another reason, for layin up with the oppressor's woe-man. The separation between black man and black woman resets, all national purpose and with that, all national spirit, broken down. A nation is a whole people. The black woman must be the one half and the black man must be the other half of our life sign, our eternal remanifestation. This has got to be easy to understand.

But as long as any *thing* separates the black man and the black woman from moving together, being together, being absolutely in tune, each doing what they supposed to, then the nation will never re-emerge. Our first step must be to reunderstand that we are simply different aspects of a single entity.

Discussion Questions

1. If we are going to judge *everything* as good or bad according to whether it advances or impedes the black revolution, isn't there a danger one might lose sight of what ultimately this revolution is *for?*

2. Beyond an appeal to "nature," is there any special reason men should do the fighting and women the educating of children?

3. Why must the goal be "complementarity" *instead of* "equality"? Can't complementary parts of a whole also be equal?

4. Is Baraka's view of education closed-minded?

Violence, Liberation, and Social Justice

One who breaks an unjust law must do it openly, lovingly (*not hatefully as the white mothers did in New Orleans when they were seen on television screaming "nigger, nigger, nigger"*) . . . .

MARTIN LUTHER KING, JR.

Be peaceful, be courteous, obey the law, respect everyone; but if someone puts his hand on you, send him to the cemetery.

MALCOLM X

At the level of individuals, violence is a cleansing force; it frees the colonized from his inferiority complex and from his despair and inaction; it makes him fearless and restores his self-respect.

FRANTZ FANON

Blacks as a group have been wronged, and are disadvantaged, by slavery and discrimination. Consequently, blacks as a group deserve compensation.

BERNARD BOXILL

Suffering can be endured and overcome, it cannot be repaid. Blacks cannot be repaid for the injustice done to the race, but we can be corrupted by society's guilty gestures of repayment.

SHELBY STEELE

This chapter is broadly concerned with issues of social (including racial) justice and the possible role of violence in attaining it. There are a number of other ethically important issues concerning violence—concerning violent crime, for instance. Thus, for many whites the notions of "violence" and "race" conjure up images of violence perpetrated against them by blacks. They forget, or do not know, that most violence is within racial groupings. Our focus here, however, is on *political* violence. We have heard the chant "No justice, no peace," but, philosophically speaking, what would constitute "justice"? Is *violence,* as opposed to peaceful civil disobedience, the better response to injustice?

In his famous "Letter from Birmingham Jail," Martin Luther King outlines the philosophy of "nonviolence," explaining both the circumstances under which society's rules may be validly broken and the code of conduct which properly governs such actions. Others, however, both in Dr. King's own time and in ours, have rejected his nonviolence, offering a number of justifications for violence. Malcolm X, for instance, points out that nonviolence has seldom been thought reasonable when confronting a violent foe. The French, the Russian, and even the American revolutions, Malcolm observes, were anything but nonviolent and could not have succeeded if they were.

In his contribution, Howard McGary, a professor of philosophy at Rutgers, explores one aspect of Malcolm X's thought: violence justified by self-defense. Here McGary is interested in the concept of "psychological violence" and its possible applications to the justification of self-defense. The basic elements of such justification are present, McGary argues, in the case of the physical and psychological violence done to African Americans in this country.

However, revolutionary violence and the nonviolence of Martin Luther King's program are not the only possible roads to social justice. In his contribution, (black Jewish) philosopher Laurence Mordekhai Thomas argues that the most lasting deficit caused by slavery is the loss of "group autonomy." Such autonomy concerns whether a group is understood by others to be the "foremost interpreters of their historical-cultural traditions." Thomas suggests that such autonomy depends on a group's having a common "narrative," a "set of stories which defines values and entirely positive goals." He argues that the absence of this common narrative for African Americans has had a crippling effect, contrasting this with the situation of the Jews following the Holocaust.

Today one of the main issues concerning social justice for African Americans is the justification of affirmative action programs. These programs are widely seen in the African American community as having been important in the progress of the past three decades and as essential for continued progress. At the same time, the critics of such programs have condemned them for violating what they claim to be the main idea originally of the civil rights movement: that individuals should be judged according to their character and abilities, not according to their race.

In his essay, Bernard Boxill defends affirmative action both as being justified compensation for past wrongs and as helping ensure the desirable future goals of a more equal society, with less poverty and suffering. On the other side, Shelby Steele sees affirmative action as a kind of devil's bargain, in which its beneficiaries opt for the limited goods it yields them, not realizing that, in the long run, affirmative action is no substitute for the genuine development of skills and qualifications.

22   Letter from Birmingham Jail

MARTIN LUTHER KING, JR.

Study Questions

1. Why is "tension" not necessarily a bad thing, according to Dr. King?
2. Describe the various factors that can make a law "unjust," according to Dr. King.
3. How must one go about breaking an unjust law?
4. How does Dr. King respond to the charge that his actions, while not violent, have "precipitated violence"?

My dear Fellow Clergymen,

While confined here in the Birmingham city jail, I came across your recent statement calling our present activities "unwise and untimely." Seldom, if ever, do I pause to answer criticism of my work and ideas. If I sought to answer all of the criticisms that cross my desk, my secretaries would be engaged in little else in the course of the day, and I would have no time for constructive work. But since I feel that you are men of genuine good will and your criticisms are sincerely set forth, I would like to answer your statement in what I hope will be patient and reasonable terms.

I think I should give the reason for my being in Birmingham, since you have been influenced by the argument of "outsiders coming in." I have the honor of serving as president of the Southern Christian Leadership Conference, an organization operating in every southern state, with headquarters in Atlanta, Georgia. We have some eighty-five affiliate organizations all across the South—one being the Alabama Christian Movement for

Human Rights. Whenever necessary and possible we share staff, educational and financial resources with our affiliates. Several months ago our local affiliate here in Birmingham invited us to be on call to engage in a nonviolent direct-action program if such were deemed necessary. We readily consented and when the hour came we lived up to our promises. So I am here, along with several members of my staff, because we were invited here. I am here because I have basic organizational ties here.

Beyond this, I am in Birmingham because injustice is here. Just as the eighth century prophets left their little villages and carried their "thus saith the Lord" far beyond the boundaries of their hometowns; and just as the Apostle Paul left his little village of Tarsus and carried the gospel of Jesus Christ to practically every hamlet and city of the Graeco-Roman world, I too am compelled to carry the gospel of freedom beyond my particular hometown. Like Paul, I must constantly respond to the Macedonian call for aid.

Moreover, I am cognizant of the interrelatedness of all communities and states. I cannot sit idly by in Atlanta and not be concerned about what happens in Birmingham. Injustice anywhere is a threat to justice everywhere. We are caught in an inescapable network of mutuality, tied in a single garment of destiny. Whatever affects one directly affects all indirectly. Never again can we afford to live with the narrow, provincial "outside agitator" idea. Anyone who lives in the United States can never be considered an outsider anywhere in this country.

You deplore the demonstrations that are presently taking place in Birmingham. But I am sorry that your statement did not express a similar concern for the conditions that brought the demonstrations into being. I am sure that each of you would want to go beyond the superficial social analyst who looks merely at effects, and does not grapple with underlying causes. I would not hesitate to say that it is unfortunate that so-called demonstrations are taking place in Birmingham at this time, but I would say in more emphatic terms that it is even more unfortunate that the white power structure of this city left the Negro community with no other alternative.

You may well ask, "Why direct action? Why sit-ins, marches, etc.? Isn't negotiation a better path?" You are exactly right in your call for negotiation. Indeed, this is the purpose of direct action. Nonviolent direct action seeks to create such a crisis and establish such creative tension that a community that has constantly refused to negotiate is forced to confront the issue. It seeks so to dramatize the issue that it can no longer be ignored. I just referred to the creation of tension as a part of the work of the nonviolent resister. This may sound rather shocking. But I must confess that I am not afraid of the word tension. I have earnestly worked and preached against violent tension, but there is a type of constructive nonviolent tension that is necessary for growth. Just as Socrates felt that it was necessary to create a tension in the mind so that individuals could rise from the bondage of myths and half-truths to the unfettered realm of creative analysis and objective appraisal, we must see the need of having nonviolent gadflies to create the kind of tension in society that will help men to rise from the dark depths of prejudice and racism to the majestic heights of understanding and brotherhood. So the purpose of the direct action is to create a situation so crisis-packed that it will inevitably open the door to negotiation. We, therefore, concur with you in your call for negotiation. Too long has our beloved Southland been bogged down in the tragic attempt to live in monologue rather than dialogue.

We know through painful experience that freedom is never voluntarily given by the oppressor; it must be demanded by the oppressed. Frankly, I have never yet engaged in a [direct-action] movement that was "well-timed," according to the time table of those who have not suffered unduly from the disease of segregation.

For years now I have heard the word "Wait!" It rings in the ear of every Negro with a piercing familiarity. This "Wait" has almost always meant "Never." It has been a tranquilizing thalidomide, relieving the emotional stress for a moment, only to give birth to an ill-formed infant of frustration. We must come to see with the distinguished jurist of yesterday that "justice too long delayed is justice denied." We have waited for more than 340 years for our constitutional and God-given rights. The nations of Asia and Africa are moving with jetlike speed toward the goal of political independence, and we still creep at horse and buggy pace toward the gaining of a cup of coffee at a lunch counter. I guess it is easy for those who have never felt the stinging darts of segregation to say, "Wait." But when you have seen vicious mobs lynch your mothers and fathers at will and drown your sisters and brothers at whim; when you have seen hate-filled policemen curse, kick, brutalize and even kill your black brothers and sisters with impunity; when you see the vast majority of your twenty million Negro brothers smothering in an airtight cage of poverty in the midst of an affluent society; when you suddenly find your tongue twisted and your speech stammering as you seek to explain to your six-year-old daughter why she can't go to the public amusement park that has just been advertised on television, and see tears welling up in her little eyes when she is told that Funtown is closed to colored children, and see the depressing clouds of inferiority begin to form in her little mental sky, and see her begin to distort her little personality by unconsciously developing a bitterness toward white people; when you have to concoct an answer for a five-year-old son asking in agonizing pathos: "Daddy, why do white people treat colored people so mean?"; when you take a cross-country drive and find it necessary to sleep night after night in the uncomfortable corners of your automobile because no motel will accept you; when you are humiliated day in and day out by nagging signs reading "white" and "colored"; when your first name becomes "nigger" and your middle name becomes "boy" (however old you are) and your last name becomes "John," and when your wife and mother are never given the respected title ".Mrs."; when you are harried by day and haunted by night by the fact that you are a Negro, living constantly at tiptoe stance never quite knowing what to expect next, and plagued with inner fears and outer resentments; when you are forever fighting a degenerating sense of "nobodiness"; then you will understand why we find it difficult to wait. There comes a time when the cup of endurance runs over, and men are no longer willing to be plunged into an abyss of injustice where they experience the blackness of corroding despair. I hope, sirs, you can understand our legitimate and unavoidable impatience.

You express a great deal of anxiety over our willingness to break laws. This is certainly a legitimate concern. Since we so diligently urge people to obey the Supreme Court's decision of 1954 outlawing segregation in the public schools, it is rather strange and paradoxical to find us consciously breaking laws. One may well ask, "How can you advocate breaking some laws and obeying others?" The answer is found in the fact that there are two types of laws: there are *just* and there are *unjust* laws. I would agree with Saint Augustine that "An unjust law is no law at all."

Now what is the difference between the two? How does one determine when a law is just or unjust? A just law is a man-made code that squares with the moral law or the law of God. An unjust law is a code that is out of harmony with the moral law. To put it in the terms of Saint Thomas Aquinas, an unjust law is a human law that is not rooted in eternal and natural law. Any law that uplifts human personality is just. Any law that degrades human personality is unjust. All segregation statutes are unjust because segregation distorts the soul and damages the personality. It gives the segregator a false sense of superiority, and the segregated a false sense of inferiority. To use the words of Martin Buber, the great Jewish philosopher, segregation substi-

tutes an "I-it" relationship for the "I-thou" relationship, and ends up relegating persons to the status of things. So segregation is not only politically, economically and sociologically unsound, but it is morally wrong and sinful. Paul Tillich has said that sin is separation. Isn't segregation an existential expression of man's tragic separation, an expression of his awful estrangement, his terrible sinfulness? So I can urge men to disobey segregation ordinances because they are morally wrong.

Let us turn to a more concrete example of just and unjust laws. An unjust law is a code that a majority inflicts on a minority that is not binding on itself. This is difference made legal. On the other hand a just law is a code that a majority compels a minority to follow that it is willing to follow itself. This is sameness made legal.

Let me give another explanation. An unjust law is a code inflicted upon a minority which that minority had no part in enacting or creating because they did not have the unhampered right to vote. Who can say that the legislature of Alabama which set up the segregation laws was democratically elected? Throughout the state of Alabama all types of conniving methods are used to prevent Negroes from becoming registered voters and there are some counties without a single Negro registered to vote despite the fact that the Negro constitutes a majority of the population. Can any law set up in such a state be considered democratically structured?

These are just a few examples of unjust and just laws. There are some instances when a law is just on its face and unjust in its application. For instance, I was arrested Friday on a charge of parading without a permit. Now there is nothing wrong with an ordinance which requires a permit for a parade, but when the ordinance is used to preserve segregation and to deny citizens the First Amendment privilege of peaceful assembly and peaceful protest, then it becomes unjust.

I hope you can see the distinction I am trying to point out. In no sense do I advocate evading or defying the law as the rabid segregationist would do. This would lead to anarchy. One who breaks an unjust law must do it *openly, lovingly* (not hatefully as the white mothers did in New Orleans when they were seen on television screaming "nigger, nigger, nigger"), and with a willingness to accept the penalty. I submit that an individual who breaks a law that conscience tells him is unjust, and willingly accepts the penalty by staying in jail to arouse the conscience of the community over its injustice, is in reality expressing the very highest respect for law.

Of course, there is nothing new about this kind of civil disobedience. It was seen sublimely in the refusal of Shadrach, Meshach and Abednego to obey the laws of Nebuchadnezzar because a higher moral law was involved. It was practiced superbly by the early Christians who were willing to face hungry lions and the excruciating pain of chopping blocks, before submitting to certain unjust laws of the Roman Empire. To a degree academic freedom is a reality today because Socrates practiced civil disobedience.

We can never forget that everything Hitler did in Germany was "legal" and everything the Hungarian freedom fighters did in Hungary was "illegal." It was "illegal" to aid and comfort a Jew in Hitler's Germany. But I am sure that if I had lived in Germany during that time I would have aided and comforted my Jewish brothers even though it was illegal. If I lived in a Communist country today where certain principles dear to the Christian faith are suppressed, I believe I would openly advocate disobeying these antireligious laws. I must make two honest confessions to you, my Christian and Jewish brothers. First, I must confess that over the last few years I have been gravely disappointed with the white moderate. I have almost reached the regrettable conclusion that the Negro's great stumbling block in the stride toward freedom is not the White Citizen's Counciler or the Ku Klux Klanner, but the white moderate who is more devoted to "order" than to justice; who prefers a negative peace which is the absence of tension to a positive peace which is the presence of justice; who constantly says, "I agree with you in the goal you seek, but I can't agree with your methods of direct action"; who paternalistically feels that he can set the timetable for another man's freedom; who lives by the myth of time and who constantly advised the Negro to wait until a "more convenient season." Shallow understanding from people of good will is more frustrating than absolute misunderstanding from people of ill will. Lukewarm acceptance is much more bewildering than outright rejection.

I had hoped that the white moderate would understand that law and order exist for the purpose of establishing justice, and that when they fail to do this they become dangerously structured dams that block the flow of social progress. I had hoped that the white moderate would understand that the present tension of the South is merely a necessary phase of the transition from an obnoxious negative peace, where the Negro passively accepted his unjust plight, to a substance-filled positive peace, where all men will respect the dignity and worth of human personality. Actually, we who engage in nonviolent direct action are not the creators of tension. We merely bring to the surface the hidden tension that is already alive. We bring it out in the open where it can be seen and dealt with. Like a boil that can never be cured as long as it is covered up but must be opened with all its pus-flowing ugliness to the natural medicines of air and light, injustice must likewise be exposed, with all of the tension its exposing creates, to the light of human conscience and the air of national opinion before it can be cured.

In your statement you asserted that our actions, even though peaceful, must be condemned because they precipitate violence. But can this assertion be logically made? Isn't this like condemning the robbed man because his possession of money precipitated the evil act of robbery? Isn't this like condemning Socrates because his unswerving commitment to truth and his philosophical delvings precipitated the misguided popular mind to make him drink the hemlock? Isn't this like condemning Jesus because His unique God-consciousness and never-ceasing devotion to his will precipitated the evil act of crucifixion? We must come to see, as federal courts have consistently affirmed, that it is immoral to urge an individual to withdraw his efforts to gain his basic constitutional rights because the quest precipitates violence. Society must protect the robbed and punish the robber.

In spite of my shattered dreams of the past, I came to Birmingham with the hope that the white religious leadership of this community would see the justice of our cause, and with deep moral concern, serve as the channel through which our just grievances would get to the power structure. I had hoped that each of you would understand. But again I have been disappointed. I have heard numerous religious leaders of the South call upon their worshippers to comply with a desegregation decision because it is the *law,* but I have longed to hear white ministers say, "Follow this decree because integration is morally *right* and the Negro is your brother." In the midst of blatant injustices inflicted upon the Negro, I have watched white churches stand on the sideline and merely mouth pious irrelevancies and sanctimonious trivialities. In the midst of a mighty struggle to rid our nation of racial and economic injustice, I have heard so many ministers say, "Those are social issues with which the gospel has no real concern," and I have watched so many churches commit themselves to a completely otherworldly religion which made a strange distinction between body and soul, the sacred and the secular.

I must close now. But before closing I am impelled to mention one other point in your statement that troubled me profoundly. You warmly commended the Birmingham police force for keeping "order" and "preventing violence." I don't believe you would have so warmly commended the police force if you had seen its angry violent dogs literally biting six unarmed, nonviolent Negroes. I don't believe you would so quickly commend the policemen if you would

observe their ugly and inhuman treatment of Negroes here in the city jail; if you would watch them push and curse old Negro women and young Negro girls; if you would see them slap and kick old Negro men and young boys; if you will observe them, as they did on two occasions, refuse to give us food because we wanted to sing our grace together. I'm sorry that I can't join you in your praise for the police department.

It is true that they have been rather disciplined in their public handling of the demonstrators. In this sense they have been rather publicly "nonviolent." But for what purpose? To preserve the evil system of segregation. Over the last few years I have consistently preached that nonviolence demands that the means we use must be as pure as the ends we seek. So I have tried to make it clear that it is wrong to use immoral means to attain moral ends. But now I must affirm that it is just as wrong, or even more so, to use moral means to preserve immoral ends. Maybe Mr. Connor and his policemen have been rather publicly nonviolent, as Chief Pritchett was in Albany, Georgia, but they have used the moral means of nonviolence to maintain the immoral end of flagrant racial injustice. T. S. Eliot has said that there is no greater treason than to do the right deed for the wrong reason.

Discussion Questions

1. In what sense is an unjust law "no law at all"?
2. At several places in this letter, Dr. King approvingly cites the example of Socrates, but, in fact, Socrates refused to *disobey* the laws of the state and chose to accept his punishment (death), even though he and his followers perceived that punishment to be as very unjust. What would Dr. King say on this point?
3. Which, in your view, has been a more effective instrument of positive social change: nonviolence or violence?
4. Do you think that Dr. King would approve of the actions of those who peacefully block the entrance to abortion clinics?

23   Message to the Grass Roots

MALCOLM X

Study Questions

1. What is the difference between the "black revolution" and the "Negro revolution"?
2. On what grounds might violence be justified in America?
3. What is the basis of revolution and what criticisms does Malcolm X raise of the civil rights movement?
4. On what basis does Malcolm X say, "If you love black nationalism, you love revolution"?
5. Under what circumstances does Malcolm X's religion justify violence?

We want to have just an off-the-cuff chat between you and me, us. We want to talk right down to earth in a language that everybody here can easily understand. We all agree tonight, all of the speakers have agreed that America has a very serious problem. Not only does America have a very serious problem, but our people have a very serious problem. America's problem is us. We're her problem. The only reason she has a problem is she doesn't want us here. And every time you look at yourself, be you black, brown, red, or yellow, a so-called Negro, you represent a person who poses such a serious problem for America because you're not wanted. Once you face this as a fact, then you can start plotting a course that will make you appear intelligent, instead of unintelligent.

What you and I need to do is learn to forget our differences. When we come together, we don't come together as Baptists or Methodists. You don't catch hell because you're a Baptist and you don't catch hell because you're a Methodist. You don't catch hell because you're a Methodist or a Baptist, you don't catch hell because you're a Democrat or a Republican, you don't catch hell because you're a Mason or an Elk, and you sure don't catch hell because you're an American; because if you were an American, you wouldn't catch hell. You catch hell because you're a black man. You catch hell, all of us catch hell for the same reason.

So we're all black people, so-called Negroes, second class citizens, ex-slaves. You're nothing but an ex-slave. You don't like to be told that. But what else are you? You are ex-slaves. You didn't come here on the "Mayflower." You came here on a slave ship. In chains, like a horse, or a cow, or a chicken. And you were brought here by the people who came here on the "Mayflower," you were brought here by the so-called Pilgrims, or Founding Fathers. They were the ones who brought you here.

We have a common enemy. We have this in common. We have a common oppressor, a common exploiter, and a common discriminator. But once we all realize that we have a common enemy, then we unite—on the basis of what we have in common. And what we have foremost in common is that enemy—the white man. He's an enemy to all of us. I know some of you all think that some of them aren't enemies. Time will tell.

In Bandung back in, I think, 1954, was the first unity meeting in centuries of black people. And once you study what happened at the Bandung conference, and the results of the Bandung conference, it actually serves as a model for the same procedure you and I can use to get our problems solved. At Bandung all the nations came together, the dark nations from Africa and Asia. Some of them were Buddhists, some of them were Muslims, some of them were Christians, some were Confucianists, some were atheists. Despite their religious differences, they came together. Some were communists, some were socialists, some were capitalists—despite their economic and political differences, they came together. All of them were black, brown, red or yellow.

The number one thing that was not allowed to attend the Bandung conference was the white man. He couldn't come. Once they excluded the white man, they found that they could get together. Once they kept him out, everybody else fell right in and fell in line. This is the thing that you and I have to understand. And these people who came together didn't have nuclear weapons, they didn't have jet planes, they didn't have all of the heavy armaments that the white man has. But they had unity.

They were able to submerge their little petty differences and agree on one thing: That there one African came from Kenya and was being colonized by the Englishman, and another African came from the Congo and was being colonized by the Belgian, and another African came from Guinea and was being colonized by the French, and another came from Angola and was being colonized by the Portuguese. When they came to the Bandung conference, they looked at the Portuguese, and at the Frenchman, and at the Englishman, and at the Dutchman, and learned or realized the one thing that all of them had in common—they were all from Europe, they were all Europeans, blond, blue-eyed and white skins. They began to recognize who their enemy was. The same man that was colonizing our people in Kenya was colonizing our people in the Congo. The same one in the Congo was colonizing our people in South Africa, and in Southern Rhodesia, and in Burma, and in India, and in Afghanistan, and in Pakistan. They realized all over the world where the dark man was being oppressed, he was being oppressed by the white man; where the dark man was being exploited, he was being exploited by the white man. So they got together on this basis—that they had a common enemy.

And when you and I here in Detroit and in Michigan and in America who have been awakened today look around us, we too realize here in America we all have a common enemy, whether he's in Georgia or Michigan, whether he's in Cal-ifornia or New York. He's the same man—blue eyes and blond hair and pale skin—the same man. So what we have to do is what they did. They agreed to stop quarrelling among themselves. Any little spat that they had, they'd settle it among themselves, go into a huddle—don't let the enemy know that you've got a disagreement.

Instead of airing our differences in public, we have to realize we're all the same family. And when you have a family squabble, you don't get out on the sidewalk. If you do, everybody calls you uncouth, unrefined, uncivilized, savage. If you don't make it at home, you settle it at home; you get in the closet, argue it out behind closed doors, and then when you come out on the street, you pose a common front, a united front. And this is what we need to do in the community, and in the city, and in the state. We need to stop airing our differences in front of the white man, put the white man out of our meetings, and then sit down and talk shop with each other. That's what we've got to do.

I would like to make a few comments concerning the difference between the black revolution and the Negro revolution. Are they both the same? And if they're not, what is the difference? What is the difference between a black revolution and a Negro revolution? First, what is a revolution? Sometimes I'm inclined to believe that many of our people are using this word "revolution" loosely, without taking careful consideration of what this word actually means, and what its historic characteristics are. When you study the historic nature of revolutions, the motive of a revolution, the objective of a revolution, the result of a revolution, and the methods used in a revolution, you may change words. You may devise another program, you may change your goal and you may change your mind.

Look at the American Revolution in 1776. That revolution was for what? For land. Why did they want land? Independence. How was it carried out? Bloodshed. Number one, it was based on land, the basis of independence. And the only way they could get it was bloodshed. The French Revolution—what was it based on? The landless against the landlord. What was it for? Land. How did they get it? Bloodshed. Was no love lost, was no compromise, was no negotiation. I'm telling you—you don't know what a revolution is. Because when you find out what it is, you'll get back in the alley, you'll get out of the way.

The Russian Revolution—what was it based on? Land; the landless against the landlord. How did they bring it about? Bloodshed. You haven't got a revolution that doesn't involve bloodshed. And you're afraid to bleed. I said, you're afraid to bleed.

As long as the white man sent you to Korea, you bled. He sent you to Germany, you bled. He sent you to the South Pacific to fight the Japanese, you bled. You bleed for white people, but when it comes to seeing your own churches being bombed and little black girls murdered, you haven't got any blood. You bleed when the white man says bleed; you bite when the white man says bite; and you bark when the white man says bark. I hate to say this about us, but it's true. How are you going to be nonviolent in Mississippi, as violent as you were in Korea? How can you justify being nonviolent in Mississippi and Alabama, when your churches are being bombed and your little girls are being murdered, and at the same time you are going to get violent with Hitler, and Tojo, and somebody else you don't even know?

If violence is wrong in America, violence is wrong abroad. If it is wrong to be violent defending black women and black children and black babies and black men, then it is wrong for America to draft us and make us violent abroad in defense of her. And if it is right for America to draft us, and teach us how to be violent in defense of her, then it is right for you and me to do whatever is necessary to defend our own people right here in this country.

The Chinese Revolution—they wanted land. They threw the British out, along with the Uncle Tom Chinese. Yes, they did. They set a good example. When I was in prison, I read an article—don't be shocked when I say that I was in prison. You're still in prison. That's what America means: prison. When I was in prison, I read an article in *Life* magazine showing a little Chinese girl, nine years old; her father was on his hands and knees

and she was pulling the trigger because he was an Uncle Tom Chinaman. When they had the revolution over there, they took a whole generation of Uncle Toms and just wiped them out. And within ten years that little girl became a full-grown woman. No more Toms in China. And today it's one of the toughest, roughest, most feared countries on this earth—by the white man. Because there are no Uncle Toms over there.

Of all our studies, history is best qualified to reward our research. And when you see that you've got problems, all you have to do is examine the historic method used all over the world by others who have problems similar to yours. Once you see how they got theirs straight, then you know how you can get yours straight. There's been a revolution, a black revolution, going on in Africa. In Kenya, the Mau Mau were revolutionary; they were the ones who brought the word "Uhuru" to the fore. The Mau Mau, they were revolutionary, they believed in scorched earth, they knocked everything aside that got in their way, and their revolution also was based on land, a desire for land. In Algeria, the northern part of Africa, a revolution took place. The Algerians were revolutionists, they wanted land. France offered to let them be integrated into France. They told France, to hell with France, they wanted some land, not some France. And they engaged in a bloody battle.

So, I cite these various revolutions, brothers and sisters, to show you that you don't have a peaceful revolution. You don't have a turn-the-other-cheek revolution. There's no such thing as a nonviolent revolution. The only kind of revolution that is nonviolent is the Negro revolution. The only revolution in which the goal is loving your enemy is the Negro revolution. It's the only revolution in which the goal is a desegregated lunch counter, a desegregated theater, a desegregated park, and a desegregated public toilet; you can sit down next to white folks—on the toilet. That's no revolution. Revolution is based on land. Land is the basis of all independence. Land is the basis of freedom, justice, and equality.

The white man knows what a revolution is. He knows that the black revolution is world-wide in scope and in nature. The black revolution is sweeping Asia, is sweeping Africa, is rearing its head in Latin America. The Cuban Revolution—that's a revolution. They overturned the system. Revolution is in Asia, revolution is in Africa, and the white man is screaming because he sees revolution in Latin America. How do you think he'll react to you when you learn what a real revolution is? You don't know what a revolution is. If you did, you wouldn't use that word.

Revolution is bloody, revolution is hostile, revolution knows no compromise, revolution overturns and destroys everything that gets in its way. And you, sitting around here like a knot on the wall, saying, "I'm going to love these folks no matter how much they hate me." No, you need a revolution. Whoever heard of a revolution where they lock arms, as Rev. Cleage was pointing out beautifully, singing "We Shall Overcome"? You don't do that in a revolution. You don't do any singing, you're too busy swinging. It's based on land. A revolutionary wants land so he can set up his own nation, an Independent nation. These Negroes aren't asking for any nation—they're trying to crawl back on the plantation.

When you want a nation, that's called nationalism. When the white man became involved in a revolution in this country against England, what was it for? He wanted this land so he could set up another white nation. That's white nationalism. The American Revolution was white nationalism. The French Revolution was white nationalism. The Russian Revolution too—yes, it was—white nationalism. You don't think so? Why do you think Khrushchev and Mao can't get their heads together? White nationalism. All the revolutions that are going on in Asia and Africa today are based on what?—black nationalism. A revolutionary is a black nationalist. He wants a nation. I was reading some beautiful words by Rev. Cleage, pointing out why he couldn't get together with someone else in the city because all of them were afraid of being identified with black nationalism. If you're afraid of black nationalism, you're afraid of revolution. And if you love revolution, you love black nationalism.

To understand this, you have to go back to what the young brother here referred to as the house Negro and the field Negro back during slavery. There were two kinds of slaves, the house Negro and the field Negro. The house Negroes—they lived in the house with master, they dressed pretty good, they ate good because they ate his food—what he left. They lived in the attic or the basement, but still they lived near the master; and they loved the master more than the master loved himself. They would give their life to save the master's house—quicker than the master would. If the master said, "We got a good house here," the house Negro would say, "Yeah, we got a good house here." Whenever the master said, "we," he said, "we." That's how you can tell a house Negro.

If the master's house caught on fire, the house Negro would fight harder to put the blaze out than the master would. If the master got sick, the house Negro would say, "What's the matter, boss, *we* sick?" *We* sick! He identified himself with his master, more than his master identified with himself. And if you came to the house Negro and said, "Let's run away, let's escape, let's separate," the house Negro would look at you and say, "Man, you crazy. What you mean, separate? Where is there a better house than this? Where can I wear better clothes than this? Where can I eat better food than this?" That was that house Negro. In those days he was called a "house nigger." And that's what we call them today, because we've still got some house niggers running around here.

This modern house Negro loves his master. He wants to live near him. He'll pay three times as much as the house is worth just to live near his master, and then brag about "I'm the only Negro out here." "I'm the only one on my job." "I'm the only one in this school." You're nothing but a house Negro. And if someone comes to you right now and says, "Let's separate," you say the same thing that the house Negro said on the plantation. "What you mean, separate? From America, this good white man? Where you going to get a better job than you get here?" I mean, this is what you say. "I ain't left nothing in Africa," that's what you say. Why, you left your mind in Africa.

On that same plantation, there was the field Negro. The field Negroes—those were the masses. There were always more Negroes in the field than there were Negroes in the house. The Negro in the field caught hell. He ate leftovers. In the house they ate high up on the hog. The Negro in the field didn't get anything but what was left of the insides of the hog. They call it "chitt'lings" nowadays. In those days they called them what they were—guts. That's what you were—gut-eaters. And some of you are still gut-eaters.

The field Negro was beaten from morning to night; he lived in a shack, in a hut; he wore old, castoff clothes. He hated his master. I say he hated his master. He was intelligent. That house Negro loved his master, but that field Negro—remember, they were in the majority, and they hated the master. When the house caught on fire, he didn't try to put it out; that field Negro prayed for a wind, for a breeze. When the master got sick, the field Negro prayed that he'd die. If someone came to the field Negro and said, "Let's separate, let's run," he didn't say "Where we going?" He'd say, "Any place is better than here." You've got field Negroes in America today. I'm a field Negro. The masses are the field Negroes. When they see this man's house on fire, you don't hear the little Negroes talking about "*our* government is in trouble." They say, "*The* government is in trouble." Imagine a Negro: *Our* government"! I even heard one say "*our* astronauts." They won't even let him near the plant—and "*our* astronauts"! "*Our* Navy"—that's a Negro that is out of his mind, a Negro that is out of his mind.

Just as the slavemaster of that day used Tom, the house Negro, to keep the field Negroes in check, the same old slavemaster today has Negroes who are nothing but modern Uncle Toms, twentieth-century Uncle Toms, to keep you and me in check, to keep us under control, keep us passive and peaceful and nonviolent. That's Tom making you nonviolent. It's like when you go to the dentist, and the man's going to take your tooth. You're going to fight him when he starts pulling. So he squirts some stuff in your jaw called novocaine, to make you think they're not doing anything to you. So you sit there and because you've got all of that novocaine in your jaw, you suffer—peacefully. Blood running all down your jaw, and you don't know what's happening. Because someone has taught you to suffer—peacefully.

The white man does the same thing to you in the street, when he wants to put knots on your head and take advantage of you and not have to be afraid of your fighting back. To keep you from fighting back, he gets these old religious Uncle Toms to teach you and me, just like novocaine, to suffer peacefully. Don't stop suffering—just suffer peacefully. As Rev. Cleage pointed out, they say you should let your blood flow in the streets. This is a shame. You know he's a Christian preacher. If it's a shame to him, you know what it is to me.

There is nothing in our book, the Koran, that teaches us to suffer peacefully. Our religion teaches us to be intelligent. Be peaceful, be courteous, obey the law, respect everyone; but if someone puts his hand on you, send him to the cemetery. That's a good religion. In fact, that's that old-time religion. That's the one that Ma and Pa used to talk about: an eye for an eye, and a tooth for a tooth, and a head for a head, and a life for a life. That's a good religion. And nobody resents that kind of religion being taught but a wolf, who intends to make you his meal.

This is the way it is with the white man in America. He's a wolf—and you're sheep. Any time a shepherd, a pastor, teaches you and me not to run from the white man and, at the same time, teaches us not to fight the white man, he's a traitor to you and me. Don't lay down a life all by itself. No, preserve your life, it's the best thing you've got. And if you've got to give it up, let it be even-steven.

The slavemaster took Tom and dressed him well, fed him well and even gave him a little education—a *little* education; gave him a long coat and a top hat and made all the other slaves look up to him. Then he used Tom to control them. The same strategy that was used in those days is used today, by the same white man. He takes a Negro, a so-called Negro, and makes him prominent, builds him up, publicizes him, makes him a celebrity. And then he becomes a spokesman for Negroes—and a Negro leader.

I would like to mention just one other thing quickly, and that is the method that the white man uses, how the white man uses the "big guns," or Negro leaders, against the Negro revolution. They are not a part of the Negro revolution. They are used against the Negro revolution.

When Martin Luther King failed to desegregate Albany, Georgia, the civil-rights struggle in America reached its low point. King became bankrupt almost, as a leader. The Southern Christian Leadership Conference was in financial trouble; and it was in trouble, period, with the people when they failed to desegregate Albany, Georgia. Other Negro civil-rights leaders of so-called national stature became fallen idols. As they became fallen idols, began to lose their prestige and influence, local Negro leaders began to stir up the masses. In Cambridge, Maryland, Gloria Richardson; in Danville, Virginia, and other parts of the country, local leaders began to stir up our people at the grass-roots level. This was never done by these Negroes of national stature. They control you, but they have never incited you or excited you. They control you, they contain you, they have kept you on the plantation.

As soon as King failed in Birmingham, Negroes took to the streets. King went out to California to a big rally and raised I don't know how many thousands of dollars. He came to Detroit and had a march and raised some more thousands of dollars. And recall, right after that Roy Wilkins attacked King. He accused King and CORE [Congress Of Racial Equality] of starting trouble everywhere and then making the NAACP [National Association for the Advancement of Colored People] get them out of jail and spend a lot of money; they accused King and CORE of raising all the money and not paying it back. This happened; I've got it in documented evidence in the newspaper. Roy started attack-

ing King, and King started attacking Roy, and Farmer started attacking both of them. And as these Negroes of national stature began to attack each other, they began to lose their control of the Negro masses.

The Negroes were out there in the streets. They were talking about how they were going to march on Washington. Right at that time Birmingham had exploded, and the Negroes in Birmingham—remember, they also exploded. They began to stab the crackers in the back and bust them up 'side their head—yes, they did. That's when Kennedy sent in the troops, down in Birmingham. After that, Kennedy got on the television and said "this is a moral issue." That's when he said he was going to put out a civil-rights bill. And when he mentioned civil-rights bill and the Southern crackers started talking about how they were going to boycott or filibuster it, then the Negroes started talking—about what? That they were going to march on Washington, march on the Senate, march on the White House, march on the Congress, and tie it up, bring it to a halt, not let the government proceed. They even said they were going out to the airport and lay down on the runway and not let any airplanes land. I'm telling you what they said. That was revolution. That was revolution. That was the black revolution.

It was the grass roots out there in the street. It scared the white man to death, scared the white power structure in Washington, D.C., to death; I was there. When they found out that this black steamroller was going to come down on the capital, they called in Wilkins, they called in Randolph, they called in these national Negro leaders that you respect and told them, "Call it off." Kennedy said, "Look, you all are letting this thing go too far." And Old Tom said, "Boss, I can't stop it, because I didn't start it." I'm telling you what they said. They said, "I'm not even in it, much less at the head of it." They said, "These Negroes are doing things on their own. They're running ahead of us." And that old shrewd fox, he said, "If you all aren't in it, I'll put you in it. I'll put you at the head of it. I'll endorse it. I'll welcome it. I'll help it. I'll join it."

A matter of hours went by. They had a meeting at the Carlyle Hotel in New York City. The Carlyle Hotel is owned by the Kennedy family; that's the hotel Kennedy spent the night at, two nights ago; it belongs to his family. A philanthropic society headed by a white man named Stephen Currier called all the top civil-rights leaders together at the Carlyle Hotel. And he told them, "By you all fighting each other, you are destroying the civil-rights movement. And since you're fighting over money from white liberals, let us set up what is known as the Council for United Civil Rights Leadership. Let's form this council, and all the civil-rights organizations will belong to it, and we'll use it for fund-raising purposes." Let me show you how tricky the white man is. As soon as they got it formed, they elected Whitney Young as its chairman, and who do you think became the co-chairman? Stephen Currier, the white man, a millionaire. Powell was talking about it down at Cobo Hall today. This is what he was talking about. Powell knows it happened. Randolph knows it happened. Wilkins knows it happened. King knows it happened. Every one of that Big Six—they know it happened.

Once they formed it, with the white man over it, he promised them and gave them $800,000 to split up among the Big Six; and told them that after the march was over they'd give them $700,000 more. A million and a half dollars—split up between leaders that you have been following, going to jail for, crying crocodile tears for. And they're nothing but Frank James and Jesse James and the what-do-you-call-'em brothers.

As soon as they got the setup organized, the white man made available to them top public-relations experts; opened the news media across the country at their disposal, which then began to project these Big Six as the leaders of the march. Originally, they weren't even in the march. You were talking this march talk on Hastings Street, you were talking march talk on Lenox Avenue, and on Fillmore Street, and on Central Avenue, and 32nd Street and 63rd Street. That's where the march talk was being talked. But the white man put the Big Six at the head of it; made them the march. They became the march. They took it

over. And the first move they made after they took it over, they invited Walter Reuther, a white man; they invited a priest, a rabbi, and an old white preacher, yes, an old white preacher. The same white element that put Kennedy into power—labor, the Catholics, the Jews, and liberal Protestants; the same clique that put Kennedy in power, joined the march on Washington.

It's just like when you've got some coffee that's too black, which means it's too strong. What do you do? You integrate it with cream, you make it weak. But if you pour too much cream in it, you won't even know you ever had coffee. It used to be hot, it becomes cool. It used to be strong, it becomes weak. It used to wake you up, now it puts you to sleep. This is what they did with the march on Washington. They joined it. They didn't integrate it, they infiltrated it. They joined it, became a part of it, took it over. And as they took it over, it lost its militancy. It ceased to be angry, it ceased to be hot, it ceased to be uncompromising. Why, it even ceased to be a march. It became a picnic, a circus. Nothing but a circus, with clowns and all. You had one right here in Detroit—I saw it on television—with clowns leading it, white clowns and black clowns. I know you don't like what I'm saying, but I'm going to tell you anyway. Because I can prove what I'm saying. If you think I'm telling you wrong, you bring me Martin Luther King and A. Philip Randolph and James Farmer and those other three, and see if they'll deny it over a microphone.

No, it was a sellout. It was a takeover. When James Baldwin came in from Paris, they wouldn't let him talk, because they couldn't make him go by the script. Burt Lancaster read the speech that Baldwin was supposed to make; they wouldn't let Baldwin get up there, because they know Baldwin is liable to say anything. They controlled it so tight, they told those Negroes what time to hit town, how to come, where to stop, what signs to carry, what song to sing, what speech they could make, and what speech they couldn't make; and then told them to get out of town by sundown. And every one of those Toms was out of town by sundown. Now I know you don't like my saying this. But I can back it up. It was a circus, a performance that beat anything Hollywood could ever do, the performance of the year. Reuther and those other three devils should get an Academy Award for the best actors because they acted like they really loved Negroes and fooled a whole lot of Negroes. And the six Negro leaders should get an award too, for the best supporting cast.

Discussion Questions

1. When accused of advocating violence, Malcolm X generally replied that he advocated it only in self-defense. But is. he not in this speech advocating a violent revolution? Or can even revolution be an act of self-defense?
2. Even today, is *land* the proper basis of revolution and black nationalism? Or has the development of technology made land much less important?
3. Should the movement of the 1960s have been after land, as Malcolm X suggests, rather than such goals as the integration of public facilities?
4. Is it fair to call the leaders of the civil rights movement (in the 1960s or at present) "Uncle Toms"?

24   Psychological Violence, Physical Violence, and Racial Oppression

HOWARD McGARY

Study Questions

1. What three possible justifications of black violence does McGary cite? Which does he take most seriously, which least?
2. What two types of violence does this essay concern?
3. Describe the three conditions normally thought necessary to justify self-defense.
4. What conclusion does McGary reach regarding the justified use of violence in self-defense by African Americans?

Strong pacifists deny that violence is ever necessary in human affairs. Gandhi and Martin L. King, Jr. are seen as famous proponents of this position (Ansbro [1983]). Although Gandhi and King are well respected, most Americans reject the strong pacifist position. Most Americans believe that violence, under certain conditions, has its place. Americans disagree, however, over when it is morally appropriate to use violence in human affairs.

Violence for many theorists is evil and is only justified as a means to achieve some extremely important end. To do violence to someone is to injure that person, but persons can be injured in two basic ways: we can injure someone by physically abusing that person and we can injure someone by causing that person's psychological distress. Although Americans recognize both kinds of violence or injury, physical violence, as a response to injustice or wrongdoing is thought to require a stronger justification than the commission of an act that causes psychological violence. Psychological violence often results from the misuse of others through the manipulation of their emotions and feelings.

Even people who are weary of violence to achieve good ends are willing to accept violence if it is the only means to stop even greater physical violence. But many of these people reject using physical violence to halt psychological vio-

Reprinted by permission of the publisher from *Existence in Black*, Lewis R. Gordon, ed. (New York: Routledge, 1997), pp. 263–272.

lence when it is the only means for doing so. Of course, we could debate whether physical violence is the only means available, in particular cases, but for the purposes of this paper, we shall assume that this is the case. If this is the case, are there moral reasons for opposing the use of physical violence to prevent psychological violence? I wish to explore this question in the context of the debate over what is morally appropriate in the battle to eliminate racial oppression. Our concern will be with the moral appropriateness of the use of physical violence to thwart psychological violence, not the tactics and the political wisdom of such use.

Let us begin to examine this question by considering the following hypothetical case: suppose large numbers of innocent African Americans are randomly seized by government authorities and hauled off to concentration camps. Would these African Americans or persons acting in their behalf be justified in using physical violence if nonviolent means have been tried and failed? Most people would think so. We tend to think that physical violence is justified as a kind of self-defense against violence provided that this self-defensive violence is proportionate in kind, unavoidable, and the threat that provokes the violence is imminent. In enumerating these conditions, I am not claiming that there is total agreement about the correct theory of self-defense, but only that most theorists believe physical violence can be used to prevent physical violence when the above conditions obtain.

What about the use of physical violence to prevent psychological violence caused by oppression? Many Americans cannot answer this question in the affirmative. Why is this so? Perhaps an important part of the answer lies in our lack of understanding about the serious detrimental consequences of psychological harms. Many people tend to underestimate their seriousness. These people are reluctant to justify physical violence to prevent what they take to be questionable harms. But even some of the people who acknowledge the severity of psychological harms are reluctant to endorse the use of physical violence to prevent psychological violence. They question whether the conditions of proportionality, avoidability, and imminent danger are satisfied when we combat psychological violence with physical violence.

Juries, for example, have found it extremely difficult to acquit women who use self-defense to justify their use of physical violence against a psychologically (mentally) abusive husband. Jurors who have been interviewed in such cases often believe that the avoidability and imminent danger conditions have not been satisfied. In a number of cases, I think they are wrong in reaching this conclusion, but saying why they are wrong is no simple matter. The jurors rightfully draw a distinction in these cases between a woman who uses physical violence against a mentally abusive husband because of temporary insanity brought on by mental abuse and a self-defense plea. They recognize that it would be wrong to equate a temporary insanity plea with a self-defense plea. Logically speaking, a woman may use physical violence against a psychologically abusive husband without being insane or irrational. But given the circumstances of many abused women, the wherewithal and avenues of action available to these women are very circumscribed. So, in many cases, their violent response to abuse is rational given their circumscribed circumstances (see Bell [1993]).

Now I would like to return to the issue of racial oppression and the use of physical violence. In a paper on violence and terrorism, the philosopher Kai Nielsen ask his readers to consider the following hypothetical case:

Suppose that the members of a small, impoverished, ill-educated ethnic minority in some democratic society are treated as second-class citizens. They are grossly discriminated against in educational opportunities and jobs, segregated in specific and undesirable parts of the country, and not allowed to marry people from other ethnic groups or to mix socially with them. For years they have pleaded and argued their case but to no avail. Moreover, working through the courts has always been a dead end, and their desperate and despairing turn to nonviolent civil disobedience has been tolerated—as the powerful and arrogant can tolerate it—but utterly ignored. Their demonstrations have not been met with violence but, rather, have simply been on violently contained and then effectively ignored. And finally suppose this small, weak and desperately impoverished minority has no effective way of emigrating. (440)

Nielsen wonders whether members of this group are entitled to use violence to protect their human rights. Nielsen concludes that they are and that the telling reasons against their doing so are prudential and not moral. Is he right? Nielsen describes a case where a group of people are clearly oppressed, but it is not the case that the oppressors have used physical violence to oppress this group. Nonetheless, he rightfully concludes that the denial of important human rights can warrant self-defensive violence.

The human right that Nielsen focuses on is the right to equal opportunity. The denial of the right to equal opportunity is quite serious and according to Nielsen, may justify physical violence even when physical violence is not used to deny a group equal opportunities. Nielsen seems to believe that members of this group cannot avoid the harm caused to them and that the harm is so serious and direct to warrant the self-defensive physical violence.

But some people may be unconvinced that physical violence is the proper response in such cases because the very fact that this group lives in a democratic society means that their condition, at least in theory, can be addressed through democratic nonviolent means. The group should be patient and pursue all of the nonviolent means for changing their condition. Why is this not a correct response?

I think it fails because such a response does not appreciate the severe negative consequences that result from a denial of basic human rights. Nielsen's case focuses on a lack of opportunities, but by implication it points out that members of this group are not seen as moral equals. The kind of treatment described in Nielsen's example serves to undermine, damage, and destroy a person's sense of self. W. E. B. Du Bois spoke eloquently to what happens to the psyche of black people or any similarly oppressed people when

they are not seen or treated as moral equals by the dominant society (see Du Bois [1969]). Frantz Fanon, the celebrated psychiatrist and revolutionary, graphically explains how a system of racial oppression constitutes psychological violence against the oppressed (Fanon [1967a]; [1968]). Both Du Bois and Fanon realized that a prolonged denial of a person's right as a human being to equal concern and respect leads to a depreciation of self and quite possibly to the destruction of the moral self. So in response to those who urge patience and tolerance, these virtues may come at too great a cost; namely, a loss of self. (McGary [1992–93]: 283–5).

Earlier I claimed that there is a strong tendency to devalue the impact of psychological harm when it comes to the abuse of women. I also contend that this is the case with African Americans. There is plenty of evidence that shows that many whites ignore or underestimate the harms inflicted on African Americans (Hochschild and Herk [1990]: 310–6). Many of these harms have been physical, but there have also been serious and far-reaching psychological harms that accompany the denial of some basic human rights. These psychological harms, in some cases, are more damaging than physical harms. If this is true, then physical violence maybe a morally appropriate response to psychological violence.

If we assume that we can use physical violence to thwart physical violence under the conditions described above, then is it reasonable to think that serious psychological violence, under certain conditions, can warrant the use of physical violence? In the case of racial oppression in the United States, the harms that African Americans experienced were (and some would say still are) unavoidable because a system of racial oppression is constructed in ways that makes it next to impossible for oppressed groups to escape its damaging effects (McGary [1992–93]: 285–90). The use of physical violence to defend oneself against psychological harm in a racially oppressive system may be proportional and perhaps can be seen as such when we fully appreciate the serious destructive effects of a system of racial oppression. The threat of harm in such a system might be imminent because it is always present and pervasive, and it continues to get worse if not addressed.

I shall examine each of these conditions for when violence can be seen as self-defense in the context of racial oppression against African Americans. Hopefully, by doing so, I can shed some light on whether psychological violence brought on by a system of racial oppression can justify the use of physical violence by those who are oppressed by such a system. However, before I begin this examination, I will first explain why self-defense is the issue. One might think that a very psychologically oppressive system might cause its victims to be insane and thus their acts of violence are not acts of self-defense but merely the reactions of people who suffer from a form of socially induced mental illness.

For example, in the Colin Ferguson case in New York (the African-American male who was convicted of killing and wounding a number of people on the Long Island Railroad), Ferguson's original attorneys (before Ferguson decided to serve as his own attorney) proffered the so-called "black rage" defense. Drawing on the work of Cobbs and Grier on black rage (1969), they argued that Ferguson was not legally responsible for his conduct because he was acting out of compulsion brought on by the consuming nature of white racism. This is clearly a controversial claim. I will not discuss the merits of this claim here. I mention it only to point out one of the ways people have attempted to mitigate or excuse violent behavior associated with racial oppression.

The black rage defense, I think, should be distinguished from the classic defense of violence advanced by Frantz Fanon (see Fanon [1968]). Fanon argued that the Algerian native suffered from what he called "colonial neurosis." This neurosis resulted from Algerian peasants being treated as less than human by their French colonizers. This system of colonization caused the peasants to come to see themselves a less than human and thus not the moral equals of their colonizers. Fanon boldly asserted that violence was

a necessary means for eliminating this neurosis. In a frequently quoted passage he wrote:

At the level of individuals, violence is a cleansing force, it frees the colonized from his inferiority complex and from his despair and inaction; it makes him fearless and restores his self-respect. (Fanon [1968]: 94)

Fanon goes on to say:

. . . colonialism is not a thinking machine, nor a body endorsed with reasoning faculties. It is violence in its natural state and will only yield when confronted with greater violence. (Fanon [1968]: 61)

and

Violence alone, violence committed by the people, violence *organized and educated by its leaders,* make it possible for the masses to understand social truths and gives the key to them. (Fanon [1968]: 147)

Clearly Fanon viewed revolutionary violence by the Algerian peasants as a cleansing force. For Fanon, it was the only way the colonized peasant could restore his moral equality and self-respect. But, unfortunately, Fanon's definition of revolutionary violence is tautological in nature (Caute [1970]). He says that an action is revolutionary violence only if it rejuvenates and purifies the actor. This definition is not very helpful in our attempt to distinguish political or revolutionary violence from mere acts of violence. It is also unclear whether Fanon is offering a general theory of violence or whether he is only making contingent claims about the role of violence in the Algerian context. (I tend to think that the latter interpretation is probably what Fanon had in mind but, I will not argue for that here. However, a recent work by Lewis Gordon offers a thoughtful development of that issue [see Gordon (1995b)]. If we assume that this interpretation is correct, then colonial neurosis [which can only be cured by political violence] is specific to the Algerian situation.)

Fanon's views on the necessity of violence in the Algerian colonial context are intriguing, but very different from the black-rage defense offered in behalf of Colin Ferguson. According to the black-rage defense, Ferguson was driven by racism to a point where he snapped. He was, for all practical purposes, insane. However, for Fanon, the peasant who cures his colonial neurosis through an act of political violence makes a choice to regain his humanity through an act of political violence. The peasant is defending his humanity. So it is an act of self-defense for Fanon, not the compulsive behavior of an insane person.

I would like to make it clear that I am not claiming, as Frantz Fanon did, that physical violence is always necessary for freeing those who suffer from a system of racial oppression, but only that it may be morally permissible, under certain conditions, even when the system is not maintained through the use of physical violence. But in order to make such a view plausible we need to examine closely the conditions of valid claims to self-defense: avoidability, imminence, and proportionality.

A legitimate act of self-defense is not a preemptive strike against a dreaded aggressor or an act of retaliation against a successful aggressor. In the words of the legal scholar, George Fletcher, "self-defense must be neither too soon or too late" ([1988]: 20). In the case of an extremely racially oppressive system, the victims of this oppression cannot have the intention to act violently because they assume that some harmful event could happen when the event is not imminent. Nor can they have the intention of harming or punishing the aggressor if their action is to qualify as self-defense. The intention of the agent must be to thwart the assault or attack and not to harm the victim per se ([1988]: 19).

The case we are discussing is also complicated by the fact that we are talking about a group of people, namely African Americans. Given that our focus is a group, if self-defense is legitimate then it must be because each member of the group has acted with the appropriate intentions or that a subset of the group has the authority to act for the group. For example, a board of directors can have the legal and moral authority to act for an organization. But even if the subset is authorized to act on behalf of the group, this subset must act with the appropriate intentions.

Let us now turn to the three conditions that are thought to be necessary and sufficient for an act of self-defense.

Avoidability

This condition requires that an actor not use violence or deadly force against someone who poses a threat to them if there is some other way to avoid the imminent harm without doing so. This requirement is most often understood in terms of the alternatives or lack of alternatives available to the actor. For example, if you threaten me with bodily harm, and I can avoid the harm by running away, I should do so. In such a case, if I choose to shoot you rather than run away, then I have failed to satisfy the avoidability condition on self-defense.

In our example involving an unyielding system of racial discrimination, the oppressed group cannot simply turn to the political process for relief because they are a discrete, despised minority in a majority-rule democracy. But what if there is a political mechanism that will allow these oppressed groups to mitigate the tyrany of the majority in democratic society? Perhaps proposals like the ones offered by Lani Guinier in her book, *The Tyranny of the Majority,* can make the system more responsive to the rights and interests of all, including a despised minority.

Guinier recommends the following: (1) Cumulative voting: "Voters get the same number of seats or options as to vote for, and they can then distribute their votes in combination to reflect their preferences. Like-minded votes can form a solid block, or instead form strategic cross-racial coalitions to gain mutual benefits" (Guinier: 15). (2) Race-Conscious Districting: legislative districts are constructed in a way such that certain groups who have historically not had their interests fairly represented can do so. It makes it possible for members of a discreet minority to elect representatives who are members of their group or to elect candidates that articulate their interests. Districts are based upon ensuring equal opportunity rather than geography (Guinier: 135). Guinier believes that when both of these proposals are combined together, we can achieve political procedures that are fair to all. In theory proposals like the ones offered by Guinier are instructive, and might solve the problem, but in reality her proposals have been met with strong opposition by some very powerful members of the majority. It is doubtful that her proposals in the present political climate will become law. The avoidability condition should focus on real alternatives, not alternatives that are just in theory possible.

Of course, Guinier's proposals are not the only ones offered to eliminate racial oppression. A frequent recommendation offered by some members of the majority is the proposal "love it or leave it." A generous interpretation of this recommendation is that the minority citizens are free to emigrate to other countries if they find this system so oppressive. Putting aside that this response is often just a polite way of expressing racial animosity, it fails to appreciate that the avoidability condition only requires people to take reasonable and practical alternatives that are available to them.

It is unreasonable and impractical to expect people with modest means who have lived all of their lives in this country to move to a foreign country where they have few, if any, prospects for securing a livelihood. Of course, wealthy African Americans might find this option more realistic, but wealthy African Americans are less likely to need to take such drastic measure because they are in a better position to ward off the damaging effects of systematic racial discrimination. The idea that the victims of racial oppression can eliminate this oppression by leaving the society or by forming their own separate communities within American society is not new. The reasonableness of these proposals have been vigorously debated for hundreds of years (McGary [1983]).

Whether an alternative open to the actor is reasonable is crucial in deciding whether or not the avoidability condition has been satisfied (Gillespie [1989]: 93). Is there some reasonable alternative to the use of physical violence to combat prolonged systematic racism? If the answer is yes, then morality would require that such an alternative be adopted. However, a reasonableness criteria is always culturally specific. Conduct that might be judged to be reasonable in one culture would not be so judged in a radically different culture. There are numerous examples that illustrate this point.

Certain legal scholars have also argued that what counts as reasonable can also be influenced by things like the gender of the actors. Cynthia K. Gillespie has pointed out that the courts still rely on "the reasonable man test." This is a standard for measuring what a reasonable person in like circumstances would do. But Gillespie argues that this test is unfair to women because it imposes, "a masculine standard against which to measure a woman's behavior" (Gillespie [1989]: 99). Gillespie's point is what the typical man might view as threatening is different from the typical woman given the norms in our society and the ways in which men and women are socialized. She argues that we need a culturally enlightened and gender sensitive standard for judging what is reasonable behavior (Gillespie [1989]: 100–22).

In a similar vein, scholars have argued that the experiences of black and white Americans are so different that generalizations based upon the experiences of the typical white American may not apply to the typical black American (Hochschild and Herk 1990). If this is so, what might be reasonable for a person who has experienced the alienation of the African American experience might be different from a white person from the same economic background (see McGary [1992–93]). Therefore where physical violence might be viewed as unreasonable by mainstream white America, it might be viewed as clearly reasonable by African Americans who have experienced acute and prolonged alienation and racial oppression.

Imminent Danger

The word imminent means appearing as if about to happen, impending, menacing, and threatening. As a condition of justified self-defense, the imminent danger condition requires that an assault must be about to happen if a person is justified in using violence against his attacker. An apparent problem with claiming that a person can use violence as a form of self-defense against a pervasive system of racial discrimination is the identity of the source of the assault. In such a case, who qualifies as the agents of harms?

With more oppressive systems different people occupy varied roles. Some may be the architects of harm, some may execute the harmful acts, others may condone and encourage the harm, and some may be bystanders. Does the existence of these varied roles mean that self-defensive violence can never be justified in such cases?

I do not think so. Clearly the mere fact that people occupy different roles in an oppressive system does not mean that the victim of this oppression cannot identify the various sources of the assault. Nor does it imply that the source of the assault is not apparent, menacing or threatening. I reject the contention that prolonged oppressive institutions can operate without the existence of faulty agents. The idea that a pervasive system of racial oppression can be comprised of totally innocent persons is a bit farfetched. This is not to deny that it may be extremely difficult in some cases to identify those who have acted in wrongful ways, but in theory and practice such identifications are possible.

The imminent danger condition is closely connected with the avoidability condition, but they are logically distinct. The close connection between the two conditions often means that when one condition is satisfied, so is the other condition. If it is true that a pervasive system of racial oppression is unavoidable for its victims, then there is a very good chance the dangers that these victims confront are imminent.

Proportionality

The proportionality condition requires that the self-defensive act must be only enough to stop or prevent the assault. For instance, you should not kill an aggressor when wounding him would stop the assault. The proportionality condition requires that we only use the minimal force necessary to stop or prevent an assault. This condition demands that we weigh the competing interests of the potential victim as well as the aggressor.

Given this condition, if the self-defense plea is used to justify the use of physical violence in our racial oppression case, then physical violence used to thwart the assault must be proportional to psychological violence used against the victims. Since the proportionality condition requires that we balance the interests of the victims as well as the aggressors, one might conclude that we can't properly balance these interests because we are dealing with apples and oranges. However, this belief is based upon the erroneous assumption that there is no adequate way to compare psychological and physical harms. But if we only reflect for a moment, we will see that this is a mistake. We often make such comparisons. For example, we judge that the pain caused by the death of a loved one is far less harmful than a serious cut on our finger. And many people would prefer to experience some physical harm than to be rejected by a love interest.

Psychological harms are real and people can cause them. Furthermore, these harms can be compared or balanced against physical harms. To claim otherwise is to raise a red herring. Acts of violence committed by members of a group who have experienced prolonged and acute systematic discrimination may be justifiable as a kind of self-defense, provided that their conduct satisfies the three conditions of justified self-defense.

Hopefully, in a preliminary way, I have offered some good reasons for thinking that these conditions can be satisfied. I am not arguing for violence. My task was to show that if violence can be justified on grounds of self-defense, then a pervasive system of racial oppression that causes serious psychological harms to its victims could warrant the use of physical violence.

Discussion Questions

1. Do you think that "psychological violence" (as McGary defines it) can justify *physical* violence in self-defense? Might it only justify psychological violence in return?
2. As in the Colin Ferguson case, can "white racism" yield a valid legal defense for a violent act against whites, even those who are apparently not doing anything threatening?

3. Explain the difference between the "black rage" defense and the justification of violence offered by Fanon in *The Wretched of the Earth.*

4. Does violence as a valid response to *oppression* have to be understood as a form of self-defense? Or is there a better justification for it?

Bibliography

Ansbro, J. J. [1983] *Martin Luther King, Jr.: The Making of a Mind* (New York: Orbis).

Bell, L. [1993] *Rethinking Ethics in the Midst of Violence* (Boston: Rowman & Littlefield).

DuBois, W. E. B. [1969] *Souls of Black Folk* (New York: Signet).

Fanon, F. [1967] *Black Skin, White Masks* (New York: Grove Press).

———[1968] *The Wretched of the Earth* (New York: Grove Press).

Fletcher, G. P. [1988] *The Crime of Self-Defense: Bernard Goetz and the Law on Trial* (New York: Free Press).

Gillespie, C. K. [1989] *Justified Homicide: Battered Women, Self-Defense, and the Law* (Columbus: Ohio State University Press).

Gordon, L. [1995] *Fanon and the Crisis of European Man* (New York: Routledge).

Grier, W. H. and Cobbs, P. [1969] *Black Rage* (New York: Basic Books).

Hochchild, J. L. and Herk, M. [1990] "Yes, but: Caveats in American Racial Attitudes," *Nomos* 32.

McGary, H. [1983] "Racial Integration and Racial Separation" in Leonard Harris, ed., *Philosophy Born of Struggle* (Dubuque, IA: Kendall/Hunt).

———[1992–93] "Alienation and the African-American Experience," *Philosophical Forum* 24.

25 Group Autonomy and Narrative Identity

LAURENCE M. THOMAS

Study Questions

1. What is meant by "group autonomy" and why is it a good thing?

2. What is a "narrative" and how is it related to group autonomy?

3. How does the absence of a narrative work to the disadvantage of a group?

4. Why doesn't a common culture provide blacks with a narrative identity? Why not a common history of discrimination?

5. Why does the kind of "structural equality" presently existing make having a narrative even more important than during periods of legal discrimination?

Originally appeared in *Color, Class, Identity: The New Politics of Race,* John Arthur and Amy Shapiro, eds. (Boulder, CO: Westview Press, 1996), pp. 179–190. Reprinted by permission of the author.

Any attempt to compare the suffering of blacks and Jews would seem likely to be felled by the waves of invidious comparisons. That is because any such comparison is likely to be seen, however obliquely, as an endeavor to answer the question: Which group has suffered more—blacks or Jews? And the feeling, of course, is that the suffering of both has been (and is) so heinous that to be concerned with answering that question is to embark upon a most despicable kind of moral enterprise. Be that as it may, there can be instructive comparisons regarding the suffering of Jews and blacks. I shall attempt such a comparison in this essay. At the very end of this essay, I shall speak to why it has seemed so natural to compare Jews and blacks.

I.

My thesis is that *despite* the Holocaust contemporary Jews have group autonomy, whereas *on account of* American slavery contemporary blacks do not. An identifiable group of people has group autonomy when its members are generally regarded by others not belonging to the group as the foremost interpreters of their own historical-cultural traditions. I take it to be obvious that group autonomy, understood in that way, is a moral good of enormous importance. On an individual level the most significant indication that others take us seriously is that they regard us as the foremost interpreters of who we are: our desires, aims, values, beliefs, and so on. Suppose I were to ask a person about her aims and so forth—but only as a matter of courtesy, it being evident that I have already satisfied myself as to what the person is like. If the person has any self-respect at all, she would rightly feel insulted, resentful, and angry. The importance of group autonomy is analogous. Normally, it is only because a group has an extraordinary command of its own history and experiences that it has group autonomy. It is logically possible that a group could have such autonomy and yet lack a command of these things, if the group is regarded as having mastery of its historical-cultural traditions when, in actuality, it does not. On the other hand, it is not sufficient for group autonomy that a group has such mastery, since having the mastery is quite compatible with other groups not acknowledging that it does.

To be sure, it is a consequence of my account that group autonomy is contingent upon being held in a certain regard by others. This is true of self-regarding attitudes in general. Insofar as we respect ourselves as individuals, it is precisely because we have been respected often enough by others. If respect from others has been adequate at the very formative stages of our lives, then it is possible to endure a considerable amount of disrespect from others for a period of time without losing our respect for ourselves, even if our self-respect shows signs of wearing out. And massive displays of respect after the ordeal would be cru-

cial to repairing the damage done—to strengthening the paths of self-respect that had worn thin. Our own self-respect is not thereby diminished because it is anchored in the respect that we receive from others. By parity of reasoning, then, group autonomy is not diminished because it is anchored in the respect that a group receives from other groups.

I maintain that despite the Holocaust contemporary Jews have group autonomy, whereas on account of American slavery contemporary blacks do not. At any rate, blacks have considerably less group autonomy than Jews. What fuels my thinking are the following considerations: 1) Given the evil of the Holocaust for Jews and the evil of slavery for blacks, if any two groups should interact in harmony with one another it is Jews and blacks. 2) It is clear that they do not. And 3) I do not find the prevailing explanation that there is enormous economic disparity between blacks and Jews to be a complete explanation for the disharmony between the two groups. I do not wish to discount the reality of the economic disparity between blacks and Jews as a factor in black-Jewish tensions; rather, I believe that the disharmony between the two groups can be explained in a different and morally more satisfying way.

I suggest that some of the negative feelings toward Jews that are so prevalent among blacks can be attributed to the fact that Jews have considerably more group autonomy than blacks. This difference has given rise to resentment born of envy on the part of blacks toward Jews. At the end of this essay, I shall say something about racism on the part of Jews toward blacks.

Group autonomy is an indisputable moral good. It is understandable that every group should want to have it. Likewise, if a group which has been egregiously wronged should fail to have it, then it is understandable, though in no way justifiable, that the members of that group should be envious of the members of groups which have it, especially the members of groups which have also been egregiously wronged. For envy is a function of the uncomfortably small distance that we find between ourselves and others who possess goods that we prize. It does not require any wrongdoing on anyone's part. As social beings, we inevitably have a comparative conception of ourselves, and sometimes we cannot prevent or blunt the force of a stark comparison between ourselves and those who possess a prized good. It is perfectly understandable, for instance, that a person without legs might experience envy from time to time toward persons with legs. Envy is no less understandable when it can be attributed to a prized good that is moral, as group autonomy certainly is.

When we see the negative feelings that blacks have toward Jews derives, in large part, from the disparity in group autonomy between the two groups rather than from the economic disparity between them, we thereby view those negative feelings from a different part of the moral landscape. Of course, understandable envy is no less envy, and we should do all that we can to dissipate it. But our attitude toward understandable envy should be different from our attitude toward envy born of rapaciousness. And this holds all the more when the envy can be attributed to a failure to possess the prized moral good of group autonomy owing to social victimization. I do not want to deny the existence of anti-Semitism on the part of blacks toward Jews. It is very real indeed. Rather, I have tried to show that not all negative feelings that blacks might have toward Jews are properly characterized as anti-Semitic. I take it to be obvious that resentment on the part of blacks toward Jews owing to the differential between them with respect to group autonomy is far more morally palatable than resentment owing to the economic success of Jews.

Needless to say, I am no more blaming blacks for lacking group autonomy than I am crediting Jews for having it. Neither situation can be construed as a matter of choice.

It is perhaps tempting to suppose that group autonomy comes in the wake of economic success. This temptation should be resisted, however. In *A Certain People* (1986), Charles E. Silberman paints a glowing picture of the success of American Jews. Well, the success of Jews should not blind us to the reality that in general Jews did not arrive in America well-off. On the contrary, many were quite poor when they came here. Yet they had group autonomy.

It was not too long ago that Jews had considerable difficulty getting into so venerable an institution as Harvard University, as Bruce Kuklick has shown in *The Rise of American Philosophy* (1977). Indeed, the Harvard philosophy department has come a very long way since the days of Harvard University's president, Lawrence Lowell, who wrote that "Cambridge could make a Jew indistinguishable from an Anglo-Saxon; but not even Harvard could make a black man white." But even in those days—when Harvard philosophy professors could write, in a letter on behalf of a Jew, that "he has none of the traits calculated to excite prejudice" (Ralph Perry), and that his Jewishness is "faintly marked and by no means offensive" (James Wood)—the Jews, I submit, still had group autonomy.

On the other hand, it is far from obvious that economically well-off blacks have group autonomy. In the area of sports and entertainment, numerous blacks are making millions upon millions of dollars. All the same, there is no reason to suppose that, collectively or individually, blacks in sports and entertainment have more group autonomy than other blacks. Together, these considerations show that economic good fortune is neither a necessary basis for group autonomy nor a sufficient basis for it. What then is? The answer, I suggest, is a narrative.

II.

By a narrative, I mean a set of stories which defines values and entirely positive goals, which specifies a set of fixed points of historical significance, and which defines a set of ennobling rituals to be regularly performed. A goal is entirely positive only if it is not in any way defined in terms of avoiding some harm. Thus, simply eliminating sexism, or racism, or anti-Semitism does not constitute a positive goal, as important as these objectives are. Learning Swahili, by contrast, can be a positive goal, even if it turns out to help one avoid some harm, since the goal itself can be entirely specified independently of avoiding any harm. A narrative can be understood as a group's conception of its good. The stories which constitute a narrative may very well be true, but they need not be—though perhaps they cannot be blatantly inconsistent with the facts. For example, the Jewish narrative (as well as the Muslim one) holds that Abraham circumcised himself in his old age, with a stone no less. Can this be true? Well, it simply does not matter at this point. For circumcision has been required of Jewish males down through the ages. What Abraham actually did does not change one iota the fact that this has been an ennobling ritual among Jewish males down through the ages.

Now, given the character of American slavery, it can hardly be surprising that this institution and its racist legacy left blacks bereft of a narrative, and so of group autonomy. The Holocaust did not leave Jews bereft of a narrative, and so of their conception of the good. This is not because the Holocaust was a less nefarious institution than American slavery, but because the Holocaust was a radically different kind of nefarious institution. The telos of American slavery was utter dependence; the telos of the Holocaust was the extermination of the Jews. The former is best achieved by depriving the victims of any sense of their history. As a matter of logic, the latter, of course, is achieved by death. But Hitler did not succeed in exterminating the Jews; and his failure made it possible for the Jewish narrative to survive. Reflection upon the extent to which he almost succeeded, and the means that he employed to achieve that end, leaves any morally decent person numb. But that he did not succeed is an unvarnished truth. The survival of the Jewish narrative owes to that fact. Many will insist that surely blacks have a narrative, as shown by black music and art. I think not, a point to which I shall return in due course (Section III).

Now, I believe that it is impossible for a people to flourish in a society that is hostile toward them without a narrative that is essentially isomorphic with respect to them. A narrative is essentially isomorphic when, taken in its totality, it cannot be shared by others, There are primarily two reasons why a narrative is crucial to the flourishing of a people in a hostile society. One is the obvious truth that genuine cooperation is necessary if a people is to be successful in the face of systematic hostility. The other is that there can be no genuine cooperation among a people in the absence of a narrative, for a narrative provides the basis for trust.

Having a common enemy does not, in and of itself, suffice to ensure cooperating among a people, precisely because it cannot be a basis for trust. If a member of an oppressed group has good reason to believe that she can entirely avoid social hostility without cooperating with others in her group, or that she can avoid as much hostility on her own as she would avoid if she cooperated, then she has no rationally compelling reason to cooperate with others like herself. For if one's only aim is to avoid harm, then it is totally irrelevant whether one does so with one's group or on one's own, since in either case one avoids the harm in question. What is more, there will always be the incentive to avoid the harm on one's own regardless of what might happen to the group. Naturally, a person could be motivated by altruistic considerations to help others in his group. But the motive of altruism is something distinct from and additional to the motive that stems purely from having a common enemy.

A common enemy makes for very unstable cooperation, if any at all, among a people. We can trust people when they have given us a good reason to believe that they will do their part, although they could refrain from doing so without bearing any loss whatsoever—that is, they will do their part whether they are being observed by others or not. A common enemy alone does not deliver such a basis for trust.

By contrast, when a people has a narrative, then their self-identity is tied to a set of goals and values that is independent of a common enemy. What is more, there is what I shall call contributory pride. Contributory pride is no more mysterious than pride itself or than the delight we generally take in doing things that reflect well upon our talents. Even when alone, and there is no chance of being heard by someone, a person who can play the piano well will want to do so because she delights in playing up to her level of competence. Likewise, we want our lives to reflect those values and goals which are dear to us, and it is a source of pleasure to us when this is so.

Because a narrative provides a basis for contributory pride, it allows for the possibility of genuine cooperation, in that others who belong to the group—and so identify with the narrative—can be counted on to do their part even if no one is observing their performances. Sometimes, in fact, people can be counted on to do their part even when this is at some cost to them. Such is the power of identification with an ideal. The moral of the story, then, is this. There can be no genuine cooperation among a people who belong to the same group simply on account of their desire to overcome the same hostile social forces, since the existence of the same social forces cannot suffice as a basis for mutual trust. What is needed is a set of positive values and goals which are constitutive of the self-identity of persons who belong to the group. For positive values and goals have their own motivational force, as the case of contributory pride makes abundantly clear.

III.

Let me now apply the account of a narrative, with its implications for group trust, directly to the situation of blacks and Jews. I take it to be obvious that there is an isomorphic narrative for Jews. Even people who do not like Jews are prepared to acknowledge that the Old Testament is primarily about the history of the Jews. What is more, there is a universal set of ennobling rituals which, when practiced, define being a good Jew or, at any rate, are the reference point against which a good Jew is defined, such as keeping kosher and mastering the Torah. These ennobling rituals are defined by the narrative and are entirely independent of the culture in which Jews happen to find themselves (the State of Israel aside). Wearing a yarmulke is an ennobling Jewish ritual. And notice that a non-Jew who outside of a synagogue generally wore what was unmistakably a yarmulke would be showing utter disrespect for Judaism. This speaks to the point that a narrative cannot be readily appropriated by nonmembers of the group.

Do blacks have a narrative, their conception of the good? Clearly, there is no denying the influence of African traditions upon the lives of black Americans. In voice, music, and dance the influence of Africa is unshakably there. Martin Luther King's speech, "I Have a Dream," surely owes some of its majesty to the cadence of voice, with its indelible African influence. It is impossible to listen to black gospel music and preaching without seeing—nay, feeling—the distinctiveness and richness. But form does not a narrative make. I want to say that blacks do not have a narrative—at least not as yet, anyway.

It is important to distinguish between culture and what I am calling a narrative. A narrative can be part of a culture, but it is quite possible to have a culture without a narrative. And even where a narrative is part of a culture, not everything in the culture is part of the narrative. Although bagels are very much identified with Jewish American culture, they are not part of the Jewish narrative. There are various Jewish cultures, but one Jewish narrative—though various disagreements over that narrative. While it is manifestly obvious that there is a black culture in America, that culture is not underwritten or guided by a narrative. Black music and style do not constitute an ennobling ritual. Neither rap music nor braids constitute ennobling rituals, although both are deep aspects of black culture. Things do not change with black gospel music and preaching. The distinctiveness here is indicative of black culture, and not to some ennobling ritual that black gospel music and preaching exemplify. Blacks have no special claim to preaching and gospel music, only to the style of performance.

Let me acknowledge the role of black Christianity in the lives of black Americans and black slaves. It stands to reason that without Christianity both American slavery and racism in general would have taken a much greater toll upon the lives of black people. Some of the great Negro spirituals such as "Swing Low, Sweet Chariot" and "Let My People Go" were surely an emotional balm in a very harsh world. Notwithstanding this moral reality, the truth of the matter is that blacks do not have any isomorphic relationship to Christianity. Christianity is a universal doctrine. Even if Jesus is given a black face, that will not change the fact that Christianity remains a universal doctrine. There are no texts in the Christian writings that blacks can claim as applying specifically to them. Nor have blacks gone on either to produce a reading of Christianity that applies specifically to blacks or to produce a set of ennobling rituals that only black Christians lay claim to performing. No basis for such rituals can be found in the Christian writings themselves.

So, in denying that blacks have a narrative, I do not mean to be taking anything away from the richness of black culture—just as in claiming that Jews do have narrative, I do not mean to be taking anything away from the suffering that Jews have endured. What is more, if it seems reasonable that blacks do not have group autonomy owing to American slavery and its racist legacy, then it should also stand to reason that blacks do not have a narrative, given the nature of slavery and racism. While I have maintained that it is possible to have a culture without a narrative, the converse is not true: a people with a narrative will have a culture. The idea that slavery robbed blacks of a narrative helps us to appreciate just how devastating the effect was that slavery had upon blacks. To be sure, there were whips and chains. There were even deaths. But the real pain of slavery, I suggest, is not to be located here but in the fact that it robbed blacks of a narrative. This makes it clear that I am using the notion of narrative in a very technical sense. The slave narratives—that is, the memoirs written by the slaves themselves—do not constitute what I have called a ritual. These are primarily accounts of the experience of slavery. The slave narratives do not specify ennobling rituals or fixed points of historical reference nor do they define a set of positive goals and values to be achieved by blacks independently of racism. As I have said, I regard the fact that black slaves were robbed of a

narrative to be the very essence of the real pain of American slavery.

On the other hand, from just the fact that Hitler failed in his attempt to exterminate the Jews, and the Jewish narrative survived, we can see the hope that can arise out of the utter ashes of despair, and so appreciate all the more Emil Fackenheim's so-called 614th Commandment: Lest Hitler be handed a posthumous victory, every Jew must continue being a Jew in practice.

Jews have both group autonomy and a narrative, whereas blacks have neither—so I have claimed. All the same, the picture is somewhat more complicated than I have allowed. It is not just that Jews have a narrative, but that the Jewish narrative is an indispensable aspect of the Christian narrative, since the Christ story is inextricably tied to the Jewish narrative. The Christian narrative, by its very own account, is conceptually tied to the Jewish narrative (see also Section V). But if the Jewish narrative is an ineliminable part of the Christian narrative, then the Jewish narrative is also an ineliminable part of the narrative of Western culture, because of the place of Christianity in Western culture. Thus, insofar as Christianity takes itself seriously, it is conceptually bound to acknowledge that at the very least Judaism once had an indisputable claim to being meritorious. So, while Christianity may insist that Jews are now quite mistaken about the importance of their rituals and traditions, it must concede the importance of these things at an earlier time. And it must concede that Jews are rightly an authority on those rituals and traditions.

By contrast, neither the Western nor the Christian narrative is conceptually required to take the black experience seriously. Lest there be any misunderstanding, I do not deny that there have been gross distortions of the contributions of blacks to Western thought. But, as I have already observed, truth as such is not the defining feature of a narrative. I am not here debating whether Christianity and Western culture have discounted the accomplishments of blacks. My point, instead, is that as these two narratives, the Christian and the Western, have been formulated, they are not conceptually bound, by their very own formulations, to take blacks seriously at any point in time, in the way that Christianity is required to take Judaism seriously.

From these considerations it might be thought to follow that Western culture has been more racist than anti-Semitic. But not so. While I shall not argue the case here, suffice it to say that having to take a people seriously is perfectly compatible with despising them to the very core. Indeed, one may despise them precisely because one has to take them seriously.

In the next section, I shall look at some of the practical implications of the account of group autonomy and narrative which I have offered.

IV.

Recall the 1967 Six-Day War, when Israel fought Egypt, Syria, and Jordan. Jews of virtually every stripe and persuasion banded together in support of Israel. This was no accident, because in the face of an imminent threat, a narrative—a group's conception of its good—orders priorities. For Orthodox Jews, kashrut laws are extremely important; for Reform Jews, nothing could be further from the truth. But during the 1967 war, a good Jew was most certainly one who supported the State of Israel, regardless of her or his other shortcomings. A common threat can be most galvanizing. But it is a narrative that gives directions that amount to more than avoiding harm.

For just about every Jew, including quite secular Jews, the existence of synagogues and the State of Israel is a good thing. It is regarded as a good thing by just about every Jew that there are Talmudic scholars and rabbis. One may define a secular Jew as one who wants nearly all aspects of Jewish life to flourish, but who does not want to be an active or regular participant in any aspect of Jewish religious life. In any case, the point that I am concerned to bring out in these observations is that there are goods that Jews want, and these goods are quite independent of a common enemy. These goods are delivered by the Jewish narrative.

Do we find a comparable set of goods among blacks? I think not. Aside from the elimination of racism, it is not clear what blacks in general can

be said to want, from the standpoint of being black. But I want to bring out the significance of a group's having a narrative, and the significance of its not having one, in another way.

Consider the black church. It is widely regarded as the most influential institution in the black community. What is more, it is relatively independent of white influence. Now, there are approximately 30 million blacks in America, and let us suppose that 4 million black adults regularly go to church each Sunday. If each were to give fifty cents to the United Negro College Fund, say, that would be $2 million. Over a year that would be $104 million to UNCF. For years now, fifty cents has been barely enough to buy a cup of coffee. And I assume that anyone who attends church regularly can afford to part with fifty cents. So, the most obvious question is: Why is something like this not being done? The answer cannot possibly be racism, if only because the black church is as independent of white influence as any institution in the black community can be. And if a common enemy—racism, in this instance—were a sufficient basis for cooperative endeavors, then one would have thought that a practice analogous to the one that I have proposed would have been in place quite some time ago.

I want to say that lack of a narrative can explain the absence of cooperative practices of the sort sketched above. In order for a people in a hostile society to flourish as a people, their self-identity must be anchored by a conception of the good that is independent of the hostility that they wish to avoid. What prevents us from seeing this, I suspect, is that there are times when eliminating a harm counts as an end in its own right, and it is irrelevant what other objectives a person might have.

To view struggling against oppression as the equivalent of eliminating an imminent life-threatening harm is to make an egregious error. By its very nature, oppression is about being deprived of some options rather than others. The struggle of a people against oppression can only be properly understood in the context of what it means for them to get on with their lives as a people. And that requires a narrative which anchors their self-identity.

Thus, we must distinguish between a racist society with overt structural inequality (such as American slavery and Jim Crow practices) and a society with structural equality that is coupled with widespread racist presuppositions of inferiority on the part of the powerful toward an identifiable group of individuals who are less well-off. In either case, we have an unjust society, and the latter, of course, may owe its origins to the former. However, combating the former does not require a narrative, whereas combating the latter does. For in the first instance, there is a rigorously specifiable set of harms or wrongs the elimination of which is called for. Their elimination is called for regardless of the aims that a people might otherwise have in society. What is more, while the elimination of the harms of overt structural inequality is no doubt a precondition for flourishing, just as being alive is a precondition for flourishing, their elimination does not constitute flourishing; nor does their elimination point to what a people's flourishing might consist of, just as being alive does not.

By contrast, eliminating the coupling of structural equality with widespread presuppositions of the other's inferiority is a different matter entirely, if only because in such an instance there is no rigorously specifiable set of harms or wrongs to be eliminated and there is no socially acceptable procedure for getting the dominant group to change their pejorative beliefs. Moreover, while it is conceptually possible to have no beliefs at all about an oppressed people, in other words a null set of beliefs, what is wanted is not a case where the null set of beliefs replaces the beliefs that a people are inferior. What is wanted, rather, is for the beliefs of inferiority to be replaced by a positive set of beliefs about the people in question. But which positive set? More to the point, who determines which positive set of beliefs replaces the beliefs about inferiority? Nothing better positions an oppressed people to answer these two questions than their having a narrative. For we have equality at its very best not simply when a people must be precisely like others in order to command the respect of others, but when a people can command the respect of others for being

who they are. Equality across sameness is one thing; equality across differences is quite another. And the virtue of equality is truly showcased only in the latter instance. The latter equality is a more affirming equality that is inescapably predicated upon a people having a narrative—not just a culture—of their own.

The role of a narrative in equality simply presupposes what we already know, namely that there is all the difference in the world between being moved to help someone out of pity and being moved to help someone out of respect for their conception of the good. The latter is a more affirming kind of assistance. Things are no different at the level of groups.

I have claimed that without a narrative a people cannot flourish in a hostile society. Initially, I focused on how a narrative provides a basis for cooperation among a people. As should be obvious, I want also to say that it is only in having a narrative that, in a hostile society, a people can have assistance born of respect instead of pity. It has been said that the Creator helps those who help themselves. It would be stunning if human beings were much different. And nothing enhances self-help like a goal. Things can be no different for a group; hence, the importance of a narrative. We can best understand the success of Jews in America if we see them as having a narrative in a society with structural equality coupled with widespread presuppositions of inferiority. In the face of widespread presuppositions of (moral) inferiority, Jews had a conception of their good—that is, a narrative. This narrative anchored their lives and provided a basis for affirmation that was (and continues to be) independent of the values of society at large, not readily appropriated by mainstream American society. Again, I submit that the pain of slavery can be seen in the fact that it robbed blacks of a narrative.

V.

A narrative is the cornerstone that secures group autonomy. In claiming that Jews, on the one hand, have both group autonomy and a narrative and that blacks, on the other, have neither, have I made an invidious comparison? It is true that I have drawn attention to a differential between blacks and Jews of extraordinary significance. But that does not make the comparison invidious. After all, it is generally agreed that Jews as a people have flourished in American society, whereas blacks as a people have languished. Yet, few would call that comparison invidious. Why? Because by any reasonable assessment, that differential between Jews and blacks would seem to be the truth of the matter—a truth that neither distorts the present social reality of either group nor requires distorting the historical experiences of either group. If this should be the guide to whether a comparison is invidious or not, then the differential between blacks and Jews regarding group autonomy and a narrative is not invidious.

Furthermore, there is the explanatory power of the account offered. Some insight is gained into why Jews have flourished and blacks have languished without denying the reality of the horrors that have occurred in the history of the Jews. If anything, some insight has been gained regarding the toll that American slavery and racism has taken upon the lives of blacks in the United States—an insight that is not gained by focusing upon the horrors of chains, whips, and lynchings or even upon the horror of how many blacks lost their lives due to slavery. These horrors are not to be diminished. Thus, those who would object to the account that I have offered as favoring Jews might want to think again; for the account gives us a better handle on the evil of racism without detracting from the horrendous evil that others have suffered.

Finally, the account sheds some light on the tension between blacks and Jews. I have already spoken to the negative feelings of blacks regarding Jews. I want to conclude with a word about racism on the part of Jews toward blacks.

Racism is the belief, immune to a wide range of evidence and explanatory considerations to the contrary, that blacks are inferior. Nothing better invites the suspicion of inferiority than the following line of reasoning: Although Jews and blacks have suffered equally, the Jews have flourished and the blacks have languished. What can explain this differential between Jews and blacks other than that blacks are lacking in some way?

In *Vessels of Evil,* I observed that there are two ways of understanding the claim that X is an ultimate evil: 1) No evil can be more horrible than X. 2) All other evils are less horrible than X. Far too often, in talking about the difference between the Holocaust and American slavery, people have said the first, but in their heart of hearts have meant the second. Blacks have often supposed that understanding American slavery in the second sense of ultimate evil helps to explain the plight of blacks in the United States today. I suggest that the account of group autonomy and narrative does much better in that regard. Let me observe that when the Holocaust is understood by Jews as an ultimate evil in the second sense, then in light of the comparative success of Jews vis-à-vis blacks, the result is an interpretation of the respective sufferings of both groups that is easily carried along by the winds of racist ideology. By contrast, the account of group autonomy and narrative is not.

But why do we think of drawing the contrast between Jews and blacks instead of Jews and some other group, or blacks and some other group? The obvious answer, it might seem, is the extraordinary suffering that both groups have endured. The problem with this answer, though, is that it does not take seriously the suffering of still other groups—Native Americans, the Armenians, and so on. I should like to conclude this essay with a different answer.

As the label suggests, American slavery stands as America's most brazen, systematic, and enduring institution of oppression. It is an evil that America actively sought to sustain. This it did, even as it took itself to be a Christian nation, which brings me to Judaism. According to the Christian narrative, Christianity is flanked by the experience of the Jews: The Jewish people gave birth to Christianity, and the fulfillment of Christianity is tied to the experience of the Jewish people. For many fundamentalist Christians, Israel's winning the Six-Day War was an occasion to rejoice, as this could only mean that the Second Coming was near.

Thus, for radically different reasons—reasons that have nothing whatsoever to do with the comparative success of Jews and blacks, these two peoples are—or at least have been—an extremely deep part of the very psyche of Americans. It is most unfortunate that this has turned into a race for the who-has-suffered-the-most award. With the accounts of group autonomy and narrative offered in this essay, I should like to think we have a basis for leaving behind that useless competition and entering into a dialogue of understanding.

Discussion Questions

1. Does having a "narrative identity" guarantee group autonomy?
2. Which of these two notions—narrative identity or group autonomy—actually is more directly relevant to explaining the different situations of blacks and Jews?
3. Even if African Americans lack the narrative identity of Jews, don't they have as much as other ethnic groups? In other words, aren't the Jews, specially favored in terms of this identity?
4. How much of anti-Jewish sentiment among blacks is due to envy? Of that, how much of this envy is over narrative identity, as opposed to material possessions and success?
5. Does a group's having a narrative identity *guarantee* there will be trust within the group?
6. Do such artistic works as the film version of Toni Morrison's *Beloved* undercut Thomas' claim that blacks lack narrative identity, or is this a matter of "too little, too late"?

Contemporary Issue: Affirmative Action

---

26   Affirmative Action

BERNARD BOXILL

Study Questions

1. What is the difference between "backward-" and "forward-" looking arguments for affirmative action?
2. What is Boxill's answer to Thomas Nagel's objection?
3. What is Boxill's argument for group preferential treatment?
4. What is the main advantage of the forward- over the backward-looking argument?

From *Blacks and Social Justice* (Totowa, NJ: Rowman and Allenfield, 1984), pp. 147–172.

Liberals into Former Liberals

As Michael Kinsley has observed in *Harper's,* "No single development of the past fifteen years has turned more liberals into former liberals than affirmative action."[1] This metamorphosis, if it is not merely an unmasking, is ostensibly due to the belief that affirmative action perverts the just goal of civil rights. That goal, protest the disillusioned liberals, is to guarantee that persons be treated as individuals and judged on their merits; but affirmative action, they complain, guarantees that individuals are treated as mere members of racial groups, and their merits disparaged and ignored.

These liberals were not appeased by Allan Bakke's victory in the Supreme Court in 1978. For although the court ruled that Bakke was wrongly denied admission to the medical school at the University of California at Davis, it allowed that race could be used as a factor in considering applicants. As *Time* announced on its cover: "What Bakke Means. Race: Yes. Quotas: No."

As with busing, the arguments for preferential treatment fell into two classes, backward-looking and forward-looking. Backward-looking arguments justify preferential treatment considered as compensation for past and present wrongs done to blacks and their effects. Forward-looking arguments justify preferential treatment considered as a means to present or future goods, particularly equality. Both the assumptions and the aims of these two kinds of argument must be carefully distinguished.

Backward-looking arguments assume that blacks have been, or are being, wronged. Forward-looking arguments assume that blacks are generally inferior to whites in status, education, and income. Backward-looking arguments aim at compensating blacks. Forward-looking arguments aim at improving the status, education, and income of blacks.

The Backward-Looking Argument

The fundamental backward-looking argument is simply stated: Black people have been and are being harmed by racists attitudes and practices. Those wronged deserve compensation. Therefore, black people deserve compensation. Preferential treatment is an appropriate form of compensation for black people. Therefore black people deserve preferential treatment.

Criticism of this argument falls into two main classes: on the one hand, critics charge that the claims to compensation of the black beneficiaries of preferential treatment are unfounded or vacuously satisfied; on the other hand, they charge that these claims are outweighed by other considerations.

The most common version of the first type always uttered by the critic with an air of having played a trump, is that, since those members of groups that have been discriminated against who benefit from preferential hiring must be minimally qualified, they are not the members of the group who deserve compensation. The philosopher Alan Goldman, for example, argues this way: "Since hiring within the preferred group still depends upon relative qualifications and hence upon past opportunities for acquiring qualifications, there is in fact a reverse ratio established between past discriminations and present benefits, so that those who most benefit from the program, those who actually get jobs, are those who least deserve to."[2] But surely a conclusion that preferential hiring is unjustified based on the argument above is a non sequitur. Let us grant that qualified blacks are less deserving of compensation than unqualified blacks, that those who most deserve compensation should be compensated first, and finally that preferential hiring is a form of compensation. How does it follow that preferential hiring of qualified blacks is unjustified? Surely the assumption that unqualified blacks are more deserving of compensation than qualified blacks does not require us to conclude that qualified blacks deserve no compensation. Because I have lost only one leg, I may be less deserving of compensation than another who has lost two legs, but it does not follow that I deserve no compensation at all.

Even Thomas Nagel, one of the country's leading philosophers and a strong defender of preferential treatment on the basis of the forward-looking argument, resorts to this criticism of the backward-looking argument. Thus he labels a "bad" argument, one that maintains that the "beneficiaries of affirmative action deserve it as compensation for past discrimination," because, he says, "no effort is made to give preference to those who have suffered most from discrimination."[3] Indeed, Nagel makes exactly the same point as Goldman: Because the blacks who benefit from preferential treatment are qualfied, "they are not necessarily, or even probably the ones who especially deserve it. Women or blacks who don't have the qualifications even to be considered are likely to have been handicapped more by the effects of discrimination than those who receive preference."[4] But for the reasons given, this criticism is bogus. Furthermore, since Nagel defends preferential treatment on forward-looking, egalitarian grounds, this puts him into deeper trouble than it does those who reject preferential treatment altogether.

For, if preferential treatment makes no effort to give preference to those who have suffered most, neither does it make an effort to give preference to those who are most unequal to whites. In other words, if the qualified have suffered least, they are also least unequal, and it seems a bad strategy, if one is aiming for equality, to prefer them. Nagel could object that preferring the qualified is a good egalitarian strategy because it will lead indirectly to equality. But a variant of the idea is open to the advocate of the backward-looking argument. He could argue that preferential treatment of the qualified also helps to compensate the unqualified insofar as it shows them that if one is qualified, being black is no longer a bar to promotion.

One claim which would make the objection to compensating qualified blacks stick, and which the critics appear not to have made, is that compensation can be made to only one section of a group—either the qualified or the unqualified—but not to both. If this were true, and if the unqualified are most deserving of compensation, then a case could be mounted for claiming that, under the circumstances, a policy of preferential hiring should not be instituted because it takes from those who are most deserving of compensation (the unqualified) to give to those who are less deserving (the qualified). But if the critics are making this assumption, they have not stated it.

But perhaps the critics mean that qualified blacks are not simply less deserving of compensation than unqualified blacks, but that they deserve no compensation at all, precisely because they are qualified.

Why should this be so? I am not questioning the possibility that, on practical grounds, we may be unable to compensate the qualified members of a group generally discriminated against. I am questioning the assumption that, just because a person has overcome his injury, he no longer has a right to compensation. If I am swindled and through time and effort retrieve my money, shouldn't I be compensated for my time and effort? And if I have plenty of money and hire a good lawyer, shouldn't I also claim from my swindlers the money I paid the lawyer?

But in their eagerness to demolish the case for preferential treatment the critics have become extraordinarily careless, and *have* moved from the claim that qualified blacks are the least harmed and wronged blacks to the unsubstantiated claim that qualified blacks are not harmed or wronged at all. Thus Goldman first made the claim in his essay, "Reparations to Individuals or Groups" that in preferential hiring of qualified minority candidates, there is "an inverse ratio established between past discrimination and present benefits." But then, almost immediately, he makes the very much stronger claim—which does not at all proceed logically from the first—that preferential hiring "singles out for benefits within a generally unjustly treated minority just that minority that has not been unjustly treated."[5] And he makes a similar error in his book, *Justice and Reverse Discrimination.* First he says that "those who are not most qualified will tend to be those who have been discriminated against least," then follows this observation with the assertion that blacks "who have altogether escaped harm from previous injustice . . . will be the ones benefitting from preference."[6] These transitions from one argument to another and others like them, embody several confusions. Most obviously, there is the submerged conflation of those least harmed or wronged, slightly harmed or wronged, and not at all harmed or wronged. Less obviously, the distinction between being harmed, and being wronged or treated unjustly, is not taken seriously enough.

The argument I am proposing in support of preferential treatment should be distinguished from another argument which, I admit, has a certain superficial attractiveness. My argument is that qualified blacks deserve compensation for discrimination because even they have been wronged and probably harmed by it, and that preferential treatment is appropriate compensation for them because it suits their objectives and abilities. The other, superficially attractive, argument is that qualified blacks deserve compensation because they are probably the very blacks who would, in the absence of discrimination, have qualified without preferential treatment. But only a moment's reflection is needed to see that this argument is flawed. As James S. Fishkin points out in *Justice, Equal Opportunity and the Family,* "There is no reason to believe that those blacks who are presently 'best prepared' offer even a remote approximation to those blacks 'who in the absence of discrimination probably would have qualified.' "[7]

But this eminently sound observation does not imply that the "best prepared" are not wronged or harmed by discrimination. That is an altogether distinct claim. The best prepared need not be the ones who would have qualified in the absence of discrimination, but they may nevertheless be disadvantaged by discrimination. Thus, I reject Fishkin's concomitant, completely unsupported, claim that, "it is far from clear that the more advantaged members of a racial minority generally are worse off than they would otherwise have been, were it not for discrimination practiced against their forebears in previous generations."[8] This assumes that discrimination does not generally disadvantage those who are discriminated against, and that is an outrageous and gratuitous conclusion.

But suppose I am wrong and many blacks have in fact escaped the effects of discrimination? This is the fundamental objection to preferential treatment, for, if so many blacks have escaped discrimination and its effects that it results in "compensation" being given large numbers of people who did not deserve it, then it would be unfair. However, even if some blacks escape discrimination altogether, it must be admitted that there is a pervasive prejudice against blacks as a group and a tendency to discriminate against them. Consequently, if as I argued in Chapter 2, the realistic threat of transgression is itself transgression, even those who escape discrimination are wronged and possibly harmed by the discrimination against other blacks. This leads us to the argument proposed by Judith Jarvis Thomson that "even those who were not themselves downgraded for being black or female have suffered the consequences of the down-grading of other blacks and women: lack of self-confidence and lack of self-respect"[9] Goldman has taken this argument as the basis for belief in the concept of a kind of "indirect," "vicarious" wrong. Thus he objects that we should reserve "vicarious compensation"— and what he means by this I do not know—"to those who suffer psychologically or vicariously from injustice toward others, and that we should draw the line [past which compensation is no longer called for] at indirect psychological pressures."[10] But his objection misses the point about the harmfulness of discrimination.

Consider, for example, how Goldman illustrates his point: "A traumatized witness," he writes, "does not suffer the harm of the real victim. Similarly, a Jewish millionaire in Scarsdale, no matter how much he suffered vicariously or psychologically from hearing of the German concentration camps, is not owed the reparations due a former inmate."[11] But Goldman fails to distinguish two kinds of witness to injustice. There is the witness who identifies with the victim, and there is the witness who the transgressors identify with the victim. The first suffers vicariously. The second may not suffer vicariously. However, it does not follow that the latter does not suffer at all. He certainly might suffer at the realization that he too was under sentence and could be next. Therefore there are two completely different kinds of suffering that a witness to the persecution of others might endure. The first stems from sympathy for the victims; it is vicarious and could be called indirect. The second stems from the witness's self-interested realization that he may under sentence too and could be the next to be harmed. But, though this suffering may be "psychological," it is not vicarious, and there is nothing indirect about it. The example of the Scarsdale Jew—the stipulation that he is a millionaire is irrelevant—obscures this. Safely ensconced in Scarsdale, any Jew, millionaire or not, was safe from Hitler. Goldman's example insinuates that the Jew who was not himself victimized could feel only vicarious suffering. To make the argument more balanced, I suggest pondering the plight of a Jewish multimillionaire in Berlin.

Failure to distinguish these two kinds of suffering is responsible for the idea that vicarious suffering is relevant to a consideration of the undermining of self-confidence and self-respect to which Judith Jarvis Thomson was presumably referring. For while the realization that, like the actual victim, the witness to discrimination is also under sentence and could be next, has everything to do with the undermining of his self-confidence and self-respect, vicarious suffering has nothing to do with it. Consequently, the vicarious suffering of middle-class blacks for lower-class blacks, if it exists to any appreciable degree, is completely irrelevant to the question of what undermines their self-confidence and self-respect. What does is the uncertainty and ambiguity of their own lives.

But the red herring of vicarious suffering is misleading in yet another way: It suggests that the undermining of self-confidence and self-respect is a consequence of "injustice toward others." Of course, one's vicarious suffering is no indication of injustice to oneself. Though a white person may suffer vicariously at the thought of discrimination against lower-class blacks, the injustice is to them and not to him. However, when black people feel threatened and insulted when other black people are discriminated against because of their color, the injustice is both to those actually discriminated against and to those who are spared. Because the blacks discriminated against are discriminated against because they are black, all black people receive a warning that they too may experience the same treatment. They are wronged, and liable to be wrongfully harmed, in two ways. First, they are wronged because the realistic threat under which they live transgresses their right to equal security. Second, they are wronged by the judgmental injustice that assumes that because they are black they deserve less consideration than others. Justice Thurgood Marshall's comment in *Bakke* is apropos: "It is unnecessary in twentieth century America to have individual Negroes demonstrate that they have been victims of racial discrimination. [It] has been so pervasive that none, regardless of wealth or position, has managed to escape its impact."[12]

To sum up to this point: The criticism of the backward-looking argument for preferential treatment under consideration is unsound in one of its forms, and irrelevant in the other. Insofar as it assumes that many blacks have escaped wrongful harm as a result of discrimination it is unsound. Even if some blacks have escaped harm this would not be sufficient to make preferential treatment unjustified, because the overwhelming majority it benefited would deserve compensation. Insofar as the criticism assumes the black preferred are less wronged or harmed than other blacks it is irrelevant. The backward-looking argument does not exclude compensating unqualified blacks, or deny that they are more deserving of compensation. Neither does it say that qualified blacks must be compensated first. It asserts only that blacks deserve compensation for the wrongful harms of discrimination. Thus, it is unaffected by the claim that qualified blacks may be the least wronged and harmed of blacks. The fact that qualified blacks are wrongfully harmed at all, and that preferential treatment is appropriate compensation, is sufficient justification for it.

Now, I have admitted that it is a weak argument which tries to justify preferential treatment of qualified blacks applying for desirable places and positions on the grounds that, had there been no discrimination, these blacks would probably have qualified for such places and positions without preferential treatment. The key assumption in this argument is simply not plausible. But if we assume that compensation is owed to blacks as a group, then a stronger version of that argument can be advanced, which goes as follows: *Blacks* as a group have been wronged, and are disadvantaged, by slavery and discrimination. Consequently, blacks as a group deserve compensation. Furthermore, had it not been for slavery and discrimination, blacks as a group would be more nearly equal in income, education, and well-being to other groups who did not suffer from slavery or the extent and kind of discrimination from which blacks have suffered. Consequently, assuming that compensating a group for wrongful disadvantages requires bringing it to the condition it would have been in had it not been wrongfully disadvantaged, compensating blacks as a group requires making them, as a group, more nearly equal to those other groups. But if blacks as a group were more nearly equal in income, education, and well-being to such groups, some blacks would then fill desirable positions. Accordingly, compensating blacks as a group requires putting some blacks in desirable positions. However, only the blacks who are now most qualified can, fittingly, be placed in desirable positions. Hence, even if those blacks are *not* the very ones who would have filled such places and positions had there been no slavery and discrimination, compensating blacks as a group may specifically require preferential treatment of qualified blacks.

Many objections can be raised to this argument. Perhaps the most obvious is that its conception of compensation differs from the conception of compensation used in the argument that blacks, as individuals, deserve compensation. In that argument, I did not contend that compensating blacks requires placing them in positions they would have occupied had there been no slavery and discrimination. I contended that blacks deserve compensation because they are wronged by discrimination, and that places in universities and professional schools are appropriate compensation for qualified blacks because of their interests and objectives. However, in outlining the group compensation argument I am saying that compensating blacks as a group requires placing them in positions they would have occupied had there been no slavery and discrimination. Is this inconsistent? I think I can demonstrate that it isn't.

I endorse the view that, ideally, compensating either individuals or groups for wrongs requires placing them in positions they would have occupied had they not been wronged. The problem is that this ideal conception of compensation cannot be applied in the case of compensation for individual blacks for the wrongs of slavery and discrimination. To place a wronged individual in a position he would have occupied had he not been wronged depends on an estimate of how much the wrong has detracted from his assets, which in turn depends on an estimate of his assets. For an individual's assets—his capacities, abilities, goals, interests, and enjoyments—determine in large part the position he will come to occupy if he is not wronged. For example, if thugs break the basketball player Dr. J's legs, he will receive more compensation than I would if they broke my legs, because it is known that his legs are a greater asset to him than are my legs to me. Similarly, some years ago the newspapers reported that a certain screen star had insured her legs with Lloyd's of London for several million pounds. Whether or not the story was true, it seemed good sense to many people because they thought the star's legs were such an enormous asset that it would take several million pounds to compensate her for them if they were flawed or lost. It should now be clear why the ideal conception of compensation cannot be used to support an argument in favor of compensating black individuals for the wrongs of slavery and discrimination. In most cases, it simply makes no sense to even try to estimate what any black individual's assets might have been before he was wronged by slavery and discrimination. For, from the very start of their lives—while they are yet in the womb—and of their parents' lives, and of the lives of their ancestors, all the way back to the first black slaves born in the New World, blacks have been wronged by slavery and discrimination. Yet the fact remains that because they have been wronged they deserve compensation. Accordingly, under the circumstances the ideal conception of compensation must be discarded. By way of compensating blacks all that can practically be done is to adopt my proposal and award them some benefit—such as preferential treatment—appropriate to their interests and objectives.

The argument for group compensation does not run into this sort of difficulty. We can form some estimate of the assets blacks as a group had before slavery and discrimination. Consequently, we can apply the ideal conception of compensation, and reasonably propose to place blacks as a group in the position they would have occupied had there been no slavery and discrimination. . . .

The Forward-Looking Argument

Whereas the backward-looking argument tried to justify preferential treatment as compensation for past wrongful harms, the forward-looking argument tries to justify preferential treatment on the grounds that it may secure greater equality or increase total social utility. Moreover, the fact that blacks were slaves and the victims of discrimination is irrelevant to the forward-looking argument, which its proponents imply, would not lose force even if blacks had never been slaves and never discriminated against. All that is relevant to the argument is that blacks are often poor, generally less than equal to whites in education, influence, and income, and preferentially treating them will alleviate their poverty, reduce their inequality, and generally increase total utility.

The forward-looking argument has one very clear advantage over the backward-looking argument. As we have seen, a persistent criticism of the backward-looking argument is that, although some blacks deserve no compensation for discrimination because they have not been harmed by discrimination, they are precisely the ones benefiting from preferential treatment. I have tried to rebut this criticism, but this is unnecessary if the forward-looking argument is adopted. For that argument does not require the assumption that the beneficiaries of preferential treatment have been harmed by discrimination, or even that they have been harmed at all. Indeed, it does not require that they be less than equal to whites, and is consistent with their being relatively privileged.

For it endorses a strategy of increasing the incomes and education even of blacks superior in those respects to most whites if, however indirectly, this will, in the long run, effectively increase blacks' equality and increase total social utility.

Now whether or not preferential treatment has such consequences is in the end an empirical question, but some critics, as I will show, insist on concocting specious a priori arguments to show that preferential treatment necessarily causes a loss in social utility.

Thus it has been argued that since, by definition, preferential treatment awards positions to the less qualified over the more qualified, and since the more qualified perform more efficiently than the less qualified, therefore preferential treatment causes a loss of utility. But suppose that less qualified blacks are admitted to medical school in preference to more qualified whites, and suppose the resulting black doctors practice in poor black neighborhoods treating serious illnesses, while if the whites they were preferred to had been admitted they would have practiced in affluent white neighborhoods, treating minor illnesses. In that sort of case, it is not at all necessarily true that preferential treatment causes a loss in utility. Some authors try to avoid the force of this argument by switching the basis of their criticism from the fact that preferential treatment may reward the less qualified to the false assertion that preferential treatment may reward the "unqualified." Thus, Goldman reminds us that "all will suffer when unqualified persons occupy many positions."[13] This is criticism of a straw man.

It has also been claimed that the forward-looking argument that preferential treatment increases utility is open to a serious philosophical objection. Thus philosopher George Sher writes that the utilitarian, or forward-looking, defence of preferential treatment is "vulnerable" to the "simple but serious" objection that "if it is acceptable to discriminate in favor of minorities and women when doing so maximises utility then it is hard to see why it should not also be acceptable to discriminate against minorities and women when that policy maximises welfare."[14] And against

Thomas Nagel who argues that racial discrimination, unlike reverse discrimination, "has no social advantages . . . and attaches a sense of reduced worth to a feature with which people are born."[15] Sher makes a similar objection. He says that Nagel gives us no reason to believe that "there could never be alternative circumstances in which racial, ethnic, or sexual discrimination had social advantages which did outweigh the sense of reduced worth it produced," and maintains that Nagel still has not shown us that such discrimination is illegitimate under "any circumstances at all."[16]

The serious utilitarian is likely to dismiss Sher's criticisms with the same impatience with which he dismisses the stock criticism that utilitarianism allows slavery. As R. M. Hare notes, it is the "strength" of the utilitarian doctrine that "the utilitarian cannot reason a priori that whatever the facts about the world and human nature, slavery is wrong. He has to show it is wrong by showing, through a study of history and other factual observation, that slavery does have the effects (namely the production of misery) that make it wrong."[17] In particular, he is not undone by the arguments of the intuitionist who thinks up "fantastic" examples which show slavery to be right according to the principles of utilitarianism, because these show only that the intuitionist has "lost contact with the actual world."[18] Much the same thing can be said about Sher's notion that there are circumstances in which racial discrimination would be legitimate according to utilitarian principles.

Finally, consider the way Sher deals with Dworkin's defence of preferential treatment. As we have seen, Dworkin's view is that if a policy is to be based on pure utilitarianism, which counts each person as equal, then it must consider only how personal preferences are affected. It cannot consider how external preferences are affected, and if it does, it fails to treat people with equal respect and concern. Dworkin's distinction between personal and external preferences may or may not be sound. I have offered emendations to the argument on which he bases it in my discussion of busing. But Sher accepts Dworkin's

distinction because he thinks that even if he does, Dworkin's argument fails. "Neither, despite his bare assertion to the contrary has Dworkin produced any reason to suppose that such [racial] discrimination could never maximize the satisfaction of purely personal preferences," he writes.[19] But Sher seems to be confused by the ambiguous nature of the expression "racial discrimination."

If discrimination is taken to mean policies based on weighing the external preferences of whites that blacks be given less, then Sher has simply misunderstood Dworkin. Dworkin does not simply say that we must maximize the satisfaction of personal preferences. He also says that we must not give any weight to external preferences. Consequently, if we grant that Dworkin is right in his theory that racial discrimination gives weight to external preferences, then, contrary to what Sher says, that theory does not permit racial discrimination even if racial discrimination did maximize the satisfaction of personal preferences.

On the other hand, "racial discrimination" may, especially if one is careless, be taken to mean policies based on something like "reverse discrimination," which does not weigh external preferences. In that case, just as reverse discrimination can prefer blacks to whites, racial discrimination can prefer whites to blacks. Now, understood in this sense, racial discrimination may, of course, maximize the satisfaction of personal preferences without weighing external preferences, and certainly Dworkin's theory does not exclude it. But, what Sher seems to overlook is that such racial discrimination, not based on weighing external preferences, would be free of the insult of racial discrimination as we now know it.

Sher also attacks the argument that preferential treatment is justified because it conduces to equality. He allows that preferential treatment may reduce inequality between the races but points out that it does not reduce inequalities between individuals. "To practise reverse discrimination," he says, is ". . . merely to rearrange the inequalities of distribution which now prevail."[20] "What the defender [of reverse discrimination] needs to show," Sher declares, "is that it is consistent to denounce whichever inequalities follow racial, ethnic or sexual lines, while at the same time not denouncing those other inequalities which reverse discrimination inevitably perpetuates."[21]

There is a well-recognized ambiguity in the term "equality" that it is relevant to consider here. "Equality" may mean equality of opportunity, or equality of result, or equality of wealth. By his championship of direct redistribution of wealth, Sher assumes that the notion of equality advanced by the forward-looking argument is equality of wealth. In this way he saves himself the trouble of considering the argument for reverse discrimination that maintains that, although it sins against a present equality of opportunity, promotes a future equality of opportunity by providing blacks with their own successful "role models."

Sher's critique is made even weaker by the fact that he concedes to Nagel his point that racial inequalities are especially wrong because they are apt to "lead to further inequalities of self-respect."[22] He thinks he can safely concede this because even if he does the egalitarian defense of reverse discrimination fails decisively. "At best," he writes, this concession allows only that racial "inequalities would have first claim on our attention if we were forced to choose among inequalities—which as we have seen, there is no reason to think we are. It does not show, and no further argument *could* show, that any consistent egalitarian could ignore the import of the other inequalities altogether."

But on what grounds has Sher managed to conclude that the advocates of reverse discrimination, presumably consistent egalitarians, "ignore the import of the other inequalities altogether"? By what bizarre train of reasoning does it follow from the fact that the advocate of reverse discrimination thinks racial inequalities particularly harmful, that he must therefore "ignore the import of the other inequalities altogether"? And granting that other inequalities have a claim on our attention, how does it follow, as Sher says, that a policy of reverse discrimination is "dubious"? Even if, *contra* our assumption, racial in-

equalities are *not* more harmful than others, since we are *not* forced to choose among inequalities, why can't we attack all inequalities at once, racial inequalities through reverse discrimination, and other inequalities through other policies?

The only argument against this would be that the other policies might make reverse discrimination superfluous. But there are obvious weaknesses in it. Stigmas are not likely to be erased just because *incomes* are equalized. Apart from the extraordinary difficulties of equalizing incomes in a capitalist context—if this is possible at all—stigmas are likely to remain attached to members of groups because of the menial work many of them do, however equal their incomes. Preferential treatment is aimed at removing such stigmas.

Discussion Questions

1. If groups are not themselves living, breathing individuals, in what sense can *they* be harmed?
2. If the only sense in which groups can be harmed is that (most) individual members of that group are harmed, then should not compensation go to those harmed—but not to the group as such?
3. In what main regard is a younger African American from an affluent background sufficiently harmed by past or present discrimination entitled to "more than equal treatment"?
4. On the assumption that Boxill's argument would also justify affirmative action for women, does it follow that black women would be entitled to "double advantages"?
5. Should affirmative action be extended to Hispanics and other more recent immigrants?

Notes

1. Michael Kinsley, "Equal Lack of Opportunity," *Harper's*, June 1983, 8.

2. Alan Goldman, "Reparations to Individuals or Groups," in *Reverse Discrimination,* ed. Barry Gross (New York: Prometheus Books, 1977), 322.

3. Thomas Nagel, "A Defense of Affirmative Action," *Report from the Center for Philosophy and Public Policy* 1, no. 4 (Fall 1981): 7.

4. Ibid.

5. Goldman, "Reparations to Individuals," 322, 323.

6. Goldman, *Justice and Reverse Discrimination* (Princeton: Princeton University Press, 1978), 90, 91.

7. James S. Fishkin, *Justice, Equal Opportunity and the Family* (New Haven: Yale University Press, 1983), 92.

8. Ibid., 97.

9. Judith Jarvis Thomson, "Preferential Hiring," in *Equality and Preferential Treatment,* 36.

10. Alan Goldman, "Reverse Discrimination and the Future: A Reply to Irving Thalberg," *The Philosophical Forum* 6, nos. 2–3 (Winter–Spring 1974–75): 324.

11. Alan Goldman, "Affirmative Action," in *Equality and Preferential Treatment,* 206.

12. 438 U.S. 265 (1978).

13. Goldman, *Justice and Reverse Discrimination,* 29.

14. George Sher, "Reverse Discrimination, the Future and the Past," *Ethics* (Oct. 1979): 83.

15. Ibid.

16. Ibid.

17. R. M. Hare, "What Is Wrong with Slavery?" *Philosophy and Public Affairs* 8, no. 2 (Winter 1979): 118.

18. Ibid.

19. Sher, "Reverse Discrimination," 84.

20. Ibid., 85.

21. Ibid., 86.

22. Ibid., 85.

27 Affirmative Action

SHELBY STEELE

Study Questions

1. Why does affirmative action constitute a "Faustian bargain"? (Faust, according to legend, sold his soul to the devil for knowledge, power, and other such advantages in this life.)

2. According to Steele, what is the "essential problem" with typical affirmative action programs?

3. What are his views on the value of "diversity"?

4. How does affirmative action contribute to the "cultural myth of black inferiority"?

5. What is Steele's argument concerning "victimization"?

6. What does Steele mean by the assertion "in education, a revolving door; in employment, a glass ceiling"?

In a few short years, when my two children will be applying to college, the affirmative action policies by which most universities offer black students

From *The Content of Our Character* (New York: Saint Martin's Press, 1990).

some form of preferential treatment will present me with a dilemma. I am a middle-class black, a college professor, far from wealthy but also well-removed from the kind of deprivation that would qualify my children for the label "disadvantaged." Both of them have endured racial insensitivity from whites. They have been called names, have suffered slights, and have experienced firsthand the peculiar malevolence that racism brings out in people. Yet, they have never experienced racial discrimination, have never been stopped by their race on any path they have chosen to follow. Still their society now tells that if they will only designate themselves as black on their college applications they will likely do better in the college lottery than if they conceal this fact. I think there is something of a Faustian bargain in this.

Of course, many blacks and a considerable number of whites would say that I was sanctimoniously making affirmative action into a test of character. They would say that this small preference is the meagerest recompense for centuries of unrelieved oppression. And to these arguments other very obvious facts must be added. In America, many marginally competent or flatly incompetent whites are hired everyday—some because their white skin suits the conscious or unconscious racial preference of their employer. The white children of alumni are often grandfathered into elite universities in what can only be seen as a residual benefit of historic white privilege. Worse, white incompetence is always an individual matter, while for blacks it is often confirmation of ugly stereotypes. The Peter Principle was not conceived with only blacks in mind. Given that unfairness cuts both ways, doesn't it only balance, the scales of history that my children now receive a slight preference over whites? Doesn't this repay, in a small way, the systematic denial under which their grandfather lived out his days?

So, in theory, affirmative action certainly has all the moral symmetry that fairness requires—the injustice of historical and even contemporary white advantage is offset with black advantage; preference replaces prejudice, inclusion answers exclusion. It is reformist and corrective, even repentant and redemptive. And I would never sneer at these good intentions. Born in the late forties in Chicago, I started my education (a charitable term in this case) in a segregated school and suffered all the indignities that come to blacks in a segregated society. My father, born in the South, only made it to the third grade before the white man's fields took permanent priority over his formal education. And though he educated himself into an advanced reader with an almost professorial authority, he could only drive a truck for a living and never earned more than ninety dollars a week in his entire life. So yes, it is crucial to my sense of citizenship, to my ability to identify with the spirit and the interests of America, to know that this country, however imperfectly, recognizes its past sins and wishes to correct them.

Yet good intentions, because of the opportunity for innocence they offer us, are very seductive and can blind us to the effects they generate when implemented. In our society, affirmative action is, among other things, a testament to white goodwill and to black power, and in the midst of these heavy investments, its effects can be hard to see. But after twenty years of implementation, I think affirmative action has shown itself to be more bad than good and that blacks—whom I will focus on in this essay—now stand to lose more from it than they gain.

In talking with affirmative action administrators and with blacks and whites in general, it is clear that supporters of affirmative action focus on its good intentions while detractors emphasize its negative effects. Proponents talk about "diversity" and "pluralism"; opponents speak of "reverse discrimination," the unfairness of quotas and set-asides. It was virtually impossible to find people outside either camp. The closest I came was a white male manager at a large computer company who said, "I think it amounts to reverse discrimination, but I'll put up with a little of that for a little more diversity." I'll live with a little of the effect to gain a little of the intention, he seemed to be saying. But this only makes him a halfhearted supporter of affirmative action. I think many people who don't really like affirmative action support it to one degree or another anyway.

I believe they do this because of what happened to white and black Americans in the crucible of the sixties when whites were confronted with their racial guilt and blacks tasted their first real power. In this stormy time white absolution and black power coalesced into virtual mandates for society. Affirmative action became a meeting ground for these mandates in the law, and in the late sixties and early seventies it underwent a remarkable escalation of its mission from simple anti-discrimination enforcement to social engineering by means of quotas, goals, timetables, set-asides and other forms of preferential treatment.

Legally, this was achieved through a series of executive orders and EEOC guidelines that allowed racial imbalances in the workplace to stand as proof of racial discrimination. Once it could be assumed that discrimination explained racial imbalances, it became easy to justify group remedies to presumed discrimination, rather than the normal case-by-case redress for proven discrimination. Preferential treatment through quotas, goals, and so on is designed to correct imbalances based on the assumption that they always indicate discrimination. This expansion of what constitutes discrimination allowed affirmative action to escalate into the business of social engineering in the name of anti-discrimination, to push society toward statistically proportionate racial representation, without any obligation of proving actual discrimination.

What accounted for this shift, I believe, was the white mandate to achieve a new racial innocence and the black mandate to gain power. Even though blacks had made great advances during the sixties without quotas, these mandates, which came to a head in the very late sixties, could no longer be satisfied by anything less than racial preferences. I don't think these mandates in themselves were wrong, since whites clearly needed to do better by blacks and blacks needed more real power in society. But, as they came together in affirmative action, their effect was to distort our understanding of racial discrimination in a way that allowed us to offer the remediation of preference on the basis of mere color rather than actual injury. By making black the color of preference, these mandates have reburdened society with the very marriage of color and preference (in reverse) that we set out to eradicate. The old sin is reaffirmed in a new guise.

But the essential problem with this form of affirmative action is the way it leaps over the hard business of developing a formerly oppressed people to the point where they can achieve proportionate representation on their own (given equal opportunity) and goes straight for the proportionate representation. This may satisfy some whites of their innocence and some blacks of their power, but it does very little to truly uplift blacks.

A white female affirmative action officer at an Ivy League university told me what many supporters of affirmative action now say: "We're after diversity. We ideally want a student body where racial and ethnic groups are represented according to their proportion in society." When affirmative action escalated into social engineering, diversity became a golden word. It grants whites an egalitarian fairness (innocence) and blacks an entitlement to proportionate representation (power). *Diversity* is a term that applies democratic principles to races and cultures rather than to citizens, despite the fact that there is nothing to indicate that real diversity is the same thing as proportionate representation. Too often the result of this on campuses (for example) has been a democracy of colors rather than of people, an artificial diversity that gives the appearance of an educational parity between black and white students that has not yet been achieved in reality. Here again, racial preferences allow society to leapfrog over the difficult problem of developing blacks to parity with whites and into a cosmetic diversity that covers the blemish of disparity—a full six years after admission, only about 26 percent of black students graduate from college.

Racial representation is not the same thing as racial development, yet affirmative action fosters a confusion of these very different needs. Representation can be manufactured; development is always hard-earned. However, it is the music of innocence and power that we hear in affirmative action that causes us to cling to it and to its distracting emphasis on representation. The fact is that after twenty years of racial preferences, the gap between white and black median income is greater than it was in the seventies. None of this is to say that blacks don't need policies that ensure our right to equal opportunity, but what we need more is the development that will let us take advantage of society's efforts to include us.

I think that one of the most troubling effects of racial preferences for blacks is a kind of demoralization, or put another way, an enlargement of self-doubt. Under affirmative action the quality that earns us preferential treatment is an implied inferiority. However this inferiority is explained—and it is easily enough explained by the myriad deprivations that grew out of our oppression—it is still inferiority. There are explanations, and then there is the fact. And the fact must be borne by the individual as a condition apart from the explanation, apart even from the fact that others like himself also bear this condition. In integrated situations where blacks must compete with whites who may be better prepared, these explanations may quickly wear thin and expose the individual to racial as well as personal self-doubt.

All of this is compounded by the cultural myth of black inferiority that blacks have always lived with. What this means in practical terms is that when blacks deliver themselves into integrated situations, they encounter a nasty little reflex in whites, a mindless, atavistic reflex that responds to the color black with alarm. Attributions may follow this alarm if the white cares to indulge them, and if they do, they will most likely be negative—one such attribution is intellectual ineptness. I think this reflex and the attributions that may follow it embarrass most whites today; therefore, it is usually quickly repressed. Nevertheless, on an equally atavistic level, the black will be aware of the reflex his color triggers and will feel a stab of horror at seeing himself reflected in this way. He, too, will do a quick repression, but a lifetime of such stabbings is what constitutes his inner realm of racial doubt.

The effects of this may be a subject for another essay. The point here is that the implication of inferiority that racial preferences engender in both the white and black mind expands rather than contracts this doubt. Even when the black sees no implication of inferiority in racial preferences, he knows that whites do, so that—consciously or unconsciously—the result is virtually the same. The effect of preferential treatment—the lowering of normal standards to increase black representation—puts blacks at war with an expanded realm of debilitating doubt, so that the doubt itself becomes an unrecognized preoccupation that undermines their ability to perform, especially in integrated situations. On largely white campuses, blacks are five times more likely to drop out than whites. Preferential treatment, no matter how it is justified in the light of day, subjects blacks to a midnight of self-doubt, and so often transforms their advantage into a revolving door.

Another liability of affirmative action comes from the fact that it indirectly encourages blacks to exploit their own past victimization as a source of power and privilege. Victimization, like implied inferiority, is what justifies preference, so that to receive the benefits of preferential treatment one must, to some extent, become invested in the view of one's self as a victim. In this way, affirmative action nurtures a victim-focused identity in blacks. The obvious irony here is that we become inadvertently invested in the very condition we are trying to overcome. Racial preferences send us the message that there is more power in our past suffering than our present achievements—none of which could bring us a *preference* over others.

When power itself grows out of suffering, then blacks are encouraged to expand the boundaries of what qualifies as racial oppression, a situation that can lead us to paint our victimization in vivid colors, even as we receive the benefits or preference. The same corporations and institutions that give us preference are also seen as our oppressors. At Stanford University minority students—some of whom enjoy as much as $15,000 a year in financial aid—recently took over the president's office demanding, among other things, more financial aid. The power to be found in victimization, like any power, is intoxicating and can lend itself to the creation of a new class of supervictims who can feel the pea of victimization under twenty mattresses. Preferential treatment rewards us for being underdogs rather than for moving beyond that status—a misplacement of incentives that, along with its deepening of our doubt, is more a yoke than a spur.

But, I think, one of the worst prices that blacks pay for preference has to do with an illusion. I saw this illusion at work recently in the mother of a middle-class black student who was going off to his first semester of college. "They owe us this, so don't think for a minute that you don't belong there." This is the logic by which many blacks, and some whites, justify affirmative action—it is something "owed," a form of reparation. But this logic overlooks a much harder and less digestible reality, that it is impossible to repay blacks living today for the historic suffering of the race. If all blacks were given a million dollars tomorrow morning it would not amount to a dime on the dollar of three centuries of oppression, nor would it obviate the residues of that oppression that we still carry today. The concept of historic reparation grows out of man's need to impose a degree of justice on the world that simply does not exist. Suffering can be endured and overcome, it cannot be repaid. Blacks cannot be repaid for the injustice done to the race, but we can be corrupted by society's guilty gestures of repayment.

Affirmative action is such a gesture. It tells us that racial preferences can do for us what we cannot do for ourselves. The corruption here is in the hidden incentive *not* to do what we believe preferences will do. This is an incentive to be reliant on others just as we are struggling for self-reliance. And it keeps alive the illusion that we can find some deliverance in repayment. The hardest thing for any sufferer to accept is that his suffering excuses him from very little and never has enough currency to restore him. To think otherwise is to prolong the suffering.

Several blacks I spoke with said they were still in favor of affirmative action because of the "subtle" discrimination blacks were subject to once on the job. One photojournalist said, "They have ways of ignoring you." A black female television producer said, "You can't file a lawsuit when your boss doesn't invite you to the insider meetings without ruining your career. So we still need affirmative action." Others mentioned the infamous "glass ceiling" through which blacks can see the top positions of authority but never reach them. But I don't think racial preferences are a protection against this subtle discrimination; I think they contribute to it.

In any workplace, racial preferences will always create two-tiered populations composed of preferreds and unpreferreds. This division makes automatic a perception of enhanced competence for the unpreferreds and of questionable competence for the preferreds—the former earned his way, even though others were given preference, while the latter made it by color as much as by competence. Racial preferences implicitly mark whites with an exaggerated superiority just as they mark blacks with an exaggerated inferiority. They not only reinforce America's oldest racial myth but, for blacks, they have the effect of stigmatizing the already stigmatized.

I think that much of the "subtle" discrimination that blacks talk about is often (not always) discrimination against the stigma of questionable competence that affirmative action delivers to blacks. In this sense, preferences scapegoat the very people they seek to help. And it may be that at a certain level employers impose a glass ceiling, but this may not be against the race so much as against the race's reputation for having advanced by color as much as by competence. Affirmative action makes a glass ceiling virtually necessary as a protection against the corruptions of preferential treatment. This ceiling is the point at which corporations shift the emphasis from color to competency and stop playing the affirmative action game. Here preference backfires for blacks and becomes a taint that holds them back. Of course, one could argue that this taint, which is, after all, in the minds of whites, becomes nothing more than an excuse to discriminate against blacks. And certainly the result is the same in either case—blacks don't get past the glass ceiling. But this argument does not get around the fact that racial preferences now taint this color with a new theme of suspicion that makes it even more vulnerable to the impulse in others to discriminate. In this crucial yet gray area of perceived competence, preferences make whites look better than they are and blacks worse, while doing nothing whatever to stop the very real discrimination that blacks may encounter. I don't wish to justify the glass ceiling here, but only to suggest the very subtle ways that affirmative action revives rather than extinguishes the old rationalizations for racial discrimination.

In education, a revolving door; in employment, a glass ceiling.

I believe affirmative action is problematic in our society because it tries to function like a social program. Rather than ask it to ensure equal opportunity we have demanded that it create parity between the races. But preferential treatment does not teach skills, or educate or instill motivation. It only passes out entitlement by color, a situation that in my profession has created an unrealistically high demand for black professors. The social engineer's assumption is that this high demand will inspire more blacks to earn Ph.D.'s and join the profession. In fact, the number of blacks earning Ph.D.'s has declined in recent years. A Ph.D. must be developed from preschool on. He requires family and community support. He must acquire an entire system of values that enables him to work hard while delaying gratification. There are social programs, I believe, that can (and should) help blacks *develop* in all these areas, but entitlement by color is not a social program; it is a dubious reward for being black.

It now seems clear that the Supreme Court, in a series of recent decisions, is moving away from racial preferences. It has disallowed preferences except in instances of "identified discrimination," eroded the precedent that statistical racial imbalances are *prima facie* evidence of discrimination, and in effect granted white males the right to challenge consent degrees that use preference to achieve racial balances in the workplace. One civil rights leader said, "Night has fallen on civil rights." But I am not so sure. The effect of these decisions is to protect the constitutional rights of everyone rather than take rights away from blacks. What they do take away from blacks is the special entitlement to more rights than others that preferences always grant. Night has fallen on racial preferences, not on the fundamental rights of black Americans. The reason for this shift, I believe, is that the white mandate for absolution from past racial sins has weakened considerably during the eighties. Whites are now less willing to endure unfairness to themselves in order to grant special entitlements to blacks, even when these entitlements are justified in the name of past suffering. Yet the black mandate for more power in society has remained unchanged. And I think part of the anxiety that many blacks feel over these decisions has to do with the loss of black power they may signal. We had won a certain specialness and now we are losing it.

But the power we've lost by these decisions is really only the power that grows out of our victimization—the power to claim special entitlements under the law because of past oppression. This is not a very substantial or reliable power, and it is important that we know this so we can focus more exclusively on the kind of development that will bring enduring power. There is talk now that Congress will pass new legislation to compensate for these new limits on affirmative action. If this happens, I hope that their focus will be on development and anti-discrimination rather than entitlement, on achieving racial parity rather than jerry-building racial diversity.

I would also like to see affirmative action go back to its original purpose of enforcing equal opportunity—a purpose that in itself disallows racial preferences. We cannot be sure that the discriminatory impulse in America has yet been shamed into extinction, and I believe affirmative action can make its greatest contribution by providing a rigorous vigilance in this area. It can guard constitutional rather than racial rights, and help institutions evolve standards of merit and selection that are appropriate to the institution's needs yet as free of racial bias as possible (again, with the understanding that racial imbalances are not always an indication of racial bias). One of the most important things affirmative action can do is to define exactly what racial discrimination is and how it might manifest itself within a specific institution. The impulse to discriminate *is* subtle and cannot be ferreted out unless its many guises are made clear to people. Along with this there should be monitoring of institutions and heavy sanctions brought to bear when actual discrimination is found. This is the sort of affirmative action that America owes to blacks and to itself. It goes after the evil of discrimination itself, while preferences only sidestep the evil and grant entitlement to its *presumed* victims.

But if not preferences, then what? I think we need social policies that are committed to two goals: the educational and economic development of disadvantaged people, regardless of race, and the eradication from our society—through close monitoring and severe sanctions—of racial, ethnic, or gender discrimination. Preferences will not deliver us to either of these goals, since they tend to benefit those who are not disadvantaged—middle-class white women and middle-class blacks—and attack one form of discrimination with another. Preferences are inexpensive and carry the glamour of good intentions—change the numbers and the good deed is done. To be against them is to be unkind. But I think the unkindest cut is to bestow on children like my own an advantage while neglecting the development of those disadvantaged children on the East Side of my city who will likely never be in a position to benefit from a preference. Give my children fairness; give disadvantaged children a better shot at development—better elementary and secondary schools, job training, safer neighborhoods, better financial assistance for college, and so on. Fewer blacks go to college today than ten years ago; more black males of college age are in prison or under the control of the criminal justice system than in college. This despite racial preferences.

The mandates of black power and white absolution out of which preferences emerged were not wrong in themselves. What was wrong was that both races focused more on the goals of these mandates than on the means to the goals. Blacks can have no real power without taking responsibility for their own educational and economic development. Whites can have no racial innocence without earning it by eradicating discrimination and helping the disadvantaged to de-

velop. Because we ignored the means, the goals have not been reached, and the real work remains to be done.

Discussion Questions

1. In terms of Boxill's distinction between forward- and backward-looking arguments on affirmative action, how would Steele's argument be classified?

2. Steele argues that affirmative action "stigmatizes" its beneficiaries as incompetent (or less competent) than whites. But, on balance, if such stigmatization were worse for African Americans than the advantages accruing to them from affirmative action, would they not *oppose* it? Polls indicate that African Americans generally support affirmative action. How would Steel reply to this argument?

3. Steele suggests that his own children are not entitled to take advantage of affirmative action programs. Would you agree?

4. Steele suggests that, instead of affirmative action, we need programs that will *develop* African Americans' skills and talents. How would a defender of affirmative action respond?

Ethics and Value Theory

In de-throning our absolutes, we must take care not to exile our imperatives, for after all, we live by them.

ALAIN LOCKE

A deep friendship need not be one that transcends ethnic differences; but owing to their texture, a deep friendship that does transcend such differences produces an element of richness that is not to be had otherwise.

NASRI ABEL-AZIZ AND LAURENCE M. THOMAS

Nihilism is not new in black America. The first African encounter with the New World was an encounter with a distinctive form of the Absurd. . . . In fact, the major enemy of black survival in American has been and is neither oppression nor exploitation but rather the nihilistic threat—that is, loss of hope and absence of meaning.

CORNEL WEST

No race can prosper till it learns that there is as much dignity in tilling a field as in writing a poem.

BOOKER T. WASHINGTON

The object of all true education is not to make men carpenters, it is to make carpenters men.

W.E.B. DuBOIS

It may be helpful to begin this chapter on ethics and values with some points of terminology. Sometimes in ordinary life "ethics" is distinguished from "morality." (Cheating in business may be "unethical," but cheating on one's spouse is *immoral*.) The branch of philosophy, however, concerned with these matters is generally referred to *either* as "ethics" or as "moral philosophy." This subject is typically divided into two main areas of inquiry: questions of right and wrong and questions of value—that is, good and bad. Depending on which of these areas of inquiry one gives priority to, one gets a different ethical theory. Thus, *deontologists* treat questions of "doing what is right" as primary and questions of "bringing about the best possible result" as secondary. One is not justified in doing what is wrong, they insist, even to produce a greater good. By contrast, *teleological* ethics treats the right as secondary to the good. The right act, this view holds, is the one that brings about the most good.

In our selections, we begin with a difficult piece, yet one of great historical importance, especially for black professional philosophers: Alain Locke's "Values and Imperatives." Locke, who would later become a central figure in the artistic movement known as the Harlem Renaissance, was the first black American to receive a Ph.D. in philosophy (Harvard University, 1918) and began his career concerned with certain difficult problems at the foundation of any system of values. Locke's essay is part of what is called "axiology" (i.e., the theory of value). His own theory is an attempt to explain both the plurality of values and their objectivity—without resorting to what he calls "absolutism" (e.g., the postulation of certain values as coming from "reason" or "God" and as necessarily valid for all times, places, and peoples). To this end, he tries to link different fundamental values to different states of feeling or emotion.

Michele M. Moody-Adams is a young African American philosopher whose research is connected to social and value issues. In her contribution, she seeks to show how philosophical clarity concerning the nature of self-respect (and how it differs from self-esteem) is helpful in understanding the deepest effects of racial discrimination and negative stereotyping.

Laurence Thomas is an extremely influential philosopher whose work draws on the history of ethics, contemporary analytical philosophy, and his own distinctive experiences as a Jewish African American. Thomas' discussion of friendship and its relation to morality (and the "self") is supplemented by an appendix, written by Thomas and his Arab friend Nasri Abdel-Aziz, on the possibility of friendship bridging traditional ethnic animosities.

Cornel West is another African American philosopher especially featured in this collection. In this essay from his best-selling (for a book of philosophical essays) *Race Matters,* West offers a diagnosis of the value problems of the black community, as an alternative to typical liberal and conservative views. On West's analysis, the deepest effect of America's racial failures is seen in the rampant nihilism in the black community—that is, nihilism understood as "the lived experience of coping with a life of horrifying meaninglessness, hopelessness, and (most important) lovelessness."

In her essay, theologian and black womanist ethicist Katie Cannon speaks to the virtue of "unctuousness" as seen in the life of novelist and folklorist Zora Neale Hurston. For Hurston, certainly, fending off the nihilism of which Cornel West speaks was dependent on her creative efforts and the relation to the black (especially the Southern black) community. Cannon addresses the kind of compromises, or limitations, the need for white financial support placed on Hurston's efforts—how she was able to live, and even thrive, in this situation—and how her life came to the tragic end it did.

The final readings in this section concern the well-known disagreement between the two leading African American theorists at the beginning of the twentieth century: W. E. B. DuBois and Booker T. Washington. The issues dividing Washington and DuBois are not merely ones of political expediency or even of educational strategy. They concern fundamental values insofar as they concern not just educational priorities but also the very meaning and goal of education. For Washington, economic participation (and eventual prosperity) are the main goals of African American education. For DuBois, such an emphasis is both self-defeating (individuals with higher cultural education are necessary for the transmission of economically useful skills) and inherently limiting—for the individual and for the race.

28   Values and Imperatives

ALAIN LOCKE

Study Questions

1. According to Locke, what have been some of the negative consequences of the recognition that absolute values do not exist?
2. What would be the middle ground Locke is seeking between scientific objectivity and "Protagorean" subjectivity?
3. According to Locke, what is the basis of values?
4. What four modes of feeling determine the four basic types of value?
5. How does Locke's theory explain conflicts of values—for example, between the religious mystic and the practical reformer?
6. How is it that Locke's value theory, if accepted, would lead to greater recognition of the diversity of values associated with the different races?

All philosophies, it seems to me, are in ultimate derivation philosophies of life and not of abstract, disembodied "objective" reality; products of time, place and situation, and thus systems of timed history rather than timeless eternity. They need not even be so universal as to become the epitomized *rationale* of an age, but may merely be the lineaments of a personality, its temperament and dispositional attitudes projected into their systematic rationalizations. But no conception of philosophy, however relativistic, however opposed to absolutism, can afford to ignore the question of ultimates or abandon what has been so aptly though skeptically termed "the quest for certainty." To do that is not merely to abdicate traditional meta-

Appeared in *American Philosophy Today and Tomorrow*, Sidney Hook and Horace Kallen, ed. (New York: Lee Furman, 1935).

physics with its rationalistic justification of absolutes but also to stifle embryonic axiology with its promising analysis of norms. Several sections of American thought, however, have been so anxious to repudiate intellectualism and escape the autocracy of categoricals and universals that they have been ready to risk this. Though they have at times discussed the problems of value, they have usually avoided their normative aspects, which has led them into a bloodless behaviorism as arid as the intellectualism they have abandoned or else resulted in a completely individualistic and anarchic relativism which has rightly been characterized recently as "philosophic Nihilism." In de-throning our absolutes, we must take care not to exile our imperatives, for after all, we live by them. We must realize more fully that values create these imperatives as well as the more formally super-imposed absolutes, and that norms control our behavior as well as guide our reasoning. Further, as I shall later point out, we must realize that not in every instance is this normative control effected indirectly through judgmental or evaluational processes, but often through primary mechanisms of feeling modes and dispositional attitudes. Be that as it may, it seems that we are at last coming to the realization that without some account of normative principles, some fundamental consideration of value norms and "ultimates" (using the term in a non-committal sense), no philosophical system can hope to differentiate itself from descriptive science or present a functional, interpretive version of human experience.

Man does not, cannot, live in a valueless world. Pluralism has merely given temporary surcease from what was the central problem of monism,—the analysis and justification of these "ultimates," and pragmatism has only transposed the question from the traditional one of what ends should govern life to the more provocative one of how and why activity creates them. No philosophy, short of the sheerest nominalism or the most colorlessly objective behaviorism, is so neutral that it has not some axiological implications. Positivism least of all; for in opposing the traditional values, positivism has set up counter-values bidding us find meaning in the act rather than project meaning from the plane of reason and the subjective approach; and further, as pragmatism and instrumentalism, has set up at the center of its philosophy a doctrine of truth as itself a functional value. So, by waiving the question of the validity of value ultimates as "absolutes," we do not escape the problem of their functional categorical character as imperatives of action and as norms of preference and choice.

Though this characteristically American repudiation of "ultimates" was originally made in the name of the "philosophy of common sense," common sense and the practical life confronts us with the problem all the more forcefully by displaying a chronic and almost universal fundamentalism of values in action. Of this, we must at least take stock, even if we cannot eventually justify it or approve of it. The common man, in both his individual and group behavior, perpetuates the problem in a very practical way. He sets up personal and private and group norms as standards and principles, and rightly or wrongly hypostasizes them as universals for all conditions, all times and all men. Whether then on the plane of reason or that of action, whether "above the battle" in the conflict of "isms" and the "bloodless ballet of ideas" or in the battle of partisans with their conflicting and irreconcilable ways of life, the same essential strife goes on, and goes on in the name of eternal ends and deified ultimates. Our quest for certainty, motivated from the same urge, leads to similar dilemmas. The blind practicality of the common man and the disinterested impracticality of the philosopher yield similar results and rationalizations. Moreover, such transvaluations of value as from time to time we have, lead neither to a truce of values nor to an effective devaluation; they merely resolve one dilemma and set up another. And so, the conflict of irreconcilables goes on as the devisive and competitive forces of our practical imperatives parallel the incompatibilities of our formal absolutes.

We cannot declare for value-anarchism as a wishful way out, or find a solution in that other alternative blind alley of a mere descriptive analysis of interests. That but postpones the vital problems of ends till the logically later consideration of evaluation and post-valuational rationalizations. To my thinking, the gravest problem of contemporary philosophy is how to ground some normative principle or criterion of objective validity for values without resort to dogmatism and absolutism on the intellectual plane, and without falling into their corollaries, on[1] the plane of social behavior and action, of intolerance and mass coercion. This calls for a functional analysis of value norms and a search for normative principles in the immediate context of valuation. It raises the question whether the fundamental value modes have a way of setting up automatically or dispositionally their end-values prior to evaluative judgment. Should this be the case, there would be available a more direct approach to the problem of value ultimates, and we might discover their primary normative character to reside in their functional rôle as stereotypes of feeling-attitudes and dispositional imperatives of action-choices, with this character reenforced only secondarily by reason and judgment about them as "absolutes." We should then be nearer a practical understanding of the operative mechanisms of valuation and of the grounds for our agreements and conflicts over values.

Normally, one would expect a philosophical tradition dominated, as contemporary American thought has been, by an activist theory of knowledge, to have made a problem like this central. We might very profitably pause for a moment to take stock of the reasons why this has not been so. In the first place, in the reaction away from academic metaphysics, there has been a flight to description and analysis too analogous to science and too committed to scientific objectivism. It is impossible to reach such problems as we have before us effectively in terms of pure positivism, of the prevalent objectivism, or of the typical view that until quite recently has dominated American value theory,—the view namely that end-values exist only in so far as values are rationalized and mediated by processes of evaluation and formal value judgments. Added to this, is our characteristic preoccupation with theories of meaning limited practically to the field of truth and knowledge. Because of this logico-experimental slant, we again have made common cause with the current scientific attitude; making truth too exclusively a matter of the correct anticipation of experience, of the confirmation of fact.[2] Yet truth may also sometimes be the sustaining of an attitude, the satisfaction of a way of feeling, the corroboration of a value. To the poet, beauty is truth; to the religious devotee, God is truth; to the enthused moralist, what ought-to-be overtops factual reality. It is perhaps to be expected that the typical American philosophies should concentrate almost exclusively on thought-action as the sole criterion of experience, and should find analysis of the emotional aspects of human behavior uncongenial. This in itself, incidentally, is a confirming example of an influential value-set, amounting in this instance to a grave cultural bias. When we add to this our American tradition of individualism, reflecting itself characteristically in the value-anarchism and *laissez faire* of which we have already spoken, it is easy to explain why American thought has moved tangent to the whole central issue of the normative aspects and problems of value.

In saying this, do we say anything more than that values are important and that American philosophy should pay more attention to axiology? Most assuredly;—we are saying that but for a certain blindness, value-theory might easily have been an American forte, and may still become so if our predominantly functionalist doctrines ever shed their arbitrary objectivism and extend themselves beyond their present concentration on theories of truth and knowledge into a balanced analysis of values generally. Ironically enough, the very type of philosophy which has insisted on truth as a value has, by rigid insistence on the objective criterion and the experimental-instrumental aspects of thought, disabled itself for pursuing a similarly functional interpretation of the other value modes and their normative principles.

Human behavior, it is true, is experimental, but it is also selectively preferential, and not always in terms of outer adjustments and concrete

results. Value reactions guided by emotional preferences and affinities are as potent in the determination of attitudes as pragmatic consequences are in the determination of actions. In the generic and best sense of the term 'pragmatic,' it is as important to take stock of the one as the other.

Fortunately, within the last few years a decided trend toward axiology and the neglected problems of value has developed, properly enough under the aegis of the *International Journal of Ethics,* promising to offset this present one-sidedness of American philosophical interests. Once contemporary American thought does turn systematically to the analysis of values, its empirical and functionalist approach will be considerably in its favor. Such a philosophic tradition and technique ought to come near to realizing the aim of Brentano, father of modern value-theory, to derive a functional theory of value from a descriptive and empirical psychology of valuation and to discover in value-experience itself the source of those normative and categorical elements construed for centuries so arbitrarily and so artificially in the realm of rational absolutes.

There is little or no hope that this can be obtained *via* a theory of value which bids us seek whatever objectivity and universality values may have outside the primary processes of valuation, whether in the confirmations of experience or the affirmations of evaluative judgments. For these positions lead only, as far as the direct apprehension of value goes, to Protagorean relativism,— each man the measure and each situation the gauge of value, and then an abysmal jump to the objective criterion of the truths of science, valid for all situations, all men and all times.

What seems most needed is some middle ground between these extremes of subjectivism and objectivism. The natural distinctions of values and their functional criteria surely lie somewhere in between the atomistic relativism of a pleasure-pain scale and the colorless, uniformitarian criterion of logic,—the latter more of a straight-jacket for value qualities than the old intellectualist trinity of Beauty, Truth and Good. Flesh and blood values may not be as universal or objective as logical truths and schematized judgments, but they are not thereby deprived of some relative objectivity and universality of their own. The basic qualities of values should never have been sought in logical classes, for they pertain to psychological categories. They are not grounded in types of realms of value, but are rooted in modes or kinds of *valuing*.

In fact, the value-mode establishes for itself, directly through feeling, a qualitative category which, as discriminated by its appropriate feeling-quality, constitutes an emotionally mediated form of experience. If this be so, the primary judgments of value are emotional judgments—(if the inveterate Austrian term "*feeling-judgments*" is not allowable philosophical English), and the initial reference for value predication is based on a form-quality revealed in feeling and efficacious in valuation through feeling. Though finally validated in different ways and by different criteria, beauty, goodness, truth (as approval or acceptance), righteousness are known in immediate recognitions of qualitative apprehension. The generic types of value are basic and fundamental feeling-modes, each with its own characteristic form criterion in value perception. For the fundamental kinds, we can refer to inveterate commonsense, which discriminates them with approximate accuracy—the moral and ethical, the aesthetic, the logical and the religious categories with their roughly descriptive predicates. For an empirical psychology of values, however, they need to be approached directly from the side of feeling and value-attitudes, and re-discriminated not in terms of formal definition but in terms of technical description of their affective-volitional dimensions and factors.

Normally a value-mode is conveyed while the value is being apprehended. Otherwise the quality of the value would be indeterminate, and this is usually contrary to fact. Though we may still be in doubt regarding its validation, its quantity, place in the value series and other specific issues of the value situation, we are usually certain of the value-mode. This is why we should think of a value-quality primarily in terms of feeling or attitude and not of predicates of judgment; why we should speak of a value-reference rather

than a value claim. And if the value type is given in the immediate apprehension of the particular value, some qualitative universal is given. It supplies the clue to the functional value norm,—being felt as good, beautiful, etc.—and we have this event in mind when we say that in the feeling-reference to some value-mode, some value ultimate becomes the birthmark of the value. If values are thus normatively stamped by form-qualities of feeling in the original value experience, then the evaluative judgment merely renders explicit what was implicit in the original value sensing, at least as far as the modal quality of the value is concerned. This could only be true on one of two assumptions, *viz.,* that some abstract feeling-character functioned dispositionally as a substitute for formal judgment, or that the feeling-attitude itself moulded the value-mode and reflected sympathetically its own pattern. If the latter be the case, a value-type or category is a feeling-mode carved out dispositionally by a fundamental attitude.

Of course, this notion of a feeling-reference or form-quality constituting the essential identity and unity of a value-mode is not easily demonstrable; it may be just a hypothetical anticipation of what an experimental analysis of valuation might later establish and prove. However, the main objection to such a conception of value form–character has been undermined, if not overthrown, by the Gestalt psychology, which has demonstrated the factual reality of a total configuration functioning in perceptual recognition, comparison and choice. There is therefore nothing scientifically impossible or bizarre in assuming a form-quality felt along with the specific value context and constituting its modal value-quality and reference. In the absence of direct evidence of this configurational element in valuation, the most corroborative circumstantial evidence is to be found in the interchangeability or rather the convertibility of the various kinds of value. The further we investigate, the more we discover that there is no fixity of content to values, and the more we are bound, then, to infer that their identity as groups must rest on other elements. We know that a *value-genre* often evades its definition and breaks through its logical barriers to include content not usually associated with it. The awe-inspiring scene becomes "*holy,*" the logical proof, "*beautiful,*" creative expression, a "duty," and in every case the appropriate new predicates follow the attitude and the attitude cancels out the traditionally appropriate predicates. For every value coupled by judgmental predication, thousands are linked by identities of feeling-mode; for every value transformed by change of logical presuppositions, scores are switched by a radical transformation of the feeling-attitude. We are forced to conclude that the feeling-quality, irrespective of content, makes a value of a given kind, and that a transformation of the attitude effects a change of type in the value situation.

In this connection, a competent analyst concludes[3]: "We are compelled to recognize that in the aesthetic value situation anything animate or inanimate, natural or artificial, deed or doer, may be the object. This consideration alone makes it clear that beauty and goodness cannot always, if ever, be the same." Yet with all this qualitative distinctness, the artist may feel duty toward his calling, obligation toward his unrealized idea, because when he feels conflict and tension in that context, he occupies an entirely different attitude toward his aesthetic material. Instead of the repose or ecstasy of contemplation or the exuberant flow of creative expression, he feels the tension and pull of an unrealized situation, and feeling obligation and conflict, senses along with that a moral quality. The changed feeling-attitude creates a new value; and the type-form of the attitude brings with it its appropriate value category. These modes co-assert their own relevant norms; each sets up a categorical imperative of its own, not of the Kantian sort with rationalized universality and objectivity, but instead the psychological urgency (shall we say, necessity?) to construe the situation as of a particular qualitative form-character. It is this that we term a functional categorical factor, since it operates in and through feeling, although it is later made explicit, analyzed, and validated by evaluative processes of judgment and experiential test.

The traditional way of accounting for the various kinds of value, on the other hand, starting out as it does from the side of evaluation, leans too heavily upon logical definition. It substitutes the terminology of predicates for the real functional *differential.* A comparison, even in incomplete, suggestive outline, between a logical and a psychological classification of values will show how much more neatly a schematization of values in terms of the mechanics of value-feelings fits the facts than the rough approximations of the traditional logical classification. More than this, such a classification not only states the basis on which the primary value groups generically rest, but reveals the process out of which they genetically arise.

Taking feeling-modes as the basic factor of differentiation, the religious and ethical, moral, logical and aesthetic types of value differentiate very neatly on the basis of four fundamental feeling-modes of exaltation, tension, acceptance, and repose or equilibrium. There are subdivisions for each value-mode determined by the usual polarity of positive and negative values, and also for each mode a less recognized but most important sub-division related to the directional drive of the value-feeling. This latter discriminates for each type of value an "introverted" and an "extroverted" variety of the value, according as the feeling-reference refers the value inward toward an individualized value of the self or projects it outward toward value-sharing and the socialized plane of action. We may illustrate first in terms of the moral values. Every definition of the moral or ethical situation recognizes the characteristic element of conflict between alternatives and the correlated sense of tension. The classification we are discussing would transpose a typical pragmatic definition such as "the conflict of mentally incompatible goods defines a moral situation" into a psychological category of value grounded in the form-feeling of tension, inducing the moral attitude toward the situation irrespective of content. Where the value reference is introverted or directed inwardly toward the self, this tension expresses itself as a compulsion of inner restraint or as "conscience": where an extroverted reference directs the tension toward a compulsion outward to action, the tension becomes sensed as "duty" or obligation. Or, to illustrate again, in the mode of the religious values, we have the mechanisms of introverted exaltation determining positively the ecstasy and sense of union of the religious mystic and negatively his sense of sin and separation, with the outward or extroverted form of the religious value expressing itself in the convictions of "conversion" and salvation (active union with God) and the salvationist crusade against evil (the fear and hate of Satan).

Tabular illustration follows.

This view, if correct, leads to the conclusion that there is a form-feeling or form-quality characteristic of each fundamental value-type, and that values are discriminated in terms of such feeling factors in the primary processes of valuation. The view further regards these modalities of feeling as constituting the basic kinds of value through the creation of stereotyped and dispositional attitudes which sustain them. The substan-

tial agreement of such a table with the traditional classification of values merely indicates that the established scheme of value judgments has traced the basic value modes with fair correctness. However, there are differences more significant than the similarities. These differences not only make possible a more accurate classification of the types of value, but make evident a genetic pattern of values by which we may trace more accurately their interrelations, both of correlation and of opposition.

Over and above greater descriptive accuracy in value analysis, then, this view may be expected to vindicate itself most effectively in the field of the genetics and the dynamics of values. Here it is able to account for value conversions and value opposition in terms of the same factors, and thus apply a common principle of explanation to value mergings, transfers and conflicts. It is with this range of phenomena that the logical theories of value experience their greatest difficulties. We are aware of instances, for example,

Modal Quality Form-Quality and Feeling Reference	Value Type or Field	Value Predicates	Value Polarity	
			Postive	*Negative*
EXALTATION: (Awe Worship) a. Introverted: (Individualized): Inner Ectasy b. Extroverted: (Socialized): Religious Zeal	Religious	Holy—Unholy	Holiness	Sin
		Good—Evil	Salvation	Damnation
TENSION: (Conflict-Choice) a. Inner Tension of "Conscience" b. Extrovert: Outer Tension of Duty	Ethical Moral	Good—Bad Right—Wrong	Conscience Right	Temptation Crime
ACCEPTANCE or AGREEMENT: (Curiosity—Intellectual Satisfaction) a. Inner Agreement in Thought	Logical Truth	True (Correct) and Incorrect	Consistency	Contradiction
b. Outer Agreement in Experience	Scientific Truth	True—False	Certainty	Error
REPOSE or EQUILIBRIUM a. Consummation in Contemplation b. Consummation in Creative Activity	Aesthetic Artistic	Beautiful—Ugly Fine—Unsatisfactory	Satisfaction Joy	Disgust Distress

a: Value: introverted type.
b: Value: extroverted type.

where a sequence of logical reasoning will take on an aesthetic character as a "beautiful proof" or a "pretty demonstration," or where a moral quality or disposition is appraised not as "good" but as "noble," or again, where a religious ritual is a mystical "reality" to the convinced believer but is only an aesthetic, symbolic show to the non-credal spectator. The logical way of explaining such instances assumes a change of the judgmental pre-suppositions mediating the values, or in other cases, puts forward the still weaker explanation of the transfer of value predicates through metaphor and analogy. But by the theory that values are constituted by the primary modal quality of the actual feeling, one does not have to go beyond that to explain the accurate appropriateness of the unusual predicates or the actuality of the attitude in the valuation. They are in direct functional relation and agreement. As a *quod erat demonstrandum,* the proof or demonstration is an enjoyed consummation of a process, and is by that very fact aesthetic in quality. Likewise, the contemplation of an ethical deed, when the tension of the act is not shared, becomes a detached appreciation, though it needs only the sharing of the tension to revert to the moral type of valuation. In fact, moral behavior, when it becomes dispositional, with the smooth feeling-curve of habit and inner equilibrium, normally takes on a quasi-aesthetic quality, as reflected in the criterion of taste and *noblesse oblige* rather than the sterner criterion of "must" and of "duty." And of course, to the disinterested spectator, the religious ritual is just like any other work of art,—an object of reposeful, equilibrated projection. Once a different form-feeling is evoked, the situation and the value type are, *ipso facto,* changed. Change the attitude, and, irrespective of content, you change the value-type; the appropriate new predicates automatically follow.

The same principles hold, moreover, in explaining the conflicts and incompatibilities of values as value-groups. Of course, there are other types of value conflicts, means-ends and value-series problems, but what concerns us at this point are those graver antinomies of values out of which our most fundamental value problems arise. One needs only to recall the endless debate over the *summum bonum* or the perennial quarrel over the respective merits of the value Trinity. How, even after lip service to the parity of Beauty, Truth and Good, we conspire for the priority of one pet favorite, which usually reflects merely our dominant value interest and our own temperamental value bias. The growth of modern relativism has at least cooled these erstwhile burning issues and tempered the traditional debate. Indeed from our point of view, we see these grand ultimates, for all their assertion of fraternal harmony, as doomed to perpetual logical opposition because their basic value attitudes are psychologically incompatible. Repose and action, integration and conflict, acceptance and projection, as attitudes, create natural antinomies, irresolvable orders of value; and the only peace a scientific view of value can sanction between them is one based not upon priority and precedence but upon parity and reciprocity.

As we dispose of this traditional value feud, we become aware of the internal value conflicts within the several value fields, those schisms within common value loyalties which are becoming all the more serious as the traditional value quarrel subsides. There is the feud between the mystic and the reformer in religion, between the speculative logician and the inductive experimentalist in the pursuit of truth, yes,—even the one, less sharp and obvious, between the aesthete and the artist. An affective theory of valuation throws these internal dilemmas into an interesting and illuminating perspective. In each of these cases, the modal value-feeling is, of course, held in common and the same ideological loyalties shared, but these sub-groups are still divided by the basic difference in their orientation toward their common values. Here we see the functional importance of that distinction in feeling-reference or feeling-direction which so closely parallels the Jungian polarity of introversion and extroversion that these terms have been adopted to describe it. These directional drives, determined emotionally in the majority of cases, deciding whether the value is focussed inwardly or outwardly, individuated or socialized, are of the utmost practical importance. For they are the root of those civil feuds within the several value provinces between the saint and the prophet, the mystic and the reformer, the speculative theorist and the practical experimentalist in the search for truth, the aesthete and dilettante versus the creative and professional artist, and finally between the self-righteous moral zealot and the moral reformer. And as each of these attitude-sets becomes dispositional and rationalized, we have the scientific clue to that pattern of value loyalties which divides humanity into psychological sub-species, each laying down rationalizations of ways of life that, empirically traced, are merely the projections of their predominant value tendencies and attitudes.

Thus our varied absolutes are revealed as largely the rationalization of our preferred values and their imperatives. Their tap-root, it seems, stems more from the will to power than from the will to know. Little can be done, it would appear, either toward their explanation or their reconciliation on the rational plane. Perhaps this is the truth that Brentano came near laying hands on when he suggested a love-hate dimensionality as fundamental to all valuation. Certainly the fundamental opposition of value modes and the attitudes based upon them has been one of the deepest sources of human division and conflict. The role of feeling can never be understood nor controlled through minimizing it; to admit it is the beginning of practical wisdom in such matters. As Hartmann[4] has well observed,—"Every value, when once it has gained power over a person, has a tendency to set itself up as a sole tyrant of the whole human *ethos,* and indeed at the expense of other values, even of such as are not inherently opposed to it." We must acknowledge this, though not to despair over it, but by understanding how and why, to find principles of control from the mechanisms of valuation themselves. Without doubt many value attitudes as separate experiences are incompatible and antithetic, but all of us, as individuals, reconcile these incompatibilities in our own experience when we shift, for variety as often as for necessity, from one mode of value to the other. The effective antidote to value absolutism lies in a systematic and realistic demonstration that values are rooted in atti-

tudes, not in reality, and pertain to ourselves, not to the world. Consistent value pluralism might eventually make possible a value loyalty not necessarily founded on value bigotry, and impose a truce of imperatives, not by denying the categorical factors in valuation, which, as we have seen, are functional, but by insisting upon the reciprocity of these norms. There is not necessarily irresolvable conflict between these separate value modes if, without discounting their emotional and functional incommensurability, we realize their complementary character in human experience.

At the same time that it takes sides against the old absolutism and invalidates the *summum bonum* principle, this type of value pluralism does not invite the chaos of value-anarchy or the complete *laissez faire* of extreme value individualism. It rejects equally trying to reduce value distinctions to the flat continuum of a pleasure-pain economy or to a pragmatic instrumentalism of ends-means relations. Of course, we need the colorless, common-denominator order of factual reality and objectivity (although that itself serves a primary value as a mechanism of the coordination of experience), but values simply do not reduce to it. To set values over against facts does not effectively neutralize values. Since we cannot banish our imperatives, we must find some principle of keeping them within bounds. It should be possible to maintain some norms as functional and native to the process of experience, without justifying arbitrary absolutes, and to uphold some categoricals without calling down fire from heaven. Norms of this status would be functional constants and practical sustaining imperatives of their correlated modes of experience; nothing more, but also nothing less.

Such "ends" totalize merely an aspect of human experience and stand only for a subsistent order of reality. They should not confuse themselves with that objective reality nor attempt to deny or disparage its other value aspects and the subsistent orders they reflect. This totalizing character is purely functional in valuation, and it is a mockery of fact either to raise it to the level of transcendental worship or to endow it with objective universality. This conceded, there is little sense and less need to set facts and values over against each other as antagonistic orders; rather should we think of reality as a central fact and a white light broken up by the prism of human nature into a spectrum of values. By proposing these basic value-modes as coordinate and complementary, value pluralism of this type proposes its two most important corollaries,—the principles of reciprocity and tolerance. As derivative aspects of the same basic reality, value orders cannot reasonably become competitive and rival realities. As creatures of a mode of experience, they should not construe themselves in any concrete embodiment so as to contradict or stultify the mode of which they are a particularized expression.

Should such a view become established,—and I take that to be one of the real possibilities of an empirical theory of value, we shall then have warrant for taking as the proper center of value loyalty neither the worship of definitions or formulae nor the competitive monopolizing of value claims, but the goal of maximizing the value-mode itself as an attitude and activity. The attitude will itself be construed as the value essence,—which it really is, and not as now the intellectualized *why* or the traditional and institutionalized *how* associated with the value category. In such a frame of reference, for example, romanticism and classicism could not reasonably think of themselves as monopolizing the field of art, nor Protestantism, Catholicism or even Christianity conceive themselves the only way to salvation. In such a perspective, Nordicism and other rampant racialisms might achieve historical sanity or at least prudential common-sense to halt at the natural frontiers of genuinely shared loyalties and not sow their own eventual downfall through forced loyalties and the counter-reactions which they inevitably breed. Social reciprocity for value loyalties is but a new name for the old virtue of tolerance, yet it does bring the question of tolerance down from the lofty thin air of idealism and chivalry to the plane of enlightened self-interest and the practical possibilities of effective value-sharing. As a working principle, it divorces proper value loyalty from unjustifiable value bigotry, releases a cult from blind identification with creed and dogma, and invests no value interest with monopoly or permanent priority.

However, no one can sensibly expect a sudden or complete change in our value behavior from any transformation, however radical, in our value theory. Relativism will have to slowly tame the wild force of our imperatives. There will be no sudden recanting of chronic, traditional absolutisms, no complete undermining of orthodoxies, no huge, overwhelming accessions of tolerance. But absolutism is doomed in the increasing variety of human experience. What over a century ago was only an inspired metaphorical flash in the solitary universal mind of a Goethe,—that phrase about civilization's being a fugue in which, voice by voice, the several nations and peoples took up and carried the interwoven theme, could in our day become a systematic philosophy of history like Pareto's. His historical and functional relativism of cultural values, with persistent normative constants ("residues") and variable and contingent specific embodiments ("derivatives"), is but an indication of the possibilities of relativism extended to historical and social thought. Cultural relativism, to my mind, is the culminating phase of relativistic philosophy, and it is bound to have a greater influence than any other phase of relativism upon our conception and practise of values.

Our present way of socializing values on the basis of credal agreement, dogmatic orthodoxies, and institutionally vested interests is fundamentally unsound and self-contradictory. As a practise, it restricts more than it protects the values that have called institutions into being. Organized for value-sharing and value promotion, they often contradict their own primary purposes. One way of reform undoubtedly is to combat the monopolistic tradition of most of our institutions. This sounds Marxian, and is to an extent. But the curtailing of the struggle over the means and instrumentalities of values will not eliminate our quarrels and conflicts about ends, and long after the possible elimination of the profit motive, our varied imperatives will still persist. Economic classes may be absorbed, but our psychological tribes will not thereby be dissolved. So, since there may be monopolistic attitudes and policies with respect to ends and ideals just as well as monopolies of the instrumentalities of human values—(and of this fact the ideological dogmatism of contemporary communism is itself a sad example), it may be more effective to invoke a non-Marxian principle of maximizing values.

Contrary to Marxian logic, this principle is non-uniformitarian. It is the Roycean principle of "loyalty to loyalty," which though idealistic in origin and defense, was a radical break with the tradition of absolutism. It called for a revolution in the practise of partisanship in the very interests of the values professed. In its larger outlines and implications it proclaimed a relativism of values and a principle of reciprocity. Loyalty to loyalty transposed to all the fundamental value orders would then have meant, reverence for reverence, tolerance between moral systems, reciprocity in art, and had so good a metaphysician been able to conceive it, relativism in philosophy.

But if reciprocity and tolerance on the large scale are to await the incorporation of the greater community, the day of our truce of values is far off. Before any such integrations can take place, the narrowness of our provincialisms must be broken down and our sectarian fanaticisms lose some of their force and glamor. A philosophy aiding this is an ally of the larger integration of life. Of this we may be sure, such reconstruction will never bring us to a basis of complete cultural uniformity or common-mindedness about values. Whatever integrations occur, therefore, whether of thought or social system,—and undoubtedly some will and must occur,—cultural and value pluralism of some sort will still prevail. Indeed in the atmosphere induced by relativism and tolerance, such differentiation is likely to increase rather than just continue. Only it is to be hoped that it will be less arbitrary, less provincial and less divisive.

One thing is certain,—whatever change may have occurred in our thinking on the subject, we are still monists and absolutists mainly in our practise of value, individual as well as social. But a theoretical break has come, and seems to have set in simultaneously from several quarters. Panoramically viewed, the convergence of these trends indicates a new center for the thought and insight of our present generation, and that would seem to be a philosophy and a psychology, and perhaps too, a sociology, pivoted around functionalistic relativism.

Discussion Questions

1. Explain Locke's opening statement that all philosophies are "of life" and not of "objective reality."
2. If values are rooted in our emotions, how can they be in any way objective or universal?
3. One can understand how the feeling of "exaltation" is directly connected to religious value, but is there anything like this direct connection in the case of "tension" and moral value?
4. How might Locke's views concerning value pluralism contribute to racial harmony?

Notes

1. Compare Professor Frank H. Knight's comment on Charner Perry's, "The Arbitrary as Basis for Rational Morality," *International Journal of Ethics* 53 (1933), 148: "In the present situation of the western mind, the crying need is to substantiate for social phenomena a middle ground between scientific objectivity and complete skepticism. On the one hand, as Scylla, is the absurdity of Behaviorism. . . . On the other side is the Charybdis of Nihilism, perhaps momentarily the nearer and more threatening of the two reefs. Of course, the two are related; nihilism is a natural correlate of 'scientificism.' . . . In any case, there is no more vital problem (pragmatically) than that of distinguishing between utterance that is true or sound and that which is effective in influencing behavior."

2. Compare Dewey, *The Quest for Certainty*, p. 21: "Are the objects of desire, effort, choice, that is to say, everything to which we attach value, real? Yes,—if they can be warranted by knowledge; if we can know objects having their value properties we are justified in thinking them real. But as objects of desire and purpose they have no sure place in Being until they are approached and validated through knowledge."

3. Herbert E. Cory, "Beauty and Goodness," *International Journal of Ethics* 36 (1926), p. 396.

4. Hartmann, N., *Ethics*, Vol. II (London, 1932), p. 423.

29   Race, Class, and the Social Construction of Self-Respect

MICHELE M. MOODY-ADAMS

Study Questions

1. What are the two main elements of self-respect?
2. How does Moody-Adams distinguish self-respect from self-esteem?
3. In what main ways is self-respect "socially constructed"?
4. How and under what circumstances does discrimination erode self-respect?
5. Describe the two main ways in which segregation distorts the self-respect of its victims, according to Moody-Adams' analysis.
6. According to Moody-Adams, why doesn't membership in street gangs promote self-respect?

Introduction

In the mid-1950s, when Kenneth Clark first investigated the influence of racial prejudice on children, discrimination appeared to pose a serious threat to the self-conception of many Black American children.[1] Clark's famous "doll study" of racial preferences in children tested black and white children in several age groups to determine which of two dolls—black or white—they preferred. A majority of Black children in every age group studied expressed a preference for the white doll and rejected the black doll. Of course, not every child who grew up during this period would have displayed such a response, but the self-conceptions of those who did seemed to have been distorted by the complex consequences of discrimination. Many social theorists hoped that social reforms of

the 1960s might help remedy the problem. Yet when the study was recently repeated, the results were surprisingly similar to Clark's original findings: a majority of the Black children studied expressed the same kind of racial preferences as those of similar children in the 1950s.[2]

Anecdotal accounts suggest that the increasing economic isolation of some Black children in American cities may compound the effects of discrimination. A public teacher in a major American city recently reported a disturbing conversation with a ten-year-old Black child who was asked to explain his disruptive classroom behavior. When this student was cautioned that he was preventing his classmates (all of whom were Black) from learning, he replied that it didn't matter, since they were "nothing." Reminded that he was disrupting his own education, he answered that he, too, was "nothing," and added "my mother told me I ain't nothing."[3]

This article describes and defends a new way of understanding the notion of self-respect, as a contribution to philosophical psychology and as an attempt to understand why the relevant social reforms seem to have failed the child in my example—and others like him. The first section defines and describes the two distinct components of self-respect and discusses the influence of social conditions on each component. I also distinguish self-respect from self-esteem and discuss the complicated relation between the two phenomena. The second section shows how socially developed expectations about persons and their capacities help shape self-conceptions and ultimately influence the ability to have and affirm self-respect and self-esteem. I show, further, how socially developed expectations—especially those bound up with class and race—sometimes undermine the capacity to develop a *robust* sense of self-respect. Finally, the third section discusses

From *The Philosophical Forum* 24 (1992), pp. 251–266. Reprinted with permission of Blackwell Publishers.

the most important social bases of self-respect. Social reforms may be a necessary component of any effort to ensure the socially widespread emergence of robust self-respect. Yet we can restore the social bases of self-respect only if we also seek to revise destructive expectations about persons and their characteristics—including many self-regarding expectations—that have supported unreformed social practices.

What Is Self-Respect?

Self-respect, or due respect for one's own worth, has two fundamental components. The first, more fundamental, component involves the conviction that one best affirms one's own value by using one's abilities and talents to contribute to one's survival. One who fails to act on this conviction fails to affirm self-respect, while one who lacks the conviction fails to have self-respect. Yet the conviction and the readiness, together, are just the minimum content of self-respect; a *robust* sense of self-respect is far more than simply a concern to use one's talents in the interest of self-preservation. Further, even the minimum content of self-respect is itself more than simply a concern for one's survival. A person might care about her own survival and yet be unwilling to try to contribute to it: such a person places some value on her own existence but lacks the attitude properly called self-respect. A person has self-respect only when the value she places on her own survival is sufficient to make her willing to contribute to it.

What constitutes contributing to one's survival will always be relative to the specific circumstances of an individual life. For instance, what might be a significant affirmation of the minimum content of self-respect for a hostage bound and gagged in a dark cell would be relatively insignificant for a person not confined in this way.[4] But virtually no human beings who are capable of consciousness and reflection are incapable of having and actively affirming the minimum content of self-respect. A mentally handicapped person who seeks employment, a young child who wants to be allowed to choose what to

wear to school, even a person wishing to end some addictive behavior by first acknowledging a need for the assistance of others—all of these people affirm their possession of the minimum content of self-respect. Finally, most people have a tenacious and regularly observable tendency to seek, and to try to protect, the minimum content of self-respect. As I suggest below, even people who have suffered severe economic and social deprivation typically bear out this observation.

The second component of self-respect is a willingness to do whatever is within one's power to enhance or develop one's abilities and talents. A person who must travel long distances to work, for instance, might need to learn to drive if she cannot take public transport to work. The willingness to develop one's talents initially emerges because, usually, one can best exercise one's abilities when these abilities have been adequately developed.

The relation between the two aspects of self-respect is typically unproblematic—it is generally easy to reconcile concerns that might be generated by the two aspects of self-respect. However, certain circumstances may complicate the relation between the two components of self-respect, making it difficult to reconcile their demands. The first complication arises because human beings have the capacity to place intrinsic value on the development and exercise of some kinds of abilities—such as artistic abilities and moral capacities. Concerns generated by the development and exercise of such abilities may even take priority over concerns associated with the minimum content of self-respect. When this happens, self-forgetfulness and even self-sacrifice can be transformed into manifestations of self-respect.[5] A great writer who works to exhaustion to complete her book, or a lifeguard who risks his life to save a child from drowning, both illustrate this kind of transformation.

But a second, very different kind of complication arises when a person is consistently thwarted in her efforts to develop or exercise her talents and abilities. Such a person may begin to mistrust her abilities; severe frustration and disappointment can make the exercise of one's abilities and talents seem antithetical to self-preservation. One may even come to believe that one's misfortune and unhappiness actually result from the exercise of one's talents and abilities—even when, as a matter of fact, one is not responsible for the unhappiness suffered. Thus children who suffer extreme abuse, for example, can come to hate the exercise of their distinctive talents and abilities—with dire consequences for their sense of self-respect.

Of course the relation between the two components of self-respect can be more harmonious: indeed, a robust sense of self-respect must comfortably combine the two components (to some degree) over a lifetime. Moreover, a robust sense of self-respect is a central ingredient of a satisfying life. To see why, we must understand, first, that the two components of self-respect are often mutually reinforcing. The satisfaction that often accompanies the development of one's distinctive talents and abilities typically increases one's enjoyment of life. This increase may in turn strengthen one's conviction of the importance to one's self-respect of using and developing those abilities. Second, a robust sense of self-respect typically generates a wish to formulate and pursue an effective life plan rather than to seek self-preservation merely by means of ad hoc reactions to circumstances. One is likely to lead a better life in virtue of having and acting upon such a wish than if one never developed, or acted upon, such a wish. Thus John Rawls is right to view self-respect as a good that any rational person will want, whatever else she might want.[6] Finally, a robust sense of self-respect generally makes one better able, and more willing, to engage in the social cooperation that makes possible the rational pursuit of life plans. Since it is in general rational to want to encourage such cooperation, it is also rational to want every member of one's society to be given the fullest possible chance to develop a robust sense of self-respect.[7]

I distinguish self-respect from self-esteem. My account thus departs substantially from Rawls's claims about the content of self-respect. Rawls contends that "a person's sense of his own value" is equivalent to that person's "secure conviction that his conception of his good, his plan of life, is worth carrying out" (TJ 440). Rawls also claims

that "self-respect implies a confidence in one's ability, so far as it is within one's power, to fulfill one's intentions" (TJ 440). Like other critics of this claim, I think that what Rawls describes here is not self-respect but the phenomenon of self-esteem.[8] Moreover, the distinction between self-esteem and self-respect is crucial. How else can we understand that a person might lose confidence in the worth of some particular life plan without at the same time questioning her value as a person?[9] People can sometimes refine, revise, or relinquish a life plan (or some portion of it) should circumstances require them to do so. This is because self-respect is both more fundamental, and less fragile, than self-esteem.

But while self-esteem—confidence in one's life plan—is distinct from self-respect—a due sense of one's own worth—severe diminutions in self-esteem may nonetheless have devastating effects on self-respect. Such effects are most likely when a loss of confidence in one's plans causes a further loss of confidence in one's abilities to attend to one's own preservation. For instance, a person might attribute some drastic failure of his plans to his own mistakes (correctly or incorrectly) rather than to bad fortune or human malevolence. Should such a belief diminish his confidence in his abilities—and, especially if the failure is extreme enough—his self-respect will be severely diminished. In a very different sort of case, a person's response to misfortune (rather than to her own mistakes) might diminish her self-esteem so severely as eventually to diminish her confidence in her abilities and talents. Repeated or extreme bad fortune forges a particularly close link between the fragility of self-esteem and the fragility of self-respect. To be sure, we can neither insulate people from all imaginable misfortune nor prevent them from making mistakes. Yet we can support a socially sanctioned scheme of education that teaches people how to avoid those mistakes most likely to undermine self-respect. We can also try to remedy at least some accidents of fortune that pose the gravest danger to self-esteem and hence to self-respect. But once we have sought the appropriate remedies, we must leave people free to make mistakes. A robust sense of self-respect develops only if one is allowed to learn the extent and the limits of one's own powers; here, experience is the best teacher.

While some circumstances threaten self-respect indirectly through self-esteem, a variety of circumstances can pose a *direct* threat to self-respect. Every society gradually develops a set of mechanisms—social, political, and economic institutions and practices—through which its members typically learn to seek constructive affirmations of self-respect. Yet one's access to mechanisms for the constructive affirmation of self-respect can be artificially limited. For instance, societies with a tradition of discrimination (de jure or de facto) against some groups of people may effectively exclude those people from the typical mechanisms for affirming self-respect. The mere fact of discrimination alone (however arbitrary or unjust its basis) is unlikely to pose a direct threat to the self-respect of its victims. Self-respect is rarely so fragile. But when a scheme of discrimination is rooted in a complex network of degrading and dehumanizing fictions about its victims it can become truly dangerous to self-respect. The more entrenched this network of fictions, the more likely discrimination is to pose a threat to the self-respect of those subjected to it.

Such a scheme demands of those whose choices it restricts that they learn to reconcile two conflicting messages: (1) that self-respect is affirmed and experienced through participation in a particular set of social practices, but (2) that one is nonetheless effectively excluded from these practices. Some who are affected by such a scheme may also fail to discover alternative constructive means to affirm their worth, and they may not recognize the destructive cultural fictions as fictions. For such people, social exclusion is almost certain to weaken self-respect. Moreover, the responses of those who are continually excluded may have powerfully damaging consequences for themselves and their societies. Of course, we cannot ensure that all those who are able to participate in constructive social practices will actually choose to do so; it would be wrong to try if we are to protect the personal liberty that is central to self-respect. Yet we can identify those lingering effects of discrimination that continue to prevent people from choosing to accept or reject the relevant mechanisms. Though these effects are more complex than is often acknowledged, they can be remedied once we understand them.

The Social Construction of Self-Respect

I have so far assumed that the ability to have and affirm a robust sense of self-respect is greatly influenced by social circumstances. Important facts about the contexts in which people initially develop self-conceptions support this assumption. First, the vocabulary in which one learns to give expression to one's self-conception, and even the concepts that initially shape that self-conception, are products of the linguistic conventions of a given community. These conventions embody that community's normative expectations about emotion, thought, and action, and as these expectations change or become more complex so, too, will the self-conceptions of the members of that community. For instance, changes in the way American society views women's choices about work and marriage have changed the way women view themselves and have produced a variety of new and complex expectations about women and their sense of self-worth. Second, a society's normative expectations about emotion, thought, and action have an especially powerful influence on the development of self-respect. Every society gradually develops intricate patterns of normative expectations about what talents and abilities one ought to use in the service of self-preservation—even about what really constitutes survival or self-preservation. A complex society will produce intricate and overlapping patterns of such expectations. Further, self-contained communities within complex societies sometimes produce their own self-contained expectations about selves and self-respect. The self-conceptions of those in such communities will overlap very little with the self-conceptions of those outside such groups. Consider, for instance, the self-contained expectations that shape life in America's Old Order Amish communities.[10]

Socially developed patterns of expectations about self-preservation, and about the acceptable means to that end, constitute what I call the *social construction of self-respect*. The social construction of self-respect is so important because it sets down the parameters within which we initially learn to evaluate our own worth. In twentieth-century America, for example, a powerful set of normative expectations encourages Americans to link their worth as persons to the kind of work they do. As we might expect, people who conform to such expectations find that their self-respect tends to rise and fall with the character of their employment prospects. But complex societies produce overlapping patterns of expectations governing self-worth. Thus some Americans are more influenced by expectations linking self-worth with material possessions than with honest and productive work. In this regard, the Wall Street stockbroker whose bumper sticker announces that "Whoever dies with the most toys wins" bears important similarities to the urban high-school student preoccupied with getting the latest running shoes or a bigger piece of gold jewelry. Finally, the overlapping patterns of expectations that gradually evolve in complex societies—especially in their coarser adaptations—may conflict with each other. Contemporary American society provides striking examples of the very common conflict between the pursuit of honest work and the pursuit of material possessions. The stockbroker who turns to insider trading in pursuit of his "toys"—and the urban high-school student who sells drugs in pursuit of his—reveal the complexity of the social construction of self-respect in America.

One's ability to conform to any pattern of expectations about appropriate ways to affirm self-respect will be affected by one's social, political, and economic circumstances. A variety of circumstances can be relevant—including geographical location, religion, or native language, as well as class and race. The relevance of any particular circumstance is a function of each society's history and traditions. In a society with a long history of relative ethnic and racial homogeneity, for instance, one's class position may be the most important such circumstance. But in many societies, including American society, there are two such circumstances: class position and membership in a particular racial, ethnic, or religious group. Moreover, in such a society the influence of class position is usually registered most directly on the phenomenon of self-esteem—affecting one's confidence in the worth and attainability of one's life plans. In contrast, the influence of race designations (like that of ethnic or religious group membership) is typically registered most directly on self-respect.

The influence of class is due partly to the typically close connection between life plans and economic resources, but its influence also depends upon each person's understanding of how this connection affects her own life. Awareness of one's class position tends to have the most immediate effects on self-esteem, particularly on one's confidence in one's ability actually to carry out one's life plans. This awareness often determines a young person's sense of what *sort* of life plan she ought to pursue. Indeed, a young person's conviction of severe economic limitations on her life plans may even diminish her confidence in the worth of her most valued plans. Such a loss of confidence, as Rawls has suggested, can have devastating consequences—including apathy and cynicism about the worth of pursuing any constructive projects (TJ 440). Finally, the effects of class on self-esteem and motivation may be compounded by geographical isolation or by membership in a historically disfavored racial group—as the lives of some people in America's Appalachian region, and of some in America's urban underclass, reveal.[11]

Though the loss of self-esteem need not diminish self-respect, those who believe themselves confined in an unfavorable class position may find that circumstances directly affecting self-esteem ultimately pose a threat to their self-respect. The experience of one who believes himself economically confined may even be *phenomenologically* like the experience of legally enforced discrimination: it may be felt as exclusion from accepted social mechanisms for affirming self-respect. To be sure, families can sometimes mitigate the potentially destructive effects of economic limitations. Thus many political philosophers—especially in the liberal tradition—view the family as a private buffer against an array of potential assaults on self-esteem and self-respect.[12] But even in societies where laws protect the internal operations of the family as private, the family is a social and economic institution that registers the effects of social and economic isolation. The strain of membership in economically marginal positions may take a severe toll on the structure and well-being of the family itself. When social and economic marginality persist for several generations of one family, the family may even be the principal vehicle for conveying the belief that social isolation is a permanent fact of experience. As in my example of the child whose mother believes that he is "nothing," the economic isolation of a family may reinforce the tendency for diminutions in self-esteem to be transformed into challenges to self-respect.

The direct influence of racial designations—of "race"—on self-conceptions is registered in different and somewhat more complex ways. Not surprisingly, these designations can have especially damaging effects if a society has ever given explicit legal protection (and implicit social support) to racial discrimination. In such a society, merely outlawing discrimination will be unlikely to immediately undo its effects. For in a country not subject to authoritarian rule, legal rules persist for several generations only if there is relatively widespread acceptance of those rules. In order to understand obedience to law as something more than mere observable regularities in behavior, we must acknowledge the existence of what H. L. A. Hart has called an "internal perspective" on the rules of a legal system.[13] According to Hart, an adequate account of a legal system must recognize the existence of a perspective from which agents subject to legal rules take demands for conformity to the rules, and criticisms of breaches of the rules, to be justified. But if we accept Hart's view, as I think we should, we shall have to relinquish the notion that changing discriminatory laws might

automatically eliminate discrimination—or its lingering structural consequences.

Yet accepting the plausibility of this view commits us to two important conclusions about discrimination in America. First, we must acknowledge the existence of a complex internal perspective on the legally supported exclusion of Black people from the social mechanisms for affirming self-respect. A complex set of beliefs and attitudes, transmitted from one generation to another for at least three hundred years, helped shore up the institution of American slavery, and the legally protected discrimination of subsequent periods. Second, it is simply implausible that this internal perspective on the exclusion of Black Americans might have magically ceased to exist with the bitterly contested end of legally-sanctioned discrimination in America.[14] In the "Letter from Birmingham Jail," Martin Luther King vividly described some of the ways in which legally enforced segregation "distorts the soul and degrades human personality" for both the segregator and those subjected to segregation.[15] I contend that many of the relevant distortions will still be transmitted from one generation to another, as part of the social construction of self-respect, long after the "official" end of segregation.

Thus I claim that, in America, the social construction of self-respect continues to bear the complex and often unacknowledged stamp of racial discrimination. What does it mean to claim this? First, in subtle—and sometimes blatant—ways, any group that has been legally excluded from American mechanisms for affirming self-respect will remain a disfavored group for some time. The "conceptual space" that a society historically marks out for a disfavored group places very definite boundaries on what those not in that group will think of them. Changing laws will not automatically alter these boundaries, and many people will unreflectively continue to accept the conceptual boundaries that have been imposed upon the disfavored group. In such a context, even some who actively try not to be "racists" may nonetheless perpetuate the very distortions used to justify discrimination. One of the most dangerous—and least questioned—distortions is the notion that the disfavored group has some psychological and behavioral "essence" that is allegedly genetically transmitted and inescapably possessed by all members of the group.[16] Moreover, beliefs about the alleged essence of some group need not be primarily negative in order to have destructive consequences. For the notion is destructive principally in the way it blinds those who believe in it to the obvious diversity to be found within each group. The Asian American student who neither likes nor excels at mathematics, and the Black American student who prefers physics to basketball alike suffer from the notion of racial essence. Nor is this notion any less destructive when it is unreflectively accepted by the disfavored group themselves as a self-conception. It is particularly destructive when they unreflectively accept a notion of their own "essence" that remains entangled in distortions bound up with the tradition of discrimination. Indeed, to accept such a notion, as I show below, is to participate in one's own victimization.

But the social construction of self-respect typically sustains discriminatory attitudes in yet a second way. For the social transmission of norms of self-respect continues to encourage many people to believe that they must measure their worth primarily by *comparison* with those in the disfavored group. In particular, some social norms governing self-respect lead many persons to believe that preserving their sense of self-respect depends upon being able to prove that they are "superior" to members of some disfavored group. The more precarious the class position of such people, the more they will learn to fear any changes in the "inferior" status of the disfavored group as challenges to the alleged certainties that shore up their sense of self-respect. This phenomenon obviously informs much recent racial discord in the urban centers of America. The more complex the hierarchies of class and ethnicity in a community—and the greater the sense of economic uncertainty there—the more complicated these fears and the resultant conflicts become.

Yet the distorting lessons of discrimination and exclusion are not always manifested in violent conflict: they continually deform and distort the most ordinary social interactions. Consider a college mathematics professor who unreflectively continues to accept unfounded preconceptions about the intellectual capacities of Black students. How might such a professor respond to a Black student's expression of confusion on some point in her class lecture? Coming from a white student, such a confusion would probably be viewed as a simple error, or even as a request for help. But this professor is likely to interpret the Black student's comment as though it were evidence of basic intellectual weakness. If the Black student has expressed confusion on previous occasions, his comments may then become evidence that Black students in general can't "keep up," or even won't try—that they are, in short, "inferior." Similar conduct from a white student would not be taken to support any analogous generalization about all white students. It would simply be a sign that this individual student can't, or even won't, keep up with the class. Moreover, the professor's preconceptions imply that the Black student who has in fact excelled is somehow suspect. Because this professor expects Black students to be weak at mathematics, she will regard a Black student's mathematical success as somehow a "fluke"—she may even question the student's honesty. Crucial social interactions can thus be shaped—one might say deformed—by discriminatory attitudes that commit those who hold them to profoundly *irrational* judgments about the abilities of those in some disfavored group.

Such distortions have consequences that transcend any single social interaction. To understand these consequences, we must take note of two important phenomena identified by social scientists. Robert Merton has described the phenomenon of the "self-fulfilling prophecy" whereby expectations of certain behavior in others often tend to evoke that very behavior.[17] For instance, a Black student might cease to put effort into a class taught by a professor who expects him to be inferior; the student may well presume (correctly) that his effort won't be taken seriously. Of course, he would then do poorly or even fail, thereby seeming to bear out the professor's prediction of failure. But this phenomenon calls attention to a second, described by Gordon Allport as the "reciprocal conduct of human beings in interaction."[18] Allport notes that in social interactions our expectations of others, and the behavior they then tend to display, will constantly reinforce each other in a complex reciprocal fashion. To be sure, sometimes the effects of this reciprocal process are benign or even beneficial. But when the process begins either with racial exclusion, or with open expression of hatred based on ethnic or religious group membership, dangerous consequences may follow. The experience of hatred and exclusion will sometimes produce extreme anger and bitterness in its victims. Further, those who—for various reasons—come to believe that there is nothing to be gained by restraining their anger may openly display such feelings. But of course, behavioral manifestations of these feelings may then be taken by those not in the disfavored group to "confirm" the culture's reasons for hate and exclusion. Racial and ethnic hatred and exclusion thus initiate processes that distort and deform social interactions by generating mistrust and suspicion, and sometimes violent conflict.

I have so far discussed attitudes that devalue the *abilities* of those in the disfavored group. Yet in many contexts discrimination embodies an effort to devalue, degrade, or discount the worth of persons themselves—not just their talents and abilities. Consider the following example. A dispatcher in an urban police station who has been taught to believe that Black people are not fully human will very likely treat Black victims of crime with less seriousness than victims who are not Black. For instance, he may view a Black person's call for emergency police assistance as relatively unimportant, with potentially disastrous consequences for those who seek that assistance. He may even attempt to rationalize the low priority he gives to emergency calls from Black callers: he might claim that statistics about violence in the caller's neighborhood support his belief that Black people "don't really care" about violence or that giving the call greater priority "won't do any good." The prevalence of such rationalizations, in turn, will have destructive reciprocal effects. People who expect to be viewed with less seriousness when they are victims of crime will learn to mis-

trust the institutions that view them in this way, and their mistrust can have devastating effects.

Yet the distorting effects of discrimination do not simply shape the attitudes of "outsiders" toward the disfavored group or vice-versa. Discrimination may also have a profound influence on the self-conceptions, and the sense of self-respect, of some within the disfavored group. Of course, even in the face of the cruelest racism, many people are able to affirm a robust sense of their own worth—and of any group with which they identify—in a variety of satisfying ways. Understanding their success, as I suggest below, yields invaluable lessons about the social bases of self-respect. Yet, like King and Clark, I contend that segregation can distort the self-conception of the segregated as well as of the segregator. The analysis of self-respect introduced in the first section allows me to show *how* some of these distortions take place. The principal distortions of self-respect take two forms: (1) the mutually reinforcing relation between the two components of self-respect may be undermined, or (2) the minimum content of self-respect may itself be distorted. Ironically, the most important distortions reveal just how valiantly people will fight to retain a minimum degree of self-respect, even in the face of challenges to their sense of self-worth.

The first kind of distortion occurs when one's wish to preserve oneself is somehow pried apart from the willingness to develop one's abilities and talents. This separation most often takes place when a person experiences severe disappointment and frustration in the exercise of her abilities. Surprisingly, this process begins as a perfectly ordinary tendency to risk-aversion: in particular, it starts as an aversion to the psychological discomfort of severe disappointment. People with weak voices, for instance, seldom like to sing in public. But what starts as fairly ordinary risk-aversion can develop into extreme self-mistrust, and it may then take on a markedly self-destructive character. Familiar, but distressing, examples of this self-destructive process are common in settings where social and economic isolation compounds the lingering effects of discrimination.

The two components of self-respect are strikingly separated in the tendency of some Black school-aged children in poor urban areas to gradually lower their expectations of themselves, until they effectively relinquish any ambitions of academic success. Hence, the high drop-out rate in these areas. Of course, some students who drop out may have lowered expectations not of themselves but of the society that they believe excludes them. They may simply lose confidence that it is prudent for them to continue in school. Still others may drop out principally because they mistrust the facilities available to them. But caring and hardworking teachers—many of whom are also Black—conclude that many Black students who drop out have learned to mistrust *themselves* because they have gradually internalized prejudicial assumptions that they cannot succeed. Such students provide distressing evidence of the pervasiveness of the self-fulfilling prophecy: the student who believes that he shouldn't even try certainly will not succeed. Moreover, such a student is liable to mistrust students who excel (or simply try to excel), branding them with the label of what he mistrusts most: they are "trying to be white." Students who make such comments are reluctant to identify successful students as "really Black" because they have come to identify being Black with failure. They have thus internalized the very preconceptions that historically have been used to exclude Black Americans from constructive affirmations of self-respect.

But accepting a view of oneself as intrinsically bound for failure can wreak havoc even on the *minimum content* of self-respect. The student who claims to believe that he is "nothing" provides unfortunate evidence of this second kind of distortion of self-respect. Now it is unlikely that this student consistently believes that he really is "nothing." Rather, his efforts to understand his experience lead him to suffer moments of extreme self-doubt and self-mistrust. Yet few children who experience this degree of self-mistrust could emerge with the minimum content of their sense of self-respect untouched. As I suggested earlier, we are unlikely to find any person totally lacking in self-respect. But one can certainly become unable to distinguish self-destructive behavior from behavior that actually promotes one's well-being. Such a confusion between self-destructive and

self-preserving behavior is manifested in the disruptive and ultimately self-destructive classroom behavior of the young boy in my example. His behavior prevents him from learning how to read well or how to manipulate the mathematical concepts he requires to survive economically.

As he develops into a young man, he will become increasingly aware of a set of expectations about selves and self-respect that govern much of his daily life. Some of these expectations will differ very little from those in the larger society: a Wall Street stockbroker and an inner city youth alike may be tempted to measure self-worth by means of their possessions. A second group of expectations will differ radically from those of the larger social group—insofar as they embody a rejection of some of the discriminatory attitudes toward Black Americans. But often, a third category of expectations unintentionally incorporates the exclusion and marginalization that most people in his community would, on reflection, obviously prefer to reject. Familiar patterns of behavior manifest the relevant structure of expectations: membership in youth gangs that promise as great a risk of death as they do protection and camaraderie, drug abuse, and various kinds of violent crime. These patterns of behavior are rooted in dangerous and destructive expectations concerning selves and self-respect.

But the appeal to a Black American teenager of membership in an urban street gang provides an important lesson. For as Rawls once argued, one's sense of one's worth is often bound up with one's sense that one is valued by others; ties of membership in associations and communities typically encourage and support one's sense of self-respect (TJ 440–42). The distressing irony of the urban street gang is that instead of providing a real remedy for the social isolation and exclusion of its members—as a college fraternity, for instance, might—it actually *intensifies* that isolation. Like the young Black student who identifies "Black" with "failure," an older gang member comes to identify "Black" with "marginal." But in viewing his membership in a gang as an affirmation of self-respect, the gang member reveals just how completely he has internalized society's effort to marginalize him. For he has come to see himself precisely as he is seen by those who wish to exclude him: as essentially a threatening "outlaw," a permanent possibility of danger. Moreover, he will sometimes act on that self-conception in a self-destructive fashion and will often wreak havoc on his community in the process. The gang member's self-conception provides a powerful example of the way in which—even in an effort at self-assertion—one can accept a vision of oneself that remains too entangled in a tradition of discrimination and exclusion to be a constructive category for self-reflection.

The Social Bases of Self-Respect

But how might a young child who claims to think that he is "nothing" learn to seek more constructive categories for self-reflection and self-understanding? An important part of the answer requires reflection on the experience of Black Americans who have been able to disentangle their self-conceptions from a conceptual scheme that threatens to confine them to marginality and failure. Such people have relied upon two principal vehicles to disentangle their sense of self-worth from the legacy of discrimination. First, their experience has typically included membership in various communities and associations that *constructively* affirm their worth as persons. For many, of course, the most important such community has been the family. But associative ties outside of a family may supplement the family's influence—or sometimes even remedy the effects of a damaged family.[19] Second, the sense of self-worth of many Black Americans has been sustained by a sense of history and social traditions. Of course, one consequence of American slavery is that many Black Americans have no detailed or particular knowledge of the national (as opposed to continental and geographical) origins of their families. Moreover, discriminatory policies bound up with slavery—and its long aftermath—have often made it difficult, it not impossible, for Black Americans to have access to written history. But the kind of oral history that is seldom preserved in formal educational institutions (for any group)

was often an important and constructive alternative. Black Americans who, for many years, managed to develop constructive means for affirming self-respect—often in spite of great hardship—were once a prominent presence in Black communities. Their successes and their failures were an important source of knowledge of how one might preserve one's self-respect—not just in response to exclusion and discrimination but in spite of it. The greater mobility of some Black Americans thus unwittingly deprives other Black people of access to those parts of their history that they may need most.[20] Further, as successful Black residents leave Black communities, many of the communal associations that provided constructive ties of membership leave with them or die off altogether. To be cut off from membership in associations that constructively affirm one's value and to be cut off from an appreciation of how others have found constructive categories for self-reflection and choice in spite of hardship is to be cut off from the two most important social bases of self-respect. Finding ways to develop the social bases of self-respect in communities set apart by class and race will surely require the participation of Black people who have learned to resist internalizing assumptions about marginality and failure. Even small-scale social programs that vividly display the concern of "sucessful" Black Americans might help provide models of constructive affirmations of self-respect—even if only as an incentive to seek altogether new models.[21]

But no social order can command the respect of people whom it continually fails to respect and for whom (as a consequence) both self-mistrust and widespread mistrust of social institutions come to seem a rational adaptation to circumstances. The possibility of social cooperation thus also imposes an *obligation* on those not in the disfavored group to relinquish the discriminatory attitudes that persist. As I have shown, this requires far more self-scrutiny—and, ultimately, a more serious revision of self-conceptions—than is acknowledged in most discussions of social reform. The police dispatcher who encourages mistrust of the police, and the professor who encourages mistrust of her students' abilities, both endanger the complex social cooperation that underwrites the pursuit of rational life plans for everyone. Still further, restoring the social bases of self-respect will require social policies that recognize the important fact that no human being is ever *simply* a victim. Even a victim retains the fundamental human need to exercise and develop his own abilities and talents in the effort to help remedy his suffering. One develops the self-trust that is fundamental to a robust sense of self-respect only by means of experiences that also require that one take responsibility for the consequences of one's choices—to an extent compatible with one's knowledge and experience. Some social "reforms" of recent years have treated the recipients of assistance simply as victims, thus encouraging the reformers, and those people whom they sought to aid, to ignore important facts about the nature of self-respect.[22]

Finally, as William Julius Wilson has suggested, efforts to encourage a robust sense of self-respect can succeed only alongside efforts to remedy the structural causes of economic and social isolation that seriously endanger self-respect (TD 1987). I have argued that some of the people who most need the benefits of economic reform have become deeply mistrustful of social institutions and—even worse—sometimes, of themselves. Their lack of trust may well hinder their capacity to take advantage of opportunities that might arise with structural changes in the economy. Finding the remedy for this mistrust will require a concerted effort to reshape the social construction of self-respect—not just for the disadvantaged but for any group whose sense of self-worth seems to "require" them to accept the isolation of the truly disadvantaged (of any race or ethnic group) as an unrevisable fact of experience.

Discussion Questions

1. Consider Jane, who has a very high opinion of herself, deflects all criticisms with an attitude of "what's your problem?" but who never accomplishes, or really ever tries to accomplish, much of anything. Does Jane have "self-esteem"? Does she have true "self-respect"? What does Moody-Adams say is the difference?

2. What about someone who has little ability to do anything (of any particular note) and is aware of this? Does such an individual possess a "due sense of his worth"? Does he possess self-respect, on Moody-Adams' account?

3. May not Moody-Adams be criticized for uncritically accepting our society's value judgment that use of one's talents lies at the essence of what constitutes a satisfactory human life? Must the person who most values material possessions and the enjoyments they bring be lacking in self-respect?

4. Does racial discrimination more affect self-esteem or self-respect?

Notes

*An earlier version of this paper was read at a conference at Brown University. Helpful comments on that version were provided by Howard McGary, Lucius Outlaw, and Laurence Thomas.

1. Kennth B. Clark, *Prejudice and Your Child* (Boston: Beacon Press, 1963).

2. Daniel Goleman, "Black Child's Self-View Is Still Low, Study Finds," *New York Times*. Aug. 31, 1987, p. A 13.

3. I am indebted to Shirley Moody for this example.

4. A hostage might vigorously attempt to protect her sanity, or her memory of the past, or even simply to keep track of the passage of time—thus exercising, relatively speaking, a significant degree of control over the conditions of her own survival.

5. On some understanding of the self—say, on which one's identity is partly constituted by one's membership in a group—a willingness to sacrifice one's physical body might be required to reveal one's self-respect. See Karl Duncker, "Ethical Relatively? (An Enquiry Into the Psychology of Ethics)," *Mind,* vol. 48: 39–57, for a discussion of the moral consequences of this view of the self.

6. John Rawls, *A Theory of Justice* (Cambridge, Mass.: Harvard University Press, 1971), p. 440 (hereafter abbreviated TJ).

7. Many important human ends and purposes can be fulfilled only in a context of social cooperation. Thus I reject the libertarian notion that social cooperation is somehow incidental to self-preservation.

8. See Bernard Boxill, *Blacks and Social Justice* (Totowa, N.J.: Rowman and Allenheld, 1984), p. 189.

9. Rawls's analysis thus encourages ambiguity: he sometimes treats "self-respect" and "self-esteem" as equivalent expressions (TJ 440–42).

10. For an intriguing discussion of an Old Order Amish community, see Donald Kraybill, *The Riddle of*

Amish Culture (Baltimore: Johns Hopkins University Press, 1989).

11. See David Looff, *Appalachia's Children* (Lexington: University Press of Kentucky, 1971); Douglas Glasgow, *The Black Underclass: Poverty, Unemployment and Entrapment of Ghetto Youth* (New York: Vintage Books, 1980); and William Julius Wilson, *The Truly Disadvantaged: The Inner City, the Underclass and Public Policy* (Chicago: University of Chicago Press, 1987) (hereafter abbreviated TD).

12. See James Fishkin, *Justice, Equal Opportunity and the Family* (New Haven, Conn.: Yale University Press, 1983), for discussion of some problematic consequences of this view for liberal theorists.

13. H. L. A. Hart, *The Concept of Law* (Oxford: Oxford University Press, 1961).

14. Even the Austinian or Benthamite legal positivist must explain the persistence of legally protected segregation in America. This theorist may appeal to the notion of entrenched "habits of obedience"—but *entrenched* habits, as we all know, do not magically disappear.

15. Martin Luther King, "Letter from Birmingham Jail," in King, *Why We Can't Wait* (New York: Mentor Books, 1964), p. 82.

16. This and other difficulties with the genetic notion of race are discussed in several of the essays in Ashley Montagu, ed., *The Concept of Race* (New York: The Free Press, 1964).

17. Robert Merton, "The Self-Fulfilling Prophecy," *The Antioch Review,* vol. 8: 193–210.

18. Gordon Allport, *The Nature of Prejudice* (Reading, Mass.: Addison-Wesley, 1954).

19. As a matter of historical fact, Black churches and their associated organizations (choirs, youth groups, and so forth) have often been a powerful force in the lives of many Black Americans. Though an organization need not be rooted in shared religious beliefs in order to successfully underwrite self-respect, the experience of the Old Order Amish provides interesting reflection. When a community is largely self-contained (whether as a result of unchosen external forces, or—as in the case of the Amish—as a result of choice), shared religious beliefs often provide a more coherent and more constructive self-conception than any other phenomenon.

20. Critics of W. J. Wilson's stance in *The Truly Disadvantaged* would do well to consider this fact.

21. Douglas Glasgow (1980) urged similar participation by Black Americans.

22. I discuss the topic of responsibility and victims of economic and social deprivation in M. M. Moody-Adams, "On the Old Saw That Character Is Destiny," in O. Flanagan and A. O. Rorty, ed., *Identity, Character and Morality: Essays in Moral Psychology* (Cambridge, Mass.: Massachusetts Institute of Technology Press, 1990).

---

30   Friendship*

LAURENCE M. THOMAS

Study Questions

1. What are some of the main features of "companion friendship"?

2. "One of the important ways companion friends exhibit understanding is that they help us to construct sound ameliorative explanations of our mistakes." Explain.

3. How does self-disclosure in friendship differ from self-disclosure in sex?

4. Why, in reference to the notion of honesty, is companion friendship necessary for a full human life?

5. How is the fact that we are more likely to forgive ourselves (than others) for wrongdoing related to the fact that we are more likely to forgive companion friends (than others) for wrongdoing?

6. How does friendship create a "tension" with respect to morality?

Friendship from *Encyclopedia of Applied Ethics* (San Diego, CA: Academic Press, 1998) vol. 2, pp. 323–333.
*See also "A Note on Friendship and Diversity," page 275.

In importance, friendship is rivaled, if at all, only by romantic love. And some would finesse the difference between the two by insisting that romantic love is at its best only when the lovers are also the best of friends. Aristotle observed that a life without friendship was an incomplete life, though a person possessed all the riches in the world. Two thousand years later, Aristotle's observation still strikes a responsive chord in our hearts.

Although there is, these days, a rather loose use of the word friend whereby people who barely know each other might refer to one another as friends (bar scenes come quickly to mind here), absolutely no one is oblivious to the difference between, at one end, friends who are mere acquaintances or who interact socially from time to time—casual friends, let us say—and, at the other end, friends who constitute a deep friendship—that is, individuals who are the best of friends. Aristotle's observation, of course, is about deep friendships, commonly referred to in the philosophical literature as character or companion friendship. No one today would be inclined to think that his observation applies equally well to individuals who are casual friends. In fact, the term friendship, itself, is generally reserved for individuals who are the best of friends. Thus, while we may use the casual sense of the word friend in ordering another beer for the person whom we have just met and with whom we are enjoying a conversation, it will most likely take more than the animated conversation that is taking place before we think of ourselves as having a friendship with that person. Common wisdom has it that casual friends are easy to come by, whereas companion friendships are rare.

I. Features of Companion Friendship

What are the features of companion or character friendship that so recommends this relationship to our lives? It is illuminating to listen to how people describe their best friend. Let Leslie and Marion, who may be female or male, be companion friends. Here are several commonplace claims: "We always spend lots of time together." "Leslie would do anything for me." "I could tell Leslie anything, for no one understands me like Leslie does." "We often know how one another feels without having to say much of anything." Even if

there is some hyperbole here, the fact that people express their feelings in such strong terms is itself significant. These claims speak to four very important things. Respectively, they are delight in one another's company, aid, self-disclosure, and understanding. Let me comment briefly upon each one.

Deep friends take enormous pleasure in one another's company, as is beautifully described by St. Augustine. Sometimes friends want to be in the proximity of one another even as they engage in different activities. Just knowing that the other is nearby—within room's reach, say—is often satisfying. Interestingly, in spite of the many obvious differences between the parent—child relationship and friendship, we have with this observation about friendship a striking similarity, for the young child takes enormous comfort in knowing that its parents are nearby even as she or he engages in independent exploration.

Turning to the next consideration, we expect our close friends to be willing to aid us in ways that go significantly beyond what the morally decent person might do. While this includes material aid, such aid is rarely the centerpiece of companion friendship, which is in keeping with Aristotle's observation that a person who has everything still needs friendship. Once material aid is set aside, the primary way in which companion friends aid one another comes through self-disclosure and understanding. Still, there are obligations of friendship which do not seem to have their source in the demands of morality. Character friends can make demands on one another's time that no casual friend could make, which is very much in keeping with the first observation. Indeed, even if a casual friend were to make an appearance during a person's time of need, the appearance would not have the same comforting results as that of a character friend, although the individual's showing up would be profoundly appreciated. From the other direction, deep friendship pushes the limits of morality without actually encouraging moral slothfulness. It goes without saying that heinous acts of immorality cannot be justified in the name of friendship. But between heinous acts of immorality and complete moral rectitude, there is a lot of moral space.

And we might tolerate a deep friend's impropriety, though we would never tolerate a like impropriety from a stranger. I shall say more about this in Section IV. However, the point leads us to the topics of self-disclosure and understanding.

Companion friends know things about one another that others do not know, because companion friends self-disclose personal information about themselves to one another. Now, while telling someone personal information about oneself is obviously a way of self-disclosing, it is not the only way. We may do so indirectly. Companion friend Marion may know enough about Leslie that a piece of behavior on Leslie's part which is of little significance in the eyes of others is quite revealing in the eyes of Marion. And Leslie may so behave in front of Marion and others fully cognizant of the fact that Leslie, and no one else, will draw an inference about his personal life that is very poignant, indeed.

Now, there is a fundamental difference between understanding why a person behaved in a certain way and justifying that behavior. In many cases, we expect our companion friend to understand why we made our mistakes even if our behavior cannot in any way be justified. It is this consideration, I want to say, that explains the willingness of friends to engage in self-disclosure. Suppose that Leslie had an extramarital affair. She may self-disclose this to Marion, not with the thought that Marion will see her as not having done wrong, but with the sense that Marion will understand how she might have succumbed in this way. Two general points about human beings are quite relevant here. One is the ever so obvious but far from trivial truth that no one is infallible. The other is the truth that there can be better and worse explanations for even the wrongs that we do. One kind of explanation—which I shall call an excoriating one—reveals us to be utterly indifferent to the wrong that we do. Another kind of explanation—which I shall call an ameliorative one—reveals us to be concerned to do what is morally right but momentarily lacking in moral fortitude. One of the important ways in which companion friends exhibit understanding is that they help us to construct sound ameliorative ex-

planations of our mistakes. Thus, in the case of Leslie's affair, if the available facts supported an ameliorative explanation, Leslie could count on Marion to see this or to help her in constructing such an explanation. It is most significant that persons are sometimes in need of help in constructing an ameliorative explanation concerning a moral failure on their part. In some cases, surely, this is because sometimes we are so stunned and overwhelmed by our mistakes that we lose our perspective.

Summing up, then, the deep, deep trust between character friends manifests itself not only in the high level of self-disclosure between character friends, but also in the conviction that each will endeavor to portray the other in the best moral light. Although such portrayals to third parties may come naturally to mind, the fact of the matter is that often enough a character friend does an invaluable task in portraying the other to himself.

While I do not want to enter into a discussion of the difference between ties of friendship and romance, it will be useful to conclude this section with a remark that speaks to the relative importance of self-disclosure vis-à-vis the sexual bonding that we associate with romance.

It is commonplace to say that sexual bonding is the deepest form of bonding that two human beings can experience, and the ultimate form of self-disclosure. But is this really so? Notice that the person who knows the most about us need not be our sexual partner. In fact, we can have ever so meaningful sex with a person and yet be deeply afraid of self-disclosing things about ourselves to that person. Sex at its best invariably involves a certain kind of affirmation and trust. Yet, sex at its best is nothing like the window to our soul that significant self-disclosure is. If a woman should self-disclose to her lover that she was repeatedly raped by her father when she was age 6, she will have displayed a level of trust in her lover that has no equal in the sexual realm. Self-disclosure at its best is anchored in a profound trust, and no other form of social interaction seems to be tied to this level of trust. And if trust is rightly thought to constitute a form of bonding, then suffice it to say that the rich bonding that sexual intercourse yields neither equals nor necessarily serves as a precursor to the bond of trust cemented by self-disclosure.

II. Self-Disclosure, Choice, and Self-Knowledge in Friendship

What underlies these three aspects of companion friendship—and, self-disclosure, and understanding? No doubt an answer that comes readily to mind is that companion friends deeply love one another. While that is certainly true, love cannot be the answer to the question just posed. To be sure, we are generally willing to aid those whom we love. However, self-disclosure and understanding do not follow simply in love's wake, as the parent-child relationship readily reveals. Parents and children often go to great lengths to hide important aspects of their lives from one another, although the love between them is extraordinary. Or, there can be deep, deep failures of understanding between the two.

Nowadays, a classic example would be the child who is gay or dating a member of a different ethnic group. It is common enough for such a child, who has no doubt whatsoever about the enormous love which his parents have for him, to say that it would hurt his parents enormously if they knew that he was gay or dating an X (a member of a different ethnic group). Or, to go in the other direction, adult children who love their parents dearly may nonetheless be unable to understand why their parents are getting a divorce—so much so that the children actually become angry at the parents. By contrast, friends of the parents may understand all too well why the parents are divorcing.

It might seem appropriate to respond here that the love between parent and child is in a category unto itself. So the fact that self-disclosure and understanding do not follow simply in the wake of this love tells us nothing about the character of love outside of that context, the love of friendship in particular. There is a fundamental insight here that needs to be brought into sharper focus.

A significant asymmetry between the love between character friends on the one hand, and the love between parent and child on the other, is choice. We choose a friend because we find her or his character appealing to us, whereas we choose neither our parents nor our children at all. To be sure, we choose to have children, but that is very different from choosing the child itself. And while adopting a child is, indeed, an instance of choosing a child, infant adoptions still represent choosing a substantially unknown entity, in terms of both physical and, in particular, character development, for it is impossible to extrapolate from an infant child's appearances and behavior what its appearance and character will be when it is a 10-year-old child. However, although we choose neither our parents nor our children, the general thought is that parents should love their children regardless of the children's behavior and children should likewise love their parents. It would almost never be argued that a person's moral character has become so heinous that the person's parents or children are morally blameworthy for maintaining their love for him, although it may be understandable that they cease to love the person.

We may think of the love between child and parent as purely role-based: "X has the role of being child of so-and-so," or "X has the role of parent of so-and-so." By contrast, we may consider the love between character friends as choice-based, where the choice is based upon the person's character. Thus, even if Marion and Leslie represent companion friendship at its very best, they would not have been open to moral criticism merely on account of not having become companion friends. And if both were morally decent individuals when they became companion friends, and Marion, say, changed for the worse, embarking upon a life of crime, we would expect the companion friendship, and so the love, between them to end. More precisely, we would expect Leslie to move on. And if she did not, the explanation, "We are companion friends," would neither seem convincing nor strike us as appropriate, whereas "That is my child" or "That is my parent" would be both convincing and appropriate in a parallel situation.

The only other form of love that also seems to be purely role-based is sibling love, though I suspect that its force, at least socially, is not equal to the love between parent and child. Many ancient texts which speak to the importance of honoring the father and mother and to the importance of caring for children say nothing about sibling relations, save that there should not be sexual intercourse between them. It is hardly accidental, I suspect, that we have role-based love only in the context of biological ties (or their social analogue, as with adoptions and children raised as siblings), for the nature of biological ties (1st or 2nd cousin to X, child/ parent of X, and so on) is absolutely unalterable by social conventions and is extinguishable, if that is the word for it, only by death (it being only upon X's death that a person who was the child/parent or cousin of X is no longer that). Religion has often sought to turn marital love into purely role-based love. Yet, it concedes from the outset the relevance of behavior, since religion has generally regarded infidelity as suitable grounds for divorce.

In any event, one would expect a love that is choice-based, where the choice is based upon the person's character, to be tied to understanding and self-disclosure, whereas one would expect these two features to play a significantly subordinate role in a love that is role-based.

Whenever one makes a choice, one can ask whether it was a good one. This is so even in matters of little or no consequence. Suppose I decide to try a new ice cream flavor and from the list of flavors which I have not yet tasted I request coconut apple. I will consider myself to have made a very good choice if I like it enormously, a bad choice if I really dislike it, and a so-so choice if I find it more or less satisfactory. In terms of significance, clearly, the choice of a companion friend is on a much higher plane. Moreover, one wants to make a good choice from the very start. This requires having some insight into the person's character that goes beyond the person's public self-presentation, which is usually what first catches our attention.

Typically, character friendships have their beginning in a conversation that focuses on something important which is of mutual interest to the individuals involved. They find either that they have similar views or that their disagreements are remarkably constructive. In either case, both find each other quite appreciative of one another's views. After all, people with similar views can learn a lot from one another.

With a companion friendship in-the-making, a conversation will often have what I shall call a distant self-disclosure. On the one hand, a distant self-disclosure is revealing without leaving the speaker particularly vulnerable or requiring supportive behavior on the part of the listener. On the other, a distant self-disclosure often allows ample opportunity to gauge the listener's reaction and understanding of the matter. An example of a distant self-disclosure would be that 20 years ago one smoked marijuana to get through a certain crisis, or that while in the army as a teenager one engaged in a certain form of criminal behavior. With a companion friendship in place, the self-disclosures will invariably cease to be distant.

At this juncture, it is worth mentioning another observation by Aristotle, namely that having a companion or character friend is rather like having another self for a friend. What Aristotle most certainly did not mean is that companion friends are mutual sycophants merely parroting one another's sentiments. For the author who observed that a life without friendship was incomplete surely did not think that what made a person's life incomplete is that he lacked someone who merely parroted his views. The best way to appreciate Aristotle's second observation is to consider the difference between honesty and self-honesty.

A person can be honest in his remarks without telling the entire story. Suppose a student asks me about how well he performed on his essay. I answer honestly if I truthfully tell him that he did not do well and that his paper actually needs enormous work if it is to measure up. I answer honestly, although my considered judgment is that his essay was the worst that I had read in 20 years. Honesty does not require me to add this further assessment. In fact, many would regard my doing so as rather mean-spirited. Most questions have a point to them, and in many cases that point can be spoken to, and so the question can be answered honestly, without offering a full description of things. If you merely ask me was John home last night, I answer honestly if I truthfully tell you that he was not, although I also know that he spent the night at someone's house having an affair. If you are his lover, then the question immediately becomes more complicated. When a lover asks that question, the point is rarely innocuous. Then, an honest answer depends, in part, on the kind of information about John that I realize you correctly take me to have about him. Things can get very complicated here. For I may know that the point of your question is whether John was out having an affair; what is more, it may be that it is entirely by accident that I know that he was (say my cordless phone picked up the conversation as the matter was being discussed). Finally, I may know that you do not really expect me to know the answer, but that you were merely asking me in desperation (I could have been just about anyone). Fortunately, this matter need not be settled here, since offering an account of honest behavior is not the aim of this essay. Yet, this last discussion nicely leads us to the topic of self-honesty.

As a purely conceptual matter, it is not true that a person always knows more about himself than another does. For instance, a person can be infatuated with another or depressed and not realize it, though someone else does. What self-honesty requires, however, is not that a person know more about himself than anyone else, but that he acknowledges to himself his beliefs and feelings such as he understands them to be, regardless of how pleasant or unpleasant they are (where beliefs and feelings are understood to cover intentions, motivations, and emotions). While self-honesty is perhaps easier to achieve than honesty, self-honesty is by no means an inevitable feature of life, as the phenomenon of self-deception makes abundantly clear. And short of outright self-deception there are a multitude of ways in which a person can avoid giving full acknowledgment to his beliefs and feelings. Self-honesty, then, is no small accomplishment, often calling for a certain level of courage.

It is in this light that we should understand Aristotle's claim that a character friend is rather like another self. Imagine a person who is masterfully self-honest. If that person has a character friend, then the extent to which that person will be forthcoming in discussions with her character friend will approach the level of self-honesty that she has attained in her life. Bearing in mind that an honest answer often does not require a full description, then the idea here is that with one another character friends are forthcoming about themselves in ways that significantly exceed the demands of honesty alone. What is more, the character friend will play an active role in getting the other to appreciate her own actions or those contemplated; and this, in turn, will be part of the reason why the other is forthcoming.

So, to recall our two companion friends, Marion and Leslie, if the next door neighbor were to ask Leslie about the banquet for her 25th reunion, a perfectly honest answer could be that she had a great time and reacquainted herself with a number of former classmates. Leslie is not being dishonest by failing to add that she ran into an old flame and there were sparks again. Nor is Leslie being dishonest if she fails to add this when Marion asks her about the banquet. All the same, in responding to Marion, not only would it be quite natural for Leslie to add this, Marion would be unpleasantly surprised if she learned of this from someone else other than Leslie. Of course, Leslie need not tell the whole story right at that moment. Or, if the inquiry about the reunion banquet is made in a public setting, a piece of nonverbal behavior or a code word may accompany Leslie's reply that signals to Marion, and no one else, that there is more to the story. But Marion remembers just how painful Leslie's relationship with that old flame was, and when they have a chance to discuss the matter in private, Marion forcefully reminds Leslie of this, which proves to be another instance of why Leslie is so grateful for their friendship.

Thus, insofar as companion friends are mirrors to one another's soul, a gloss is in order. Contrary to what the metaphor of a mirror perhaps unwittingly invites, companion friends are far from passive in the role which they play in one another's life. A mirror reflects, but the verb "to reflect" has two meanings, one of which pertains to the reasoning that is involved in weighing considerations. Character friends, then, are not just mirrors, but mirrors of insight into one another's soul, thereby helping each other to live up to her or his moral ideals and, at least from time to time, improving upon those ideals. Understanding the mirror metaphor in this way is in keeping with the idea that character friends help one another to see whether an excoriating or ameliorative explanation applies to a serious moral failing. And if an excoriating explanation holds, a character friend will make the case without in any way being self-righteous.

Now, these last remarks speak to the question of what is the gain in having a friend where the level of self-disclosure would invite the idea that the friend is rather like another self? The gain is moral and personal flourishing, an essential ingredient of which is the practical knowledge to interact in the social world in just the right way, given who one is. Consider that a person with all the theoretical knowledge in the world concerning what pregnancy is like does not, thereby, have any practical knowledge about the matter. To have practical knowledge here, there is one, and only one, thing that will do, namely having been pregnant.

To live well is not just to have theoretical knowledge about what is morally right and wrong and personally good or bad for one, but practical knowledge about such matters. And that knowledge is unattainable in the absence of social interaction. But this does not require that one interact with everyone, but only with the right individuals. And no one is better placed for such interaction than a friend who is rather like another self. Let me explain, starting with an illustration.

No matter how well one rehearses a speech that one is going to give, that will never be tantamount to actually giving the speech. A speech that has only been rehearsed can always be revised, whereas a speech that has been given can never be rendered a speech that has not been given. It is only in giving the speech that one can feel, say, ei-

ther relief (or pleasure) for having gotten that out of the way (for having done a wonderful job) or regret for not having gotten things just right. Quite simply, feelings developed in isolation are characteristically too much infected by our hopes and fears. What is more, no matter how self-aware we are concerning the impact which our behavior has upon others, there is no substitute for the actual reactions of others—their praise, criticism, or even indifference, which in some instances can be more haunting than criticism.

Companion friendship often provides the much needed social space between words rehearsed and words spoken to their intended hearer. To our companion friends, we express our feelings about people and situations in ways that we would never express to others, and often enough it is only in so doing that often we learn or appreciate more fully that, indeed, we should never express our feelings in those ways to others. A remark may prove too hostile or too familiar. Sometimes the friend draws this to our attention; sometimes merely uttering the remark to the friend suffices for us to see this. Expressing our most intimate feelings with our companion friend and matching our feelings with theirs is an indispensable moral exercise. This moral exercise yields insights that cannot be had in any other way, even by self-reflection at its very best. Because, as a result of self-disclosure, companion friends have a commanding perspective of one another's life, they are in the position to offer advice, constructive criticism, and running commentary that is profoundly informed, but yet has distance from the person's life. Even as having a character friend approximates having another self, the fact remains that the friend's feelings and reactions will always be those of another person, and self-knowledge, for all of its importance and significance, is no substitute for the knowledge that is given by another's feelings and reactions.

Of course, the very fact that a deep friend so identifies with us can itself be a reason to seek the reactions of others, since we expect that our friend will readily grasp the proper point of our endeavors, and what may rightly be of concern to us is whether those who take no interest in our endeavors, as such, will readily enough correctly grasp the point of our endeavors. A striking difference between companion friendship and the parent-child relationship comes to mind here. It is that in general companion friends never seek the kind of independence from the opinions of one another that children often seek from their parents. At least part of the explanation for this is that, in the eyes of the child, even an adult child, the opinions of parents never entirely lose their authoritative force, owing to the authority that parents properly have over their child in its youth, whereas from the start friends do not have authority over one another, although they certainly have considerable influence with one another. This points to the subtlety of social interaction. A friend's influence can be utterly considerable, making all the difference in what we do; yet we may find this infinitely preferable to even the mere vestiges of authority that remain with our parents. And this, I suspect, is because moral behavior and related concerns are one of the central aspects of friendship, a topic which I take up next.

III. Friendship and the Tensions of Morality

We can quickly get at some of the issues that arise concerning friendship and morality by looking at a particular reading of morality that no doubt has its inspiration in Kantian thought. The view is that a person is not entitled to set aside the demands of morality when it comes to his own behavior. What is morally required of others, in a given set of circumstances, is no less required of that person in like circumstances. Thus, if a person finds $10,000, and morality requires that anyone who finds $10,000 should report the discovery, then that person is not morally permitted to regard his circumstances as different and not report the loss. While technical maneuvers can be made regarding what counts as similar circumstances, the general insight seems relatively secure.

Now, everyone knows that they commit moral errors, including egregious ones from time to time. Some who make egregious moral errors engage in quite substantial acts of self-flagellation. And as I noted in Section I, it sometimes happens that people fail to construct the veritable ameliorative explanation for their moral failure, thinking much worse of themselves than the circumstances warrant. These situations are common enough, though perhaps most people do not react to their grave moral failures in this way.

In most instances, people feel terribly guilty for a period of time, and then get on with living their lives. Rarely do people subject themselves to any of the excoriating blame to which they subject others who make similar egregious moral errors. This is often the case even among people who are quite demanding of themselves (at least when the moral error does not yield lasting damage). While, in the case of people who are morally demanding of themselves, there are a number of explanations for this that operate in concert, I shall focus upon self-knowledge. Having committed an egregious moral error, a person who is morally demanding of herself may have such a poignant sense of moral failure that, with good reason, she is certain that she will never commit that error again. This person would gain very little from acts of self-flagellation. Self-knowledge enables the person to put the wrong behind him without, in any way, condoning the wrong that he has done. Incidentally, this brings out that, in some though hardly all cases, the value of the institution of punishment may lie more in the role it plays in the public's eye than the good that it does for the person being punished.

At any rate, there is another side to the coin of self-knowledge, perhaps a more slippery side. Suppose that what makes a piece of morally objectionable behavior particularly so is that it is done for ignoble reasons, say, a married person's having an affair to test her or his sexual prowess. But suppose that Johnson recently had an affair because her husband has been completely paralyzed for 10 years. Johnson could say, with some justification, that while having an affair is morally wrong, her reason for doing so is considerably less open to moral criticism than numerous other reasons which people give for having an affair; and let us also suppose that she rightly holds that but for the circumstances of her husband's permanent physical impairment she would have done no such thing, since she dearly loves her husband. Accordingly, she may be able to forgive herself for having deliberately done what she regards and continues to regard as morally wrong, for she thinks that if ever it were understandable that a person had an extramarital affair, it is so in her case. Whether in the end Johnson is open to the same level of moral criticism as is any other person who has an affair is a matter that I shall not discuss. What I mean to be drawing attention to is that as people view their personal lives, a Johnson-like line of reasoning is often deemed efficacious to permit moral self-pardoning: X is morally wrong, but I committed X for reason R, and R is a considerably less morally objectionable reason for X-ing than most other reasons why people X; indeed, doing X for reason R is forgivable.

We should be clear about what has been claimed here. I have not argued that people are naturally inclined to be more forgiving of themselves than of others, although that may be true generally. Instead, the claim is that owing to self-knowledge, a person has access to exculpatory reasons for his morally inappropriate behavior which are not readily available to others, and the problem is that a person might succumb to rationalization, taking something as an exculpatory reason when (reflection would reveal that) it is no such thing. The idea here is that because a person knows himself well, he is aware of the kind of reasons that will work for him, psychically, to get him to assuage his conscience.

No doubt one can immediately see the relevance of the preceding discussion to the issue of friendship and morality. Companion friends have enormous knowledge of one another's lives. The point I wish to make, which surely has been anticipated, is that from the standpoint of moral assessment, the knowledge which friends have of one another functions in roughly the same way as self-knowledge does in the individual case.

Returning to companion friends Leslie and Marion, I offer a two-step example of a moral wrong, speaking first to the case where a person is too self-critical and then to the case where a person perhaps has an exculpatory reason.

Leslie may know that Marion had an affair with a 26-year-old student who had been pursuing him, and that Marion is so devastated over the fact that he did this that nothing good whatsoever would be gained by reporting Marion—a brilliant instructor—to the administration, which Leslie has done in other cases. In tears, Marion tells Leslie that he is so terribly ashamed of himself—that not having ever done such a thing before had been a tremendous source of moral pride. In fact, Marion has written his letter of resignation. To now give this example the flavor of the previous Johnson scenario, Leslie may also know that were it not for Marion having just lost both of his parents, he would never have been so emotionally vulnerable as to succumb to such a thing, for Leslie knows that the opportunity (with others) has forcefully presented itself on numerous occasions. I am supposing that in the first instance Marion has no exculpatory reason for his inappropriate behavior, but that he does in the second one. Without adding the loss of parents, Leslie may know that Marion is profoundly sincere and remorseful for what he has done, and from past experience Leslie may know that when Marion exhibits such profound remorse over some behavior the chances of Marion's engaging in that behavior again are next to zero. To be sure, Leslie could scold Marion for having done this thing and file a report against Marion, but I trust that, as I am telling the story, filing a report would hardly seem to serve any purpose. Moreover, I trust that scolding him would seem pointless as well, for the issue is not one of Marion failing to have the appropriate moral ideal here; nor is it one of his failing to have and show appropriate remorse for his wrongdoing. Accordingly, would it not be far more natural for Leslie to want to comfort Marion, to let him know that this one mistake does not render him morally bankrupt, to point out that many a person would have succumbed much earlier on to the student's advances, and so on. In fact, were Leslie to scold Marion as if Marion were but a lecher we might think that Leslie was being rather harsh.

So without adding the loss of parents to the scenario, Leslie's posture is not that Marion has an excuse for his impropriety, but one of understanding without condoning. If we add the loss of both parents, then Leslie's posture becomes all the more one of understanding without condoning. The difference is that in one case the understanding is tied to the simple truth that even morally decent human beings are fallible, whereas with the addition of the loss of both parents, the understanding is also tied to the realization that a traumatic emotional loss can render a person extremely vulnerable emotionally. Of course, the tragic loss of parents or not, Leslie could rightly insist that, in having that affair with that 26-year-old, Marion had violated a most important principle of the academy. But, given Marion's character and Leslie's familiarity with it, I trust that, even without this addition, such a stance on Leslie's part reeks of fulsome moral self-righteousness rather than a justified invocation of moral standards, which is not to say that we have self-righteous behavior whenever a friend holds the moral line with a friend. By contrast, were the offender simply another member of the faculty, we would not expect Leslie even to attempt to be as understanding, although this other faculty member could be just like Marion in every way.

Of course, we can be horrified that a friend behaved in a certain way, especially if the person's behavior reflects negatively upon us. In any case, such behavior usually has to be particularly egregious in some way. The very wrongdoing itself goes beyond the pale or, for instance, the act showed a flagrant indifference to the feelings of others. Suppose everyone in a room failed a most important examination, save one's friend. Or suppose that she passed the examination and it is announced that a person's mother just passed away. In either context it would be most inappropriate for her to make much of her success, perhaps saying nothing unless she is directly asked about her performance on the examination, although she is rightly proud of this success. It is important to bear in mind the difference between explaining a friend's behavior and apologizing for it.

Others may find our friend's behavior strange, whereas we appreciate and admire it. Here, we do not apologize for how she behaves, since we do not concede any inappropriate behavior on her part; indeed, we may chastise others for being judgmental. We apologize for inappropriate, especially wrongful, behavior, and for reasons that I shall give below in this section, occasions of this sort should be few and far between.

We are now in the position to appreciate more fully the claim made in the introduction that friendship pushes the limits of morality. Limiting ourselves to innocent people who have been wronged, it is natural for morally decent persons to experience, on behalf of the victim, indignation toward the perpetrator of the wrongful behavior. And if the victim is a companion friend, then it is common enough to experience enormous resentment as well toward the perpetrator. But here is the rub. When the perpetrator turns out to be a companion friend, we do not experience a like level of indignation toward the friend—certainly not immediately and often never—on behalf of the innocent victim. On the contrary, as I have indicated with the example of Leslie and Marion, we seek to understand the friend's behavior, to put his wrongdoing in perspective, with the result being that the innocent victim fails to receive his moral due, if you will, in terms of our moral reaction to his having been wronged. This is of enormous significance because if indignation and resentment motivate us to press for what is right on behalf of those who have been wronged, then friendship can be a substantial barrier in this regard, when the wrongdoer is a deep friend.

Another way of getting at the tension between morality and friendship is by looking at the phenomenon of loyalty in friendship. In moral theory, objectivity and impartiality are highly valorized. A wrong is a wrong whether it is done by a friend or a stranger. But this kind of moral stance can be at odds with the demands of loyalty in friendship. Although as with honesty, kindness, and so on, a person can certainly be loyal to a fault, merely being willing to plant one's feet firmly on the soil of available circumstantial evidence is not generally a sign of loyalty, as one can presumably expect that of anyone. If the loyal soldier is one who, up to a point, continues to stand by his captain even when the evidence on the battlefield would point to her defeat, then a loyal friend, presumably, is one who holds fast to the belief that his friend is of good character, even though strong circumstantial evidence would suggest otherwise. As a result of loyalty, not only does a friend give the benefit of the doubt to a friend when it would be reasonable for a stranger not to, but a friend will often distance her- or himself from reasonable acts of public criticism of a friend. Of course, it is arguable that anyone should be given the benefit of the doubt where this is possible. Perhaps. But the point is that the motivation to do so would seem to be anchored in loyalty rather than morality.

All the same, none of previous discussion should be mistaken for the view that friends are tolerant of moral squalor on one another's part. I have not made any such claim; nor does a claim of this sort follow from what has been said, including the remarks about loyalty, for a quite loyal friend may nonetheless be concerned to get at the very truth of the matter. Without ever engaging in anything like a display of righteous moral indignation toward a friend on account of the wrong that he has done to an innocent person, one can take a very hard moral stance with him on account of the wrong that he has done. One can indicate the pain that his wrongdoing has caused one, because one has held him in such high moral esteem. One can go on to express how such wrongdoing even jeopardizes the friendship, if only because one does not want to be associated with a person who so behaves. Still, this will be very different from acting on the victim's behalf against the friend. Except incidentally, an argument that a friendship has been jeopardized by wrong done to another leaves unaddressed the harm that the innocent person has suffered.

The reader will notice that I have been careful not to offer an assessment of whether there should be this tension between friendship and morality. There are those who would insist that all personal relations, no matter what level of affection they may attain, are properly subsumable under the principles of morality. All that I want to say here is that this view of the priority of the right cannot, it seems, be squared with the psychological makeup of human beings, where profound ties of affection are involved. Within a rather wide range, a person would have to be capable of extraordinary compartmentalization in order to be capable of responding to a friend's wronging of an innocent third party with the same kind of wrath and resentment with which he would respond to any stranger's wronging of an innocent third-party. And such compartmentalization does not make for a psychologically healthy self nor for wholesome friendship. In the *New Testament*, there is the saying that love hides a multitude of faults. Taken literally, this may be far too strong. But a gloss on this saying would be that love carries in its wake an understanding of the faults of others that is rarely achieved in its absence. And the psychology of understanding a person for whom one has great affection may be such that, up to a point, any rate, it calms the storm of moral indignation that we would otherwise have.

On the other hand, our understanding of the wrongdoing of a friend would seem to hit a most impenetrable wall when we turn out to be the victim of the friend's wrongdoing. This should come as no surprise. This is because if anyone should be fortified with reasons not to harm us, a character friend should. Not only are there the ever-present moral considerations, which should be reason enough, but there is the love of the friendship itself, which one supposes should serve as a fail-safe measure. When we are wronged by a friend, the question is never simply, "How could you have done that?" Rather, it is, "How could you have done that to *me?*" What cries out for an explanation is not as much the wrongdoing as it is the target of the wrongdoing. These considerations indirectly complement our preceding discussion. In friendship, we expect love to reign and to govern interactions to a degree that far exceeds the demands of morality.

This love should serve as a safety net for us against even the very temptation to wrong us, and it should give us understanding in many instances where morality would render a verdict of guilty.

In bringing this section to a close, let me return briefly to the subject of friendship and moral squalor. As I have indicated, the tension that I have spelled out between morality and friendship does not entail that companion friendship is a matter of tolerating moral squalor. On the other hand, companion friends tend to maintain the same level of moral rectitude in their lives, whatever that level might be. Thus, take two companion friends at the same level of moral rectitude. If one became a more morally upright person than the other or, conversely, one became a more ignoble person than the other, then either the friendship would terminate or the other friend would change accordingly. There are two reasons why this is so.

One of these has to do with the importance of self-disclosure between friends. In general, aside from matters involving counseling, we are uneasy self-disclosing to people whom we regard as morally superior to us because it is simply impossible to avoid the feeling that the person is sitting in judgment of us, although the friend may assure us that nothing of the sort is going on. The second reason is related to the first.

While saints and heroes are a wonderful reminder of the potential for goodness that exists in human beings, the fact remains that most us of are neither, nor are we much concerned to be either. Most of us are rather content to be ordinary human beings with, if at all, moments of excellence here and there. More poignantly, most of us are inclined to think that this is all that can be rightly expected of us; hence, it is unreasonable to expect people to realize their full moral potential. If two individuals start at the same level of moral rectitude and one goes on to a much higher level, then this becomes, as it were, a moral challenge to the other friend, which he must either accept or decline—for if one could have made the change for the better than the other could have as well, since they supposedly had the same kind of moral timbre. On the other

hand, if one descends to a much lower level of moral rectitude, then in addition to the problem of self-disclosing which the person who has descended will have, the one who has not descended will find the friendship increasingly unsatisfying.

On the one hand, there will be the tensions that come with having a close friend who constantly engages in moral behavior that one finds unacceptable. If the friend does not make a turnaround in his behavior, then one loses one's moral leverage with that person, since he can rightly point out that his behavior is no different from that which one has been tolerating all along. To be sure, one can talk about limits having been reached, and so on. But to make this move is, in effect, to issue an ultimatum: change or lose a friend. On the other hand, there will be the issue of one's own moral reputation, which will become sullied by association: either one engages in certain immoral behavior or one is tolerant of it in (at least certain) others. Either way, one's reputation has been sullied, though undoubtedly more so in the first instance. But the second instance is hardly trivial; to be known as one who is tolerant of such-and-such immoral behavior when committed by X and Y is invariably to lose one's moral leverage with others. Thus, the one who sustains the level of moral rectitude with which the two parties started their friendship will become disenchanted with the friendship.

I have not addressed the topic of friendship where both individuals are immoral. This case raises special problems insofar as immoral persons can be viewed as egoists. How can two people, each of whom is primarily concerned with promoting only her or his self-interests, have genuine affection for another? And if each claims that the other is an exception, what reason does the other have to place much confidence in this claim? I shall not pursue these issues except to note that if there can be genuine friendship among the immoral, the argument in the preceding two paragraphs concerning the importance of parity of moral rectitude between friends applies equally well to such cases. Just as moral goodness admits of considerable range, so does moral badness. And the absence of parity pertains to there being a significant distance in quality between the moral character of two people, a distance which can be anywhere along the spectrum of moral goodness and badness. So suppose that Leslie and Marion are both immoral friends who engage in the immoral behavior of defrauding the elderly, but that, after awhile, Leslie moves on to murder. If Marion were to protest that Leslie had gone too far, Marion's protest would make sense notwithstanding the fact that Marion's own moral behavior is quite reprehensible.

IV. Conclusion: Friendship and the Ideal Society

As a most fitting way of bringing this essay to a close, the preceding discussion suggests a very profound way in which friendship can push morality to its limit. If the account just sketched of the equality of moral rectitude between friends is correct, then a most interesting question arises, bearing in mind just these considerations: Might a person refrain from becoming a morally better person in order to maintain a friendship with a person, where the friends are morally decent to begin with? Could the good that flows from a friendship be preferable to the good that flows from being a morally better person? In *The Politics,* Aristotle observed that those who have no need of others are either gods or beasts. So we can ask whether a person could have a proper understanding of the value of others if she or he were prepared to forsake all ties of human affection in the ascent toward moral perfection. It is difficult to see how such a person could. Alas, it would seem that if a friendship is rich enough then morality's claim to continual moral self-development may, at some point, fall upon deaf ears. None of this may be justified; but, alas, it may all be more understandable than we had been inclined to suppose. And if so, then Aristotle's observation about friendship may be so enduring because it speaks to a deep deep insight concerning what it is like to be a human being: Even with all the riches in the world a life without friendship is incomplete. Why? Because neither morality nor all the riches in the world can take the place of the affirmation, the understanding, and the reflection of ourselves that we all need from time to time in order to flourish and which companion friendship—that is, friendship at its best—affords us. I have not argued that the affection and affirmation of friendship is always preferable to moral betterment. Rather, I have challenged the converse, namely that moral betterment is always preferable to these things. Although there are few, if any, instances when a person might be open to criticism for eschewing friendship in order to achieve moral betterment, I have suggested that in view of the nature of human psychology, it is untenable to hold that in choosing friendship over moral betterment a person is thereby, and always, open to moral criticism. The quality of some friendships may be worth the trade-off. Thus, we may find in friendship a formidable challenge to moral perfectionism, understood as the idea that human beings should have as their sole goal the moral perfection of their lives.

So to conclude with a most speculative remark regarding a society replete with friendship at its best, this society would be an association of individuals for whom each serves as a mirror of insight for another, who in turn serves as a mirror of insight for that person. Accordingly, even if each friendship in and of itself does not represent a life of morality at its best, this association of individuals taken together would nonetheless yield an outcome, among individuals who are neither gods nor beasts, whereby the quality of the whole of moral life in society would nonetheless achieve a moral good that could never be reached by single pairs of friends living in isolation of one another.

Discussion Questions

1. Do you agree that companion-friendship must always be based on "character"?
2. Persons tend to be less "judgmental" with respect to friends, Thomas suggests, in virtue of the much greater knowledge they possess, especially of their friends' reasons and motives. Why are *spouses* so typically judgmental,

even possessing the knowledge they have of each other?

3. Ideally, one knows one's enemy extremely well. Why does this have no seeming tendency to lead to "ameliorative" judgments?

4. Can friendship justify what would otherwise be immoral? Explain your point with an example.

5. In what ways does Aziz and Thomas' discussion of friendship across ethnic lines draw on Thomas' earlier discussion of friendship (in general)? *See* "A Note on Friendship and Diversity." What other aspects of "interethnic" friendship do you see as important?

Acknowledgments

I thank Michele Moody-Adams, Neera Kapur Badhwar, Lawrence A. Blum, David Kim, Alasdair MacIntyre, and Howard McGary for their instructive comments upon earlier versions of this essay.

Bibliography

Badhwar, N. K. (Ed.) (1993). "Friendship: A Philosophical Reader." Cornell Univ. Press, Ithaca, NY.

Badhwar, N. K. (1996). The limited unity of virtue. *Nous,* 30, 306–329.

Blum, L. (1980). "Friendship, Altruism, and Morality." Routledge and Kegan Paul, London.

Cooper, J. M. (1980). Aristotle on friendship. In "Essays on Aristotle's Ethics" (A. Rorty, Ed.). Univ. of California Press, Berkeley.

MacIntyre, A. (1981). "After Virtue: A Study in Moral Theory." The Univ. of Notre Dame Press, Notre Dame, IN.

Railton, P. (1984). Alienation, consequentialism, and the demands of morality. *Philos. Public Affairs* 13(2), 134–171.

Schwarzenbach, S. (1996). On civic friendship. *Ethics* 107(1), 97–128.

Sherman, N. (1989). "The Fabric of Character: Aristotle's Theory of Virtue." Oxford Univ. Press, New York.

Stocker, M. (1990). "Plural and Conflicting Values." Clarendon Press, Oxford.

Thomas, L. (1989). "Living Morally: A Psychology of Moral Character." Temple Univ. Press, Philadelphia, PA.

A Note on Friendship and Diversity*

We were both attending a lecture at Syracuse University. It is quite plain to the naked eye that LMT is black; whereas NAA could be either Middle Eastern or Hispanic, depending perhaps on who is doing the observing. When NAA speaks, however, his accent rules out the latter as an option. At any rate, as we were walking across the campus after the lecture, NAA indicated that he is an Arab who was born in Jerusalem; and quite unexpectedly from NAA's perspective, LMT commented that he is a Jew who hails from a Sephardic community that had once thrived in South Carolina in the 1700s.

Needless to say, the walk across the campus after the lecture was suddenly transformed. An Arab and a Jew, what now were we supposed to do? Clearly enough, the moment was either going to be lost to the never-ending struggles between Arabs and Jews in the Middle East, or it was going to be salvaged. The moment, far from being lost, was resoundly redeemed. What follows is our explanation for why the moment was not lost, and so how friendship can transcend potentially explosive ethnic differences.

Friendship at its best, we believe, requires a certain kind of moral disposition, namely that of being naturally responsive to the moral goodness of others. We think of this as a kind of innocence, responsive innocence is perhaps the term for it; and we believe that responsive innocence is exhibited most fully by infants. Infants are quite uninterested in the skin color, and other physical features, of the persons who love them. Instead, infants simply delight in being the object of love. As adults, it is possible to be so fixated with the shortcomings of others that their acts of goodness are either discounted or ignored entirely. In a non-ideal world fraught with hostilities, this is especially likely to occur across ethnic differences because for adults ethnic differences represent historical legacies: A person of such-and-such

_____

*Nasri Abdel-Aziz and Laurence M. Thomas

ethnic group has this kind of character and personality; accordingly, this person is inclined to behave in certain undesirable ways. In the unfortunate cases, this historical legacy is superimposed with such relentlessness that the person's actual behavior is not seen for what it is.

Interestingly, then, we believe that friendship across ethnic differences requires a high degree of self-knowledge concerning one's ability to detect moral goodness in unusual encounters and contexts. For there is no greater impediment to the development of such friendships, than that the two parties allowing their thinking about the other to be so informed by prevailing social images regarding the group to which the other is a member that the other's actual behavior is distorted by these images. While these images may themselves be mistaken, our point is simply that images about a group, whether these images are true or not, do not always apply, without exception, to each and every member of the group. A friendship across ethnic differences will flounder if, in the endeavor to understand the other, one or both parties to the friendship rely more heavily upon the social images of the group to which the person belongs rather than the particular actions of the other individual.

No less important is a considerable measure of courage. This is because, with friendship across ethnic differences, each friend must be prepared to encounter suspicions, doubts, or perhaps outright threats of rejection from those of his own group on account the friendship with the person from the other group. To begin with, there will often be the shrill and incredulous "What does that person have to offer that you cannot find among your own kind?" This will be followed by solemn reminders of the disaster that ensued when so-and-so befriended a person of such-and-such ethnicity. Then there will be the avowals about differences that simply cannot be bridged; and admonishments about how prudence dictates that a person not try to change the world.

In our own case, there was not only the long history of struggles between Arabs and Jews, but our religious differences: Islam and Judaism. In both of our communities, some wondered how, in the first place, did it happen that we managed a non-volatile conversation.

Here is how we managed. While both of us take our religious traditions and ethnic identity to be defining features of our lives, both of us are also quite self-conscious about the fact that none of these things are exhaustive of who we are—of our identity as persons Nor does either of us think that his religion's traditions has a monopoly on moral goodness. This gave us plenty of moral and personal space for that conversation.

In this non-ideal world, friendship across ethnic differences requires a certain moral vision, if you will, born of self-knowledge and courage. On the one hand, one must never deny the moral pain of anyone's life. But, just as surely, on the other hand, one must never deny those aspects of innocence which are also part of a person's life. Prevailing social attitudes in a community often facilitate trivializing the moral pain of another or discounting the innocence of that person's motives; and a quite unfortunate fact about human beings is that most of us are unwilling to risk group alienation in order to do what is right by those who are members of a different ethnic group. All the same, the person who is willing to take such a risk cannot afford to be mistaken, which is why self-knowledge with respect to one's own moral judgments regarding the moral qualities of another is so very important.

As has been noted, one of Aristotle's most striking claims is that friendship at its best is rather like having another self for a friend. Surely one of the ways in which this turns out to be true is when we endeavor to give as much weight to the moral pain and innocence of another as we give to our own moral pain and innocence. This is a form of selflessness that is not about self-denial. And while similarities in life-style and experiences may facilitate the end of giving as much weight to moral pain and innocence of another as we give to our own, there is perhaps no better indication that an Aristotelian-like friendship has been achieved than when this end is realized across differences. A deep friendship need not be one that transcends ethnic differences; but owing to their texture, a deep friendship that does transcend such differences produces an element of richness that is not to be had otherwise.

31 Nihilism in Black America

CORNEL WEST

Study Questions

1. What are the limitations of the liberal structuralist and the conservative behaviorist accounts of the problems of black America?
2. How does West understand, and not understand, "nihilism"?
3. What are the main causes of today's nihilism in the black community?
4. What can be done to overcome this nihilism?

We black folk, our history and our present being, are a mirror of all the manifold experiences of America. What we want, what we represent, what we endure is what America is. If we black folk perish, America will perish. If America has forgotten her past, then let her look into the mirror of our consciousness and she will see the living *past living in the present, for our memories go back, through our black folk of today, through the recollections of our black parents, and through the tales of slavery told by our black grandparents, to the time when none of us, black or white, lived in this fertile land. The differences between black folk and white folk are not blood or color, and the ties that bind us are deeper than those that separate us. The common road of hope which we all traveled has brought us into a stronger kinship than any words, laws, or legal claims.*

RICHARD WRIGHT,
12 MILLION BLACK VOICES (1941)

Recent discussions about the plight of African Americans—especially those at the bottom of the social ladder—tend to divide into two camps. On

Reprinted by permission of the publisher from *Race Matters* (Boston: Beacon Press, 1993), pp. 17–31. © 1993 by Cornel West.

the one hand, there are those who highlight the *structural* constraints on the life chances of black people. Their viewpoint involves a subtle historical and sociological analysis of slavery, Jim Crowism, job and residential discrimination, skewed unemployment rates, inadequate health care, and poor education. On the other hand, there are those who stress the *behavioral* impediments on black upward mobility. They focus on the waning of the Protestant ethic—hard work, deferred gratification, frugality, and responsibility—in much of black America.

Those in the first camp—the liberal structuralist—call for full employment, health, education, and child-care programs, and broad affirmative action practices. In short, a new, more sober version of the best of the New Deal and the Great Society: more government money, better bureaucrats, and an active citizenry. Those in the second camp—the conservative behaviorists—promote self-help programs, black business expansion, and non-preferential job practices. They support vigorous "free market" strategies that depend on fundamental changes in how black people act and live. To put it bluntly, their projects rest largely upon a cultural revival of the Protestant ethic in black America.

Unfortunately, these two camps have nearly suffocated the crucial debate that should be taking place about the prospects for black America. This debate must go far beyond the liberal and conservative positions in three fundamental ways. First, we must acknowledge that structures and behavior are inseparable, that institutions and values go hand in hand. How people act and live are shaped—though in no way dictated or determined—by the larger circumstances in which they find themselves. These circumstances can be changed, their limits attenuated, by positive actions to elevate living conditions.

Second, we should reject the idea that structures are primarily economic and political creatures—

an idea that sees culture as an ephemeral set of behavioral attitudes and values. Culture is as much a structure as the economy or politics; it is rooted in institutions such as families, schools, churches, synagogues, mosques, and communication industries (television, radio, video, music). Similarly, the economy and politics are not only influenced by values but also promote particular cultural ideals of the good life and good society.

Third, and most important, we must delve into the depths where neither liberals nor conservatives dare to tread, namely, into the murky waters of despair and dread that now flood the streets of black America. To talk about the depressing statistics of unemployment, infant mortality, incarceration, teenage pregnancy, and violent crime is one thing. But to face up to the monumental eclipse of hope, the unprecedented collapse of meaning, the incredible disregard for human (especially black) life and property in much of black America is something else.

The liberal/conservative discussion conceals the most basic issue now facing black America: *the nihilistic threat to its very existence.* This threat is not simply a matter of relative economic deprivation and political powerlessness—though economic well-being and political clout are requisites for meaningful black progress. It is primarily a question of speaking to the profound sense of psychological depression, personal worthlessness, and social despair so widespread in black America.

The liberal structuralists fail to grapple with this threat for two reasons. First, their focus on structural constraints relates almost exclusively to the economy and politics. They show no understanding of the structural character of culture. Why? Because they tend to view people in egoistic and rationalist terms according to which they are motivated primarily by self-interest and self-preservation. Needless to say, this is partly true about most of us. Yet, people, especially degraded and oppressed people, are also hungry for identity, meaning, and self-worth.

The second reason liberal structuralists overlook the nihilistic threat is a sheer failure of nerve. They hesitate to talk honestly about culture, the realm of meanings and values, because doing so seems to lend itself too readily to conservative conclusions in the narrow way Americans discuss race. If there is a hidden taboo among liberals, it is to resist talking *too much* about values because such discussions remove the focus from structures and especially because they obscure the positive role of government. But this failure by liberals leaves the existential and psychological realities of black people in the lurch. In this way, liberal structuralists neglect the battered identities rampant in black America.

As for the conservative behaviorists, they not only misconstrue the nihilistic threat but inadvertently contribute to it. This is a serious charge, and it rests upon several claims. Conservative behaviorists talk about values and attitudes as if political and economic structures hardly exist. They rarely, if ever, examine the innumerable cases in which black people do act on the Protestant ethic and still remain at the bottom of the social ladder. Instead, they highlight the few instances in which blacks ascend to the top, as if such success is available to all blacks, regardless of circumstances. Such a vulgar rendition of Horatio Alger in blackface may serve as a source of inspiration to some—a kind of model for those already on the right track. But it cannot serve as a substitute for serious historical and social analysis of the predicaments of and prospects for all black people, especially the grossly disadvantaged ones.

Conservative behaviorists also discuss black culture as if acknowledging one's obvious victimization by white supremacist practices (compounded by sexism and class condition) is taboo. They tell black people to see themselves as agents, not victims. And on the surface, this is comforting advice, a nice cliché for downtrodden people. But inspirational slogans cannot substitute for substantive historical and social analysis. While black people have never been simply victims, wallowing in self-pity and begging for white giveaways, they have been—and are— *victimized.* Therefore, to call on black people to be agents makes sense only if we also examine the dynamics of this victimization against which their agency will, in part, be exercised. What is particularly naive and peculiarly vicious about the conservative behavioral outlook is that it tends to deny the lingering effect of black history—a history inseparable from though not reducible to victimization. In this way, crucial and indispensable themes of self-help and personal responsibility are wrenched out of historical context and contemporary circumstances—as if it is all a matter of personal will.

This ahistorical perspective contributes to the nihilistic threat within black America in that it can be used to justify right-wing cutbacks for poor people struggling for decent housing, child care, health care, and education. As I pointed out above, the liberal perspective is deficient in important ways, but even so liberals are right on target in their critique of conservative government cut-backs for services to the poor. These ghastly cutbacks are one cause of the nihilist threat to black America.

The proper starting point for the crucial debate about the prospects for black America is an examination of the nihilism that increasingly pervades black communities. *Nihilism is to be understood here not as a philosophic doctrine that there are no rational grounds for legitimate standards or authority; it is, far more, the lived experience of coping with a life of horrifying meaninglessness, hopelessness, and, (most important) lovelessness.* The frightening result is a numbing detachment from others and a self-destructive disposition toward the world. Life without meaning, hope, and love breeds a coldhearted, mean-spirited outlook that destroys both the individual and others.

Nihilism is not new in black-America. The first African encounter with the New World was an encounter with a distinctive form of the Absurd. The initial black struggle against degradation and devaluation in the enslaved circumstances of the New World was, in part, a struggle against nihilism. In fact, the major enemy of black survival in America has been and is neither oppression nor exploitation but rather the nihilistic threat—that is; loss of hope and absence of meaning. For as long as hope remains and meaning is preserved, the possibility of overcoming oppression stays alive. The self-fulfilling prophecy of the nihilistic threat is that without hope there can be no future, that without meaning there can be no struggle.

The genius of our black foremothers and forefathers was to create powerful buffers to ward off the nihilistic threat, to equip black folk with cultural armor to beat back the demons of hopelessness, meaninglessness, and lovelessness. These buffers consisted of cultural structures of meaning and feeling that created and *sustained communities;* this armor constituted ways of life and struggle that embodied values of service and sacrifice, love and care, discipline and excellence. In other words, traditions for black surviving and thriving under usually adverse New World conditions were major barriers against the nihilistic threat. These traditions consist primarily of black religious and civic institutions that sustained familial and communal networks of support. If cultures are, in part, what human beings create (out of antecedent fragments of other cultures) in order to convince themselves not to commit suicide, then black foremothers and forefathers are to be applauded. In fact, until the early seventies black Americans had the lowest suicide rate in the United States. But now young black people lead the nation in the rate of increase in suicides.

What has changed? What went wrong? The bitter irony of integration? The cumulative effects of a genocidal conspiracy? The virtual collapse of rising expectations after the optimistic sixties? None of us fully understands why the cultural structures that once sustained black life in America are no longer able to fend off the nihilistic threat. I believe that two significant reasons why the threat is more powerful now than ever before are the saturation of market forces and market moralities in black life and the present crisis in black leadership. The recent market-driven shattering of black civil society—black families, neighborhoods, schools, churches, mosques—leaves more and more black people vulnerable to daily lives endured with little sense of self and fragile existential moorings.

Black people have always been in America's wilderness in search of a promised land. Yet many black folk now reside in a jungle ruled by a cutthroat market morality devoid of any faith in deliverance or hope for freedom. Contrary to the superficial claims of conservative behaviorists,

these jungles are not primarily the result of pathological behavior. Rather, this behavior is the
tragic response of a people bereft of resources in
confronting the workings of U.S. capitalist society. Saying this is not the same as asserting that
individual black people are not responsible for
their actions—black murderers and rapists should
go to jail. But it must be recognized that the nihilistic threat contributes to criminal behavior. It
is a threat that feeds on poverty and shattered cultural institutions and grows more powerful as the
armors to ward against it are weakened.

But why is this shattering of black civil society
occurring? What has led to the weakening of
black cultural institutions in asphalt jungles? Corporate market institutions have contributed
greatly to their collapse. By corporate market institutions I mean that complex set of interlocking
enterprises that have a disproportionate amount
of capital, power, and exercise a disproportionate
influence on how our society is run and how our
culture is shaped. Needless to say, the primary
motivation of these institutions is to make profits,
and their basic strategy is to convince the public
to consume. These institutions have helped create
a seductive way of life, a culture of consumption
that capitalizes on every opportunity to make
money. Market calculations and cost-benefit
analyses hold sway in almost every sphere of U.S.
society.

The common denominator of these calculations and analyses is usually the provision, expansion, and intensification of *pleasure.* Pleasure
is a multivalent term; it means different things to
many people. In the American way of life pleasure involves comfort, convenience, and sexual
stimulation. Pleasure, so defined, has little to do
with the past and views the future as no more
than a repetition of a hedonistically driven present. This market morality stigmatizes others as
objects for personal pleasure or bodily stimulation. Conservative behaviorists have alleged that
traditional morality has been undermined by radical feminists and the cultural radicals of the sixties. But it is clear that corporate market institutions have greatly contributed to undermining

traditional morality in order to stay in business
and make a profit. The reduction of individuals to
objects of pleasure is especially evident in the
culture industries—television, radio, video,
music—in which gestures of sexual foreplay and
orgiastic pleasure flood the marketplace.

Like all Americans, African-Americans are influenced greatly by the images of comfort, convenience, machismo, femininity, violence, and sexual
stimulation that bombard consumers. These seductive images contribute to the predominance of the
market-inspired way of life over all others and
thereby edge out nonmarket values—love, care,
service to others—handed down by preceding
generations. The predominance of this way of life
among those living in poverty-ridden conditions,
with a limited capacity to ward off self-contempt
and self-hatred, results in the possible triumph of
the nihilistic threat in black America.

A major contemporary strategy for holding the nihilistic threat at bay is a direct attack on the sense
of worthlessness and self-loathing in black America. This *angst* resembles a kind of collective clinical depression in significant pockets of black
America. The eclipse of hope and collapse of
meaning in much of black America is linked to
the structural dynamics of corporate market institutions that affect all Americans. Under these circumstances black existential *angst* derives from
the lived experience of ontological wounds and
emotional scars inflicted by white supremacist
beliefs and images permeating U.S. society and
culture. These beliefs and images attack black intelligence, black ability, black beauty, and black
character daily in subtle and not-so-subtle ways.
Toni Morrison's novel, *The Bluest Eye,* for example, reveals the devastating effect of pervasive European ideals of beauty on the self-image of
young black women. Morrison's exposure of the
harmful extent to which these white ideals affect
the black self-image is a first step toward rejecting
these ideals and overcoming the nihilistic self-
loathing they engender in blacks.

The accumulated effect of the black wounds
and scars suffered in a white-dominated society is
a deep-seated anger, a boiling sense of rage, and

a passionate pessimism regarding America's will to justice. Under conditions of slavery and Jim Crow segregation, this anger, rage, and pessimism remained relatively muted because of a well-justified fear of brutal white retaliation. The major breakthroughs of the sixties—more physically than politically—swept this fear away. Sadly, the combination of the market way of life, poverty-ridden conditions, black existential *angst,* and the lessening of fear of white authorities has directed most of the anger, rage, and despair toward fellow black citizens, especially toward black women, who are the most vulnerable in our society and in black communities. Only recently has this nihilistic threat—and its ugly inhumane outlook and actions—surfaced in the larger American society. And its appearance surely reveals one of the many instances of cultural decay in a declining empire.

What is to be done about this nihilistic threat? Is there really any hope, given our shattered civil society, market-driven corporate enterprises, and white supremacism? If one begins with the threat of concrete nihilism, then one must talk about some kind of *politics of conversion.* New models of collective black leadership must promote a version of this politics. Like alcoholism and drug addiction, nihilism is a disease of the soul. It can never be completely cured, and there is always the possibility of relapse. But there is always a chance for conversion—a chance for people to believe that there is hope for the future and a meaning to struggle. This chance rests neither on an agreement about what justice consists of nor on an analysis of how racism, sexism, or class subordination operate. Such arguments and analyses are indispensable. But a politics of conversion requires more. Nihilism is not overcome by arguments or analyses; it is tamed by love and care. Any disease of the soul must be conquered by a turning of one's soul. This turning is done through one's own affirmation of one's worth—an affirmation fueled by the concern of others. A love ethic must be at the center of a politics of conversion.

A love ethic has nothing to do with sentimental feelings or tribal connections. Rather it is a last attempt at generating a sense of agency among a downtrodden people. The best exemplar of this love ethic is depicted on a number of levels in Toni Morrison's great novel *Beloved.* Self-love and love of others are both modes toward increasing self-valuation and encouraging political resistance in one's community. These modes of valuation and resistance are rooted in a subversive memory—the best of one's past without romantic nostalgia—and guided by a universal love ethic. For my purposes here, *Beloved* can be construed as bringing together the loving yet critical affirmation of black humanity found in the best of black nationalist movements, the perennial hope against hope for transracial coalition in progressive movements, and the painful struggle for self-affirming sanity in a history in which the nihilistic threat *seems* insurmountable.

The politics of conversion proceeds principally on the local level—in those institutions in civil society still vital enough to promote self-worth and self-affirmation. It surfaces on the state and national levels only when grass-roots democratic organizations put forward a collective leadership that has earned the love and respect of and, most important, has proved itself *accountable* to these organizations. This collective leadership must exemplify moral integrity, character, and democratic statesmanship within itself and within its organizations.

Like liberal structuralists, the advocates of a politics of conversion never lose sight of the structural conditions that shape the sufferings and lives of people. Yet, unlike liberal structuralism, the politics of conversion meets the nihilistic threat head-on. Like conservative behaviorism, the politics of conversion openly confronts the self-destructive and inhumane actions of black people. Unlike conservative behaviorists, the politics of conversion situates these actions within inhumane circumstances (but does not thereby exonerate them). The politics of conversion shuns the limelight—a limelight that solicits status seekers and ingratiates egomaniacs. Instead, it stays on the ground among the toiling everyday people, ushering forth humble freedom fighters—both followers and leaders—who have the audacity to take the nihilistic threat by the neck and turn back its deadly assaults.

Discussion Questions

1. Is the "nihilism" West describes more characteristic of the young than of the black community?
2. Why does capitalism as an economic system, and pleasure as a motivation, produce something as devastating as complete despair and hopelessness? Is West's explanation of the causes of nihilism adequate?
3. Why are the black institutions (e.g., the churches) that were responsible in the past for combating nihilism no longer able to?
4. Does the "Afrocentric" movement, in your view, offer a good chance of combating nihilism in the black community (by offering a different set of values)?
5. Is there anything *wrong* with African Americans' accepting the consumerist outlook of Americans today?

32   Unctuousness as Virtue: According to the Life of Zora Neale Hurston

KATIE G. CANNON

Study Questions

1. What is "unctuousness"?
2. How does Zora Neale Hurston's life help us understand how unctuousness is a virtue?
3. Describe the primary tension in Hurston's life, concerning the role of her "Godmother."
4. Why was Hurston criticized by many black male artists and critics?
5. Why did Hurston oppose forced integration?

Reprinted by permission of the publisher from *Katie's Canon: Womanism and the Soul of the Black Community* (New York: Continuum, 1995), pp. 91–100.

It may surprise some readers that a study in virtue would focus on the life of Zora Neale Hurston. To be sure, Hurston did not write as a formal exponent of ethics, but she clarifies the moral values that are central in the Black community in the very life she lived. As a Black-woman-artist, who was subjected to the violence of White supremacy, of male superiority, and of economic poverty, Zora Neale Hurston offers a concrete frame of reference for understanding the Black woman as a moral agent. Hurston's life serves as a prophetic paradigm for understanding the modes of behavior and courses of action that are passed from generation to generation by the most oppressed segments of the Black population.

Hurston, like Black women generally, understood suffering not as a moral norm or as a desirable ethical quality, but rather as the typical state of affairs. Virtue is not in the experiencing of suffering, nor in the survival techniques for enduring. Rather, the quality of moral good is that which allows Black people to maintain a feistiness about life that nobody can wipe out, no matter how hard they try.

Even though suffering is all but universal, Black women establish a relationship with suffering in their lives in order to endure. Due to Black women's widespread intimate acquaintance with suffering they do not assess suffering as the chief end of creation. It is not a natural condition. Nor is it a spiritual accompaniment of their life story that supposedly causes them to grow to maturity. Instead, suffering is the normal state of affairs.

The Black female community connects the entire range and spectrum of Black suffering to the history of this country, a history grounded in slavery, a history whose purpose and intent is denying Black people their full humanity. Suffering primarily arises from the inevitable trials and tribulations that come with being Black and female in a society that despises both. Such suffering occurs in many degrees of intensity, from that which is specifiable to that which constitutes an unimaginable anguish. Black women have suffered in fields and kitchens, their bodies freely used, their children taken from them, their men castrated before their eyes, "and yet in the mind of white America this abuse, this outrage, was somehow not serious, was in fact justified."[1]

In light of such suffering, what counsel of action is central for Blacks? Very specifically, the primary ethical principle or action guide is "unctuousness."[2] What Hurston makes clear is that it is the quality of steadfastness, akin to fortitude, in the face of formidable oppression that serves as the most conspicuous feature in the construction of Black women's ethics. My thesis is that Hurston portrays this moral quality of life not as an ideal to be fulfilled but as a balance of complexities so that suffering will not overwhelm and endurance is possible. The moral premises and assumptions that are inherited from the Black community's oral tradition, accentuated by Hurston's life, emphasize the continual struggle and interplay of contradictory opposites as the highest good. Creatively straining against the external restraints in one's life is virtuous living.

After her brief research fellowship expired in 1928, Zora Neale Hurston returned to New York City with the little bit of folklore she had collected, no money, and no job. She was able to continue her data-gathering for several more years under the auspices of Charlotte Osgood Mason, a White Park Avenue dowager of enormous wealth and influence. Some of Hurston's critics mercilessly discredited her as a respectable artist because she "got money from white folks." More often than not, these same critics, who caricatured Hurston as a charming, manipulative minion, "who lived up to the whites' notion of what a 'darky' should be," were financially backed by the same White patrons.

In spite of the ridicule, Hurston acted with unctuousness in this racist financial arrangement. Implicit in her contract, as in all of Mason's contracts with Black artists—Alain Locke, Langston Hughes, Richard Wright, Miguel Covarrubias, Aaron Douglas, Raymond Barthe and Louise Thompson—was an understanding that their work ought to reflect unalloyed primitivism. Mason wanted her protégées to "slough off white culture—using it only to clarify the thoughts that surge in your being." Mason also insisted that her Harlem beneficiaries never mention her name to others. They were only to refer to her as "Godmother." Mason had strict control over all of Hurston's work. She forbade Hurston to display in revues or publish any of the information, data, or music transcripts she gathered without her permission. Hurston knew that she needed Mason's financial sponsorship in order to preserve the Black cultural heritage, and at the same time she was aware of the razor-blade tension between obsequious accommodation to "Godmother" and fidelity to her own values.

A Black woman writer who was never able to make a living from her craft, Hurston experienced her situation as a moral dilemma and as a yoke around her neck. On the one hand, she celebrated the value of the rich reservoir of materials passed along in the oral tradition of her parents, neighbors, and common everyday people. On the other hand, Hurston had to confront the almost universal understanding outside of the context of Black culture itself: that of Black folkways as inferior, comic, and primitive.

During this period, Zora Neale Hurston coined the term "Negrotarian" for Whites such as Charlotte Mason, Carl Van Vechten, Fannie Hurst, Florenz Ziegfeld, Clarence Darrow, Pearl Buck, and Amy and Joe Springarn, all of whom specialized in "uplifting" all areas of Negro life. Negrotarians not only patronized Blacks and socialized with them, but sometimes used their White privileges to lionize Black artists in the most elite social circles. They would feature Black writing in leading national magazines, invite Blacks to participate in lecture series at Ivy League institutions, and publish Black manuscripts through the most notable publishing houses.

Karla Holloway described this type of WASP and Jewish philanthropy as New York's own form of the "peculiar institution." Holloway contends that the criteria for defining Black art, literature, and music as "truly Black" were determined by the economic imbalance between the wealthy White patrons and the poverty of the struggling Black artists. Thus, Black culture was commercialized and perverted. David L. Lewis, who described and analyzed the Negrotarians in significant detail in *When Harlem Was in Vogue,* said that the premise for the uplift mentality among Whites was a combination of "inherited abolitionism, Christian charity and guilt, social manipulation, political eccentricity and a certain amount of persiflage."[3] Jeanne Noble's comment on this "peculiar institution" within the Harlem Renaissance is that even though Black writers were inspired by the Black experience, they were almost completely dependent on Whites for public exposure and financial help, a dependency that sucked the vitality and creativity from Black artists. Whites either co-opted Black writers' ideas and style in an attempt to transfuse new and vigorous creativity into their own culture, or when awareness struck that what Black writers were communicating was not all fun and games they repressed the literary movement.[4] Harold Cruse suggests that the Black intellectual "must deal intimately with the white power structure and America's cultural institutions while dealing as a spokesperson for the inner realities of the black world at one and the same time."[5]

Hurston had to deal intimately with the White power structure while dealing with the inner realities of the Black world. She was constantly caught between the rock and the hard place, accepting financial assistance from wherever it was offered so that Black culture would survive. Considering the implications of accepting the financial backing of Negrotarians, Hurston concluded that it was more important to uncover Black folk culture in all its rare beauty than to reject the financial support. Hurston understood the rich resources in the Black cultural heritage for her on-going process of determining who she was and who she would become.

Gender discrimination as a complex social force had a profound negative impact in Zora Neale Hurston's career as well. Black men, such as Alain Locke, the leader and chief interpreter of the cultural revitalization in Harlem during the 1920s, believed that by virtue of their gender they were in charge of the infrastructures in the Black community. As the prime movers of the Harlem Renaissance, Claude McKay, Countee Cullen, Langston Hughes, Arna Bontemps, and W. E. B. Du Bois used their privileged positions and monopoly of power to identify, nurture, and promote the artists who best represented their interests. As "godfathers" of the Black Art Movement, these men used their eminence to give a rubber stamp to some and to filter out other young artists. As males, subtly socialized to perpetuate superiority over females, most of these men were unaware of the pervasive ideologies they harbored that subordinated, distorted, and devalued Black women. Zora Neale Hurston, both in the life she lived and in the writings she produced, challenged the assumptions of men. Hurston tapped her inner strength and pushed against the structural limits that did not adhere to her own standards of self-fulfillment. Hurston's modus operandi of unctuousness was a genuine threat to her male colleagues.

Hurston was twice stigmatized—once for race and once for gender. Yet Hurston refused to fit into a male mold. She would not succumb to the subtle, debilitating pressures to conform to the norms and values of the Black male literary tradition. While some of Hurston's contemporaries were busily proving that well-bred, intelligent Blacks could mimic the attitudes, behavior, and standards dictated by well-bred, intelligent Whites, Hurston invested her energies into entertaining Whites, and all who would listen, with vivid, metaphorical stories of the Black oral tradition. While Hurston's colleagues focused on White antagonism as the cause for the poverty of the masses who supposedly languished in despair, anger, and defeatism, Hurston was trekking through the South collecting the Black classics in music, art, dance, and literature with hopes of eventually correcting dominant misconceptions about the quality of life in the Black context.

The moral wisdom that Hurston received from her all-Black southern context encouraged her to "jump at de sun," not to bend to the demanding will of her critics, most of whom were members of a self-selected male sanctioning body. Thus, Hurston's behavior was seen as an "unnatural" anomaly. The more successful she became as a writer, researcher, and critic, the more her motives were subjected to misinterpretation.

The men in the literary guild had difficulty accepting the seriousness Hurston brought to her work. She made it clear to everyone that her writings were an integral part of her life. She was unwilling to be defined by others or limited in exchange for male endorsement and support. Hurston fought hard. She faced rigorous demands and obstacles. Her professional aspirations posed such a threat that in her obituary she was attacked by a male writer for "shuttling between the sexes, the professions and the races as if she were a man and a woman, scientists and, creative writer, white and colored."[6] Hurston's "unctuousness" trespassed on something that her critics felt was exclusively theirs. The Black male literary guild picked apart Hurston's person and viciously satirized her work.[7] Hurston, the most prolific Black woman writer in the United States between 1920 and 1950, was "lauded by the white world, but suspiciously regarded and often lampooned by the black."[8]

When Zora Hurston wrapped her hair in beautiful cloth turbans, her critics charged that she was trying to pass for an African queen.[9] When she dared divorce, not one, but two husbands, with rumor alluding to the possibility of a third marriage, her critics portrayed her as indecent.[10] However, Hurston refused to take a defensive posture about acting in ways that were not acceptable for women until decades later.[11]

In 1938, while working with the Florida Federal Writers Project, Hurston was described as "flighty" because she loved to show off, refused to cooperate with her co-workers, and hated to stay inside at her desk, Carl Van Vechten, a White critic and one of her closest friends, assessed Hurston not as "flighty" but as a woman with a "magnetic" personality:

What it comes down to is the fact that Zora was put together entirely different from the rest of mankind. Her reactions were always original because they were always her own. When she breezed into a room (she never merely entered), tossed a huge straw hat (as big as a cart wheel) on the floor and yelled "I am the queen of the 'niggerati,' " you knew you were in the presence of an individual of the greatest magnitude.[12]

One of the most damning and damaging charges against Hurston focused upon her fight against integration. When most Black leaders were organizing around integration as a goal, Zora Hurston was a lonely frontrunner who saw the implementation of integration as an affront and threat to the Black community. Hurston believed that the integration of schools was needed only if "some residual, some inherent and unchangeable quality in white schools were impossible to duplicate anywhere else."

The Supreme Court would have pleased [her] more if they had concerned themselves about enforcing the compulsory education provisions for Negroes in the South as is done for white children.[13]

Hurston, busy affirming Black values and Black life, saw no benefit in forsaking the Black reality under the pretense of being bleached into acceptance in a so-called superior White world. Hurston wrote in that same article:

The whole matter revolves around the self-respect of my people. How much satisfaction can I get from a court order for somebody to associate with me who does not wish me near them. . . . It is a contradiction in terms to scream race pride and equality while at the same time spurning Negro teachers and self-associations.

Hurston personally believed in the principle of an integrated society, but she did not support the invidious comparisons that implied that Black people were divergent deviants from the "norm."[14] She did not believe that Black people were a negligible factor in the thought of the world. Instead, her life was committed to redressing ignorance about Black culture. Her work was an affirmation of the Black race as one of the great human races, inferior to none in its accomplishments and in its ability.

Hurston's social relationships put her in close contact with her male colleagues. Her apartment was always open, with a communal pot on the stove. Zora entertained entire parties with stories, group singing, and stand-up comedy routines mimicking snobbish Park Avenue Whites who she called "Astorperious." Discovering that there was to be no support when these peers put their critic hats on to review her work, Hurston refused to behave in ways that conformed to the status quo.

Hurston's emphasis on "the Negro farthest down" brought criticism from many quarters. Richard Wright condemned Hurston for being unconcerned with racism, class struggle, and the revolutionary tradition of Black people. Roy Wilkins, after reading Hurston's article on Jim Crow, went so far as to say:

Now is no time for tongue-wagging by Negroes for the sake of publicity. The race is fighting a battle that may determine its status for fifty years. Those who are not for us, are against us.[15]

Lester B. Granger of the *California Eagle* responded to some of Hurston's articles in this manner:

Miss Hurston has written seldom in recent years and so far as her public is concerned, when she has come out with a production it has been readily evident that she "shoulda stayed in bed."[16]

In 1932, Wallace Thurman wrote an elaborate satire on himself and his colleagues of the Harlem Renaissance entitled *Infants of the Spring.* Unfortunately his "bas-relief" caricature of Zora Hurston as Sweetie May Carr, "a short story writer, more noted for her ribald wit and effervescence than any actual literary work," has haunted the authentic Hurston up to the present time.[17] As recently as 1971, Black men like Darwin Turner still depicted Zora Neale Hurston as

superficial and shallow in her artistic and social judgements. . . . Always, she remained a wandering minstrel. It was eccentric but perhaps appropriate for her to return to Florida to take a job as a cook and maid for a white family and to die in poverty. She had

not ended her days as she once had hoped—a farmer among growing things she loved. Instead she had returned to the level of life which she proposed for her people.[18]

While the *Saturday Review* was praising Hurston's autobiography as a significant contribution to the field of race relations, Arna Bontemps denounced her life story:

Miss Hurston deals very simply with the more serious aspects of Negro life in America—she ignores them. She has done well by herself in the kind of world she has found.[19]

Harold Preece, writing for *Crisis,* dismissed Hurston's autobiography as no more than

the tragedy of a gifted, sensitive mind, eaten up by an egocentrism fed on the patronizing admiration of the dominant white world.[20]

Hurston's scientific study of folklore in novelistic form, *Mules and Men,* was of such quality that it resulted in invitations for her to become a member of three prestigious organizations: the American Folklore Society, the American Ethnological Society, and the American Anthropological Society. By direct contrast, Sterling Brown's review of this work found the characters "naive, quaint, complacent and bad enough to kill each other in looks, but meek otherwise, and socially unconscious."[21]

Some critics lauded Hurston's third novel: "If Hurston had written nothing else she would deserve recognition for *Moses, Man of the Mountain,*" but Alain Locke called it "a caricature instead of portraiture."[22] Ralph Ellison claimed that "for Negro fiction, it did nothing."[23]

Robert Bone, a White critic of Black literature, heralded Hurston's *Their Eyes Were Watching God* as a "classic of Black literature, one of the finest novels of the period,"[24] while Richard Wright reviewed this work and found it to be a "shallow romance, lacking in protest value."[25]

Poor reviews also shut down in fast order the song-dance revues *Fast and Furious, Jungle Scandals,* and *Spunk,* which Hurston had arranged from her exclusive collection of folklore material. Hall Johnson, of *Run Little Chillun* fame, summed up the popular sentiments toward Hurston's colorful revues among the Renaissance artists:

The world was not ready for Negro music unless it was highly arranged. The barbaric melodies and harmonies were simply not fit for musical ears.[26]

George Antheil, a U.S. composer known internationally for his ultramodern music, attended one of the revues Hurston had arranged, *The Great Day,* when it was performed at the New School for Social Research in 1932. Antheil insisted that the quality of Hurston's revue was so superb that she would be the most plagiarized Black person in the world for at least a decade.

This sort of thievery in unavoidable. Unpleasant, of course, but at the bottom a tribute to one's originality.[27]

In 1948, Zora Neale Hurston was falsely charged with sexually molesting a ten-year-old-boy. Hurston was able to prove that she was not in the country when the alleged crimes were supposed to have happened. The charges were dropped but not before the Black press in Baltimore, Chicago, and New York had exploited the scandal to the hilt. This was the straw that broke Hurston's back. In a letter to Carl Van Vechten dated October 30, 1948, Hurston described the devastating catastrophe in this manner:

The thing is too fantastic, too evil, too far from reality for me to conceive it. . . . One inconceivable horror after another swept over me. I went out of myself, I am sure, though no one seemed to notice. It seemed that every hour some other terror assailed me, the last thing being the Afro-American filth. I care nothing for anything anymore. My country has failed me utterly. My race has seen fit to destroy me without reason, and with the vilest tools conceived of by men so far. A society, eminently Christian, and supposedly devoted to super-democracy has gone so far from its announced purpose, not to protect children, but to exploit the gruesome fancies of a pathological case and do this thing to human decency. Please do not forget that this thing was not done in the South, but in the so-called liberal North. Where shall I look in the country for justice?

All that I have ever tried to do has proved useless. All that I have believed in has failed me. I have resolved to die. It will take a few days for me to set my affairs in order, and then I will go. . . . No acquittal will persuade some people that I am innocent. I feel hurled down a filthy privy hole.[28]

As we have seen, Zora Neale Hurston captured the integrity of Black people who buttressed themselves with the community's moral wisdom in her effort to hold on to the essence of her humanity. Hurston lived out of a Black consciousness and political/social awareness that provided realistic assessment of the nature of virtuous living in situations of oppression.

So the question now before us is, What caused this creative, vibrant, and astute Black woman to acquiesce into neurotic passivity after the false sodomy charges of 1948? Why did she let go of everything she previously valued? What was missing in the Black woman's wisdom tradition that caused Zora Hurston to sink into unreboundable brokenness when the sex slander was circulated by, to, and through the Black community?

Hurston's entire life had been grounded in an uncompromising struggle to fulfill her human capacity against incredible odds. In all of her work she adamantly opposed a defensive, reactionary posture for Black people. Yet Hurston assumed such a stance as her only recourse in her fight to reclaim her dignity and self-worth. Since the politics of justice was not on the horizon for her and the experience of community was denied to her, were there any resources that would have helped Hurston recover from this traumatic attack against her personhood?

There are two main criticisms lodged against Zora Neale Hurston: political conservatism and obsessive individualism. I believe that both of these criticisms are valid and highly accurate when they are evaluated within the context of Hurston's own time. In the throes of betrayal, Hurston responded in opposite ways from her previous approach of unctuousness.

However, much of the critical commentary tends to minimize the devastating impact of the false charge that she had committed an immoral act with a ten-year-old-boy. Hurston was an intensely proud woman. Her whole life was committed to a defiant affirmation of the cultural practices manifested in the Black community. Hemenway's biography documents how Hurston's professional career was spent "trying to show that normality is a function of culture, that an Afro-American culture exists, and that its creators lead lives rich with ideological and esthetic significance."[29] And yet it was a Black court employee who peddled the inaccurate and sensationalized story to the Black press, which, in turn, circulated lurid coverage to the Black community. Hurston referred to this betrayal of her as "the Afro-American sluice of filth." In the prime of her career, she felt that her world had collapsed, unfairly, unreasonably, in the ugliest possible way.

After the case was dropped and the indictment dismissed, Hurston commented that she didn't think that she could even endure the sight of a Black person. Dispirited and broken, Hurston was occasionally suspicious and paranoid. Questioning the motives behind her moral and intellectual lynching, Hurston even wondered if the charges against her in 1948 were part of some kind of Communist frame-up. Always struggling to remain solvent, Hurston sold articles and essays to White magazines, knowing that they would be heavily edited. She also campaigned for conservative Republicans such as Taft.

Barbara Christian provides a critical analysis of Hurston's situation:

One cannot help but note the similarities between Larsen [Nella] and Hurston's disappearances from the world. Although very different writers, they were both assaulted by the prejudices of the other society. Larsen's writing ability was challenged and Hurston's sex life was used, consciously or unconsciously, as a means of diminishing her effectiveness as a writer and as an anthropologist. Both charges are indicative of the vulnerable position of black women writers. Their sexual morality and intellectual capacity are seen as tentative, not only by their fellow countrymen but by members of their own race as well. Both writers fell prey to the racial and sexual stereotypes inflicted upon the black woman.[30]

I maintain that this virtue of unctuousness was directly responsible for Zora Neale Hurston's brief periods of professional notoriety and also for her professional demise. Living under a system of triple oppression, Hurston's unprecedented strength to endure could not ward off the precedented assaults on her as a Black woman. The defeat of Hurston's "unctuousness" was not due to its importance as a virtue in Black women's lives, but to the viciousness of the assault on her. Without communal recognition that unctuousness is a virtue, even it is not enough to sustain Black women. In other words, if the Black community cannot recognize and celebrate its Zora Hurstons more in their ongoing struggle against race, sex, and class oppression and if Black women are forced to embrace the conventional morality of middle-class American ideals, which twists their virtue into a vice, then Black women face the gravest danger yet.

Discussion Questions

1. Many blacks in her own time evidently resented Hurston for playing to a white audience. From the perspective of a half-century later, how should we view their resentment?

2. In the past, many middle-class blacks were uncomfortable even with some of the classics of black literature, because they did not always present black people in the best possible light. Is this a justified attitude? How does it relate to the reception of Hurston's work?

3. Why do you suppose the white patrons of the Harlem Renaissance artists were so concerned that their work display genuinely "primitivist" tendencies—and never follow European artistic models? How would you compare this with the attitude of *black* "Afro-centrists" today?

4. Did Zora Neale Hurston have a right to be "entirely herself," or does a black artist have a special responsibility to conduct herself in more "dignified" ways?

5. How would you compare the attacks against Hurston with those against Clarence Thomas in our own day?

Notes

1. Pat Crutchfield Exum, ed., *Keeping the Faith: Writings by Contemporary Black Women* (Greenwich, Conn.: Fawcett Publications, 1974), 34–35.

2. Alice Walker, foreword to Robert Hemenway, *Zora Neale Hurston: A Literary Biography* (Urbana:

University of Illinois Press, 1977), xvii. The moral agency of Zora Neale Hurston culminates in a quality that Alice Walker identifies as "unctuousness." On her own from the age of nine and a runaway from the age of fourteen, Hurston repeatedly had to act sincere in the most insincere situations.

3. David L. Lewis, *When Harlem Was in Vogue* (New York: Alfred A. Knopf, 1981), 99.

4. Jeanne Noble, *Beautiful, Also, Are the Souls of My Black Sisters: A History of the Black Woman in America* (Englewood Cliffs, N.J.: Prentice-Hall, 1978), 148.

5. Harold Cruse, *The Crisis of the Negro Intellectual* (New York: William Morrow & Co., 1967), 9–10.

6. Karla F. C. Holloway, "Critical Investigation of Literary and Linguistic Structures in the Fiction of Zora Neale Hurston" (Ph.D. diss., Michigan State University, 1978), 36.

7. Mary Helen Washington, "Zora Neale Hurston: A Woman Half in Shadow," Introduction to *I Love Myself When I Am Laughing. . .: A Zora Neale Hurston Reader,* ed. Alice Walker (Old Westbury, N.Y.: Feminist Press, 1979, 8: "To a large extent, the attention focused on Zora Hurston's controversial personality and lifestyle have inhibited any objective critical analysis of her work. Few male critics have been able to resist sly innuendos and outright attacks on Hurston's personal life, even when the work in question was not affected by her disposition or her private affairs. But these controversies have loomed so large in the reviews of her work that once again the task of confronting them must precede any reappraisal or reevaluation of her highly neglected work."

8. Robert Hemenway, *Zora Neale Hurston: A Literary Biography* (Urbana: University of Illinois Press, 1977), 218–20.

9. Walker, Foreword to Hemenway, *Zora Neale Hurston,* xv.

10. Hemenway, *Zora Neale Hurston,* 93–94, 308, 314 (first marriage to Herbert Sheen); 273–74, 314 (second marriage to Albert Price III).

11. Alice Walker, Foreword to Hemenway, *Zora Neale Hurston,* xv, writes, "They [Hurston's critics] disliked her apparent sensuality: the way she tended to marry or not marry men, but enjoyed them anyway, while never missing a beat in her work. They hinted slyly that Zora was gay, or at least bi-sexual—how else could they account for her drive?—though there is not a shred of evidence that this was true. The accusation becomes humorous—and, of course, at all times irrelevant—when one considers that what she *did* write was some of the most healthily rendered heterosexual loving in our literature."

12. Carl Van Vechten to Fannie Hunt, July 5, 1960 James Weldon Johnson Memorial Collection of American Literature, Beinecke Rare Book and Manuscript Library, Yale University.

13. Zora Neale Hurston to the *Orlando Sentinel,* August 11, 1955, in response to the Supreme Court desegregation decision in 1954.

14. Hemenway, *Zora Neale Hurston,* 338, points out that Zora Hurston objected to the implied pathological stereotype in the desegregation decision wherein it was thought that Black students could learn only if they were in close proximity with Whites. Black students would be "uplifted" to White standards and a White way of life. "The Supreme Court ruling," she said, "implied that just like mules being led by a white mare, black students had to be led by white pupils and white teachers."

15. Roy Wilkins, "The Watchtower," *New York Amsterdam News,* February 27, 1943.

16. Lester Granger, *California Eagle,* December 20, 1951.

17. Wallace Thurman, *Infants of the Spring* (New York: Macaulay, 1932), 239–40.

18. Darwin Turner, *In a Minor Chord* (Carbondale: Southern Illinois University Press, 1971), 120.

19. Arna Bontemps, "From Eatonville, Fla. to Harlem," review of *Dust Tracks on a Road,* by Zora Neale Hurston, *New York Herald Tribune,* November 23, 1942.

20. Harold Preece, "The Negro Folk Cult," review of Zora Neale Hurston, *Dust Tracks on a Road,* in *Crisis* 43 (1936): 364.

21. Sterling Brown, "Old Time Tales," review of *Mules and Men* (1936), a clipping in the James Weldon Johnson Memorial Collection of American Literature, Beinecke Rare Book and Manuscript Library, Yale University.

22. Alain Locke, "Dry Fields and Green Pastures," review of Zora Neale Hurston, *Moses, Man of the Mountain* in *Opportunity* 18 (January 1940): 7.

23. Ralph Ellison, "Recent Negro Fiction," review of Zora Neale Hurston, *Moses, Man of the Mountain,* in *New Masses,* August 5, 1941, 211.

24. Robert Bone, *The Negro Novel in America* (New Haven: Yale University Press, 1965), 41.

25. Hemenway, *Zora Neale Hurston,* 241.

26. Zora Neale Hurston's manuscript chapter "Concert," *Dust Tracks on a Road,* James Weldon Johnson Memorial Collection of American Literature, Beinecke Rare Book and Manuscript Library, Yale University.

27. Zora Neale Hurston to Charlotte Osgood Mason, September 25, 1931, and October 15, 1931, Locke Collection, Howard University.

28. Zora Neale Hurston to Carl Van Vechten, October 30, 1948, James Weldon Johnson Memorial Collection of American Literature, Beinecke Rare Book and Manuscript Library, Yale University.

29. Hemenway, *Zora Neale Hurston,* 332.

30. Barbara Christian, *Black Women Novelists: The Development of a Tradition, 1892–1976* (Westport, Conn.: Greenwood Press, 1980), 61.

A Classic Question of Values, Rights, and Education

33   Atlanta Exposition Address

BOOKER T. WASHINGTON

Study Questions

1. What is the meaning Washington is trying to get across by "Cast down your bucket where you are"?
2. In what way is Washington's message the same for whites as for blacks? In what way is it different?
3. What argument concerning progress does Washington offer to white Southerners?

One third of the population of the South is of the Negro race. No enterprise seeking the material, civil, or moral welfare of this section can disregard this element of our population and reach the highest success. I but convey to you, Mr. President and Directors, the sentiment of the masses of my race when I say that in no way have the value and manhood of the American Negro been more fittingly and generously recognized than by the managers of this magnificent exposition at every stage of its progress. It is a recognition that will do more to cement the friendship of the two races than any occurrence since the dawn of our freedom.

Not only this, but the opportunity here afforded will awaken among us a new era of industrial progress. Ignorant and inexperienced, it is not strange that in the first years of our new life we began at the top instead of at the bottom; that a seat in Congress or the State Legislature was more sought than real estate or industrial skill; that the political convention or stump-speaking

had more attraction than starting a dairy farm or truck garden.

A ship lost at sea for many days suddenly sighted a friendly vessel. From the mast of the unfortunate vessel was seen a signal: "Water, water; we die of thirst!" The answer from the friendly vessel at once came back: "Cast down your bucket where you are." A second time the signal, "Water, water; send us water!" ran up from the distressed vessel, and was answered: "Cast down your bucket where you are." And a third and fourth signal for water was answered, "Cast down your bucket where you are." The captain of the distressed vessel, at last heeding the injunction, cast down his bucket, and it came up full of fresh, sparkling water from the mouth of the Amazon River. To those of my race who depend upon bettering their condition in a foreign land, or who underestimate the importance of cultivating friendly relations with the Southern white man who is their next-door neighbor, I would say: "Cast down your bucket where you are"—cast it down in making friends, in every manly way, of the people of all races by whom we are surrounded.

Cast it down in agriculture, mechanics, in commerce, in domestic service, and in the professions. And in this connection it is well to bear in mind that whatever other sins the South may be called to bear, when it comes to business, pure and simple, it is in the South that the Negro is given a man's chance in the commercial world, and in nothing is this Exposition more eloquent than in emphasizing this chance. Our greatest danger is that in the great leap from slavery to freedom we may overlook the fact that the masses of us are to live by the productions of our hands, and fail to keep in mind that we shall prosper in proportion as we learn to dignify and

Speech given at the opening of the Cotton States and International Exposition at Atlanta, September 1865.

glorify common labor, and put brains and skill into the common occupations of life; shall prosper in proportion as we learn to draw the line between the superficial and the substantial, the ornamental gewgaws of life and the useful. No race can prosper till it learns that there is as much dignity in tilling a field as in writing a poem. It is at the bottom of life we must begin, and not at the top. Nor should we permit our grievances to overshadow our opportunities.

To those of the white race who look to the incoming of those of foreign birth and strange tongue and habits for the prosperity of the South, were I permitted, I would repeat what I say to my own race, "Cast down your bucket where you are." Cast it down among the eight million Negroes whose habits you know, whose fidelity and love you have tested in days when to have proved treacherous meant the ruin of your firesides. Cast down your bucket among these people who have without strikes and labor wars tilled your fields, cleared your forests, builded your railroads and cities, brought forth treasures from the bowels of the earth, and helped make possible this magnificent representation of the progress of the South. Casting down your bucket among my people, helping and encouraging them as you are doing on these grounds, and, with education of head, hand, and heart, you will find that they will buy your surplus land, make blossom the waste places in your fields, and run your factories. While doing this, you can be sure in the future, as in the past, that you and your families will be surrounded by the most patient, faithful, law-abiding, and unresentful people that the world has seen. As we have proved our loyalty to you in the past, in nursing your children, watching by the sick bed of your mothers and fathers, and often following them with tear-dimmed eyes to their graves, so in the future, in our humble way, we shall stand by you with a devotion that no foreigner can approach, ready to lay down our lives, if need be, in defense of yours, interlacing our industrial, commercial, civil, and religious life with yours in a way that shall make the interests of both races one. In all things that are purely social we can be as separate as the fingers, yet one as the hand in all things essential to mutual progress.

There is no defense or security for any of us except in the highest intelligence and development of all. If anywhere there are efforts tending to curtail the fullest growth of the Negro, let these efforts be turned into stimulating, encouraging, and making him the most useful and intelligent citizen. Effort or means so invested will pay a thousand per cent interest. These efforts will be twice blessed—"Blessing him that gives and him that takes."

There is no escape through law of man or God from the inevitable:

> The laws of changeless justice bind
>   Oppressor with oppressed;
> And close as sin and suffering joined
>   We march to fare abreast.

Nearly sixteen millions of hands will aid you in pulling the load upward, or they will pull, against you, the load downward. We shall constitute one third and more of the ignorance and crime of the South, or one third its intelligence and progress; we shall contribute one third to the business and industrial prosperity of the South, or we shall prove a veritable body of death, stagnating, depressing, retarding every effort to advance the body politic.

Gentlemen of the Exposition, as we present to you our humble effort at an exhibition of our progress, you must not expect overmuch. Starting thirty years ago with ownership here and there in a few quilts and pumpkins and chickens (gathered from miscellaneous sources), remember, the path that has led from these to the inventions and production of agricultural implements, buggies, steam engines, newspapers, books, statuary carving, paintings, the management of drugstores and banks, has not been trodden without contact with thorns and thistles. While we take pride in what we exhibit as a result of our independent efforts, we do not for a moment forget that our part in this exhibition would fall far short of your expectations but for the constant help that has come to our educational life, not only from the Southern states, but especially from Northern philanthropists, who have made their gifts a constant stream of blessing and encouragement.

The wisest among my race understand that the agitation of questions of social equality is the extremest folly, and that progress in the enjoyment of all the privileges that will come to us must be the result of severe and constant struggle rather than of artificial forcing. No race that has anything to contribute to the markets of the world is long, in any degree, ostracized. It is important and right that all privileges of the law be ours, but it is vastly more important that we be prepared for the exercise of those privileges. The opportunity to earn a dollar in a factory just now is worth infinitely more than the opportunity to spend a dollar in an opera house.

In conclusion, may I repeat that nothing in thirty years has given us more hope and encouragement, and drawn us so near to you of the white race, as this opportunity offered by the Exposition; and here bending, as it were, over the altar that represents the results of the struggles of your race and mine, both starting practically empty-handed three decades ago, I pledge that, in your effort to work out the great and intricate problem which God has laid at the doors of the South, you shall have at all times the patient, sympathetic help of my race; only let this be constantly in mind, that while, from representations in these buildings of the product of field, of forest, of mine, of factory, letters, and art, much good will come, yet far above and beyond material benefits will be that higher good, that, let us pray God, will come in a blotting out of sectional differences and racial animosities and suspicions, in a determination to administer absolute justice, in a willing obedience among all classes to the mandates of law. This, coupled with our material prosperity, will bring into our beloved South a new heaven and a new earth—September 18, 1895.

Discussion Questions

1. What is Washington's general theory of social progress for disadvantaged groups?
2. What is Washington's vision for the South? How would it compare, in its dual emphasis on social separation and economic progress, with that of the black nationalists?
3. Washington is often condemned as an "Uncle Tom." Based on this speech, is this a fair criticism?
4. Is there "as much dignity in tilling a field as writing a poem"? Assuming that there is, does this mean that Washington's program for black progress was the right one?

34   The Talented Tenth

W. E. B. DuBOIS

Study Questions

1. What is, and what is not, the proper object of education, according to DuBois?
2. In what way, does DuBois suggest, was slavery a means of avoiding "the survival of the fittest"?
3. "All men cannot go to college but some men must." Why, according to DuBois?
4. According to DuBois, what must a system of education do in order to raise the Negro's "scale of civilization"?
5. DuBois observes that one limitation of an exclusive emphasis on industrial training is that it will not produce the individuals needed as teachers and "teachers of teachers." What other limitation of such a system does he stress?

Originally published by James Pott & Co., 1903.

The Negro race, like all races, is going to be saved by its exceptional men. The problem of education, then, among Negroes must first of all deal with the Talented Tenth; it is the problem of developing the Best of this race that they may guide the Mass away from the contamination and death of the Worst, in their own and other races. Now the training of men is a difficult and intricate task. Its technique is a matter for educational experts, but its object is for the vision of seers. If we make money the object of man-training, we shall develop money-makers but not necessarily men; if we make technical skill the object of education, we may possess artisans but not, in nature, men. Men we shall have only as we make manhood the object of the work of the schools—intelligence, broad sympathy, knowledge of the world that was and is, and of the relation of men to it—this is the curriculum of that Higher Education which must underlie true life. On this foundation we may build bread winning, skill of hand and quickness of brain, with never a fear lest the child and man mistake the means of living for the object of life.

If this be true—and who can deny it—three tasks lay before me; first to show from the past that the Talented Tenth as they have risen among American Negroes have been worthy of leadership; secondly, to show how these men may be educated and developed; and thirdly, to show their relation to the Negro problem.

You misjudge us because you do not know us. From the very first it has been the educated and intelligent of the Negro people that have led and elevated the mass, and the sole obstacles that nullified and retarded their efforts were slavery and race prejudice; for what is slavery but the legalized survival of the unfit and the nullification of the work of natural internal leadership? Negro leadership, therefore, sought from the first to rid the race of this awful incubus that it might make way for natural selection and the survival of the fittest. In colonial days came Phillis Wheatley and Paul Cuffe striving against the bars of prejudice; and Benjamin Banneker, the almanac maker, voiced their longings when he said to Thomas Jefferson, "I freely and cheerfully acknowledge that I am of the African race, and in colour which is natural to them, of the deepest dye; and it is under a sense of the most profound gratitude to the Supreme Ruler of the Universe, that I now confess to you that I am not under that state of tyrannical thraldom and inhuman captivity to which too many of my brethren are doomed, but that I have abundantly tasted of the fruition of those blessings which proceed from that free and unequalled liberty with which you are favored, and which I hope you will willingly allow, you have mercifully received from the immediate hand of that Being from whom proceedeth every good and perfect gift.

"Suffer me to recall to your mind that time, in which the arms of the British crown were exerted with every powerful effort, in order to reduce you to a state of servitude; look back, I entreat you, on the variety of dangers to which you were exposed; reflect on that period in which every human aid appeared unavailable, and in which even hope and fortitude wore the aspect of inability to the conflict, and you cannot but be led to a serious and grateful sense of your miraculous and providential preservation, you cannot but acknowledge, that the present freedom and tranquility which you enjoy, you have mercifully received, and that a peculiar blessing of heaven.

"This, sir, was a time when you clearly saw into the injustice of a state of Slavery, and in which you had just apprehensions of the horrors of its condition. It was then that your abhorrence thereof was so excited, that you publicly held forth this true and invaluable doctrine, which is worthy to be recorded and remembered in all succeeding ages: 'We hold these truths to be self evident, that all men are created equal; that they are endowed with certain inalienable rights, and that among these are life, liberty and the pursuit of happiness.' "

Then came Dr. James Derham, who could tell even the learned Dr. Rush something of medicine, and Lemuel Haynes, to whom Middlebury College gave an honorary A. M. in 1804. These and others we may call the Revolutionary group of distinguished Negroes—they were persons of marked ability, leaders of a Talented Tenth, standing conspicuously among the best of their time. They strove by word and deed to save the color line from becoming the line between the bond and free, but all they could do was nullified by Eli Whitney and the Curse of Gold. So they passed into forgetfulness.

But their spirit did not wholly die; here and there in the early part of the century came other exceptional men. Some were natural sons of un-natural fathers and were given often a liberal training and thus a race of educated mulattoes sprang up to plead for black men's rights. There was Ira Aldridge, whom all Europe loved to honor; there was that Voice crying in the Wilderness, David Walker, and saying:

"I declare it does appear to me as though some nations think God is asleep, or that he made the Africans for nothing else but to dig their mines and work their farms, or they cannot believe history, sacred or profane. I ask every man who has a heart, and is blessed with the privilege of believing—Is not God a God of justice to all his creatures? Do you say he is? Then if he gives peace and tranquility to tyrants and permits them to keep our fathers, our mothers, ourselves and our children in eternal ignorance and wretchedness to support them and their families, would he be to us a God of Justice? I ask, O, ye Christians, who hold us and our children in the most abject ignorance and degradation that ever a people were afflicted with since the world began—I say if God gives you peace and tranquility, and suffers you thus to go on afflicting us, and our children, who have never given you the least provocation—would He be to us a God of Justice? If you will allow that we are men, who feel for each other, does not the blood of our fathers and of us, their children, cry aloud to the Lord of Sabaoth against you for the cruelties and murders with which you have and do continue to afflict us?"

This was the wild voice that first aroused Southern legislators in 1829 to the terrors of abolitionism.

In 1831 there met that first Negro convention in Philadelphia, at which the world gaped curiously but which bravely attacked the problems of race and slavery, crying out against persecution and declaring that "Laws as cruel in themselves as they were unconstitutional and unjust, have in many places been enacted against our poor, un-friended and unoffending brethren (without a shadow of provocation on our part), at whose bare recital the very savage draws himself up for fear of contagion—looks noble and prides himself because he bears not the name of Christian." Side by side this free Negro movement, and the movement for abolition, strove until they merged into one strong stream. Too little notice has been taken of the work which the Talented Tenth among Negroes took in the great abolition crusade. From the very day that a Philadelphia colored man became the first subscriber to Garrison's "Liberator," to the day when Negro soldiers made the Emancipation Proclamation possible, black leaders worked shoulder to shoulder with white men in a movement, the success of which would have been impossible without them. There was Purvis and Remond, Pennington and Highland Garnett, Sojourner Truth and Alexander Crummell, and above all, Frederick Douglass—what would the abolition movement have been without them? They stood as living examples of the possibilities of the Negro race, their own hard experiences and well wrought culture said silently more than all the drawn periods of orators—they were the men who made American slavery impossible. As Maria Weston Chapman once said, from the school of anti-slavery agitation "a throng of authors, editors, lawyers, orators and accomplished gentlemen of color have taken their degree! It has equally implanted hopes and aspirations, noble thoughts, and sublime purposes, in the hearts of both races. It has prepared the white man for the freedom of the black man, and it has made the black man scorn the thought of enslavement, as does a white man, as far as its influence has extended. Strengthen that noble influence! Before its organization, the country only saw here and there in slavery some faithful Cudjoe or Dinah, whose strong natures blossomed even in bondage, like a fine plant beneath a heavy stone. Now, under the elevating and cherishing influence of the American Anti-slavery Society, the colored race, like the white, furnishes Corinthian capitals for the noblest temples."

Where were these black abolitionists trained? Some, like Frederick Douglass, were self-trained, but yet trained liberally; others, like Alexander Crummell and McCune Smith, graduated from famous foreign universities. Most of them rose up through the colored schools of New York and Philadelphia and Boston, taught by college-bred men like Russworm, of Dartmouth, and college-bred white men like Neau and Benezet.

After emancipation came a new group of educated and gifted leaders: Langston, Bruce and Elliot, Greener, Williams and Payne. Through political organization, historical and polemic writing and moral regeneration, these men strove to uplift their people. It is the fashion of to-day to sneer at them and to say that with freedom Negro leadership should have begun at the plow and not in the Senate—a foolish and mischievous lie; two hundred and fifty years that black serf toiled at the plow and yet that toiling was in vain till the Senate passed the war amendments; and two hundred and fifty years more the half-free serf of to-day may toil at his plow, but unless he have political rights and righteously guarded civic status, he will still remain the poverty-stricken and ignorant plaything of rascals, that he now is. This all sane men know even if they dare not say it.

And so we come to the present—a day of cowardice and vacillation, of strident wide-voiced wrong and faint hearted compromise; of double-faced dallying with Truth and Right. Who are to-day guiding the work of the Negro people? The "exceptions" of course. And yet so sure as this Talented Tenth is pointed out, the blind worshippers of the Average cry out in alarm: "These are exceptions, look here at death, disease and crime—these are the happy rule." Of course they are the rule, because a silly nation made them the rule: Because for three long centuries this people lynched Negroes who dared to be brave, raped black women who dared to be virtuous, crushed dark-hued youth who dared to be ambitious, and encouraged and made to flourish servility and lewdness and apathy. But not even this was able to crush all manhood and chastity and aspiration from black folk. A saving remnant continually survives and persists, continually aspires, continually shows itself in thrift and ability and character. Exceptional it is to be sure, but this is its chiefest promise; it shows the capability of Negro blood, the promise of black men. Do Americans ever stop to reflect that there are in this land a million men of Negro blood, well-educated, owners of homes, against the honor of whose womanhood no breath was ever raised, whose men occupy positions of trust and usefulness, and who, judged by any standard, have reached the full measure of the best type of modern European culture? Is it fair, is it decent, is it Christian to ignore these facts of the Negro problem, to belittle such aspiration, to nullify such leadership and seek to crush these people back into the mass out of which by toil and travail, they and their fathers have raised themselves?

Can the masses of the Negro people be in any possible way more quickly raised than by the effort and example of this aristocracy of talent and character? Was there ever a nation on God's fair earth civilized from the bottom upward? Never; it is, ever was and ever will be from the top downward that culture filters. The Talented Tenth rises and pulls all that are worth the saving up to their vantage ground. This is the history of human progress; and the two historic mistakes which have hindered that progress were the thinking first that no more could ever rise save the few already risen; or second, that it would better the unrisen to pull the risen down.

How then shall the leaders of a struggling people be trained and the hands of the risen few strengthened? There can be but one answer: The best and most capable of their youth must be schooled in the colleges and universities of the land. We will not quarrel as to just what the university of the Negro should teach or how it should teach it—I willingly admit that each soul and each race-soul needs its own peculiar curriculum. But this is true: A university is a human invention for the transmission of knowledge and culture from generation to generation, through the training of quick minds and pure hearts, and for this work no other human invention will suffice, not even trade and industrial schools.

All men cannot go to college but some men must; every isolated group or nation must have its yeast, must have for the talented few centers of training where men are not so mystified and befuddled by the hard and necessary toil of earning a living, as to have no aims higher than their bellies, and no God greater than Gold. This is true training, and thus in the beginning were the favored sons of the freedmen trained. . . .

[Training and Education]

The problem of training the Negro is to-day immensely complicated by the fact that the whole question of the efficiency and appropriateness of our present systems of education, for any kind of child, is a matter of active debate, in which final settlement seems still afar off. Consequently it often happens that persons arguing for or against certain systems of education for Negroes, have these controversies in mind and miss the real question at issue. The main question, so far as the Southern Negro is concerned, is: What under the present circumstance, must a system of education do in order to raise the Negro as quickly as possible in the scale of civilization? The answer to this question seems to me clear: It must strengthen the Negro's character, increase his knowledge and teach him to earn a living. Now it goes without saying, that it is hard to do all these things simultaneously or suddenly, and that at the same time it will not do to give all the attention to one and neglect the others; we could give black boys trades, but that alone will not civilize a race of ex-slaves; we might simply increase their knowledge of the world, but this would not necessarily make them wish to use this knowledge honestly; we might seek to strengthen character and purpose, but to what end if this people have nothing to eat or to wear? A system of education is not one thing, nor does it have a single definite object, nor is it a mere matter of schools. Education is that whole system of human training within and without the school

house walls, which molds and develops men. If then we start out to train an ignorant and unskilled people with a heritage of bad habits, our system of training must set before itself two great aims—the one dealing with knowledge and character, the other part seeking to give the child the technical knowledge necessary for him to earn a living under the present circumstances. These objects are accomplished in part by the opening of the common schools on the one, and of the industrial schools on the other. But only in part, for there must also be trained those who are to teach these schools—men and women of knowledge and culture and technical skill who understand modern civilization, and have the training and aptitude to impart it to the children under them. There must be teachers, and teachers of teachers, and to attempt to establish any sort of a system of common and industrial school training, without *first* (and I say *first* advisedly) without *first* providing for the higher training of the very best teachers, is simply throwing your money to the winds. School houses do not teach themselves—piles of brick and mortar and machinery do not send out *men*. It is the trained, living human soul, cultivated and strengthened by long study and thought, that breathes the real breath of life into boys and girls and makes them human, whether they be black or white, Greek, Russian or American. Nothing, in these latter days, has so dampened the faith of thinking Negroes in recent educational movements, as the fact that such movements have been accompanied by ridicule and denouncement and decrying of those very institutions of higher training which made the Negro public school possible, and make Negro industrial schools thinkable. It was Fisk, Atlanta, Howard and Straight, those colleges born of the faith and sacrifice of the abolitionists, that placed in the black schools of the South the 30,000 teachers and more, which some, who depreciate the work of these higher schools, are using to teach their own new experiments. If Hampton, Tuskegee and the hundred other industrial schools prove in the future to be as successful as they deserve to be, then their success in training black artisans for the South, will be due primarily to the white colleges of the North and the black colleges of the South, which trained the teachers who to-day conduct these institutions. There was a time when the American people believed pretty devoutly that a log of wood with a boy at one end and Mark Hopkins at the other, represented the highest ideal of human training. But in these eager days it would seem that we have changed all that and think it necessary to add a couple of saw-mills and a hammer to this outfit, and, at a pinch, to dispense with the services of Mark Hopkins.

I would not deny, or for a moment seem to deny, the paramount necessity of teaching the Negro to work, and to work steadily and skillfully; or seem to depreciate in the slightest degree the important part industrial schools must play in the accomplishment of these ends, but I *do* say, and insist upon it, that it is industrialism drunk with its vision of success, to imagine that its own work can be accomplished without providing for the training of broadly cultured men and women to teach its own teachers, and to teach the teachers of the public schools.

But I have already said that human education is not simply a matter of schools; it is much more a matter of family and group life—the training of one's home, of one's daily companions, of one's social class. Now the black boy of the South moves in a black world—a world with its own leaders, its own thoughts, its own ideals. In this world he gets by far the larger part of his life training, and through the eyes of this dark world he peers into the veiled world beyond. Who guides and determines the education which he receives in his world? His teachers here are the group-leaders of the Negro people— the physicians and clergymen, the trained fathers and mothers, the influential and forceful men about him of all kinds; here it is, if at all, that the culture of the surrounding world trickles through and is handed on by the graduates of the higher schools. Can such culture training of group leaders be neglected? Can we afford to ignore it? Do you think that if the leaders of thought among Negroes are not trained and educated thinkers, that they will have no leaders?

On the contrary a hundred half-trained demagogues will still hold the places they so largely occupy now, and hundreds of vociferous busybodies will multiply. You have no choice; either you must help furnish this race from within its own ranks with thoughtful men of trained leadership, or you must suffer the evil consequences of a headless misguided rabble.

I am an earnest advocate of manual training and trade teaching for black boys, and for white boys, too. I believe that next to the founding of Negro colleges the most valuable addition to Negro education since the war, has been industrial training for black boys. Nevertheless, I insist that the object of all true education is not to make men carpenters, it is to make carpenters men; there are two means of making the carpenter a man, each equally important: the first is to give the group and community in which he works, liberally trained teachers and leaders to teach him and his family what life means; the second is to give him sufficient intelligence and technical skill to make him an efficient workman; the first object demands the Negro college and college-bred men—not a quantity of such colleges, but a few of excellent quality; not too many college-bred men, but enough to leaven the lump, to inspire the masses, to raise the Talented Tenth to leadership; the second object demands a good system of common schools, well-taught, conveniently located and properly equipped. . . .

Thus, again, in the manning of trade schools and manual training schools we are thrown back upon the higher training as its source and chief support. There was a time when any aged and wornout carpenter could teach in a trade school. But not so to-day. Indeed the demand for college-bred men by a school like Tuskegee, ought to make Mr. Booker T. Washington the firmest friend of higher training. Here he has as helpers the son of a Negro senator, trained in Greek and the humanities, and graduated at Harvard; the son of a Negro congressman and lawyer, trained in Latin and mathematics, and graduated at Oberlin; he has as his wife, a woman who read Virgil and Homer in the same class room with me; he has as college chaplain, a classical graduate of Atlanta

University; as teacher of science, a graduate of Fisk; as teacher of history, a graduate of Smith,—indeed some thirty of his chief teachers are college graduates, and instead of studying French grammars in the midst of weeds, or buying pianos for dirty cabins, they are at Mr. Washington's right hand helping him in a noble work. And yet one of the effects of Mr. Washington's propaganda has been to throw doubt upon the expediency of such training for Negroes, as these persons have had.

Men of America, the problem is plain before you. Here is a race transplanted through the criminal foolishness of your fathers. Whether you like it or not the millions are here, and here they will remain. If you do not lift them up, they will pull you down. Education and work are the levers to uplift a people. Work alone will not do it unless inspired by the right ideals and guided by intelligence. Education must not simply teach work—it must teach Life. The Talented Tenth of the Negro race must be made leaders of thought and missionaries of culture among their people. No others can do this work and Negro colleges must train men for it. The Negro race, like all other races, is going to be saved by its exceptional men.

Discussion Questions

1. DuBois is sometimes accused of being an "elitist." Is there any basis for this in his discussion here?

2. In DuBois' view (and in your own), what is the purpose of studying such indirectly useful things as Greek, Latin, and philosophy? Do they produce "civilization"? (What is "civilization"?) Do they produce "character"? If so, how?

3. As DuBois suggests, why should teachers at technical schools be possessed of more than merely technical knowledge?

4. In the passage quoted at the start of this section, DuBois insists that the purpose of education is to make "men" (and not mere carpenters). What do you think he means by "men"? Can formal education produce men? (Does knowing Greek, Chinese, or philosophy make one more of a man?)

PHILOSOPHY AND RELATED DISCIPLINES

Philosophy and Legal Theory

For blacks, therefore, the battle is not deconstructing rights, in a world of no rights; nor of constructing statements of need, in a world of abundantly apparent need. Rather, the goal is to find a political mechanism that can confront the denial of need.

PATRICIA J. WILLIAMS

Given the current tenuous status of African Americans, the desperate condition of those on the bottom, and the growing resentment of the successes realized by those who are making gains despite the odds, one wonders how this country would respond to a crisis in which the sacrifice of the most basic rights of blacks would result in the accrual of substantial benefits to all whites?

DERRICK BELL

If the purpose of the First Amendment is to foster the greatest amount of speech, racial insults disserve that purpose. Assaultive racist speech functions as a preemptive strike. The invective is experienced as a blow, not as a proffered idea. And once the blow is struck, a dialogue is unlikely to follow.

CHARLES LAWRENCE

If there is any principle of the Constitution that more imperatively calls for attachment than any other it is the principle of free thought—not free thought for those who agree with us but freedom for the thought that we hate.

OLIVER WENDELL HOLMES

The law—and the legal and moral rights it has been thought to embody—has long been of prime concern to African American thinkers. In the history of this African American concern with the law, one finds alienation and idealism, in roughly equal measure. There is great alienation from much of the actual law and its interpretation but also a persistent idealism in the refusal to give up on the law or the Constitution, as the last best hope of peaceful change in America.

This legal idealism is certainly not new, and it may be traced at least as far back as Frederick Douglass, who rejected the very negative view of the Constitution put forward by many white abolitionists. Douglass chose to understand the Constitution as a progressive document and a repository of certain basic rights. Although fellow abolitionists, such as William Lloyd Garrison, saw the Constitution as almost a criminal document, for Douglass, the real crime was that its ideals were not being followed.

Today one finds a similar contrast between the views of leading African American legal theorists—the so-called Critical Race Studies movement—and what is called the "Critical Legal Studies" movement. The latter has aimed to show that legal principles, rules, decisions, and even rights need to be understood in the context of social power relations. Like their ancestors—the American "legal realists" of the 1930s and 1940s—the "Crits" stress the need to see the law not as a set of logical, rationally organized and grasped set of principles but as a social instrument. Critical Legal Studies, however, goes beyond Realism in taking a politically radical stance—for example, in seeing the law and legal decisions as mainly an instrument of corporate capitalism. Critical Race theorists, while not rejecting the Crit's political radicalism, tend to part company with Critical Legal Studies insofar as the latter includes in its critique of American law the very notion of a legal *right*. As Patricia J. Williams eloquently brings out in her essay, this "critique of rights discourse" leaves minority group members more than uneasy.

Beyond this critique of their fellow radicals, however, the Critical Race Theory movement has aimed to show how American law *continues* almost a half-century after such "landmark decisions" as the *Brown* case to subvert the interests of African Americans. We include here some leading examples of this line of thought. In her contribution, for instance, Regina Austin opposes a decision upholding the firing of a young black woman who, contrary to the rules of the "Girls Club" for which she worked, had gotten pregnant. To some, it would seem only reasonable that a "role model" for young black women should not become pregnant (out of wedlock). Austin, however, argues that such court decisions need to be understood as part of a long and inglorious history of attempts control black women and their reproductive rights.

In his paper, Derrick Bell, probably the leading figure of this movement, addresses what he sees as the fundamental problem: namely, the white majority is unmoved by, and uninterested in, black aspirations for more than a marginal role in American life. For Bell, "racial realism" means at least calling attention to this problem and developing realistic ways of addressing it.

In his contribution, John Arthur discusses some of the connections between the Critical Legal Studies and Critical Race theory movements, criticizing the view, shared by both movements, that the law is itself indeterminate and therefore apt to be used for political purposes by those in power. Arthur goes on to raise a number of criticisms of Critical Race theory, especially on the question of whether race is as important an explanatory factor as Critical Race theorists suppose.

The final essays constitute a debate between two noted constitutional scholars on racist "hate speech." Black law professor Charles Lawrence, while strongly upholding the right to dissent, sees hate speech as creating a climate in which free thought is stifled, not enhanced. Despite (and because) of his own experiences with hatred of Jews in Nazi Germany, Gerald Gunther takes a different view: upholding a broad right to express even the most hateful, and hated, racist speech.

35 Alchemical Notes: Reconstructing Ideals from Deconstructed Rights

PATRICIA J. WILLIAMS

Study Questions

1. What is Williams' parable supposed to tell us about the Critical Legal Studies (CLS) movement?
2. How did Williams' experience as a working lawyer help make her skeptical about the CLS position?
3. For Williams' discussion of CLS and blacks, what is the relevance of her story about the lease?
4. Why would a switch from talk of "rights" to talk of "needs" not serve any useful purpose?
5. What conclusions does Williams reach regarding the "sorcery" of rights?

Once upon a time, there was a society of priests who built a Celestial City whose gates were secured by Word-Combination locks. The priests were masters of the Word, and, within the City, ascending levels of power and treasure became accessible to those who could learn ascendingly intricate levels of Word Magic. At the very top level, the priests became gods; and because they then had nothing left to seek, they engaged in games with which to pass the long hours of eternity. In particular, they liked to ride their strong, sure-footed steeds, around and around the perimeter of heaven: now jumping word-hurdles, now playing polo with the concepts of the moon and of the stars, now reaching up to touch that pinnacle, that fragment, that splinter of Refined Understanding which was called Superstanding, the brass ring of their merry-go-round.

In time, some of the priests-turned-gods tired of this sport, denounced it as meaningless. They donned the garb of pilgrims, seekers once more, and passed beyond the gates of the Celestial City. In this recursive passage, they acquired the knowledge of Undoing Words.

From *Harvard Civil Rights and Liberties Law Review* 22 (1987), pp. 401–433.

Beyond the walls of the City lay a Deep Blue Sea. The priests built themselves small boats and set sail, determined to explore the uncharted courses, the open vistas of this new and undefined domain. They wandered for many years in this manner, until at last they reached a place that was half-a-circumference away from the Celestial City. From this point, the City appeared as a mere shimmering illusion; and the priests knew that at last they had reached a place which was Beyond the Power of Words. They let down their anchors, the plumb lines of their reality, and experienced godhood once more.

The Story

Under the Celestial City, dying mortals called out their rage and suffering, battered by a steady rain of sharp hooves whose thundering, sound-drowning path described the wheel of their misfortune.

At the bottom of the Deep Blue Sea, drowning mortals reached silently and desperately for drifting anchors dangling from short chains far, far overhead, which they thought were life-lines meant for them.

I wrote the above parable in response to a friend who asked me what Critical Legal Studies was *really* all about; the Meta-Story was my impressionistic attempt to explain. Then my friend asked me if there weren't lots of blacks and minorities, organizers and grass-roots types in an organization so diametrically removed from tradition. Her question immediately called to mind my first days on my first job out of law school: armed with fresh degrees and shiny new theories, I walked through the halls of the Los Angeles Criminal and Civil Courthouses, from assigned courtroom to assigned courtroom. The walls of every hall were lined with waiting defendants and families of defendants,[1] almost all poor, Hispanic and/or black. As I passed, they stretched out their arms and asked me for my card; they asked me if I were a lawyer, they called me 'sister' and 'counselor.' The power of that memory is fused with my concern about the disproportionately low grass-roots membership in or input to CLS. CLS wields significant power in shaping legal strategies which affect—literally from on high—the poor and oppressed. The irony of that reproduced power imbalance prompted me to complete 'The Brass Ring and the Deep Blue Sea' with the Story.

In my experience, most non-corporate clients looked to lawyers almost as gods. They were frightened, pleading, dependent (and resentful of their dependence), trusting only for the specific purpose of getting help (because they had no choice), and distrustful in a global sense (again, because they most often had no choice). Subservience is one way I have heard the phenomenon described (particularly by harried, well-meaning practitioners who would like to see their clients be more assertive, more responsible, and more forthcoming), but actually I think its something much worse, and more complexly worse.

I think what I saw in the eyes of those who reached out to me in the hallways of the courthouse was a profoundly accurate sense of helplessness—a knowledge that without a sympathetically effective lawyer (whether judge, prosecutor, or defense attorney) they would be lining those halls and those of the lockup for a long time to come. I probably got more than my fair share of outstretched arms because I was one of the few people of color in the system at that time; but just about every lawyer who has frequented the courthouse enough has had the experience of being cast as a saviour. I have always tried to take that casting as a real request—not as a literal message that I am a god, but as a rational demand that I work the very best of whatever theory-magic I learned in law school on their behalves. CLS has a good deal of powerful theory-magic of its own to offer; but I think it has failed to make its words and un-words tangible, *reach*-able and applicable to those in this society who need its powerful assistance most.

In my Story, the client-mortals reached for help because they needed help; in CLS, I have sometimes been left with the sense that lawyers and clients engaged in the pursuit of 'rights' are viewed as foolish, 'falsely conscious,' benighted, or misled. Such an attitude indeed gives the courthouse scenario a cast not just of subservience but of futility. More important, it may keep CLS from reaching back; or, more ironically still, keep CLS reaching in the wrong direction, locked in refutation of formalist legal scholarship.

This chapter is an attempt to detail my discomfort with that part of CLS which rejects rights-based theory, particularly that part of the debate and critique which applies to the black struggle for civil rights.

I by no means want to idealize the importance of rights in a legal system in which rights are so often selectively invoked to draw boundaries, to isolate, and to limit. At the same time, it is very hard to watch the idealistic or symbolic importance of rights being diminished with reference to the disenfranchised, who experience and express their disempowerment as nothing more or less than the denial of rights. It is my belief that blacks and whites do differ in the degree to which rights-assertion is experienced as empowering or disempowering. The expression of these differing experiences creates a discourse boundary, reflecting complex and often contradictory societal understandings. It is my hope that in redescribing the historical alchemy of rights in black lives, the reader will experience some reconnection with that part of the self and of society whose story unfolds beyond the neatly staked bounds of theoretical legal understanding.

A Tale with Two Stories

Mini-Story (In Which Peter Gabel and I Set Out to Teach Contracts in the Same Boat While Rowing in Phenomenological Opposition)

Some time ago, Peter Gabel[2] and I taught a contracts class together. Both recent transplants from California to New York, each of us hunted for apartments in between preparing for class and ultimately found places within one week of each other. Inevitably, I suppose, we got into a discussion of trust and distrust as factors in bargain relations. It turned out that Peter had handed over a $900 deposit, in cash, with no lease, no exchange of keys, and no receipt, to strangers with whom he had no ties other than a few moments of pleasant conversation. Peter said that he didn't need to sign a lease because it imposed too much formality. The handshake and the good vibes were for him indicators of trust more binding than a distancing form contract. At the time, I told Peter I thought he was stark raving mad, but his faith paid off. His sublessors showed up at the appointed time, keys in hand, to welcome him in. Needless to say, there was absolutely nothing in my experience to prepare me for such a happy ending.

I, meanwhile, had friends who found me an apartment in a building they owned. In *my* rush to show good faith and trustworthiness, I signed a detailed, lengthily negotiated, finely printed lease firmly establishing me as the ideal arm's length transactor.

As Peter and I discussed our experiences, I was struck by the similarity of what each of us was seeking, yet in such different terms, and with such polar approaches. We both wanted to establish enduring relationships with the people in whose houses we would be living; we both wanted to enhance trust of ourselves and to allow whatever closeness, whatever friendship, was possible. This similarity of desire, however, could not reconcile our very different relations to the word of law. Peter, for example, appeared to be extremely self-conscious of his power potential (either real or imagistic) as a white or male or lawyer authority figure. He therefore seemed to go to some lengths to overcome the wall which that image might impose. The logical ways of establishing some measure of trust between strangers were for him an avoidance of conventional expressions of power and a preference for informal processes generally.[3]

I, on the other hand, was raised to be acutely conscious of the likelihood that, no matter what degree of professional or professor I became,

people would greet and dismiss my black femaleness as unreliable, untrustworthy, hostile, angry, powerless, irrational, and probably destitute. Futility and despair are very real parts of my response. Therefore it is helpful for me, even essential for me, to clarify boundary; to show that I can speak the language of lease is my way of enhancing trust of me in my business affairs. As a black, I have been given by this society a strong sense of myself as already too familiar, too personal, too subordinate to white people. I have only recently evolved from being treated as three-fifths of a human,[4] a subpart of the white estate. I grew up in a neighborhood where landlords would not sign leases with their poor, black tenants, and *demanded* that rent be paid in cash; although superficially resembling Peter's transaction, such 'informality' in most white-on-black situations signals distrust, not trust. Unlike Peter, I am still engaged in a struggle to set up transactions at arms' length, as legitimately commercial, and to portray myself as a bargainer of separate worth, distinct power, sufficient *rights* to manipulate commerce, rather than to be manipulated as the object of commerce.

Peter, I speculate, would say that a lease or any other formal mechanism would introduce distrust into his relationships and that he would suffer alienation, leading to the commodification of his being and the degradation of his person to property. In contrast, the lack of a formal relation to the other would leave me estranged. It would risk a figurative isolation from that creative commerce by which I may be recognized as whole, with which I may feed and clothe and shelter myself, by which I may be seen as equal—even if I am stranger. For me, stranger-stranger relations are better than stranger-chattel.

The unifying theme of Peter's and my experiences (assuming that my hypothesizing about Peter's end of things has any validity at all) is that one's sense of empowerment defines one's relation to the law, in terms of trust-distrust, formality-informality, or rights-no rights (or 'needs'). In saying this I am acknowledging and affirming points central to CLS literature: that rights may be unstable[5] and indeterminate.[6] Despite this recognition, however, and despite a mutual struggle to reconcile freedom with alienation, and solidarity with oppression, Peter and I found the expression of our social disillusionment lodged on opposite sides of the rights/needs dichotomy.

On a semantic level, Peter's language of circumstantially defined need—of informality, of solidarity, of overcoming distance—sounded dangerously like the language of oppression to someone like me who was looking for freedom through the establishment of identity, the *form*-ation of an autonomous social self. To Peter, I am sure, my insistence on the protective distance which rights provide seemed abstract and alienated.

Similarly, while the goals of CLS and of the direct victims of racism may be very much the same, what is too often missing from CLS works is the acknowledgment that our experiences of the same circumstances may be very, very different; the same symbol may mean different things to each of us. At this level, for example, the insistence of Mark Tushnet, Alan Freeman, and others[7] that the 'needs' of the oppressed should be emphasized rather than their 'rights' amounts to no more than a word game. It merely says that the choice has been made to put 'needs' in the mouth of a rights discourse—thus transforming 'need' into a new form of right. 'Need' then joins 'right' in the pantheon of reified representations of what it is that you, I, and we want from ourselves and from society.

While rights may not be ends in themselves, it remains that rights rhetoric has been and continues to be an effective form of discourse for blacks. The vocabulary of rights speaks to an establishment that values the guise of stability, and from whom social change for the better must come [whether it is given, taken, or smuggled). Change argued for in the sheep's clothing of stability [i.e., 'rights') can be effective, even as it destabilizes certain other establishment values [i.e., segregation). The subtlety of rights' real instability thus does not render unusable their persona of stability.

What is needed, therefore, is not the abandonment of rights language for all purposes, but an attempt to become multilingual in the seman-

tics of each other's rights-valuation. One summer when I was about six, my family drove to Maine. The highway was very straight and hot and shimmered darkly in the sun. My sister and I sat in the back seat of the Studebaker and argued about what color the road was. I said black. My sister said purple. After I had successfully harangued her into admitting that it was indeed black, my father gently pointed out that my sister still saw it as purple. I was unimpressed with the relevance of that at the time, but with the passage of years, and much more observation, I have come to see endless overheated highways as slightly more purpley than black. My sister and I will probably argue about the hue of life's roads forever. But, the lesson I learned from listening to her wild perceptions is that it really is possible to see things—even the most concrete things—simultaneously yet differently; and that seeing simultaneously yet differently is more easily done by two people than one; but that one person can get the hang of it with lots of time and effort.

In addition to our differing word usage, Peter and I had qualitatively different *experiences* of rights. For example, for me to understand fully the color my sister saw when she looked at a road involved more than my simply knowing that her 'purple' meant my 'black.' It required as well a certain 'slippage of perception' that came from my finally experiencing how much her purple *felt* like my black.

In Peter's and my case, such a complete transliteration of each other's experiences is considerably harder to achieve. If it took years for me to understand fully my own sister, probably the best that Peter and I can do—as friends and colleagues, but very different people—is to listen intently to each other so that maybe our respective children can bridge the experiential distance. Bridging such gaps requires listening at a very deep level to the uncensored voices of others. To me, therefore, one of the most troubling positions advanced by some in CLS is that of rights' actual disutility in political advancement. That position seems to discount entirely the voice and the experiences of blacks in this country, for whom politically effective action has occurred mainly in connection with asserting or extending rights.

For blacks, therefore, the battle is not deconstructing rights, in a world of no rights; nor of constructing statements of need, in a world of abundantly apparent need. Rather, the goal is to find a political mechanism that can confront the *denial* of need. The argument that rights are disutile, even harmful, trivializes this aspect of black experience specifically, as well as that of any person or group whose genuine vulnerability has been protected by that measure of actual entitlement which rights provide.

For many white CLSers, the word 'rights' seems to be overlaid with capitalist connotations of oppression, universalized alienation of the self, and excessive power of an external and distancing sort. The image of the angry bigot locked behind the gun-turreted, barbed wire walls of his white-only enclave, shouting 'I have my rights!!' is indeed the rhetorical equivalent of apartheid. In the face of such a vision, 'token bourgeoisification'[8] of blacks is probably the best—and the worst—that can ever be imagined. From such a vantage point, the structure of rights is akin to that of racism in its power to constrict thought, to channel broad human experience into narrowly referenced and reified stereotypes. Breaking through such stereotypes would naturally entail some 'unnaming' process.

For most blacks, on the other hand, running the risk—as well as having the power—of 'stereotyping' (a misuse of the naming process; a reduction of considered dimension rather than an expansion) is a lesser historical evil than having been unnamed altogether. The black experience of anonymity, the estrangement of being without a name, has been one of living in the oblivion of society's inverse, beyond the dimension of any consideration at all. Thus, the experience of rights-assertion has been one of both solidarity and freedom, of empowerment of an internal and very personal sort; it has been a process of finding the self.

The individual and unifying cultural memory of black people is the helplessness, the uncontrollability of living under slavery. I grew up living in

the past: the future, some versions of which had only the sheerest possibility of happening, was treated with the respect of the already-happened, seen through the expansively prismatic lenses of what had already happened. Thus, when I decided to go to law school, my mother told me that 'the Millers were lawyers so you have it in your blood.' Now the Millers were the slaveholders of my maternal grandmother's clan. The Millers were also my great-great-grandparents and great-aunts and who knows what else. My great-great-grandfather Austin Miller, a thirty-five-year-old lawyer, bought my eleven-year-old great-great-grandmother, Sophie, and her parents (being 'family Negroes,' the previous owner sold them as a matched set). By the time she was twelve, Austin Miller had made Sophie the mother of a child, my great-grandmother Mary. He did so, according to family lore, out of his desire to have a family. Not, of course, a family with my great-great-grandmother, but with a wealthy white widow whom he in fact married shortly thereafter. He wanted to *practice* his sexual talents on my great-great-grandmother. In the bargain, Sophie bore Mary, who was taken away from her and raised in the Big House as a house servant, an attendant to his wife, Mary (after whom Sophie's Mary, my great-grandmother, had been named), and to his legitimated white children.

In ironic, perverse obeisance to the rationalizations of this bitter ancestral mix, the image of this self-centered child molester became the fuel for my survival during the dispossessed limbo of my years at Harvard; the *Bakke* years, the years when everyone was running around telling black people that they were very happy to have us there, but after all they did have to lower the standards and readjust the grading system, but Harvard could *afford* to do that because Harvard was Harvard. And it worked. I got through law school, quietly driven by the false idol of the white-man-within-me, and I absorbed a whole lot of the knowledge and the values which had enslaved me and my foremothers.

I learned about images of power in the strong, sure-footed arms' length transactor. I learned about unique power-enhancing lands called Whiteacre and Blackacre, and the mystical fairy rings which encircled them, called restrictive covenants. I learned that excessive power overlaps generously with what is seen as successful, good, efficient, and desirable in our society.

I learned to undo images of power with images of powerlessness; to clothe the victims of excessive power in utter, bereft naiveté; to cast them as defenseless supplicants raising—*pleading*—defenses of duress, undue influence, and fraud. I learned that the best way to give voice to those whose voice had been suppressed was to argue that they had no voice.

Some time ago, a student gave me a copy of *Pierson v. Post*[9] as reinterpreted by her six-year-old, written from the perspective of the wild fox. In some ways it resembled Peter Rabbit with an unhappy ending; most importantly it was a tale retold from the doomed prey's point of view, the hunted reviewing the hunter. I had been given this story the same week that my sister had gone to the National Archives and found something which may have been the contract of my great-great-grandmother Sophie's sale (whether hers or not, it was someone's) as well as the census accounting which listed her, along with other, inanimate evidence of wealth, as the 'personal property' of Austin Miller.

In reviewing those powerfully impersonal documents, I realized that both she and the fox shared a common lot, were either owned or unowned, never the owner. And whether owned or unowned, rights over them never filtered down *to* them; rights to their persons never vested in them. When owned, issues of physical, mental, and emotional abuse or cruelty were assigned by the law to the private tolerance, whimsy, or insanity of an external master. And when unowned—i.e., free, freed, or escaped—again their situation was uncontrollably precarious, for as objects *to be* owned, they and the game of their conquest were seen only as potential enhancements to some other self. They were fair game from the perspective of those who had rights; but from their own point of view, they were objects of a murderous hunt.

This finding of something which could have been the contract of sale of my great-great-grandmother irretrievably personalized my analysis of the law of her exchange. Repeatedly since then, I have tried to analyze, rationalize, and rescue her fate, employing the tools I learned in law school: adequacy of valuable consideration, defenses to formation, grounds for discharge and remedies (for whom?). That this was to be a dead-end undertaking was all too obvious, but it was interesting to see how the other part of my heritage, Austin Miller, the lawyer, and his confreres had constructed their world so as to nip quests like mine in the bud.

The very best I could do for my great-great-grandmother was to throw myself, in whimpering supplication, upon the mercy of an imaginary, patriarchal court and appeal for an exercise of its extraordinary powers of conscionability and 'humanitarianism.'[10] I found that it helped to appeal to that courts' humanity, and not to stress the fullness of her own. I found that the best way to get anything for her, whose needs for rights were so compellingly, overwhelmingly manifest, was to argue that she, poor thing, had no rights.[11] It is this experience of having, for survival, to argue our own invisibility in the passive, unthreatening rhetoric of 'no-rights' which, juxtaposed with the CLS abandonment of rights theory, is both paradoxical and difficult for minorities to accept.

To say that blacks never fully believed in rights is true; yet it is also true that blacks believed in them so much and so hard that we gave them life where there was none before. We held onto them, put the hope of them into our wombs, and mothered them—not just the notion of them. We nurtured rights and gave rights life. And this was not the dry process of reification, from which life is drained and reality fades as the cement of conceptual determinism hardens round—but its opposite. This was the resurrection of life from 400-year-old ashes; the parthenogenesis of unfertilized hope.

The making of something out of nothing took immense alchemical fire: the fusion of a whole nation and the kindling of several generations. The illusion became real for only a very few of us; it is still elusive and illusory for most. But if it took this long to breathe life into a form whose shape had already been forged by society and which is therefore idealistically if not ideologically accessible, imagine how long would be the struggle without even that sense of definition, without the power of that familiar vision. What hope would there be if the assignment were to pour hope into a timeless, formless futurism? The desperate psychological and physical oppression suffered by black people in this society makes such a prospect either unrealistic (i.e., experienced as unattainable) or other-worldly (as in the false hopes held out by many religions of the oppressed).

It is true that the constitutional foreground of 'rights' was shaped by whites, parcelled out to blacks in pieces, ordained in small favors, as random insulting gratuities. Perhaps the predominance of that imbalance obscures the fact that the recursive insistence of those rights is also defined by black desire for them, desire not fueled by the sop of minor enforcement of major statutory schemes like the Civil Rights Act, but by knowledge of, and generations of existing in, a world without any meaningful boundaries. And 'without boundary' for blacks has meant not untrammelled vistas of possibility, but the crushing weight of totalistic—bodily and spiritual—*intrusion.* 'Rights' feels so new in the mouths of most black people. It is still so deliciously empowering to say. It is a sign for and a gift of selfhood that is very hard to contemplate reconstructing (deconstruction is too awful to think about!) at this point in history. It is the magic wand of visibility and invisibility, of inclusion and exclusion, of power and no-power. The concept of rights, both positive and negative, is the marker of our citizenship, our participatoriness, our relation to others.

In many mythologies, the mask of the sorcerer is also the source of power. To unmask the sorcerer is to depower.[12] So CLS' unmasking rights mythology in liberal America is to reveal the source of much powerlessness masquerading as strength. It reveals a universalism of need and oppression among whites as well as blacks.

In those ancient mythologies, however, unmasking the sorcerer was only part of the job. It was impossible to destroy the mask without destroying the balance of things, without destroying empowerment itself. Therefore, the mask had to be donned by the acquiring shaman, and put to good ends. As rulers range from despotic to benign, as anarchy can become syndicalism, so the power mask in the right hands can transform itself from burden into blessing.

The task for CLS, therefore, is not to discard rights, but to see through or past them so that they reflect a larger definition of privacy, and of property: so that privacy is turned from exclusion based on *self*-regard into regard for another's fragile, mysterious autonomy; and so that property regains its ancient connotation of being a reflection of that part of the self which by virtue of its very externalization is universal. The task is to expand private property rights into a conception of civil rights, into the right to expect civility from others.[13]

In discarding rights altogether, one discards a symbol too deeply enmeshed in the psyche of the oppressed to lose without trauma and much resistance. Instead, society must give them away. Unlock them from reification by giving them to slaves. Give them to trees. Give them to cows. Give them to history. Give them to rivers and rocks. Give to all of society's objects and untouchables the rights of privacy, integrity, and self-assertion; give them distance and respect. Flood them with the animating spirit which rights-mythology fires in this country's most oppressed psyches, and wash away the shrouds of inanimate object status, so that we may say not that we own gold, but that a luminous golden spirit owns us.

Discussion Questions

1. At the end of the film *Annie Hall,* Woody Allen tells the story of his uncle, who thought he was a chicken. Asked why the family never sent the man to a psychiatrist, Allen responds simply, "We needed the

eggs." Comment with respect to Williams' discussion of rights.

2. What is the difference between "rights" discourse and "needs" discourse?

3. To what extent does Williams agree with the CLS position on rights? At what point do they ultimately differ?

Notes

1. Few plaintiffs ever seemed to wait around as much as defendants did. In part, this was due to the fact that, in the courts in which I practiced, unlike, for example, a family court, the plaintiffs were largely invisible entities—like the state or a bank or a corporate creditor—whose corporeal manifestations were their lawyers.

2. Peter Gabel was one of the first to bring critical theory to legal analysis; as such he is considered one of the 'founders' of Critical Legal Studies.

3. *See generally* R. Delgado et al., *Fairness and Formality: Minimizing the Risk of Prejudice in Alternative Dispute Resolution,* 1985 Wis. L. Rev. 1359 [hereinafter *Fairness and Formality*]

4. *See* U.S. Const. art. I, § 2.

5. 'Can anyone seriously think that it helps either in changing society or in understanding how society changes to discuss whether [someone is] exercising rights protected by the First Amendment? It matters only whether they engaged in politically effective action.' M. Tushnet, *An Essay on Rights,* 62 Tex. L. Rev. 1363, 1370–71 (1984); *see also* The Politics of Law: A Progressive Critique (D. Kairys ed., 1982); G. Frug, *The Ideology of Bureaucracy in American Law,* 97 Harv. L. Rev. 1276 (1984); P. Gabel, *Reification in Legal Reasoning,* 3 Res. in L. & Soc. 25 (1980); P. Gabel & P. Harris, *Building Power and Breaking Images: Critical Legal Theory and the Practice of Law,* 11 N.Y.U. Rev. L. & Soc. Change 369 (1982–83); D. Kennedy, *The Structure of Blackstone's Commentaries,* 28 Buff. L. Rev. 205 (1979); D. Kennedy, *Form and Substance in Private Law Adjudication,* 89 Harv. L. Rev. 1685 (1976).

6. *See* Tushnet, *supra* note 5, at 1375; *see also* R. Gordon, *Historicism in Legal Scholarship,* 90 Yale L.J. 1017 (1981); R. Unger, *The Critical Legal Studies Movement,* 96 Harv. L. Rev. 561 (1983).

7. *See* Tushnet, *supra* note 5; A. Freeman, *Legitimizing Racial Discrimination Through Anti-Discrimination Law: A Critical Review of Supreme Court Doctrine,* 62 Minn. L. Rev. 1049 (1978); *see also* D. Hay, et al., *Albion's Fatal Tree* (1975).

8. A. Freeman, *Antidiscrimination Law: A Critical Review,* in The Politics of Law: A Progressive Critique 96, 114 (D. Kairys ed., 1982).

9.

Post, being in possession of certain dogs and hounds under his command, did, 'upon a certain wild and uninhabited, unpossessed and waste land, called the beach, find and start one of those noxious beasts called a fox,' and whilst there hunting, chasing and pursuing the same with his dogs and hounds, and when in view thereof, Pierson, well knowing the fox was so hunted and pursued, did, in the sight of Post, to prevent his catching the same, kill and carry it off.

3 Cai. R. 175, 175 (N.Y. Sup. Ct. 1805).

10. *See* S. Elkins, Slavery: A Problem in American Institutional and Intellectual Life 237 (2d ed. 1963), in which the 'conduct and character' of slave traders is described as follows: 'Between these two extremes [from 'unscrupulous' to 'guilt-ridden'] must be postulated a wide variety of acceptable, genteel, semi-personalized, and doubtless relatively *humane* commercial transactions whereby slaves in large numbers could be transferred in exchange for money' (emphasis added).

11. *See* D. Bell, *Social Limits on Basic Protections for Blacks, in* Race, Racism and American Law 280 (1980).

12. The 'unmasking' can occur in a number of less-than-literal ways: killing the totemic animal from whom the sorcerer derives power; devaluing the magician as merely the village psychotic; and, perhaps most familiarly in our culture, incanting sacred spells backwards. C. Lévi-Strauss, The Raw and the Cooked 28 (1979); M. Adler, Drawing Down the Moon 321 (1979); W. La Barre, The Ghost Dance 315–19 (1970). Almost every culture in the world has its share of such tales: Plains Indian, Eskimo, Celtic, Siberian, Turkish, Nigerian, Cameroonian, Brazilian, Australian and Malaysian stories—to name a few—describe the phenomenon of the power mask or power object. *See generally* L. Andrews, Jaguar Woman and the Wisdom of the Butterfly Tree, 151–76 (1985); J. Halifax, Shamanic Voices (1979); A. Kamenskii, *Beliefs About Spirits and Souls of the Dead, in* Ravens Bones 67 (A. Hope III, ed. 1982); J. Frazer, The Golden Bough 810 (1963).

13.

He had to choose. But it was not a choice
Between excluding things. It was not a choice
Between, but of. He chose to include the things
That in each other are included, the whole,
The complicate, the amassing harmony.

W. Stevens, *Notes Toward a Supreme Fiction, in* The Collected Poems of Wallace Stevens 403 (1981).

36   Sapphire Bound!

REGINA AUSTIN

Study Questions

1. What is Austin's answer to the question of how we should come to terms with "Sapphire"?
2. Explain the court's reasoning in the case of *Chambers v. Omaha Girls Club.*
3. On what questionable assumption does Austin see the decision as based?
4. How does Austin contrast the stereotypes of the "Jezebel" and the "Mammy"? How does she try to show the relevance of these to the Chambers case?
5. What conclusions does Austin reach with respect to the regulation of black female sexuality?

I. "Write-ous" Resistance

I grew up thinking that "Sapphire" was merely a character on *Amos 'n' Andy,* a figment of a white man's racist, sexist comic imagination.[1] Little did I suspect that Sapphire was a more generally employed appellation for the stereotypical *Black Bitch*—tough, domineering, emasculating, strident, and shrill.[2] Sapphire is the sort of person you look at and wonder how she can possibly stand herself. All she does is complain. Why doesn't that woman shut up?

Black bitch hunts are alive and well in the territory where minority female law faculty labor. There are so many things to get riled about that keeping quiet is impossible. We really cannot function effectively without coming to terms with Sapphire. Should we renounce her, rehabilitate her, or embrace her and proclaim her our own?

I think the time has come for us to get truly hysterical, to take on the role of "professional

Sapphires" in a forthright way, to declare that we are serious about ourselves, and to capture some of the intellectual power and resources that are necessary to combat the systematic denigration of minority women. It is time for Sapphire to testify on her own behalf, in writing, complete with footnotes.

"To testify" means several different things in this context: to present the facts, to attest to their accuracy, and to profess a personal belief or conviction. The minority feminist legal scholar must be a witness in each of these senses. She must document the material legal existences of minority women. Her work should explore their concrete problems and needs, many of which are invisible even to minority lawyers because of gender and class differences. Moreover, a synthesis of the values, traditions, and codes that bind women of the same minority group to one another and fuel their collective struggle is crucial to the enterprise. The intellectual product of the minority feminist scholar should incorporate in a formal fashion the ethical and moral consciousnesses of minority women, their aspirations, and their quest for liberation. Her partisanship and advocacy of a minority feminist jurisprudence should be frankly acknowledged and energetically defended. Because her scholarship is to be grounded in the material and ideological realities of minority women and in their cultural and political responses, its operative premises must necessarily be dynamic and primarily immanent; as the lives of minority women change, so too should the analysis.

Finally, the experiential is not to be abandoned by the minority female legal scholar. She must be guided by her life, instincts, sensibility, and politics. The voice and vision reflected in her work should contain something of the essence of the culture she has lived and learned; imagine, if you can, writing a law review article embodying

Reprinted with permission from the publisher of the *Wisconsin Law Review* (1989), pp. 539–578.

the spontaneity of jazz, the earthiness of the blues, or the vibrancy of salsa.

I have given some thought to the tenets that a black feminist or "womanish" legal jurisprudence might pursue or embrace. We must write with an empowered and empowering voice. The chief sources of our theory should be black women's critiques of a society that is dominated by and structured to favor white men of wealth and power. We should also find inspiration in the modes of resistance which black women mount, individually and collectively, on a daily basis in response to discrimination and exploitation. Our jurisprudence should amplify the criticism and lend clarity and visibility to the positive, transformative cultural parries that are overlooked unless close attention is given to the actual struggles of black women. In addition, our jurisprudence should create enough static to interfere with the transmission of the dominant ideology and jam the messages that reduce our indignation, limit our activism, misdirect our energies, and otherwise make us the (re)producers of our own subordination. By way of an alternative, a black feminist jurisprudence should preach the justness of the direct, participatory, grassroots opposition black women undertake despite enormous material and structural constraints.

The mechanics of undertaking a research project based on the concrete material and legal problems of black women are daunting.

The problems these projects involve are difficult because they do not begin with a case and will not necessarily end with a new rule. The world with which many legal scholars deal is that found within the four corners of judicial opinions. If the decisions and the rubrics they apply pay no attention to race, sex, and class—and insurance and malpractice cases generally do not—then the material conditions of minority females are nowhere to be found, and the legal aspects of the difficulties these conditions cause are nearly impossible to address as a matter of scholarly inquiry. It is thus imperative that we find a way to portray, almost construct for a legal audience, the contemporary reality of the disparate groups of minority women about whom we write. We re-

ally cannot do this without undertaking field research or adopting an interdisciplinary approach, relying on the empirical and ethnographic research of others. The latter route is the one that I have taken in this article and elsewhere.[3]

Implementation of an agenda for black feminist legal scholarship, and the expanded study of the legal status of minority women in general, will require the right sort of environmental conditions, such as receptive or at least tolerant nonminority publishers and a network of established academics engaged in similar pursuits. We minority female scholars must devote a bit of our sass to touting the importance of the perspective of minority women and the significance of their concerns to any list of acceptable law review topics. If anyone asks you to talk or write about anything related to your race or your sex, turn the opportunity into one for exploring the legal concerns of women of color.

II. A Sapphire Named Crystal

The task of articulating and advancing distinctive minority feminist jurisprudential stances will become easier as those of us interested in the status of minority women begin to analyze concrete cases and legal problems. To substantiate my point that a black feminist perspective can and must be manifest, I have attempted to apply the rough, tentative thesis I advance above to the examination of a particular decision, *Chambers v. Omaha Girls Club.*[4]

The plaintiff, Crystal Chambers, was employed by the defendant Girls Club of Omaha as an arts and crafts instructor at a facility where approximately 90 percent of the program participants were black. Two years later, Chambers, an unmarried black woman in her early twenties, was discharged from her job when she became pregnant. Her dismissal was justified by the club's so-called "negative role model rule," which provided for the immediate discharge of staff guilty of "[n]egative role modeling for Girls Club Members" including "such things as single parent pregnancies."[5]

In her lawsuit, Chambers attacked the role model rule on several grounds. In her Title VII claims, for example, she maintained that the rule would have a disparate impact on black women because of their significantly higher fertility rate. She further asserted that her discharge constituted per se sex discrimination barred by the Pregnancy Discrimination Act of 1978. Although soundness of these arguments was acknowledged, they were effectively countered by the business necessity[6] and the bona fide occupational qualification of defenses.[7]

The district court ruled against Crystal Chambers because it concluded that the club's role model rule was the product of its dedication to the goal of "helping young girls reach their fullest potential."[8] Programmatic concerns provided adequate support for the rule. According to the findings, the club's activities were characterized by a "high staff to member ratio," "extensive contact" and "close relationships" between the staff and members, and an "open, comfortable atmosphere." Thus, "model" behavior by the staff and imitation by the members were essential to the club's agenda:

Those closely associated with the Girls Club contend that because of the unique nature of the Girls Club's operations, each activity, formal or informal, is premised upon the belief that the girls will or do emulate, at least in part, the behavior of staff personnel. Each staff member is trained and expected to act as a role model and is required, as a matter of policy, to be committed to the Girls Club philosophies so that the messages of the Girls Club can be conveyed with credibility.

The club's goal was to expose its members "to the greatest number of available positive options in life"; "teenage pregnancy [was] contrary to this purpose and philosophy," because it "severely limit[s] the available opportunities for teenage girls." Citing plaintiff's expert, the court stated that "[t]eenage pregnancy often deprives young women of educational, social and occupational opportunities, creating serious problems for both the family and society."[9] The club had several programs that related to pregnancy prevention.

In the opinion of the district court, the club "established that it honestly believed that to permit single pregnant staff members to work with the girls would convey the impression that the Girls Club condoned pregnancy for the girls in the age group it serves."[10] Furthermore, "[w]hile a single pregnant working woman may, indeed, provide a good example of hard work and independence, the same person may be a negative role model with respect to the Girls Club objective of diminishing the number of teenage pregnancies."[11] The club pointed to the reaction of two members to the earlier pregnancies of other single staffers in accounting for the genesis of the rule. In one case, a member who stated "that she wanted to have a baby as cute" as that of a staff member became pregnant shortly thereafter; in the second, a member became upset upon hearing of the pregnancy of an unmarried staff member.

As painted by the court, there were numerous indications that the operative animus behind the role model rule was paternalistic, not racist or sexist. The North Omaha facility was "purposefully located to better serve a primarily black population."[12] Although the club's principal administrators were white, the girls served were black, the staff was black, and Crystal Chamber's replacements were black; "sensitivity" was shown to the problems of the staff members, including those who were black, pregnant, and unmarried. Plaintiff was even offered help in finding other employment after she was fired.

The district court concluded its opinion as follows:

This Court believes that the policy is a legitimate attempt by a private service organization to attack a significant problem within our society. The evidence has shown that the Girls Club did not intentionally discriminate against the plaintiff and that the policy is related to the Girls Club's central purpose of fostering growth and maturity of young girls. . . . The Court emphasizes, however, that this decision is based upon the unique mission of the Girls Club of Omaha, the age group of the young women served, the geographic locations of the Girls Club facilities, and the comprehensive and historical methods the organization has employed in addressing the problem of teenage pregnancy.[13]

There were dissenting views among the Eighth Circuit judges who considered the case. In opposing the judgment in the club's favor, Judge McMillian demanded hard evidence to support the legality of the negative role model rule:

Neither an employer's sincere belief, without more, nor a district court's belief, that a discriminatory employment practice is related to and necessary for the accomplishments of the employer's goals is sufficient to establish a (BFOQ) or business necessity defense. The fact that the goals are laudable and the beliefs sincerely held does not substitute for data that demonstrate a relationship between the discriminatory practice and the goals.

A.

For those who have no understanding of the historical oppression of black women and no appreciation of the diversity of their contemporary cultural practices, the outcome of *Chambers* might have a certain policy appeal, one born of sympathy for poor black youngsters and desperation about stemming "the epidemic" of teenage pregnancy that plagues them. According to such an assessment, the club's hope that its members could be influenced by committed counselors who, by example, would prove that life offers more attractive alternatives than early pregnancy and single parenthood was at worst benign, if it was not benevolent.

However, for better informed, more critical evaluators, the opinions are profoundly disturbing. Firing a young, unmarried, pregnant black worker in the name of protecting other young black females from the limited options associated with early and unwed motherhood is ironic, to say the least. The club managed to replicate the very economic hardships and social biases that, according to the district court, made the role model rule necessary in the first place. Crystal Chambers was not much older than some of the club members, and her financial and social status after being fired was probably not that much different from what the members would face if they became pregnant at an early age, without the benefit of a job or the assistance of a fully employed helpmate. On the other hand, she was in many respects better off than many teen mothers: she was in her early twenties and had a decent job. Chambers's condition became problematic because of the enforcement of the role model rule.

The material consequences that befell Chambers—which plague other black women who have children despite their supposed role modeling responsibilities—are not inherent byproducts of single pregnancy and motherhood. The condemnation and the economic hardships that follow in its wake are politically and socially contingent. Furthermore, they are not the product of a consensus that holds across race, sex, and class boundaries.

Implicit in the *Chambers* decision is an assumption that the actual cultural practices and articulated moral positions of the black females who know the struggles of early and single motherhood firsthand are both misguided and destructive. The older women are apparently so outrageous that they represent a grave threat to their own daughters. Yet, for some of us, their portrayal in the *Chambers* opinions is more flattering than the authors intended. Grounded in a culture that turns "bad" (pronounced "baaad") on its head and declares as wily, audacious, and good all conduct that offends the white, male, and middle-class establishments, a black feminist scholar has to wonder whether the villainous black women one discerns lurking in the interstices of the opinions are not doing something right. A black feminist jurisprudential analysis of *Chambers* must seriously consider the possibility that young, single, sexually active, fertile, and nurturing black women are being viewed ominously because they have the temerity to attempt to break out of the rigid economic, social, and political categories that a racist, sexist, and the class-stratified society would impose upon them.

Although the outcome hinged upon it, the opinions are awfully vague about the adverse effect that continued employment of an unmarried pregnant arts and crafts instructor would have had in promoting teenage pregnancy among the young black club members. I want to suggest a few possible relationships whose plausibility is attributable to a deep suspicion of black women's sexuality and an intense desire to control their "excessive" promiscuity and fecundity. The first is reminiscent of a bad joke. The club and the courts conceivably subscribe to a theory of reproduction—one that can only be termed "primitive"—which posits that simply seeing an unmarried pregnant woman can have such a powerful impact on adolescent females that they will be moved to imitate her by becoming pregnant themselves.[14] If the girls are poor, and they and the woman are black, such a hypothesis might be given credence in some quarters. Under it, Crystal Chambers's mere pregnant presence at the club would be considered a corrupting influence in light of the club's goals. Surely, the club and the courts do not believe that black teenage pregnancy is the product of social voyeurism or a female variant of "reckless eyeballing."[15]

It is more likely that unmarried, pregnant Crystal was thought to be a problem because she functioned as an icon, a reminder of a powerful culture from which the club members had to be rescued. The club was supposed to be a wholesome haven where young black girls would be introduced to an alternative array of positive life choices. Crystal Chambers tainted the environment by introducing into it the messy, corrupting cultural orientations that were the target of the club's "repress and replace" mission.

There is a widespread belief that poor black women who raise children alone in socially and economically isolated enclaves encourage teenage pregnancy by example, subsidize it through informal friendship and extended family networks, and justify it by prizing motherhood, devaluing marriage, and condoning welfare dependency. Operating on similar assumptions, the club set about exposing (literally, it seems) its young members to counterimages that would act as antidotes to the messages they absorbed at home. In a newspaper story concerning Chambers's lawsuit, the attorney for the club stated that

while there was no intent "to condemn any parent of these girls or any of the parent's life decisions," the club did undertake to introduce the young members to alternatives that were different from those of the "girl's home life."[16] The attorney continued, "We're trying to say that at age 14, girls aren't necessarily emotionally mature enough to make the decision to voluntarily get pregnant. Their parents may have been."[17] The *Omaha World-Herald* ran an editorial in support of the firing which continued the theme. The editorial states: "The absence of strong family structures among many poor blacks has long been identified as a major obstacle to blacks' entering the mainstream. A high rate of out-of-wedlock pregnancies among poor blacks contributes both to the perpetuation of the poverty cycle and to the weakness of families caught in that cycle."

The editorial further argues that if, as Crystal Chambers asserted, "half the girls at the club have mothers who aren't married," then that is "one of the reasons the dismissal policy makes sense."[18]

This assessment of the danger posed by the ranks of mothers which Crystal was about to join attributes to black teenagers a level of passivity not often associated with adolescence. Looking to their parent's cultural orientations to explain teenage pregnancy may be giving the teens too little credit for attempting to shape the course of their own lives. It also attributes too much power to parents whose economic and social standing renders them impotent to control either their children's life chances or lives.

Furthermore, the club's conduct is indicative of the way in which the battle to curb black teenage pregnancy via the use of role models has become a pretext for continuing and expanding the economic and ideological wax on unwed black mothers. This emphasis on the impact on teenage pregnancy of single middle-class role models who opt to have children furnishes continued opportunity to add a new twist to the historical efforts to ridicule and control black women's sexuality and reproduction.

Although Crystal Chambers's firing was publicly justified on the ground that she would have an adverse impact on the young club members, it is likely that the club sacked her in part because she resisted its effort to model her in conformity with white and middle-class morality. In its struggles against the culture of the girls' mothers, Chambers, employee and instructor, was supposed to be on the club's side. Like a treasonous recruit, though, she turned up unmarried and pregnant: as such, she embodied the enemy. If the club could not succeed in shaping and restraining the workers whose economic welfare it controlled, how could it expect to win over the young members and supplant their mothers' cultural legacy[?] The requirement that one allow oneself to be modeled in order to keep one's job is not limited to blacks who are young fertile females. To a certain extent, the trouble that Crystal Chambers encountered is a generic infliction suffered by black role models of both sexes and all ages who reject the part and become rebellious renegades or traitors to the cause of black cultural containment. In sum, then, faulty conceptions of "role modeling" lie at the heart of the policy basis of the *Chambers* decision.

In this article, I explore the contemporary effort to control the sexual and reproductive freedom of those single black mothers who are said to be role models by blaming them for increased black teenage pregnancy. I explore parallels between the parts that "model" black women are supposed to play and historical stereotypes of black females as workers and sexual beings. I then go on to question the propriety of blacks' accepting the guise of model assimilationists.

Aside from the occasional piece that accuses black adolescents of absolute perversity,[19] news accounts and academic literature generally portray black teens who are pregnant or already parents as pursuing private, ad hoc solutions to pervasive systemic economic and political powerlessness. Teenage pregnancy is the product of the complex interaction not only of culture and individual adjustment but also of material conditions that present black teens with formidable obstacles to survival and success. Black adolescents whose families are of low socioeconomic status are at greater risk of becoming teenage mothers than their middle- and upper-class peers.[20] Teenage pregnancy is correlated with the lack of success these black adolescents experience in dealing with institutions that should provide them with an entrée to the society beyond the confines of their communities. Blame for black teenage pregnancy must be shared by an educational system that fails to provide black youngsters with either the desire or the chance to attend college,[21] a labor market that denies them employment that will supply the economic indicia of adulthood,[22] and a health care system that does not deliver adequate birth control, abortion, or family planning services.[23]

The impact of these structural factors does not make the problems constricting the lives of black adolescents entirely beyond their locus of control, however. The cultures of poor young blacks play a role in the reproduction of their material hardship; their cultures also have strengths and virtues. Yet even persons sympathetic to black females like the club members, their mothers, and Crystal Chambers may have a hard time identifying anything positive and liberating about the modes and mores that produce black teen pregnancy and single motherhood. The need to highlight the affirmative while conceding the negative is quite pressing. "Strong and complex identification with one's culture and community is necessary not only for survival but for a positive sense of self, and for the making of an involved and active community member."[24] To be efficacious, that identification must be critical of all the elements that prevent black teens from improving their economic, social, and political circumstances. To the extent that it is, it deserves affirmation from sympathetic supporters. In addition, it is imperative that those who broadly denigrate poor young black mothers be engaged in debate. A critical perspective held by the mothers themselves would provide the strongest possible basis for a counterattack.

The condemnation of black unwed motherhood is so deeply embedded in mainstream thought that its invocation in connection with teenage pregnancy may be considered uncontroversial. Single black mothers get blamed for so much that there is little reason not to blame them for teenage pregnancy as well.

At bottom, unmarried black women workers who have babies are being accused of carrying on like modern-day Jezebels when they should be acting like good revisionist Mammies. Though not totally divorced from reality, Jezebel and Mammy were largely ideological constructs that supported slavery. Each pertained to black female slaves' intertwined roles as sexual beings and workers. Each justified the economic and sexual exploitation of black female slaves by reference to their character traits rather than to the purposes of the masters. Jezebel was the wanton, libidinous black woman whose easy ways excused white men's abuse of their slaves as sexual "partners" and bearers of mulatto off-spring.[25] Jezebel was both "free of the social constraints that surrounded the sexuality of white women," to whom she represented a threat, and "isolated from the men of her own community."[26]

In contrast, Mammy was "asexual," "maternal," and "deeply religious."[27] Her principal tasks were caring for the master's children and running the household.[28] Mammy was said to be so enamored of her white charges that she placed their welfare above that of her own children.[29] She was "the perfect slave—a loyal, faithful, contented, efficient, conscientious member of the family who always knew her place; and she gave the slaves a white-approved standard of black behavior."[30] She was "the personification of the ideal slave, and the ideal woman. . . . An ideal symbol of the patriarchal tradition. She was not just a product of the 'cultural uplift' theory," which touted slavery as a means of civilizing blacks, "but she was also a product of the forces that in the South raised motherhood to sainthood."[31]

Commentators have emphasized the negative implications of the Mammy stereotype. Elizabeth Fox-Genovese writes:

If implicitly the idea of the Mammy referred to motherhood and reproduction, it also claimed those privileges for the masters rather than for the slaves themselves. Just as Buck signaled the threat [to] master-slave relations, Mammy signaled the wish for organic harmony and projected a woman who suckled and reared white masters. The image displaced sexuality into nurture and transformed potential hostility into sustenance and love. It claimed for the white family the ultimate devotion of black women, who reared the children of others as if they were their own. Although the image of the Mammy echoed the importance that black slaves attached to women's roles as mothers, it derived more from the concerns of the master than from those of the slave.[32]

bell hooks sounds a similar theme:

The mammy image was portrayed with affection by whites because it epitomized the ultimate sexist-racist vision of ideal black womanhood—complete submission to the will of whites. In a sense whites created in the mammy figure a black woman who embodied solely those characteristics they as colonizers wished to exploit. They saw her as the embodiment of woman as passive nurturer, a mother figure who gave all without expectation of return, who not only acknowledged her inferiority to whites but who loved them.[33]

The critique of the images of black women which whites have historically promoted is relevant to the assessment of the treatment accorded contemporary role models. Role models are supposed to forgo the vices of Jezebel and exhibit the many virtues of Mammy. The case of Crystal Chambers illustrates this quite well: when she refused to subordinate her interest in motherhood to the supposed welfare of the club girls, she essentially rejected the club's attempt to impose upon her the "positive" stereotype of the black female as a repressed, self-sacrificing, nuturing woman whose heart extends to other people's children because she cannot (or should not) have kids of her own. Instead, like a Jezebel, Crystal Chambers "flaunted" her sexuality and reproductive capacity, but, unlike her counterpart in slavery, she did so in furtherance of her own ends, in defiance of her white employers, and in disregard of a rule that forbade her from connecting with a man outside of the marriage relationship.

As if to resemble the role model that Fox-Genovese says Mammy could have been, Chambers was supposed to expose the young club members, the beneficiaries of white benevolence, to images congruent with traditional notions of patriarchy which were not entirely consistent with the norms of the black community. She was supposed to be an accomplice in regulating the sexuality of other young black females, in much the same way that she was expected to tolerate the regulation of her own. The courts would have us believe that the club acted for the good of the girls who would miss out on a host of opportunities if they became teen mothers—yet the distinction between paternalism and oppression is hardly crisper now than it was during slavery. It may be that the young women of the club set are not fully informed that there is an increasing demand for their labor and are misreading the material landscape. On the other hand, they could be well informed and reaching more negative assessments of their actual economic prospects. If their options are indeed no greater than they imagine, the effort to repress their fertility may stem from its being dysfunctional for the larger society. Declining to live out the myth of the modern Mammy, Crystal Chambers refused to accept the yoke of paternalism or of oppression for herself and thereby freed the club girls, to a small extent, from manipulation of their productive and reproductive capacities. She then became valueless to her employers and was, in essence, expelled from the big house and returned to the field.

Breaking the hold of ideological shackles that have restricted black women's sexuality and fertility will not be easy. Hortense Spillers, a black female literary critic, has argued that "sexual experience among black people . . . is so boundlessly imagined that it loses meaning and becomes, quite simply, a medium through which the individual is suspended."[34] Jezebel and Mammy, harlot and nun, "whore" and "eunuch" have "acquire[d] mystical attribution . . . divested of specific reference and dispersed over time and space in blind disregard for the particular agents on which it lands."[35] Spillers likens this process to a mugging.[36] She challenges feminist literary critics to find words that embody "differentiated responsiveness,"[37] words that enable us "to imagine women in their living and pluralistic

confrontation with experience."[38] Her charge is equally relevant to black feminist jurisprudes.

Some of the black women who are not married yet have babies may be young and wise; others may be poor and brave; and yet a third group may be rich and selfish. Whether they confirm or confound the stereotypes, all of them deserve a measure of freedom with regard to their sexuality that the dominant culture withholds. All of them have the potential for being guerrilla fighters in a war that is being waged on three fronts. Struggles to control sexual expression and reproduction pit the combined hegemonic power of whites, males, and the middle class against overlapping constituencies of women, people of color, and ordinary working folks. Black values regarding individual family formation and parenthood decisions, as befits a community under siege, should facilitate, not interfere with, the critical vision that promotes the "seeing that negotiates at every point a space for living."[39] In other words, black women who attempt to express their sexuality and control their reproduction should not have to travel through a minefield of stereotypes, clichés, and material hardships with the handicap of a restriction that they keep to the right. Black women must be permitted to exercise their judgments without fear of reprisals from patriarchal, bourgeois, and culturally repressive elements within the black community.

There are significant norms that bind and cage a basis for a community of concern among black men and women of various classes and outlooks. They support an agenda of systemic changes to strengthen minority families. Thus, economic resources should be available to both black men and black women who want to maintain families with children. Black teenagers of both sexes should be given the means and the support required to delay parenthood until the time is best for them. Everybody else should be allowed to do what they want to do, with the admonition that they give their offspring the advantages of the prenatal care, schools, and health programs that an ethical society would make available to assure its future.

B.

It is hard to think of Crystal Chambers, arts and crafts instructor, as a role model, as powerless and vulnerable as she ultimately proved to be. Her skills and natural behavior were not particularly valued by the people running the club. Rather than being a role model by virtue of doing her job and living her own life, Chambers was supposed to perform the role of model, play a part that was not of her own design. She was a model in the sense that a model is "something made in a pliable material ([such] as clay or wax) [that is] intended to serve as a pattern of an object or figure to be made in a more permanent material."[40] When she deviated from the club's philosophy and engaged in a practice that was common to the community of black women from which she and the members came, she was fired.

Chambers's experience is emblematic of the political significance of the professional "black role model" (including many of us lawyers and law professors) in this, the post–civil rights, post–black power era.[41] Blacks are deluged with role models. Our attention is constantly being directed to some black person who is, should, or wants to be a role model for others.[42] Many of these role models are black people who have achieved stature and power in the white world because they supposedly represent the interests of the entire black community. Such role models gain capital (literally and figuratively) to the extent that they project an assimilated persona that is as unthreatening to white people as it is (supposed to be) intriguing to our young. They become embodiments of the liberal image of "the successful Negro" with perhaps a bit of "cutup"[43] thrown in to keep them credible. By their sheer visibility, they are of service to those left behind: they are functionally useful in providing images for emulation, and their legitimacy should be unquestioned. Because the emphasis on role modeling suggests that motivation and aspirations are the cure for the problems of poor minority people, those who accept the appellation "role model" help to contain demands from below for further structural changes and thereby assist in

the management of other blacks. Insofar as doing more for the poor is concerned, the service that role models perform is regrettably distinguishable from mentoring or power brokering: role models really do not have very much clout to wield on behalf of other blacks, racial and sexual discrimination and exploitation being what they are.

There are conceptions of "role modeling" that are not quite so alien to the political and cultural heritage of African-American women.[44] As far as I am concerned, Crystal Chambers became more nearly a role model when she fought back, when she became a Sapphire. Her legal protest brought the club's contempt for the values of the population it served into the open. Her behavior and her lawsuit challenged the hegemony of the club's white, patriarchal, and middle-class orientation. Her single motherhood represented an alternative social form that one might choose deliberately, rationally, and proudly. She made manifest the critique that is "life as it is lived" by ordinary black single mothers. Refusing to go along with the program, she joined the host of nonelite black women who every day mount local, small-scale resistance grounded in indigenous cultural values—values whose real political potential is often hidden even from those whose lives they govern.

Nonetheless, there are times when low-volume defiance must give way to all-out "mouthing off." Crystal Chambers's rebellion was ended not because Title VII doctrine could not be manipulated in her favor but because the presiding judges did not respect her normative framework. Her position should have been "out there, vocalized affirmatively, coherently, and vehemently by black women and others before she got to court. History suggests that black people's recourse to conventional warfare on the legal terrain proceeds more smoothly when the positions underlying their claims of entitlement have achieved some positive visibility via skirmishes in the cultural and political domains. Of course, concrete legal cases that prove to be losing efforts may nonetheless provide an opportunity for lawyers and law professors to get their acts together, to engage the enemy, and to refine their arguments. Although the front line may remain in a distant realm, ideas do percolate from one sphere to another, and those of us who are daring may move about as well. Next time we should all be better prepared.

III. For Kanti and Asia and Fatima . . . and Ruth[45] (Which Is to Say, Sapphires by Another Name)

Back in the sixties, when Aretha Franklin demanded respect ("R-E-S-P-E-C-T")[46] and admonished her listeners to "think about what you're trying to do me,"[47] black people knew she was talking to white America. Times have changed. In 1988, vocal innovator Bobby McFerrin ambiguously sings "Don't Worry, Be Happy" with a Caribbean lilt,[48] and the Bush-Quayle campaign tries to steal the song for its anthem.[49] Somewhere along the line, we lost confidence in the political efficacy of cultural critique as a basis for the continuing struggle for black liberation. Perhaps we came to doubt the propriety of our distinctive cultural production,[50] or we foolishly thought that we would be better off if we dispensed with social protest for a while and just relied on the law.

Poor black women have especially suffered as a result. Their enemies have entrapped them in a quagmire of soft variables by challenging their morals and chiding them for looking to the government for relief from economic hardship instead of relying on individual initiative and self-help. The nonsense has deflected attention from the fact that their material circumstances have eroded.[51]

The reign of President Reagan was blessed with unusual legal and political quiescence among black women, but the signs of dissent are there. I have often wondered why black women give their daughters the names they do. Names like Kanti, Asia, Fatima, Rashiah, Tamika, Latoya, Chauntel, Ebony, and DaJuvetta (for David).[52] The mothers, in naming them, and the girls, in being so named, share a bond with other distinc-tively named black women—a bond that extends backward in time to slavery. Desperation born of material and political powerlessness may be operating here. Perhaps the mothers are trying to give to their daughters a mark of distinction that will otherwise be denied them because they are black and female. Uncommon names can generate hostility that can be a severe handicap. I like to think that the names are in part an expression of group solidarity and self-affirmation, and not the by-product of the mothers' unfamiliarity with and isolation from the dominant culture. Whether the naming practices represent a tactic of opposition, a critique of a society that typically chooses to call its female children Ashley, Jessica, Amanda, and the like, and a form of cultural resistance, I do not know. The possibility should be fully explored. It is my fondest hope, however, that whatever their mothers' motivations, the little black girls will grow up to see the positive potential of what their mothers did and relish being Sapphires by another name.

Discussion Questions

1. Were the actions of the Girls Club board unreasonable?
2. Do teenagers—black or white—have the "right to express their sexuality and control their reproduction"?
3. How can society discourage single motherhood without seeming to disparage those women who are *already* single mothers?
4. Imagine that the "Ida B. Wells Girls Club" (a black-run organization) took a similar stand; do you suppose that Austin would object?

Notes

1. R. Chapman, ed., *New Dictionary of American Slang,* 368 (1986). *Amos 'n' Andy* originated as a radio comedy program about two black males; B. Andrews and A. Juilliard, *Holy Mackerel! The* Amos 'n' Andy *Story,* 15–16 (1986). It was first broadcast in 1928, and the characters were played by the program's white originators; *id. Amos 'n' Andy* came to CBS television in 1951 (*id.* at 60–61) with a cast of carefully chosen black actors; *id.* at 45–59. Various black civil rights

organizations condemned the television version as "insulting to blacks" and as portraying blacks "in a stereotyped and derogatory manner." The sponsor withdrew from the show, and it was dropped by the network in 1953; *id.* at 61, 101. It lived on in syndication until 1966; *id.* at 118, 121–22.

Several of my contemporaries who watched *Amos 'n' Andy* have told me that they considered Sapphire a sympathetic character, the justifiably exasperated spouse of a trifling husband. Their comments suggest the potential for subversive interpretations of mass cultural forms.

2. b. hooks, *Ain't I a Woman: Black Women and Feminism,* 85–86 (1981); Scott, "Debunking Sapphire: Toward a Non-racist and Non-sexist Social Science," in G. Hull, P. Scott, and B. Smith, eds., *All the Women Are White, All the Blacks Are Men, but Some of Us Are Brave,* 85 (1982).

3. See Austin, "Employer Abuse, Worker Resistance, and the Tort of Intentional Infliction of Emotional Distress," 41 *Stan L. Rev.,* 1 (1988).

4. 629 F. Supp. 925 (D.Neb. 1986), aff'd, 834 F.2d 697 (8th Cir. 1987), reh'g denied, 840 F.2d 583 (1988).

5. 834 F.2d at 699 n. 2.

6. 834 F.2nd at 701–3. The burden of persuasion with regard to this defense is now clearly on the Title VII claimant; *Wards Cove Packing Co. v. Atonio,* 57 U.S.L.W. 4583 (U.S. June 5, 1989).

7. 834 F.2d at 703–5.

8. 629 F. Supp. at 943.

9. *Id.* at 928–29.

10. *Id.* at 950.

11. *Id.* at 951.

12. *Id.* at 934.

13. *Id.* at 951–52.

14. See *supra* text accompanying note II.

15. I. Reed, *Reckless Eyeballing* (1986). In Reed's novel, the term refers to the offense committed by a black man who "stares at a white woman too long"; *id.* at 25.

In *Ponton v. Newport News School Board,* 632 F.Supp. 1056 (E.D. Va. 1986), the court rejected the notion that "the mere sight of an unmarried, pregnant teacher would have a sufficiently undesirable influence on schoolchildren to justify excluding the teacher from the classroom"; *id.* at 1062. The court in *Ponton,* however, assumed that the plaintiff's students would not be close enough to her to know her marital status and that her single pregnancy would not interfere with her ability to teach the prescribed curriculum; *id.* at 1062–63.

16. "Unwed Mothers Challenge Firing at Omaha Girls Club," *Omaha World-Herald* (Dec. 1, 1982), 1:1.

17. *Id.*

18. "Dismissal of Two Girls Club Staffers Was Logical," *Omaha World-[Herald]* Dec. 11, 1982, at 20, col. 1.

19. See Read, "For Poor Teen-agers, Pregnancies Become New Rite of Passage," *Wall Street J.* (Mar. 17, 1988), 1.1:1.

20. See Hogan and Kitagawa, "The Impact of Social Status, Family Structure, and Neighborhood on the Fertility of Black Adolescents," 90 *Am. J. Soc.,* 825, 846 (1985); A. Abrahamse, P. Morrison, and L. Waite, *Beyond Stereotypes: Who Becomes a Single Teenage Mother,* 57–60 (1988).

21. A study conducted by the Rand Corporation found that "the presence of college plans inhibits single childbearing for blacks by nearly 10 percentage points . . . the strongest [effect] . . . measured"; A. Abrahmase, P. Morrison, and L. Waite, *supra* note 20, at 62. See also K. Moore, M. Simms, and C. Betsey, *Choice and Circumstance: Racial Differences in Adolescent Sexuality and Fertility,* xii–xiii, 67–86 (1986) (suggesting that desperately low educational goals are not a significant factor affecting black fertility, although frustration in fulfilling them might be).

22. There is little statistical data concerning the correlation between unemployment and rates of black teenage pregnancy; see K. Moore, M. Simms, and C. Betsey, *supra* note 21, at 87–101. Interview accounts, however, suggest that the inability to procure employment motivates teens, particularly males, to prove their maturity through the conception of children; see *id.* at 90; D. Frank, *Deep Blue Funk and Other Stories: Portraits of Teenage Parents,* II, 158 (1983); Anderson, "Sex Codes and Family Life among Poor Inner-City Youths," *Annals* (Jan. 1989), 59, 77.

23. See K. Moore, M. Simms, and C. Betsey, *supra* note 21, at 58–59, 62–64; L. Schorr, *Within Our Reach: Breaking the Cycle of Disadvantage,* 40–55 (1988).

24. Fine and Zane, "Bein' Wrapped Too Tight: When Low Income Women Drop Out of High School," in L. Weis, ed., *Dropouts from Schools: Issues, Dilemmas and Solutions* (forthcoming 1989).

25. D. White, *Ar'n't I a Woman? Female Slaves in the Plantation South,* 46, 61 (1985).

26. E. Fox-Genovese, *Within the Plantation Household: Black and White Women of the Old South,* 292 (1988).

27. D. White, *supra* note 25, at 46.

28. E. Genovese, *Roll, Jordan, Roll: The World the Slaves Made,* 353–56 (1972).

29. See *id.* at 356–57 (suggesting that mammies' regard for their masters' children was of strategic significance to their own families).

30. *Id.* at 356.

31. D. White, *supra* note 25, at 58.

32. E. Fox-Genovese, *supra* note 26, at 291–92.

33. b. hooks, *supra* note 2, at 84–85.

34. Spillers, "Interstices: A Small Drama of Words," in *Pleasure and Danger: Exploring Female Sexuality* 73, 85 (C. Vance ed. 1984).

35. *Id.* at 94–95.

36. *Id.* at 95.

37. *Id.*

38. *Id.* at 94.

39. *Id.* at 84.

40. Webster's Third New International Dictionary 1451 (1981).

41. *See generally* Reed, "The 'Black Revolution' and the Reconstitution of Domination", in *Race, Politics, and Culture: Critical Essays on the Radicalism of the 1960's* at 61 (A. Reed ed. 1986).

42. *See, e.g.,* B. Reynolds, And Still We Rise: Interviews with 50 Blacks Role Models (1988); Raspberry, *"No-Choice" Role-Models Can Be Countered,* Chic. Trib., Oct. 27, 1987, § 1, at 21, col. 2; Arnold & Pristin, *The Rise and Fall of Maxine Thomas,* L.A. Times, May 6, 1988, § 2, at 1, col. 2; Hofman, *Ebony Fashion Fair Raises $15,000 for Black Actors Theatre,* L.A. Times, Apr. 14, 1988, § 9, at 4, col. 2 (Orange Cty, ed.) (theatre group and fashion show "gives audiences a chance to see more blakc role models").

43. "Outspolen" and "militant" are the terms usually employed to described vocal elite champions of the causes of the black masses.

44. *See* Gilkes, *Successful Rebellious Professionals: The Black Woman's Professional Identity and Community Commitment,* 6 Psychology of Women Q. 289 (1982).

45. Kanti is graduating from high school in Washington, D.C. Asia and Fatima are among the apples of their grandmother's eye. Ruth is the daughter of Crystal Chambers, 629 F.Supp. at 929 n.6.

46. A. Franklin, "Respect," on *Aretha's Gold* slide 1, track 3 (1969).

47. A. Franklin, *Think,* on Aretha's Gold, *supra* note 46, at side 2, track 3; *see also A. Franklin, Think (1989),* on Through the Storm side 2, track 2 (1989).

48. B. McFerrin, *Don't Worry, Be Happy,* on Simple Pleasures side 1, track 1 (1988).

49. Philadelphia Inquirer, Oct. 23, 1988, at 3A, col. 3.

50. I use the term expansively. It includes "the collective, creative use of discourses, meanings, materials, practices and group processes to explore, understand and creatively occupy particular positions, relations and sets of material possibilities." Willis, *supra* note 107, at 114.

51. See Simms, "Black Women Who Head Families: An Economic Struggle"; in *Slipping Through the Cracks: The Status of Black Women* 141, 143–148 (M. Simms and J. Malveaux eds. 1986).

52. *See* J. McGregory, Aareck to Zsaneka: African American Names in an Urban Community, 1945–1980 (1985) (master's thesis, Cornell University).

37 Racial Realism—After We're Gone: Prudent Speculations on America in a Post-Racial Epoch

DERRICK BELL

Study Questions

1. What reaction does the space travelers' proposal receive from whites?

2. According to Bell, why do whites who are not rich not protest the maldistribution of income? Do you think that they would protest more once the "space travelers' proposal" was carried out?

3. What is Bell's view of such landmark civil rights decisions as *Brown v. Board of Education*?

Reprinted with permission of the publisher from the *St. Louis University Law Journal* 34 (1990).

It is time—as a currently popular colloquialism puts it—to "Get Real" about race and the persistence of racism in America. The very visible social and economic progress made by some African Americans can no longer obscure the increasingly dismal demographics that reflect the status of most of those whose forebears in this country were slaves. Statistics on poverty, unemployment, and income support the growing concern that the slow racial advances of the 1960s and 1970s have ended, and retrogression is well under way.

Perhaps Thomas Jefferson had it right after all. When musing on the future of Africans in this country, he expressed the view that blacks should be free, but he was certain that "the two races, equally free, cannot live in the same government."[1] Jefferson suspected that blacks, whether originally a distinct race, or made distinct by time and circumstances, are "inferior to the whites in the endowments both of body and mind."[2] Such differences prompted Jefferson to warn that "[i]f the legal barriers between the races were torn down, but no provision made for their separation, 'convulsions' would ensue, which would 'probably never end but in the extermination of the one or the other race.'"[3]

Jefferson's views were widely shared. In his summary of how the Constitution's framers came to include recognition and protection of human slavery in a document that was committed to the protection of individual liberties, Professor Staughton Lynd wrote: "Even the most liberal of the Founding Fathers were unable to imagine a society in which whites and Negroes would live together as fellow-citizens. Honor and intellectual consistency drove them to favor abolition; personal distaste, to fear it."[4]

In our era, the premier precedent of *Brown v. Board of Education* promised to be the twentieth century's Emancipation Proclamation. Both policies, however, served to advance the nation's foreign policy interests more than they provided actual aid to blacks. Nevertheless, both actions inspired blacks to push for long-denied freedoms. Alas, the late Alexander Bickel's dire prediction has proven correct. He warned that the *Brown* decision would not be reversed but "[could] be headed for—dread word—irrelevance."[5]

Given the current tenuous status of African Americans, the desperate condition of those on the bottom, and the growing resentment of the successes realized by those who are making gains despite the odds, one wonders how this country would respond to a crisis in which the sacrifice of the most basic rights of blacks would result in the accrual of substantial benefits to all whites? This primary issue is explored in a fictional story that could prove to be prophetic.

The Chronicle of the Space Traders

The first surprise was not their arrival—they had sent radio messages weeks before advising that they would land 1,000 space ships along the Atlantic coast on January 1, 2000. The surprise was the space ships themselves. Unlike the Star Wars variety, the great vessels, each the size of an aircraft carrier, resembled the square-shaped landing craft used to transport troops to beachhead invasion sites during World War II.

The great ships entered the earth's atmosphere in a spectacular fiery display that was visible throughout the western hemisphere. After an impressive, cross-continental "fly by," they landed in the waters just off the Atlantic coast. The lowered bows of the mammoth ships exposed cavernous holds that were huge, dark, and impenetrable.

Then came the second surprise. The welcoming delegation of government officials and members of the media covering the event could hear and understand the crew as they disembarked. They spoke English and sounded like the former President Ronald Reagan, whose recorded voice, in fact, they had dubbed into their computerized language translation system. The visitors, however, were invisible—at least they could not be seen by whites who were present or by television viewers to the special coverage that, despite howls of protest, had preempted football bowl games. American blacks were able to see them all too well. "They look like old South sheriffs, mean and ugly," some said. They were, according to others, "more like slave drivers and overseers." Particularly frantic reports claimed, "The visitors are dressed in white sheets and hoods like the Ku Klux Klan." In whatever guise they saw them, blacks all agreed that the visitors embodied the personification of racist evil.

The space visitors cut short the long-winded welcoming speeches, expressed no interest in parades and banquets, and made clear that their long journey was undertaken for one purpose, and one purpose only: trade. Here was the third surprise. The visitors had brought materials that they knew the United States needed desperately:

gold to bail out the almost bankrupt federal, state, and local governments; special chemicals that would sanitize the almost uninhabitable environment; and a totally safe nuclear engine with fuel to relieve the nation's swiftly diminishing fossil fuel resources.

In return, the visitors wanted only one thing. This demand created more of a shock than a surprise. The visitors wanted to take back to their home star all African Americans (defined as all citizens whose birth certificates listed them as black). The proposition instantly reduced the welcoming delegation to a humbling disarray. The visitors seemed to expect this reaction. After emphasizing that acceptance of their offer was entirely voluntary and would not be coerced, they withdrew to their ships. The Traders promised to give the nation a period of sixteen days to respond. The decision would be due on January 17, the national holiday commemorating Dr. Martin Luther King, Jr.'s birthday.

The Space Traders' proposition immediately dominated the country's attention. The President called the Congress into special session, and governors did the same for state legislatures that were not then meeting. Blacks were outraged. Individuals and their leaders cried in unison, "You have not seen them. Why don't you just say no?" Although for many whites the trade posed an embarrassing question, the Space Traders' offer proved to be an irresistible temptation. Decades of conservative, laissez-faire capitalism had taken their toll. The nation that had funded the reconstruction of the free world a half-century ago following World War II was now in a very difficult state. Massive debt had debilitated all functioning. The environment was in shambles, and crude oil and coal resources were almost exhausted.

In addition, the race problem had greatly worsened in the last decade. A relatively small group of blacks had survived the retrogression of civil rights protection that marked the 1990s. Perhaps twenty percent managed to make good in the increasingly technologically oriented society. But more than one-half of the group had sunk to an unacknowledged outcast status. They were confined in former inner-city areas that had been divorced from their political boundaries. High walls surrounded these areas, and entrance and exit were carefully controlled. No one even dreamed anymore that this mass of blacks and dark-complexioned Hispanics would ever "overcome."

Supposedly, United States officials tried in secret negotiations to get the Space Traders to exchange only those blacks locked in the inner cities, but the visitors made it clear that this was an all-or-nothing offer. During these talks, the Space Traders warned that they would withdraw their proposition unless the United States halted the flight of the growing numbers of blacks who—fearing the worst—were fleeing the country. In response, executive orders were issued and implemented, barring blacks from leaving the country until the Space Traders' proposition was fully debated and resolved. "It is your patriotic duty," blacks were told, "to allow this great issue to be resolved through the democratic process and in accordance with the rule of law."

Blacks and their white supporters challenged these procedures in the courts, but their suits were dismissed as "political questions" that must be determined by co-equal branches of government. Even so, forces that supported the proposition took seriously blacks' charges that if the nation accepted the Space Traders' proposition it would violate the Constitution's most basic protections. Acting swiftly, supporters began the necessary steps to convene a constitutional convention. In ten days of feverish work, the quickly assembled convention drafted and, by a substantial majority, passed an amendment that declared:

Every citizen is subject at the call of Congress to selection for special service for periods necessary to protect domestic interests and international needs.

The amendment was scheduled for ratification by the states in a national referendum. If ratified, the amendment would validate previously drafted legislation that would induct all blacks into special service for transportation under the terms of the Space Traders' offer. In the brief but intense pre-election day campaign, pro-ratification groups' major argument had an appeal that surprised even those who made it. Their message was straightforward:

The framers intended America to be a white country. The evidence of their intentions is present in the original Constitution. After more than 137 years of good faith efforts to build a healthy, stable interracial nation, we have concluded that our survival today—as the framers did in the beginning—requires that we sacrifice the rights of blacks in order to protect and further the interests of whites. The framers' example must be our guide. Patriotism and not pity must govern our decision. We should ratify the amendment and accept the Space Traders' proposition.

To their credit, many whites worked hard to defeat the amendment. Nevertheless, given the usual fate of minority rights when subjected to referenda or initiatives, the outcome was never really in doubt. The final vote tally confirmed the predictions. By a vote of seventy percent in favor—thirty percent opposed—Americans accepted the Space Traders' proposition. Expecting this result, government agencies had secretly made preparations to facilitate the transfer. Some blacks escaped, and many thousands lost their lives in futile efforts to resist the joint federal and state police teams responsible for the roundup, cataloguing, and transportation of blacks to the coast.

The dawn of the last Martin Luther King holiday that the nation would ever observe illuminated an extraordinary sight. The Space Traders had drawn their strange ships right up to the beaches, discharged their cargoes of gold, minerals, and machinery, and began loading long lines of silent black people. At the Traders' direction, the inductees were stripped of all but a single undergarment. Heads bowed, arms linked by chains, black people left the new world as their forebears had arrived.

And just as the forced importation of those African ancestors had made the nation's wealth and productivity possible, so their forced exodus saved the country from the need to pay the price of its greed-based excess. There might be other unforeseen costs of the trade, but, like their colonial predecessors, Americans facing the twenty-first century were willing to avoid those problems as long as possible.

Discussion

It is not a futile exercise to try to imagine what the country would be like in the days and weeks after the last space ship swooshed off and disappeared into deep space—beyond the reach of our most advanced electronic tracking equipment. How, one might ask, would the nation bear the guilt for its decision? Certainly, many white Americans would feel badly about the trade and the sacrifice of humans for economic well-being. But the country has a 200-year history of treating black lives as property. Genocide is an ugly, but no less accurate, description of what the nation did, and continues to do, to the American Indian. Ignoring the Treaty of Guadalupe Hidalgo was only the first of many betrayals by whites toward Americans of Spanish descent. At the time of writing, Japanese Americans who suffered detention during World War II and lost hard-earned property and status were still awaiting payment of the small compensation approved, but not yet funded, by Congress. The country manages to carry on despite the burden of guilt that these injustices impose against our own people. In all likelihood, the country would manage the Space Trader deal despite recriminations, rationalizations, and remorse. Quite soon, moreover, the nation could become preoccupied with problems of social unrest based on class rather than race.

The trade would solve the budget deficit, provide an unlimited energy source, and restore an unhealthy environment. The new resources, however, would not automatically correct the growing income disparities between blacks and whites as reflected in the growing income gap between upper and lower income families in the nation as a whole. According to the Center on Budget and Policy Priorities: "In 1985, 1986 and 1987, the poorest fifth of American families received only 4.6 percent of the national family income. . . ."[6] The poorest two-fifths of American families received 15.4 percent of the national family income in 1986 and 1987.[7] In contrast, "the richest fifth of all families received 43.7 percent of the national family income in 1986 and 1987, the highest percentage on record."[8] The top two-fifths of all families' share was 67.8 percent, which broke another record.[9] The poorest two-fifths of American families received a smaller share of the national family income in 1986 and 1987 than in any other year since the Census Bureau began collecting data in 1947.[10] Meanwhile, the richest two-fifths of American families received a larger share of the national income in 1987 than in any year since 1947.[11]

These statistics are shocking, but they are certainly not a secret. Even more shocking than the serious disparities in income is the relative silence of whites about economic gaps that should constitute a major political issue. Certainly, it is a matter of far more importance to voters than the need either to protect the American flag from "desecration" by protesters or to keep the "Willie Hortons" of the world from obtaining prison furloughs. Why the low level of interest about so critical a pocketbook issue? Why is there no political price to pay when our government bails out big businesses like savings and loans, Chrysler, Lockheed, and even New York City for mistakes, mismanagement, and thinly veiled theft that are the corporations' fault? Why is there no public outrage when thousands of farmers go under due to changes in economic conditions that are not their fault? Why does government remain on the sidelines as millions of factory workers lose their livelihood because of owners' greed—not the workers' fault? Why is there no hue and cry at a tax structure that rewards builders who darken the skies with gigantic, expensive condominiums for the rich while the working class spend up to one-half of their minimum-wage incomes for marginal housing, and as our poor live on the streets?

The reasons are likely numerous and complex. One substantial factor, however, seems to be the unstated understanding by the mass of whites that they will accept large disparities in economic opportunity in comparison to other whites as long as they have a priority over blacks and other people of color for access to those opportunities. On any number of occasions in American history, whites have acquiesced in—when they were not pressuring for—policy decisions that subordinated the rights of blacks in order to further some other interest. One might well ask, what do the masses of working class and poor whites gain from this continued sacrifice of black rights that justifies such acquiescence when so often the policies limit whites' opportunities as well as those of blacks?

The answer is as unavoidable as it is disturbing. Even those whites who lack wealth and power are sustained in their sense of racial superiority by policy decisions that sacrifice black rights. The subordination of blacks seems to reassure whites of an unspoken, but no less certain, property right in their "whiteness." This right is recognized by courts and society as all property rights are upheld under a government created and sustained primarily for that purpose. With blacks gone, the property right in "whiteness" goes with them. How long will the masses of whites remain silent about their puny share of the nation's wealth?

The film *Resurgence* shows a poor southern white, mired in poverty, who nevertheless declares: "Every morning I wake up and thank God I'm white." But after we're gone, we can be fairly sure, this individual will not shout, "Thank God, I'm poor." What will he and millions like him shout when the reality of his real status hits him? How will the nation's leaders respond to discontent that has been building for so long and that has been so skillfully misdirected toward a group no longer here? It will be too late to call off the trade—too late to bring back African Americans to fill their traditional role. Indeed, even without an extraterrestrial trade mission, the hour is growing late for expecting that black people will always keep the hope of racial equality alive. For millions in what is now designated the underclass, that hope has already died in the devastation of their lives. The cost of this devastation is not limited to the ghetto. As manifestations of self-hate and despair turn to rage and retaliation against the oppressors, those costs will rise dramatically and frightfully.

When I ask audiences how Americans would vote on the Space Traders' offer, rather substantial majorities express the view that the offer would be accepted. That is a present day measure of an almost certain future decision—one that will be required whether or not we have trade-oriented visitors from outer space. The century-long cycles of racial progress and reform cannot continue, and should not. Those subordinated on the basis of color cannot continue forever in this status, and will not. Politics, the courts, and self-help have failed or proved to be inadequate. Perhaps the prospect of black people removed from the American landscape will bring a necessary reassessment of who has suffered most from our subordination.

Discussion Questions

1. Bell contends that race is the main factor why poorer whites do not protest poverty and social injustice. What would he say about the fact that poorer whites do not rebel, even in virtually all-white societies?
2. Bell views the United States as undergoing a period, possibly a very long period, of retrenchment on questions of race. In your estimation, what kinds of factors might end this period? If it does not end, what can be done?
3. If Bell is right, what general conclusions should we reach regarding the power of the law to effect social change?

Notes

1. Quoted in Staughton Lynd, *Slavery and the Founding Fathers, in* Black History 115, 129 (M. Drimmer ed., 1968) (citations omitted).
2. Robinson, Slavery in the Structure of American Politics, 1765–1820, at 91 (1971) (quoting Notes on the State of Virginia (Abernethy ed., 1964)).
3. *Id.* at 90.
4. Lynd, *supra* note 1, at 129.
5. Alexander Bickel, The Supreme Court and the Idea of Progress 151 (1978).
6. Center on Budget and Policy Priorities, Still Far from the Dream: Recent Developments in Black Income, Employment and Poverty 21 (Oct. 1988).
7. *Id.*
8. *Id.* at 22.
9. *Id.*
10. *Id.* at 21.
11. *Id.* at 22.

38 Critical Race Theory: A Critique

JOHN ARTHUR[1]

Study Questions

1. Explain what is meant by "legal indeterminacy" and then indicate the reason that Critical Race Theorists believe it is inevitably going to be found in the law.
2. What is a "checkboard statute" and how does Arthur think it gives a reason to reject legal indeterminacy?
3. Explain the importance of race in American law, according to Critical Race Theory.
4. What arguments does Arthur give that race is not as important a factor as Critical Race Theory believes?
5. What is Austin's central claim and why does Arthur reject it?

My objective in this essay is first to identify, and then to comment critically on, some of the basic assumptions behind Critical Race Theory or CRT.

Critical Race Theory is a movement of mainly minority legal scholars that grew out of another, politically similar movement of the 1980s called Critical Legal Studies or CLS. CRT accepts much of the legal and jurisprudential view of CLS, and so I will begin with a brief discussion [of] the CRT/CLS view of law itself. Then I discuss the importance of race in contemporary American political and legal practices, asking whether CRT is right in its claim that racial equality is a myth and that racism is central to understanding American law and politics.

From Critical Legal Studies to Critical Race Theory

CLS rests on the assumption that the dominant ideology in the U.S. and the legal/political institutions it supports are oppressive, hierarchical, and unjust. Woven into these charges is a second series of claims, about the ideal of the rule of law and legal objectivity. Critical Legal Studies believes that law is generally *indeterminate:* neither the general language of statutes and constitutional rules nor concern with earlier precedents restrains judges' wide discretion. Judges are free to rule as they wish, without the constraining force of legal materials and argument. In reality, writes Derrick Bell, judges "can use abstract concepts, such as equality, to mask policy choices and value judgments" and so hide the "result oriented, value laden nature of judicial decision-making."[2]

Explaining the role of precedents and their inability to limit judges' discretion. David Kairys writes that past decisions are "largely reduced to rationalizations, not factors meaningfully contributing to the result; they support rather than determine the principles and outcomes adopted by judges."[3]

Nor do legal or interpretive *principles* embedded in the language of statutes or constitutions provide judges with the road map to correct legal answers. Stanley Fish, for example, writes of those who invoke general legal principles in defense of their decision that

at the moment of their invocation, "principles" would be doing rhetorical, not theoretical, work, contributing to an argument rather than presiding over it. Such principles (and there are loads of them) form part of the arsenal available to a lawyer or judge . . . and the skill of deploying them is the skill of knowing . . . just when to pull them off the shelf and insert them in your discourse. Once inserted, they are just like other items in the storehouse, pieces of verbal artillery whose effectiveness will be a function of the discursive moment.[4]

What are normally thought to be various elements of law—precedents, concepts, principles—are in reality just rationalizations used to justify what is essentially a political decision by a judge. Legal arguments, in Fish's terminology, are nothing more than the "arsenal" a judge has available to deploy in whatever way and toward whatever political end the judge chooses. While for CLS, a *particular* judge's specific attitudes are important to understanding how the judge will decide a case, so too should we appreciate the larger political *ideologies* that compete just under the surface of legal opinions and argument. To understand law requires looking beyond a judge's psychology to the underlying ideological, class, and other conflicts that are fought out in law and that find expression in the law's on-going development.

That then is the first key CLS claim, that law is the site of warring ideological struggle and that it is "indeterminate" in the sense that judges are generally (in interesting, hard cases at least) free to choose among the different, competing ideological viewpoints. Precedents, legal language found in statutes and the constitution, and even the underlying moral principles and ideals do not "control" judges but instead are the raw material out of which judges are left to fashion their own decisions.

CLS's analysis of law does not end there, however, for wedded to the thesis of legal indeterminacy is a second, more explicitly political claim about the role of law. While there are different, competing ideologies found in law, CLS also claims that all these serve to *legitimize* the existing power relationships. Low-level criminal courts are the site where *power* is exercised by police and the courts in the service of the dominant political ideology, while judicial opinions (especially "higher level" ones from places like the U.S. Supreme Court) serve the function of legitimizing and rationalizing the law's exercise of that power. Law's ideological power supports its monopoly over political power.

So, for example, when the Supreme Court explains that it cannot allow affirmative actions programs giving preferences to minorities because they violate a white male's Constitutional right to "equal protection of the laws" two things are going on. First, the Court is acting as if it were being forced to reach that conclusion by the language of the Constitution and by past decisions when in fact it is not and, second, in explaining its reasons the Court is legitimizing that exercise of power, claiming that the Constitution gives the neutral, impartial judges no choice except to go along with the weight of reason found embedded in the law itself.

Law professor Mari Matsuda summarized the CLS position this way: it pursues the work of "unmasking: unmasking a grab for power disguised as science, unmasking a justification for tyranny disguised as history, unmasking an assault on the poor disguised as law."[5] Critical Race Theory accepts this general approach, believing law is indeterminate and that it serves the function of legitimizing the illegitimate, oppressive use of power. Our next question, then, is whether this claim is true.

Is Legal Indeterminacy True?

The most straightforward argument *for* legal indeterminacy is based on where the law comes from and how it is made.[6] Two points are important here. First, legislatures vary from year to year, sometimes dominated by one ideology and other times by another. Given that, it is only reasonable to expect that statutory law will itself tend toward incoherence since it will be the product of different political coalitions with varying amounts of strength. Civil rights and welfare laws passed by

Congress when Johnson was President and Democrats controlled Congress will inevitably reflect a different political perspective from laws passed by a conservative Congress under Reagan. This tendency toward indeterminacy is compounded by the fact that law is also interpreted by different judges at different periods. During the 1960s, the Supreme Court was dominated by more liberal judges; now its membership is much more conservative, which means that the opinions will vary and, therefore, that case law presents another source of indeterminacy.

This CLS argument moves too quickly, however, for in addition to the forces they describe that tend toward incoherence are other factors that will tend to force law in the opposite direction, toward consistency. What I have in mind is the familiar thought that besides seeking to express their political ideals in law, judges might also seek—again as a matter of political morality—to *avoid* legal incoherence. This would be the case if judges had a sense that contradictions in law are to be avoided for their own sake, in order to protect consistency and the rule of law.

But do lawmakers and judges have such a sense? Ronald Dworkin suggests they do, using as an illustration what he terms a "checkerboard statute."[7] Imagine a law that strikes a compromise between pro-choice and pro-life forces by allowing women born in odd years to get abortions while those born in even years are denied them. Legislators, we may well suppose, would tend to reject such a statute. Forced to choose between it and a law that gives no protection to a fetus (or women's choice) a legislator might reluctantly accept such a compromise as the lesser of the two evils—but the point is that it would, in fact, be regarded as an evil by almost everybody. Or consider other examples: suppose the law provided for women prisoners to vote and not male prisoners, or required negligent heart doctors to pay full compensation while eye surgeons enjoyed caps on their liability. These and other laws are objectionable not just that they treat two groups differently—laws do that all the time—but because they make arbitrary and rationally indefensible distinctions among them.

The lesson is that if, as seems likely, both judges and legislators would be inclined against passage of such laws, then CLS is wrong to infer that because statutes and cases grow out of conflicting ideology the law must therefore inevitably be deeply and pervasively incoherent. If coherence is regarded as an *independent* virtue by lawmakers and judges, then judges would be motivated to avoid incoherence and there would be a counter-balance working against the tendency toward indeterminacy. We needn't conclude, therefore, that law is indeterminate, though we cannot know without investigation that it is not incoherent, either.

So finally we've reached the center of the problem: why should we care if we are under the authority of arbitrary power, or of the rule of law. Does it matter? I think it does matter, because there are important moral stakes in the debate. What I mean is this. Following John Rawls, suppose we think of law as, roughly, a system of rules and other standards, backed by the coercive power of the state, that are addressed to persons in order to enable and encourage them to regulate their conduct.[8] Laws inform people how fast they may go on the highways, how much to pay in taxes, how to make a will or contract, and what are the extent and limits of their free speech rights, to give only a few examples.[9] They also specify the consequences of failure to follow those rules, whether they be fines, prison, payment of compensation to people whom we injure, or simply failure to create a binding, legally valid contract or will.

The connection between these thoughts about law in general and legal indeterminacy is pretty obvious. For a legal rule to succeed in addressing persons for purposes of providing guidance, it *must* exhibit to a sufficient extent the characteristics of constancy, clarity of definition and publicity. Otherwise, at least in the extreme, there can be no legal system at all.[10] A system of secret rules, for example, could not serve as a guide for citizens; nor could a system of constantly changing rules or rules that are inconsistent or so vague that they fail to provide guidance constitute a genuine system of law.[11] The specter of legal in-

determinacy and unpredictability means the absence of law itself. The rule of law is thus a condition of the existence of law at all. In an entirely indeterminate system in which judges act independently of previous judicial decisions and enactments of legislatures or other political bodies not only would democratic rule be impossible but the law itself would cease to exist. The CLS claim of indeterminacy therefore cuts more deeply than may at first appear: it follows from at least the more radical versions of the indeterminacy thesis that law is, in fact, a myth.

This conclusion that, in the extreme, indeterminacy destroys law itself leads then to a final question: So what? Why should we care about the rule of law? Rightly understood, I want to suggest, the rule of law actually expresses *two* important moral ideals. The first is "formal" justice or what might be termed equality of citizenship. Here the idea, deeply rooted in the law, is that all citizens are entitled to fair and impartial treatment at the hands of government. For example, if one person is not prosecuted for an act, then the principle of fair equality requires that no one else be prosecuted *unless* there is a relevant difference in the cases. Similarly, if one person receives compensation for damages caused by a negligent doctor, then fair equality requires that another citizen on whom similar malpractice was performed also be compensated. If government fails to live up to this ideal, arbitrarily punishing some or compensating others without regard to how those similarly situated are treated, then the government's claim to political legitimacy is compromised.

The second moral ideal that is expressed by the rule of law is often termed "fair notice," and it applies primarily in the criminal context. It is the notion that people should be held liable for actions only where they could have been expected to behave as the law expects. This means, however, that the legal system must state clearly what it requires and forbids so that people can act accordingly. But obviously if as CLS thinks the law is deeply and pervasively incoherent and judges exercise unbounded authority to rule in whatever fashion their own political ideology would recommend then fair notice can never be achieved.

Legal indeterminacy is not, therefore, to be welcomed. In the extreme, indeterminacy jeopardizes the very existence of law and the legal system. And even in less extreme forms, it undermines two values inherent in the ideal of the rule of law: equal citizenship and due process. Insofar as CRT has followed CLS in accepting the thesis that law is indeterminate, CRT has accepted an unsound argument leading to a conclusion that nobody should wish to accept in any event.

That said, however, it remains possible that CRT may still be right in a larger sense. All I have shown so far is that we need not embrace radical legal indeterminacy and give up on the ideal of the rule of law as an achievable, worthy goal. But that says nothing about whether the ideal will actually be achieved in practice, nor whether racial equality and social justice accompany the rule of law. It is possible, in other words, that while CRT is wrong in thinking legal indeterminacy is inevitable and the rule of law a myth, it is nonetheless right in emphasizing the central importance of racial prejudice and oppression in contemporary American politics. I now turn to that second claim of Critical Race Theory.

Critical Race Theory and Racial Dominance

CRT agrees with the key CLS claim that as practiced today law legitimizes oppression and rationalizes the use of power. American *ideals* of equality, including equality before the law, and the *reality* of its racial politics are in radical conflict. Racism and racial oppression, reinforced by law, are at the heart of the problems confronted by African-Americans.

Critical Race Theory, says Kimberle Crenshaw, "focuses on the relationship between law and racial subordination in American society."[12] Derrick Bell, usually thought to be among the founders of CRT, writes that

In spite of dramatic civil rights movements and periodic victories in the legislatures, black Americans by no means are equal to whites . . . The reality is that

blacks still suffer disproportionately higher rates of poverty, joblessness, and insufficient health care than other ethnic populations in the U.S. The ideal is that law, through racial equality, can lift them out of this trap. I suggest we abandon this ideal . . . Racial equality is, in fact, not a realistic goal. . . . The racial realism we must seek is simply a hard-eyed view of racism as it is and our subordinate role in it.[13]

Tying this idea to earlier, CLS views about the ways law serves to rationalize oppression, he adds that law rarely serves as a "refuge for oppressed people" but instead works in general as a means for "preserving the status quo."[14]

On what basis does CRT make these claims? What is the evidence for charges by Bell, Crenshaw, and others of the persistence of racism at the foundation of U.S. politics and law? In what follows I look critically at a range of possible answers, arguing that this key assumption behind all Critical Race Theory is mistaken.

First, it is clear that the racism and racial oppression alleged by CRT to exist at the heart of U.S. law cannot be shown by simply pointing to random acts of violence by murderous white racists, such as the white supremacist recently condemned to be executed for dragging a black man to death behind his truck. Whites and blacks alike were appalled by the crime, and furthermore the legal system has in this and other cases shown itself willing to punish racists who commit crimes more severely than others for the same crimes. (Hate crime legislation that requires additional punishment when racism motivates the criminal illustrates this.) Nobody denies that racists exist, or that they sometimes commit horrible crimes. But it is also well to remember that over half of the victims of violent crimes by blacks were white, and that 89% of inter-racial crime is committed by black perpetrators against white victims.[15] Nor, second, should we conclude the law is racist based on individual atrocities committed by government employees such as police, unless it can be shown that such acts are either implicitly or explicitly condoned.

Perhaps, then, the CRT claim of racism's importance in law could be shown by whites' attitudes toward blacks. But what attitudes? It's true that police and others often assume, for example, that black males are more likely to be criminals. But is that racist? Figures show that beginning in the 1960s the U.S. experienced a huge increase in crime—what two sociologists describe as the "worst crime wave in its history"—and young black males were responsible for a disproportionate share of reported offenses. In 1995 over half of those arrested for murder and robbery were black (54% and 59% respectively) despite the fact they represent about 12% of the population.[16] Blacks are also much more likely to be victims of crime: 93% of blacks who are murdered are killed by another African-American.[17] In a survey in 1991 by the University of California, more blacks than whites said blacks are "aggressive or violent" while many more blacks (52%) than whites (31%) also reported being afraid to walk out alone at night.[18] "Fear of blacks," writes Norman Podhoretz in 1993, "has become the dirty little secret of our political culture."[19] Believing the truth about crime and race cannot make one a racist.

The fact is that despite these figures the racial attitudes of whites toward blacks have improved markedly in the last decades. Since the 1940s the U.S. has moved from a racist, segregated society affording little opportunity to blacks (or other minorities) to one that is far more tolerant. From 1944 to 1963, for example, the percentage of white Americans saying that blacks should "have as good a chance as white people to get any kind of job" went from 42 to 83%.[20] By 1972 that figure had gone to 97%. Similarly, by 1972 84% of whites favored integrated schools and 85% expressed no reservation about having a black neighbor. Changes since then have continued that trend.[21]

Charges of racism can also be assessed by comparing U.S. whites with citizens of other countries. Compared with other countries around the world, the evidence is that Americans are the least racist. While 13% of Americans responded in 1991 that they have an "unfavorable attitude" toward the principal domestic minority (blacks), that figure was lower than the comparable ones in every country in Europe. Only in Great Britain

(where the minority group was the Irish) and Spain (the Catalans) were the figures less than *twice* as high as in the U.S., while in East Germany (where the minority was Poles), Czechoslovakia (Hungarians) and Russia (Azerbaijanis) the percentages of people reporting negative attitudes were all over 40%.[22] I don't have figures for non-European countries, but there's no reason to think China, Japan, Brazil or Nigeria would be less intolerant than Europeans or people in the U.S. I am of course not saying that the U.S. is free of racial prejudice; it is and will continue to be a problem that must be faced. It's also possible that people are lying when they respond to surveys. But the question to be asked is which situation is more likely to be true: that since 1940 racial attitudes have improved, as the surveys indicate, or that people have merely decided to lie more and hide their true feelings? And even if the latter were true, we still would have moved into a situation in which people feel guilty about their racial attitudes, sense that racism is condemned by the larger society, and therefore are unwilling to admit to it—another indication of improvement.

If racism is not shown in the occasional acts of racists or the belief shared by blacks and whites about crime, and if surveys show steady and substantial reductions in racist attitudes generally, then what reasons *do* defenders of CRT rely on to prove their claim that racial oppression is the central, dominant fact about American legal and political practices?

Economic Inequality and Racism

The most frequent argument offered by defenders of Critical Race Theory relies on economic inequalities and especially the black "underclass." Again quoting Crenshaw:

Material subordination . . . refers to the ways that discrimination and exclusion economically subordinated blacks to whites and subordinated the life chances of blacks to those of whites on almost every level. . . . where poverty, anxiety, poor health care, and crime create a life expectancy for blacks that is five or six years shorter than white.[23]

The myth of race neutrality, she concludes, "creates the illusion that racism is no longer the primary factor responsible for the condition of the black underclass."[24] Racism, then, is not just one problem but, she asserts, is the *primary* cause of the black underclass. Indeed, for her any significant difference in group performance, income level, and poverty by itself proves racism. The "expansive" view of equality, which she favors,

stresses *equality as a result,* and it looks to real consequences for African-Americans. It interprets the objective of anti-discrimination law as the eradication of the substantive conditions of black subordination . . . and the effects of racial oppression. [emphasis added][25]

So on this way of understanding race and law, wherever we see differences in "life expectancy" or in "poverty, anxiety, health care, and crime" correlated with group membership then we have reason to believe we have also found racial subordination and racial oppression. Until parity among groups is achieved, we have proof of a racist legal system. According to Crenshaw and others, all cultural or other factors should be set aside in favor of the view that white power and white racism determine the position of African-Americans. The question, of course, is whether any of this is true. Is racism the exclusive or even primary cause of the problems of the black under-class? And if not racism, then what is the explanation? The fact of the matter is that there is no simple answer here, except that the claim of Crenshaw, Bell and others is almost entirely wrong.

First, it's important to note that major economic disparities exist among many groups, not just between blacks and whites; indeed, those other disparities are often *greater* than the black/white one. The figures are striking. Overall, the average family income for native-born whites is $35,975 and that of blacks is $20,209. But look more closely. Americans of Japanese and Chinese descent earn an average of $52,728 and $56,762, far above the average for whites. Those of Cuban descent also earn more than whites ($37,452). And among whites there is also wide variation:

Greek-Americans, for instance, do much better than both Scottish and Polish Americans.

Turning to the economic position of blacks in the U.S., what we see rather than racism holding people back is a complex picture involving many other much more important factors. First, we should note that many blacks have made substantial economic progress in the last few decades. Today almost half of all African-Americans describe themselves as middle class, and since 1970 the proportion of blacks living in suburbs has almost doubled.[26] The proportion of blacks who have attended college went from about 15% in 1965 to nearly half in 1995, and the percentage graduating rose from less than 7% to over 15%. But it also remains true that blacks are still less likely to attend or finish college than whites—a fact that has implications for income of everybody regardless of race, as I will discuss shortly.[27] Black women with a college degree now earn 107% of what comparably educated white women earn. For males, the figures show a different pattern, with black males earning only 77% of whites.[28] It's hard to imagine that racism works only against black males, so what else might explain the difference?

One part of the answer is that fewer black male college graduates than whites go into high paying professions like medicine, law, and accounting—a fact that by itself would create a disparity. (It will also explain some of the income disparities noted earlier among other groups of Americans.) But perhaps importantly, studies show significant disparities between comparably educated black and white males on basic tests involving arithmetical reasoning, reading comprehension and vocabulary. Furthermore, when those differences are considered blacks males actually earned 19% *more* than white males having the same skill levels.[29] So once again close inspection reveals a complex picture in which racism seems to play little role.

But what, finally, of the suggestion by Crenshaw, Bell and others in CRT that the presence of a black under-class proves racism? As I have been trying to insist, the truth is very complex;

but by far the most important variables here are *not* race. In fact, the percentage of black families below the poverty line went from 87% in 1940 (when racism greatly influenced income) to about 30% in 1970 where it has remained pretty constant ever since, declining to about 26% today.[30] What was it that occurred, beginning in the 1960s, that could explain the fact that this decline in black poverty came to a standstill? The answer is clearly not that the law became more racist; the reverse is of course true, as racial attitudes have consistently improved as the civil rights laws of the 1960s and 1970s attest. And as we saw, surveys show improved racial attitudes throughout the period.

What did happen during that period of relative stagnation for the poorest blacks is (1) there was a surge in black children being born to single women; (2) there was an explosion of crime and unemployment among young black males; and (3) the economy shifted more and more toward jobs requiring high levels of skill, so that people with those skills have seen incomes grow while those lacking them have seen wage stagnation and, often, unemployment. All of these have had an impact on poverty, though just how much influence to attribute to each is much disputed.

Children growing up in households headed by single parents tend overwhelmingly to be poor. In 1995, 85% of the poor black children lived in families without a father present[31] while 70% of black births were out of wedlock.[32] That matters tremendously for poverty: the majority (62%) of black children living with only their mother are poor, while only 13% of black children living with both parents are poor. The income for female-headed black families was just over a third of the income of black married couples.[33]

As these children get older, the economic and social effects of family structure become ever clearer. With the rise of the single parent family came large increases in crime and unemployment. While it is often claimed that unemployment and poverty cause crime, the evidence is again more complicated. As we saw, crime exploded *not* during the 1930s and 1940s, when poverty was rampant, but instead during the 1960s, after a period of sustained economic progress among blacks. The crime rise continued into the 1990s, which was again a time of great economic progress for most blacks and even slight increase for the poorest. Instead of poverty causing crime, then, it's at least in part the reverse—crime causes poverty. Ghetto crime creates unemployment in many ways: (1) by encouraging the perception that young black males are not responsible employees, (2) by increasing the cost and risk of doing business in the ghetto, causing businesses to move away, and (3) by reducing the number of young black males available for employment since many are earning nothing in prison. But again we should avoid the mistake of CRT of oversimplification.

While it's no doubt partly true that crime causes unemployment, William Julius Wilson has argued that a third important cause of the persistence of black poverty and unemployment has been changes in the labor market, as more and more blue collar jobs have been replaced by ones requiring more education and other skills.[34] The effect of this has been felt among all those who lack valuable skills, but disproportionately on African-Americans.

Which brings me to the final part of the poverty cycle: added to increased crime and unemployment of the poorest black children is poor educational performance. Large gaps exist in the educational levels of black, white and Asian-American students. Black seventeen-year-olds range from three to almost six grades behind whites in educational achievement.[35] And while just over 15% of blacks complete college, 26% of whites have a college degree. Educational achievement is also, in itself, a major factor in predicting economic success, with college educated people earning more than those not finishing college, and those with high skills doing better than those who lack them.

My point here is not to resolve these disputes by demonstrating precisely *how much* of the poverty can be explained by crime, by family break-down, and by economic shifts; it's rather to emphasize that racism is not the sole factor explaining black poverty and is of second order importance to other factors. All the factors work together to maintain the black under-class: violence in the neighborhood and in school makes education more difficult and jobs more difficult to find; poor education and high unemployment lead to more crime and in turn to poor educational performance. The fact of being raised in a single-parent family is by itself a handicap in terms of education. Even ignoring the economic disadvantages associated with such families, educational achievement is lower than for children raised by two parents.[36]

Does It Matter That CRT Is Wrong?

The lesson of all this is clear, I think. While CRT is right in supposing that we are race-*conscious*—we pay perhaps too much attention to how people look—they are wrong in supposing the basic attitudes of whites towards non-whites are racist. Nor, more importantly, does racism explain much in the way of economic inequalities. The fact that CRT is so racialist, and that it is therefore wrong in its diagnosis of the problems, might seem to be of merely academic interest, without serious consequences for the people facing poverty, crime, and social disintegration. It might even seem like a good idea to encourage people to be constantly on the lookout for racism, even though it is not the major cause of poverty or other problems. But that's not the case. The truth is that emphasizing race is not just an intellectual mistake, it's also harmful and potentially self-destructive of democratic processes and of the real interests of blacks. I'll mention two examples.

One proposal, defended forcefully by Lani Guinier and other members of CRT, seeks to perfect the democratic process by designing electoral districts so as to assure minority participation. Some have even suggested giving minority legislators extra votes or a veto over legislation affecting their constituents. Such proposals present a variety of problems, however. First, which groups are to be given such special protection? If

Asian-Americans and Latinos are included along with African-Americans, should sub-groups like Korean-Americans, Chinese-Americans, Cuban-Americans, Mexican-Americans and so on also be assured proportional representation? And what about other groups that arguably do not exert their share of influence, such as women, homosexuals and the poor? Women constitute over fifty percent of the population, so should they be assured at least fifty senators? if proportional representation is the test, would Jewish judges and legislators, who constitute more than 2–3%, be forced to retire? If a history of discrimination is the test, then would Irish Americans also be assured proportional representation? Asian-Americans now make up about three percent of the U.S. population, so should they be assured of three senators and fourteen representatives? What about the fact that only one percent of Asian-Americans vote—is that irrelevant?

In addition to these difficult problems of implementation, the political assumptions and consequences of explicit adoption of these proposals must also be weighed. Defenders of racially or ethnically based voting districts tend to see the electoral process through the lens of the market, as a competition among groups with conflicting interests, and also to assume that these interests follow mainly racial and ethnic lines. Yet neither of these assumptions is entirely true. While voters obviously do sometimes vote on the basis of private *interests,* votes also express their *judgments* about major issues of public concern. Issues of equality, rights and justice are central to public debate and the electoral process, yet racial districting focuses only on political influence and power.

Nor is it true that people's interests and wishes track racial or ethnic lines. In recent years, blacks have been increasingly successful at winning elections in predominantly white districts, just as many whites have won support from black voters. There are also profound disagreements among members of various groups that cannot be ignored; Asian-Americans, Latinos and African-Americans can be found occupying the entire political spectrum. Yet none of these facts fits neatly with CRT proposals that electoral politics can be improved simply by assuring that groups are given a proportional share of representatives of their own race. Indeed I think that such racialist thinking distracts from needed reforms in campaign financing and in education, both of which could improve democracy without racial balkanization.

A more doubtful, and I will argue dangerous example of CRT racialist thinking is Regina Austin's essay "Sapphire Bound." In it, Austin criticizes a legal decision upholding the right of a girls' club to discharge an employee when she became pregnant. The woman was unmarried, and the girls' club contended that having her there would set a bad example. For Austin, however, this is another illustration of how the law fails to understand "the historical oppression of black women and . . . The diversity of their contemporary cultural practices."[37] Single mothers, she said, are being "viewed ominously because they have the temerity to attempt to break out of the rigid categories that a racist, sexist and class-stratified society would impose on them."[38] Instead, she writes, blacks should resist this "war on unwed black mothers" and reject the model of "assimilation."[39]

This argument would be silly, if it weren't so dangerous. Silly because she simply assumes that it is the right of every woman or girl to have a baby whether or not she or her family is in any position to care for it financially or emotionally. But more importantly, Austin is blinded by the race question. Unable to see clearly the economic, educational and social consequences for young women and for their children, she sees only racial oppression and cultural imperialism behind the ruling. How would the same ruling look if it had been handed down by a black judge in South Africa who made similar points about the costs of having babies out of wedlock? The answer, I am sure, is that it would look very different; Austin is prevented from seeing the truth by her assumption that racism is pervasive and that every legal opinion (at least every one written by a white that criticizes a black) is motivated by racism. In "refusing to accept the yoke of pa-

ternalism and oppression," Austin tells us, the woman may be regarded as a heroine. Imagining the women who may make this decision, she says that "Some of the black women may be young and wise; others may be poor and brave; and yet a third group may be rich and selfish."[40] But the evidence is that it is more than likely she will belong to none of these categories, let alone to a group of people throwing off the yoke of racial oppression. Describing her as a heroine ignores the breakdown of the black family, contributing to the perpetuation of poverty, crime and poor educational performance.

Discussion Questions

1. Even if we accept Arthur's claim that there are important forces pushing toward legal *coherence*, does this negate the CRT claim that the law can be used for political, even racist, purposes?

2. According to Derrick Bell, the law "is an instrument for preserving the status quo." Does Arthur's argument concerning race undercut *this* claim?

3. Arthur argues that such factors as single-mother households, not racism, are the main causes of the black underclass. But are these wholly separate factors?

4. Even if we accept Arthur's point (against Regina Austin) that single motherhood can lead to social problems, does it follow that the pregnant employee ought to be fired?

Notes

1. I wish to express my thanks to Amy Shapiro for her valuable comments on an earlier draft of this paper.

2. Derrick Bell, "Racial Realism" in *Critical Race Theory*, ed. Kimberle Crenshaw, Neil Gotanda, Gary Peller, and Kendall Thomas (New York: The New Press, 1995), p. 304.

3. David Kairys, "Legal Reasoning," in *The Politics of Law*, ed. David Kairys (New York: Pantheon Books, 1982). p. 15.

4. Stanley Fish, "Almost Pragmatism" in *Pragmatism in Law and Society*, ed. Michael Brint and William Weaver (Boulder CO: Westview Press, 1991), p. 76.

5. Mari J. Matsuda, "Voices of America: Accent, Anti-discrimination Law, and a Jurisprudence for the Last Reconstruction," 100 *Yale Law Journal* (1991), p. 1394.

6. This is a large, interesting, and complex question, so I can make only a few comments on it here. For anyone interested in a much fuller description and defense of my views on this subject, they can be found in *Words That Bind: Judicial Review and the Grounds of Modern Constitutional Theory* (Boulder, CO, and London: Westview Press, 1995), Chapter 3.

7. See Ronald Dworkin, "Integrity in Law" in *Law's Empire* (Cambridge: Harvard University Press, 1986), pp. 225–275.

8. John Rawls, *A Theory of Justice* (Cambridge: Harvard University Press, 1971), p. 235.

9. By saying laws are rules or principles that are addressed to citizens, I mean to avoid disputes about whether they include principles that cannot be equated with rules, as well as whether they are commands of the sovereign as Hobbes and others have argued.

10. As described below, no legal system can overcome all indeterminacy; but neither, I am suggesting, can it fall too far short of the rule of law without losing its character as a system of *law*.

11. For a helpful discussion of these and other ways a system may fail to achieve the status of law, see Lon Fuller, *The Morality of Law* (New Haven: Yale University Press, 1964), pp. 33–41. Fuller's list is best seen, I think, as a slightly longer and more precise conception of the rule of law.

12. Kimberle Crenshaw, "A Black Feminist Critique of Anti-discrimination Law and Politics," in *The Politics of Law*, ed. David Kairys (New York: Pantheon, rev. ed., 1990), p. 213, n. 7.

13. Derrick Bell, "Racial Realism," in Crenshaw et al. *Critical Race Theory*, pp. 302 and 308.

14. Derrick Bell, "Racial Realism," 24 *Connecticut Law Review* (1992), p. 364.

15. U.S. Department of Justice, Bureau of Justice Statistics, *Criminal Victimization in the United States, 1993* (Washington, D.C.: U.S. Department of Justice, 1996),) pp. 45 and 49. Quoted in Stephan Thernstrom and Abigail Thernstrom, *America in Black and White* (New York: Simon and Schuster, 1997). p. 272

16. U.S. Department of Justice, *Crime in the United States—1995* (Washington, D.C.: U.S. Government Printing Office, 1996), p. 226. Quoted in Thernstrom and Thernstrom, *America in Black and White*, pp. 262–264.

17. Ibid.

18. Thernstrom and Thernstrom, *America in Black and White*, p. 141. (Figures from various sources.)

19. Norman Podhoretz., "Postscript (1993)" In *Blacks and Jews: Alliances and Arguments*, ed. Paul Berman (New York: Bantam Doubleday Dell, 1994), p. 94.

20. Thernstrom and Thernstrom, *America in Black and White*, p. 141. (Figures from various sources.)

21. Thernstrom and Thernstrom, *America in Black and White*, p. 500. (Figures from various sources.)

22. Times Mirror Center for the People and the Press, *The Pulse of Europe: A Survey of Political and Social Values and Attitudes* (Washington, D.C.: Times Mirror Center, 1991), sec. VIII. Quoted in Thernstrom and Thernstrom, *America in Black and White*, p. 531.

23. Crenshaw, "Race, Reform, and Retrenchment" in Crenshaw et al. *Critical Race Theory*, p. 114.

24. Crenshaw, "Race, Reform, and Retrenchment" in Crenshaw et al. *Critical Race Theory*, p. 117.

25. Crenshaw, "Race, Reform, and Retrenchment" in Crenshaw et al. *Critical Race Theory*, p. 105.

26. Thernstrom and Thernstrom, *America in Black and White*, p. 533. (Figures from various sources.)

27. From U.S. Department of Education, *Youth Indicators 1996: Trends in the Well-Being of American Youth* (Washington, D.C.: U.S. Government Printing Office, 1996) p. 70. Quote in Thernstrom and Thernstrom, *America in Black and White*, p. 391.

28. U.S. Bureau of Census, *Current Population Reports: March 1995* (Washington, D.C.: Government Printing Office, 1996), table 9. Quoted in Thernstrom and Thernstrom, *America in Black and White*, p. 445.

29. Thernstrom and Thernstrom, *America in Black and White*, p. 446.

30. Thernstrom and Thernstrom, *America in Black and White*, p. 233. (Taken from census figures.)

31. Thernstrom and Thernstrom, *America in Black and White*, pp. 236–237. (Figures from various sources.)

32. Thernstrom and Thernstrom, *America in Black and White*, p. 237. (Figures from various sources.)

33. Thernstrom and Thernstrom, *America in Black and White*, p. 241. (Figures from various sources.)

34. William Julius Wilson, *The Truly Disadvantaged* (Chicago: The University of Chicago Press, 1987)

35. Thernstrom and Thernstrom, *America in Black and White*, p. 355. (Figures from various sources.)

36. Thernstrom and Thernstrom, *America in Black and White*, p. 358.

37. Regina Austin, "Sapphire Bound" in Crenshaw et al., *Critical Race Theory*, p. 429.

38. Regina Austin, "Sapphire Bound" in Crenshaw et al., *Critical Race Theory*, p. 430.

39. Regina Austin, "Sapphire Bound" in Crenshaw et al., *Critical Race Theory*, p. 431.

40. Regina Austin, "Sapphire Bound" in Crenshaw et al., *Critical Race Theory*, p. 433.

Contemporary Issue: Racist Hate Speech

39   Prohibiting Racist Speech: A Debate

CHARLES LAWRENCE AND GERALD GUNTHER

Study Questions

1. According to Lawrence, how has the issue of violence on campus been incorrectly framed and how should it be framed?
2. How is racist speech contrary to the purposes of the First Amendment?
3. How would Lawrence distinguish protected and unprotected (racist) speech?
4. How does Gunther differ from Lawrence regarding what the correct response to "bad speech" should be?
5. Contrast where Gunther would draw the line to where Lawrence would (see question 3)?
6. Following Justices Holmes and Brandeis, how does Gunther ultimately frame the issue of forbidding certain speech?

By Charles Lawrence

I have spent the better part of my life as a dissenter. As a high-school student, I was threatened with suspension for my refusal to participate in a civil-defense drill, and I have been a conspicuous consumer of my First Amendment liberties ever since. There are very strong reasons for protecting even speech that is racist. Perhaps the most important is that such protection reinforces our society's commitment to tolerance as a value. By protecting bad speech from government regulation, we will be forced to combat it as a community.

From "Good Speech, Bad Speech—Yes" and "Good Speech, Bad Speech—No," *Stanford Lawyer* 24 (1990), pp. 6, 8, 40 and 7, 9, 41.

I have, however, a deeply felt apprehension about the resurgence of racial violence and the corresponding increase in the incidence of verbal and symbolic assault and harassment to which blacks and other traditionally excluded groups are subjected. I am troubled by the way the debate has been framed in response to the recent surge of racist incidents on college and university campuses and in response to some universities' attempts to regulate harassing speech. The problem has been framed as one in which the liberty of free speech is in conflict with the elimination of racism. I believe this has placed the bigot on the moral high ground and fanned the rising flames of racism.

Above all, I am troubled that we have not listened to the real victims—that we have shown so little understanding of their injury, and that we have abandoned those whose race, gender, or sexual orientation continues to make them second-class citizens. It seems to me a very sad irony that the first instinct of civil libertarians has been to challenge even the smallest, most narrowly framed efforts by universities to provide black and other minority students with the protection the Constitution, in my opinion, guarantees them.

The landmark case of *Brown v. Board of Education* is not a case that we normally think of as a case about speech. But *Brown* can be broadly read as articulating the principle of equal citizenship. *Brown* held that segregated schools were inherently unequal because of the message that segregation conveyed: that black children were an untouchable caste, unfit to go to school with white children. If we understand the necessity of eliminating the system of signs and symbols that signal the inferiority of blacks, then we should hesitate before proclaiming that all racist speech that stops short of physical violence must be defended.

University officials who have formulated policies to respond to incidents of racial harassment have been characterized in the press as "thought police," even though such policies generally do nothing more than impose sanctions against intentional face-to-face insults. Racist speech that takes the form of face-to-face insults, catcalls, or other assaultive speech aimed at an individual or small group of persons falls directly within the "fighting words" exception to the First Amendment protection. The Supreme Court has held in *Chaplinsky v. New Hampshire* that words which "by their very utterance inflict injury or tend to incite an immediate breach of the peace" are not protected by the First Amendment.

If the purpose of the First Amendment is to foster the greatest amount of speech, racial insults disserve that purpose. Assaultive racist speech functions as a preemptive strike. The invective is experienced as a blow, not as a proffered idea. And once the blow is struck, a dialogue is unlikely to follow. Racial insults are particularly undeserving of First Amendment protection, because the perpetrator's intention is not to discover truth or initiate dialogue but to injure the victim. In most situations, members of minority groups realize that they are likely to lose if they fight back, and are forced to remain silent and submissive.

Courts have held that offensive speech may not be regulated in public forums (such as streets, where the listener may avoid the speech by moving on). But the regulation of otherwise protected speech has been permitted when the speech invades the privacy of the unwilling listener's home, or when the unwilling listener cannot avoid the speech. Racist posters, fliers, and graffiti in dormitories, bathrooms, and other common living spaces would seem to fall within the reasoning of these cases. Minority students should not be required to remain in their rooms in order to avoid racial insult. Minimally, they should find a safe haven in their dorms and in all other common rooms that are part of their daily routine.

I would also argue that the university's responsibility for ensuring that these students receive an equal educational opportunity provides a compelling justification for regulations that ensure them safe passage in all common areas. A minority student should not have to risk becoming the target of racially assaulting speech every time he or she chooses to walk across campus. Regulating vilifying speech that cannot be anticipated or avoided need not preclude announced speeches and rallies—situations that would give minority-group members and their allies the opportunity to organize counterdemonstrations or avoid the speech altogether.

The most commonly advanced argument against the regulation of racist speech proceeds something like this: We recognize that minority groups suffer pain and injury as the result of racist speech, but we must allow this hate mongering for the benefit of society as a whole. Freedom of speech is the lifeblood of our democratic system. It is especially important for minorities, because often it is their only vehicle for rallying support of the redress of their grievances. It will be impossible to formulate a prohibition so precise that it will prevent the racist speech you want to suppress, without catching in the same net all kinds of speech that it would be unconscionable for a democratic society to suppress.

Such arguments seek to strike a balance between our concern, on the one hand, for the continued free flow of ideas and the democratic process dependent on that flow, and, on the other, our desire to further the cause of equality. There can, however, be no meaningful discussion of how we should reconcile our commitment to equality with our commitment to free speech, until it is acknowledged that racist speech inflicts real harm, and that this harm is far from trivial.

To engage in a debate about the First Amendment and racist speech without a full understanding of the nature and extent of that harm is to risk making the First Amendment an instrument of domination rather than a vehicle of liberation. We have not all known the experience of victimization by racist, misogynist, and homophobic speech, nor do we equally share the burden of the harm it inflicts. We are often quick to say that we have heard the cry of the victims when we have not.

The *Brown* case is again instructive, because it speaks directly to the psychic injury inflicted by racist speech by noting that the symbolic message of segregation affected "the hearts and minds" of Negro children "in a way unlikely ever to be undone." Racial epithets and harassment often cause deep emotional scarring and feelings of anxiety and fear that pervade every aspect of a victim's life.

Brown also recognized that black children did not have an equal opportunity to learn and participate in the school community when they bore the additional burden of being subjected to the humiliation and psychic assault contained in the message of segregation. University students bear an analogous burden when they are forced to live and work in an environment where at any moment they may be subjected to denigrating verbal harassment and assault. The same injury was addressed by the Supreme Court when it held that, under Title VII of the Civil Rights Act of 1964, sexual harassment which creates a hostile or abusive work environment violates the ban on sex discrimination in employment.

Carefully drafted university regulations could bar the use of words as assault weapons while at the same time leaving unregulated even the most heinous of ideas provided those ideas are presented at times and places and in manners that provide an opportunity for reasoned rebuttal or escape from immediate insult. The history of the development of the right to free speech has been one of carefully evaluating the importance of free expression and its effects on other important societal interests. We have drawn the line between protected and unprotected speech before without dire results. (Courts have, for example, exempted from the protection of the First Amendment obscene speech and speech that disseminates official secrets, defames or libels another person, or is used to form a conspiracy or monopoly.)

Blacks and other people of color are skeptical about the argument that even the most injurious speech must remain unregulated because, in an unregulated marketplace of ideas, the best ones will rise to the top and gain acceptance. Experience tells quite the opposite. People of color have seen too many demagogues elected by appealing to America's racism, and too many sympathetic politicians shy away from issues that might brand them as being too closely allied with disparaged groups.

Whenever we decide that racist speech must be tolerated because of the importance of maintaining societal tolerance for all unpopular speech, we are asking blacks and other subordinated groups to bear the burden for the good of all. We must be careful that the ease with which we strike the balance against the regulation of racist speech is in no way influenced by the fact that the cost will be borne by others. We must be certain that those who will pay that price are fairly represented in our deliberations and that they are heard.

At the core of the argument that we should resist all government regulation of speech is the ideal that the best cure for bad speech is good—that ideas that affirm equality and the worth of all individuals will ultimately prevail. This is an empty ideal unless those of us who would fight racism are vigilant and unequivocal in that fight. We must look for ways to offer assistance and support to students whose speech and political participation are chilled in a climate of racial harassment.

Civil rights lawyers might consider suing on behalf of blacks whose right to an equal education is denied by a university's failure to ensure a nondiscriminatory educational climate or conditions of employment. We must embark upon the development of a First Amendment jurisprudence grounded in the reality of our history and our contemporary experience. We must think hard about how best to launch legal attacks against the most indefensible forms of hate speech. Good lawyers can create exceptions and narrow interpretations that limit the harm of hate speech without opening the floodgates of censorship.

Everyone concerned with these issues must find ways to engage actively in actions that resist and counter the racist ideas that we would have the First Amendment protect. If we fail in this, the victims of hate speech must rightly assume that we are on the bigot's side.

By Gerald Gunther

I am deeply troubled by current efforts—however well-intentioned—to place new limits on freedom of expression at this and other campuses. Such limits are not only incompatible with the mission and meaning of a university; they also send exactly the wrong message from academia to society as a whole. University campuses should exhibit greater, not less, freedom of expression than prevails in society at large.

Proponents of new limits argue that historic First Amendment rights must be balanced against "Stanford's commitment to the diversity of ideas and persons." Clearly, there is ample room and need for vigorous University action to combat racial and other discrimination. But curbing freedom of speech is the wrong way to do so. The proper answer to bad speech is usually more and better speech—not new laws, litigation, and repression.

Lest it be thought that I am insensitive to the pain imposed by expressions of racial or religious hatred, let me say that I have suffered that pain and empathize with others under similar verbal assault. My deep belief in the principles of the First Amendment arises in part from my own experiences.

I received my elementary education in a public school in a very small town in Nazi Germany. There I was subjected to vehement anti-Semitic remarks from my teacher, classmates and others—"Judensau" (Jew pig) was far from the harshest. I can assure you that they hurt. More generally, I lived in a country where ideological orthodoxy reigned and where the opportunity for dissent was severely limited.

The lesson I have drawn from my childhood in Nazi Germany and my happier adult life in this country is the need to walk the sometimes difficult path of denouncing the bigots' hateful ideas with all my power, yet at the same time challenging any community's attempt to suppress hateful ideas by force of law.

Obviously, given my own experience, I do *not* quarrel with the claim that words *can* do harm. But I firmly deny that a showing of harm suffices to deny First Amendment protection, and I insist on the elementary First Amendment principle that our Constitution usually protects even offensive, harmful expression.

That is why—at the risk of being thought callous or doctrinaire—I feel compelled to speak out against the attempt by some members of the Stanford community to enlarge the area of forbidden speech under the Fundamental Standard. Such proposals, in my view, seriously undervalue the First Amendment and far too readily endanger its precious content. Limitations on free expression beyond those established by law should be eschewed in an institution committed to diversity and the First Amendment.

In explaining my position, I will avoid extensive legal arguments. Instead, I want to speak from the heart, on the basis of my own background and of my understanding of First Amendment principles—principles supported by an ever larger number of scholars and Supreme Court justices, especially since the days of the Warren Court.

Among the core principles is that any official effort to suppress expression must be viewed with the greatest skepticism and suspicion. Only in very narrow, urgent circumstances should government or similar institutions be permitted to inhibit speech. True, there are certain categories of speech that may be prohibited; but the number and scope of these categories has steadily shrunk over the last fifty years. Face-to-face insults are one such category; incitement to immediate illegal action is another. But opinions expressed in debates and arguments about a wide range of political and social issues should not be suppressed simply because of disagreement with those views, with the content of the expression.

Similarly, speech should not and cannot be banned simply because it is "offensive" to substantial parts or a majority of a community. The refusal to suppress offensive speech is one of the most difficult obligations the free speech principle imposes upon all of us; yet it is also one of the First Amendment's greatest glories—indeed it is a central test of a community's commitment to free speech.

The Supreme Court's 1989 decision to allow flag-burning as a form of political protest, in *Texas v. Johnson,* warrants careful pondering by all those who continue to advocate campus restraints on "racist speech." As Justice Brennan's majority opinion in *Johnson* reminded, "If there is a bedrock principle underlying the First Amendment, it is that the Government may not prohibit the expression of an idea simply because society finds the idea itself offensive or disagreeable." In refusing to place flag-burning outside the First Amendment, moreover, the *Johnson* majority insisted (in words especially apt for the "racist speech" debate): "The First Amendment does not guarantee that other concepts virtually sacred to our Nation as a whole—*such as the principle that discrimination on the basis of race is odious and destructive*—will go unquestioned in the marketplace of ideas. We decline, therefore, to create for the flag an exception to the joust of principles protected by the First Amendment." (Italics added.)

Campus proponents of restricting offensive speech are currently relying for justification on the Supreme Court's allegedly repeated reiteration that "fighting words" constitute an exception to the First Amendment. Such an exception has indeed been recognized in a number of lower court cases. However, there has only been *one* case in the history of the Supreme Court in which a majority of the Justices has ever found a statement to be a punishable resort to "fighting words." That was *Chaplinsky v. New Hampshire,* a nearly fifty-year-old case involving words which would very likely not be found punishable today.

More significant is what has happened in the nearly half-century since: Despite repeated appeals to the Supreme Court to recognize the applicability of the "fighting words" exception by affirming challenged convictions, the Court has in every instance refused. One must wonder about the strength of an exception that, while theoretically recognized, has for so long not been found apt in practice. (Moreover, the proposed Stanford rules are *not* limited to face-to-face insults to an addressee, and thus go well beyond the traditional, albeit fragile, "fighting words" exception.)

The phenomenon of racist and other offensive speech that Stanford now faces is not a new one in the history of the First Amendment. In recent decades, for example, well-meaning but in my view misguided majorities have sought to suppress not only racist speech but also antiwar and antidraft speech, civil rights demonstrators, the Nazis and the Ku Klux Klan, and left-wing groups.

Typically, it is people on the extremes of the political spectrum (including those who advocate overthrow of our constitutional system and those who would not protect their opponents' right to dissent were they the majority) who feel the brunt of repression and have found protection in the First Amendment; typically, it is well-meaning people in the majority who believe that their "community standards," their sensibilities, their sense of outrage, justify restraints.

Those in power in a community recurrently seek to repress speech they find abhorrent; and their efforts are understandable human impulses. Yet freedom of expression—and especially the protection of dissident speech, the most important function of the First Amendment—is an antimajoritarian principle. Is it too much to hope that, especially on a university campus, a majority can be persuaded of the value of freedom of expression and the resultant need to curb our impulses to repress dissident views?

The principles to which I appeal are not new. They have been expressed, for example, by the most distinguished Supreme Court justices ever since the beginning of the Court's confrontations with First Amendment issues nearly seventy years ago. These principles are reflected in the words of so imperfect a First Amendment defender as Justice Oliver Wendell Holmes: "If there is any principle of the Constitution that more imperatively calls for attachment than any other it is the principle of free thought—not free thought for those who agree with us but freedom for the thought that we hate."

This is the principle most elaborately and eloquently addressed by Justice Louis D. Brandeis, who reminded us that the First Amendment rests on a belief "in the power of reason as applied through public discussion" and therefore bars "silence coerced by law—the argument of force in its worst form."

This theme, first articulated in dissents, has repeatedly been voiced in majority opinions in more recent decades. It underlies Justice Douglas's remark in striking down a conviction under a law banning speech that "stirs the public to anger": "A function of free speech [is] to invite dispute. . . . Speech is often provocative and challenging. That is why freedom of speech [is ordinarily] protected against censorship or punishment."

It also underlies Justice William J. Brennan's comment about our "profound national commitment to the principle that debate on public issues should be uninhibited, robust and wide-open, and that it may well include vehement, caustic and sometimes unpleasantly sharp attacks"—a comment he followed with a reminder that constitutional protection "does not turn upon the truth, popularity or social utility of the ideas and beliefs which are offered."

These principles underlie as well the repeated insistence by Justice John Marshall Harlan, again in the majority opinions, that the mere "inutility or immorality" of a message cannot justify its repression, and that the state may not punish because of "the underlying content of the message." Moreover, Justice Harlan, in one of the finest First Amendment opinions on the books, noted, in words that Stanford would ignore at its peril at this time:

"The constitutional right of free expression is powerful medicine in a society as diverse and populous as ours. . . . To many, the immediate consequence of this freedom may often appear to be only verbal tumult, discord and even offensive utterance. These are, however, necessary side effects of the broader enduring values which the process of open debate permits us to achieve. That the air may at times seem filled with verbal cacophony is, in this sense, not a sign of weakness but of strength."

In this same passage, Justice Harlan warned that a power to ban speech merely because it is offensive is an "inherently boundless" notion, and added that "we think it is largely because governmental officials cannot make principled distinctions in this area that the Constitution leaves matters of taste and style so largely to the individual." (The Justice made these comments while overturning the conviction of an antiwar protestor for "offensive conduct." The defendant had worn, in a courthouse corridor, a jacket bearing the words "Fuck the Draft." It bears noting, in light of the ongoing campus debate, that Justice Harlan's majority opinion also warned that "we cannot indulge in the facile assumption that one can forbid particular words without also running the substantial risk of suppressing ideas in the process.")

I restate these principles and repeat these words for reasons going far beyond the fact that they are familiar to me as a First Amendment scholar. I believe—in my heart as well as my mind—that these principles and ideals are not only established but right. I hope that the entire Stanford community will seriously reflect upon the risks to free expression, lest we weaken hard-won liberties at Stanford and, by example, in this nation.

Discussion Questions

1. It seems that Lawrence and Gunther would agree that advertised speeches are acceptable, no matter what their content, and that direct face-to-face insults ("fighting words") are not. Where might they disagree, then?
2. To what extent is racial harassment similar to sexual harassment? How are they different?
3. Some have suggested that we should forbid racist *actions* on campus but not speech. Is this a good solution?
4. Consider the case of a hypothetical English instructor who repeatedly uses the word *nigger* in connection with teaching Twain's *Huckleberry Finn* but in a way that the lone black student in class finds offensive (the instructor's example leads to a general use of the word by the student's classmates, although always in the context of the book). Should such speech be permitted?
5. How should we try to balance such fundamental rights as freedom of speech and the right to an equal education?

Aesthetics

African-American classical music is dialectical music. It recognizes a world of order, but it simultaneously embraces a world of unpredictability.

LEWIS R. GORDON

The fair are fair/and deathly white
The day will not save them
And we own the night

AMIRI BARAKA

But another strategy is to use the stereotype in profound acts of self-empowerment. . . . Black guys are, according to the stereotype, animalistic, armed, violent, out of control. Rap's reply: Hell yes we are, so get the fuck out of the way.

CRISPIN SARTWELL

On first hearing 2 Live Crew I was shocked; unlike [Henry Louis] Gates I did not "bust out laughing." One trivializes the issue by describing the images of women in As Nasty As They Wanna Be *as simply "sexually explicit."*

KIMBERLE CRENSHAW

Aesthetics concerns the theory of art and beauty. Although art and artistic expression have always been central to African American life, black aesthetics as a mode of *reflection* on the arts became particularly important during the Harlem Renaissance (mainly, the 1920s and 1930s). During this period, such poets as Langston Hughes and such novelists as Zora Neale Hurston sought to *incorporate* everyday folk idioms into their art. More generally, the distinction between so-called folk art (songs and stories of the people) and high art (formal musical compositions and novels) began to break down, yet a tension remained: some enthusiasts of the new era of black artistic expression (including Alain Locke) ignored or were critical of the use of materials such as the blues and folktales.[1] Locke differed with DuBois in giving much less stress to the importance of art as a *political* vehicle. Both of these contrasts—between popular and "high" art and between purely artistic and political goals—are reflected in this chapter.

---

[1] In one of his contributions to his own collection, *The New Negro* (New York: Atheneum, 1992), "The Negro Spirituals," Locke celebrates these as high artistic expression, though looking forward to their incorporation into a more classic form by one who would be "the musical giant of his age." In his introduction to this edition, Arnold Rampersad remarks on Locke's choosing to ignore the "lowly blues."

In the well-known essay that begins this chapter, James Baldwin speaks for a black art that is not directly tied to political protest. In so doing, he strikes a theme developed later in this volume by black theologian Victor Anderson: the seeming error of defining "black" solely in its relation to whites and their actions. Criticizing art that sacrifices truth and humanity for social protest, Baldwin sees Richard Wright's *Native Son* as part of a dubious tradition going back to *Uncle Tom's Cabin.*

A very different kind of rejection of "art as social protest" emanates from the Black Arts Movement, here represented by Larry Neal's essay. For Neal and for the leading artistic representative of this movement, Amiri Baraka (Leroi Jones), the significance of black art lies entirely in its serving, and expressing, the revolutionary aspirations of black and other oppressed people. To that extent, mere "protest" has a secondary value.

The next readings involve two "takes" on black music. Angela Y. Davis, a famous black activist and radical Marxist philosopher, emphasizes the social and political relevance of Billie Holiday's art. For his part, novelist Ralph Ellison (author of the classic *Invisible Man*), is skeptical of the very existence of a separate and an entirely non-European musical tradition of the sort that Baraka posits.

One might distinguish, then, on one side, Neal, Baraka, and Davis articulating a politicized, community-oriented view of black art and, on the other side, novelists Baldwin and Ellison as wishing to free art from a too simple and moralistic connection to politics and political mythologies. The first group sees art from a radical, political perspective; the members of the second group are skeptical of such a potentially narrow view of artistic expression.

Our final two essays debate the moral and social significance of "rap music." Crispin Sartwell, a white philosophy professor, praises rap—especially "gangsta rap"—as a form of self-empowerment. Black law professor Kimberle Crenshaw, while critical of the prosecution of 2 Live Crew, is equally critical of their misogynistic lyrics—and those who would defend them as part of a black tradition—or as mere "humor" not to be taken seriously.

40   Everybody's Protest Novel

JAMES BALDWIN

Study Questions

1. According to Baldwin, why is *Uncle Tom's Cabin* a "very bad novel"?
2. In what sense can, and should, art seek "truth"?
3. Why is Tom Harriet Beecher Stowe's "only black man" and how and why has she "robbed him of his 'humanity'"?
4. What is the avowed aim of the "protest novel" and why is it fundamentally defective, according to Baldwin?
5. Why is Bigger Thomas, different as he is, Uncle Tom's "descendant"?

In *Uncle Tom's Cabin,* that cornerstone of American social protest fiction, St. Clare, the kindly master, remarks to his coldly disapproving Yankee cousin, Miss Ophelia, that, so far as he is able to tell, the blacks have been turned over to the devil for the benefit of the whites in this world —however, he adds thoughtfully, it may turn out in the next. Miss Ophelia's reaction is, at least, vehemently right-minded: "This is perfectly horrible!" she exclaims. "You ought to be ashamed of yourselves!"

Miss Ophelia, as we may suppose, was speaking for the author; her exclamation is the moral, neatly framed, and incontestable like those improving mottoes sometimes found hanging on the walls of furnished rooms. And, like these mottoes, before which one invariably flinches, recognizing an insupportable, almost an indecent glibness, she and St. Clare are terribly in earnest. Neither of them questions the medieval morality from which their dialogue springs: black, white, the devil, the next world—posing its alternatives between heaven and the flames—were realities for them as, of course, they were for their creator. They spurned and were terrified of the darkness, striving mightily for the light; and considered

Reprinted with permission of the publisher from *Notes of a Native Son* (Boston: Beacon Press, 1983), pp. 13–23.

from this aspect, Miss Ophelia's exclamation, like Mrs. Stowe's novel, achieves a bright, almost a lurid significance, like the light from a fire which consumes a witch. This is the more striking as one considers the novels of Negro oppression written in our own, more enlightened day, all of which say only: "This is perfectly horrible! You ought to be ashamed of yourselves!" (Let us ignore, for the moment, those novels of oppression written by Negroes, which add only a raging, near-paranoiac postscript to this statement and actually reinforce, as I hope to make clear later, the principles which activate the oppression they decry.)

Uncle Tom's Cabin is a very bad novel, having, in its self-righteous, virtuous sentimentality, much in common with *Little Women.* Sentimentality, the ostentatious parading of excessive and spurious emotion, is the mark of dishonesty, the inability to feel; the wet eyes of the sentimentalist betray his aversion to experience, his fear of life, his arid heart; and it is always, therefore, the signal of secret and violent inhumanity, the mask of cruelty. *Uncle Tom's Cabin*—like its multitudinous, hard-boiled descendants—is a catalogue of violence. This is explained by the nature of Mrs. Stowe's subject matter, her laudable determination to flinch from nothing in presenting the complete picture; an explanation which falters only if we pause to ask whether or not her picture is indeed complete; and what constriction or failure of perception forced her to so depend on the description of brutality—unmotivated, senseless— and to leave unanswered and unnoticed the only important question: what it was, after all, that moved her people to such deeds.

But this, let us say, was beyond Mrs. Stowe's powers; she was not so much a novelist as an impassioned pamphleteer; her book was not intended to do anything more than prove that slavery was wrong; was, in fact, perfectly horrible. This makes material for a pamphlet but it is hardly enough for a novel; and the only question left to ask is why we are bound still within the same constriction. How is it that we are so loath to make a further journey than that made by Mrs. Stowe, to discover and reveal something a little closer to the truth?

But that battered word, truth, having made its appearance here, confronts one immediately with a series of riddles and has, moreover, since so many gospels are preached, the unfortunate tendency to make one belligerent. Let us say, then, that truth, as used here, is meant to imply a devotion to the human being, his freedom and fulfillment; freedom which cannot be legislated, fulfillment which cannot be charted. This is the prime concern, the frame of reference; it is not to be confused with a devotion to Humanity which is too easily equated with a devotion to a Cause; and Causes, as we know, are notoriously bloodthirsty. We have, as it seems to me, in this most mechanical and interlocking of civilizations, attempted to lop this creature down to the status of a time-saving invention. He is not, after all, merely a member of a Society or a Group or a deplorable conundrum to be explained by Science. He is—and how old-fashioned the words sound! —something more than that, something resolutely indefinable, unpredictable. In overlooking, denying, evading his complexity—which is nothing more than the disquieting complexity of ourselves—we are diminished and we perish; only within this web of ambiguity, paradox, this hunger, danger, darkness, can we find at once ourselves and the power that will free us from ourselves. It is this power of revelation which is the business of the novelist, this journey toward a more vast reality which must take precedence over all other claims. What is today parroted as his Responsibility—which seems to mean that he must make formal declaration that he is involved in, and affected by, the lives of other people and to say something improving about this somewhat self-evident fact—is, when he believes it, his corruption and our loss; moreover, it is rooted in, interlocked with and intensifies this same mechanization. Both *Gentleman's Agreement* and *The Postman Always Rings Twice* exemplify this terror of the human being, the determination to cut him down to size. And in *Uncle Tom's Cabin* we may find foreshadowing of both: the formula created by the necessity to find a lie more palatable than the truth has been handed down and memorized and persists yet with a terrible power.

It is interesting to consider one more aspect of Mrs. Stowe's novel, the method she used to solve the problem of writing about a black man at all. Apart from her lively procession of field hands, house niggers, Chloe, Topsy, etc.—who are the stock, lovable figures presenting no problem— she has only three other Negroes in the book. These are the important ones and two of them may be dismissed immediately, since we have only the author's word that they are Negro and they are, in all other respects, as white as she can make them. The two are George and Eliza, a married couple with a wholly adorable child—whose quaintness, incidentally, and whose charm, rather put one in mind of a darky bootblack doing a buck and wing to the clatter of condescending coins. Eliza is a beautiful, pious hybrid, light enough to pass—the heroine of *Quality* might, indeed, be her reincarnation—differing from the genteel mistress who has overseered her education only in the respect that she is a servant. George is darker, but makes up for it by being a mechanical genius, and is, moreover, sufficiently un-Negroid to pass through town, a fugitive from his master, disguised as a Spanish gentleman, attracting no attention whatever beyond admiration. They are a race apart from Topsy. It transpires by the end of the novel, through one of those energetic, last-minute convolutions of the plot, that Eliza has some connection with French gentility. The figure from whom the novel takes its name, Uncle Tom, who is a figure of controversy yet, is jet-black, wooly-haired, illiterate; and he is phenomenally forbearing. He has to be; he is black; only through this forbearance can he survive or triumph. (*Cf.* Faulkner's preface to *The Sound and the Fury:* These others were not Compsons. They were black:—They endured.) His triumph is metaphysical, unearthly; since he is black, born without the light, it is only through humility, the incessant mortification of the flesh, that he can enter into communion with God or man. The virtuous rage of Mrs. Stowe is motivated by nothing so temporal as a concern for the relationship of men to one another—or, even, as she would have claimed, by a concern for their relationship to God—but merely by a panic of being hurled into the flames, of being caught in traffic with the devil. She embraced this merciless doctrine with all her heart, bargaining shamelessly before the throne of grace: God and salvation becoming her personal property, purchased with the coin of her virtue. Here, black equates with evil and white with grace; if, being mindful of the necessity of good works, she could not cast out the blacks —a wretched, huddled mass, apparently, claiming, like an obsession, her inner eye—she could not embrace them either without purifying them of sin. She must cover their intimidating nakedness, robe them in white, the garments of salvation; only thus could she herself be delivered from ever-present sin, only thus could she bury, as St. Paul demanded, "the carnal man, the man of the flesh." Tom, therefore, her only black man, has been robbed of his humanity and divested of his sex. It is the price for that darkness with which he has been branded.

Uncle Tom's Cabin, then, is activated by what might be called a theological terror, the terror of damnation; and the spirit that breathes in this book, hot, self-righteous, fearful, is not different from that spirit of medieval times which sought to exorcize evil by burning witches; and is not different from that terror which activates a lynch mob. One need not, indeed, search for examples so historic or so gaudy; this is a warfare waged daily in the heart, a warfare so vast, so relentless and so powerful that the interracial handshake or the interracial marriage can be as crucifying as the public hanging or the secret rape. This panic motivates our cruelty, this fear of the dark makes it impossible that our lives shall be other than superficial; this, interlocked with and feeding our glittering, mechanical, inescapable civilization which has put to death our freedom.

This, notwithstanding that the avowed aim of the American protest novel is to bring greater freedom to the oppressed. They are forgiven, on the strength of these good intentions, whatever violence they do to language, whatever excessive demands they make of credibility. It is, indeed, considered the sign of a frivolity so intense as to approach decadence to suggest that these books are both badly written and wildly improbable.

One is told to put first things first, the good of society coming before niceties of style or characterization. Even if this were incontestable—for what exactly is the "good" of society?—it argues an insuperable confusion, since literature and sociology are not one and the same; it is impossible to discuss them as if they were. Our passion for categorization, life neatly fitted into pegs, has led to an unforeseen, paradoxical distress; confusion, a breakdown of meaning. Those categories which were meant to define and control the world for us have boomeranged us into chaos; in which limbo we whirl, clutching the straws of our definitions. The "protest" novel, so far from being disturbing, is an accepted and comforting aspect of the American scene, ramifying that framework we believe to be so necessary. Whatever unsettling questions are raised are evanescent, titillating; remote, for this has nothing to do with us, it is safely ensconced in the social arena, where, indeed, it has nothing to do with anyone, so that finally we receive a very definite thrill of virtue from the fact that we are reading such a book at all. This report from the pit reassures us of its reality and its darkness and of our own salvation; and "As long as such books are being published," an American liberal once said to me, "everything will be all right."

But unless one's ideal of society is a race of neatly analyzed, hard-working ciphers, one can hardly claim for the protest novels the lofty purpose they claim for themselves or share the present optimism concerning them. They emerge for what they are: a mirror of our confusion, dishonesty, panic, trapped and immobilized in the sunlit prison of the American dream. They are fantasies, connecting nowhere with reality, sentimental; in exactly the same sense that such movies as *The Best Years of Our Lives* or the works of Mr. James M. Cain are fantasies. Beneath the dazzling pyrotechnics of these current operas one may still discern, as the controlling force, the intense theological preoccupations of Mrs. Stowe, the sick vacuities of *The Rover Boys.* Finally, the aim of the protest novel becomes something very closely resembling the zeal of those alabaster missionaries to Africa to cover the nakedness of the natives, to hurry them into the pallid arms of Jesus and thence into slavery. The aim has now become to reduce all Americans to the compulsive, bloodless dimensions of a guy named Joe.

It is the peculiar triumph of society—and its loss—that it is able to convince those people to whom it has given inferior status of the reality of this decree; it has the force and the weapons to translate its dictum into fact, so that the allegedly inferior are actually made so, insofar as the societal realities are concerned. This is a more hidden phenomenon now than it was in the days of serfdom, but it is no less implacable. Now, as then, we find ourselves bound, first without, then within, by the nature of our categorization. And escape is not effected through a bitter railing against this trap; it is as though this very striving were the only motion needed to spring the trap upon us. We take our shape, it is true, within and against that cage of reality bequeathed us at our birth; and yet it is precisely through our dependence on this reality that we are most endlessly betrayed. Society is held together by our need; we bind it together with legend, myth, coercion, fearing that without it we will be hurled into that void, within which, like the earth before the Word was spoken, the foundations of society are hidden. From this void—ourselves—it is the function of society to protect us; but it is only this void, our unknown selves, demanding, forever, a new act of creation, which can save us—"from the evil that is in the world." With the same motion, at the same time, it is this toward which we endlessly struggle and from which, endlessly, we struggle to escape.

It must be remembered that the oppressed and the oppressor are bound together within the same society; they accept the same criteria, they share the same beliefs, they both alike depend on the same reality. Within this cage it is romantic, more, meaningless, to speak of a "new" society as the desire of the oppressed, for that shivering dependence on the props of reality which he shares with the *Herrenvolk* makes a truly "new" society impossible to conceive. What is meant by a new society is one in which inequalities will

disappear, in which vengeance will be exacted; either there will be no oppressed at all, or the oppressed and the oppressor will change places. But, finally, as it seems to me, what the rejected desire is, is an elevation of status, acceptance within the present community. Thus, the African, exile, pagan, hurried off the auction block and into the fields, fell on his knees before that God in Whom he must now believe; who had made him, but not in His image. This tableau, this impossibility, is the heritage of the Negro in America: *Wash me,* cried the slave to his Maker, *and I shall be whiter, whiter than snow!* For black is the color of evil; only the robes of the saved are white. It is this cry, implacable on the air and in the skull, that he must live with. Beneath the widely published catalogue of brutality—bringing to mind, somehow, an image, a memory of church-bells burdening the air—is this reality which, in the same nightmare notion, he both flees and rushes to embrace. In America, now, this country devoted to the death of the paradox—which may, therefore, be put to death by one—his lot is as ambiguous as a tableau by Kafka. To flee or not, to move or not, it is all the same; his doom is written on his forehead, it is carried in his heart. In *Native Son,* Bigger Thomas stands on a Chicago street corner watching airplanes flown by white men racing against the sun and "Goddamn" he says, the bitterness bubbling up like blood, remembering a million indignities, the terrible, rat-infested house, the humiliation of home-relief, the intense, aimless, ugly bickering, hating it; hatred smoulders through these pages like sulphur fire. All of Bigger's life is controlled, defined by his hatred and his fear. And later, his fear drives him to murder and his hatred to rape; he dies, having come, through this violence, we are told, for the first time, to a kind of life, having for the first time redeemed his manhood. Below the surface of this novel there lies, as it seems to me, a continuation, a complement of that monstrous legend it was written to destroy. Bigger is Uncle Tom's descendant, flesh of his flesh, so exactly opposite a portrait that, when the books are placed together, it seems that the contemporary Negro novelist and the dead New England woman are locked together in a deadly, timeless battle; the one uttering merciless exhortations, the other shouting curses. And, indeed, within this web of lust and fury, black and white can only thrust and counter-thrust, long for each other's slow, exquisite death; death by torture, acid, knives and burning; the thrust, the counter-thrust, the longing making the heavier that cloud which blinds and suffocates them both, so that they go down into the pit together. Thus has the cage betrayed us all, this moment, our life, turned to nothing through our terrible attempts to insure it. For Bigger's tragedy is not that he is cold or black or hungry, not even that he is American, black; but that he has accepted a theology that denies him life, that he admits the possibility of his being sub-human and feels constrained, therefore, to battle for his humanity according to those brutal criteria bequeathed him at his birth. But our humanity is our burden, our life; we need not battle for it; we need only to do what is infinitely more difficult—that is, accept it. The failure of the protest novel lies in its rejection of life, the human being, the denial of his beauty, dread, power, in its insistence that it is his categorization alone which is real and which cannot be transcended.

Discussion Questions

1. Is Baldwin saying that there are no Bigger Thomases, that Bigger Thomas is not a fit subject for a novel (even though many exist), or neither?
2. Why are Bigger's creator and Tom's "locked together in a deadly, timeless battle"?
3. What did the black slave truly want, according to Baldwin? Do you see this analysis as true or relevant today?
4. If one of the effects of slavery was to produce a demented mentality, how can a literature that proposes to deal with slavery get beyond the limitations of "the protest novel"?

41   The Black Arts Movement

LARRY NEAL

Study Questions

1. In what ways is the Black Arts Movement an "aesthetic and spiritual sister" to the Black Power concept?
2. Why does the Black Arts concept reject a literature of "protest"?
3. What are the goals of this movement?
4. What philosophy of poetry is suggested by Neal?
5. According to Neal, how does the revolutionary black theater differ from existing white theater?

From *The Black Aesthetic,* Addison Gayle, ed. (New York: Anchor Books, 1971), pp. 926–935.

1.

The Black Arts Movement is radically opposed to any concept of the artist that alienates him from his community. Black Art is the aesthetic and spiritual sister of the Black Power concept. As such, it envisions an art that speaks directly to the needs and aspirations of Black America. In order to perform this task, the Black Arts Movement proposes a radical reordering of the western cultural aesthetic. It proposes a separate symbolism, mythology, critique, and iconology. The Black Arts and the Black Power concept both relate broadly to the Afro-American's desire for self-determination and nationhood. Both concepts are nationalistic. One is concerned with the relationship between art and politics; the other with the art of politics.

Recently, these two movements have begun to merge: the political values inherent in the Black Power concept are now finding concrete expression in the aesthetics of Afro-American dramatists, poets, choreographers, musicians, and novelists. A main tenet of Black Power is the necessity for Black people to define the world in their own terms. The Black artist has made the same point in the context of aesthetics. The two movements postulate that there are in fact and in spirit two Americas—one black, one white. The Black artist takes this to mean that his primary duty is to speak to the spiritual and cultural needs of Black people. Therefore, the main thrust of this new breed of contemporary writers is to confront the contradictions arising out of the Black man's experience in the racist West. Currently, these writers are re-evaluating western aesthetics, the traditional role of the writer, and the social function of art. Implicit in this reevaluation is the need to develop a "black aesthetic." It is the opinion of many Black writers, I among them, that the Western aesthetic has run its course: it is impossible to construct anything meaningful within its decaying structure. We advocate a cultural revolution in art and ideas. The cultural values inherent in western history must either be radicalized or destroyed, and we will probably find that even radicalization is impossible. In fact, what is needed is a whole new system of ideas. Poet Don L. Lee expresses it:

. . . We must destroy Faulkner, dick, jane, and other perpetrators of evil. It's time for Du Bois, Nat Turner, and Kwame Nkrumah. As Frantz Fanon points out: destroy the culture and you destroy the people. This must not happen. Black artists are culture stabilizers; bringing back old values, and introducing new ones. Black Art will talk to the eople and with the will of the people stop impending "protective custody."

The Black Arts Movement eschews "protest" literature. It speaks directly to Black people. Implicit in the concept of "protest" literature, as

Brother Knight has made clear, is an appeal to white morality:

Now any Black man who masters the technique of his particular art form, who adheres to the white aesthetic, and who directs his work toward a white audience is, in one sense, protesting. And implicit in the act of protest is the belief that a change will be forthcoming once the masters are aware of the protestor's "grievance" (the very word connotes begging, supplications to the gods). Only when that belief has faded and protestings end, will Black art begin.

Brother Knight also has some interesting statements about the development of a "Black aesthetic":

Unless the Black artist establishes a "Black aesthetic" he will have no future at all. To accept the white aesthetic is to accept and validate a society that will not allow him to live. The Black artist must create new forms and new values, sing new songs (or purify old ones); and along with other Black authorities, he must create a new history, new symbols, myths and legends (and purify old ones by fire). And the Black artist, in creating his own aesthetic, must be accountable for it only to the Black people. Further, he must hasten his own dissolution as an individual (in the Western sense)—painful though the process may be, having been breast-fed the poison of "individual experience."

When we speak of a "Black aesthetic" several things are meant. First, we assume that there is already in existence the basis for such an aesthetic. Essentially, it consists of an African-American cultural tradition. But this aesthetic is finally, by implication, broader than that tradition. It encompasses most of the useable elements of Third World culture. The motive behind the Black aesthetic is the destruction of the white thing, the destruction of white ideas, and white ways of looking at the world. The new aesthetic is mostly predicated on an Ethics which asks the question: whose vision of the world is finally more meaningful, ours or the white oppressors? What is truth? Or more precisely, whose truth shall we express, that of the oppressed or of the oppressors? These are basic questions. Black intellectuals of previous decades failed to ask them. Further, national and international affairs demand that we appraise the world in terms of our own interests. It is clear that the question of human survival is at the core of contemporary experience. The Black artist must address himself to this reality in the strongest terms possible. In a context of world upheaval, ethics and aesthetics must interact positively and be consistent with the demands for a more spiritual world. Consequently, the Black Arts Movement is an ethical movement. Ethical, that is, from the viewpoint of the oppressed. And much of the oppression confronting the Third World and Black America is directly traceable to the Euro-American cultural sensibility. This sensibility, anti-human in nature, has, until recently, dominated the psyches of most Black artists and intellectuals; it must be destroyed before the Black creative artist can have a meaningful role in the transformation of society.

It is this natural reaction to an alien sensibility that informs the cultural attitudes of the Black Arts and the Black Power movement. It is a profound ethical sense that makes a Black artist question a society in which art is one thing and the actions of men another. The Black Arts Movement believes that your ethics and your aesthetics are one. That the contradictions between ethics and aesthetics in western society is symptomatic of a dying culture.

The term "Black Arts" is of ancient origin, but it was first used in a positive sense by LeRoi Jones [Amiri Baraka]:

> We are unfair
> And unfair
> We are black magicians
> Black arts we make
> in black labs of the heart
>
> The fair are fair
> and deathly white
>
> The day will not save them
> And we own the night

There is also a section of the poem "Black Dada Nihilismus" that carries the same motif. But a fuller amplification of the nature of the new aesthetics appear in the poem "Black Art":

> Poems are bullshit unless they are
> teeth or trees or lemons piled

on a step. Or black ladies dying
of men leaving nickel hearts
beating them down. Fuck poems
and they are useful, would they shoot
come at you, love what you are,
breathe like wrestlers, or shudder
strangely after peeing. We want live
words of the hip world, live flesh &
coursing blood. Hearts and Brains
Souls splintering fire. We want poems
like fists beating niggers out of Jocks
or dagger poems in the slimy bellies
of the owner-jews . . .

Poetry is a concrete function, an action. No more abstractions. Poems are physical entities: fists, daggers, airplane poems, and poems that shoot guns. Poems are transformed from physical objects into personal forces:

> . . . Put it on him poem. Strip him naked
> to the world. Another bad poem cracking
> steel knuckles in a jewlady's mouth
> Poem scream poison gas on breasts in green
>   berets . . .

Then the poem affirms the integral relationship between Black Art and Black people:

> . . . Let Black people understand
> that they are the lovers and the sons
> of lovers and warriors and sons
> of warriors Are poems & poets &
> all the loveliness here in the world

It ends with the following lines, a central assertion in both the Black Arts Movement and the philosophy of Black Power:

> We want a black poem. And a
> Black World.
> Let the world be a Black Poem
> And let All Black People Speak This Poem
> Silently
> Or LOUD

The poem comes to stand for the collective conscious and unconscious of Black America—the real impulse in back of the Black Power movement, which is the will toward self-determination and nationhood, a radical reordering of the nature and function of both art and the artist.

2.

In the spring of 1964, LeRoi Jones, Charles Patterson, William Patterson, Clarence Reed, Johnny Moore, and a number of other Black artists opened the Black Arts Repertoire Theatre School. They produced a number of plays including Jones's *Experimental Death Unit # One, Black Mass, Jello,* and *Dutchman.* They also initiated a series of poetry readings and concerts. These activities represented the most advanced tendencies in the movement and were of excellent artistic quality. The Black Arts School came under immediate attack by the New York power structure. The Establishment, fearing Black creativity, did exactly what it was expected to do—it attacked the theatre and all of its values. In the meantime, the school was granted funds by OEO [Office of Economic Opportunity] through HARYOU-ACT. Lacking a cultural program itself, HARYOU turned to the only organization which addressed itself to the needs of the community. In keeping with its "revolutionary" cultural ideas, the Black Arts Theatre took its programs into the streets of Harlem. For three months, the theatre presented plays, concerts, and poetry readings to the people of the community. Plays that shattered the illusions of the American body politic, and awakened Black people to the meaning of their lives.

Then the hawks from the OEO moved in and chopped off the funds: Again, this should have been expected. The Black Arts Theatre stood in radical opposition to the feeble attitudes about culture of the "War on Poverty" bureaucrats. And later, because of internal problems, the theatre was forced to close. But the Black Arts group proved that the community could be served by a valid and dynamic art. It also proved that there was a definite need for a cultural revolution in the Black community.

With the closing of the Black Arts Theatre, the implications of what Brother Jones and his colleagues were trying to do took on even more sig-

nificance. Black Art groups sprang up on the West Coast and the idea spread to Detroit, Philadelphia, Jersey City, New Orleans, and Washington, D.C. Black Arts movements began on the campuses of San Francisco State College, Fisk University, Lincoln University, Hunter College in the Bronx, Columbia University, and Oberlin College. In Watts, after the rebellion, Maulana Karenga welded the Black Arts Movement into a cohesive cultural ideology which owed much to the work of LeRoi Jones. Karenga sees culture as the most important element in the struggle for self-determination:

> Culture is the basis of all ideas, images and actions. To move is to move culturally, i.e. by a set of values given to you by your culture.
> Without a culture Negroes are only a set of reactions to white people.
> The seven criteria for culture are:
> 1. Mythology
> 2. History
> 3. Social Organization
> 4. Political Organization
> 5. Economic Organization
> 6. Creative Motif
> 7. Ethos

In drama, LeRoi Jones represents the most advanced aspects of the movement. He is its prime mover and chief designer. In a poetic essay entitled "The Revolutionary Theatre," he outlines the iconology of the movement:

> The Revolutionary Theatre should force change: it should be change. (All their faces turned into the lights and you work on them black nigger magic, and cleanse them at having seen the ugliness. And if the beautiful see themselves, they will love themselves.) We are preaching virtue again, but by that to mean NOW, toward what seems the most constructive use of the word.

The theatre that Jones proposes is inextricably linked to the Afro-American political dynamic. And such a link is perfectly consistent with Black America's contemporary demands. For theatre is potentially the most social of all of the arts. It is an integral part of the socializing process. It exists in direct relationship to the audience it claims to serve. The decadence and inanity of the contemporary American theatre is an accurate reflection of the state of American society. Albee's *Who's*

Afraid of Virginia Woolf? is very American: sick white lives in a homosexual hell hole. The theatre of white America is escapist, refusing to confront concrete reality. Into this cultural emptiness come the musicals, an up-tempo version of the same stale lives. And the use of Negroes in such plays as *Hello Dolly* and *Hallelujah Baby* does not alter their nature; it compounds the problem. These plays are simply hipper versions of the minstrel show. They present Negroes acting out the hang-ups of middle-class white America. Consequently, the American theatre is a palliative prescribed to bourgeois patients who refuse to see the world as it is. Or, more crucially, as the world sees them. It is no accident, therefore, that the most "important" plays come from Europe—Brecht, Weiss, and Ghelderode. And even these have begun to run dry.

The Black Arts theatre, the theatre of LeRoi Jones, is a radical alternative to the sterility of the American theatre. It is primarily a theatre of the Spirit, confronting the Black man in his interaction with his brothers and with the white thing.

Our theatre will show victims so that their brothers in the audience will be better able to understand that they are the brothers of victims, and that they themselves are blood brothers. And what we show must cause the blood to rush, so that pre-revolutionary temperaments will be bathed in this blood, and it will cause their deepest souls to move, and they will find themselves tensed and clenched, even ready to die, at what the soul has been taught. We will scream and cry, murder, run through the streets in agony, if it means some soul will be moved, moved to actual life understanding of what the world is, and what it ought to be. We are preaching virtue and feeling, and a natural sense of the self in the world. All men live in the world, and the world ought to be a place for them to live.

The victims in the world of Jones's early plays are Clay, murdered by the white bitch-goddess in *Dutchman,* and Walker Vessels, the revolutionary in *The Slave.* Both of these plays present Black men in transition. Clay, the middle-class Negro trying to get himself a little action from Lula, digs himself and his own truth only to get murdered after telling her like it really is:

Just let me bleed you, you loud whore, and one poem vanished. A whole people neurotics, struggling to keep from being sane. And the only thing that would cure the neurosis would be your murder. Simple as that. I mean if I murdered you, then other white people would understand me. You understand? No. I guess not. If Bessie Smith had killed some white people she wouldn't needed that music. She could have talked very straight and plain about the world. Just straight two and two are four. Money. Power. Luxury. Like that. All of them. Crazy niggers turning their back on sanity. When all it needs is that simple act. Just murder. Would make us all sane.

But Lula understands, and she kills Clay first. In a perverse way it is Clay's nascent knowledge of himself that threatens the existence of Lula's idea of the world. Symbolically, and in fact, the relationship between Clay (Black America) and Lula (white America) is rooted in the historical castration of black manhood. And in the twisted psyche of white America, the Black man is both an object of love and hate. Analogous attitudes exist in most Black Americans, but for decidedly different reasons. Clay is doomed when he allows himself to participate in Lula's "fantasy" in the first place. It is the fantasy to which Frantz Fanon alludes in *The Wretched of the Earth* and *Black Skins, White Mask:* the native's belief that he can acquire the oppressor's power by acquiring his symbols, one of which is the white woman. When Clay finally digs himself it is too late.

Walker Vessels, in *The Slave,* is Clay reincarnated as the revolutionary confronting problems inherited from his contact with white culture. He returns to the home of his ex-wife, a white woman, and her husband, a literary critic. The play is essentially about Walker's attempt to destroy his white past. For it is the past, with all of its painful memories, that is really the enemy of the revolutionary. It is impossible to move until history is either recreated or comprehended. Unlike Todd, in Ralph Ellison's *Invisible Man,* Walker cannot fall outside history. Instead, Walker demands a confrontation with history, a final shattering of bullshit illusions. His only salvation lies in confronting the physical and psychological forces that have made him and his people powerless. Therefore, he comes to understand that the world must be restructured along spiritual imperatives. But in the interim it is basically a question of *who* has power:

Easley: You're so wrong about everything. So terribly, sickeningly wrong. What can you change? What do you hope to change? Do you think Negroes are better people than whites . . . that they can govern a society better than whites? That they'll be more judicious or more tolerant? Do you think they'll make fewer mistakes? I mean really, if the Western white man has proved one thing . . . it's the futility of modern society. So the have-not peoples become the haves. Even so, will that change the essential functions of the world? Will there be more love or beauty in the world . . . more knowledge . . . because of it?

Walker: Probably. Probably there will be more . . . if more people have a chance to understand what it is. But that's not even the point. It comes down to baser human endeavor than any social-political thinking. What does it matter if there's more love or beauty? Who the fuck cares? Is that what the Western ofay thought while he was ruling . . . that his rule somehow brought more love and beauty into the world? Oh, he might have thought that concomitantly, while sipping a gin rickey and scratching his ass . . . but that was not ever the point. Not even on the Crusades. The point is that you had your chance, darling, now these other folks have theirs. [Quietly.] Now they have theirs.

Easley: God, what an ugly idea.

This confrontation between the black radical and the white liberal is symbolic of larger confrontations occurring between the Third World and Western society. It is a confrontation between the colonizer and the colonized, the slave-master and the slave. Implicit in Easley's remarks is the belief that the white man is culturally and politically superior to the Black Man. Even though Western society has been traditionally violent in its relation with the Third World, it sanctimoniously deplores violence or self-assertion on the part of the enslaved. And the Western mind, with clever rationalizations, equates the violence of the oppressed with the violence of the oppressor. So that when the native preaches self-determination, the Western white man cleverly

misconstrues it to mean hate of *all* white men. When the Black political radical warns his people not to trust white politicians of the left and the right, but instead to organize separately on the basis of power, the white man cries: "racism in reverse." Or he will say, as many of them do today: "We deplore both white and black racism." As if the two could be equated.

There is a minor element in *The Slave* which assumes great importance in a later play entitled *Jello*. Here I refer to the emblem of Walker's army: a red-mouthed grinning field slave. The revolutionary army has taken one of the most hated symbols of the Afro-American past and radically altered its meaning.* This is the supreme act of freedom, available only to those who have liberated themselves psychically. Jones amplifies this inversion of emblem and symbol in *Jello* by making Rochester (Ratfester) of the old Jack Benny (Penny) program into a revolutionary nationalist. Ratfester, ordinarily the supreme embodiment of the Uncle Tom Clown, surprises Jack Penny by turning on the other side of the nature of the Black man. He skillfully, and with an evasive black humor, robs Penny of all of his money. But Ratfester's actions are "moral." That is to say, Ratfester is getting his back pay; payment of a long over-due debt to the Black man. Ratfester's sensibilities are different from Walker's. He is *blues people* smiling and shuffling while trying to figure out how to destroy the white thing. And like the blues man, he is the master of the understatement. Or in the Afro-American folk tradition, he is the signifying Monkey, Shine, and Stagolee all rolled into one. There are no stereotypes any

---

* In Jones's study of Afro-American music, *Blues People,* we find the following observation: "Even the adjective *funky,* which once meant to many Negroes merely a stink (usually associated with sex), was used to qualify the music as meaningful (the word became fashionable and is now almost useless). The social implication, then, was that even the old stereotype of a distinctive Negro smell that white America subscribed to could be turned against white America. For this smell now, real or not, was made a valuable characteristic of 'Negro-ness.' And 'Negro-ness,' by the fifties, for many Negroes (and whites) was the only strength left to American culture."

more. History has killed Uncle Tom. Because even Uncle Tom has a breaking point beyond which he will not be pushed. Cut deeply enough into the most docile Negro, and you will find a conscious murderer. Behind the lyrics of the blues and the shuffling porter loom visions of white throats being cut and cities burning.

Jones's particular power as a playwright does not rest solely on his revolutionary vision, but is instead derived from his deep lyricism and spiritual outlook. In many ways, he is fundamentally more a poet than a playwright. And it is his lyricism that gives body to his plays. Two important plays in this regard are *Black Mass* and *Slave Ship*. *Black Mass* is based on the Muslim myth of Yacub. According to this myth, Yacub, a Black scientist, developed the means of grafting different colors of the Original Black Nation until a White Devil was created. In *Black Mass,* Yacub's experiments produce a raving White Beast who is condemned to the coldest regions of the North. The other magicians implore Yacub to cease his experiments. But he insists on claiming the primacy of scientific knowledge over spiritual knowledge. The sensibility of the White Devil is alien, informed by lust and sensuality. The Beast is the consummate embodiment of evil, the beginning of the historical subjugation of the spiritual world.

Black Mass takes place in some pre-historical time. In fact, the concept of time, we learn, is the creation of an alien sensibility, that of the Beast. This is a deeply weighted play, a colloquy on the nature of man, and the relationship between legitimate spiritual knowledge and scientific knowledge. It is LeRoi Jones's most important play mainly because it is informed by a mythology that is wholly the creation of the Afro-American sensibility.

Further, Yacub's creation is not merely a scientific exercise. More fundamentally, it is the aesthetic impulse gone astray. The Beast is created merely for the sake of creation. Some artists assert a similar claim about the nature of art. They argue that art need not have a function. It is against this decadent attitude toward art—ramified throughout most of Western society—that the play militates.

Yacub's real crime, therefore, is the introduction of a meaningless evil into a harmonious universe. The evil of the Beast is pervasive, corrupting everything and everyone it touches. The play ends with destruction of the holy place of the Black Magicians. Now the Beast and his descendants roam the earth. An off-stage voice chants a call for the Jihan to begin. It is then that myth merges into legitimate history, and we, the audience, come to understand that all history is merely someone's version of mythology.

Slave Ship presents a more immediate confrontation with history. In a series of expressionistic tableaux it depicts the horrors and the madness of the Middle Passage. It then moves through the period of slavery, early attempts at revolt, tendencies toward Uncle Tom–like reconciliation and betrayal, and the final act of liberation. There is no definite plot (LeRoi calls it a pageant), just a continuous rush of sound, groans, screams, and souls wailing for freedom and relief from suffering. This work has special affinities with the New Music of Sun Ra, John Coltrane, Albert Ayler, and Ornette Coleman. Events are blurred, rising and falling in a stream of sound. Almost cinematically, the images flicker and fade against a heavy back-drop of rhythm. The language is spare, stripped to the essential. It is a play which almost totally eliminates the need for a text. It functions on the basis of movements and energy—the dramatic equivalent of the New Music.

Slave Ship's energy is, at base, ritualistic. As a matter of fact, to see the play any other way is to miss the point. All the New York reviewers, with the possible exception of John Lahr, were completely cut off from this central aspect of the play when it was performed at the Brooklyn Academy under the brilliant direction of Gilbert Moses. One of the prime motivations behind the work is to suck the audience into a unique and very precise universe. The episodes of this "pageant" do not appear as strict interpretations of history. Rather, what we are digging is ritualized history. That is, history that allows emotional and religious participation on the part of the audience. And, like all good ritual, its purpose is to make the audience stronger, more sensitive to the historical realities that have shaped our lives and the lives of our ancestors. The play acts to extend memory. For black people to forget the realities posed by *Slave Ship* is to fall prey to an existential paralysis. History, like the blues, demands that we witness the painful events of our prior lives; and that we either confront these painful events or be destroyed by them.

Discussion Questions

1. What if the "community" properly served by the revolutionary black artist is not receptive to his or her revolutionary message. What then?
2. In his contribution in Reading 48 of this volume, black theologian Victor Anderson criti-cizes definitions of "blackness" couched in terms of common oppression by whites. He holds that this is a merely negative. To what extent can Neal be criticized along these lines?
3. Is it true that all genuine black art, or art generally, should serve a political (revolutionary) function?
4. Given its social goals and orientation, should the Black Arts Movement ignore or be critical of white art?
5. Baraka's poetry, while very much his own in content, owes much in style to the "beat poetry" of the 1950s. Arguably, it owes more to this than to any African model. Does this invalidate it as black art?

42   Billie Holiday's "Strange Fruit": Music and Social Consciousness

ANGELA Y. DAVIS

Study Questions

1. How did "Strange Fruit" mark a break with Billie Holiday's previous work?
2. How does "Strange Fruit" exemplify Davis' definition of "great art"?
3. What central event within Billie Holiday's own life personalized the issues of racism and lynching for her?
4. What dominant feeling were Holiday's performances of "Strange Fruit" trying to evoke?

Southern trees bear a strange fruit
Blood on the leaves, blood at the root
Black bodies swinging in the Southern breeze
Strange fruit hanging from the poplar trees
Pastoral scene of the gallant South
The bulging eyes and the twisted mouth
Scent of magnolia sweet and fresh

Then the sudden smell of burning flesh
Here is a fruit for the crows to pluck
For the rain to gather, for the wind to suck
For the sun to rot, for the tree to drop
Here is a strange and bitter crop.

This song, which Billie Holiday called her "personal protest" against the death-bringing ravages of racism, was destined to radically transform her status in American popular culture. If she had been previously acknowledged by the giants in her field as a brilliant innovator in jazz vocals, "Strange Fruit" would establish her as an unsurpassed aesthetic cultivator of social consciousness. Although she was only twenty-four years old when she recorded this song and integrated it into her performance repertoire, she had been striving for some time to reach beyond the circles of musicians and jazz cognoscenti who had faithfully and generously praised her work, in order to offer her art to the public at large. Yet, she staunchly refused to mar her art with tinges of commerciality which might have brought her the popular success for which she longed. She seemed to instinctively recognize that her musi-

Reprinted from *Political Affairs* 67 (1988), pp. 5–12.

cal genius was destined to serve a profound social purpose, for when she became aware of the impact of "Strange Fruit," she reconceptualized her role as a popular singer.

Prior to "Strange Fruit," the overwhelming majority of her music consisted of contemporary popular tunes, most of whose lyrics tended to be mediocre, if not downright trite. It was her unique phrasing, her striking transformations of original melodies and the timbre of her voice which elevated these songs to the status of art. She forged new content for these tunes by working wonders on the levels of form and technique. Now here was a song whose content had urgent and far-reaching implications—a song about hate, indignities and eruptions of violence which threatened every Afro-American in the country. Here was a song which could potentially awaken vast numbers of people—Black and white alike—from their apolitical slumber.

I worked like the devil on it because I was never sure I could put it across or that I could get across to a plush nightclub audience the things that it meant to me.[1]

As long as her work appeared to be without manifest social content (and indeed, it only appeared to be so), she was lavishly praised by critics, whose belief in the "universality" of art presumptuously excluded themes relating to the collective struggles of Black people. Since "Strange Fruit" was unambiguously designed to prick the consciences of those who preferred to remain oblivious to the racist malevolence afflicting this land, it was inevitable that many critics would dismiss it as blatant propaganda, undeserving of the rubric of art. However, Billie Holiday needed no complicated aesthetic theories to grasp the artistic greatness of this work and to instinctively understand that "Strange Fruit" would render explicit the social function of her music in general.

Great art never achieves its greatness through an act of absolute transcendence of socio-historical reality. On the contrary, even as it transcends specific circumstances, it is deeply rooted in social realities. Its function precisely is to fashion new perspectives on the human condition—in its specificity and in its generality. "Strange Fruit" contained very specific references to the horrors of lynching at a time when Afro-Americans were still

passionately calling for allies to assist in the campaign to eradicate this murderous manifestation of racism. At the same time, Billie Holiday's rendition expressed a universal condemnation of all assaults on the rights and lives of human beings.

During the 1930s, apologists for what was so cavalierly referred to as "American Democracy" attempted to pretend that the institution of lynching was merely a blemish on the country's past. While it was true that the lives of Afro-Americans were no longer systematically consumed by mob-violence in numbers that mounted into the thousands, as had been the case during the decades following emancipation, this did not mean that the hundreds of contemporary lynch victims could be brushed aside as insignificant. During the four years following the Stock Market crash in 1929, 150 Black people were lynched.[2] In the fall of 1934, a mere five years before Lady Day's encounter with the poem "Strange Fruit," a lynching occurred in Florida which should remain indelibly impressed on the memories of all who presume to understand the history of the United States. According to a newspaper account of the time,

An eye-witness to the lynching . . . said that [Claude] Neal had been forced to mutilate himself before he died. The eye-witnesses gave the following account of the event which took place in a swamp beside the Chattahoochee River:

". . . first they cut off his penis. He was made to eat it. Then they cut off his testicles and made him eat them and say he liked it.

"Then they sliced his sides and stomach with knives and every now and then somebody would cut off a finger or a toe. Red hot irons were used on the n-----[deletion by Ed.] to burn him from top to bottom. From time to time during the torture, a rope would be tied around Neal's neck and he was pulled over a limb and held there until he almost choked to death, when he would be let down and the torture begun all over again. After several hours of this punishment, they decided to kill him.

"Neal's body was tied to a rope on the rear of an automobile and dragged over the highway to the Cannidy home. Here a mob estimated to number somewhere between 3,000 to 7,000 people from eleven southern states was excitedly awaiting his arrival. . . .

"A woman came out of the Cannidy house and drove a butcher knife into his heart. Then the crowd came by and some kicked him and some drove their cars over him."

What remained of the body was brought by the mob to Marianna where it is now hanging from a tree on the northeast corner of the courthouse square.

Photographers say they will soon have pictures of the body for sale at fifty cents each. Fingers and toes from Neal's body are freely exhibited on streetcorners here.[3]

Billie Holiday may never have witnessed such abominations firsthand, but she certainly grasped the connections between lynching, which constitutes one extreme of the spectrum of racism, and the daily routines of biases and prejudices which affect in some way every member of the Afro-American population. She apprehended in her own way a dynamic described by Franz Fanon when he wrote:

One can not say that a given country is racist but that lynchings or extermination camps are not to be found there. The truth is that all that and still other things exist on the horizon. These virtualities, these latent tendencies circulate, carried by the life-stream of psycho-affective, economic relations.[4]

If the spectre of lynchings irrevocably conjured up other forms of racism, the lyrics of "Strange Fruit" immediately led Billie Holiday to reflect upon the circumstances of her father's death. When Lewis Allen showed her the poem he had written with the idea in mind of setting it to music, she said, "I dug it right off. It seemed to spell out all the things that had killed Pop."[5] Her father, jazz guitarist Clarence Holiday, had inhaled poison gas, during a battle in World War I, which caused him to have chronic lung problems. In March of 1937, while on tour in Texas with Don Redman's band, he developed a chest cold for which he received no treatment because of the segregation practices of the hospitals in that state. By the time the band reached Dallas, where he was able to seek medical attention, he had already contracted pneumonia and he died of a hemorrhage in the Jim Crow ward of the Veterans Hospital.[6] From Billie Holiday's perspective, to sing "Strange Fruit" was to release a passionate cry of protest against the racism which had killed her father.

Of course, Billie Holiday's gift of aesthetic communication did not simply consist in her ability to render in song the profound emotions underlying her own private woes. However skilfull she may have been in musically transmitting her own state of mind, this could never have served as the foundation for her greatness as an artist. While eloquently incorporating the emotions occasioned by her own personal tragedies in her songs, her particular condition functioned as a conduit permitting others to acquire insights about the emotional and social circumstances of their own lives. For Black people and their politically conscious white allies, "Strange Fruit" affirmed not only the existence of lynching and the web of racist institutions within which the abomination of lynching resided. It also signified the possibility and necessity of challenging and eventually eradicating this age-old oppression. For those who had not grasped the meaning of American racism, "Strange Fruit" functioned as a compelling statement of fact. As Bert Korall said of Billie Holiday in general, she

. . . so illuminated human situations as to give the listener a rare, if frightening, glimpse into the realities of experience. Where others fear to tread, she reached out and touched, where others mask their eyes, she defiantly kept hers open.[7]

Invariably, some people had been so hardened by racism as to be impervious to her message. In a Los Angeles club, a woman requested that Billie sing "Strange Fruit" by saying, ". . . why don't you sing that sexy song you're famous for? You know, the one about naked bodies swinging in the trees?"[8] Needless to say, in such situations, for the sake of preserving the song's dignity, she refused to sing it.

In general, however, "Strange Fruit" rose out of socio-historical circumstances which provided the best backdrop, since the brief period of Radical Reconstruction, for the reception of such an impassioned plea for racial justice. If the 1920s had allowed for an expanding awareness of Afro-American art and culture in the wider population (even though this awareness was marred by racist notions of Black culture as "primitive" and "exotic"), the 1930s saw the emergence of important political and multi-racial alliances.

Organized challenges to lynching dated back to the turn-of-the-century efforts of Ida B. Wells. However, the ideological climate of the period, as well as through World War I and well into the 1920s, was so poisoned by racism that substantial numbers of white people could not be drawn into the anti-lynching campaigns. Billie Holiday's "Strange Fruit" echoed through circles of people who had been sensitized both by the trans-racial economic and social tragedies of the Great Depression and by the multi-racial mass movements seeking to redress the myriad grievances of Black and white alike.

Before the great movements of the 1930s and the consequent radicalization of large sectors of the population, "Strange Fruit" as a phenomenon would have been inconceivable. Indeed, an inter-racial night club like Cafe Society, where the song was born, would not have been viable at any other time. Barney Josephson, who opened this club at a time when even in Harlem Black and white people could not listen to jazz under the same roof, told Billie that ". . . this was to be one club where there was going to be no segregation, no racial prejudice."[9] And, in fact according to Holiday's biographer, John Chilton:

The liberal atmosphere of the club, with its clientele of "New Dealers," and the humanitarian principles of its owner made it a receptive setting for the presentation of the song's dramatic anti-lynching lyrics.[10]

If white people had developed a greater sensitivity to the plight of Afro-Americans, it was perhaps because enormous numbers of them had experienced in one form or another the devastation of the Great Depression. Workers' wages were cut almost in half and, by the last crisis year, seventeen million people were unemployed. Even more essential to the development of this sensitivity were the great mass movements which emerged during the 1930s—the campaign against unemployment and the extensive organizing of industrial unions associated with the CIO. The Communist Party, the Young Communist League and the Trade Union Unity League joined forces to establish the National Unemployed Councils, which were responsible for spectacular demon-

strations throughout the country. On March 6, 1930, well over a million people participated in hunger marches in major urban centers—110,000 in New York, 100,000 in Detroit, for example. In December of 1931 and 1932, national hunger marches to Washington dramatized demands for unemployment insurance and other means of bringing relief to the unemployed.[11]

Such mass opposition to the anti-worker policies of the Hoover Administration played a pivotal role in the election of Franklin D. Roosevelt and the subsequent inauguration of the New Deal. Far from pacifying those who suffered the effects of the Great Depression, the New Deal served as a further catalyst for the organization of multi-racial mass movements. Black people, in particular, were hardly satisfied with the sedatives offered them by the New Deal Legislation. One of the most consequential of the mass organizations initiated during the Roosevelt years was the American Youth Congress (AYC), founded in 1934. Although the government was responsible for the inception of the AYC, the more than four and a half million young people who joined it before the outbreak of the war in 1939 could not be contained by the policies of the government. Young Afro-Americans, especially in the South, played an indispensable part in developing the strategic direction of this organization. The Southern Negro Youth Congress, according to William Z. Foster, was "the most important movement ever conducted by Negro youth"[12] before the era of the Civil Rights Movement.

It pioneered many of the constructive developments . . . in the South—including the right-to-vote movement, the unionization of Southern industry, the fight for the right of education and the general struggle against lynching and all forms of Jim Crow.[13]

As a result of the work of the American Youth Congress, the issue of federal anti-lynching legislation was placed on the national political agenda for the first time in the twentieth century since the thwarted efforts of the NAACP to secure the passage of an anti-lynching bill in 1921. Consequently, when Billie Holiday sang "Strange Fruit" in 1939, her message fell upon many ears that had long since been rendered receptive by the AYC's demand that the Roosevelt Administration support the enactment of a law against lynching.

This is not to say that Billie Holiday herself was necessarily aware of the political developments of the thirties which served as the backdrop for her own cultural contributions. She was not the only artist swept into the stream of political radicalization who was incognizant of all the political ramifications of her own work. The Thirties, according to Phillip Bonosky, constituted a "watershed in the American democratic tradition."

It is a period which will continue to serve both the present and the future as a reminder and as an example of how an aroused people, led and spurred by the working class, can change the entire complexion of the culture of a nation.[14]

Bonosky continues,

This period, for the first time in American history, saw the fundamental placing of the Negro and Jewish questions, which brought them out of the murky realm of private and personal ethics to their real roots in a class society. . . . [It] saw a dramatic change in every aspect of culture—its most characteristic feature being the discovery of the organic relationship between the intellectual and the people—the workers first of all.[15]

Although Billie Holiday was not directly associated with the artists' and cultural workers' movements related to the Works Progress Administration (WPA), she was clearly conscious of the need for radical change in the status of Black people in U.S. society. On countless occasions, she was herself the target of vitriolic expressions of racism. As a Black vocalist with Artie Shaw's all-white band, she encountered the crassness of Jim Crow on a daily basis when the band toured the Southern states. In Kentucky, for example, a small-town sheriff who tried his best to prevent her from performing, finally came up to the bandstand and asked Shaw, "What's Blackie going to sing?"[16] In St. Louis, the man who had hired the band to play in one of the city's largest ballrooms confronted Billie by saying, "What's that n----- [deletion by Ed.] doing there? I don't have n-----s [deletion by Ed.] to clean up around here."[17] Needless to say, there were numerous incidents

surrounding her hotel rooms and the eating establishments where she attempted to buy meals. "I got to the point where I hardly ever ate, slept or went to the bathroom without having a major NAACP-type production."[18]

Sometimes we'd make a six-hundred-mile jump and stop only once. Then it would be a place where I couldn't get served, let alone crash the toilet without causing a scene. At first I used to be ashamed. Then finally I just said to hell with it. When I had to go, I'd just ask the bus driver to stop and let me off at the side of the road. I'd rather go into the bushes than take a chance in the restaurants and towns.[19]

Billie Holiday's social consciousness was deeply rooted in her own experiences—and she had indeed experienced more than her share of racism. While she was not one to engage in any extended political analyses, she never attempted to conceal where her loyalties were. "I'm a race woman,"[20] she proclaimed on numerous occasions. According to Josh White, who developed a friendship with her after an initial collision surrounding his performance of "Strange Fruit," "she had more thought for humanity and was more race-conscious than people thought."[21]

Billie Holiday's unique ability to imbue her music with authentic human feelings and thus to touch the hearts of all who had the privilege of hearing her was more evident in her singing of "Strange Fruit" than any other song. And this song posed a number of serious problems with respect to its rendering. With its forceful metaphors, an overly dramatic rendering might have transformed its powerful emotional content into histrionics. The intent behind this song—both Allen's and Holiday's—was to invoke the emotions of solidarity with its auditors. Unfortunately sometimes, art with this intent misses the aim and instead occasions feelings of pity. If those who were touched by "Strange Fruit" exited from the experience of feeling pity for Afro-American victims of racism, instead of solidarity and compassion, the underlying dynamics of racism would have been reduplicated instead of challenged. For white people thus moved by the song, the superiority of the white race would have been implicitly affirmed. But unless one is an incurable racist, it is difficult to listen to Billie Holiday's rendering of "Strange Fruit" without sensing the plea for human solidarity—equality even in the process of challenging racist horrors and indignities. One is able to identify with the "Black bodies swinging in the southern breeze" as human beings who deserve the right to live and love. "The lyric is stark and moving," as John Chilton put it,

and Billie wrings every ounce of emotion from the terrifying description of Black bodies hanging from the trees. Billie's supreme artistry ensures that there is no melodrama.[22]

Glenn Coulter writes about

[the] uncanny expression of horror which transcends its willful lyric when Billie sings it, and becomes a frozen lament, a paralysis of feeling truer to psychology than any conventional emotionalism could be.[23]

If Billie Holiday ushered into popular music culture a new and original approach to singing, her decision to feature "Strange Fruit" as the centerpiece of her work established the basis for a tradition that was taken up later by musicians such as Nina Simone, whose "Mississippi Goddam" became an anthem of the Civil Rights era. "Strange Fruit" was a frontal challenge not only to lynching and racism, but to the policies of a government which implicitly condoned such actions, especially in its refusal thus far to secure the passage of laws against lynching. It was an undisguised rallying cry against the state. "The message of Lewis Allen's poem," in the words of jazz critic Leonard Feather,

had a meaning more vital than any of the soufflé-songs she had been handed by record producers. This was the first significant protest in words and music, the first unmuted cry against racism. It was radical and defiant at a time when Blacks and whites alike found it dangerous to make waves, to speak out against a deeply entrenched status quo.[24]

Joachim Berendt called it

the most emphatic and most impassioned musical testimony against racism to become known before Abbey Lincoln's interpretation of Max Roach's "Freedom Now Suite" of 1960.[25]

"Strange Fruit" became a permanent piece in Billie Holiday's repertoire and, of more than 350 songs she sang, this one remains inextricably connected to the prevailing image of Lady Day. However, at the time, she was unable to convince Columbia, the recording company with which she was under contract, to permit her to record it. "They won't buy it in the South," was the company's response. "We'll be boycotted. . . . It's too inflammatory."[26] Billie persisted, however, and eventually John Hammond released her for one recording date with Commodore, whose head, Milt Gabler agreed to record it.

Billie Holiday's recording of "Strange Fruit" achieved something far greater than permanent preservation of her most important song, the aesthetic centerpiece of her career. Eventually millions would hear her sing this haunting anti-lynching appeal, and few not feel edified. People of many races, cultures and nations would be moved and simultaneously educated—thus fulfilling the artist's goal of lifting her listeners' consciousness. Yet, many others would be more deeply touched by Lady Day's musical protest than she could ever imagine. Would she have predicted that "Strange Fruit" would impel people to discover within themselves a previously unawakened calling to political activism? Or could she have understood how artists with incorruptible aesthetic principles would be inspired by this song to realize how passionately political their work could be without compromising an ounce of their aesthetic integrity? And could she have even sensed that catalytic role her song would play in rejuvenating a tradition of anti-lynching and anti-racist literature which had been initiated in the nineteenth century by such great abolitionists as Frances E. W. Harper? No, Lady Day could not have begun to fathom the vast influence and imperishable prestige of her courageous song of protest. Indeed, the literary continuum extending from "Strange Fruit" consists of works that would amount to volumes of poems, songs, novels and short stories about racist violence visited upon Black people. Occupying a prominent position on that continuum is a poem entitled "Lynchsong" whose author, Lorraine Hansberry, was linked by race and gender to the creator of the ancestral song. As an Afro-American woman who was far more knowledgeable of her people's culture than most of her contemporaries, Lorraine Hansberry was certainly conscious of the literary kinship between "Lynchsong" and "Strange Fruit."

Laurel:
Name sweet like the breath of peace

Blood and blood
Hatred there
White robes and
Black robes
And a burning
Burning cross

  cross in Laurel
  cross in Jackson
  cross in Chicago

And a
Cross in front of the
City Hall
In:
New York City

Lord
Burning cross
Lord
Burning man
Lord
Murder cross

Laurel:
Name bitter like the rhyme of a lynchsong

I can hear Rosalee
See the eyes of Willie McGee
My mother told me about
Lynchings
My mother told me about

The dark nights
and dirt roads
and torch lights
and lynch robes

  sorrow night
  and a
  sorrow night

The
faces of men
Laughing white
Faces of men
Dead in the night

  sorrow night
  and a
  sorrow night.[27]

Discussion Questions

1. Is Davis saying that "Strange Fruit" is a greater art work than Billie Holiday's many unpolitical songs?
2. In what sense is all great art "political"? In what sense is it not?
3. According to Davis, how does great art pertain to social circumstances?
4. Compare, in terms of their artistic and social value, Billie Holiday singing "Strange Fruit" and Louis Robeson (famous black singer of the 1940s and 1950s) singing "Old Man River."

Notes

1. Billie Holiday (with William Dufty), *Lady Day Sings the Blues,* (New York: Penguin Books, 1984), p. 84.
2. William Z. Foster, *The Negro People in American History,* (New York: International Publishers, 1954), p. 480.
3. Ralph Ginzberg, *One Hundred Years of Lynching,* (New York: Lancer Books, 1969), p. 222.
4. Franz Fanon, "Racism and Culture," *Toward the African Revolution* (New York: Grove Press, 1964), p. 41.
5. Holiday, p. 84.
6. Ibid. pp. 68–69; John Chilton, *Billie's Blues,* (New York: Stein and Day, 1978), p. 75.
7. William Dufty, Liner Notes, *The Billie Holiday Story,* Decca DXB 161.
8. Holiday, p. 84.
9. Ibid., p. 83.
10. Chilton, p. 68.
11. Foster, p. 479.
12. Ibid. p. 480.
13. Ibid.
14. Phillip Bonosky, "The 'Thirties' in American Culture," *Political Affairs,* May 1959.
15. Ibid.

16. Holiday, p. 74.

17. Ibid.

18. Ibid.

19. Ibid. p. 76.

20. Chilton, p. 69.

21. Ibid., p. 104.

22. Ibid., p. 217.

23. Charles E. Smith, "Billie Holiday," in Nat Shapiro and Nat Hentoff, *The Jazz Makers* (New York: Da Capo Press, 1979), p. 288.

24. Leonard Feather, Liner Notes, "Billie Holiday: Strange Fruit," Atlantic Records SD 1614, 1972.

25. Joachim Berendt, *The Jazz Book: From New Orleans to Rock and Free Jazz,* (New York: Lawrence, Hill and Company, 1975), p. 310.

26. Feather, op. cit.

27. Lorraine Hansberry, "Lynchsong," *Masses and Mainstream,* Vol. 4, No. 7, July, 1951.

43   Blues People

RALPH ELLISON

Study Questions

1. Why does Ellison think that Jones places too much of a "burden" on music (in terms of black history)?

2. How is Ellison's account of the history of black music different from Jones'?

3. What does Ellison mean by "Technique was then, as today, the key to creative freedom"?

4. What gave the African "an edge in shaping the music and dance of this nation"?

5. What relation does Ellison see between art and politics?

In his Introduction to *Blues People* LeRoi Jones advises us to approach the work as

. . . a strictly theoretical endeavor. Theoretical, in that none of the questions it poses can be said to have been answered definitely or for all time (sic!), etc. In fact, the whole book proposes more questions than it will answer. The only questions it will properly move to answer have, I think, been answered already within the patterns of American life. We need only give these patterns serious scrutiny and draw certain permissible conclusions.

Reprinted by permission of the publisher from *Shadow and Act* (New York: Random House, 1964), pp. 247–258. Copyright 1953, 1964 and renewed 1981, 1992 by Ralph Ellison.

It is a useful warning and one hopes that it will be regarded by those jazz publicists who have the quite irresponsible habit of sweeping up any novel pronouncement written about jazz and slapping it upon the first available record liner as the latest insight into the mysteries of American Negro expression.

Jones would take his subject seriously—as the best of jazz critics have always done—and he himself should be so taken. He has attempted to place the blues within the context of a total culture and to see this native art form through the disciplines of sociology, anthropology and (though he seriously underrates its importance in the creating of a viable theory) history, and he spells out explicitly his assumptions concerning the relation between the blues, the people who created them and the larger American culture. Although I find several of his assumptions questionable, this is valuable in itself. It would be well if all jazz critics did likewise; not only would it expose those who have no business in the field, but it would sharpen the thinking of the few who have something enlightening to contribute. *Blues People,* like much that is written by Negro Americans at the present moment, takes on an inevitable resonance from the Freedom Movement, but it is in itself characterized by a straining for a note of militancy which is, to say the least, distracting. Its introductory mood of scholarly analysis frequently shatters into a dissonance of accusation, and one gets the impression that while Jones wants to perform a crucial task which he feels *someone* should take on—as indeed someone should— he is frustrated by the restraint demanded of the critical pen and would like to pick up a club.

Perhaps this explains why Jones, who is also a poet and an editor of a poetry magazine, gives little attention to the blues as lyric, as a form of poetry. He appears to be attracted to the blues for what he believes they tell us of the sociology of Negro American identity and attitude. Thus, after beginning with the circumstances in which he sees their origin, he considers the ultimate values of American society:

The Negro as slave is one thing. The Negro as American is quite another. But the *path* the slave took to "citizenship" is what I want to look at. And I make my analogy through the slave citizen's music—through the music that is most closely associated with him: blues and a later, but parallel, development, jazz. And it seems to me that if the Negro represents, or is symbolic of, something in and about the nature of American culture, this certainly should be revealed by his characteristic music. . . . I am saying that if the music of the Negro in America, in all its permutations, is subjected to a socio-anthropological as well as musical scrutiny, something about the essential nature of the Negro's existence in this country ought to be revealed, as well as something about the essential nature of this country, i.e., society as a whole. . . .

The tremendous burden of sociology which Jones would place upon this body of music is enough to give even the blues the blues. At one point he tells us that "the one peculiar reference to the drastic change in the Negro from slavery to 'citizenship' is in his music." And later with more precision, he states:

. . . The point I want to make most evident here is that I cite the beginning of the blues as one beginning of American Negroes. Or, let me say, the reaction and subsequent relation of the Negro's experience in this country in *his* English is one beginning of the Negro's conscious appearance on the American scene.

No one could quarrel with Mr. Jones's stress upon beginnings. In 1833, two hundred and fourteen years after the first Africans were brought to these shores as slaves, a certain Mrs. Lydia Maria Child, a leading member of the American Anti-Slavery Society, published a paper entitled: *An Appeal in Favor of that Class of Americans Called Africans.* I am uncertain to what extent it actually reveals Mrs. Child's ideas concerning the complex relationship between time, place, cultural and/or national identity and race, but her title sounds like a fine bit of contemporary ironic *signifying*—"signifying" here meaning, in the unwritten dictionary of American Negro usage, "rhetorical understatements." It tells us much of the thinking of her opposition, and it reminds us that as late as the 1890s, a time when Negro composers, singers, dancers and comedians dominated the American musical stage, popular Negro songs (including James Weldon Johnson's "Under the Bamboo Tree," now immortalized by T. S. Eliot) were commonly referred to as "Ethiopian Airs."

Perhaps more than any other people, Americans have been locked in a deadly struggle with time, with history. We've fled the past and trained ourselves to suppress, if not forget, troublesome details of the national memory, and a great part of our optimism, like our progress, has been bought at the cost of ignoring the processes through which we've arrived at any given moment in our national existence. We've fought continuously with one another over who and what we are, and, with the exception of the Negro, over who and what is American. Jones is aware of this and, although he embarrasses his own argument, his emphasis is to the point.

For it would seem that while Negroes have been undergoing a process of "Americanization" from a time preceding the birth of this nation— including the fusing of their blood lines with other non-African strains, there has persisted a stubborn confusion as to their American identity. Somehow it was assumed that the Negroes, of all the diverse American peoples, would remain unaffected by the climate, the weather, the political circumstances—from which not even slaves were exempt—the social structures, the national manners, the modes of production and the tides of the market, the national ideals, the conflicts of values, the rising and falling of national morale, or the complex give and take of acculturalization which was undergone by all others who found their existence within the American democracy. This confusion still persists and it is Mr. Jones's concern with it which gives *Blues People* a claim upon our attention.

Mr. Jones sees the American Negro as the product of a series of transformations, starting with the enslaved African, who became Afro-American slave, who became the American slave, who became, in turn, the highly qualified "citizen" whom we know today. The slave began by regarding himself as enslaved African, during the time when he still spoke his native language, or remembered it, practiced such aspects of his native religion as were possible and expressed himself musically in modes which were essentially African. These cultural traits became transmuted as the African lost consciousness of his African background, and his music, his religion, his language and his speech gradually became that of the American Negro. His sacred music became the spirituals, his work songs and dance music became the blues and primitive jazz, and his religion became a form of Afro-American Christianity. With the end of slavery Jones sees the development of jazz and the blues as results of the more varied forms of experience made available to the freedman. By the twentieth century the blues divided and became, on the one hand, a professionalized form of entertainment, while remaining, on the other, a form of folklore.

By which I suppose he means that some Negroes remained in the country and sang a crude form of the blues, while others went to the city, became more sophisticated, and paid to hear Ma Rainey, Bessie, or some of the other Smith girls sing them in night clubs or theatres. Jones gets this mixed up with ideas of social class—middle-class Negroes, whatever that term actually means, and light-skinned Negroes, or those Negroes corrupted by what Jones calls "White" culture—preferring the "classic" blues, and black, uncorrupted, country Negroes preferring "country blues."

For as with his music, so with the Negro. As Negroes became "middle-class" they rejected

their tradition and themselves. ". . . They wanted any self which the mainstream dictated, and the mainstream *always* dictated. And this black middle class, in turn, tried always to dictate that self, or this image of a whiter Negro, to the poorer, blacker Negroes."

One would get the impression that there was a rigid correlation between color, education, income and the Negro's preference in music. But what are we to say of a white-skinned Negro with brown freckles who owns sixteen oil wells sunk in a piece of Texas land once farmed by his ex-slave parents who were a blue-eyed, white-skinned, red-headed (kinky) Negro woman from Virginia and a blue-gummed, black-skinned, curly-haired Negro male from Mississippi, and who not only sang bass in a Holy Roller church, played the market and voted Republican but collected blues recordings and was a walking depository of blues tradition? Jones's theory no more allows for the existence of such a Negro than it allows for himself; but that "concord of sensibilities" which has been defined as the meaning of culture, allows for much more variety than Jones would admit.

Much the same could be said of Jones's treatment of the jazz during the thirties, when he claims its broader acceptance (i.e., its economic "success" as entertainment) led to a dilution, to the loss of much of its "black" character which caused a certain group of rebellious Negro musicians to create the "anti-mainstream" jazz style called bebop.

Jones sees bop as a conscious gesture of separatism, ignoring the fact that the creators of the style were seeking, whatever their musical intentions—and they were the least political of men—a fresh form of entertainment which would allow them their fair share of the entertainment market, which had been dominated by whites during the swing era. And although the boppers were reacting, at least in part, to the high artistic achievement of Armstrong, Hawkins, Basie and Ellington (all Negroes, all masters of the blues-jazz tradition), Jones sees their music as a recognition of his contention "that when you are black in a society where black is an extreme liability [it] is one thing, but to understand that it is the society which is lacking and is impossibly deformed because of this lack, and not *yourself,* isolates you even more from that society."

Perhaps. But today nothing succeeds like rebellion (which Jones as a "beat" poet should know) and while a few boppers went to Europe to escape, or became Muslims, others took the usual tours for the State Department. Whether this makes *them* "middle class" in Jones's eyes I can't say, but his assertions—which are fine as personal statement—are not in keeping with the facts; his theory flounders before that complex of human motives which makes human history, and which is so characteristic of the American Negro.

Read as a record of an earnest young man's attempt to come to grips with his predicament as Negro American during a most turbulent period of our history, *Blues People* may be worth the reader's time. Taken as a theory of American Negro culture, it can only contribute more confusion than clarity. For Jones has stumbled over that ironic obstacle which lies in the path of any who would fashion a theory of American Negro culture while ignoring the intricate network of connections which binds Negroes to the larger society. To do so is to attempt a delicate brain surgery with a switch-blade. And it is possible that any viable theory of Negro American culture obligates us to fashion a more adequate theory of American culture as a whole. The heel bone is, after all, connected, through its various linkages, to the head bone. Attempt a serious evaluation of our national morality and up jumps the so-called Negro problem. Attempt to discuss jazz as a hermetic expression of Negro sensibility and immediately we must consider what the "mainstream" of American music really is.

Here political categories are apt to confuse, for while Negro slaves were socially, politically and economically separate (but only in a special sense even here), they were, in a cultural sense, much closer than Jones's theory allows him to admit.

"A slave," writes Jones, "cannot be a man." But what, one might ask, of those moments when he feels his metabolism aroused by the rising of the sap in spring? What of his identity among other slaves? With his wife? And isn't it closer to the truth that far from considering themselves only in terms of that abstraction, "a slave," the enslaved really thought of themselves as *men* who had been unjustly enslaved? And isn't the true answer to Mr. Jones's question, "What are you going to be when you grow up?" not, as he gives it, "a slave" but most probably a coachman, a teamster, a cook, the best damned steward on the Mississippi, the best jockey in Kentucky, a butler, a farmer, a stud, or, hopefully, a free man! Slavery was a most vicious system and those who endured and survived it a tough people, but it was *not* (and this is important for Negroes to remember for the sake of their own sense of who and what their grandparents were) a state of absolute repression.

A slave was, to the extent that he was a *musician,* one who expressed himself in music, a man who realized himself in the world of sound. Thus, while he might stand in awe before the superior technical ability of a white musician, and while he was forced to recognize a superior social status, he would never feel awed before the music which the technique of the white musician made available. His attitude as "musician" would lead him to seek to possess the music expressed through the technique, but until he could do so he would hum, whistle, sing or play the tunes to the best of his ability on any available instrument. And it was, indeed, out of the tension between desire and ability that the techniques of jazz emerged. This was likewise true of American Negro choral singing. For this, no literary explanation, no cultural analyses, no political slogans—indeed, not even a high degree of social or political freedom—were required. For the art—the blues, the spirituals, the jazz, the dance—was what we had in place of freedom.

Technique was then, as today, the key to creative freedom, but before this came a will toward expression. Thus, Jones's theory to the contrary. Negro musicians have never, as a group, felt alienated from any music sounded within their hearing, and it is my theory that it would be impossible to pinpoint the time when they were not shaping what Jones calls the mainstream of American music. Indeed, what group of musicians has made more of the sound of the American experience? Nor am I confining my statement to the sound of the slave experience, but am saying that the most authoritative rendering of America in music is that of American Negroes.

For as I see it, from the days of their introduction into the colonies, Negroes have taken, with the ruthlessness of those without articulate investments in cultural styles, whatever they could of European music, making of it that which would, when blended with the cultural tendencies inherited from Africa, express their own sense of life—while rejecting the rest. Perhaps this is only another way of saying that whatever the degree of injustice and inequality sustained by the slaves, American culture was, even before the official founding of the nation, pluralistic; and it was the African's origin in cultures in which art was highly functional which gave him an edge in shaping the music and dance of this nation.

The question of social and cultural snobbery is important here. The effectiveness of Negro music and dance is first recorded in the journals and letters of travelers but it is important to remember that they saw and understood only that which they were prepared to accept. Thus a Negro dancing a courtly dance appeared comic from the outside simply because the dancer was a slave. But to the Negro dancing it—and there is ample evidence that he danced it well—burlesque or satire might have been the point, which might have been difficult for a white observer to even imagine. During the 1870s Lafcadio Hearn reports that the best singers of Irish songs, in Irish dialect, were Negro dock workers in Cincinnati, and advertisements from slavery days described escaped slaves who spoke in Scottish dialect. The master artisans of the South were slaves, and white Americans have been walking Negro walks, talking Negro flavored talk (and prizing it when spoken by Southern belles), dancing Negro dances and singing Negro melodies far too long to talk of a "mainstream" of American culture to which they're alien.

Jones attempts to impose an ideology upon this cultural complexity, and this might be useful if he knew enough of the related subjects to make it interesting. But his version of the blues lacks a sense of the excitement and surprise of men living in the world—of enslaved and politically weak men successfully imposing their values upon a powerful society through song and dance.

The blues speak to us simultaneously of the tragic and the comic aspects of the human condition and they express a profound sense of life shared by many Negro Americans precisely because their lives have combined these modes. This has been the heritage of a people who for hundreds of years could not celebrate birth or dignify death and whose need to live despite the dehumanizing pressures of slavery developed an endless capacity for laughing at their painful experiences. This is a group experience shared by many Negroes, and any effective study of the blues would treat them first as poetry and as ritual. Jones makes a distinction between classic and country blues, the one being entertainment and the other folklore. But the distinction is false. Classic blues were both entertainment *and* a form of folklore. When they were sung professionally in theatres, they were entertainment; when danced to in the form of recordings or used as a means of transmitting the traditional verses and their wisdom, they were folklore. There are levels of time and function involved here, and the blues which might be used in one place as entertainment (as gospel music is now being used in night clubs and on theatre stages) might be put to a ritual use in another. Bessie Smith might have been a "blues queen" to the society at large, but within the tighter Negro community where the blues were part of a total way of life, and a major expression of an attitude toward life, she was a priestess, a celebrant who affirmed the values of the group and man's ability to deal with chaos.

It is unfortunate that Jones thought it necessary to ignore the aesthetic nature of the blues in order to make his ideological point, for he might have come much closer had he considered the blues not as politics but as art. This would have still required the disciplines of anthropology and sociology— but as practiced by Constance Rourke, who was well aware of how much of American cultural expression is Negro. And he could learn much from the Cambridge School's discoveries of the connection between poetry, drama and ritual as a means of analyzing how the blues function in their proper environment. Simple taste should have led Jones to Stanley Edgar Hyman's work on the blues instead of Paul Oliver's sadly misdirected effort.

For the blues are not primarily concerned with civil rights or obvious political protest; they are an art form and thus a transcendence of those conditions created within the Negro community by the denial of social justice. As such they are one of the techniques through which Negroes have survived and kept their courage during that long period when many whites assumed, as some still assume, they were afraid.

Much has been made of the fact that *Blues People* is one of the few books by a Negro to treat the subject. Unfortunately for those who expect that Negroes would have a special insight into this mysterious art, this is not enough. Here, too, the critical intelligence must perform the difficult task which only it can perform.

Discussion Questions

1. How can Jones be guilty of considerably underestimating both the extent to which American culture was African and the extent to which African musicians freely followed the white music they heard?

2. Contrast Ellison's view of art with those who, like Angela Davis, see great art as serving an essentially political function. (What seems to be Ellison's view concerning the nature and function of art?)

3. An important contemporary viewpoint (Pinn, West) is that black music should be understood as a primary expression of the thinking, including the religious thought, of black people. Would not Ellison be skeptical of this viewpoint?

4. In an essay, Lewis R. Gordon speaks of jazz as "African American classical music" and sharply contrasts it with European classic forms. How do you suppose Ellison would react to this idea?

Contemporary Issue: Rap Music

44   Rap Music and the Uses of Stereotype

CRISPIN SARTWELL

Study Questions

1. How is the rapper's assertion that something is true different from ordinary assertion?

2. According to Sartwell, what is the relationship between the content of much of rap lyrics and white stereotypes of blacks?

3. How does the importance of being "real" differ between rap and the traditional literary movement exemplified by Dickens?

4. How does commercial success, far from comprising the rap artist, add to his or her stature (as an artist)?

5. What is Sartwell's point about Kool Moe Dee?

6. How does Sartwell respond to the charge that much of rap is an expression of self-hatred and misogyny?

Rap music, in particular the sub-genre known as gangsta rap, has been widely condemned on the ground that it confirms white stereotypes of

Reprinted with permission of the author.

African-Americans as violent and highly sexualized (see, e.g., Ro). I will argue that the matter is more complicated than that; rap often seizes the stereotype and wields it directly, self-consciously, as a weapon. Rap transforms oppression into resistance, and it does so in a way that makes the conceptual structure of that oppression absolutely clear. This is an extremely hopeful event, it seems to me, because in order for the content of our notions of race to be overcome, it must first be made visible. And it must be made visible not once or twice or here or there or in general; it must be made visible over and over again in as many locations as possible and with total specificity. Some rap *plays* with race in a way that betrays both awareness of the power of race in the American experience and an ability to wield that power, an empowerment over that power. And it does so by constituting a distinctive sort of speech act in which what is asserted and the act of asserting it become numerically identical.

I.

Rap is, often enough, precisely about power (one of the defining moments for the form was Spike Lee's use of the Public Enemy song "Fight the Power" at the opening of *Do the Right Thing*). But the content of that "about" is of interest. Rap continually asserts superiority: the superiority of black over white, man over woman (or woman over man), or the personal superiority of the rapper over other rappers, or other people in general. But as a rapper describes the superiority of her skills, she does so by displaying those very skills. Rap, then, becomes a very particular sort of speech act; it has a ceremonial force. It effects power by incantation (cf. J. L. Austin's notion of the "performative" in Austin). The fact that my voice is coming out of your speakers shows that there is a particular power in what I am doing, and that very voice as it comes out of your speakers is telling you that there's a particular power in what I am doing. If rap asserts the superiority of black over white culture, it mounts a demonstration precisely within that assertion. Another common assertion of power is the rapper's claim to move the bodies of the audience, to produce

words and rhythms that *possess* the listeners' bodies, making them dance. The creativity of the slang and word play, the profundity of the poetry, the engagement of the body by the beat: these are aspects of this particular African-American cultural production that show you, as they tell you, that black culture has power.

Thus, the rap speech act aspires to, asserts, but also enacts a reversal of cultural and personal domination. Here's a typical enactment of personal power by MC Lyte: "Gusto gusto I got so much so/ You can have some; you just lay low. . . . / Cause I flip and trip and do all that good shit./ That's why the brothers they can't get off my tip./ They know whose show this is./ Whose show is this?/ This is MC Lyte; act like you know." This passage displays, as do many rap songs, a reversal of the power/knowledge relations that have characterized the history of African-American speech. Knowledge here is not something MC Lyte wants, or wants to use to explain herself; it is *fame.* She demands that you know her, bases her claims to superiority on how well known she is (Biggie Smalls: "And if you don't know, now you know, you know"). The assertion of fame in rap, repeated over and over, requires that to know, listeners take those rappers on their own terms. Being "known" in rap terms means having your neighborhood's attention and loyalty, means having fame and fans, means *setting the terms* of representation through the power to be heard. MC Lyte *makes* you know what she *wants* you to know, and in the process takes your twenty bucks. And if you *don't* know, you better *act like* you know; if you're obviously ignorant of the power and the glory that is MC Lyte, you're going to be roundly abused.

Likewise, there is a constant cultural aggression in rap. This aspect connects rap with the African-American response to oppression that stretches back to the slave narratives. As have many others (see Baker, Gates, and Rose), Ice T in his book *The Ice Opinion,* connects rap to African-American traditions:

The main misinterpretation and misunderstanding of rap is in the dialogue—in the ghetto talk and machismo, even in the basic body language. From the nasty tales of Stagolee in the 1800s to H. Rap Brown in the '60s, most of rap is nothing more than straight-up black bravado. . . . In the ghetto, a black man will say, "I'll take my dick and wrap it around this room three times and fuck yo' mama." Now this man cannot wrap his dick around the room three times and probably doesn't want to fuck your mother, but this is how he's gonna talk to another brother. (Ice T, 94)

Notice that this both confirms and contextualizes the material of stereotype; aggressiveness and sexuality are put *in play* here in a way that is typical of rap. African-American linguistic codes and cultural traditions are centralized and their meanings explained without excuse. But here, it is precisely the elements of African-American culture that are despised and feared by white culture that are celebrated.

As expressed in rap, this aesthetic has one criterion of quality: reality. An alternate formulation of the same standard is this: blackness. KRS One (Knowledge Reigns Supreme Over Nearly Everyone), for example, raps "Let me show you whose ass is the blackest." To assert that his ass is the blackest is for KRS to assert precisely that his stuff is real, authentic, hard-core rap.

Here, to take another example, is the introduction to Guru's album *Jazzmatazz:* "Hip hop, rap music, it's real. It's musical, cultural expression based on reality. And at the same time jazz is real, and based on reality." The disk then becomes an exploration and celebration of black musical traditions, and an attempt to focus them into a single coherent synthesis that demonstrates their reality and power. It is a use and an embodiment of truth as an agent of resistance. And it gives this truth a poetic turn, as on the song "Transit Ride," which uses the recording that blares from subway trains as a figure of urban entrapment: "Watch the closing doors." Thus, much rap is a form of literary "realism," a slice of life and so forth; it is "based on reality." But the typical movement in Guru's introduction shows the distinctiveness of rap as a form (though the same thing is attributed to jazz by the Guru): it is both based on reality and is itself real. It is no mere reflection of reality, but also a real thing that takes up the antecedent reality, both the realities of black life and the manufactured realities of stereotype, into its own real enactment. This is

not the realism of Dickens or Flaubert, which attempts to achieve a plausible and elaborate description while concealing the author. Imagine Dickens interrupting his tales constantly to *tell* you that Oliver is real, and detail his authority so to tell you (by, say, claiming that he *is* Oliver, all grown up, with a record contract and an AK). Rap enters and transforms the context it also reflects: It yields no distance between art object and represented material. It is the human voice speaking out of the circumstances it sets out, and speaking (at its best) with grit and power and immediacy.

As I have argued elsewhere, white construction of blackness is an ejected dualism (and see also Ellison, Fanon). We attempt to associate ourselves with mind, you with body: with violence, sexuality, athletics, and so on. This is, I have argued, primarily an act of white self-construction; what this is about, ultimately, is our image of ourselves: our attempt to render you pure bodies is an attempt to render ourselves pure minds. Notice that, in the construction of whiteness, we white folks make of ourselves the truth. We associate knowledge and science and comprehension with ourselves and expel you from them. But notice too that comprehension also *falsifies,* that in ranging the particular fact under the general category, the jagged edges of that fact, its massed idiosyncracies, must be erased. This abandons by ejection an entire realm of truths to those who are left in the particular (behind the veil, in W. E. B. Du Bois's formulation). Developing an ethic and an aesthetic of "keeping it real" is a powerful way of reasserting these truths. And the identification of reality with blackness in rap is thus both a perfect crystallization of the racial constructions and a perfect critique of those constructions: it is an attack on whiteness for its irreality.

Ice T puts it like this: "I rap about my life, and I rap about it in the hardest, most blatant sense. I consider what I say as real. This is the way the world I come from is. This is the way I talk and live. This is the only way I can be" (Ice T, 97). In rap, then, discourse materializes, becomes a hard, solid thing. The discourse of white science, of ejected dualism, is material as well, but systematically hides that materiality and denies its effects; in rap the materiality of discourse is explicitly thematized. Rap enacts the truth and slaps you with it. The particular truth of rap is put forward by and in a particular voice. The truth is transformed into art, but the reality of the art itself becomes a mode of resistance.

A directly related theme is the rapper's claim to be "representing," in both the descriptive and political senses, some constituency. (A Tribe Called Quest: "Lincoln Boulevard represent represent. A Tribe Called Quest represent, represent.") Rap refers its authority to represent to the hood, gang, or crew, and makes an issue of whether the rapper has stayed true to that constituency or turned her back on them. Rap authorizes itself in its own embodiment; its truth can be *heard,* is inherent in its expression and the power with which the expression is bodied forth. But that power is constantly assigned to the rapper's particular history and location and his authorization to represent friends, family, and listeners; that authorization in turn depends on the rapper staying real, staying connected, "staying black." Part of the power of the assertion is also the iteration and re-iteration of the rapper's ability to speak about and for his reality, authorized by those who share it, with no reference needed to the epistemic structure of white authorization of the representation. In fact, such authorization immediately casts suspicion on the reality and authority of the music.

And the mode of dissemination is relevant here as well, because whereas most speech acts (giving a promise, say) are ephemeral, once-and-for-all events, the rap act as it appears on disk or tape is endlessly repeatable and reproducible. It exists as a constant potential assertion or claim; the rap speech act is indefatigable and is produced in a never-ending spiral of recycled and reordered recorded sound. It leaves you with its own evidence, re-asserts itself whenever you press the right button. It can be heard anywhere, everywhere, by anybody. Rap commodifies the racial signifier with absolute precision; it sells, both to blacks and to whites, the preacher, the freedom fighter, the threatening druggie, the earthy black sex bomb, the independent and powerful mama, the black man armed to the

teeth and hung like a horse, and so forth. It does this with great directness, but also, I think, often with great irony, and often with a crystalline self-awareness. The assertion of real, particular experience becomes both a commercial strategy (thus it *must* be accomplished in self-awareness) and an aesthetic and epistemological subversion.

That rap is a commodity, however, does not compromise it as an art; indeed, rap is inconceivable without commodification; it presupposes the current modes of dissemination and exploits them better than any other art form. Rap's medium is, finally, commodity, and while country music, for example, exists in an uneasy tension with its own commodification, rap revels in it, constantly makes of it an advantage. Rap circulates a set of racial signifiers through the network of commodity exchange; it permeates the white-dominated world of market economics and mass media. It is to some extent co-opted and reduced in power by its location, but its market penetration also signals a significant increase in black economic power.

Furthermore, the role of white performers and producers in rap seems to me quite different than their role in previous black musics. Though there has often been successful black/white collaboration in black pop forms (think of Leiber and Stoller's work with the Coasters, or Jerry Wexler's with the Memphis and Muscle Shoals scenes), there has also been a rough division of labor into those who authorize the art and those whose art is authorized to enter public space. But a group like the Beastie Boys, who are a great white rap act, is authorized precisely out of a black discourse of authenticity, just as Vanilla Ice is extruded and finally discredited by it. Still, Vanilla Ice sought recognition in this discourse, and hence made up a blackened autobiography out of whole cloth. One point of a good rap is, again, that it *be* black, and even white producers such as Rick Rubin learn what that means. Baker points out that "Unlike rock and roll, rap cannot be hastily and prolifically appropriated or 'covered' by white artists. For the black urbanity of the form seems to demand not only a style most readily accessible to black urban youngsters, but also a representational black urban *authenticity* of performance" (Baker, 82). This seems fundamentally right to me, though it must be pointed out that rap has entered much more widely into pop music vocabularies since Baker wrote, and is more and more part of the common language out of which pop songs can be made by anyone. But even in that case, the authorizing function has been reversed, and it is obvious that white performers hope to glean an aura of authenticity through these borrowings, even where the vocabulary now comes very "naturally."

The Beastie Boys are an interesting case. Where many black rappers play with blackness, the Beastie Boys play with whiteness: an amazing and potentially devastating turn of events, considering how elusive the content of whiteness is to white people. Try asking a white person what it means to be white and you will be met with blank stares; try asking him what it means to be black and he will tell you in great detail, and thus tell you by exclusion exactly what it *does* mean to be white (see Frankenberg). But the Beastie Boys can make the content of whiteness visible because the discourse in which they engage emerges from a black authorizing community (see Wimsatt, 107–8). White folks' invisibility to ourselves is absolutely essential if the dualism is to be formulated and wielded as a weapon in the precise way it is in American culture. If anyone in our culture has approached the parodic deconstruction of race—a sort of whiteface minstrel show—from the white side, it is the Beastie Boys, and they can only do it from a point within an ongoing black discourse. One of the funniest things about the Beastie Boys is that they *sound white* even when (as on their early albums) they rap over black beats, and it seems to me that they try to sound *extremely* white. When Vanilla Ice, and even somewhat better white rap acts such as House of Pain or Snow try to sound black, the move is appropriative, is slumming. But the Beastie Boys show themselves as white to (among others) black audiences, and parody whiteness. This is an extremely transgressive stance, but they take it up with such light-hearted enthusiasm that it is irresistible.

II.

Consider Kool Moe Dee's song "Funke Wisdom," which is typical of his output and indeed of a whole style of rap: "Take the first power, elevate to the third./ Manifest the power of the spoken word. . . . / Knowledge ain't enough, you need funky, funky wisdom." One might take this simply as a tribute to the power of wisdom. But notice that while Kool Moe extols wisdom, he remains situated in African-American traditions. Rap takes up and pushes forward an oral tradition, and a tradition in which the spoken word is a vehicle of wisdom, as against the European culture of comprehension which (Derrida's bizarre argument notwithstanding) privileges the written text—abstract, enduring, comprehensive, authoritative—above the act of speaking. Further, Kool Moe doesn't just recommend wisdom; he recommends funky, funky wisdom. That is, he recommends wisdom that emerges from and transforms the African-American context, that has funk to it, bass. This is not a recommendation that black people learn Western traditions (though it does not exclude that) but that they locate their own sources of wisdom in, among other places, spoken and musical communication. Socrates had wisdom, perhaps. But Kool Moe Dee has funky, funky wisdom.

This participates in a reversal of stereotype. But Kool Moe also shows in that very reversal what stands in excess to the stereotype: the fact that there was a real culture there with practices of wisdom that antedated the imposition of dualisms upon it in European colonialism and American slavery. Further, the antecedent culture bears within itself the possibility of a reassertion in and out of stereotyped materials. That wisdom could be "funky" is a delightful notion, and one that is designed to expose the impoverishment both of white constructions of African-Americans (the exclusion of African-Americans from the space of wisdom, of mind, of civilization), and the impoverishment of white constructions of themselves (*we* don't have a smell, much less a funk; one of the first things I learned about race as a child in D.C. was that black folks *smell funny*). Wisdom since Plato has been associated with a process of disembodiment that locates the wise man in the realm of pure concepts. If wisdom in that sense were possible, it would be a horror, and the attempt to accomplish the impossible has been horrifying: has turned us toward the world and the ejected body with violence. But funky wisdom is *embodied* wisdom; Kool Moe does not celebrate ignorance, nor does he celebrate *our* wisdom; he celebrates *his* wisdom. And in Kool Moe's work, this wisdom is explicitly associated with an African history and an Afrocentric cultural construction.

It is often asserted that rap glorifies violence. That may occasionally be true (though far less frequently, I think, than is commonly supposed) and when it *is* true one of its functions is, of course, the reassertion of what has been excluded; it is among other things a confrontation of white culture with its ejection of the body. But, as I say, this is occasional, and the bald general assertion that rap glorifies violence makes me wonder what these people have been listening to, if anything. Just a week before the release of *Doggystyle*, Snoop Doggy Dogg was arrested for murder, apparently because his bodyguard shot someone who had been threatening them with a gun. But check this lyric from "Murder Was the Case," a song which begins with Snoop getting shot:

> [They're] pumpin on my chest and I'm
>   screamin.
> I stop breathin.
> Man I see demons.
> Dear God, I wonder can you save me?
> I can't die, my boohoo's bout to have my
>   baby.
> It's too late for prayin
> Hold up, a voice spoke to me
> And it slowly started sayin:
> 'Relax your soul; let me take control.
> Close your eyes my son.'
> My eyes are closed.

This hardly celebrates violence. It describes violence, however, and obviously emerges from a situation in which people are armed and in which the threat of death is often present. But

Snoop, for one, is whole lot more interested in getting mellow and partying than killing someone, not to speak of being killed. This chilling dream of his own death is a reminder of what goes on in the heads of people who live with violence on a daily basis. In fact, there is a whole genre of rap videos that depict gang funerals, or in which the dead or injured are mourned and avenged. But one thing such works do *not* do is make death an entertaining game; the pain is palpable. The late Biggie Smalls (Notorious B.I.G.) issued an amazing disk that began with his birth and ended with his death by suicide ("I hear death calling me," he says, shortly before the shot rings out). He, or rather the character that he constructs, gives us an incredibly detailed description of why he hates himself enough to kill himself. These lyrics do not glorify violence, unless you take the position that to notice violence, to admit that it exists, is to glorify it. Rather they tell about violence, mourn it, object to it, and rage against the conditions that make violence a day to day reality. (Raekwon: "I can't believe in heaven cause I'm livin in hell.")

Rap yields narratives, including narratives about violence and death. But narrative is also containment, and hence threat. Narrative has been a weapon of white culture. It has been used, as Derrida puts it, as "white mythology," above all in the scientific explanation of the object which is ejected in the self-constructions that make "the human sciences" possible and that set up the material world, including the human body, as an object for study. Narrative containment is how we explain you to ourselves, and thus us to ourselves, while simultaneously removing ourselves from the scene of description by our "objectivity." Our story about ourselves is that our histories are not stories, but sciences: In Hegel, for instance, our story of progress becomes the entire inner truth of History and Being (significantly, as Kobena Mercer points out, Africa gets left out of history, or rather is on principle excluded (Mercer, 109)).

There is, however, a radical excess available here, and available precisely out of the materials of oppression. For there are experiences that resist being swept into narrative altogether, and some of those experiences are signs or nodes of oppression itself. Thus an excess to narrative in general can be gestured toward precisely in narrative. There is a white mythology that gives the sociological story, for example, of the underclass and its substance abuse and its poverty and its violence and its transgression of "our" values. But notice that these very experiences are constant challenges to narrative in general. There can be narratives of acts of violence. But violence as it is experienced shatters narrative structures; violence might be defined precisely as what exceeds and destroys the coherence of narrative. The "slave narrative," for example, is both narrative and an interruption of narrative; the sheer intensity of the violence depicted cannot be smoothly incorporated in a story; its intensity disturbs the experience of the narrative as story. William Andrews points out that some slave narrators "lamented the inadequacy of language itself to represent the horrors of slavery or the depth of their feelings as they reflected on their sufferings. In some cases black narrators doubted their white readers' ability to translate the words necessary to a full rendering of their experience and feeling" (Andrews, 9).

To narrate one's own death, for example—as do Snoop and Biggie Smalls—is to make oneself impossible as a narrator. Ice T says this:

Gangs have been able to get away with so much killing it just continues. The capability of violence in these kids is unimaginable. Last year, five of my buddies died. I don't even go to the funerals anymore. It's just so crazy. There are just so many people dying out there. Sometimes I sit up with my friends and think, "There will never be another time on earth where we'll all be together again." . . . You get hard after a while. You get hard. People on the outside say, "These kids are so stone-faced; they don't show any remorse or any emotion." It's because they are . . . conditioned, like soldiers in war, to deal with death. You just don't know what it's like until you've been around it. (Ice T, 31)

Rap constantly enacts transgression. It flouts the law; it flouts taboos about what words to use and taboos about racial signifiers; it flouts sexual mores and drug prohibitions and polite language. Violence is transgression *per se:* a sheer violation.

No story contains or captures violence; no story expresses the oblivion out of which it emerges or the oblivion it imposes. Violence is the Kantian thing in itself about which we can say nothing positively or wholly true. Even violence that fits into the most recognizable stories of white culture does so uneasily, and there is a penumbra of excess about it. Violence is something into which we are forced, or into which we are seduced; thus violence calls to the self for its oblivion. Often it makes this call precisely through an intensification of self to the point of collapse; shooting someone is an assertion of self, indeed the most pointed and extreme assertion of self; but it pulls at the self by a vertigo into a vortex. Violence is a destroyer of selves, and hence of every attempt to contain or explain the self.

White culture is obsessed with the task of constructing a narrative of black culture, an "explanation." Partly it does this in various attempts at self-absolution, self-abasement, or self-accusation. But in all cases it allocates to itself the right to tell the story of African-American culture, perhaps as a preliminary to "solving its problems" for it. Rap insists that black folks are, and must be, telling their own stories. And it tells stories even of what exceeds story itself.

III.

We now return to our initial theme, but we return with more conceptual equipment. Rap music has been criticized by black leaders and by many white moralists for reinforcing racial stereotypes. The widespread use of words such as "bitch," "ho," and "nigger" is taken as an expression of self-hatred now extended into hatred of whatever resembles oneself (see Sister Souljah, 350 ff.). This charge is not without force. Da Brat, for example, refers to herself as a bitch and a ho. It is sometimes said that rap denigrates education, celebrates violence and substance abuse, and confirms white America's image of African-Americans as ignorant, threatening crackheads (or whatever the latest drug of choice happens to be). If this were offered as a general critique of rap, it would be ridiculously overgeneralized. But it is not without force.

Sherley Anne Williams gives a quite typical argument:

[B]lack people have to ask ourselves why so much [rap] has become so vehemently misogynistic, violent, and sexually explicit, so soaked in black self-hatred? Why, given that we are so ready to jump on Hollywood, the Man, the Media, and black women writers for negative and distorted portrayals of black people, have black academics, critics, and intellectuals been so willing to talk about the brilliant and innovative form of rap? Proclaiming rap's connection to traditional wells of black creativity and thus viewing even its most pornographic levels as "art," intellectuals have been slow to analyze and critique rap's content. We have, by and large, refused to call that content, where appropriate, pathological, anti-social, and anti-community. And by our silence, we have allowed what used to be permissible only in the locker room or at stag parties, among consenting adults, to become the norm among our children. (Williams, 167–68)

Now I have quite a hostile response to this passage, which is notable above all for its prissiness, for its unquestioning assumption that what is art cannot be obscene, and for its assumption that *describing* the realities of some black lives amounts to self-hatred. Williams adds that "the best rap is characterized by . . . innocuous messages and funky beats" (Williams, 216), which is colossally wrong. But again, it is obvious that the criticism has bite in that it refers to the actual content of many raps.

The charge of misogyny, for example, is hardly misplaced. Here is Claude Brown on the term "bitch":

Johnny was always telling us about bitches. To Johnny, every chick was a bitch. Of course, there were some nice bitches, but they were still bitches. And a man had to be a dog in order to handle a bitch.
Johnny said once, "If a bitch ever tells you she's only got a penny to buy the baby some milk, take it. You take it, 'cause she's gon git some more. Bitches can always git some money." He really knew about bitches. Cats would say, "I saw your sister today, and she is a fine bitch." Nobody was offended by it. That's just the way things were. It was easy to see all women as bitches. (Brown, 109)

Here, the use of the term "bitch" is related directly to the predation of women by men, which is a predominant theme of *Manchild in the Promised Land*. So the last thing I want to do is simply to suggest that such speech is not problematic.

But one question that remains is: problematic to whom? The assumption that the meaning of words is set by one particular history of meaning encodes a certain cultural assumption of superiority. No matter what you say about what you mean by certain terms, or what those terms mean in your community in practice, cultural commentators are likely to dismiss your claim about meaning in the name of what the words "really" mean—that is, what they would mean in the white community and what practices they support in the white community. As I explore this, I want it to be understood that I take seriously the fact that black figures such as Sister Souljah, Queen Latifah, and Sherley Anne Williams also attack such forms of words. Ice T, in an interview on National Public Radio in which the interviewer sought to confront him with his "misogynistic" use of the word "bitch," tried to show her that it could be used as a term of affection, in a speech that started out "Say you were *my* bitch," and finished off with "Oh baby, quit trippin. You know I love you. But you're still my bitch." This reduced the interviewer to silence, though I suspect to enraged silence. And of course, had the interviewer been a man, Ice T could not have reduced him to silence in just this way. The question of who gets to say what words mean, however, is central to the possibility of a discourse that resists white hegemony of the sign. And typically, in the white discourse, it is words themselves as abstract objects that are supposed to be holders of power, as if the sheer phonemes in "bitch" or "nigger" carried the same meaning whenever or wherever or by whomever they are uttered, as if to expunge them from the language would actually be concretely to remedy sexist or racist oppression.

IV.

I am going to try, however, to give an analysis of the sort Williams demands. Seizing upon and turning around stereotypes is a weapon of subversion.

In his memoir *Colored People,* Henry Louis Gates, Jr. writes:

I used to reserve my special scorn for those Negroes who were always being embarrassed by someone else in the race. Someone too dark, too "loud," someone too "wrong." Someone who dared to wear red in public. Loud and wrong: we used to say that to each other. Nigger is loud and wrong. "Loud" carried a triple meaning: speaking too loudly, dressing too loudly, and just *being* too loudly.

   I do know that, when I was a boy, many Negroes would have been the first to censure other Negroes once they were admitted into all-white neighborhoods or schools or clubs. "An embarrassment to the race"— phrases of that sort were bandied about. Accordingly, many of us in our generation engaged in strange antics to flout those strictures. Like eating watermelon in public, eating it loudly and merrily, and spitting the seeds into the middle of the street, red juice running down the sides of our cheeks, collecting under our chins. (Gates, xiii–xiv)

Where assimilation may be a form of cultural erasure, and where what makes a culture resistant to assimilation is its loudness; where integration means the production of the appearance of whiteness and hence the minting of double consciousness; where the non-assimilated culture is constructed by stereotype: there, the stereotype becomes a weapon of resistance to hegemonic power. Nigger is loud and wrong, hence dangerous and recalcitrant. Gates says that he eventually tried to stop telling people how to be black. But meanwhile being *extremely* black precisely by the standards of the stereotype is a way of asserting cultural existence and cultural difference.

   It is one thing for a white moviemaker to portray black men as dangerous, violent addicts; it is quite another for Spike Lee to present such characters (as he did, for example, in *Mo Better Blues* and *Clockers*). Even if the portrayals coincided precisely (and they do not), they have exactly opposite positions in the power structure. One way to try to destroy the power of stereotype is to defy it, to go get a Ph.D., for example. This has its advantages, and of course is not only a strategy for racial empowerment, but for personal development. But *as* a strategy for racial empowerment, it has its disadvantages as well. For, first of all, stereotypes stand up remarkably well to "excep-

tions"; stereotypes are not really generalizations, even bad generalizations, but rather templates through which we interpret experience. (That is, the character of the generalization is *given* in the antecedent taxonomy, and the generalization can break down while the taxonomy remains unquestioned.) It is very easy for me to see a black professor as a racial anomaly; worse, the blackness of the black professor is in danger of disappearing in my eyes; he may walk like me and talk like me, and perhaps I can make of him an honorary white guy. And notice, too, that the Ph.D. may be seen by African-Americans as being purchased at the price of racial identification; it may be seen as a racial betrayal; one may be told to "stay black." I am certain that this is a maddening thing to be told, particularly in a situation such as (say) academia, which is fraught with racial tensions, and in which the color of the professor is not, ultimately, forgettable. It is, I am certain, a maddening thing to be told to stay black when there is really no choice in the matter. Nevertheless, the black professor at Harvard or wherever is operating in the white-dominated world, and may be doing so in part by creating a white surface. This compromises stereotypes, but only locally, and it also raises the threat of cultural annihilation by assimilation.

   But another strategy is to use the stereotype in profound acts of self-empowerment: "If you think this is what I am, I'll give it to you (so to speak) in spades." And notice the potential of the stereotype, particularly of the black man, as a weapon against the power that creates it: Black guys are, according to the stereotype, animalistic, armed, violent, out of control. Rap's reply: Hell yes we are, so get the fuck out of the way. (Consider MC Eiht's song "Niggaz That Kill," which ends up being more or less a simple list of niggaz that kill; it says: there's a whole bunch of us out here, and we're coming.) Ice T says:

Crime is an equal-opportunity employer. It never discriminates. Anybody can enter the field. You don't need a college education. You don't need a G.E.D. You don't have to be any special color. You don't need white people to like you. You're self-employed. As a result, criminals are very independent people. They don't like to take orders. That's why they get into this business. There are no applications to fill out, no special dress codes. In crime you need only one thing: heart. (Ice T, 53)

This is something of an explanation. But it is also a demonstration of the power of transgression, a demonstration of how transgression becomes a form of economic and characterological resistance. It confirms the stereotype, but with a self- and other-awareness that are incompatible with the supposed neutrality of the values that make and enforce the stereotype, and with a skill and self-consciousness that are incompatible with the stereotype itself. It says: *this* is what you have made by stereotype.

Furthermore, this leads to a heightened romanticism of black culture by whites; every confirmation that black people are earthy, ignorant, violent, criminal, sexy, drunk calls out both a greater fear and a greater yearning toward that culture on the part of people whose lives have been designed to omit or simply fail to acknowledge these things. So white parents find their children listening to and dressing like Snoop (and maybe sipping on gin and juice or smoking chronic), and face a racial situation that has been to some extent transformed. "Bitch" animalizes the person to whom it is applied. "Ho" sexualizes, or equates person with sexual body. "Nigger" carries with it the weight of the entire white cultural construction of black people as savages. There's no doubt that such terms are "degrading," and so forth. But there is, equally, no doubt of the capacity of reversal and subversion that lies in those terms when they are appropriated by black people and shoved at or sold to white people.

In rap music, by a magical reversal, the instrument of oppression, the stereotype, becomes in the hands of those against whom it used an instrument of resistance. Critics who read rap as a manifestation of self-hatred are supposing that the words and images must mean what they would mean if they proceeded from white mouths, under the auspices of white authority. But the shift in voice and authority fundamentally changes the speech act. It is not too much to say that rap, by a sort of alchemy, converts oppres-sion itself into resistance. Like a martial art, it turns the attacker's energy against him and threatens him with his own violence.

This is appropriate to the particular mode of oppression in which we white folks are now engaged. For we have become inaudible as oppressors; we have learned not to say the wrong words. Our oppression has been continually subtilized until it is maddeningly elusive; as the oppressed turn their thoughts to resistance, they find it difficult to finger any particular individual as directly responsible. (There are, of course, exceptions to this, such as the LAPD.) Racism has been subtilized to the point at which no *persons* seem responsible for it; it seems to be matter of fudged vocabularies and implicit standards, a sort of linguistic logjam of domination assignable to nobody's act or control. But rap has invented a manner of resistance that employs the submerged energy of oppression that still flows palpably in the direction of African-Americans; rap hijacks the language of oppression itself and both attacks and uses the constructions of its imaginary locations. Tupac Shakur said "I'm not a gangster; I'm a thug." He had "Thug Life" tattooed on his stomach. Then the oppressor feels threatened even if he is not aware that he *is* an oppressor.

The stereotype is, in the first place and as we have seen, a mode of ejection: It is an attempt to insulate the culture from aspects of its own humanity that it perceives as threatening or bizarre. The stereotype in this sense is conceptual segregation. It functions the same way in individuals: Bigotry is an attempt to eject from oneself aspects of oneself one finds intolerable. For such reasons, bigotry has been at its most explicit in segments of white culture that are in fact closest to black culture: in poor southern whites, for example. Here the conceptual exclusion of the other is at its most tenuous, and so extreme methods of insulation must be developed. With regard to rap, this ejection has been quite explicit and quite extreme: rap is continually censored. Many artists make one version of their songs for CD and another for radio and television. Words such as "nigger," "bitch," and "ho" are omitted, bleeped, or replaced.

What must be rejected or expunged are, to repeat, the parts of oneself one finds intolerable (above all, violence and desire, the violence of desire, the desire for violence). The content of the stereotype, thus, is *per se* what threatens the self-image of the bigot and, more widely, what threatens the image that white culture makes of itself. So the stereotype can be utilized as an absolutely precise weapon against the dominant culture: What we've tried to make of you is precisely what compromises us most deeply. The over-sexed and overdrugged black gangster is the perfect "shadow" self of white culture, its absolutely intolerable negative image. Thus, the stereotype is invested with a preternatural power to threaten white culture and white personality; it can be used as a weapon.

The amazingly shrill white response to rap is a desperate clinging to life lived in ejected dualism, but of course that desperate clinging is itself desire: desire turned against desire, the desire not to desire. That is why rap is invested with a preternatural power as art, as culture, as cultural critique, as the confirmation of stereotype. In it, we really do watch the threat of violence to ourselves as white people. But what we do not understand is that this violence is our own violence, returning to us from the ghetto into which we sought to confine it. Our lack of self-knowledge makes this threat incredibly intense, gives it the air of something surreal; in making ourselves what we are, we have made this violence, returned upon us, incomprehensible to ourselves. And since our self-construction is precisely a comprehension, we are threatened at our core by a violence we cannot understand or contain. It is for precisely that reason that rap is censored. Bizarrely, for example, MTV blanks out all guns from rap videos, and bleeps out words that refer to guns. But of course guns are ubiquitous on television in general; the policy applies *only* to black popular music. Violence and its signifiers are permissible in the "right" hands, and those hands belong to Sylvester Stallone, not to Doctor Dre.

Ice T, star of disk, book, screen, and lecture circuit, has had particular success in transforming his life into art. (He says of the lecturing: "I'm going to Harvard or someplace to teach these people how to be real. Isn't that stupid?" Well, no. The people at Harvard *need* to be taught how to be real very badly.) Here is "Straight Up Nigga," which plumbs all of the themes I have been discussing.

> Yo check this out. A lot of people be gettin mad cause I use the word nigger, know what I'm sayin? . . . They say I'm a black man. I tell them I'm a nigger; they don't understand that. I'm gonna say what I wanna say. I call myself what I want to call myself. Know what I'm sayin? They need to stay off my dick, you know? . . .

I'm a nigger, a stand-up nigger from a hard school.
Whatever you are I don't care; that's you, fool.
I'm loud and proud, well-endowed with a big beef.
Out on the corner I hang out like a horse thief.
So you can call me dumb or crazy,
Ignorant, inferior, stupid, or lazy,
Silly and foolish but I'm bad and I'm bigger.
But most of all I'm a straight-up nigger. . . .
I'm a steak and lobster-eating billionaire.
Those who hate me, I got something for ya.
I'm a nigger with cash, a nigger with a lawyer.
No watermelon, chitlin-eatin nigger down south,
But a nigger that'll slap the taste from your mouth.
A contemplatin, best-champagne drinkin,
Ten-inch-givin, extra large livin,
Mercedes Benz drivin, thrivin, survivin,
All the way live and kickin, high-fivin,
Strokin, rappin, happenin, deal doin,
Fly in from Cali to chill with the crewin,
Grindin, groovin, fly-girl grabbin,
Horny, gun-shootin, long-hair-havin
Nigger, straight up nigger. . . .

Now you keep me in a constant sweat.
But I'm a nigger that you'll never forget.
A black, bad, ironclad, always-mad
Fly nigger takin off from a helipad.

Rolex stylin, buck whilin, cash pilin,
Sportin chain links and medallions,
Intellectual, high-tech,
Cashin seven-figure checks and still breakin
  necks.
The ultimate male supreme, white woman's
  dream,
Big dick straight up nigger.

Ice T says: "If some square Tom politician is not a nigger, then I *am* a nigger, you understand? I am not what you want me to be" (Ice T, 105). For this reason, the upwelling of black culture into the mass media and swirl of commodity exchange takes the form of a reinforcement of stereotype. In fact, and typically, though with particular gusto and sheer verbal agility, Ice T goes beyond confirming stereotypes to revelling in them and deploying them with perfect strategy.

This song intensifies the stereotype and makes it even more threatening than it is on its own. The black guy hanging on the corner like a horse thief, armed and every white woman's dream, is bad enough. But when that black guy has a lawyer and is cashing seven-figure checks—in short when he has the resources to burst out of the ghetto and into your face—*that's* a threat. This figure of the rapper as simultaneously hoodlum, poet, and successful entrepreneur is unprecedented in American history and is deeply subversive. This black man is, first, operating within white America's capitalist structures with complete success, in part by selling his product to white consumers. He's rich, and it's obvious that he's smart, and so forth. But he's also got ten inches for the bitches; he's also hooked into the gang structure in LA; he's also potentially violent. And it must be pointed out that he's supremely conscious of what he's doing: like many rappers, he's utterly at play in the racial signifier.

Discussion Questions

1. Sartwell suggests that the exaggeration of a stereotype can be an effective weapon against it. Besides rap, can you think of any instances in which this has proven true or might prove true in the future?

2. Even if we grant Sartwell's point that rappers' use of the term "nigger" does not express self-hatred, is it also plausible that use of the terms "ho" and "bitch" do not reflect any degree of misogyny—hatred of women?

3. Since Sartwell is not a black woman, how much credence should we put in his defense of male rappers against the charges of some black women—such as Sherley Ann Williams and Kimberle Crenshaw?

4. What is the difference between knowledge and "funky, funky wisdom"? What is the difference between the latter and just plain wisdom?

References

Andrews, William L. 1986. *To Tell a Free Story*. Urbana: University of Illinois Press.

Austin, J. L. 1962. *How to Do Things with Words*. Cambridge Mass.: Harvard University Press.

Baker, Houston. 1993. *Black Studies, Rap, and the Academy*. Chicago: University of Chicago Press.

Brown, Claude. 1965. *Manchild in the Promised Land*. New York: Macmillan.

Ellison, Ralph. "Change the Joke and Slip the Yoke." *Shadow and Act*. New York: Random House.

Fanon, Frantz. 1967. *Black Skin, White Masks*, trans. C. L. Markmann. New York: Grove.

Frankenberg, Ruth. 1993. *White Women, Race Matters: The Social Construction of Whiteness*. Minneapolis: University of Minnesota Press.

Gates, Henry Louis Jr. 1989. *The Signifying Monkey: A Theory of African-American Literary Criticism*. New York: Oxford University Press.

———. 1994. *Colored People*. New York: Knopf.

Ice T as told to Heidi Siegmund. 1994. *The Ice Opinion: Who Gives a Fuck?* New York: St. Martin's.

Mercer, Kobena. 1994. *Welcome to the Jungle: New Positions in Black Cultural Studies*. New York: Routledge.

Ro, Ronin. 1996. *Gangsta: Merchandising the Rhymes of Violence*. New York: St. Martin's.

Rose, Tricia. 1993. *Black Noise: Rap Music and Black Culture in Contemporary America*. New York: Wesleyan University Press.

Sherley Anne Williams. 1992. "Two Words on Music: Black Community." in *Black Popular Culture*. Gina Dent, ed. Seattle: Dia/Bay Press.

Sister Souljah. 1994. *No Disrespect*. New York: Random House.

Wimsatt, William Upski. 1994. *Bomb the Suburbs*. Chicago: The Subway and Elevated Press Company.

45   Beyond Racism and Misogyny: Black Feminism and 2 Live Crew

KIMBERLE CRENSHAW

Study Questions

1. On what grounds might it be plausibly held that the 2 Live Crew performance was not legally obscene?
2. On what grounds is George Will's apparent concern for black women suspect, according to Crenshaw?
3. What two defenses does Henry Louis Gates offer for 2 Live Crew's lyrics? How does Crenshaw respond to each of these?
4. In the end, what should be the relation between black feminists and black cultural practices, according to Crenshaw?

The prosecution of 2 Live Crew began several months after the release of their *As Nasty As They Wanna Be* album. In the midst of the Mapplethorpe controversy and Tipper Gore's campaign to label offensive rock music, the Broward County sheriff, Nick Navarro, began investigating 2 Live Crew's *Nasty* recording at the behest of Jack Thompson, a fundamentalist attorney in Miami, Florida. The sheriff obtained an ex parte order declaring the recording obscene and presented copies of the order to local store owners, threatening them with arrest if they continued to sell the recording. 2 Live Crew filed a civil rights suit, and Sheriff Navarro sought a judicial determination labeling 2 Live Crew's *Nasty* recording obscene.[1] A federal court ruled that *Nasty* was obscene but granted 2 Live Crew permanent injunctive relief because the sheriff's action had subjected the recording to unconstitutional prior restraint. Two days after the judge declared the recording obscene, 2 Live Crew members were charged with giving an obscene performance at

Reprinted with permission of the publisher from *Words That Wound*, Mari J. Matsuda et al., eds. (Boulder, CO: Westview Press, 1993), pp. 120–131.

a club in Hollywood, Florida. Additionally, deputy sheriffs arrested a merchant who was selling copies of the *Nasty* recording. These events received national attention and the controversy quickly polarized into two camps. Writing in *Newsweek*, political columnist George Will staked out a case for the prosecution. He argued that *Nasty* was misogynistic filth. Will characterized the performance as a profoundly repugnant "combination of extreme infantilism and menace" that objectified Black women and represented them as suitable targets for sexual violence.[2]

The most prominent defense of 2 Live Crew was advanced by Professor Henry Louis Gates, Jr., an expert on African-American literature. In a *New York Times* op-ed piece and in testimony at the criminal trial, Gates contended that 2 Live Crew were literary geniuses operating within and inadvertently elaborating distinctively African-American forms of cultural expression.[3] Furthermore, the characteristic exaggeration featured in their lyrics served a political end: to explode popular racist stereotypes in a comically extreme form. Where Will saw a misogynistic assault on Black women by social degenerates, Gates found a form of "sexual carnivalesque" with the promise to free us from the pathologies of racism.

As a Black feminist, I felt the pull of each of these poles but not the compelling attractions of either. My immediate response to the criminal charges against 2 Live Crew was a feeling of being torn between standing with the brothers against a racist attack and standing against a frightening explosion of violent imagery directed to women like me. This reaction, I have come to believe, is a consequence of the location of Black women at the intersection of racial and sexual subordination. My experience of sharp internal division—if dissatisfaction with the idea that the "real issue" is race or gender is inertly juxtaposed—is characteristic of that location. Black feminism offers an intellectual and political response to that experience. Bringing together the different aspects of an otherwise divided sensibility, Black feminism argues that racial and sexual subordination are mutually reinforcing, that Black women are marginalized by a politics of race and of gender, and that a political response to each form of subordination must at the same time be a political response to both. When the controversy over 2 Live Crew is approached in light of such Black feminist sensibilities, an alternative to the dominant poles of the public debate emerges.

At the legal bottom line I agree with the supporters of 2 Live Crew that the obscenity prosecution was wrongheaded. But the reasons for my conclusion are not the same as the reasons generally offered in support of 2 Live Crew. I will come to those reasons shortly, but first I must emphasize that after listening to 2 Live Crew's lyrics along with those of other rap artists, my defense of 2 Live Crew, however careful, did not come easily.

On first hearing 2 Live Crew I was shocked; unlike Gates I did not "bust out laughing." One trivializes the issue by describing the images of women in *As Nasty As They Wanna Be* as simply "sexually explicit." We hear about cunts being fucked until backbones are cracked, asses being busted, dicks rammed down throats, and semen splattered across faces. Black women are cunts, bitches, and all-purpose "hos." Images of women in some of the other rap acts are even more horrifying: battering, rape, and rape-murder are often graphically detailed. Occasionally, we do hear Black women's voices, and those voices are sometimes oppositional. But the response to opposition typically returns to the central refrain: "Shut up, bitch. Suck my dick."

This is no mere braggadocio. Those of us who are concerned about the high rates of gender violence in our communities must be troubled by the possible connections between such images and violence against women. Children and teenagers are listening to this music, and I am concerned that the range of acceptable behavior is being broadened by the constant propagation of anti-women imagery. I'm concerned, too, about young Black women who together with men are learning

that their value lies between their legs. Unlike that of men, however, women's sexual value is portrayed as a depletable commodity: By expending it, boys become men and girls become whores.

Nasty is misogynist, and a Black feminist response to the case against 2 Live Crew should not depart from a full acknowledgment of that misogyny. But such a response must also consider whether an exclusive focus on issues of gender risks overlooking aspects of the prosecution of 2 Live Crew that raise serious questions of racism. And here is where the roots of my opposition to the obscenity prosecution lie.

An initial problem concerning the prosecution was its apparent selectivity. Even the most superficial comparison between 2 Live Crew and other mass-marketed sexual representations suggest the likelihood that race played some role in distinguishing 2 Live Crew as the first group to ever be prosecuted for obscenity in connection with a musical recording, and one of only a handful of recording groups or artists to be prosecuted for a live performance. Recent controversies about sexism, racism, and violence in popular culture point to a vast range of expression that might have provided targets for censorship, but that were left untouched. Madonna has acted out masturbation, portrayed the seduction of a priest, and insinuated group sex on stage. But she has never been prosecuted for obscenity. Whereas 2 Live Crew was performing in an adult's-only club in Hollywood, Florida, Andrew Dice Clay was performing nationwide on HBO. Well known for his racist "humor," Clay is also comparable to 2 Live Crew in sexual explicitness and misogyny. In his show, for example, Clay offers: "Eeny, meeny, miney, mo, suck my [expletive] and swallow slow," or "Lose the bra bitch." Moreover, graphic sexual images—many of them violent—were widely available in Broward County where 2 Live Crew's performance and trial took place. According to the trial testimony of a vice detective named McCloud, "Nude dance shows and adult bookstores are scattered throughout the county where 2 Live Crew performed."[4] But again, no obscenity charges were leveled against the performers or producers of these representations.

In response to this charge of selectivity, it might be argued that the successful prosecution of 2 Live Crew demonstrates that its lyrics were uniquely obscene. In a sense, this argument runs, the proof is in the prosecution—if they were not uniquely obscene, they would have been acquitted. However, the elements of 2 Live Crew's performance that contributed initially to their selective arrest continued to play out as the court applied the obscenity standard to the recording. To clarify this argument, we need to consider the technical use of "obscenity" as a legal term of art. For the purposes of legal argument, the Supreme Court in the 1973 case of *Miller v. California* held that a work is obscene if and only if it meets each of three conditions: (1) "the average person, applying community standards, would find that the work, taken as a whole, appeals to the prurient interest"; (2) "the work depicts or describes, in a patently offensive way, sexual conduct specifically defined by the applicable state law"; and (3) "the work, taken as a whole, lacks serious literary, artistic, political, or scientific value."[5] The Court held that it is consistent with first amendment guarantees of freedom of expression for states to subject work that meets each of the three prongs of the *Miller* test to very restrictive regulations.

Focusing first on the prurient interest prong of the *Miller* test, we might wonder how 2 Live Crew could have been seen as uniquely obscene by the lights of the "community standards" of Broward County. After all, as Detective McCloud put it, "Patrons [of clubs in Broward] can see women dancing with at least their breasts exposed" and bookstore patrons can "view and purchase films and magazines that depict vaginal, oral and anal sex, homosexual sex and group sex."[6] In arriving at its finding of obscenity, the court placed little weight on the available range of films, magazines, and live shows as evidence of the community's sensibilities. Instead, the court apparently accepted the sheriff's testimony that the decision to single out *Nasty* was based on the number of complaints against 2 Live Crew, "communicated by telephone calls, anonymous messages, or letters to the police."[7]

Evidence of this popular outcry was never substantiated. But even if it were, the case for selectivity would remain. The history of social repression of Black male sexuality is long, often violent, and all too familiar. Negative reactions against the sexual conduct of Black males have traditionally had racist overtones, especially where that conduct threatens to "cross over" into the mainstream community. So even if the decision to prosecute did reflect a widespread community perception of the purely prurient character of 2 Live Crew's music, that perception itself might reflect an established pattern of vigilante attitudes directed toward the sexual expression of Black males. In short, the appeal to community standards does not undercut a concern about racism; rather, it underscores that concern.

A second troubling dimension of the case against 2 Live Crew was the court's apparent disregard for the culturally rooted aspects of 2 Live Crew's music. Such disregard was essential to a finding of obscenity given the third prong of the *Miller* test, requiring that obscene material lack any literary, artistic, or political value. 2 Live Crew argued that this test was not met because the recording exemplified such African-American cultural modes as "playing the dozens," "call and response," and "signifying." As a storehouse of such cultural modes, it could not be said that *Nasty* could be described as completely devoid of literary or artistic value. In each case the court denied the group's claim of cultural specificity by recharacterizing those modes claimed to be African-American in more generic terms. For example, the court reasoned that playing the dozens is "commonly seen in adolescents, especially boys, of all ages." "Boasting," the court observed, appears to be "part of the universal human condition." And the court noted that the cultural origins of one song featuring call and response—a song about fellatio in which competing groups chanted "less filling" and "tastes great"—were to be found in a Miller beer commercial, not in African-American cultural tradition. The possibility that the Miller beer commercial may have itself evolved from an African-American cultural tradition was lost on the court.

In disregarding this testimony the court denied the artistic value in the form and style of *Nasty* and, by implication, rap music more generally. This disturbing dismissal of the cultural attributes of rap and the effort to universalize African-American modes of expression flattens cultural differences. The court's analysis here manifests in the law a frequently encountered strategy of cultural appropriation. African-American contributions accepted by be mainstream culture are considered simply "American" or found to be "universal." Other modes associated with African-American culture that resist absorption and remain distinctive are neglected or dismissed as "deviant."

An additional concern has as much to do with the obscenity doctrine itself as with the court's application of it in this case. The case illustrates the ways in which obscenity doctrine asks the wrong questions with respect to sexual violence and facilitates the wrong conclusions with respect to racially selective enforcement. As I mentioned earlier, obscenity requires a determination that the material be intended to appeal to the prurient interest. In making this determination, the court rejected the relevance of 2 Live Crew's admitted motives—both their larger motive of making money and their secondary motive of doing so through the marketing of outrageous sexual humor. Although the prurient interest requirement eludes precise definition—re call Potter Stewart's infamous declaration that "I know it when I see it"—it seems clear that it must appeal in some immediate way to sexual desire. It would be difficult to say definitively what does or does not constitute an appeal to this prurient interest, but one can surmise that the twenty-five-cent peep shows that are standard fare in Broward County rank considerably higher on this scale than the sexual tall tales told by 2 Live Crew.

2 Live Crew is thus one of the lesser candidates in the prurient interest sweepstakes mandated by the obscenity standard, and it is also a lesser contender by another measure that lies explicitly outside the obscenity doctrine: violence. Compared to groups such as N.W.A., Too Short, Ice Cube, and the Geto Boys, 2 Live Crew's misogynistic hyperbole sounds minor league. Sometimes called gangsta' rap, the lyrics offered by these other groups celebrate violent assault, rape, rape-murder, and mutilation. Had these other groups been targeted rather than the comparatively less offensive 2 Live Crew, they may have been more successful in defeating the prosecution. The graphic violence in their representations militates against a finding of obscenity by suggesting an intent to appeal not to prurient interests but instead to the fantasy of the social outlaw. Indeed, these appeals might even be read as political. Against the historical backdrop in which the image of the Black male as social outlaw is a prominent theme, gangsta' rap might be read as a rejection of a conciliatory stance aimed at undermining fear through reassurance in favor of a more subversive form of opposition that attempts to challenge the rules precisely by becoming the very social outlaw that society has proscribed. Thus, so long as obscenity remains preoccupied with finding prurient interests and violent imagery is seen as distinct from sexuality, obscenity doctrine is ineffectual against more violent rappers.

Yet even this somewhat formal dichotomy between sex, which obscenity is concerned about, and violence, which lies beyond its purview, may provide little solace to the entire spectrum of rappers ranging from the Geto Boys to 2 Live Crew. Given the historical linkages between Black male sexuality and violence, the two are likely to be directly linked in the prurient interest inquiry, even if subconsciously. In fact, it may have been the background images of Black male sexual violence that rendered 2 Live Crew an acceptable target for obscenity in a lineup that included many stronger contenders.

My point here is not to suggest that the distinction between sex and violence should be maintained in obscenity, nor more specifically, that the more violent rappers ought to be protected. To the contrary, these groups trouble me much more than 2 Live Crew. My point instead is to suggest that the obscenity doctrine does nothing to protect the interests of those who are most directly implicated in such rap—Black women. On a formal level, obscenity separates out sexuality and violence, thus shielding the more violently misogynist groups from prosecution. Yet the historical linkages between images of Black male sexuality and violence simultaneously single out lightweight rappers for prosecution among all other purveyors of explicit sexual imagery. Neither course furthers Black women's simultaneous interests in opposing racism and misogyny.

Although Black women's interests were quite obviously irrelevant in this obscenity judgment, their bodies figured prominently in the public case supporting the prosecution. George Will's *Newsweek* essay provides a striking example of how Black women's bodies were appropriated and deployed in the broader attack against 2 Live Crew. In "America's Slide into the Sewers," Will told us, "America today is capable of terrific intolerance about smoking, or toxic waste that threatens trout. But only a deeply confused society is more concerned about protecting lungs than minds, trout than black women. We legislate against smoking in restaurants; singing 'Me So Horny' is a constitutional right. Secondary smoke is carcinogenic; celebration of torn vaginas is 'mere words.' "[8]

Notwithstanding these expressions of concern about Black women, Will's real worry is suggested by his repeated references to the Central Park jogger. He writes, "Her face was so disfigured a friend took 15 minutes to identify her. 'I recognized her ring.' Do you recognize the relevance of 2 Live Crew?" Although the connection between the threat of 2 Live Crew and the image of the Black male rapist was suggested subtly in the public debate, it is manifest throughout Will's discussion and in fact bids to be its central theme. "Fact: Some members of a particular age and societal cohort—the one making 2 Live Crew rich—stomped and raped the jogger to the razor edge of death, for the fun of it." Will directly indicts 2 Live Crew in the Central Park jogger rape through a fictional dialogue between himself and the defendants. Responding to one defendant's alleged confession that the rape was fun, Will asks: "Where can you get the idea that sexual violence against women is fun? From a music store, through Walkman earphones, from boom boxes

blaring forth the rap lyrics of 2 Live Crew"; because the rapists were young Black males and *Nasty* presents Black men celebrating sexual violence, surely 2 Live Crew was responsible. Apparently, the vast American industry that markets misogynistic representation in every conceivable way is irrelevant to understanding this particular incident of sexual violence.

Will invokes Black women—twice—as victims of this music. But if he were really concerned with the threat to Black women, why does the Central Park jogger figure so prominently in his argument? Why not the Black woman from Brooklyn who, within weeks of the Central Park assault, was gang-raped and then thrown down an air shaft? What about the twenty-eight other women—mostly women of color—who were raped in New York City the same week the Central Park jogger was raped? Rather than being centered in Will's display of concern, Black women appear to function as stand-ins for white women. The focus on sexual violence played out on Black women's bodies seems to reflect concerns about the threat to Black male violence against the strategy of the prosecutor in Richard Wright's novel *Native Son*.[9] Bigger Thomas, the Black male protagonist, is on trial for killing Mary Dalton, a white woman. Because Bigger burned her body, however, it cannot be established whether Mary was raped. So the prosecutor brings in the body of Bessie, a Black woman raped by Bigger and left to die, to establish that Bigger had raped Mary.

Further evidence that Will's concern about sexual imagery and rape is grounded in familiar narratives of Black sexual violence and white victimhood is suggested by his nearly apoplectic reaction to similar attempts to regulate racist speech. In his assault on 2 Live Crew, Will decries liberal tolerance for lyrics that "desensitize" our society and that will certainly have "behavioral consequences." Proponents of campus speech regulations have made arguments that racist speech facilitates racist violence in much the same way that Will links rap to sexual violence. Yet Will has excoriated such proponents.

Despite his anguish that sexual lyrics "coarsen" our society and facilitate a "slide into the sewer," in Will's view,[10] racist speech is situated on a much higher plane. Apparently, the "social cohort" that is most likely to engage in racial violence—young white men—has sense enough to distinguish ideas from action whereas the "social cohort" that identifies with 2 Live Crew is made up of mindless brutes who will take rap as literal encouragement to rape. Will's position on racist speech not only indicates how readily manipulable the link between expression and action is, but suggests further reasons why his invocation of Black women seems so disingenuous. One can't help but wonder why Will is so outraged about attacks on Black women's vaginal walls and not concerned about attacks on our skin.

These concerns about selectivity in prosecution, about the denial of cultural specificity, and about the manipulation of Black women's bodies convince me that race played a significant if not determining role in the shaping of the case against 2 Live Crew. While using antisexist rhetoric to suggest a concern for women, the attack simultaneously endorsed traditional readings of Black male sexuality. The fact that most sexual violence involves intraracial assault fades to the background as the Black male is represented as the agent of sexual violence and the white community is represented as his victim. The subtext of the 2 Live Crew prosecution thus becomes a re-reading of the sexualized racial politics of the past.

Although concerns about racism fuel my opposition to the obscenity prosecution, I am also troubled by the uncritical support for and indeed celebration of 2 Live Crew by other opponents of that prosecution. If the rhetoric of antisexism provided an occasion for racism, so too, the rhetoric of antiracism provided an occasion for defending the misogyny of Black male rappers.

The defense of 2 Live Crew took two forms, one political and one cultural, both of which were advanced most prominently by Henry Louis Gates, Jr. The political argument was that 2 Live Crew represents an attack against Black sexual stereotypes. The strategy of the attack is, in Gates's words, to "exaggerate [the] stereotypes" and thereby "to show how ridiculous the portrayals are."[11] For the strategy to succeed, it must of course highlight the sexism, misogyny, and violence stereotypically associated with Black male sexuality. But far from embracing that popular mythology, the idea is to fight the racism of those who accept it. Thus, the argument goes, 2 Live Crew and other rap groups are simply pushing white society's buttons to ridicule its dominant sexual images.

I agree with Gates that the reactions by Will and others to 2 Live Crew confirm that the stereotypes still exist and still evoke basic fears. But even if I were to agree that 2 Live Crew intended to explode these mythic fears, I still would argue that its strategy was wholly misguided. These fears are too active and African Americans are too closely associated with them not to be burned when the myths are exploded. More fundamentally, however, I am deeply skeptical about the claim that the Crew was engaged—either in intent or effects—in a post-modern guerrilla war against racist stereotypes.

Gates argues that when one listens to 2 Live Crew, the ridiculous stories and the hyperbole make the listener "bust out laughing." Apparently, the fact that Gates and many other people react with laughter confirms and satisfies the Crew's objective of ridiculing the stereotypes. The fact that the Crew is often successful in achieving laughter neither substantiates Gates's reading, nor forecloses serious critique of its subordinating dimensions.

In disagreeing with Gates, I do not mean to suggest that 2 Live Crew's lyrics are to be taken literally. But rather than exploding stereotypes as Gates suggests, I believe that the group simply uses readily available sexual images in trying to be funny. Trading in racial stereotypes and sexual hyperbole are well-rehearsed strategies for achieving laughter; the most extreme representations often do more to reinforce and entrench the image than to explode it. 2 Live Crew departs from this tradition only in its attempt to up the ante through more outrageous boasts and more explicit manifestations of misogyny.

The acknowledgement, however, that the Crew was simply trying to be funny should not be interpreted as constituting a defense against its misogyny. Neither the intent to be funny nor Gates's loftier explanations negate the subordinating qualities of such humor. An examination of the parallel arguments in the context of racist humor suggests why neither claim functions as a persuasive defense for 2 Live Crew.

Gates's use of laughter as a defensive maneuver in the attack on 2 Live Crew recalls similar strategies in defense of racist humor. Racist humor has sometimes been defended as antiracist—an effort to poke fun at or to show the ridiculousness of racism. More simply, racist humor has often been excused as just joking; even racially motivated assaults are often defended as simple pranks. Thus, the racism and sexism of Andrew Dice Clay could be defended either as an attempt to explode the stereotypes of white racists or more simply as simple humor not meant to be taken seriously. Implicit in these defenses is the assumption that racist representations are injurious only if they are devoid of any other objective or are meant to be taken literally. Although these arguments are familiar within the Black community, I think it is highly unlikely that they would be viewed as a persuasive defense of Andrew Dice Clay. Indeed, the historical and ongoing criticism of such humor suggests widespread rejection of such disclaimers. Operating instead under a premise that humor can be nonliteral, perhaps even well intended, but racist nonetheless, African Americans have protested such humor. This practice of opposition suggests a general recognition within the Black community that "mere humor" is not inconsistent with subordination. The question of what people find humorous is of course a complicated one that includes considerations of aggression, reinforcement of group boundaries, projection, and other issues. The claim of intending only a joke may be true, but representations function as humor within a specific social context and frequently reinforce patterns of social power. Even though racial humor may sometimes be intended to ridicule racism, the close relationship between the stereotypes and the prevailing images of marginalized people as well as a presumed connection between the humorist and the dominant audience complicates this strategy. Clearly, racial humor does not always undermine the racism of the character speaking or indict the wider society in which the jokes have meaning. The endearment of Archie Bunker seems to suggest at least this much.

Thus, in the context of racist humor, neither the fact that people actually laughed at racist humor nor the usual disclaimer of intent have functioned to preclude incisive and often quite angry criticism of such humor within the African-American community. Although a similar set of arguments could be offered in the context of sexist humor, images marketed by 2 Live Crew were not condemned, but as Gates illustrates, defended, often with great commitment and skill. Clearly, the fact that the Crew is Black, as are the women it objectifies, shaped this response. There is of course an ongoing issue of how one's positioning vis-à-vis a targeted group colors the way the group interprets a potentially derisive stereotype or gesture. Had 2 Live Crew been whites in blackface, for example, all of the readings would have been different. Although the question of whether one can defend the broader license given to Black comedians to market stereotypical images is an interesting one, it is not the issue here. 2 Live Crew cannot claim an in-group privilege to perpetuate misogynistic humor against Black women. Its members are not Black women, and more important, they enjoy a power relationship over them.

Sexual humor in which women are objectified as packages of bodily parts to serve whatever male-bonding/male-competition the speakers please subordinates women in much the same way that racist humor subordinates African Americans. That these are "just jokes" and are not taken as literal claims does little to blunt their demeaning quality—nor, for that matter, does it help that the jokes are told within a tradition of intragroup humor.

Gates offered a second, cultural defense of 2 Live Crew: the idea that *Nasty* is in line with distinctively African-American traditions of culture. It is true that the dozens and other forms of verbal boasting have been practiced within the Black community for some time. It is true as well that raunchy jokes, insinuations, and boasts of sexual prowess were not meant to be taken literally. Nor, however, were they meant to disrupt conventional myths about Black sexuality. They were meant simply to be laughed at and perhaps to gain respect for the speaker's word wizardry.

Ultimately, however, little turns on whether the "wordplay" performed by 2 Live Crew is a post-modern challenge to racist sexual mythology or simply an internal group practice that has crossed over into mainstream U.S. society. Both versions of the defense are problematic because both call on Black women to accept misogyny and its attendant disrespect in the service of some broader group objective. Whereas one version argues that accepting misogyny is necessary to antiracist politics, the other argues that it is necessary to maintain the cultural integrity of the community. Neither presents sufficient justification for requiring Black women to tolerate such misogyny. The message that these arguments embrace—that patriarchy can be made to serve antiracist ends—is a familiar one, with proponents ranging from Eldridge Cleaver in the 1960s to Shahrazad Ali in the 1990s. In Gates's variant, the position of Black women is determined by the need to wield gargantuan penises in efforts to ridicule racist images of Black male sexuality. Even though Black women may not be the intended targets, they are necessarily called to serve these gargantuan penises and are thus in the position of absorbing the impact. The common message of all such strategies is that Black women are expected to be vehicles for notions of "liberation" that function to preserve Black female subordination.

To be sure, Gates's claim about the cultural aspects of 2 Live Crew's lyrics do address the legal issue about the applicability of the obscenity standard. As I indicated earlier, the group's music does have artistic and potentially political value; I believe the court decided this issue incorrectly and Will was all too glib in his critique. But these criticisms do not settle the issue within the

community. Dozens and other wordplays have long been within the Black oral tradition, but acknowledging this fact does not eliminate the need to interrogate either the sexism within that tradition or the objectives to which that tradition has been pressed. To say that playing the dozens, for example, is rooted in a Black cultural tradition or that themes represented by mythic folk heroes such as Stagolee are Black does not settle the question of whether such practices are oppressive to women and others within the community. The same point can be made about the relentless homophobia in the work of Eddie Murphy and many other comedians and rappers. Whether or not the Black community has a pronounced tradition of homophobic humor is beside the point; the question instead is how these subordinating aspects of tradition play out in the lives of people in the community, people who are otherwise called upon to share the benefits and the burdens of a common history, culture, and political agenda. Although it may be true that the Black community is more familiar with the cultural forms that have evolved into rap, that familiarity should not end the discussion of whether the misogyny within rap is acceptable.

Moreover, we need to consider the possible relationships between sexism in our cultural practices and violence against women. Violence against women of color is not centered as a critical issue in either the antiracist or antiviolence discourses. The "different culture" defense may contribute to a disregard for women of color victimized by rape and violence that reinforces the tendency within the broader community not to take intraracial violence seriously. Numerous studies have suggested that Black victims of crime can count on less protection from the criminal justice system than whites receive. This is true for Black rape victims as well—their rapists are less likely to be convicted and on average serve less time when they are convicted. Could it be that perpetuating the belief that Blacks are different with respect to sexuality and violence contributes to the disregard of Black female rape victims like Bessie in *Native Son* or the woman thrown down an air shaft in Brooklyn?

Although there are times when Black feminists should fight for the integrity of Black culture, this does not mean that criticism must end when a practice or form of expression is traced to an aspect of culture. We must also determine whether the practices and forms of expression are consistent with other interests that we must define. The legal question of obscenity may be settled by finding roots in the culture. But traditional obscenity is not our central issue. Performances and representations that do not appeal principally to "prurient interests" or that may reflect expressive patterns that are culturally specific may still encourage self-hatred, disrespect, subordination, and various other manifestations of intragroup pathology. These problems require an internal group dialogue. Although we have no plenary authority to grapple with these issues, we do need to find ways of using group formation mechanisms and other social spaces to reflect upon and reformulate our cultural and political practices.

I said earlier that the political goals of Black feminism are to construct and empower a political sensibility that opposes misogyny and racism simultaneously. Merging this double vision in an analysis of the 2 Live Crew controversy makes clear that despite the superficial defense of the prosecution as being in the interests of women, nothing about the anti–2 Live Crew movement is about Black women's lives. The political process involved in legal prosecution of 2 Live Crew's representational subordination of Black women does not seek to empower Black women; indeed, the racism of that process is injurious to us.

The implication of this conclusion is not that Black feminists should stand in solidarity with the supporters of 2 Live Crew. The spirited defense of 2 Live Crew was no more about defending the Black community than the prosecution was about defending women. After all, Black women—whose assault is the very subject of the representation—are part of that community. Black women can hardly regard the right to be represented as rape-deserving bitches and whores as essential to their interests. Instead the defense primarily functions to protect the cultural and political prerogative of male rappers to be as misogynistic as they want to be.

The debate over 2 Live Crew illustrates how the discursive structures of race and gender politics continue to marginalize Black women, rendering us virtually voiceless. Fitted with a Black feminist sensibility, one uncovers other issues in which the unique situation of Black women renders a different formulation of the problem than the version that dominates in current debate. Ready examples include rape, domestic violence, and welfare dependency. A Black feminist sensibility might also provide a more direct link between the women's movement and traditional civil rights movements, helping them both to shed conceptual blinders that limit the efficacy of their efforts. In the recent controversy over the nomination of Clarence Thomas to the U.S. Supreme Court, for example, organized groups in both camps—in particular women's groups—initially struggled to produce evidence showing Thomas's negative disposition toward their respective constituencies. Thomas's repeated derogatory references to his sister as the quintessential example of welfare dependency might have been profitably viewed from a Black feminist framework as the embodiment of his views on race, gender, and class, permitting an earlier formulation of a more effective coalition.

The development of a Black feminist sensibility is no guarantee that Black women's interests will be taken seriously. For that sensibility to develop into empowerment, Black women will have to make it clear that patriarchy is a critical issue that negatively impacts the lives of not only African-American women, but men as well. Within the African-American political community, this recognition might reshape traditional practices so that evidence of racism would not constitute sufficient justification for uncritical rallying around misogynistic polities and patriarchal values. Although collective opposition to racist practice has been and continues to be crucially important in protecting Black interests, an empowered Black feminist sensibility would require that the terms of unity no longer reflect priorities premised upon the continued marginalization of Black women.

Discussion Questions

1. Explain how Crenshaw's reply to Gates' first point might also be considered an answer to Sartwell. How, though, is Sartwell's point somewhat different from Gates'?

2. Is it wrong of Crenshaw to reject the support of such "allies" as George Will? If black feminists are going to isolate themselves from both white feminist and white conservative criticisms of rap, can they validly complain that they stand alone in their fight?

3. Many young black women say they are not offended by talk of "hos" and "bitches" on the grounds that it may apply to others but not to them. Is this a reasonable response—or naive in underestimating the possible effects of rap?

Notes

1. Santoro, *How 2B Nasty: Rap Musicians 2 Live Crew Arrested,* The Nation, July 2, 1990, at 4.
2. Will, *America's Slide into the Sewer,* Newsweek, July 30, 1990, at 64.
3. Gates, *2 Live Crew Decoded,* N.Y. Times, June 19, 1990, at A23.
4. *2 Live Crew,* UPI (Oct. 19, 1990).
5. 413 U.S. 15, 24 (1973).
6. *2 Live Crew,* UPI (Oct. 19, 1990).
7. 739 F. Supp. 578, 589 (S.D. Fla. 1990).
8. Will, *supra* note 2.
9. R. Wright, Native Son (1966).
10. Will, *supra* note 2.
11. *An Album Is Judged Obscene; Rap: Slick, Violent, Nasty and, Maybe Helpful,* N.Y. Times, June 17, 1990, at 1.

Philosophy and Theology

The blackness of God, and everything implied by it in a racist society, is the heart of the black theology doctrine of God. There is no place in black theology for a colorless God in a society where human beings suffer precisely because of their color. The black theologian must reject any conception of God which stifles black self-determination by picturing God as a God of all peoples. Either God is identified with the oppressed to the point that their experience becomes God's experience, or God is a God of racism.

JAMES H. CONE

Black experience is defined [by Cone] as the experience of suffering and rebellion against whiteness. . . . Whiteness appears to be the ground of black experience, and hence of black theology and its new black being. Therefore, while black theology justifies itself as radically oppositional to whiteness, it nevertheless requires whiteness, white racism, and white theology for the self-disclosure of its new black being and its legitimacy.

VICTOR ANDERSON

In spite of what Black theologians have traditionally argued, Black experience does not suggest teleological certainties. More accurately, Black struggle may suggest the presence of God working with humans to overcome evil; or, it may connote God's maliciousness and genocidal plans for the African-American population.

ANTHONY PINN

In the experience of the cross and resurrection, we know not only that black suffering is wrong but that it has been overcome in Jesus Christ.

JAMES H. CONE

Black theology has always been rooted in the black experience and the human problems that arose therefrom. Faith in God and Christian faith generally have been inextricably tied to the kind of practical, human faith it has necessary to survive. Perhaps for this reason, the validity of religion in general and Christianity in particular has rarely been subject to question; what has mainly been questioned is the religious *hypocrisy* of racist whites. Even in their most powerful attacks on the religion of the slave master, David Walker and Frederick Douglass did not question the truth of Christianity itself.

Still, African American theology has not been without its questioning voices. Douglass himself was critical of the *reliance* on prayer and religion. Such recent authors as William R. Jones and Anthony Pinn raise the question of how African Americans can reconcile their faith in an all-good and all-powerful God, with the evils that have befallen them.

The readings in this chapter are organized around two major philosophical issues for contemporary black theology. In both cases, James H. Cone—the theological counterpart of Amiri Baraka (leader of the Black Arts Movement, discussed in the previous chapter)—plays a central role. For Cone, as for David Walker, a true Christian theology must be a *liberation theology*—that is, a doctrine by which the oppressed can find not just spiritual comfort but also material victory over their oppressors. God is on *their* side. To quote abolitionist Walker, "God Almighty will tear up the very face of the earth."

Cone's theology of black liberation has been criticized by contemporary "humanistic" black theologians in two fundamental ways. In his contribution, Victor Anderson questions whether Cone's focus on black suffering and oppression can yield anything like a *positive* black theology of "fulfillment" or human "flourishing." Is it not paradoxical, Anderson asks, that blackness would be defined solely in terms of its relation to white oppression?

In his contribution, Anthony Pinn takes up the question raised by the aforementioned black philosopher and theologian, William R. Jones, in his provocatively titled book *Is God a White Racist?* Pinn and Jones are not satisfied that the evidence of history supports the traditional faith that God is working to end oppression in general, let alone the specific oppression of black people. Whereas Cone appeals to the resurrection of Jesus Christ as demonstrating God's work in the triumph over oppression, Pinn (following Jones) observes that the suffering and oppression of African peoples has largely come *after* that event.

In her contribution, Cheryl J. Sanders offers a view different from those of such currently influential black womanist theologians as Katie Cannon and Delores Williams. Sanders questions whether Alice Walker's womanism—because of its secularism, its friendliness to lesbianism, and its general lack of explicit concern for Jesus Christ—is an appealing doctrine for the preponderance of black Christians. Sanders wishes to side with the value system of the traditional black church (and churchgoer), in opposition to certain new radical voices. In her contribution, Delores Williams takes a much more critical view of these dominations and their leadership, arguing that there is much with which to find fault—morally and politically—in the black church and in its leadership.

46   David Walker's Appeal to the Colored Citizens of the World, and Very Expressly, to Those of the United States

DAVID WALKER

Study Questions

1. What historical evidence does Walker cite to show that God punishes oppression and injustice?
2. Apart from actual incidents, how we do know that God will avenge himself against the slaveholders?
3. What historical evidence does Walker cite to show that American slavery is far worse than Egyptian slavery?
4. How has Christianity led to the oppression of Africans?

Preamble

My dearly beloved Brethren and Fellow Citizens:

Having travelled over a considerable portion of these United States, and having, in the course of my travels taken the most accurate observations of things as they exist—the result of my observations has warranted the full and unshakened conviction, that we, (colored people of these United States) are the most degraded, wretched, and abject set of beings that ever lived since the world began, and I pray God, that none like us ever may live again until time shall be no more. They tell us of the Israelites in Egypt, the Helots in Sparta, and of the Roman Slaves, which last, were made up from almost every nation under heaven, whose sufferings under those ancient and heathen nations were, in comparison with ours, under this enlightened and christian nation, no more than a cypher—or in other words, those heathen nations of antiquity, had but little more

among them than the name and form of slavery, while wretchedness and endless miseries were reserved, apparently in a phial, to be poured out upon our fathers, ourselves and our children by *christian* Americans!

These positions, I shall endeavour, by the help of the Lord, to demonstrate in the course of this *appeal,* to the satisfaction of the most incredulous mind—and may God Almighty who is the father of our Lord Jesus Christ, open your hearts to understand and believe the truth.

The *causes,* my brethren, which produce our wretchedness and miseries, are so very numerous and aggravating, that I believe the pen only of a Josephus or a Plutarch, can well enumerate and explain them. Upon subjects, then, of such incomprehensible magnitude, so impenetrable, and so notorious, I shall be obliged to omit a large class of, and content myself with giving you an exposition of a few of those, which do indeed rage to such an alarming pitch, that they cannot but be a perpetual source of terror and dismay to every reflecting mind.

I am fully aware, in making this appeal to my much afflicted and suffering brethren, that I shall not only be assailed by those whose greatest earthly desires are, to keep us in abject ignorance and wretchedness, and who are of the firm conviction that heaven has designed us and our children to be slaves and *beasts of burden* to them and their children.—I say, I do not only expect to be held up to the public as an ignorant, impudent and restless disturber of the public peace, by such avaricious creatures, as well as a mover of insubordination—and perhaps put in prison or to death, for giving a superficial exposition of our miseries, and exposing tyrants. But I am persuaded, that many of my brethren, particularly those who are ignorantly in league with slaveholders or tyrants, who acquire their daily bread

From *David Walker's Appeal,* originally published 1848, J. H. Tobbitt, printer.

by the blood and sweat of their more ignorant brethren—and not a few of those too, who are too ignorant to see an inch beyond their noses, will rise up and call me cursed—Yea, the jealous ones among us will perhaps use more abject subtlety by affirming that this work is not worth perusing; that we are well situated and there is no use in trying to better our condition, for we cannot. I will ask one question here.—Can our condition be any worse?—Can it be more mean and abject? If there are any changes, will they not be for the better, though they may appear for the worse at first? Can they get us any lower? Where can they get us? They are afraid to treat us worse, for they know well, the day they do it they are gone. But against all accusations which may or can be preferred against me, I appeal to heaven for my motive in writing—who knows that my object is, if possible, to awaken in the breasts of my afflicted, degraded and slumbering brethren, a spirit of enquiry and investigation respecting our miseries and wretchedness in this *Republican Land of Liberty! ! ! ! !*

The sources from which our miseries are derived and on which I shall comment, I shall not combine in one, but shall put them under distinct heads and expose them in their turn; in doing which, keeping truth on my side, and not departing from the strictest rules of morality, I shall endeavor to penetrate, search out, and lay them open for your inspection. If you cannot or will not profit by them, I shall have done *my* duty to you, my country and my God.

And as the inhuman system of *slavery,* is the *source* from which most of our miseries proceed, I shall begin with that *curse to nations;* which has spread terror and devastation through so many nations of antiquity, and which is raging to such a pitch at the present day in Spain and in Portugal. It had one tug in England, in France, and in the United States of America; yet the inhabitants thereof, do not learn wisdom, and erase it entirely from their dwellings and from all with whom they have to do. The fact is, the labor of slaves comes so cheap to the avaricious usurpers, and is (as they think) of such great utility to the country where it exists, that those who are actuated by sordid avarice only, overlook the evils, which will

as sure as the Lord lives, follow after the good. In fact, they are so happy to keep in ignorance and degradation, and to receive the homage and the labor of the slaves, they forget that God rules in the armies of heaven and among the inhabitants of the earth, having his ears continually open to the cries, tears and groans of his oppressed people; and being a just and holy Being will at one day appear fully in behalf of the oppressed, and arrest the progress of the avaricious oppressors; for although the destruction of the oppressors God may not effect by the oppressed, yet the Lord our God will bring other destructions upon them—for not unfrequently will he cause them to rise up one against another, to be split and divided, and to oppress each other, and sometimes to open hostilities with sword in hand. Some may ask, what is the matter with this enlightened and happy people?—Some say it is the cause of political usurpers, tyrants, oppressors, &c. But has not the Lord an oppressed and suffering people among them? Does the Lord condescend to hear their cries and see their tears in consequence of oppression? Will he let the oppressors rest comfortably and happy always? Will he not cause the very children of the oppressors to rise up against them, and oftimes put them to death? "God works in many ways his wonders to perform."

I will not here speak of the destructions which the Lord brought upon Egypt, in consequence of the oppression and consequent groans of the oppressed—of the hundreds and thousands of Egyptians whom God hurled into the Red Sea for afflicting his people in their land—of the Lord's suffering people in Sparta or Lacedemon, the land of the truly famous Lycurgus—nor have I time to comment upon the cause which produced the fierceness with which Sylla usurped the title, and absolutely acted as dictator of the Roman people—the conspiracy of Cataline—the conspiracy against, and murder of Cæsar in the Senate house—the spirit with which Marc Antony made himself master of the commonwealth—his associating Octavius and Lipidus with himself in power,—their dividing the provinces of Rome among themselves—their attack and defeat on the plains of Phillipi the last defenders of their liberty, (Brutus and Cassius)—the tyranny of Tiberius, and from him to the final overthrow of Constantinople by the Turkish Sultan, Mahomed II., A.D. 1453. I say, I shall not take up time to speak of the *causes* which produced so much wretchedness and massacre among those heathen nations, for I am aware that you know too well, that God is just, as well as merciful!—I shall call your attention a few moments to that *christian* nation, the Spaniards, while I shall leave almost unnoticed that avaricious and cruel people, the Portuguese, among whom all true hearted christians and lovers of Jesus Christ, must evidently see the judgments of God displayed. To show the judgments of God upon the Spaniards I shall occupy but little time, leaving a plenty of room for the candid and unprejudiced to reflect.

All persons who are acquainted with history, and particularly the Bible, who are not blinded by the God of this world, and are not actuated solely by avarice—who are able to lay aside prejudice long enough to view candidly and impartially, things as they were, are, and probably will be, who are willing to admit that God made man to serve him *alone,* and that man should have no other Lord or Lords but himself—that God Almighty is the *sole proprietor* or *master* of the WHOLE human family, and will not on any consideration admit of a colleague, being unwilling to divide his glory with another.—And who can dispense with prejudice long enough to admit that we are men, notwithstanding our *improminent noses* and *woolly heads,* and believe that we feel for our fathers, mothers, wives and children as well as they do for theirs.—I say, all who are permitted to see and believe these things, can easily recognize the judgments of God among the Spaniards. Though others may lay the cause of the fierceness with which they cut each other's throats, to some other circumstances, yet they who believe that God is a God of justice, will believe that SLAVERY *is the principal cause.*

While the Spaniards are running about upon the field of battle cutting each other's throats, has not the Lord an afflicted and suffering people in the midst of them whose cries and groans in consequence of oppression are continually pouring into the ears of the God of justice? Would they not cease to cut each other's throats if they could? But how can they? The very support which they draw from government to aid them in perpetrating such enormities, does it not arise in a great degree from the wretched victims of oppression among them? And yet they are calling for *Peace!—Peace! !* Will any peace be given unto them? Their destruction may indeed be procrastinated awhile, but can it continue long while they are oppressing the Lord's people? Has He not the hearts of all men in His hand? Will he suffer one part of his creatures to go on oppressing another like brutes always, with impunity? And yet those avaricious wretches are calling for *Peace! ! ! !* I declare it does appear to me, as though some nations think God is asleep, or that he made the Africans for nothing else but to dig their mines and work their farms, or they cannot believe history, sacred or profane. (I ask every man who has a heart and is blessed with the privilege of believing—Is not God a God of justice to all his creatures? Do you say he is? Then if he gives peace and tranquility to tyrants, and permits them to keep our fathers, our mothers, ourselves and our children in eternal ignorance and wretchedness to support them and their families, would he be to us a God of *justice?*) I ask O ye *christians! ! !* who hold us and our children, in the most abject ignorance and degradation, that ever a people were afflicted with since the world began—I say, if God gives you peace and tranquility, and suffers you thus to go on afflicting us and our children, who have never given you the least provocation,—Would he be to us *a God of justice?* If you will allow that we are MEN who feel for each other, does not the blood of our fathers and of us their children, cry aloud to the Lord of Sabaoth against you, for the cruelties and murders with which you have, and do continue to afflict us. But it is time for me to close my remarks on the suburbs, just to enter more fully into the interior of this system of cruelty and oppression.

Article I.

Our Wretchedness in Consequence of Slavery

My beloved brethren: The Indians of North and of South America—the Greeks—the Irish subjected under the king of Great Britain—the Jews that ancient people of the Lord—the inhabitants of the islands of the sea—in fine, all the inhabitants of the earth, (except however, the sons of Africa) are called *men,* and of course are, and ought to be free. But we, (coloured people) and our children are *brutes! !* and of course are and ought to be SLAVES to the American people and their children forever! to dig their mines and work their farms; and thus go on enriching them, from one generation to another with our blood and our tears! !

I promised in a preceding page to demonstrate to the satisfaction of the most incredulous, that we, (colored people of these United States of America) are the *most wretched, degraded* and abject set of beings that ever *lived* since the world began, and that the white Americans having reduced us to the wretched state of *slavery,* treat us in that condition *more cruel* (they being an enlightened and christian people) than any heathen nation did any people whom it had reduced to our condition. These affirmations are so well confirmed in the minds of all unprejudiced men who have taken the trouble to read histories, that they need no elucidation from me. But to put them beyond all doubt, I refer you in the first place to the children of Jacob, or of Israel in Egypt, under Pharaoh and his people. Some of my brethren do not know who Pharaoh and the Egyptians were—I know it to be a fact that some of them take the Egyptians to have been a gang of *devils,* not knowing any better, and that they (Egyptians) having got possession of the Lord's people, treated them *nearly* as cruel as *christians Americans* do us, at the present day. For the information of such, I would only mention that the Egyptians, were Africans or colored people, such as we are—some of them yellow and others dark—a mixture of Ethiopians and the natives of Egypt—about the same as you see the colored people of the United States at the present day,—I say, I call your attention then, to the children of Jacob, while I point out particularly to you his son Joseph among the rest, in Egypt.

"And Pharaoh, said unto Joseph, thou shalt be over my house, and according unto thy word shall all my people be ruled; only in the throne will I be greater than thou."*

"And Pharaoh said unto Joseph, see, I have set thee over all the land of Egypt."†

"And Pharaoh said unto Joseph, I am Pharaoh, and without thee shall no man lift up his hand or foot in all the land of Egypt."‡

Now I appeal to heaven and to earth, and particularly to the American people themselves who cease not to declare that our condition is not *hard,* and that we are comparatively satisfied to rest in wretchedness and misery, under them and their children. Not, indeed, to show me a colored President, a Governor, a Legislator, a Senator, a Mayor, or an Attorney at the Bar.—But to show me a man of color, who holds the low office of a Constable, or one who sits in a Juror Box, even on a case of one of his wretched brethren, throughout this great Republic! !—But let us pass Joseph the son of Israel a little further in review, as he existed with that heathen nation.

"And Pharaoh called Joseph's name Zaphnath-paaneah; and he gave him to wife Asenath the daughter of Potipherah priest of On. And Joseph went out over all the land of Egypt."§

Compare the above, with the American institutions. Do they not institute laws to prohibit us from marrying among the whites? I would wish, candidly, however, before the Lord, to be understood, that I would not give *a pinch of snuff* to be married to any white person I ever saw in all the days of my life. And I do say it, that the black man, or man of color, who will leave his own color (provided he can get one who is good for any thing) and marry a white woman, to be a double slave to her just because she is *white,* ought to be treated by her as he surely will be, viz; as a NIGER! ! ! It is not indeed what I care

---

*See Genesis, chap. xli. v. 40, †v. 41, ‡v. 44. §v. 45

about intermarriages with the whites, which in-duced me to pass this subject in review; for the Lord knows, that there is a day coming when they will be glad enough to get into the company of the blacks, notwithstanding, we are, in this gener-ation, levelled by them almost on a level with the brute creation; and some of us they treat even worse than they do the brutes that perish. I only made this extract to show how much lower we are held, and how much more cruel we are treated by the Americans, than were the children of Jacob, by the Egyptians. We will notice the suf-ferings of Israel some further, under *heathen Pharaoh,* compared with ours under the *enlight-ened christians of America.*

"And Pharaoh spake unto Joseph, saying, thy father and thy brethren are come unto thee:"

"The land of Egypt is before thee: in the best of the land make thy father and brethren to dwell; in the land of Goshen let them dwell; and if thou knowest any men of activity among them, then make them rulers over my cattle."*

I ask those people who treat us so *well,* Oh! I ask them, where is the most barren spot of land which they have given unto us? Israel had the most fertile land in all Egypt. Need I mention the very notorious fact, that I have known a poor man of color, who labored night and day, to ac-quire a little money, and having acquired it, he vested it in a small piece of land, and got him a house erected thereon, and having paid for the whole, he moved his family into it, where he was suffered to remain but nine months, when he was cheated out of his property by a white man, and driven out of door!—And is not this the case gen-erally? Can a man of color buy a piece of land and keep it peaceably? Will not some white man try to get it from him even if it is in a *mud hole?* I need not comment any farther on a subject, which all, both black and white, will readily admit. But I must, really, observe that in this very city, when a man of color dies, if he owned any real estate it must generally fall into the hands of some white person. The wife and children of the

deceased may weep and lament if they please, but the estate will be kept snug enough by its white posessors. . . .

Article III.

Our Wretchedness in Consequence of the Preachers of the Religion of Jesus Christ

Religion, my brethren, is a substance of deep consideration among all nations of the earth. The Pagans have a kind, as well as the Mahometans, the Jews and the Christians. But pure and unde-filed religion, such as was preached by Jesus Christ and his apostles, is hard to be found in all the earth. God, through his instrument, Moses, handed a dispensation of his divine will to the children of Israel after they had left Egypt for the land of Canaan, or of Promise, who through hypocrisy, oppression, and unbelief, departed from the faith. He then, by his apostles handed a dispensation of his, together with the will of Jesus Christ, to the Europeans in Europe, who, in open violation of which, have made *merchandize* of us, and it does appear as though they take this very dispensation to aid them in their infernal depredations upon us. Indeed, the way in which religion was and is conducted by the Europeans and their descendants, one might believe it was a plan fabricated by themselves and the *devils* to oppress us. But hark! my master has taught me better than to believe it—he has taught me that his gospel as it was preached by himself and his apostles remains the same, notwithstanding Eu-rope has tried to mingle blood and oppression with it.

It is well known to the Christian world that Bartholomew Las Casas, that very notoriously avaricious Catholic priest or preacher, and ad-venturer with Columbus in his second voyage, proposed to his countrymen, the Spaniards in Hispaniola, to import the Africans from the Por-tuguese settlement in Africa, to dig up gold and silver, and work their plantations for them, to ef-fect which, he made a voyage thence to Spain, and opened the subject to his master, Ferdinand, then in declining health, who listened to the plan;

*Genesis, chap. xlvii. v. 5, 6.

but who died soon after, and left it in the hands of his successor, Charles V.*—This wretch, (" Las Cassas, the Preacher,") succeeded so well in his plans of oppression, that in 1503, the first blacks had been imported into the new world. Elated with this success, and stimulated by sordid avarice only, he importuned Charles V. in 1511, to grant permission to a Flemish merchant to import 4000 blacks at one time. Thus we see, through the instrumentality of a pretended preacher of the gospel of Jesus Christ our common master, our wretchedness first commenced in America—where it has been continued from 1503 to this day, 1829. A period of three hundred and twenty-six years. But two hundred and nine, from 1620—when twenty of our fathers were brought into James-town, Virginia, by a Dutch man-of-war, and sold off like brutes to the highest bidders; and there is not a doubt in my mind, but that tyrants are in hopes to perpetuate our miseries under them and their children until the final consummation of all things. But if they do not get dreadfully, deceived, it will be because God has forgotten them.

The Pagans, Jews and Mahometans try to make proselytes to their religions, and whatever human beings adopt their religions, they extend to them their protection. But Christian Americans not only hinder their fellow creatures, the Africans, but thousands of them will *absolutely beat a coloured person nearly to death, if they catch him on his knees, supplicating the throne of grace.* This barbarous cruelty was by all the heathen nations of antiquity, and is by the Pagans, Jews and Mahometans of the present day, left entirely to Christian Americans to inflict on the Africans and their descendants that their cup which is nearly full may be completed. I have known tyrants or usurpers of human liberty in different parts of this country take their fellow creatures, the colored people, and beat them until they would scarcely leave life in them; what for? Why they say, "The black devils had the audacity to be "found *making prayers and supplications to* the *"God made them! ! !"* Yes, I have known small collections of coloured people to have convened together, for no other purpose than to worship God Almighty, in spirit and in truth, to the best of their knowledge; when tyrants, calling themselves *patrols,* would also convene and wait almost in breathless silence for the poor coloured people to commence singing and praying to the Lord our God, and as soon as they had commenced the wretches would burst in upon them and drag them out and commence beating them as they would rattle-snakes—many of whom, they would beat so unmercifully, that they would hardly be able to crawl for weeks and sometimes for months.—Yet the American ministers send out missionaries to convert the heathen, while they keep us and our children sunk at their feet in the most abject ignorance and wretchedness that ever a people was afflicted with since the world began. Will the Lord suffer this people to proceed much longer? Will he not stop them in their career? Does he regard the heathens abroad, more than the heathens among the Americans? Surely the Americans must believe that God is partial, notwithstanding his Apostle Peter, declared before Cornelius and others that he has no respect to persons, but in every nation he that feareth God and worketh righteousness is accepted with him.—"The word," said he, "which God sent unto the children of Israel, preaching peace, by Jesus Christ, (he is the Lord of all.)"* Have not the Americans the Bible in their hands? Do they believe it? Surely they do not. See how they treat us in open violation of the Bible! ! They no doubt will be greatly offended with me, but if God does not awaken them, it will be, because they are superior to other men, as they have represented themselves to be. Our divine Lord and Master said "all things whatsoever ye would that men should do unto you, do ye even so unto them." But an American minister, with the Bible in his hand, holds us and our children in the most abject slavery and wretchedness. Now I ask them, would they like for us to hold them and their children in

---

*See Butler's History of the United States, vol. 1, page 24. See also, page 25.

*See the Acts of the Apostles, chap. x. v.—25—26.

abject slavery and wretchedness? No says one, that never can be done—you are too abject and ignorant to do it—you are not men—you were made to be slaves to us, to dig up gold and silver for us and our children. Know this, my dear sirs, that although you treat us and our children now, as you do your domestic beasts—yet the final result of all future events are known but to God Almighty alone, who rules in tke armies of heaven and among the inhabitants of the earth, and who dethrones one earthly king and sits up another, as it seemeth good in his holy sight. We may attribute these vicissitudes to what we please, but the God of armies and of justice rules in heaven and in earth, and the whole American people shall see and know it yet, to their satisfaction. I have known pretended preachers of the gospel of my Master, who not only held us as their natural inheritance, but treated us with as much rigor as any Infidel or Deist in the world—just as though they were intent only on taking our blood and groans to glorify the Lord Jesus Christ. The wicked and ungodly, seeing their preachers treat us with so much cruelty, they say: our preachers, who must be right, if any body are, treat them like brutes, and why cannot we?—They think it is no harm to keep them in slavery and put the whip to them, and why cannot we do the same!—They being preachers of the gospel of Jesus Christ, if it were any harm, they would surely preach against their oppression and do their utmost to erase it from the country; not only in one or two cities, but one continual cry would be raised in all parts of this confederacy, and would cease only with the complete overthrow of the system of slavery, in every part of the country. But how far the American preachers are from preaching against slavery and oppression, which have carried their country to the brink of a precipice; to save them from plunging down the side of which, will hardly be effected, will appear in the sequel of this paragraph, which I shall narrate just as it transpired. I remember a Camp Meeting in South Carolina, for which I embarked in a Steam Boat at Charleston, and having been five or six hours on the water, we at last arrived at the place of hearing, where was a very great con-

course of people, who were no doubt, collected together to hear the word of God, (that some had collected barely as spectators to the scene, I will not here pretend to doubt, however, that is left to themselves and their God.) Myself and boat companions, having been there a little while, we were all called up to hear; I among the rest, went up and took my seat—being seated, I fixed myself in a complete position to hear the word of my Saviour and to receive such as I thought was authenticated by the Holy Scriptures; but to my no ordinary astonishment, our Reverend gentleman got up and told us (colored people) that slaves must be obedient to their masters—must do their duty to their masters or be whipped—the whip was made for the backs of fools, &c. Here I pause for a moment, to give the world time to consider what was my surprise, to hear such preaching from a minister of my Master, whose very gospel is that of peace and not of blood and whips, as this pretended preacher tried to make us believe. What the American preachers can think of us, I aver this day before my God, I have never been able to define. They have newspapers and monthly periodicals, which they receive in continual succession, but on the pages of which, you will scarcely ever find a paragraph respecting slavery, which is ten thousand times more injurious to this country than all the other evils put together; aud which will be the final overthrow of its government, unless something is very speedily done; for their cup is nearly full.—Perhaps they will laugh at, or make light of this; but I tell you Americans! that unless you speedily alter your course, *you* and your *Country are gone! ! ! ! !* For God Almighty will tear up the very face of the earth! ! ! ! Will not that very remarkable passage of Scripture be fulfilled on Christian Americans? Hear it Americans! ! " He that is unjust, let him be unjust still:—and he which is filthy, let him be filthy still: and he that is righteous, let him be righteous still; and he that is holy, let him be holy still."* I hope that the Americans may hear, but I am afraid that they have done us so much injury, and are so firm in the belief that our Creator

*See Revelation, chap. xxii. v. 11.

made us to be an inheritance to them forever, that their hearts will be hardened, so that their destruction may be sure.—This language, perhaps is too harsh for the American's delicate ears. But Oh Americans! Americans! ! I warn you in the name of the Lord, (whether you will hear, or forbear,)to repent and reform, or you are ruined !!!!!! Do you think that our blood is hidden from the Lord, because you can hide it from the rest of the world by sending out missionaries, and by your charitable deeds to the Greeks, Irish, &c.? Will he not publish your secret crimes on the house top? Even here in Boston, pride and prejudice have got to such a pitch, that in the very houses erected to the Lord, they have built little places for the reception of colored people, where they must sit during meeting, or keep away from the house of God; and the preachers say nothing about it—much less, go into the hedges and highways seeking the lost sheep of the house of Israel, and try to bring them in, to their Lord and Master. There are hardly a more wretched, ignorant, miserable, and abject set of beings in all the world, than the blacks in the Southern and Western sections of this country, under tyrants and devils. The preachers of America cannot see them, but they can send out missionaries to convert the heathens, notwithstanding. Americans! unless you speedily alter your course of proceeding, if God Almighty does not stop you, I say it in his name, that you may go on and do as you please for ever, both in time and eternity—never fear any evil at all! ! ! ! ! ! ! !

Addition—The preachers and people of the the United States form societies against Free Masonry and Intemperance, and write against Sabbath breaking, Sabbath mails, Infidelity, &c. &c. But the fountain head,* compared with which all those other evils are comparatively nothing, and from the bloody and murderous head of which, they receive no trifling support, is hardly noticed by the Americans. This is a fair illustration of the state of society in this country—it shows what a bearing *avarice* has upon a people, when they

are nearly given up by the Lord to a hard heart and a reprobate mind, in consequence of afflicting their fellow creatures. God suffers some to go on until they are ruined for ever! ! Will it be the case with our brethren the whites of the United States of America? We hope not—we would not wish to see them destroyed, notwithstanding they have and do now treat us more cruel than any people have treated another, on this earth since it came from the hands of its creator (with the exception of the French and the Dutch, they treat us nearly as bad as the Americans of the United States.) The will of God must however, in spite of us, *be done.*

The English are the best friends the colored people have upon earth. Tho' they have oppressed us a little, and have colonies now in the West Indies, which oppress us *sorely,*—Yet notwithstanding they (the English) have done one hundred times more for the melioration of our condition, than all the other nations of the earth put together. The blacks cannot but respect the English as a nation, notwithstanding they have treated us a little cruel.

There is no intelligent *black man* who knows any thing, but esteems a real English man, let him see him in what part of the world he will—for they are the greatest benefactors we have upon earth. We have here and there, in other nations, good friends. But as a nation, the English are our friends.

How can the preachers and people of America believe the Bible? Does it teach them any distinction on account of a man's color? Hearken, Americans! to the injunctions of our Lord and Master, to his humble followers.

*"And Jesus came and spake unto them saying, "all power is given unto me in heaven and in earth. "Go ye, therefore, and teach all nations, baptizing them in the name of the Father, and of the Son, and of the Holy Ghost,

"Teaching them to observe all things whatsoever I have commanded you; and lo, I am with you alway, even unto the end of the world. Amen."

---

*Slavery and oppression.

*See St. Matthew's Gospel, chap. xxviii. v. 18—19—20. After Jesus was risen from the dead.

I declare, that the very face of these injunctions appears to be of God and not of man. They do not show the slightest degree of distinction. "Go ye, therefore," (says my divine Master) "and teach all nations," (or in other words, all people) "baptizing them in the name of the Father, and of the Son, and of the Holy Ghost." Do you understand the above, Americans? We are a people, notwithstanding many of you doubt it. You have the Bible in your hands, with this very injunction. Have you been to Africa, teaching the inhabitants thereof the words of the Lord Jesus? "Baptizing them in the name of the Father, and of the Son, and of the Holy Ghost." Have you not, on the contrary, entered among us, and learnt us the art of throat-cutting, by setting us to fight, one against another, to take each other as prisoners of war, and sell to you for small bits of calicoes, old swords, knives, &c. to make slaves for you and your children? This being done, have you not brought us among you, in chains and handcuffs, like brutes, and treated us with all the cruelties and rigour your ingenuity could invent, consistent with the laws of your country, which (for the blacks) are tyrannical enough? Can the American preachers appeal unto God, the Maker and Searcher of hearts, and tell him, with the Bible in their hands, that they make no distinction on account of men's colour? Can they say, O God! thou knowest all things—thou knowest that we make no distinction between thy creatures to whom we have to preach thy Word? Let them answer the Lord; and if they cannot do it in the affirmative, have they not departed from the Lord Jesus Christ, their master? But some may say, that they never had or were in possession of a religion, which makes no distinction, and of course they could not have departed from it. I ask you then, in the name of the Lord, of what kind can your religion be? Can it be that which was preached by our Lord Jesus Christ from Heaven? I believe you cannot be so wicked as to tell him that his Gospel was that of *distinction*. What can the American preachers and people take God to be?—Do they believe his words? If they do, do they believe that he will be mocked? Or do they

believe because they are whites and we blacks, that God will have respect to them? Did not God make us as it seemed best to himself? What right, then, has one of us, to despise another and to treat him cruel, on account of his colour, which none but the God who made it can alter? Can there be a greater absurdity in nature, and particularly in a free republican country? But the Americans, having introduced slavery among them, their hearts have become almost seared, as with an hot iron, and God has nearly given them up to believe a lie in preference to the truth! ! ! and I am awfully afraid that pride, prejudice, avarice and blood, will, before long, prove the final ruin of this happy republic, or land of liberty! ! ! Can any thing be a greater mockery of religion than the way in which it is conducted by the Americans? It appears as though they are bent only on daring God Almighty to do his best—they chain and handcuff us and our children and drive us around the country like brutes, and go into the house of the God of justice to return Him thanks for having aided him in their infernal cruelties inflicted upon us. Will the Lord suffer this people to go on much longer, taking his holy name in vain? Will he not stop them, PREACHERS and all? O Americans! Americans! ! I call God—I call angels—I call men, to witness, that your DESTRUCTION *is at hand,* and will be speedily consummated unless you REPENT. . . .

Discussion Questions

1. More recent African American theologians, such as James Cone, have spoken of the Christian God as a "God of the oppressed." Other Christian authors stress the idea of God as loving all of his creation, without any special regard for those who might judged "oppressors." What reason would Walker give, do you think, for favoring the first of these two views?

2. Do you think that a slave owner is *worse* for also being a Christian? (After all, is a Christian not supposed to be better than the common lot of humankind?)

3. Why, do you think, as Frederick Douglass and David Walker maintain, the slave owners who were the most fervent Christians were also the *most* cruel? Is this a reflection on Christianity?

4. For his part, Frederick Douglass always insisted that we must never wait for God to free us (that "he who would be free must strike the first blow"). Do you think Walker has a different view, as witnessed by his assurance that God will avenge the oppressor?

47   God and Black Theology

JAMES H. CONE

Study Questions

1. How do we know that God is the God of the "oppressed"?
2. In what ways does black theology remain Christian?
3. How has "white theology" failed blacks and thereby not qualified as Christian at all?
4. Why is talk of "God" difficult?
5. Why is God "black"?

THE CONTENT OF THEOLOGY

Liberation as the Content of Theology

Christian theology is a theology of liberation. It is *a rational study of the being of God in the world in light of the existential situation of an oppressed community, relating the forces of liberation to the essence of the gospel, which is Jesus Christ.* This means that its sole reason for existence is to put into ordered speech the meaning of God's activity in the world, so that the community of the oppressed will recognize that its inner thrust for liberation is not only *consistent with* the gospel but *is* the gospel of Jesus Christ. There can be no Christian theology that is not identified unre-

servedly with those who are humiliated and abused. In fact, theology ceases to be a theology of the gospel when it fails to arise out of the community of the oppressed. For it is impossible to speak of the God of Israelite history, who is the God revealed in Jesus Christ, without recognizing that God is the God *of* and *for* those who labor and are over laden.

The perspective and direction of this study are already made clear. The reader is entitled to know at the outset what is considered to be important. My definition of theology and the assumptions on which it is based are to be tested by the working out of a theology which can then be judged in terms of its consistency with a communitarian view of the ultimate. We begin now by exploring some preliminary considerations in my definition.

The definition of theology as the discipline that seeks to analyze the nature of the Christian faith in the light of the oppressed arises chiefly from biblical tradition itself.

(1) Though it may not be entirely clear why God elected Israel to be God's people, one point is evident. The election is inseparable from the event of the exodus:

You have seen what I did to the Egyptians, and how I bore you on eagles' wings and brought you to myself. Now therefore, if you will obey my voice and keep my covenant, you shall be my own possession among all peoples . . . [Exodus 19:4–5a].

Certainly this means, among other things, that God's call of this people is related to its oppressed

Reprinted with permission of the publisher from *A Black Theology of Liberation* (Maryknoll, NY: Orbis Books, 1990), pp. 1–11, 55–57, 63–66.

condition and to God's own liberating activity already seen in the exodus. *You have seen what I did!* By delivering this people from Egyptian bondage and inaugurating the covenant on the basis of that historical event, God is revealed as the God of the oppressed, involved in their history, liberating them from human bondage.

(2) Later stages of Israelite history also show that God is particularly concerned about the oppressed within the community of Israel. The rise of Old Testament prophecy is due primarily to the lack of justice within that community. The prophets of Israel are prophets of social justice, reminding the people that Yahweh is the author of justice. It is important to note in this connection that the righteousness of God is not an abstract quality in the being of God, as with Greek philosophy. It is rather God's active involvement in history, making right what human beings have made wrong. The consistent theme in Israelite prophecy is Yahweh's concern for the lack of social, economic, and political justice for those who are poor and unwanted in society. Yahweh, according to Hebrew prophecy, will not tolerate injustice against the poor; God will vindicate the poor. Again, God is revealed as the God of liberation for the oppressed.

(3) In the New Testament, the theme of liberation is reaffirmed by Jesus himself. The conflict with Satan and the powers of this world, the condemnation of the rich, the insistence that the kingdom of God is for the poor, and the locating of his ministry among the poor—these and other features of the career of Jesus show that his work was directed to the oppressed for the purpose of their liberation. To suggest that he was speaking of a "spiritual" liberation fails to take seriously Jesus' thoroughly Hebrew view of human nature. Entering into the kingdom of God means that Jesus himself becomes the ultimate loyalty of humankind, for *he is the kingdom.* This view of existence in the world has far-reaching implications for economic, political, and social institutions. They can no longer have ultimate claim on human life; human beings are liberated and thus free to rebel against all powers that threaten human life. That is what Jesus had in mind when he said:

The Spirit of the Lord is upon me, because he has anointed me to preach good news to the poor. He has sent me to proclaim release to the captives and recovering of sight to the blind, to set at liberty those who are oppressed, to proclaim the acceptable year of the Lord [Luke 4:18–19].

In view of the biblical emphasis on liberation, it seems not only appropriate but necessary to define the Christian community as the community of the oppressed which joins Jesus Christ in his fight for the liberation of humankind. The task of theology, then, is to explicate the meaning of God's liberating activity so that those who labor under enslaving powers will see that the forces of liberation are the very activity of God. Christian theology is never just a rational study of the being of God. Rather it is a study of God's liberating activity in the world, God's activity in behalf of the oppressed.

If the history of Israel and the New Testament description of the historical Jesus reveal that God is a God who is identified with Israel because it is an oppressed community, the resurrection of Jesus means that all oppressed peoples become his people. Herein lies the universal note implied in the gospel message of Jesus. The resurrection-event means that God's liberating work is not only for the house of Israel but for all who are enslaved by principalities and powers. The resurrection conveys hope in God. Nor is this the "hope" that promises a reward in heaven in order to ease the pain of injustice on earth. Rather it is hope which focuses on the future in order to make us refuse to tolerate present inequities. To see the future of God, as revealed in the resurrection of Jesus, is to see also the contradiction of any earthly injustice with existence in Jesus Christ. That is why Camilo Torres was right when he described revolutionary action as "a Christian, a priestly struggle."[1]

The task of Christian theology, then, is to analyze the meaning of hope in God in such a way that the oppressed community of a given society will risk all for earthly freedom, a freedom made possible in the resurrection of Jesus. The language of theology challenges societal structures because it is inseparable from the suffering community.

Theology can never be neutral or fail to take sides on issues related to the plight of the oppressed. For this reason it can never engage in conversation about the nature of God without confronting those elements of human existence which threaten anyone's existence as a person. Whatever theology says about God and the world must arise out of its sole reason for existence as a discipline: to assist the oppressed in their liberation. Its language is always language about human liberation, proclaiming the end of bondage and interpreting the religious dimensions of revolutionary struggle.

Liberation and Black Theology

Unfortunately, American white theology has not been involved in the struggle for black liberation. It has been basically a theology of the white oppressor, giving religious sanction to the genocide of Amerindians and the enslavement of Africans. From the very beginning to the present day, American white theological thought has been "patriotic," either by defining the theological task independently of black suffering (the liberal northern approach) or by defining Christianity as compatible with white racism (the conservative southern approach). In both cases theology becomes a servant of the state, and that can only mean death to blacks. It is little wonder that an increasing number of black religionists are finding it difficult to be black *and* be identified with traditional theological thought forms.

The appearance of black theology[2] on the American scene then is due primarily to the failure of white religionists to relate the gospel of Jesus to the pain of being black in a white racist society. It arises from the need of blacks to liberate themselves from white oppressors. Black theology is a theology of liberation because it is a theology which arises from an identification with the oppressed blacks of America, seeking to interpret the gospel of Jesus in the light of the black condition. It believes that the liberation of the black community *is* God's liberation.

The task of black theology, then, is to analyze the nature of the gospel of Jesus Christ in the light of oppressed blacks so they will see the gospel as inseparable from their humiliated condition, and as bestowing on them the necessary power to break the chains of oppression. This means that it is a theology of and for the black community, seeking to interpret the religious dimensions of the forces of liberation in that community.

There are two reasons why black theology is Christian theology. First, there can be no theology of the gospel which does not arise from an oppressed community. This is so because God is revealed in Jesus as a God whose righteousness is inseparable from the weak and helpless in human Society. The goal of black theology is to interpret God's activity as related to the oppressed black community.

Secondly, black theology is Christian theology because it centers on Jesus Christ. There can be no Christian theology which does not have Jesus Christ as its point of departure. Though black theology affirms the black condition as the primary datum of reality to be reckoned with, this does not mean that it denies the absolute revelation of God in Jesus Christ. Rather it affirms it. Unlike white theology, which tends to make the Jesus-event an abstract, unembodied idea, black theology believes that the black community itself is precisely where Jesus Christ is at work. The Jesus-event in twentieth-century America is a black-event—that is, an event of liberation taking place in the black community in which blacks recognize that it is incumbent upon them to throw off the chains of white oppression by whatever means they regard as suitable. This is what God's revelation means to black and white America, and why black theology is an indispensable theology for our time.

It is to be expected that some will ask, "Why black theology? Is it not true that God is color-blind? Is it not true that there are others who suffer as much as, if not in some cases more than, blacks?" These questions reveal a basic misunderstanding of black theology, and also a superficial view of the world at large. There are at least three points to be made here.

First, in a revolutionary situation there can never be nonpartisan theology. Theology is always identified with a particular community. It is either identified with those who inflict oppression or with those who are its victims. A theology of the latter is authentic Christian theology, and a theology of the former is a theology of the Antichrist. Insofar as black theology is a theology arising from an identification with the oppressed black community and seeks to interpret the gospel of Jesus Christ in the light of the liberation of that community, it is Christian theology. American white theology is a theology of the Antichrist insofar as it arises from an identification with the white community, thereby placing God's approval on white oppression of black existence.

Secondly, in a racist society, God is never color-blind. To say God is color-blind is analogous to saying that God is blind to justice and injustice, to right and wrong, to good and evil. Certainly this is not the picture of God revealed in the Old and New Testaments. Yahweh takes sides. On the one hand, Yahweh sides with Israel against the Canaanites in the occupancy of Palestine. On the other hand, Yahweh sides with the poor within the community of Israel against the rich and other political oppressors. In the New Testament, Jesus is not for *all,* but for the oppressed, the poor and unwanted of society, and against oppressors. The God of the biblical tradition is not uninvolved or neutral regarding human affairs; God is decidedly involved. God is active in human history, taking sides with the oppressed of the land. If God is not involved in human history, then all theology is useless, and Christianity itself is a mockery, a hollow, meaningless diversion.

The meaning of this message for our contemporary situation is clear: the God of the oppressed takes sides with the black community. God is not color-blind in the black-white struggle, but has made an unqualified identification with blacks. This means that the movement for black liberation is the very work of God, effecting God's will among men.

Thirdly, there are, to be sure, many who suffer, and not all of them are black. Many white liberals derive a certain joy from reminding black militants that two-thirds of the poor in America are white. Of course I could point out that this means that there are five times as many poor blacks as there are poor whites, when the ratio of each group to the total population is taken into account. But it is not my intention to debate white liberals on this issue, for it is not the purpose of black theology to minimize the suffering of others, including whites. Black theology merely tries to discern the activity of the Holy One in achieving the purpose of the liberation of humankind from the forces of oppression.

We *must* make decisions about where God is at work so we can join in the fight against evil. But there is no perfect guide for discerning God's movement in the world. Contrary to what many conservatives would say, the Bible is not a blueprint on this matter. It is a valuable symbol for pointing to God's revelation in Jesus, but it is not self-interpreting. We are thus placed in an existential situation of freedom in which the burden is on us to make decisions without a guaranteed ethical guide. This is the risk of faith. For the black theologian God is at work in the black community, vindicating black victims of white oppression. It is impossible for the black theologian to be indifferent on this issue. Either God is for blacks in their fight for liberation from white oppressors, or God is not. God cannot be both for us and for white oppressors at the same time.

In this connection we may observe that black theology takes seriously Paul Tillich's description of the symbolic nature of all theological speech.[3] We cannot describe God directly; we must use symbols that point to dimensions of reality that cannot be spoken of literally. Therefore to speak of black theology is to speak with the Tillichian understanding of symbol in mind. The focus on blackness does not mean that *only* blacks suffer as victims in a racist society, but that blackness is an ontological symbol and a visible reality which best describes what oppression means in America.

The extermination of Amerindians, the persecution of Jews, the oppression of Mexican-Americans, and every other conceivable inhumanity done in the name of God and country—these brutalities can be analyzed in terms of the white American inability to recognize humanity in persons of color. If the oppressed of this land want to challenge the oppressive character of white society, they must begin by affirming their identity in terms of the reality that is antiwhite. Blackness, then, stands for all victims of oppression who realize that the survival of their humanity is bound up with liberation from whiteness.[4]

This understanding of blackness can be seen as the most adequate symbol of the dimensions of divine activity in America. And insofar as this country is seeking to make whiteness the dominating power throughout the world, whiteness is the symbol of the Anti-christ. Whiteness characterizes the activity of deranged individuals intrigued by their own image of themselves, and thus unable to see that they are what is wrong with the world. Black theology seeks to analyze the satanic nature of whiteness and by doing so to prepare all nonwhites for revolutionary action.

In passing, it may be worthwhile to point out that whites are in no position whatever to question the legitimacy of black theology. Questions like "Do you think theology is black?" or "What about others who suffer?" are the product of minds incapable of *black* thinking. It is not surprising that those who reject blackness in theology are usually whites who do not question the blue-eyed white Christ. It is hard to believe that whites are worried about black theology on account of its alleged alienation of other sufferers. Oppressors are not genuinely concerned about *any* oppressed group. It would seem rather that white rejection of black theology stems from a recognition of the revolutionary implications in its very name: a rejection of whiteness, an unwillingness to live under it, and an identification of whiteness with evil and blackness with good.

Black Theology and the Black Community

Most theologians agree that theology is a church discipline—that is, a discipline which functions within the Christian community. This is one aspect which distinguishes theology from philosophy of religion. Philosophy of religion is not committed to a community; it is an individualistic attempt to analyze the nature of ultimate reality through rational thought alone, using elements of many religions to assist in the articulation of the ultimate.

Theology by contrast cannot be separated from the community which it represents. It assumes that *truth* has been given to the community at the moment of its birth. Its task is to analyze the implications of that truth, in order to make sure that the community remains committed to that which defines its existence. Theology is the continued attempt of the community to define in every generation its reason for being in the world. A community that does not analyze its existence theologically is a community that does not care what it says or does. It is a community with no identity.

Applying this description, it is evident that white American theology has served oppressors well. Throughout the history of this country, from the Puritans to the death-of-God theologians, the theological problems treated in white churches and theological schools are defined in such a manner that they are unrelated to the problem of being black in a white, racist society. By defining the problems of Christianity in isolation from the black condition, white theology becomes a theology of white oppressors, serving as a divine sanction from criminal acts committed against blacks.

No white theologian has ever taken the oppression of blacks as a point of departure for analyzing God's activity in contemporary America. Apparently white theologians see no connection between whiteness and evil or blackness and God. Even those white theologians who write books about blacks invariably fail to say anything relevant to the black community as it seeks to break the power of white racism. They usually think that writing books makes them experts on black humanity. As a result they are as arrogant as George Wallace in telling blacks what is "best" for them. It is no surprise that the "best" is always nonviolent, posing no threat to the political and social interests of the white majority.

Because white theology has consistently preserved the integrity of the community of oppressors, I conclude that it is not Christian theology at all.[5] When we speak about God as related to humankind in the black-white struggle, Christian theology can only mean black theology, a theology that speaks of God as related to black liberation. If we agree that the gospel is the proclamation of God's liberating activity, that the Christian community is an oppressed community that participates in that activity, and that theology is the discipline arising from within the Christian community as it seeks to develop adequate language for its relationship to God's liberation, then black theology is Christian theology.

It is unthinkable that oppressors could identify with oppressed existence and thus say something relevant about God's liberation of the oppressed. In order to be Christian theology, white theology must cease being *white* theology and become black theology by denying whiteness as an acceptable form of human existence and affirming blackness as God's intention for humanity. White theologians will find this difficult, and it is to be expected that some will attempt to criticize black theology precisely on this point. Such criticism will not reveal a weakness in black theology but only the racist character of the critic.

Black theology will not spend too much time trying to answer its critics, because it is accountable only to the black community. Refusing to be separated from that community, black theology seeks to articulate the theological self-determination of blacks, providing some ethical and religious categories for the black revolution in America. It maintains that all acts which participate in the destruction of white racism are Christian, the liberating deeds of God. All acts which impede the struggle of black self-determination—black power—are anti-Christian, the work of Satan.

The revolutionary context forces black theology to shun all abstract principles dealing with what is the "right" and "wrong" course of action. There is only one principle which guides the thinking and action of black theology: an unqualified commitment to the black community as that community seeks to define its existence in the light of God's liberating work in the world. This means that black theology refuses to be guided by ideas and concepts alien to blacks. It assumes that whites encountering black thought will judge it "irrational." Not understanding what it means to be oppressed, the oppressor is in no position to understand the methods which the oppressed use in liberation. The logic of liberation is always incomprehensible to slave masters. From their position of power, masters never understand what slaves mean by "dignity." The only dignity they know is that of killing slaves, as if "superior" humanity depended on the enslavement of others. Black theology does not intend to debate with whites who have this perspective. Speaking for the black community, black theology says with Eldridge Cleaver, "We shall have our manhood. We shall have it, or the earth will be leveled by our attempts to gain it." . . .

GOD IN BLACK THEOLOGY

The reality of God is presupposed in black theology. Black theology is an attempt to analyze the nature of that reality, asking what we can say about the nature of God in view of God's self-disclosure in biblical history and the oppressed condition of black Americans.

If we take the question seriously, it becomes evident that there is no simple answer to it. To speak of God and God's participation in the liberation of the oppressed of the land is a risky venture in any society. But if the society is racist and also uses God-language as an instrument to further the cause of human humiliation, then the task of authentic theological speech is even more dangerous and difficult.

It is *dangerous* because the true prophet of the gospel of God must become both "anti-Christian" and "unpatriotic." It is impossible to confront a racist society, with the meaning of human existence grounded in commitment to the divine, without at the same time challenging the very existence of the national structure and all its institutions, especially the established churches. All national institutions represent the interests of society as a whole. We live in a nation which is committed to the perpetuation of white supremacy, and it will try to exterminate all who fail to support this ideal. The genocide of the Amerindian is evidence of that fact. Black theology represents that community of blacks who refuse to cooperate in the exaltation of whiteness and the degradation of blackness. It proclaims the reality of the biblical God who is actively destroying everything that is against the manifestation of black human dignity.

Because whiteness by its very nature is against blackness, the black prophet is a prophet of national doom. He proclaims the end of the "American Way," for God has stirred the soul of the black community, and now that community will stop at nothing to claim the freedom that is three hundred and fifty years overdue. The black prophet is a rebel with a cause, the cause of over twenty-five million American blacks and all oppressed persons everywhere. It is God's cause because God has chosen the blacks as God's own people. And God has chosen them not for redemptive suffering but for freedom. Blacks are not elected to be Yahweh's suffering people. Rather we are elected because we are oppressed against our will and God's, and God has decided to make our liberation God's own undertaking. We are elected to be free now to do the work for which we were called into being—namely, the breaking of chains. Black theologians must assume the dangerous responsibility of articulating the revolutionary mood of the black community. This means that their speech about God, in the authentic prophetic tradition, will always move on the brink of treason and heresy in an oppressive society.

The task of authentic theological speech is *difficult* because all religionists in society claim to be for God and thus for humankind. Even executioners are for God. They carry out punitive acts against certain segments of society because "decent" citizens need protection against undesirables. That is why blacks were enslaved and Amerindians exterminated—in the name of God and freedom. That is why today blacks are forced into ghettos and shot down like dogs if they raise a hand in protest.

When George Washington, Thomas Jefferson, Lyndon Johnson, Richard Nixon, and other "great" Americans can invoke the name of God at the same time that they are shaping society for whites only, then black theology knows it cannot approach the God-question too casually. It must ask, "How can we speak of God without being associated with oppressors?" White racism is so pervasive that oppressors can destroy the revolutionary mood among the oppressed by introducing a complacent white God into the black community, thereby quelling the spirit of freedom.

Therefore if blacks want to break their chains, they must recognize the need for going all the way if liberation is to be a reality. The white God will point to heavenly bliss as a means of detouring blacks away from earthly rage. Freedom comes when we realize that it is against our interests, as a self-determining black community, to point out the "good" elements in an oppressive structure. *There are no assets to slavery!* Every segment of society participates in black oppression. To accept the white God, to see good in evil, is to lose sight of the goal of the revolution—the destruction of everything "masterly" in society. "All or nothing" is the only possible attitude for the black community. . . .

God Is Black

Because blacks have come to know themselves as *black,* and because that blackness is the cause of their own love of themselves and hatred of whiteness, the blackness of God is the key to our knowledge of God. The blackness of God, and everything implied by it in a racist society, is the heart of the black theology doctrine of God. There is no place in black theology for a colorless God in a society where human beings suffer precisely because of their color. The black theologian must reject any conception of God which stifles black self-determination by picturing God as a God of all peoples. Either God is identified with the oppressed to the point that their experience becomes God's experience, or God is a God of racism.

As Camus has pointed out, authentic identification

[Is not] a question of psychological identification—a mere subterfuge by which the individual imagines that it is he himself who is being offended. . . . [It is] identification of one's destiny with that of others and a choice of sides.[6]

Because God has made the goal of blacks God's own goal, black theology believes that it is not only appropriate but necessary to begin the doctrine of God with an insistence on God's blackness.

The blackness of God means that God has made the oppressed condition God's own condition. This is the essence of the biblical revelation. By electing Israelite slaves as the people of God and by becoming the Oppressed One in Jesus Christ, the human race is made to understand that God is known where human beings experience humiliation and suffering. It is not that God feels sorry and takes pity on them (the condescending attitude of those racists who need their guilt assuaged for getting fat on the starvation of others); quite the contrary, God's election of Israel and incarnation in Christ reveal that the *liberation* of the oppressed is a part of the innermost nature of God. Liberation is not an afterthought, but the essence of divine activity.

The blackness of God means that the essence of the nature of God is to be found in the concept of liberation. Taking seriously the Trinitarian view of the Godhead, black theology says that as Creator, God identified with oppressed Israel, participating in the bringing into being of this people; as Redeemer, God became the Oppressed One in order that all may be free from oppression; as Holy Spirit, God continues the work of liberation. The Holy Spirit is the Spirit of the Creator and the Redeemer at work in the forces of human libera-

tion in our society today. In America, the Holy Spirit is black persons making decisions about their togetherness, which means making preparation for an encounter with whites.

It is the black theology emphasis on the blackness of God that distinguishes it sharply from contemporary white views of God. White religionists are not capable of perceiving the blackness of God, because their satanic whiteness is a denial of the very essence of divinity. That is why whites are finding and will continue to find the black experience a disturbing reality.

White theologians would prefer to do theology without reference to color, but this only reveals how deeply racism is embedded in the thought forms of their culture. To be sure, they would *probably* concede that the concept of liberation is essential to the biblical view of God. But it is still impossible for them to translate the biblical emphasis on liberation to the black-white struggle today. Invariably they quibble on this issue, moving from side to side, always pointing out the dangers of extremism on both sides. (In the black community, we call this "shuffling.") They really cannot make a decision, because it has already been made for them.

How scholars would analyze God and blacks was decided when black slaves were brought to this land, while churchmen sang "Jesus, Lover of My Soul." Their attitude today is no different from that of the bishop of London who assured slaveholders that:

Christianity, and the embracing of the Gospel, does not make the least Alteration in Civil property, or in any Duties which belong to Civil Relations; but in all these Respects, it continues Persons just in the same State as it found them. The Freedom which Christianity gives, is a Freedom from the Bondage of Sin and Satan, and from the dominion of Man's Lust and Passions and inordinate Desires; but as to their outward Condition, whatever that was before, whether bond or free, their being baptized and becoming Christians, makes no matter of change in it.[7]

Of course white theologians today have a "better" way of putting it, but what difference does that make? It means the same thing to blacks.

"Sure," as the so-called radicals would say, "God is concerned about blacks." And then they would go on to talk about God and secularization or some other white problem unrelated to the emancipation of blacks. This style is a contemporary white way of saying that "Christianity . . . does not make the least alteration in civil property."

In contrast to this racist view of God, black theology proclaims God's blackness. Those who want to know who God is and what God is doing must know who black persons are and what they are doing. This does not mean lending a helping hand to the poor and unfortunate blacks of society. It does not mean joining the war on poverty! Such acts are sin offerings that represent a white way of assuring themselves that they are basically "good" persons. Knowing God means being on the side of the oppressed, becoming *one* with them, and participating in the goal of liberation. *We must become black with God!*

It is to be expected that whites will have some difficulty with the idea of "becoming *black* with God." The experience is not only alien to their existence as they know it to be, it appears to be an impossibility. "How can whites become black?" they ask. This question always amuses me because they do not really want to lose their precious white identity, as if it is worth saving. They know, as everyone in this country knows, blacks are those who say they are black, regardless of skin color. In the literal sense a black person is anyone who has "even one drop of black blood in his or her veins."

But "becoming black with God" means more than just saying "I am black," if it involves that at all. The question "How can white persons become black?" is analogous to the Philippian jailer's question to Paul and Silas, "What must I do to be saved?" The implication is that if we work hard enough at it, we can reach the goal. But the misunderstanding here is the failure to see that blackness or salvation (the two are synonymous) is the work of God, not a human work. It is not something we accomplish; it is a gift. That is why Paul and Silas said, "Believe in the Lord Jesus and you will be saved."

To *believe* is to receive the gift and utterly to reorient one's existence on the basis of the gift. The gift is so unlike what humans expect that when it is offered and accepted, we become completely new creatures. This is what the Wholly Otherness of God means. God comes to us in God's blackness, which is wholly unlike whiteness. To receive God's revelation is to become black with God by joining God in the work of liberation.

Even some blacks will find this view of God hard to handle. Having been enslaved by the God of white racism so long, they will have difficulty believing that God is identified with their struggle for freedom. Becoming one of God's disciples means rejecting whiteness and accepting themselves as they are in all their physical blackness. This is what the Christian view of God means for blacks.

Discussion Questions

1. Should Christianity and Christian theology be concerned *only* with the oppressed?
2. How does Cone reply to the objection that the kind of "liberation" Christianity promises is only "spiritual"? Is his reply satisfactory to you?
3. If one is going to be a social revolutionary like Cone, why not go the whole road, like the Marxists, who deny God altogether, maintaining that religion is the "opiate of the masses"?
4. Is Cone adequately sensitive to the difference between a "colorless God" and a "colorblind God?"
5. To what extent was Jesus a social revolutionary on a par with Mao, Lenin, or Malcolm X?

Notes

1. Quoted in José Míguez Bonino, "Christians and the Political Revolution," in S. C. Rose and P. P. Van Lelyveld, eds., *Risk*, spec. ed., *The Development Apocalypse*, 1967, p. 109.
2. See James Cone, *Black Theology and Black Power* (New York: The Seabury Press, 1969).
3. See Paul Tillich, *Dynamics of Faith* (New York: Harper and Brothers, 1957).

4. I do not intend to qualify this statement, because too much is at stake—the survival of the black community. But perhaps some clarification is needed here. Some critics will undoubtedly ask, "How can you dismiss out of hand any criticisms that white theologians or others in traditional white Christianity might raise concerning your interpretation of black theology, and at the same time use quotations from white theologians, both European and American, with approval? If white theology is as bad as you say, why not dismiss them altogether, without any reference to their work?" Of course, these are challenging questions, and I can see whites milking this idea for all that it is worth.

There are essentially two responses. First, those who press this point have taken too seriously the American definition of white. When I say that white theology is not Christian theology, I mean the theology that has been written without any reference to the oppressed of the land. This is not true of Karl Barth and certainly not true of Dietrich Bonhoeffer. Reinhold Niebuhr's *Moral Man and Immoral Society* moves in the direction of blackness. To verify the blackness of a particular perspective, we need only ask, "For whom was it written, the oppressed or oppressors?" If the former, it is black; if the latter, it is white. I do not condemn all persons who happen to look like white Americans; the condemnation comes when they act like them.

Secondly, it is characteristic of the oppressed to be limited to the thought forms of those who call themselves the masters. Oppression refers not only to economic, social, and political disfranchisement; there is the disfranchisement of the mind, of the spiritual and moral values that hold together one's identity in a community. To be oppressed is to be defined, located, or set aside according to another's perspective. This is pre-cisely what has happened to black persons in America. If they would be free, they must use the thought forms of the master and transform them into ideas of liberation. If blacks clearly understood the meaning of their spirituality, from their own vantage point, they would not be oppressed. The task of black theology is to take Christian tradition that is so white and make it black, by showing that whites do not really know what they are saying when they affirm Jesus as the Christ. He who has come to redeem us is not white but black; and the redemption of which he speaks has nothing to do with stabilizing the status quo. It motivates the redeemed to be what they are—creatures endowed with freedom.

5. The reader should take note of two characteristics of the definition of blackness. First, blackness is a *physiological* trait. It refers to a particular black-skinned people in America, a victim of white racist brutality. The scars of its members bear witness to the inhumanity committed against them. Black theology believes that they are the *only* key that can open the door to divine revelation. Therefore, no American theology can even tend in the direction of Christian theology without coming to terms with the black-skinned people of America. Secondly, blackness is an *ontological* symbol for all those who participate in liberation from oppression. This is the universal note in black theology. It believes that all human beings were created for freedom, and that God always sides with the oppressed against oppressors.

6. Albert Camus, *The Rebel*, trans. by Anthony Bower, Vintage Book V30 (New York: Random House, 1956), pp. 16, 17.

7. Quoted in H. Richard Niebuhr, *The Social Sources of Denominationalism* (Cleveland: Meridian Books, 1929), p. 249.

48   Ontological Blackness in Theology

VICTOR ANDERSON

Study Questions

1. What are the main elements of Cone's black theology?
2. For Anderson, what is the relevance of the distinction between "struggle, resistance, and survival" and "thriving, flourishing, or fulfillment"?
3. What basic difficulty does Anderson pose for Cone's notion of black theology as grounded in "black experience"?
4. What second criticism does Anderson raise in terms of Tillich's theory of religious language?
5. What is Hopkins' project "of the hermeneutics of return" and what criticisms does Anderson raise of this?

Reprinted with permission of the publisher from *Beyond Ontological Blackness* (New York: Continuum, 1995), pp. 86–104.

In 1969, a revolutionary moment in black American culture, James H. Cone wrote: "What is needed is not integration but a sense of worth in being black, and only black people can teach that. Black consciousness is the key to the Black man's emancipation from his distorted self-image" (1989, 19). The juxtaposition of black revolutionary consciousness (as the subject of liberation) and hope (as the ground motive of liberation) frame the argument of this chapter. The black theology project was born out of the chaos of deferred cultural fulfillment. A new revolutionary racial consciousness was ascending among an emergent educated class of black intellectuals and black theology sought to defend this revolutionary agenda.

Black theology would take its point of departure from black life and experience, which constitute the exceptional social location for a theology of black power. If white theology was viewed as an ideology of oppression, then black theology would become the ideology of liberation (127). Black theology's method is correlational. The task of the black theologian is to show the critical correlations existing between black life/experience and traditional theological categories (God, humanity, Christ, eschatology, and so forth), between black religion and black radicalism Wilmore, 1983), and the correlations between the black church and black theology. The sources of black theology are black history, black faith, and black cultural activities. And the ultimate end of black theology is the construction of a "new black being" (134).

The argument of this chapter is that black theology constructs its new being on the dialectical structures that categorical racism and white racial ideology bequeathed to African American intellectuals (notwithstanding its claims for privileging black sources). However, the new being of black theology remains an alienated being whose mode of existence is determined by crisis, struggle, resistance, and survival—not thriving, flourishing, or fulfillment. Its self-identity is always bound by white racism and the culture of survival. The motive of transcendence from this unresolved matrix of struggle and survival recedes into the background as oppression is required for the self-disclosure of the oppressed. I suggest that as long as black theology remains determined by ontological blackness, it remains not only a crisis theology but also a theology in a crisis of legitimation.

The Black Theology Project

The expressive elements of black heroic genius in African American theology peaked in 1969 and the 70s in the black theology project. James H. Cone is its unsurpassed representative. In the preface to his 1986 edition of *A Black Theology of Liberation* (1991), first published in 1970, Cone framed his discourse under the idea of ontological blackness. Cone suggests that the theological problem for blacks as well as the entire problem of American culture is subsumed under white racism. And in the matrix of black existence and white racism, Cone explicates the meaning of ontological blackness in terms of an emergent collective black revolutionary consciousness (23). The critical task of black theologians is to disclose the "essential religious and theological meaning" of this new black collective consciousness in light of the black experience, black history, and black culture. Black experience is a "totality of black existence in a white world where babies are tortured, women are raped, and men are shot. . . . The black experience is existence in a system of white racism" (24). Such an experiential matrix is symbolized by Cone as a *Symbolic Blackness* (7). It expresses itself in:

The power to love oneself precisely because one is black and a readiness to die if whites try to make one behave otherwise. It is the sound of James Brown singing, "I'm Black and I'm Proud" and Aretha Franklin demanding "respect." The black experience is catching the spirit of blackness and loving it. It is hearing black preachers speak of God's love in spite of the filthy ghetto, and black congregations responding Amen, which means that they realize that ghetto existence is not the result of divine decree but of white inhumanity. (25)

The black theology project seeks to disclose the essential meanings of black faith in the black

God revealed in the black Christ from the perspective of the black experience. Cone writes in a later work:

When I speak of black faith, I am referring only secondarily to organized religion and primarily to black people's collective acknowledgment of the spirit of liberation in their midst, a Spirit who empowers them to struggle for freedom even though the odds are against them. This is the historical matrix out of which my hermeneutical perspective has been formed. (1986, 43)

The essential meaning of the black collective consciousness (ontological blackness) is the resolve of two cultural motifs, both of which are reconfigurations of the classical black aesthetic: black survivalist culture and black revolutionary self-assertion.

Survival "is a way of life for the black community," says Cone. And C. Eric Lincoln and Lawrence Mamiya would write twenty years after Cone, in their monumental work on the black church, that black "culture is the sum of the options for creative survival" (1990, 3). "Black theology is a theology of survival," Cone argued, "because it seeks to interpret the theological significance of the being of a community whose existence is threatened by the power of non-being" (1991, 16). Moreover, it seeks to elicit the essential theological meaning of black self-assertion as "an event of liberation taking place in the black community in which blacks recognize that it is incumbent upon them to throw off the chains of white oppression by whatever means they regard as necessary" (5). And, for Cone, any means necessary might mean "attacking the enemy of black humanity by throwing a Molotov cocktail into a white-owned building and watching it go up in flames" (25). Although such a position seems revolutionary enough, such an act of racial frustration is not likely to transact cultural fulfillment.

It is only insofar as Cone extends these essentialized meanings of the new black revolutionary consciousness to black cultural productions themselves that ontological blackness climaxes in the absurdity that "the black experience is possible only for black persons":

[The black experience] means having natural hair cuts, wearing African dashikis, and dancing to the sound of Johnny Lee Hooker or B. B. King, knowing that no matter how hard whitey tries there can be no real duplication of black "soul." Black soul is not learned; *it comes from the totality of black experience,* the experience of carving out an existence in a society that says you do not belong. (25; emphasis mine)

For Cone, the essential theological meanings of black experience, black history, and black culture—all of which represent the black collective consciousness—emerge in a symbolic expressive play of the heroic survivalist culture of the black community, the pain and joy it derives from "reacting to whiteness and affirming blackness" and "the mythic power inherent in [its historical] symbols for the present revolution against white racism" (28). When the theological meaning of ontological blackness is accented, black theology approaches an identification of black culture with the Christ event in which "God's revelation comes to us in and through the cultural situation of the oppressed" (28). And black culture (art, music, literature, and theology) is the expressive vehicle of black liberation by the black messiah.

A number of problems plagued Cone's project from the beginning. These problems centered around the relation of black theology to the black churches. Early critics, particularly those who pressed internal criticisms as black church theologians, asked how black theology could be a theology of the black churches if it fundamentally disentangles itself from the creeds and confessions, as well as the liturgical practices that structure the black churches. To some, black theology appeared to posit within itself a revolutionary consciousness that looked more like the mirror of white racism and less like an expression of the evangelical gospel that characterized most black churches. Was black theology, then, an academic project in theology rather than an ecclesiastical project? Others asked, in what sense could black theology be black since its theological method was derived from white European theologians, notably Karl Barth and Paul Tillich, and European philosophers such as Albert Camus and Jean Paul Sartre?

In subsequent writings throughout the 70s and 80s, Cone tried to answer many of the problems that center around the relation of black theology to the black churches and to black culture in books such as *A Black Theology of Liberation* (1970), *The Spirituals and the Blues* (1972), *God of the Oppressed* (1975), and *Speaking the Truth* (1986). The fundamental difficulty lies in Cone's call for the radical disentanglement of black theology from white theology and European religious sources.

Cone's radically oppositional rhetoric leaves him with this dilemma: he could either capitulate his claims for exceptionalism in the production of black theology by acknowledging the indebtedness of black theology to the west European manuscript tradition in the theological formation of the black churches, or he might insist on the radical disjunction of black theology from European sources and remain a theologian alienated from the theology of the churches and their evangelical roots. Cone chose the latter. He attempted to overcome his academic alienation from the black churches by emphasizing the necessity of black sources for the construction of black theology. But this apologetic preoccupation with black sources creates more contradictions in the project than it solves.

Most of Cone's problems center around the category of symbolic blackness. Cone's problems are matters of internal contradiction. First, black theology, as Cone formulated it, risks self-referential inconsistency when it sees itself as radically oppositional to white racism and white theology. Because Cone collapses metaphysics into ontology, blackness is reified into a totality or a unity of black experience. At the same time, blackness is regarded as symbolic, so that anyone who can participate in its meaning can also be said to be black (1990, 9). However, black theology exceptionally circumscribes the meaning of symbolic blackness in terms of black oppression and suffering.

The difficulty arises here: (a) blackness is a signification of ontology and corresponds to black experience. (b) Black experience is defined as the experience of suffering and rebellion against whiteness. Yet (c) both black suffering and rebellion are ontologically created and provoked by whiteness as a necessary condition of blackness. (d) Whiteness appears to be the ground of black experience, and hence of black theology and its new black being. Therefore, while black theology justifies itself as radically oppositional to whiteness, it nevertheless requires whiteness, white racism, and white theology for the self-disclosure of its new black being and its legitimacy. In this way, black theology effectively renders whiteness identifiable with what is of ultimate concern. "Our ultimate concern is that which determines our being or not being," says Tillich (1967, 14).

The cogency of black theology, in its classical formulation, also appears performatively contradictory. Cone defined blackness in terms of Tillich's semiotics (1990, 7). On Tillich's terms, then, symbolic blackness must point to something other than itself. According to Tillich, revelatory word-symbols have a basic correlation to the ultimate mystery signified by the symbol. However, the symbolic correlation of our ordinary language and ultimate mystery is asymtotic. Thus, while theological words are not identifiable with ultimate mystery, they nevertheless may have "a denotative power that points through the ordinary meaning to us." They also have an "expressive power which points through ordinary expressive possibilities of language to the unexpressible and its relations to us," says Tillich (1967, 124).

Whether denotatively or expressively, on Tillich's account, revelatory word-symbols reflexively point beyond their ordinary meanings to the unexpressible. Therefore, theological symbols approximate what is of ultimate concern but are not identifiable with ultimate concern. "When speaking of the ultimate, of being and meaning, ordinary language brings it down to the level of the preliminary, the conditioned, the finite, thus muffling its revelatory power," says Tillich (124). Theological symbols are idolatrous when they are taken for the ground of being or nonbeing.

In black theology, blackness has become a totality of meaning. It cannot point to any transcendent meaning beyond itself without also fragmenting. Because black life is fundamentally determined by black suffering and resistance to whiteness (the power of nonbeing), black existence is without the possibility of transcendence from the blackness that whiteness created. Without transcendence from the determinancy of whiteness, black theology's promise of liberation remains existentially a function of black self-consciousness (to see oneself as black, free, and self-determined). However, since as Cone argues it is whiteness, white racism, and white theology that threatens the nonbeing of blacks, the promise of black liberation remains bracketed both existentially and politically.

Existentially, the new black being remains bound by whiteness. Politically, it remains unfulfilled because blackness is ontologically defined as the experience of suffering and survival. Any amelioration of these essential marks of blackness performatively contradicts ontological blackness in black theology. Insofar as it is predicated ontologically on symbolic blackness, black theology remains alienated from black interests in not only surviving against suffering but also thriving, flourishing, and obtaining cultural fulfillment.

Subsequent projects of thinkers such as Dwight Hopkins, James Evans, and womanist thinkers, such as Katie Cannon, Jacquelyn Grant, and Delores Williams, have tried to reassure the ecclesiastical and public relevancy of black theology. In the remaining pages of this chapter, I make clear how these subsequent formulations of the black theology project differ from the classical formulation but, at the same time, remain under the burden of ontological blackness. The decisive turn occurs in these later theologians' intentions to reassure the exceptional and essential sources legitimizing the project under *the hermeneutics of return* to black sources and the expansion of experiential matrices for rethinking ontological blackness in light of black women's experience.

"The hermeneutics of return," as I retrieve the idea from Said (1993, xii–xiii), is a narrative return to distinctively black sources for the purpose of establishing and reassuring the legitimacy of black theology in a postrevolutionary context.

The theological gaze here returns to African traditional religions and slave narratives, autobiography, and folklore in order to assure the vitality of the black church (church theology) and the cultural solidarities that transcend the individualism that drives our market culture and morality, and rob the black community of moral vitality. The hermeneutics of return is a decisive element of African American fundamental theology. As a function of fundamental theology, hermeneutics is therefore prolegomenon to African American constructive theology.

Dwight N. Hopkins has been at the forefront of this fundamental theology. In his recent book, *Shoes That Fit Our Feet: Sources for a Constructive Black Theology* (1993), Hopkins attempts to play out the systematic implications of *slave theology* for the black theology project. Hopkins gives several significations for the sort of return he proposes for constructive black theology. The return is at once to *slave theology* and *bush arbor theology*. Yet as I shall show presently, both sources are attributive to black theology in such a way that it is not clear whether they are *sources* for a constructive black theology or the *product* of constructive black theology. Slave theology and African American religious experience are hybrids. Slave theology is the synthesis of "white Christianity with the remains of African religions under slavery," says Hopkins (1993, 15). As his argument goes, African slaves maintained enough residual aspects, or what Hopkins calls *remains,* of their former religions to establish a historically effective slave religion. This religion was preserved and transmitted in an invisible institution, among bushes and trees away from the eyes and ears of white and black guardians. In that institution, these *remains* achieved some measure of coherence and a regulative content. However, one of the problems in understanding Hopkins's argument is that while slave theology is fundamentally a religious hybrid, the individuated elements (African traditional religions, on the one side, and white Christianity, on the other side) are unidentifiable from the theological content of black theology.

Let us look more closely at Hopkins's argument. Hopkins argues that "enslaved Africans, the majority coming from the African West Coast, brought a distinct perception of God to North America" (16). And "African traditional religions described their ultimate divinity as the High God" (16). Hopkins then suggests that there is a correlation between the High God (who has no name in Hopkins's discourse) and Western "theological" notions of omnipresence, omnipotence, transcendence, and immanence. However, the correlation Hopkins proposes turns out to be one between the High God of African traditional religions and Israel's God.

Hopkins sees other correlations between African traditional religions and the Hebrew God when he compares cosmologies in which the earth and human flourishing are regarded as actions of the compassion and care of the High God and Yahweh:

African indigenous religions believe in a God who cares; some call God "the Compassionate One"; others see "the God of Pity," who rescues victims in need. Even more, God is kind and "looks after the case of the poor man." In fact, God is the main hope of the poor in society. As Guardian and Keeper, God is named "the protector of the poor" by some African traditional religions. They further specify that "there is a Saviour and only he can keep our lives." As Judge, God metes out justice, punishment, and retribution. Similarly, God displays protectiveness by avenging injustice. God is a divinity of partiality to the victim; God sides with the political powerlessness of society's injured. (17)

A third correlation is also proposed in what Hopkins regards as a theological anthropology. These religions are shown to share a "dynamic and interdependent relation between the individual and the community" (17). And this correlation justifies the opposition of black theology to *individualism.*

African religions gave rise to a dynamic interplay between community and individual. Whatever happened to the communal gathering affected the individual; whatever happened to the individual had an impact on the community. Such a theological view of humanity cuts across bourgeois notions of white Christianity's individualism and "me-firstism." It seeks to forge a group solidarity and identity, beginning with God, proceeding through the ancestors to the

community and immediate family and continuing even to the unborn. One cannot be a human being unless one becomes a part of, feels a responsibility to, and serves the community. To preserve the community's well-being (through liberation) in African religions is to preserve the individual's well-being (through salvation). Thus salvation and liberation become a holistic individual-collective and personal-systemic ultimate concern. (17)

Hopkins argues that there are possible correlations between the High God of African traditional religions and the Hebrew God at the levels of both formal and moral utterances. And there are possible correlations between the formal and moral utterances concerning humanity at the level of theological anthropology. However, Hopkins has the burden of showing that there is a correlation between the *remains* of African traditional religions, *Africanism(s)* and *slave religion.* He must also show that the elements in correspondence are genetically independent for a successful argument for hybridity. He argues that the biblical faith of the slaves effects the synthesis:

Enslaved Africans took the remnant of their traditional religious structures and meshed them together with their interpretation of the Bible. All of this occurred in the "Invisible Institution," far away from the watchful eyes of white people. Only in their own cultural idiom and political space could black slaves truly worship God. (18)

Bush arbor theology (the theology slaves created hidden among bushes and trees away from the eyes and ears of their masters) signifies a distinctive discursive site for the formation of a slave theology. Hopkins argues that among trees and bushes, slaves achieved "a remarkable clarity concerning the cultural dimension of their theology" (19). And the distinctive formation of their religious experience was materially manifest in ecstatic religious expressions and a political space from which they defined their humanity and established creative forms of resistance (19). Slave theology defines the content of its faith in terms of the egalitarian principle, absolute justice, and divine preference for the poor. Its content echoes both incarnational and resurrection triumphalism; and the mark of authenticity in religious experience is religious immediacy.

When I examine the claims that Hopkins makes for slave religion as a hybrid religion, I am left asking whether the hermeneutics of narrative return does not introduce more ambiguities and contradictions into Hopkins's project than it solves. Two lines of argument seem warranted: an examination of whether the coherence of Hopkins's project is compromised by committing a performative contradiction, and an examination of whether the project's legitimacy depends on a viciously circular mode of reasoning that commits hermeneutical violence not only to the African sources but also to the narrative sources. On the first charge, for all of Hopkins's talk about privileging African sources as an effective means for reassuring the legitimacy of black theology, these sources seem to fall out of or are simply consumed into Hebraic-Christian utterances. That is, so-called Africanisms are unidentifiable from the biblical utterances of Christian slaves. And instead of slave religion manifesting a hybridity, Hopkins's African slaves baptize the African gods into Hebrew faith. Therefore, Hopkins violates his principle of correlation by collapsing correlation into identification, since African religions collapse into biblical faith.

In order to explicate the biblical faith of the slaves, Hopkins has to show how the High God(s) of African traditional religions, tending to be *deus otiosus,* is identifiable with the Hebrew God of slave religions without also committing violence against the former God(s). Failure to demonstrate correlation constitutes a performative contradiction. Hopkins's argument for hybridity collapses in a performative contradiction for several reasons. Hopkins begs the question of whether the belief systems of African traditional religions are translatable (notwithstanding whatever family resemblances may exist between them and slave religion) into the languages of Hebrew/Christian faith without also committing violence against traditional religions.

Hopkins also does not show how the differences already signaled in the notion of African traditional *religions* (plural) are reducible to the sort of categorical simplicities which he calls

Africanisms. Hopkins calls these categories *remains.* But the misnomer seems ironically quite appropriate. For in the interest of forcing not only a correlation but also an identification of African traditional religions with slave religion, Hopkins has his slave theologians carrying the *remains* of their African gods into their invisible institution and disposing of the *remains* in the inauguration of slave religion. The performative contradiction renders the return to African traditional religions a moot point if, in the end, there are no recognizable differences that would count as independent sources for black theology.

This brings me to my second criticism: that Hopkins's hermeneutics of narrative return ends up justifying the black theology project by a vicious circularity of reasoning that renders the legitimacy of slave religion coterminous with black theology and the legitimacy of black liberation theology coterminous with slave religion. When comparing the utterances properly ascribed to the slave narratives with those characteristic of the black theology project, there appears to be no significant differences that would suggest that the latter (black theology) is effectively indebted to the former sources (African traditional religion and slave theology). Both antecedent sources tend to be identified as liberation utterances. This is to say that there appears to be no difference between a source (antecedent) and its effect (consequent).

The slave narratives are rendered as just so much *proto-black liberation theology.* At its best, this is an anachronism, and at its worst, this is hermeneutical violence for the sake of reassuring the identity of the black theology project by grounding it in authentic African American religious experience. By identifying the legitimacy of black theology with that of slave religion (authentic African American religious experience and practices), Hopkins *connotatively* overcomes one of the problems that has plagued the black theology project from its inception: How is black theology an authentic expression of the black churches and their theology, and not the ideological invention of black middle-class academic theologians (mostly heterosexual males) seeking to come to terms with their alienation from the everyday, routinized functions of the churches and their members?

My criticisms try to disclose intentions in the hermeneutics of return that distinguish the recent emphasis in the black theology project from its classical formulation in the 70s. I contend that the controlling intention is to reassure, in contemporary African American public life, the ideological position of the black theology project. In other words, the return to black sources is attributive to an ideological function that is culturally apologetic. It is apologetic insofar as black theology must assure its relevance for African American public life as a project that effectively contributes to the formation of a contemporary black cultural consciousness. Its cultural relevance is not self-evident. The *return* is also an attempt to place the black theology project in solidarity with the pressing problems of the urban underclass and its culture of poverty, and to construct a position that can effectively speak to the crisis of black nihilism and its culture of violence.

The hermeneutics of return projects a grand narrative that evokes a great cloud of witnesses whose heroic legacy of survival, resistance, and hope can mediate the fragility of African American public life today and bind together our alienated generation that is so much in need of a heroic black faith. But the consequence of such a hermeneutic is that whatever claims are made for African American identity in terms of black subjectivity, these are subsumed under a black collective consciousness definable in terms of black faith. So not only are the *remains* of the African gods disposed of under the totalizing hermeneutics of black theology, but black subjectivity itself is also subjugated under the totality of black faith.

The recent systematic theology by James H. Evans, Jr., *We Have Been Believers: An African American Systematic Theology* (1992), is another attempt to reassure the project of black theology in our postmodern context of African American cultural life. Like Hopkins, Evans also continues to legitimize the project of black academic theol-

ogy almost singularly in terms of ontological blackness and a cult of black heroic genius. Evans's project is also fundamentally justified in terms of a hermeneutic of return in which theology is primarily a church-dependent discourse that "is essentially the church's response to the autobiographical impulse, and it grows out of the need to proclaim with authority and commitment the identity and mission of the church in the world" (1992, 1).

However, a problem of academic black theology is its tendency toward alienation from the existential pathos and crises of the church as a community. The primary directive of Evans's book is to suggest ways in which the alienation of professional black theologians from church members can be overcome and how their mutual relation can be "strengthened so that it becomes clear that black theology is rooted in the faith of the church and that the faith of the church is given intellectual clarity and expression in black theology" (1).

Such clarity is predicated on hermeneutics more than on ritual performances, which are routinized in the everyday practices of the church. African American theology "requires a praxeological commitment to the community of faith" (1). And the faith that occupies the black theologian's tasks is that which African Americans *constructed* out of their unprecedented experience of African chattel slavery. In this context,

> They created distinctive ways of conceptualizing and speaking about ultimate concerns. Black theology is a continuation of that discursive tradition. Therefore, African-American theological development can be best understood as the convergence of an African-derived world view, the complexities of the experience of slavery, oppression, survival, rebellion, and adjustment in the New World, and the encounter with the biblical text. These realities shaped the African-American intellect and spirit. (2)

African American theology is grounded both by the theologian's recognition that his or her project is historically derivative from the economy of slavery and also expressive of the passions, feelings, and rationality that constitutes African-American Christianity.

Already some of the marks of the classical black aesthetic begin to resurface as the creative matrix from which black theology's self-understanding occurs. Through ecstatic reason, black theology correlates the economy of slavery and the heroic impetuses of survival, rebellion, and adjustment with Christian faith. Ecstatic reason is privileged as a distinctive mark of black rationality. It connects the project of black theology with the classical black aesthetics. As Evans puts it, an authentic African American theology must be "in touch with the 'guts' of Black religion. Without this quality, it would forfeit its claim to authenticity" (2). While black theology must have some occupation with "formal, self-conscious, systematic attempt[s] to interpret that faith," its mode of conceptualization is regarded as oppositional, nonlinear, and non-Western. The black theology project is not only epistemologically oppositional in its Afrocentric ideology. As an Afrocentric discourse, black theology is ontologically oppositional. The marks of Western ontology are the devaluing of community, the idolization of individuality, and "private property and individual rights as the basis of social and political organization." In distinction from these essential marks, Evans says that:

The cultural matrix of the African tended to affirm the infinite worth of the African as a human being in relation to other human beings and under the auspices of a benevolent creator God. The community (the no longer living, the living, and the yet to be born) was affirmed as the basic social unit and the social framework in which the individual was defined. All creation, including nature, was seen as infused with the spiritual presence of God. (5)

What fundamentally guides the "hermeneutics of return" to black sources among the recent black theologians? Evans wants black theology to speak to the problems of contemporary black Christianity—namely, the threat of black cultural fragility and nihilism. On the one side, African Americans are caught in a crisis of faith in which they "struggle with the pull of a secular materialistic, hedonistic, narcissistic, and pessimistic culture." And on the other side, they also struggle to "experience, to varying degrees, the magnetic hold of a spiritual, integrated, communal, and hopeful, counter-culture" of black faith (6). The oppositional tension between nihilism and faith tends to push Evans normatively to affirm and reassure the communal focus in black theology and to minimize individuality.

The legitimacy for such a focus is found in the hermeneutics of narrative return. The kernel beliefs that identify African American religious faith involve a selective retrieval of the *canonical story* of God's divine interventions into the affairs of oppressors in order to effect the liberation of the oppressed in both the exodus and the Christ events. But there is also a selective reception of "folk stories" that drives black theologians to the slave narratives. The heart of these stories centers on their "fears, frustrations and struggle as well as the determination for freedom from existential anxiety, political oppression, and cultural exploitation that constitutes our experience" (7). The theologian as storyteller has a difficult task of overcoming the vicious circularity between oppression and liberation. The black theologian has to reassure the canonical gospel story as an effective liberating story in the context of black suffering. One would hope therefore that suffering can be ameliorated or transcended. At the same time, liberation is the correlate of black experience, but black experience is essentially the experience of unrelenting crisis. The oppression-liberation circle remains viciously closed to cultural transcendence.

Although Hopkins and Evans try to reassure the black theology project in terms of an Afrocentric narrative return, it remains a crisis theology in two senses. First, it is a theology of crisis insofar as it identifies ontological blackness with *black experience* and black experience as the experience of suffering and black rebellion. Where either term (suffering or rebellion) is existentially mitigated or ameliorated so that suffering and rebellion are no longer the *way of life* for black people, then the ontological matrix of such a theology must enter into a crisis of legitimacy. This is the second sense in which black theology is a theology in a crisis of legitimation. It is a theology in crisis insofar as social and cultural elements of differentiation genuinely occur among African Americans, which are sufficient to call into question any reasonable assent to such ideological totalities as *the black church, the black faith,* or *the black sacred cosmos.*

Where radical differentiation occurs among African Americans, such ideological totalities are relativized by a pluralism of quasi-religious and not so religious organizations (street gangs, black gay and lesbian clubs, military service, fraternities and sororities). They are relativized by a multitude of faith traditions including non-Christian ones (Judaism, traditional orthodox Islam, African traditional religions, and new religions). And they are relativized by the plurality of world and life views held by African Americans who occupy varying social positions of class, gender, sex, and ethnicity. Under such differentiations, suffering, rebellion, and survival cannot be categorically descriptive of black experience. Many African Americans experience privileges and benefits of social mobilization within black culture itself. To make suffering, rebellion, and survival essential marks of black existence, it seems to me, trivializes the nature of oppression many blacks genuinely experience by the absurdity that anyone who is black is also oppressed.

Both Hopkins and Evans remain honest in their intentions to reassure the viability of the black faith in our market culture by privileging black community over black subjectivity. As a community of resistance, survival, and rebellion, however, the black community subjugates black subjectivity under ontological blackness. Since ontological blackness is identifiable with black experience, it is defined by and coterminous with black resistance and black suffering. Black theology—both in its classical and Afro-

centric varieties—fails to show how cultural transcendence over white racism is possible. It also fails to disclose what forms existential amelioration of black suffering and resistance will take. If suffering and resistance and white racism are ontologically constitutive of black life, faith, and theology, then transcendence from ontological blackness puts at risk the cogency of black theology.

Discussion Questions

1. Must a theology based, like Cone's, on "the black experience" inevitably be limited, and mainly negative, in the way Anderson suggests?
2. Will there be an inevitable split between "intellectual" liberation theologians and the functioning black church?
3. To what extent do, and should, black Christians seek a theology specifically rooted in African sources?
4. In your own words, explain how Hopkins' project fails to provide independent evidence of African remains out of which a black theology might be constructed.

References

Cone, James H. 1986. *Speaking the Truth.* Grand Rapids: Eerdmans. 1989. *Black Theology and Black Power.* New York: Harper/Collins. 1991. *A Black Theology of Liberation.* Maryknoll: Orbis.

Evans, James H. 1992. *We Have Been Believers: An African American Systematic Theology.* Minneapolis: Fortress.

Hopkins, Dwight. 1993. *Shoes that Fit Our Feet: Sources for a Constructive Black Theology.* Maryknoll: Orbis.

Lincoln, C. Eric, and Mamiya, Lawrence. 1990. *The Black Church in the African American Experience.* Durham: Duke University Press.

Said, Edward. 1993. *Culture and Imperialism.* New York: Knopf.

Tillich, Paul. 1967. *Systematic Theology.* Chicago: University of Chicago Press.

Wilmore, Gayraud. 1983. *Black Religion and Black Radicalism.* Maryknoll: Orbis.

49 Alternative Perspectives and Critiques

ANTHONY PINN

Study Questions

1. Explain William R. Jones' view of "divine racism." Is he saying that God *is* a white racist?
2. What is Cone's response to Jones and Jones' reply to him?
3. What conclusions does Jones ultimately reach regarding the role of God in black theology ("humanocentric theism")?
4. What criticism(s) does Pinn raise against Jones?
5. What is Williams' final position, especially regarding the Hagar story. According to Pinn, how is it ultimately similar to Jones' on the question of suffering?

Not convinced by the theological apologetic of popular Black theologians such as James Cone, Albert Cleage, Major Jones, Joseph Washington, and J. Deotis Roberts, William R. Jones wrote his first major work, *Is God a White Racist?*, as a prolegomenon to Black religious reflection. That is, Jones seeks to stimulate thought on the present condition of and inconsistencies in Black theology. The logically and historically unsound theological map offered by major Black religious thinkers makes this corrective necessary. That is to say, Black theologians have constructed a theological system which is full of deficiencies in logic and format.[1] The presence of unbending theological presuppositions has rendered silent questions concerning God's involvement in suffering. Accordingly, many theologians

started [their] work in theodicy with a specific and assumed concept of God. Thus the view that God is one, creator, benevolent, etc. is the presupposed framework into which the evil is forced.

Reprinted with permission of the publisher from *Why Lord?* (New York: Continuum, 1995) pp. 91–111.

This traditional approachX has a dual effect: It obviously eliminates by definition other explanations of suffering and evil, for example dualism. . . . The accumulated effect of this traditional approach is to create a theological climate hostile to the consideration of categories such as divine racism.[2]

Jones' critique centers on an analysis of Black theology's response to the issue of evil[3] because the theodic issue is the foundation (recognized or not) of Black theological thought. In fact, the centrality of oppression within Black theology combined with talk of a sovereign God makes Black theology an extended Black "theodicy."[4] Concerning this, Black theologians assume God is concerned with the welfare of the oppressed and is working toward their liberation. Consequently, "their [Black theologians'] own presuppositions and conclusions make the question 'Is God a White racist?' and its refutation the necessary point of departure for the construction of their respective systems."[5] With this statement, one begins to see the degree to which Jones' critique rests upon the fourth possible resolution to the problem of evil, i.e., rethinking God's goodness/righteousness.

Black experience has many layers and is open to a host of possible interpretations. This being the case, feasible resolutions to the vexing paradox of the problem of evil, with respect to Black Americans, are not restricted to mysterious yet honorable divine intentions. It is also plausible that God's concern lies outside of the Black community. And so, for Black liberation theology to legitimately speak of liberation it must acknowledge and disprove divine misconduct regarding African-Americans.[6] Thoughtful theological treatments therefore must demonstrate an awareness of the "multi-evidential quality of material" and the resulting interpretations.[7] In short, Jones contends that Black thinkers must not be so wed to their theological assumptions and structures that they are unwilling to raise hard questions about oppression and God's relationship to it. They must first disprove divine malevolence prior to proclaiming divine compassion for the oppressed.[8]

In spite of what Black theologians have traditionally argued, Black experience does not suggest teleological certainties. More accurately, Black struggle may suggest the presence of God working with humans to overcome evil; or, it may connote God's maliciousness and genocidal plans for the African-American population. Therefore:

. . . in the face of human suffering, whatever its character, we must entertain the possibility that it is an expression of divine hostility. Moreover, if it is allowed that the general category of human suffering raises the possibility of a demonic deity, then the particular category of black suffering—and this is the crucial point for the argument—at least suggests the possibility of divine racism, a particular form of hostility.[9]

The notion of divine racism is premised upon a certain set of assumptions: (1) there is a hierarchy of human value instituted and orchestrated by God; (2) this hierarchy directly relates to levels of suffering ordained by God; and, (3) God favors the "in" group—the group with less suffering. As a note, this triadic system (particularly item three) is complicated by the potential for certain groups to serve a limited function which appears oppressive but is in reality a much-needed lesson. With respect to this, Jones argues that suffering is shrouded in complexity, and types of suffering are often indistinguishable. Suffering can be beneficial, harmful, or a combination of the two. Hence, it is difficult to determine whether it is a sign of divine "favor or disfavor."[10] In light of the possibility of both beneficial and harmful suffering, some type of structure for distinguishing them—ethnic or limited suffering—is needed. (Ethnic suffering entails the following elements: (1) maldistribution of suffering; (2) negative quality of suffering; (3) enormity of suffering; and, (4) suffering of long duration.[11]) This structure or proof can be nothing less than a full liberation event. Essentially, anything less than total liberation leaves questions concerning God's intent and does not preclude the possibility of divine racism. Underlying this assertion is the premise that God is the sum of

God's actions. With regard to Black suffering then, God must want to remove it and cannot, or is able to remove it but desires not to. Jones asks, where is the liberation-exaltation event that suggests Blacks are God's "suffering servants" or that God is involved in their liberation? Many Black theologians, Jones acknowledges, point to the Christ event as proof of God's work towards the liberation of the oppressed.

James Cone certainly makes this argument in his texts and in his response to Jones' critique. His most explicit and forthright response to William Jones is contained in an extended footnote to chapter eight of *God of the Oppressed*.[12] Here, Cone argues for the Christ event as the ultimate proof positive of God's historical siding with the oppressed. Through the activities of Christ, God says "yes" to human freedom and fulfillment:

The coming of God in Jesus breaks open history and thereby creates an experience of truth-encounter that makes us talk in ways often not understandable to those who have not had the experience. . . . [I]n the experience of the cross and resurrection, we know not only that black suffering is wrong but that it has been overcome in Jesus Christ. . . . [13]

The acceptance of this faith stance is an essential component of Cone's argument. Furthermore, Jones' failure to understand the importance of the Christ event for Black Christian faith-praxis keeps him from appreciating the nature of Black faith. Without this appreciation, Jones cannot, according to Cone, accurately respond to Cone's Christ-centered perspective. Consequently Jones provides an external critique:

To do internal criticism is to think as another thinks and to criticize on the basis of another's presuppositions. In this case, Jones claimed to be thinking my thoughts [Cone's] on the basis of my frame of reference, and he concludes that my perspective on divine liberation of blacks from bondage demands that I produce the decisive liberating event. Apparently he has completely overlooked the *christological* orientation of my theology.[14]

Although an external critique—one outside the "tradition"—Cone believes that Jones deserves a reply:

. . . Therefore, to William Jones's question, What is the decisive event of liberation? We respond: Jesus Christ![15]

Jones counters this evidence of God's liberative activity by first arguing that the Christ event is situated, in time, prior to the suffering of Black Americans; therefore, it cannot be used as a marker of God's concern for African-Americans:

In point of fact, does not the continued suffering of blacks *after* the Resurrection raise the essential question all over again: Is God for blacks? We must not forget that black misery, slavery, and oppression—the very facts that make black liberation necessary—are all *post-*Resurrection events.[16]

Jones argues that Biblical stories such as the Exodus and Christ event merely point to God's favoring of the Hebrews and Children of Israel. Jones' counsel to Cone is to weigh the implications and ramifications of Cone's claim that:

Divine truth is not an idea but an event breaking into the brokenness of history, bestowing wholeness in wretched places. Only one who has experienced and is experiencing the truth of divine liberation can tell the story of how God's people shall overcome.[17]

The resurrection does not speak directly—if at all—to Blacks.[18] Traditional Black theological formulation (based upon the Exodus and Christ event) is unable to adequately refute the charge of divine racism.

Having established traditional Black theology's relevant defects, Jones undertakes the constructive portion of his prolegomenon[19] by delineating a "theodicy" which addresses the question of divine racism. With this in mind, Jones suggests that the "rigid monolithic theism" of dominant Black theology must be reformulated in light of Black experience and the question of divine racism.[20] The doctrine of God corresponding to this "theodicy" is humanocentric theism. Jones argues that only this human centered theism or secular humanism can provide the necessary polemic regarding the presence of Black suffering. On this point, Jones chooses to only outline the former approach because of the dominance of theism (monotheism) within the Black religious tradition. Accordingly:

[A] movement away from theism should come only if it is convincingly demonstrated that it is a hindrance to black liberation. Disregarding for the moment the issue

of theological accuracy, the black theologian, for pragmatic reasons, should develop initially a theistic framework for theodicy.[21]

Any viable "theodicy," i.e., one resolving divine racism charges, must explain Black suffering in light of theological anthropology and a doctrine of God (e.g., character and activity of God). For Black theology, all of the above must support the human struggle for liberation and *confirm* Black experience.[22] Humanocentric theism alone (a hybrid of humanism and theism) fits the Black tradition of theism and meets the stated criteria.[23]

An essential element of humanocentric theism is human ultimacy which entails men and women freely determining the course of events within history. In a word, the human is supreme; even God's encounter with the world must be measured by human reaction to it. God is no longer the functional center. To clarify his argument, Jones distinguishes two types of ultimacy: (1) functional; and, (2) ontological. The former involves the human ability to operate freely. However, this freedom is not absolute because it was externally granted by the Creator who maintains ontological supremacy:

Humanocentric theism does assign an exalted status to man, particularly to human freedom, but this status—and here we come to its theistic ground—is the consequence of God's will, and it conforms to His ultimate purpose and plan for humankind.[24]

God has, in giving humans free will, limited God's own range of activity within history. That is to say, God placed a restriction upon God's transforming contact with humanity. A consequence of this self-imposed limitation is the inability to assist humans through divine coercion. Rather, God involves God's self with humanity through the art of persuasion and in this way remains an integral and vital presence. Persuasion, borrowing from Howard Burkle and Harvey Cox, entails God's acting to influence (without force of any kind) humans to move toward the fulfillment of their best potentials:[25]

. . . God communicates, solicits, and tries by rational means to affect our choices. We are always responding to influences which are encouraging us to think, weigh and choose. Whenever a man seizes the possibilities of freedom and acts from within his own being, he is certifying the persuasive activity of God.[26]

To extend God's activity beyond persuasion would entail a form of omnipotence which allows for the divine racism charge. That is,

the concept of divine persuasion and the functional ultimacy of man leads to a theory of human history in which the interplay of human power centers and alignment is decisive. In this context, racism is traced, causally, to human forces. Divine responsibility for the crimes of human history is thus eliminated.[27]

This self-imposed reduction in divine power makes it necessary for humans to serve as God's co-workers in the liberation struggle. Furthermore, humanocentric theism's emphasis on human freedom of will) requires increased human accountability and responsibility for world conditions.[28] In other words, God is not accountable for oppression, it is the consequence of human misconduct—the perversion of human freedom.[29] Furthermore, Jones sees the pinning of human suffering on the activity of humans as a safeguard against quietism. He is convinced the oppressed will be more willing to fight humans for their freedom than to fight God. Albeit, passivity may occur, ". . . it is decidedly easier to validate the character of suffering vis-a-vis other men than vis-a-vis the divine."[30] In a word, Jones avoids charges of divine racism by removing God's responsibility for oppression. God is limited.

Although there are some notable differences, there are also similarities between this humanocentric theism and the positions held by other Black theologians. Regarding these similarities, Jones writes that:

Only Washington's emphatic description of God's overruling sovereignty seems to oppose it at all points, though his theological development after *The Politics of God* may belie this conclusion.[31]

Theological similarities belie similar theodical dilemmas which relate to: (1) the continuing issue of divine racism; and, (2) the resulting possibility of redemptive suffering within humanocentric theism. Jones argues in his text that the divine racism charge is an ad absurdum argument. Therefore, he must simply demonstrate that traditional Black theology raises the issue of divine racism but cannot refute it. Maintaining this type of criterion for a functional "theodicy," Jones' humanocentric theism should raise and refute this charge in order to prove viable.

Does Jones in actuality challenge the assumed positive intentions of God? It appears humanocentric theism implicitly suggests good intentions on the part of God. One gleans this in Jones' use of supporting documents, during the construction of his "limited God" concept, which hold to this perspective. Some might argue that my remark is at best guilt by association. However, if Jones in fact constructs his notion of persuasion on works he disagrees with (i.e., those positing strictly good persuasive endeavors on the part of God) and fails to note this, his research is shoddy. Yet, the care he has taken in developing his agreement and disagreement with scholars/concepts in other areas of the text make this type of oversight hard to fathom. Within the materials taken from Burkle, notice that only positive forms of persuasion are attributable to God:

God is the efficient cause of the world in that he is the agent, mover or source by which the world receives its being. There is no question of persuasion here; forbearance would mean non-existence for the world. . . . Efficient causality, as the activity which grounds all being, must therefore be a sovereign or originating act. . . . Efficient causality . . . is the first step which the Persuader must take in order to have before Him someone to persuade. . . . Even though the creature exists whether or not he wishes to, . . . suicide is always possible. Also nihilism and other attitudes which deny the importance and reality of existence are possible. The creature retains a veto even though he had nothing to do with the determination that gave him being.[32]

Jones argues that humanocentric theism sufficiently resolves the issue of divine racism: God is good-intentioned but cannot act through coercive means. Therefore, questions concerning God's intentions surface because of faulty theologizing not because of God's actual movements in history.

What evidence does Jones provide for this other than the persistence of suffering and the visible role of humans in it? Such evidence is insufficient when one recalls that Jones does not believe suffering can do more than demonstrate the importance of the question; it cannot be used to refute divine racism because of the multievidential nature of experience.[33] Where then are the acts of persuasion which allow the reader to believe God is not malicious? Until these are presented, does not this self-limiting act of God betray the possibility of a well-masked racism? That is, for the good of humanity God has prevented divine intervention—is this respect for freedom or a back-handed form of racism? A reduction in God's authority out of respect for humanity does not suggest positive intentions on God's part. This is particularly true when one considers that this human freedom, granted by God, directly corresponds to human oppression and environmental destruction. Furthermore, divine malicious intentions are certainly a real possibility if one holds to Jones' premise of counterevidence.[34] In other words, the counterevidence and multievidentiality Jones argues for could just as easily suggest that God has determined to allow humans to do God's work—the destruction of unwanted groups. Perhaps God's self-limitation is the ultimate slight of hand, the supreme alibi—with human abusers of freedom as the fall guys. Perhaps evil is not the result of human misdeeds against divine persuasion. Rather, it is possible that God is persuading white Americans to act in oppressive ways.

If Jones is able to sense this type of trickery regarding the Christ event, why does this possibility elude him with respect to the self-limiting scenario? The words from Camus he refers to have relevance here:

For as long as the Western world has been Christian, the Gospels have been the interpreter between heaven and earth. Each time a solitary cry of rebellion against human suffering was uttered, the answer came in the form of an even more terrible suffering. In that Christ had suffered and had suffered voluntarily, suffering was no longer unjust. . . . From this point of view the New Testament can be considered as an attempt to

answer, in advance, every [rebel] by painting the figure of God in softer colors and by creating an intercessor between God and man.[35]

If there is any merit (or truth) to Camus' analysis of the Christ event as a divine cover-up, then it is possible that God has performed the same maneuver with respect to human freedom. That is, under the cover of human freedom, God condones the suffering of Black Americans without being held responsible for it. Granted, the actual acts are the result of human misconduct; yet, who made this misconduct possible? God. It must be noted that Jones argues for the neutrality of God with regard to coercive actions; but, he does not rule out the possibility of God taking sides with regard to persuasion: "The concept of God as for the oppressed must be relinquished if this means that the oppressed are the unique object of God's activity *in a manner that differs from persuasion*" [emphasis added].[36] This suggests God's evil designs worked out by willing human accomplices. In a word, the reduction of God's authority and the bolstering of human responsibility do not sufficiently alter the possibility of an evil (though limited) God or a God who persuades others to perform evil acts. If the latter is taken seriously, there is also the possibility of divinely approved and redemptive suffering.

When one rejects the possibility of an evil God as Jones seems to do, the possibility of redemptive suffering resurfaces. If a good-intentioned God limits God's self (in order to foster human freedom) even in light of the evil resulting from this freedom, there is something ultimately useful about suffering. That is, the existence of a benevolent God who allows suffering (through an act of restraint) suggests the possibility of the permitted suffering being redemptive. The biblical account of Job is an example of suffering permitted by God which serves to clarify my point. The book of Job is a theodical treatment[37] of a righteous man's seemingly unmerited sufferings. At the outset of this biblical story, the reasons for Job's loyalty to God are questioned on two occasions by Satan. With the first attack upon Job's integrity Satan is allowed to take Job's possessions and family:

And Jehovah said unto Satan, "Behold, all that he has is in your power; only upon himself do not put forth your hand. . . ."[38]

Notice that Jehovah does not *directly* inflict this suffering; yet, Jehovah does *indirectly* participate in it. Nonetheless, Job is not conquered by his pain; he remains faithful to God. Satan suggests that Job's loyalty is based on physical health. And so, Jehovah gives Satan permission to touch Job's body:

And the Lord said to Satan, "Behold, he [Job] is in your power; only spare his life."[39]

Over the course of the remaining chapters in the Book of Job, the possible reasons for Job's pain are outlined by his friends. Their reasons are incorrect. At the end of the story, Job realizes that the undeserved sufferings of the righteous do not bring into question the goodness of God. God's purpose for this suffering is eventually made clear and suffering is rendered beneficial:

And the Lord restored the fortunes of Job, when he had prayed for his friends; and the Lord gave Job twice as much as he had before.[40]

In short, the Book of Job suggests the possibility of a good-intentioned God indirectly participating in the affliction of suffering for justifiable reasons. Due to the presence of a situation similar to Job's—unmerited suffering—it is plausible to consider Black Americans modern Job figures. If this is correct, there are grounds for African-Americans perceiving suffering as redemptive. They must only wait for the restoration of all they have lost.

Finally, Jones argues that God does not take sides;[41] this alone can foster the quietism he seeks to avoid. Many choose passivity because God's role is uncertain, and so it is best to accept one's fate as divinely orchestrated. In this respect, humanocentric theism has the flaw cited in theocentric theism—uncertainty of divine intentionality resolved through unsubstantiated and psychologically comforting assertions:

This [commitment to the oppressed demonstrated through omnipotence] may seem like a lot to give up, but consider the other alternative: If the black

theologians emphasize the theocentric side of their thought, if God's overruling sovereignty is affirmed, then they are forced to account for the maldistribution of black suffering in the face of His coercive sovereignty. They must answer these questions: Why has God not eliminated black suffering: Why are the oppressed always with us?[42]

According to Jones, it is better to have a limited God who attempts to work good through persuasion than a God whose goodness is brought into question by human suffering. Yet, neither position escapes the trappings of redemptive suffering.

Theology done by Black men fails to include the full spectrum of Black experience. And so, Black women have argued for its reformulation. Jacquelyn Grant gives voice to this task in one of her early publications (1979):

Just as White women formerly had no place in white theology—except as the receptors of White men's theological interpretations, Black women have had no place in the development of Black theology. By self-appointment, or by the sinecure of a male-dominated society, Black men have deemed it proper to speak for the entire Black community, male and female.[43]

In addition to stating the problem, Grant suggests a resolution which serves to clarify the intellectual excavation she and other scholars seek to perform. In a word, Grant argues that theologizing must be sensitized to forgotten communities and their experiences. Through this conscientization, the patriarchal and sexist theological norms are debilitated, and theology is free to learn from the experiences of the larger community. In this respect, Black women theologians bring to the theological discussion alternative sources (e.g., Black women's literature) and objectives (e.g., freedom from sexism, racism, and classism) based upon the life of Black women.[44] According to Grant:

There is a tradition which declares that God is at work in the experience of the Black woman. This tradition, in the context of the total Black experience, can provide data for the development of a wholistic Black theology. Such a theology will repudiate the God of classical theology who is presented as an absolute Patriarch, a deserting father who created Black men and women and then "walked out" in the face of responsibility.

Such a theology will look at the meaning of the total Jesus Christ Event; it will consider not only how God through Jesus Christ is related to the oppressed men, but to women as well. . . . This theology will exercise its prophetic function, and serve as a "self test" in a church characterized by the sins of racism, sexism, and other forms of oppression.[45]

Black women involved in the restructuring of disciplines including theology have used the term womanist[46] as a description of their enterprise and its character. These scholars have taken upon themselves the defining essentials of "womanish" behavior—strength, daring, and hard questioning:

1. From *womanish* (opp. of "girlish," i.e., frivolous, irresponsible, not serious) A black feminist of color. From the black folk expression of mother to female children, "you acting womanish," i.e., like a woman. Usually referring to outrageous, audacious, courageous or *willful* behavior. Wanting to know more and in greater depth than is considered "good" for one. Interested in grown-up doings. Acting grown up. Being grown up. Interchangeable with another black folk expression: You trying to be grown: Responsible. In charge. *Serious.* 2. Also: A woman who loves other women, sexually and/or nonsexually. Appreciates and prefers women's culture, women's emotional flexibility (values tears as natural counterbalance of laughter), and women's strength. Sometimes loves individual men, sexually and/or nonsexually. Committed to revival and wholeness of entire people, male and female. Not a separatist, except periodically, for health. Traditionally universalist, as in: "Mama, why are we brown, pink, and yellow, and our cousins are white, beige, and black?" Ans.: "Well, you know the colored race is just like a flower garden, with every color flower represented." Traditionally capable, as in: "Mama, I'm walking to Canada and I'm taking you and a bunch of other slaves with me." Reply: "It wouldn't be the first time."[47]

One of the best examples of womanist thought is found in the work of Delores S. Williams.

In *Sisters in the Wilderness,*[48] Williams brings to Black theology the forgotten experiences of Black women. With her "female identity fixed firmly in her Consciousness," Williams recognizes that biblical and other resources speak to a much larger perspective than that presented by Black males. In other words, the "second tradition of African-American Biblical appropriation" (the first being the norm of God as liberator gleaned by Black men) points to the place of Black women in this liberation tradition.[49] Fundamentally, such an appropriation requires rereading the Bible from the perspective of the most oppressed—Black women and their religiosity.

Some argue that Black women's reliance upon religion is a problem. More precisely, male writers such as Richard Wright have argued, according to Williams, that a strong reliance on religion fosters a contentment with suffering (e.g., abuse and pain).[50] Williams refers to *Native Son*[51] in which Wright records a conversation between Bigger Thomas and Reverend Hammond which is rather revealing. Christians such as Bigger Thomas' mother find comfort, Wright suggests, in the words of ministers such as Reverend Hammond:

Look son Ah'm holdin' in mah hands a wooden cross taken from a tree. A tree is the worl' son. 'N nailed t' this tree is a sufferin' man. Th's whut life is, son. Sufferin'. How kin yuh keep from b'levin' the word of Gawd when Ah'm, holdin' befo' yo' eyes the only thing tha' gives a meanin' t' yo' life?[52]

According to Wright, religiosity easily lends itself to resignation, the strength to gratefully accept life's hardships. It produces a martyr complex by which one's worth is measured in terms of pain endured. Williams notes that for writers such as Alice Walker, an important and powerful sense of self does not necessitate nor precipitate a rejection of religious devotion. Rather, a sense of self may entail a rethinking of religious images and a placing of them within the context of Black women's experience (particularly as care providers). One sees this in Alice Walker's characters Shug and Celie in *The Color Purple.*[53] Concerning these characters, Williams says: "Shug helps Celie to reexamine certain religious values Celie has held all her life—religious values supporting her bondage rather than her empowerment as a new, liberated woman. This reexamination centers on notions of God, man and church."[54] Celie establishes a constructive relationship with God once she no longer imagines God in the form of a man. With Shug's assistance, Celie begins to perceive God as connected to the environment—Celie, Shug, trees—life. And from this liberating doctrine of God, Celie forges a new love and respect for herself. This, in turn, transforms her familial relations. Williams writes,

Celie's change of consciousness about "God-as-man" frees her psychologically from the fear of her husband, who was as stern as any God she had imagined. After years of silently suffering, Celie "enters into creation."[55]

In short, the map of Black women's religiosity is complex. It often contains markings left by abuse and manipulation; however, it points to liberative paths of faith and spiritual values carved out of wilderness.

Using Hagar's encounters with motherhood, surrogacy, and ethnicity (Genesis 16), Williams suggests the wilderness can be a place of both transformation and hardship which analogously speaks to Black life in America. On the one hand, the wilderness marks a state of rejection:

And Sarai said to Abram, "May the wrong done to me be on You! I gave my maid to your embrace, and when she saw that she had conceived, she looked on me with contempt. May the Lord judge between you and me!" But Abram said to Sarai, "Behold, your maid is in your power; do to her as you please." Then Sarai dealt harshly with [Hagar], and she fled from her.[56]

On the other hand, the wilderness encompasses a place of divine—liberating—encounter. It is a place where one's faith in God is tested and rewarded:

The angel of the Lord said to her [Hagar], "Return to your mistress, and submit to her. . . . I will so greatly multiply your descendants that they cannot be numbered for multitude."[57]

According to Williams, Hagar, like African-American women, navigates the world certain only of God's help. In examining the wilderness experience of Black women, Delores Williams provides surrogacy—forced and coerced—as an analogy for the economic, sexual, and care-giving forms of oppression historically encountered by Black women.

Williams begins her exploration of surrogacy in the article "Black Women's Surrogacy Experience and the Christian Notion of Redemption."[58] Here she defines surrogacy as the unique character of Black women's experience involving substitute labor. On one level, surrogacy (i.e., forced surrogacy) entails the roles Black women played as coerced care givers through domestic service, child care, physical field labor (man's work), and sexual exploitation. Within these antebellum roles, Black women were categorized as "jezebels," "mammies," or "work mules." This usurping of Black women's energy

illustrate[s] a unique kind of oppression only black women experienced in the slavocracy. Only black women were mammies. Only black women were permanently assigned to field labor. Only black women permanently lost control of their bodies to the lust of white men. During slavery, black women were bound to a system that had respect for neither their bodies, their dignity, their labor, nor their motherhood except as it was put to the service of securing the well-being of ruling class white families.[59]

The ending of slavery did not mean the demise of oppressive "substitute" labor situations. Regrettably, efforts by Black men and women to end surrogacy activities often fell victim to economic realities.[60] Furthermore, not all African-Americans worked toward the elimination of surrogacy roles. In order to demonstrate the strength of their familial structures, some African-American men attempted to mimic patriarchal patterns they observed in the homes of white Americans. The surrogacy role considered most appropriate for this emulation was that of the mammy, complete with child nurturing and household management skills.[61] While surrogacy activity transverses the Civil War, postbellum years mark changes associated with the mammy figure. Most noticeably, within Black families, female care givers were referred to as mother as opposed to the stereotype latent term mammy.[62] In addition, the protector role played by antebellum mammies with respect to white children was increasingly superceded by Black male protection of Black women and children.[63]

A consequence of continuing surrogacy has been the perpetuation of negative stereotypes which encourage and sustain abusive, sexist, and misogynistic attitudes. In many cases these stereotypes fostered the model of Black women as superwomen.[64] Status as superwomen entails Black women facing expectations—of labor and care—which extend beyond those held over other groups. The negative effect of surrogacy and superwoman status is tremendous. In short, these roles foster a subsumption of Black women's personality and worth under others they care for. This underexplored form of exploitation, "gives black women's oppression its unique character and raises challenging questions about the way redemption is imagined in a Christian context."[65]

Williams is forced by her use of scripture (the Hagar account) and the theological assumptions contained therein to address God's role in this surrogacy process. That is, what does one make of God's presence in the wilderness experience?

The angel of the Lord found her by a spring of water in the wilderness. . . . And he said, "Hagar, maid of Sarai, where have you come and where are you going?" She said, "I am fleeing from my mistress Sarai." The angel of the Lord said to her, "Return to your mistress, and submit to her."[66]

Does this request suggest that God condones Hagar's oppression? Is there some inherently valuable lesson that Hagar can learn only through such an ordeal? Furthermore, is Black women's surrogacy an issue God is concerned with? Although these questions are legitimate in light of what scripture seemingly says, Williams vehemently opposes all suggestions that God approves of the oppressive surrogacy roles held by Black women. For Williams, God is on the side of the oppressed and such a God cannot orchestrate suffering. However, this is contradicted by traditional perceptions of the Christ event as an act of redemption through suffering. In Christ, the ultimate instance of suffering is elevated to its highest possible redemptive level: atonement resulting from pain and torture. Christians who emphasize death as the focal point of the Christ event implicitly suggest a strong connection between suffering and the will of God. It is then logical for Christians—imitators of Christ—to find divine approval in their hardships and sufferings. In this respect, an avenue is opened through which righteousness or closeness to God is measured by affliction endured; to be Christlike is to be in misery: "No Cross, No Crown." Williams rightly fears that the acceptance of suffering as Christlike will

result in the oppressed supporting their oppression. Specifically, it entails Black women bolstering the surrogacy they face because Christ was also a surrogate.

Finding the traditional Christian interpretation inadequate and inaccurate, Williams recasts God's involvement in history:

Perhaps not many people today can believe that evil and sin were overcome by Jesus' death on the cross; that is, that Jesus took human sin upon himself and therefore saved humankind. Rather, it seems more intelligent and more scriptural to understand that redemption had to do with God, through Jesus, giving humankind new vision to see the resources for positive, abundant relational life. Redemption had to do with God, through the *ministerial* vision, giving humankind the ethical thought and practice upon which to build positive, productive quality of life.[67]

The cross is separated from redemption, and the life and ministry of Jesus become the foci of liberative, salvific influence, and power. The victory over evil occurs in the wilderness when Jesus resists the tempter. In this refusal to surrender, and not in the shame of the crucifixion, Jesus defeats evil/sin through a radical commitment to life. That is to say:

Jesus' own words in Luke 4 and his ministry of healing the human body, mind and spirit (described in Matthew, Mark, and Luke) suggest that Jesus did not come to redeem humans by showing them God's "love" manifested in the death of God's innocent child on the cross erected by cruel, imperialistic, patriarchal power. Rather, the texts suggest that the spirit of God in Jesus came to show humans life. . . . [68]

In this manner, the death of Christ illustrates what *not* to do. Emphatically put, "there is nothing divine in the blood of the Cross."[69] As with the Christ event, the importance of Black women's wilderness experience (as a time of temptation/ pain and triumph) is its affirmation of life. God does not condone the abuse of Black women in the same way that God's actions through Christ did not glorify surrogacy.

The objective of the Christ event is a demonstration of life properly lived. However, there is another lesson: death indicates the depravity and misdeeds of humanity. It sums up the human tendency to destroy those persons who suggest an alternative to greed, fear, and oppressive relations. Therefore, to place emphasis upon death is to raise serious questions:

Surrogacy, attached to this divine personage, thus takes on an aura of the sacred. It is therefore fitting and proper for black women to ask whether the image of a surrogate-God has salvific power for black women or whether this image supports and re-enforces the exploitation that has accompanied their experience with surrogacy. If black women accept this idea of redemption, can they not also passively accept the exploitation that surrogacy brings?[70]

And furthermore:

Black women should never be encouraged to believe that they can be united with God through this kind of suffering. There are quite enough black women bearing the cross by rearing children alone, struggling on welfare, suffering through poverty, experiencing inadequate health care, domestic violence and various forms of sexism and racism.[71]

Yet, is Williams implying that God sustains but humans must liberate? If God is working against surrogacy, what can be made of continued oppression?

When one looks closely at the biblical story of Hagar and expands it to include the experiences of women of color in general, questions such as the one above are raised. In fact,

when non-Jewish people—like many African-American women who now claim themselves to be economically enslaved—read the entire Hebrew testament from the point of view of the non-Hebrew slave, there is no clear identification that God is against their perpetual enslavement.[72]

Obviously, there is a tension between communal claims of liberation and the biblical silence of God during certain cases of oppression.[73] Williams suggests an interpretative tool capable of respecting the collective experiences of Black women—experience of pain, struggle, and survival. When searching scripture, Williams suggests that thinkers make use of a new hermeneutical approach—hermeneutic of identification-ascertainment—which brings to the surface the hidden issues of oppression. This hermeneutic entails a three-layered approach to interpretation. First, a subjective reading, followed by a reading

geared toward the "faith journey of the Christian commmunity with which they are affliated." Finally, it entails an objective look at the phenomena writers identify with and phenomena these same writers ignore.[74] It takes account of the ways in which African-Americans (particularly Black mothers) have traditionally read the Bible in light of their existential realities of oppression and their efforts at survival. By means of this interpretative process, a critical rethinking of scriptural appropriations takes place. Using this new hermeneutic, one can ask again an important question without damaging God's reputation: "What is God's word about survival and quality of life formation for oppressed and quasi-free people struggling to build community in the wilderness?"[75]

Williams believes God's relationship with humans is beneficial for humans. She argues that God's involvement with oppressed women corresponds to the development of heeded "survival strategies."[76] In a word, survival, not liberation, is what God promises the oppressed. Therefore, God's reputation is secured in that God fosters the continued existence of those who are oppressed:[77]

When they and their families get into serious social and economic straits, black Christian women have believed that God helps them make a way out of no way. This is precisely what God did for Hagar and Ishmael when they were expelled from Abraham's house and were wandering in the desert without food and water. God opened Hagar's eyes and she saw a well of water that she had not seen before. In the context of the survival struggle of poor African-American women this translates into God providing Hagar [read also African-American women] with *new vision* to see survival resources where she saw none before.[78]

Williams' position is questionable in part because of her reliance on the Hagar story. Firstly, it is not self-evident in the biblical story of Hagar that God does not enjoy or ordain the suffering of the oppressed. The survival of Ishmael and the fostering of a great nation through him is contingent upon Hagar's return to the suffering inflicted by Sarah. That is, God tells Hagar to go back to Sarah and thereby continue within an oppressive situation. Williams notes that, "God is clearly partial to Sarah. Regardless of the way one interprets

God's command to Hagar to submit herself to Sarah, God does not liberate her."[79] Is this a sign of love for Hagar? To use Williams' terminology, it is through the "tragic" nature of the wilderness that ultimate "health" is achieved:

Yet wilderness was a place where the slave underwent intense struggle before gaining a spiritual/religious identity, for example, as a Christian. But the struggle itself was regarded as positive, leading to a greater good than the slave ordinarily realized.[80]

This certainly is reminiscent of earlier arguments concerning redemptive suffering; in a word, good things occur as a consequence of unmerited suffering. That is to say, if God is good and on the side of the oppressed, their continued oppression must have a divine reason. As a result, unmerited and intrinsically evil suffering is transmuted into something good. This is the case when one considers Williams' claim that God is concerned with the survival of the oppressed rather than their liberation. If their suffering was ultimately useless, would not a concerned and able God work toward their liberation rather than survival? Williams apparently answers "no" to this and consequently raises the possibility of redemptive suffering.

Delores Williams would disagree with my assessment of her position. In fact, she ideologically separates herself from the redemptive suffering philosophies. Lining up with feminists who also reject this thought, she writes:

Brown and Parker claim, as I do, that most of the history of atonement theory in Christian theology supports violence, victimization and undeserved suffering. The earlier discussion of atonement in chapter 6 [of *Sisters in the Wilderness*] above agrees with Brown and Parker's assertion that "the central image of Christ on the cross as the savior of the world communicates the message that suffering is redemptive.[81]

Williams is careful to note the possibility of Black thought leading to passivity in the face of suffering. She does not want this opinion to be connected with her work on Hagar and surrogacy. To prevent this, Williams voices her disagreement with Black leaders such as King in that his opinions on Black experience require an oppressive interpretation of Black suffering. Once again, with reference to Brown and Parker she says:

Their critique of Martin Luther King, Jr.'s idea of the value of the suffering of the oppressed in oppressed-oppressor confrontations accords with my assumption that African-American Christian women can, through their religion and its leaders, be led passively to accept their own oppression and suffering—if the women are taught that suffering is redemptive.[82]

Even in light of the above considerations, Black women's surrogacy experiences do not call into question the intentions of God. The focus of blame for evil rests with human misconduct. (Jones suggests that the divine racism dilemma is rectified by rethinking the divine-human makeup of liberative activity.) And reminiscent of this, Williams argues for a rereading or a new vision regarding Christ's purpose and God's agenda for the oppressed. Hagar and Black women's experiences teach that God provides the oppressed with survival skills and improved life options, *not* liberation. If one follows Williams' reasoning, "theodicy" is only an issue for those who misunderstand God's intentions and assume liberation is God's objective. Otherwise, the suffering of the oppressed does not require a questioning of God because the measuring stick of God's worth is no longer liberation. It is survival—the basic necessities such as sustenance, shelter, and hope. Hence, to the extent the oppressed survive, workings of God are confirmed. With survival granted, it becomes the responsibility of the oppressed to seek their liberation.[83] The continuing question is this: should Christians devote their time and worship to a God who merely points out the already present elements of survival? Is this position substantially better than explicit redemptive suffering arguments? Although Williams attributes survival to contact with the divine, cannot survival just as easily point to humanly fostered tenacity of spirit?

It turns out, then, that even the two thinkers—Jones and Williams—who question traditional theological assumptions in actuality maintain them: the activity and responsibilities of God are given new packaging. Things required of God are adjusted so as not to contradict an unchanging reality of Black oppression. That is, Jones resolves the problem of evil by limiting God and making humans responsible for evil. Williams manages the same effect by limiting God's responsibility to the area of survival. In both cases suffering persists while God's intentions remain good, and this allows for the continuing feasibility of redemptive suffering.

Once again, the problem of evil can be resolved in four ways: (1) rethinking the nature of evil; (2) rethinking the power of God (humans become God's coworkers); (3) questioning of God's goodness/ righteousness; (4) questioning/denial of God's existence. To this point, the arguments examined reveal the use of the first two resolutions to Black suffering (i.e., rethinking the nature of evil and rethinking the power of God), with some limited use (by Jones) of option three. However, dialogue concerning the problem of evil within the Black community should extend itself to a full exploration of all four resolutions. I initiate this type of dialogue by outlining a resource (i.e., Black humanism) in Black thought for the questioning/denial of God's existence as a response to the problem of evil. Furthermore, I begin the exploration of a method beyond "theodicy" by which to adequately explore the resolution offered by Black humanism as a religious option. I label this alternative methodology nitty-gritty hermeneutics.

Discussion Questions

1. James Cone (among others) distinguishes "good" from "bad" suffering: the first comes from fighting oppression, the second from oppression itself. God approves of the one but not the other, according to Cone. Is this a tenable distinction?

2. Is it inconceivable that God would favor one group over another? Did God do this in favoring the Jews?

3. Why suppose that God has *only* the power to persuade? Is it not more reasonable to hold that God could do more than persuade but prefers to allow humans to work out their own destiny?

4. Is Jones not ultimately subject to the same flaw he criticizes in others—namely, insisting that God must be on the side of the oppressed, without any evidence that this is so?

5. As Jones puts it, if God is "the sum of his acts," what does this say about his nature as good or evil?

Notes

1. See William R. Jones, *Is God a White Racist?: A Preamble to Black Theology* (Garden City, N.Y.: Anchor Press, 1973), xiii; 169–72. It should be noted that Black Process thought has addressed this issue. However, Black Process thinkers such as Henry Young and Theodore Walker find the Process God anemic and weak on racism and classism. Their alternative approach involves a partnership with God to combat such evils. I find this very similar to the partnership proposed by James Cone. See *Process Thought,* 18/4 (Winter, 1989); Henry Young, "Black Theology: Providence and Evil," *Duke Divinity School Review* 40 (Spring 1975): 87–96; Henry Young, *Hope in Process: A Theology of Social Pluralism* (Minneapolis: Fortress Press, 1990). The earliest example of Black Process theology is Eulalio R. Baltazar, *The Dark Center: A Process Theology of Blackness* (New York: Paulist Press, 1973).

2. Ibid., 66.

3. For an earlier analysis of this issue in which Jones establishes the natural centrality of the problem of evil for Black theology of liberation see: William Jones, "Theodicy and Methodology in Black Theology: A Critique of Washington, Cone, and Cleage," *Harvard Theological Review* 64 (October 1971): 541–57; "Theodicy: The Controlling Category for Black Theology," *Journal of Religious Thought* 30/1 (Summer 1973): 28–38.

4. Regarding this Jones says: "The general issue of theodicy and the particular issue of divine racism are central because of the status black theologians assign to black suffering. Theodicy and divine racism are controlling issues because black oppression and suffering are made the starting point for theological analysis" (Jones, *Is God a White Racist?,* 73).

5. Ibid., 61. For material on theology's "threshold question" see 62–64. Also in the same volume, see "Divine Racism: Explicit and Implicit," 72–78.

6. Ibid., 65.

7. Ibid.

8. Ibid., 75. Jones argues that Black theologians must involve themselves in a "reconstruction" effort which seeks to obliterate harmful concepts and beliefs, and provides more useful paradigms. He labels this process "Gnosiological conversion":

> Gnosiological here means the shift is primarily one of concepts and beliefs it relates to one's "knowledge." Thus the object of the theologian's analysis should be what his black sisters and brothers believe to be true about themselves and the universe of nature and society, for it is this knowledge that regulates their actions (67).

9. Ibid., 9.

10. Ibid., 16–17.

11. See ibid., 20–22.

12. Cone, *God of the Oppressed* (New York: Harper & Row, 1975), n. 23, 267–68.

13. Ibid., 191–92.

14. Ibid., n.23, 268. For evidence of what Jones means by internal criticism, see *Is God a White Racist?*, chap. 4; "Purpose and Method in Liberation Theology: Implications for an Interim Assessment," in *Liberation Theology: North American Style,* ed. Deane William Ferm (New York: International Religious Foundation, 1987), 137–64; "The Religious Legitimation of Countervillance; Insights from Latin American Liberation Theology," in *The Terrible Meek: Religion and Revolution in Cross Cultural Perspective,* ed. Lonnie D. Kliever (New York: Paragon House, 1987), 189–215. Also of interest: "Toward an Interim Assessment of Black Theology," *The Christian Century,* May 3, 1972, 513–17.

15. Cone, *God of the Oppressed,* 191–92. For additional responses to Jones which suggest this same rationale see for example: Major Jones, *The Color of G.O.D.: The Concept of God in African-American Thought* (Macon, Ga.: Mercer University Press, 1987), chap. 6; Roberts, "Liberation Theism," in *Black Theology II: Essays on the Formulation and Outreach of Contemporary Black Theology,* ed. Calvin Bruce and William Jones (Lewisburg, Pa.: Bucknell University Press, 1978), chap. 9; James Evans, *We Have Been Believers: An African-American Systematic Theology* (Minneapolis: Fortress Press, 1992), 58–78. For a process perspective see Henry Young's "Black Theology and the Work of William R. Jones," *Religion in Life,* 44 (Spring 1975):14–28.

16. Jones, *Is God a White Racist?,* 119.

17. Ibid., 92.

18. Ibid., 118.

19. For the nature of the Prolegomenon, see ibid., 169–72.

20. William Jones, "The Case for Black Humanism," in *Black Theology II: Essays on the Formation and Outreach of Contemporary Black Theology,* ed. Calvin Bruce and William Jones (Lewisburg, Pa.: Bucknell University Press, 1978).

21. Jones, *Is God a White Racist?,* 172.

22. Ibid., 173.

23. However Jones does admit that humanocentric theism does not fulfill all demands (ibid., 185–86). It is not a flawless system, yet is "more trustworthy than the theological models that inform the extant black theologies" (186).

24. Ibid., 187.

25. Ibid., 186–94. Howard Burkle, *The Non-Existence of God* (New York: Herder and Herder, 1969); Harvey Cox, *The Secular City* (New York: Macmillan Co., 1968).

26. Jones, *Is God a White Racist?,* 192; citing Burkle 1969, 207.

27. Ibid., 195.

28. William Jones, "Is Faith in God Necessary for a Just Society? Insights from Liberation Theology," in *The Search for Faith and Justice in the Twentieth Century,* ed. Gene G. James (N.Y.: Paragon House, 1987), 82–96.

29. Jones, *Is God a White Racist?,* 195.

30. Ibid., 196.

31. Ibid., 200.

32. Cited in ibid., 193; Burkle, 214–16.

33. See Jones, *Is God a White Racist?,* 15–20.

34. Ibid., 64–67.

35. Cited in ibid., 7–8; Albert Camus, *The Rebel,* trans. by Anthony Bower (New York: Alfred A. Knopf, 1956), 32–34.

36. Jones, *Is God a White Racist?,* 196–97; 201.

37. Terrence Tilley's *The Evils of Theodicy* (Washington, D.C.: Georgetown University Press, 1991) argues against viewing the Book of Job as a theodicy. Tilley asserts that the Book of Job argues against the feasibility of theodicy. Nonetheless, in addition to the Book of Job, I would suggest that the story of Abraham and the potential sacrifice of his son also support my contention (Gen. 22:1–19).

38. Job 1:12, RSV.

39. Ibid., 2:6.

40. Ibid., 42:10, RSV.

41. Jones, *Is God a White Racist?,* 196.

42. Ibid., 201.

43. Jacquelyn Grant, "Black Theology and the Black Woman," in *Black Theology: A Documentary History, 1966–1979* (Maryknoll, N.Y.: Orbis Books, 1979), 420–21.

44. See Delores Williams "Womanist Theology: Black Women's Voices," 267–70, in *Black Theology: A Documentary History, 1980–1993,* vol. II, ed. James Cone and Gayraud Wilmore (Maryknoll, N.Y.: Orbis Books, 1993).

45. Jacquelyn Grant, "Black Theology and the Black Woman," 1979, 430–31.

46. A notable exception to the overwhelming support of this term comes from Cheryl Sanders, who questions the feasibility of this "secular" term for Black church related efforts. This term she argues may have damaging consequences if Black theology is to foster a relationship with Black church morality and ethics. See her article in Jones and Wilmore, *Black Theology* vol. II, first published as "Christian Ethics and Theology in Womanist Perspective," *Journal of Feminist Studies in Religion* 5/2 (Fall 1989): 83–91. The same volume of this journal contains responses to Dr. Sanders from Emilie Townes, Katie Cannon, Cheryl Gilkes, M. Shawn Copeland, and bell hooks.

47. Alice Walker, *In Search of our Mother's Gardens: Womanist Prose* (New York: Harcourt Brace Jovanovich, 1982), xi.

48. Delores Williams, *Sisters in the Wilderness* (Maryknoll, N.Y.: Orbis Books, 1993).

49. Because of its commitment to the maintenance of Black life, this tradition can also be called the "survival/quality-of-life tradition of African-American biblical appropriation" (Williams, *Sisters,* 6).

50. In her biography of Richard Wright (for example, see chap. 25), Margaret Walker states that Richard Wright held a very low opinion of Black women in general and that this attitude is prevalent in his writings:

> There is not one whole black woman in Wright's fiction whom he feels deserves respect. . . . One feels he hates black women; one senses early in his writing an unconscious hatred of black women (Margaret Walker, *Richard Wright, Daemonic Genius: A Portrait of the Man, a Critical Look at His Work* (New York: Warner Books, 1988), 179.

With this in mind and combined with his harsh feelings towards religion, one begins to understand the background for his statements concerning the effect of religion on Black women.

51. Richard Wright, *Native Son* (New York: Harper & Row, 1940). For this dissertation, I have made use of the Perennial Library (1987) ed..

52. Williams, *Sisters,* 48; citing Wright, *Native Son,* 246.

53. Alice Walker, *The Color Purple: A Novel* (New York: Harcourt Brace Jovanovich, 1982).

54. Williams, *Sisters,* 53.

55. Ibid., 54; citing Alice Walker *The Color Purple,* 170.

56. Gen. 16:5–6, RSV.

57. Gen. 16:9–10, RSV.

58. Delores Williams, "Black Women's Surrogacy Experience and the Christian Notion of Redemption," 1–14, in *After Patriarchy: Feminists Transformation of the World Religions,* ed. Cooey et al., (Maryknoll, N.Y.: Orbis Books, 1991).

59. Ibid., 5.

60. Williams, *Sisters,* 73.

61. Ibid., 78.

62. Ibid., 79.

63. Ibid., 80.

64. Of interest: Michele Wallace's *Black Macho and the Myth of the Superwoman* (New York: Dial; London: John Calder, 1979).

65. Williams, "Black Women's Surrogacy," 1, 8.

66. Gen. 16:7–9, RSV.

67. Williams, *Sisters,* 165, 166.

68. Ibid., 164.

69. Ibid., 167.

70. Ibid., 162.

71. Ibid., 169.

72. Ibid., 146.

73. Ibid., 148.

74. Ibid., 144–53.

75. Ibid., 161.

76. Ibid., 196–99.

77. Ibid., 197.

78. Ibid., 198.

79. Ibid., 145.

80. Ibid., 113.

81. Ibid., 200; Joanee Carlson Brown and Rebecca Parker, "For God So Loved the World?" 1–30, in *Christianity, Patriarchy, and Abuse,* ed. Joanne Carlson Brown and Carole R. Bolin (New York: The Pilgrim Press, 1989).

82. Williams, *Sisters,* 200.

83. Ibid., 198.

Contemporary Issue: Womanist Theology and the Traditional Black Church

---

50 Christian Ethics and Theology in Womanist Perspective

CHERYL J. SANDERS

Study Questions

1. What have been the basic activities of "womanist" scholars in theology?

2. To what extent is "lesbian" part of the meaning of "womanist" in Alice Walker's definition?

3. What explanation and criticism does Sanders have of the tendency to emphasize just two features of Walker's definition of "womanist"?

4. What is wrong with using the term "womanist" to apply to all "theological claims that have been extracted from the testimony of black women"?

5. What three criticisms does Sanders raise of current work being done in the name of "womanism"?

From the *Journal of Feminist Studies in Religion* 5 (1989), pp. 83–91. Copyright Cheryl Jo Sanders.

One of the most exciting developments in the theological scholarship of the 1980s has been the emergence of womanist ethics and theology. *Womanist* refers to a particular dimension of the culture of black women that is being brought to bear upon theological, ethical, biblical and other religious studies. These new interpretations of black women's religious experience and ideas have been sparked by the creative genius of Alice Walker. She defines the term womanist in her 1983 collection of prose writings *In Search of Our Mother's Gardens.*[1] In essence, womanist means black feminist.

As early as 1985, black women scholars in religion began publishing works that used the womanist perspective as a point of reference. The major sources for this work are the narratives, novels, prayers and other materials that convey black women's traditions, values and struggles, especially during the slavery period. Methodologically, womanist scholars tend to process and interpret these sources in three ways: (1) the celebration of black women's historical struggles and strengths; (2) the critique of various manifestations of black women's oppression; and (3) the construction of black women's theological and ethical claims. The content of womanist ethics and theology bears the distinctive mark of black women's assertiveness and resourcefulness in the face of oppression. The womanist ideal impels the scholars who embrace it to be outrageous, audacious and courageous enough to move beyond celebration and critique to undertake the difficult task of practical constructive work, toward the end of black women's liberation and wholeness.

Does the term *womanist* provide an appropriate frame of reference for the ethical and theological statements now being generated by black women? To answer this question, it is necessary first to examine critically Walker's own understanding and use of the term, and then to construct some basis for assessing its adequacy as a rubric for Christian ethical and theological discourse.

In 1981 Alice Walker wrote a review of *Gifts of Power: The Writings of Rebecca Jackson* for *The Black Scholar.*[2] The review lifts up the spiritual legacy of the nineteenth-century black Shaker, Rebecca Jackson, who had an unusual conversion experience, left her husband for a life of celibacy, and lived thereafter in close relationship with a Shaker sister, Rebecca Perot. Walker gives high praise to editor Jean McMahon Humez, but takes exception to Humez's suggestion that Jackson was a lesbian. Walker identifies at least three errors in judgment by Humez with respect to Jackson's sexual orientation: (1) her disregard of Jackson's avowed celibacy; (2) her questionable interpretation of Jackson's dreams about Perot as erotic; and (3) her attempt to "label something lesbian that the black woman in question has not." Walker's own position regarding Jackson's sexual orientation is that it would be "wonderful" either way. Having thus disclaimed the moral significance of Jackson's alleged lesbianism, she then goes on to suggest that lesbian would be an inappropriate word in any case, not only for Jackson, but for all black women who choose to love other women sexually. Walker offers her own word *womanist* as a preferred alternative to *lesbian* in the context of black culture. Her concern is to find a word that affirms connectedness rather than separation, in view of the fact that Lesbos was an island whose symbolism for blacks "is far from positive." Furthermore, Walker concludes that "the least we can do," and what may well be for black women in this society our only tangible sign of personal freedom, is to name our own experience after our own fashion, selecting our own words and rejecting those words that do not seem to suit.

Walker gives a more complete definition of womanist as a preface to *In Search of Our Mothers' Gardens,* her 1983 collection of womanist prose that includes the *Gifts of Power* review. This definition has four parts, the first showing the word's derivation from *womanish* (opposite of *girlish*) and its primary meaning "black feminist" or "feminist of color." The second part conveys the sense of the word as explained in the book review; as a woman who loves other women but is committed to the survival and wholeness of entire people; who is not separatist, but is "traditionally" universalist and capable (these traits being illustrated with excerpts of dialogue between mother and daughter). The third part celebrates what the womanist loves—music, dance, the moon, the Spirit, love, food, roundness, struggle, the Folk, herself—ending with the word "regardless," presumably an allusion to Walker's earlier call in the review for a word that affirms connectedness to the community and the world "*regardless* of who worked and slept with whom." The fourth and final part of the definition compares womanist to feminist as purple to lavender, expressing in vivid terms the conclusion that womanist has a deeper and fuller meaning than feminist.

Walker's definition of womanist represents a shift in emphasis from her earlier discussion of womanist in the book review. In the first instance womanist carries the connotation of black *lesbian,* and in the second it denotes black *feminist,* a designation that includes women who love women and those who love men. In both cases, however, her point is to name the experience of audacious black women with a word that acknowledges their sensibilities and traditions in ways that the words *lesbian* and *feminist* do not. Walker's womanist definition and writings send a clear and consistent signal to celebrate the black woman's freedom to choose her own labels and lovers.

It is apparent that a few black women have responded to this call for celebration by writing womanist theology and womanist ethics and by calling themselves womanist scholars.[3] Those who have made use of the term womanist in their writing have cited the definition that Walker gives in her preface to *In Search of Our Mothers' Gardens* generally without giving attention to Walker's explanation of womanist in her review of *Gifts of Power.* Walker's definition has been subjected each time to the writer's own editing and interpretation, partly because each writer seems compelled to construe its meaning in light of her own thought. This process of appropriation and adaptation merits close scrutiny. In our efforts to tailor Walker's definition to suit our own purposes, have we misconstrued the womanist concept and its meaning? Is the word womanist being co-opted because of its popular appeal and used as a mere title or postscript for whatever

black women scholars want to celebrate, criticize or construct? Are we committing a gross conceptual error when we use Walker's descriptive cultural nomenclature as a foundation for the normative discourse of theology and ethics? On what grounds, if any, can womanist authority and authenticity be established in our work? In other words, what is the necessary and sufficient condition for doing womanist scholarship? To be a black woman? A black feminist? A black lesbian?

One approach to resolving these concerns would be to devise some reasonable categories for evaluating the event to which womanist theological and ethical thought conforms to (or deviates from) Walker's basic concern for black women's freedom to name their own experience and to exercise prerogatives of sexual preference. If we assume, rather boldly, that Walker never intended to reserve exclusive authority to use the word as her own private vehicle of expression, it can be argued that the authority to label one's work as a womanist derives directly from one's ability to set forth an authentic representation of Walker's concept in that work. Three categories are suggested here as grounds for comparison and evaluation: context, criteria, and claims.

The context of the womanist perspective is set forth quite clearly in Walker's long definition of the word. While its general context is the folk culture of black women, its specific context is the intergenerational dialogue between black mothers and their daughters in an oppressive society. The origin of the word *womanist* is a traditional warning given by black mothers to their daughters, "You acting womanish," in response to their precocious behavior (i.e., "You trying to be grown"). The behavior in question is further described as outrageous, audacious, courageous, and willful, words suggesting rebellion against the mother's authority, as well as resistance to oppressive structures that would limit knowledge and self-realization. However, it is evident that Walker's concern is to include the mother in the womanist context by ascribing to her the role of teacher and interpreter, and by portraying her as resigned to the daughter's assertion of her womanhood. This can be seen in the mother-daughter dialogues cited to illustrate the meaning of "traditionally universalist," with reference to the diversity of skin tones among blacks, and "traditionally capable," i.e., the determination of slaves to persist in their pursuit of freedom.

The criteria of the womanist perspective are very clearly spelled out in Walker's definition. To summarize, the womanist is a black feminist who is audacious, willful and serious; loves and prefers women, but also may love men; is committed to the survival and wholeness of entire people, and is universalist, capable, all loving, and deep. Perhaps it is unrealistic to expect complete compliance with all of these criteria as a prerequisite for employing womanist nomenclature. But it is intellectually dishonest to label a person, movement or idea as womanist on the basis of only one or two of these criteria to the exclusion of all the others. Two of these criteria tend to have the broadest appeal in theological-ethical statements: commitment to the survival and wholeness of entire people and love of the Spirit. The reason for this should be obvious; these two criteria point directly to the self-understanding of the black church. However, they would seem not to merit the prominence theologians and ethicists ascribe to them, especially in view of the fact that they are not given any particular priority within the definition itself. In other words, it may be a distortion of Walker's concept to lift up these two criteria because they resonate with black church norms, while quietly dismissing others that do not. The fact is that womanist is essentially a secular cultural category whose theological and ecclesial significations are rather tenuous. Theological content too easily gets "read into" the womanist concept, whose central emphasis remains the self-assertion and struggle of black women for freedom, with or without the aid of God or Jesus or anybody else. The womanist concept does lend itself more readily to ethical reflection, given that ethics is often done independently of theology, as philosophical discourse with greater appeal to reason than to religious dogma. Walker's definition comprises an implicit ethics of moral autonomy, liberation, sexuality and love that is not contingent

upon the idea of God or revelation. In any case, to be authentically "womanist," a theological or ethical statement should embrace the full complement of womanist criteria without omissions or additions intended to sanctify, de-feminize or otherwise alter the perspective Walker intended the word *womanist* to convey.

Despite the proliferation of theological claims that have been issued under the authority of the womanist rubric, Walker's womanist nomenclature makes only one claim—that black women have the right to name their own experience. This claim is inclusive of the prerogative of sexual preference; to choose one's own labels and lovers is a sign of having fully come into one's own. It may be understood theologically as the right to name one's own deity and sources of revelation, but to do so is to move beyond interpretation to the more dubious task of interpolation. Moreover, neither Walker's definition nor her discussion of womanist addresses the nature and purpose of God in relation to the plight of the oppressed, as blacks and/or as women. So it appears that womanist theology, with its liberatory theological claims, has been built upon a cultural foundation that not only was not intended to sustain theological arguments, but actually was fashioned to supplant ideas and images, theological or otherwise, that might challenge the supremacy of self-definition. This is not to deny the possibility of a genuine congruence between womanist theological-ethical discourse and the claim of personal and collective self-definition. The real problem here is the appropriation of the womanist concept as the prime ground and source for theological claims that have been extracted from the testimony of black women whose theology and ethics rested upon other foundations, and who, given the opportunity to choose labels, might have rejected womanist even as a name for their own experience.

It would seem that to do ethics in womanist perspective presents less of a problem, insofar as the construction of ethical claims can be pursued independently of theological considerations. Even so, one must take care not to force the ethical statements of one era into the ethical categories of another, nor to ascribe to our black foremothers womanist sensibilities shaped by a modernist impulse that they might not have endorsed or understood.

The necessary and sufficient condition for doing womanist scholarship has to be adherence to the context, criteria, and claims inherent in Walker's definition; it would be a mistake to recognize anything that any black woman writes with a womanist title or reference as womanist discourse simply because the author is black and female. Ultimately, the authority to determine what qualifies as womanist discourse rests with Alice Walker, who has defined and demonstrated the meaning of the word in her writing with great skill and consistency. However, given the fact that so many black female scholars have already taken the liberty of using her word in our work, we need to come to terms with the responsible exercise of the authority we have claimed.

I am fully convinced of the wisdom of Walker's advice to black women to name our own experience after our own fashion and to reject whatever does not suit. It is upon the authority of this advice that I want to explore further the suitability of the term womanist for theological-ethical discourse. The context, criteria, and claims of the womanist perspective provide an appropriate basis for raising critical questions concerning the suitability of this label for the work black women scholars are currently doing in theology and ethics.

First, there are contextual problems, beginning with tensions inherent in the dialogues presented in Walker's definition. There is an intergenerational exchange where the traditional piety of the acquiescent mother is in conflict with the brash precociousness of the womanish daughter. The definition conveys a spirit of celebration, evoking approval of the daughter's rebellion and the mother's resignation to it. This push to be "womanish" or "grown" also bears a hint of self-assertion in a sexual sense, where sexual freedom is a sign of moral autonomy. Thus, the context of womanist self-assertion includes two apparently inseparable dimensions; the personal struggle for sexual freedom and the collective struggle for

freedom in the political-social sense. Yet, in the theological-ethical statements womanist is used to affirm the faith of our mothers principally in the collective sense of struggle, that is, for freedom from racist and sexist oppression. Further, it should be noted that although the question of Rebecca Jackson's sexual orientation is Walker's point of departure for discussing the meaning of womanist, she refrains from applying the term to Jackson. Walker chides Humez for not taking seriously Jackson's description of herself as celibate, but Jackson's choice of celibacy (i.e., not to love either women or men sexually, not even her own husband) as an act of submission to a spiritual commitment to follow Jesus Christ evidently is not regarded by Walker as a womanist assertion of sexual freedom. Thus it would seem inappropriate to label as womanist those saintly rebels (e.g., Sojourner Truth) whose aim was not to assert their sexual freedom but rather to work sacrificially toward the liberation of their people as followers of Jesus Christ. To designate a historic figure as womanist solely on the basis of political-social engagement without addressing the personal-sexual dimension is a contextual error typical of womanist theological-ethical discourse. To be authentically grounded in the womanist context, these statements cannot be simply celebrations of black women's assertiveness, but must also give attention to the inherent dialogical and intergenerational tensions within the black woman's struggle for freedom, and to both dimensions of that struggle, the personal-sexual and the political-social.

A further contextual problem stems from the fact that Walker's definition gives scant attention to the sacred. Womanist is defined in secular terms, centered on a worldly premise of self-assertion and self-sufficiency. The womanist's concern for the sacred is demonstrated in the definition by italicizing the verb in the statement that she "*loves* the Spirit," but otherwise finds no distinctiveness among her loves for other aspects of nature and culture (she also "*loves* the folk"). The term *womanist theology* is in my view a forced hybridization of two disparate concepts and may come to resemble another familiar hybrid, the mule, in being incapable of producing offspring. Novelist Zora Neale Hurston once declared in the voice of one of her characters that the black woman is "the mule of the world," but unlike the mule the black woman has often sought to cast upon the Lord those burdens too hard for her to bear, and has reproduced herself, body and spirit, through many generations. Not only does this scant attention to the sacred render the womanist perspective of dubious value as a context for theological discourse, but it ultimately subverts any effort to mine the spiritual traditions and resources of black women. The use of black women's experience as a basis for theology is futile if that experience is interpreted apart from a fully theistic context. One might argue here that it is inappropriate to make such an issue of the distinctiveness of the sacred in black theological discourse in view of our African heritage that allegedly draws no such distinctions, at least not the way they are drawn in the West. In the African tradition, however, the basis for denial of the distinction between sacred and secular is the notion that the sacred pervades everything. By contrast, Western modernity exalts the secular to the point of disregarding or circumscribing the sacred in unhealthy ways. African American Christians, poised historically in a peculiar position between two incompatible world views, have tended to resolve this dilemma by fashioning for ourselves a world view that derives its power, character, and spirit from the sacred realm, from which we have drawn wisdom and hope to survive within the profane world of those who have oppressed us in the name of God and mammon. Thus it would appear incongruous to try to do black women's theology, or even just to articulate it in words, within a context that marginalizes the sacred within black women's existence. The search for our mothers' gardens, and our own, seems pointless if we remain oblivious to our mothers' gods.

The womanist concept sets forth a variety of criteria that convey specific moral values, character traits and behavior, especially with regard to sexuality. One important question to raise is whether or not the sexual ethics implied by the womanist concept can serve the best interests of the black family, church, and community. Part of Walker's original intent was to devise a spiritual, concrete, organic, characteristic word, consistent with black cultural values, that would describe black women who prefer women sexually, but are connected to the entire community. *Womanist* is a preferred alternative to *lesbian* because it connotes connectedness and not isolation, and a womanist is one who loves other women, sexually and/or nonsexually, and who appreciates and prefers women's culture. Clearly, in Walker's view, sexual preference is not a morally or ethically significant factor in determining whether or not one is "committed to the survival and wholeness of entire people, male *and* female." But the affirmation of the connectedness of all persons within the black community regardless of sexual preference is not the only issue at stake with respect to the well-being of black people. In my view there is a fundamental discrepancy between the womanist criteria that would affirm and/or advocate homosexual practice, and the ethical norms the black church might employ to promote the survival and wholeness of black families. It is problematic for those of us who claim connectedness to and concern for the black family and church to engage these criteria authoritatively and/or uncritically in the formulation of theological-ethical discourse for those two institutions. If black women's ethics is to be pertinent to the needs of our community, then at least some of us must be in a position to offer intellectual guidance to the church as the principal (and perhaps only remaining) advocate for marriage and family in the black community. There is a great need for the black churches to promote a positive sexual ethics within the black community as one means of responding to the growing normalization of the single-parent family, and the attendant increases in poverty, welfare dependency, and a host of other problems. Moreover, it is indisputably in the best interest of black children for the church not only to strengthen and support existing families, but also to educate them ethically for marriage and parenthood. The womanist nomenclature, however, conveys a sexual ethics that is ambivalent at best with respect to the value of heterosexual monogamy within the black community.

Thirdly, it is problematic for black women who are doing womanist scholarship from the vantage point of Christian faith to weigh the claims of the womanist perspective over against the claims of Christianity. The womanist perspective ascribes ultimate importance to the right of black women to name our own experience; in the Christian perspective, Christ is the incarnation of claims God makes upon us as well as the claims we make upon God. While there may be no inherent disharmony between these two assertions, the fact remains that there are no references to God or Christ in the definition of womanist. For whatever reason, christology seems not to be directly relevant to the womanist concept. And if we insist upon incorporating within the womanist rubric the christological confessions of black women of faith, or discerning therein some hidden or implicit christology, then we risk entrapment in the dilemma of reconciling Christian virtues such as patience, humility and faith, with the willful, audacious abandon of the womanist. Walker only obscures the issue by making vague references to the spirit instead of naming Christian faith and practice. For example, she uses terms like *general power* and *inner spirit* to describe Rebecca Jackson's motive for leaving husband, home, family, friends and church to "live her own life." Yet it seems obvious that Jackson would name her own experience simply as a call to follow Christ. I suspect that it is Christianity, and not womanism, that forms the primary ground of theological and ethical identity with our audacious, serious foremothers.

In conclusion, the womanist perspective has great power, potential and limitations; it may be useful as a window to the past, but a truly womanist tradition has yet to be fully created and understood. I have raised some questions concerning the suitability of womanist as a rubric for black women's ethics and theology, yet I have no better word to offer, nor do I feel especially compelled to come up with one. I am aware that many of my colleagues in theological scholarship are wholly committed to the womanist perspective, and my principal aim has been to prod us all further in the direction of critique and construction. If we are going to be serious about the constructive task, then we must be celebrative and critical at the same time, neither letting ourselves become so enraptured in celebrating our heroines and ideals that we sweep aside the critical questions, nor allowing the critical process to dampen our zeal for the content of our work. I have great faith that black female theologians and ethicists are on target to give significant direction to both church and society by further exposing the roots of oppression in all its forms and manifestations, and by discovering more keys to our personal and collective survival, regardless of which labels we embrace.

Discussion Questions

1. A "womanist," Sanders argues, is not the same as a "black female Christian." In what way?

2. Is Sanders criticizing Alice Walker? If so, on what grounds? If not, whom is she criticizing?

3. Is it inconsistent for a philosophy that celebrates black womanhood and black female bonding to draw the line and specifically repudiate sexual bonding (lesbianism)?

4. Sanders points to womanism as a kind of "secular" philosophy based on "a worldly premise of self-assertion and self-sufficiency." Other womanists (e.g., Katie Cannon and Delores Williams), however, would say that self-assertion and self-sufficiency, among black women at least, has *not* been primarily a secular thing. Is this a valid criticism of Sanders?

Notes

1. Alice Walker, *In Search of Our Mothers' Gardens* (San Diego and New York: Harcourt Brace Jovanovich, 1983).

2. Jean McMahon, ed., *Gifts of Power: The Writings of Rebecca Jackson (1795–1871), Black Visionary, Shaker Eldress* (Amherst: Univ. of Massachusetts Press. 1981); Alice Walker, review of *Gifts of Power: The*

Writings of Rebecca Jackson (1795–1871), Black Visionary, Shaker Eldress, edited with an introduction by Jean McMahon Humez, in *Black Scholar* (November-December 1981): 64–67. Reprinted in Alice Walker, *In Search of Our Mothers' Gardens,* 71–82.

3. See, for example, Katie Geneva Cannon, *Black Womanist Ethics* (Atlanta: Scholars Press; 1988); Toinette M. Eugene, "Moral Values and Black Womanists," *Journal of Religious Thought* 44 (Winter-Spring 1988): 23–34; Jacquelyn Grant, "Womanist Theology: Black Women's Experience as a Source for Doing Theology, with Special Reference to Christology," *Journal of the Interdenominational Theological Center* 13 (Spring 1986): 195–212; Renita J. Weems, *Just a Sister Away* (San Diego: LuraMedia, 1988); and Delores S. Williams, "Womanist Theology: Black Women's Voices," *Christianity and Crisis* (July 14, 1986): 230–232.

51   Womanist Reflections on "the Black Church," the African-American Denominational Churches and the Universal Hagar's Spiritual Church

DELORES WILLIAMS

Study Questions

1. How does Williams characterize the "black church"?
2. What is the difference between the black church and the African American *denominational* churches?
3. What are some of the main sins of the African American denominational churches against women?
4. What is the main unfinished business as far as the doctrinal beliefs of the black denominational church are concerned?

Any attempt to discern the meaning of African-American women's faith and action would be incomplete without reflection upon "The Black Church" and the African-American denominational churches in which African-American women have, through the years, invested much care, commitment, time and money. It is therefore appropriate at this point to provide womanist reflections on the black church, the African-American denomina-

tional churches and the Universal Hagar's Spiritual Church, given some of the insights in this book.

"The Black Church" Invisible

The black church does not exist as an institution. Regardless of sociological, theological, historical and pastoral attempts, the black church escapes precise definition.[1] As many discussions of it as there are, there will be that many (and more) different definitions. Some believe it to be rooted deeply in the soul of the community memory of black folk. Some believe it to be the core symbol of the four-hundred-year-old African-American struggle against white oppression with God in the struggle providing black people with spiritual and material resources for survival and freedom. Others believe it to be places where black people come to worship God without white people being present.

I believe the black church is the heart of hope in the black community's experience of oppression, survival struggle and its historic efforts toward complete liberation. It cannot be tampered with or changed by humans to meet human expectations and goals. The black church cannot be made respectable because it is already sacralized by the pain and resurrection of thousands upon

Reprinted with permission of the publisher from *Sisters in the Wilderness* (Maryknoll, NY: Orbis Books, 1993), pp. 204–209, 215–219.

thousands of victims. It cannot be made elite because it is already classless. In America it came first to the community of slaves. It cannot be made racial because it is too real for false distinctions. It cannot be made more male than female because it is already both, equally. It cannot be made heterosexist because it is a "homo-hetero" amalgam. It cannot be made political because it is perfect justice.

We cannot confine the black church to one special location because it can move everywhere faster than a bird in flight, faster than a rocket soaring, faster than time—but slowly enough to put spiritual songs in our burdened souls—slowly enough to put love in our broken lives—slowly enough to bring moments of liberation to our troubled people.

The black church is invisible, but we know it when we see it: our daughters and sons rising up from death and addiction recovering and recovered; our mothers in poverty raising their children alone, with God's help, making a way out of no way and succeeding; Harriet Tubman leading hundreds of slaves into freedom; Isabel, the former African-American slave, with God's help, transforming destiny to become Sojourner Truth, affirming the close relation between God and woman; Mary McLeod Bethune's college starting on a garbage heap with one dollar and fifty cents growing into a multimillion dollar enterprise; Rosa Parks sitting down so Martin Luther King, Jr., could stand up. The black church is invisible, but we know it when we see oppressed people rising up in freedom. It is community essence, ideal and real as God works through it in behalf of the survival, liberation and positive, productive quality of life of suffering people.

It has neither hands nor feet nor form, but we know when we feel it in our communities as neither Christianity, nor Islam, nor Judaism, nor Buddhism, nor Confucianism, nor any human-made religion. Rather, it comes as God-full presence to our struggles quickening the heart, measuring the soul and bathing life with the spirit from head to toe. It comes as moral wisdom in the old folks saying, "You give out one lemon, God gonna give you a dozen back!" It comes as folk-analysis in the old people claiming, "White folks and us both Christians, but we ain't got the same religion." It comes as folk-faith nevertheless believing that "*all* God's children got wings to soar." The black church gave us spiritual songs and blues and gospel and rap and a singing way to justice, fighting. It is invisible, but we know when we see, hear and feel it quickening the heart, measuring the soul and bathing life with the spirit in time.

Then There Are African-American Denominational Churches

The womanist thought in this book makes a distinction between the black church as invisible and rooted in the soul of community memory and the African-American denominational churches as visible. Contrary to the nomenclature in current black theological, historical and sociological works, in this book *the black church* is not used to name *both* the invisible black church and the African-American denominational churches. To speak of the African-American denominational churches as the black church suggests a unity among the denominations that does not consistently exist.

The fallacious merging of the black church and African-American denominational churches hides a multitude of sins against black women prevalent in the African-American denominational churches on a daily basis. Some of these sins are:

- The sexism that denies black women equal opportunity in the churches' major leadership roles. Such action opposes God by denying God's call to black women to preach. This sin has existed in the African-American denominational churches and among black male leadership in the denominations for more than one hundred years. Jarena Lee, whose narrative appeared in 1836, tells of Richard Allen's refusal to ordain her. Allen founded the African Methodist Episcopal Church. Old Elizabeth, a former slave whose narrative appeared in 1863, tells of black men prohibiting her from preaching.[2]

The sin of sexism dies slowly in some African-American denominational structures and hangs on tenaciously in others. The male-dominated black Baptist ministerial association, which has met on Mondays for years at Convent Baptist Church in New York City, only last year voted to accept black female ministers. But a female minister working as an associate pastor at one of the most prominent and prosperous Baptist churches in Brooklyn, New York, tells of other male associate ministers (her colleagues) who put obstacles in her way by trying to refuse her even the space in which to work. She tells of not receiving her paycheck on time and feeling as if she has to beg to be paid for the work she has done. Finally, the major minister of this famous African-American Baptist church told her she was a "pain in the bu—" and fired her when she asked for the pay that was due her at Christmas time.

Another fully ordained black woman says her incentive to pastor would die were she not called by God who supports her courage to stay in ministry. Having grown up in Baptist churches associated with the National [black] Baptist Convention, she has received no support for her ministry from that convention while black males receive much support. In fact, some black Baptist women, whose memberships were in denominational churches associated with the black National Baptist Convention, have had to seek ordination in the denominational churches connected with the American Baptist Convention, an integrated convention where white power is obvious. This means that black males, through the sexist practices in their churches, have left it to white men to affirm black women and to acknowledge black women's call from God while they (black male ministers) reject both black women and the women's call from God. Time and again, black women have told me some of their male colleagues try to "set them up" to fail in their ministries.

- The immoral models of male leadership at the helm of too many of the black denominational churches[3] (even in the nineteenth century, Ida B. Wells spoke of "corrupt" black ministers);[4]
- Collusion that often exists between some black male preachers and the political forces in America oppressing black women and all black people;[5]
- The sexual exploitation of black women in the denominational church by some preachers;[6]
- The tendency of the proclamation and teachings of the denominational churches to be so spiritualized and "heaven-directed" that women parishioners are not encouraged to concentrate on their lives in this world and to fight for their own survival, liberation and productive quality of life. They are not encouraged to develop a self-concept and build female self-esteem. Rather they are indoctrinated to be self-sacrificing and emotionally dependent upon males including male gods sacralizing the male image and making the feminine in Jesus invisible. They are encouraged to disregard and even work against freedom movements afoot in the culture to secure the rights of women;
- The failure of African-American denominational churches on a consistent and large scale, to pool their resources (across all denominational and class lines) in order to deal effectively with the poverty, drug-addiction, homelessness, hunger and health problems such as AIDS sweeping through the black communities in the United States;
- The leadership in the denominational churches encouraging homophobia;
- Responding to the AIDS crisis with denial;
- The emotional exploitation of black female parishioners as ministers provoke emotional reactions to proclamation and ministry rather than thoughtful questions and responses;
- Building and purchasing elaborate church edifices while thousands of black people live in dire poverty—buildings that are often open only on Sunday and for prayer meeting or

Bible study during the week—buildings without viable programs to meet the needs of black women and the black community;

- Failure of the denominational churches to pool their resources in order to develop a powerful, effective and extensive prison ministry working in both female and male prisons on a consistent basis to help black prisoners shape goals and begin to make and realize dreams for their lives—a prison ministry that works as effectively to rehabilitate the health, consciousness and lives of prisoners as the Black Islamic forces often do.[7]

However, it must be pointed out here that some African-American denominational churches are providing outstanding work in some of these areas. Among them are Glide Memorial United Methodist Church in San Francisco, California; Allen A.M.E. Church in Queens, New York; Bridge Street A.M.E. Church in Brooklyn. In *The Black Church in the African American Experience,* C. Eric Lincoln and Lawrence H. Mamiya mention several churches in different parts of the country with effective ministries in the black communities.[8]

Though problems in the church regarding women's freedom, faith and self-concept are old and legion, there have been moments in African-American history when some of the denominational churches have been effective instruments of freedom, survival and positive quality of life formation for all black people. This is when the black church emerges from the soul of community memory.[9] For the black church—having neither denominational commitment nor religious bias—acts as the great judging, healing, fighting, holy Godforce. It breathes compassion and power in the black community as community groups strip systems of oppression down to the core human essential of justice-bearing in the midst of oppressed people's economic, educational, freedom and survival struggles.

Out of the black church Godforce, the black denominations have founded schools for black people; built housing for the poor; birthed great civil rights movements; birthed black salvation-bearers like Harriet Tubman, Sojourner Truth, Milla Granson, Ida Wells Barnett, Fredrick Douglass, Martin Luther King, Jr., Medgar Evers and many other ordinary black women and men. The black church has been the holy Godforce holding black people together body, soul and spirit as the perpetrators of genocide tried to exterminate the community.

Both in slavery and shortly after they came out of bondage, African Americans survived and were welded together as a community by the black church in solidarity with the mutual aid societies and the black extended family.[10] As African Americans became more and more "Americanized" by appropriating white American values of individualism, capitalist economics and classism, the solidarity between the black church, the mutual aid societies and the extended family disappeared.[11] The mainline African-American denominational churches[12] supported the adoption of these white values, and the black church retreated to the deep recesses of the soul of community memory. Many mutual aid societies went out of existence or changed to organizations of lesser importance in the economic structure of the African-American denominational churches. Black people were duped into believing that their economic interests could be served by a white-dominated American capitalist economy and capitalist institutions. The black extended family passed away. Black people, in their effort to be "Americanized," began to believe that the white model of the nuclear family could more adequately service the bonding and the wisdom-transmitting tasks absolutely necessary for the survival of generations of black people: women, men and children. Nothing, of course, could have been farther from the truth. In actuality, the old folks (the grandmothers, grandfathers, great aunts and great uncles: the ancestors) were the carriers of the wisdom and traditions effective for survival and community building. The old folks were alienated from the nuclear family structure. They were isolated from black children who needed, along with their parents, the wisdom of the ancestors. They needed this wisdom in order to learn the strategies in black everyday life, which had worked over time for survival, liberation and for developing a positive, productive quality of life.

Discussion Questions

1. If the essence of the black church does not lie in the black denominations, where *does* it exist?

2. The black church, Williams insists, cannot make a distinction between hetero- and homosexual because it is an "amalgam." Sanders would apparently hold otherwise, as she cites the persistent objection to lesbianism among typical black churchgoers. Who is right? Or is there a way of reconciling the views of Williams and Sanders?

3. It might be objected that the black church, as Williams defines it, is basically those views congruent with *her own* (and other black womanists). Is there any place for dialogue within Williams' black church on such issues as homosexuality and women's liberation?

Notes

1. For sociological attempts to define the black church, see C. Eric Lincoln and Lawrence Mamiya, *The Black Church in the African American Experience* (Durham, North Carolina: Duke University Press, 1991); W. E. B. Du Bois, *The Negro Church* (Atlanta: Atlanta University Press, 1903); E. Franklin Frazier, *The Negro Church in America* (Chicago: University of Chicago Press, 1969); E. Franklin Frazier and C. Eric Lincoln, *The Negro Church in America: The Black Church Since Frazier* (New York: Schocken Books, 1974). Also see Hart M. Nelson and Anne Kusener Nelson, *Black Church in the Sixties* (Lexington: University of Kentucky Press, 1975); see Peter Paris, *Social Teaching of the Black Churches* (Philadelphia: Fortress Press, 1985). For theological responses to the black church see James Cone, *For My People: Black Theology and the Black Church* (Maryknoll, New York: Orbis Books, 1984); James Deotis Roberts, *Roots of a Black Future: Family and Church* (Philadelphia: Westminster Press, 1980). For historical perspectives on the black church, see Albert Raboteau, *Slave Religion: The "Invisible Institution" in the Antebellum South* (New York: Oxford

University Press, 1978); Gayraud Wilmore, *Black Religion and Black Radicalism,* 2d ed. (Maryknoll, New York: Orbis Books, 1983); James M. Washington, *Frustrated Fellowship: The Black Baptist Quest for Social Power* (Macon, Georgia: Mercer University Press, 1986). For pastoral perspectives on the black church, see Wyatt T. Walker, Harold A. Carter and William Jones, *The Black Church Looks at the Bicentennial: A Minority Report* (Elgin, Illinois: Progressive National Baptist Publishing House, 1976).

2. See Jarena Lee, "The Life and Religious Experience of Jarena Lee, A Coloured Lady, Giving an Account of Her Call to Preach the Gospel," in William L. Andrews, ed., *Sisters of the Spirit;* (Bloomington, Indiana: Indiana University Press, 1986), pp. 25–48. Also see Old Elizabeth, "Memoir of Old Elizabeth, a Colored Woman."

3. Immorality here refers to preachers exploiting the financial resources and emotional needs of black women in order to increase the preacher's personal financial resources and to build a strong power base for himself so that he becomes a power broker in the community. He uses this power primarily for self-advancement and not to advance the survival, liberation and struggle for a positive, productive quality of life for the black community.

4. See her letter to Booker T. Washington dated November 30, 1890, contained in *The Booker T. Washington Papers,* vol. 3, ed. Raymond Smock, Louis Harlan and Stuart Kaufman (Urbana, Illinois: University of Illinois Press, 1974).

5. There are serious questions black people must ask about the American national political forces (for example, political parties and surveillance forces like CIA) and the African-American denominational churches which are purported to be the only viable institutions in the African-American community. Why have the oppressive white power structures allowed these church groups to exist in the black community for over a hundred years while they (the white power structures) consistently destroyed other black groups that have the ability to become powerful and long-lasting in the black community? A case in point here is the Black Panther Party, which was consistently harassed and finally all but destroyed. Another case was Marcus Garvey's Universal Negro Improvement Association. I cannot help but wonder if Martin Luther King, Jr., and Malcolm X were, in part, assassinated because they were fast becoming institutions in the African-American community supported by the organizations they were founding. These organizations were operating beyond the power range of either the denominational churches or the black Muslim movement. Yet the organizations of Martin and Malcolm were based on spiritual foundations deriving from the religious ethos of African Americans, and these organizations together

had one insistent political intent: the full liberation of African-American people. We black people have bought into the idea (fostered by white politicians, media and power structures) that the black denominational churches are the only viable "institutions" in the black community. We are indoctrinated to believe that they alone determine the way black people think and vote. Thus black preachers easily become the power brokers between the black community and white power and just as easily can become corrupted by the "tid-bits" offered to them by oppressive white power structures. The liberation interests of the black community become highly compromised as the preacher's personal ambitions are rewarded by the collusive white power structures. (I suppose one of our problems as African-American people is that we depend so much upon white definitions for the meaning we assign to our cultural realities. We do not see, name appropriately or emphasize other avenues through which black culture is transmitted. Therefore we think the word *institution,* as defined by white sociologists, aptly identifies our cultural realities. What if black people began to identify beauty shops, barber shops, street corners and other non-church places as also major "funnels" through which black culture was transmitted—instead of thinking in "institutional" terms as defined by white sociologists? Would we not get an expanded sense of the interconnectedness of our cultural "funnels" and see more clearly how our communities could be organized to foster a consistent culture of survival, resistance and liberation? And if our cultural ideas become thoroughly non-sexist, non-homophobic and Afrocentric, would it not be to our advantage to have all of these places—the denominational churches, the beauty shops, the barber shops, the street corners—as the "funnels" for African-American culture?)

6. Consider where sexual exploitation of a woman led in the following account: Some years ago, when I lived in a Tennessee town, a black man there killed his wife. When the reasons for this husband's actions surfaced, it was learned that the wife, a leading usher in one of the black denominational churches, had become sexually involved with the preacher. The preacher convinced the woman to take her and her husband's savings out of the bank and give the money to the church. The husband had worked a long time at a rather stable job and had, for many years, diligently put aside most of the money that was in savings. When he learned what the wife had done, he tried to get the money back but could not. In a fit of rage he killed the wife. The preacher left town until the husband's trial was held. The husband was convicted and put in prison. Then the preacher came back to town and resumed his pastorate.

There is also the case of the denominational church in Massachusetts where the preacher's girlfriend came into the church to fight the preacher's wife, and the preacher ran out the back door of the church. Many, many instances exist of the sexual exploitation of black women in these churches. Black women and entire congregations have kept silent about these matters and have not often disciplined the preachers for their actions. In too many cases business in the church went on as usual. This sets a terrible example for young black people who need moral models of responsible and honest leadership guiding our people. I am convinced that this kind of activity in the denominational churches will only stop when black women open their mouths and tell their stories. We black women need to quit thinking about how good or bad white people will think we are if we tell the stories about our abuse and exploitation. White people and white churches hardly have the moral rectitude and moral fitness that would allow them to be judges of anybody's morality. Centuries and centuries of slave holding and their continuing racism have forfeited the right of white people to make moral judgments about black people. We black women must tell our stories of sexual and financial exploitation within the denominational churches *for the benefit of black people, so that the churches can be cleaned up within, so that the salvation and liberation of black women in the churches can occur.* God will surely judge the African-American denominational churches for oppressing women just as some of our black theology insists that [God] judges the white churches for practicing and affirming racism.

7. When I visited the Edgecombe Correctional Facility in New York City in 1991, I saw the woeful failure of the African-American denominations to have meaningful ministry among the prisoners who were about 98 percent black and Hispanic—more black than Hispanic. All male, these prisoners had been brought down to the Edgecombe facility from Rikers Island, a full-fledged prison. These men were eligible to be released from Rikers Island *if they could find a job on the outside.* The prison system gave these men fifteen days to find a job in New York. Many of the men had been in prison for some time. There was no assistance program to help the men in the job-finding process. They were to do it all on their own. If they could not find a job in fifteen days, they were sent back to Rikers Island. It seems to me that this is an area in which the African-American denominations, through a well-planned and well-supported ecumenical effort, could work to help prisoners. As I talked with these men, I learned that they had not given up on the denominational churches, but they were highly critical of them. Several talked about the way the preachers had exploited their mothers by encouraging the mothers to give their money to the denominational church, even when there was no food on the women's tables at home. Others talked about the need of denominational members and ministry

to come from behind denominational walls and bring an effective ministry into the streets and territories beyond the church grounds.

8. Lincoln and Mamiya, *The Black Church in the African American Experience,* chap. 13, "The Black Church and the Twenty-First Century: Challenges to the Black Church," pp. 382–404.

9. The black church emerges from the soul of community memory when community is centered by the inseparable inter-connected struggles for survival, liberation and positive quality of life formation for poor and oppressed peoples.

10. See Lincoln's and Mamiya's discussion of the mutual aid societies in *The Black Church in the African American Experience,* chap. 9, "The American Dream and the American Dilemma: The Black Church and Economics," pp. 236–73. Also see treatments of mutual societies in August Meier and Elliott Rudwick, *From Plantation to Ghetto* (New York: Hill and Wang, 1970).

11. In this context the term *Americanized* refers to the transformation of patterns of slave culture and sanctioned ways of behaving to patterns of dominant American culture and ways of behaving sanctioned by the Anglo-American status quo.

12. *Mainline* here means the same as it does among whites, that is, Baptist, Methodist, Episcopal, Presbyterian, Lutheran. Catholicism can also be considered mainline.

Suggestions for Further Reading

Part I Foundations
Race and Racism

Allen, Ernest, Jr. "On the Reading of Riddles: Rethikning DuBoisian ` Double Consciousness,' " in Lewis R. Gordon, ed., *Existence in Black: An Anthology of Black Existentialist Writing* (New York: Routledge, 1997).

Appiah, Kwame Anthony. "But Would That Still Be Me?: Notes on Gender, ` Race,' Ethnicity as Sources of Identity," *The Journal of Philosophy* 77 (1990), 493–99.

———."Race, Culture, Identity," in Kwame Anthony Appiah and Amy Gutman, eds., *Color Consciousness: The Political Morality of Race* (Princeton, N.J.: Princeton University Press, 1996), 3–75.

DuBois, W. E. B. *Dusk of Dawn* (New York: Harcourt Brace, 1940).

Fanon, Frantz. *Black Skin, White Masks* (New York: Grove Press, 1967).

Goldberg, David Theo. *Racist Culture: Philosophy and the Politics of Meaning* (Oxford: Blackwell, 1993).

Gordon, Lewis. *Bad Faith and Antiblack Racism* (Atlantic Highlands, N.J.: Humanities Press, 1995).

McGary, Howard. "Alienation and the African-American Experience," *Philosophical Forum* 24 (1992), 282–96.

Zack, Naomi. *Mixed Race* (Philadelphia: Temple University Press, 1993).

Part II Moral and Political Philosophy
Nationalism, Separatism, and Assimilation

Appiah, Kwame Anthony. *In My Father's House: Africa in the Philosophy of Culture* (New York: Oxford University Press, 1992).

Asante, Molefi K. *Afrocentricity* (Trenton, N.J.: Africa World, 1988).

Boxill, Bernard. "Separation or Assimilation," in *Blacks and Social Justice* (Lanham, Md.: Rowman and Allenheld, 1984).

Crummell, Alexander. *Destiny and Race: Selected Writings 1848–1898*, W. J. Moses, ed. (Amherst: University of Massachusetts Press, 1992).

Diop, Anta. *The African Origins of Civilization: Myth or Reality*, Mercer Cook, trans. (Westport, Conn.: L. Hill, 1974).

Howell, Stephen. *Afrocentrism: Mythical Pasts and Imagined Homes* (New York: Verso, 1998).

Outlaw, Lucious. "Africana Philosophy," *The Journal of Ethics* 1 (1997), 265–90.

Van DeBurg, William L., ed. *Modern Black Nationalism* (New York: New York University Press, 1997).

Wiredu, Kwasi. *Philosophy and an African Culture* (Cambridge: Cambridge University Press, 1980).

Feminism, Womanism, and Gender Relations

Cannon, Katie. *Black Womanist Ethics* (Atlanta: Scholars Press, 1988).

Clarke, Cheryl. "The Failure to Transform Homophobia in the Black Community, in Barbara Smith, ed., *Home Girls: A Black Feminist Anthology* (New York: Kitchen Table Press, 1983).

Cooper, Anna Julia. *A Voice from the South* (Xenia, Ohio: Aldine, 1892).

Davis, Angela. *Women, Race and Class* (New York: Random House, 1981).

hooks, bell. *Ain't I a Woman: Black Woman and Feminism* (Boston: South End Press, 1981).

Lorde, Audre. *Sister Outsider* (Truansburg, N.Y.: Crossing Press, 1984).

Morrison, Toni. *The Bluest Eye* (New York: Holt, Rinehart and Winston, 1970).

Staples, Robert. "The Myth of Black Macho: A Response to Angry Black Feminists," *The Black Scholar* (1979), 24–32.

Thomas, Laurence. "Sexism and Racism: Some Conceptual Differences," *Ethics* 90 (1980), 239–50.

Walker, Alice. *In Search of Our Mothers' Garden* (San Diego: Harcourt Brace Jovanovich, 1967).

Zack, Naomi, ed. *Race/Sex: Their Sameness, Difference, and Interplay* (New York: Routledge, 1996).

Violence, Liberation, and Social Justice

Boxill, Bernard. "The Morality of Reparation," *Social Theory and Practice* 2 (1972), 113–22.

———. "Self-Respect and Protest," *Philosophy and Public Affairs* (1976).

Dyson, Michael Eric. *Making Malcolm: The Myth and Meaning of Malcolm X* (New York: Oxford University Press, 1995).

Fanon, Frantz. *The Wretched of the Earth* (New York: Grove Press, 1963).

Gordon, Jill. "By Any Means Necessary: John Locke and Malcolm X on the Right to Revolution," *Journal of Social Philosophy* 26 (1995), 53–85.

Gordon, Lewis. *Fanon and the Crisis of European Man: An Essay on Philosophy and the Human Sciences* (New York: Routledge, 1995).

Lawson, Bill E., ed. *The Underclass Question* (Philadelphia: Temple University Press, 1992).

Thomas, Laurence. *Vessels of Evil* (Philadelphia: Temple University Press, 1993).

Young, Iris. *The Politics of Difference* (Princeton: Princeton University Press, 1990).

Ethics and Value Theory

Boston, Thomas, ed. *A Different Vision: African-American Economic Thought* (New York: Routledge, 1997).

Harris, Leonard, ed. *The Philosophy of Alain Locke: Harlem Renaissance and Beyond* (Philadelphia: Temple University Press, 1989).

James, Joy. *Transcending the Talented Tenth* (New York: Routledge, 1997).

Washington, Booker T. *Up from Slavery: An Autobiography* (Williamstown, Mass.: House Publishers, 1971).

Washington, Johnny. *A Journey into the Philosophy of Alain Locke* (Westport, Conn.: Greenwood Press, 1994).

West, Cornel, "The Crisis of Black Leadership," in *Race Matters* (New York: Random House, 1993).

Part III Philosophy and Related Disciplines
Philosophy and Legal Theory

Bell, Derrick. *And We Are Not Saved* (New York: Basic Books, 1987).

———. *The View from the Bottom of the Well: The Permanence of Racism* (New York: Basic Books, 1992).

Carter, Stephen. *The Culture of Disbelief: How American Law and Politics Trivialize Religious Devotion* (New York: Basic Books, 1993).

Crenshaw, Kimberle et al., eds. *Critical Race Theory: The Key Writings That Formed the Movement* (New York: New Press, 1995).

Delgado, Richard, ed. *Critical Race Theory: The Cutting Edge* (Philadelphia: Temple University Press, 1995).

Douglass, Frederick. "The Constitution of the U.S.: Is It Pro-Slavery or Anti-Slavery?" in Philip S. Foner, ed., *The Life and Writings of Frederick Douglass,* vol. II (New York: International Publishers, 1950).

Guinier, Lani. *The Tyranny of the Majority* (New York: Free Press, 1994).

Lawson, Bill. "Property or Persons," *Journal of Ethics* 1 (1997), 291–303.

Matsuda, Mari et al., eds. *Words That Wound: Critical Race Theory, Assaultive Speech, and the First Amendment* (Boulder, Col.: Westview Press, 1993).

Sowell, Thomas. *Civil Rights: Rhetoric and Reality* (New York: William Morrow, 1984).

Williams, Patricia J. *The Alchemy of Race and Rights* (Cambridge: Harvard University Press, 1991).

Aesthetics

Baker, Houston. *Black Studies, Rap, and the Academy* (Chicago: University of Chicago Press, 1993).

Baldwin, James. *Nobody Knows My Name: More Notes of a Native Son* (New York: Dial Press, 1961).

Davis, Angela. *Blues Legends and Black Feminism: Gertrude "Ma" Rainey, Bessie Smith, and Billie Holiday* (New York: Pantheon, 1998).

Ellison, Ralph. *Shadow and Act* (New York: Random House, 1964).

Fabre, Michael. "Richard Wright, French Existentialism, and the Outsider," in Yoshinobu Hakutani, ed., *Critical Essays on Richard Wright* (Boston: E.K. Hall, 1982).

Gates, Henry Louis. *The Signifying Monkey: A Theory of Afro-American Literary Criticism* (New York: Oxford University Press, 1988).

Gordon, Lewis. "Sketches of Jazz" in *Her Majesty's Other Children* (Lanham, Md.: Rowman and Littlefield, 1997).

Harris, Will J., ed. *The LeRoi Jones/Amiri Baraka Reader* (New York: Thunder's Mouth Press, 1991).

Johnson, Charles. *Being and Race: Black Writing Since 1970* (Indianapolis: Indiana University Press, 1988).

Kent, George E. "Blackness and the Adventure of Western Civilization," in Richard Macksey and Frank E. Moorer, eds., *Richard Wright: A Collection of Critical Essays* (Englewood Cliffs, N.J.: Prentice Hall, 1984).

Locke, Alain, ed. *The New Negro: Voices of the Harlem Renaissance* (New York: Atheneum, 1992).

Rose, Tricia. *Black Noise: Rap Music and Black Culture in Contemporary America* (Hanover, N.H.: University Press of New England, 1994).

Sartwell, Crispin. *Act Like You Know* (Chicago: University of Chicago Press, 1998).

Philosophy and Theology

Cone, James H. *God of the Oppressed,* revised edition (Maryknoll, N.Y.: Orbis, 1997).

Gordon, Lewis. "Can Men Worship? Reflections on Male Bodies in Bad Faith and a Theology of Authenticity," in Bjorn Krondorfer, ed., *Men's Bodies, Men's Gods: Male Identities in a (Post-) Christian Culture* (New York: New York University Press, 1996).

Grant, Jacqueline. *White Woman's Christ and Black Woman's Jesus* (Atlanta: Scholars Press, 1989).

Jones, William R. *Is God a White Racist? Prolegomenon to Black Theology* (New York: Doubleday, 1973).

Lincoln, Eric, and Mamiya Lawrence. *The Black Church and the African American Experience* (Durham: Duke University Press, 1993).

West, Cornel. *Prophecy Deliverance! An Afro-American Revolutionary Christianity* (Philadelphia: Westminster Press, 1982).

———. *Prophetic Fragments* (Grand Rapids, Mich: Erdmans, 1988).